# Projecting
# Capitalism

# PROJECTING CAPITALISM

## A History of the Internationalization of the Construction Industry

Marc Linder

*Contributions in Economics and Economic History, Number 158*

**Greenwood Press**
Westport, Connecticut • London

HD
9715
A2
L498
1994

**Library of Congress Cataloging-in-Publication Data**

Linder, Marc.
    Projecting capitalism : a history of the internationalization of
the construction industry / Marc Linder.
       p.  cm.— (Contributions in economics and economic history,
ISSN 0084–9235 ; no. 158)
    Includes bibliographical references and index.
    ISBN 0–313–29293–0 (alk. paper)
    1. Construction industry—History.  2. Engineering firms—History.
3. International business enterprises—History.  4. Railroads,
Colonial—History.  5. Capitalism—History.  6. Technology transfer—
History.  7. International economic relations—History.  I.  Title.
II.  Series.
HD9715.A2L498   1994
338.8′872—dc20       93–50546

British Library Cataloguing in Publication Data is available.

Library of Congress Catalog Card Number: 93–50546
ISBN: 0–313–29293–0
ISSN: 0084–9235

First published in 1994

Greenwood Press, 88 Post Road West, Westport, CT   06881
An imprint of Greenwood Publishing Group, Inc.

Printed in the United States of America

The paper used in this book complies with the
Permanent Paper Standard issued by the National
Information Standards Organization (Z39.48–1984).

10 9 8 7 6 5 4 3 2 1

[T]here is nothing more brutal than the world market....

A. Sartorius Freiherr von Waltershausen, *Das volkswirtschaftliche*
*System der Kapitalanlage im Auslande* 82 (1907)


[T]he railway is a strategic tool of a foreign power and not a means, except incidentally, of developing the country through which it passes.

"A European-Asiatic Railway Problem,"
86 *Engineering News-Record* 411 (1921)

# Contents

# Tables and Figures

## Tables

## Figures

# Preface

From the transnational building of railways in the 1840s to that of petrochemical plants at the end of the twentieth century, construction firms have played a crucial but little-appreciated role in creating the prerequisites of the world market and propagating capitalism to what were once the ends of the earth. In facilitating the global radiation of a system of international profit-driven production for exchange, these firms only gradually forged a world market for their own industry—construction. This book seeks to place the interaction of the formative processes of this universal world market and its submarket in an adequate political-economic and historical perspective.

Much of the current discussion of industrial construction and economic development is ahistorical, or at least concerns itself with narrow, local historical issues and not with the contours of internationalization over time. This book addresses the larger history first. How has construction-engineering influenced the migration of capital across political and geographical boundaries? What has been the relationship of construction to capital allocation, first in construction decisions and then in the production and marketing of transnational industries? How does historical analysis promote understanding of the construction industry's role in international development?

Persistently penetrating puzzles peskily propounded by Larry Zacharias, Gail Hollander, and John Houghton helped articulate some of the questions that gave rise to this book. Michael ''deus ex machina'' Saks, interceding to tame the most user-inimical software, produced the graphs. The circulation staff at The University of Iowa Library considerately permitted an interloper to forage in storage, thus making instantaneously and massively accessible tons of nineteenth-century construction, engineering, and railway trade journals before they go the (rest of the) way of all acidic paper. Sylvia Linder, from her end of the earth, made this book (and several others) possible by expediting several whole libraries across continents and oceans, while her confederate, a former antipodean prime minister, made available unpublished government documents from his.

# Abbreviations of Periodicals and Serials

| | |
|---|---|
| AAAPSS | *Annals of the American Academy of Political and Social Science* |
| AAS | *Annual Abstract of Statistics* |
| AB | *America's Builders* |
| ACDDP | *Annales de la Chambre des Députés: Documents Parlementaires* |
| AF | *Architectural Forum* |
| APCF | *Asian and Pacific Census Forum* |
| ARICC | *Annual Report of the Isthmian Canal Commission* |
| ASB | *Anlagen zu den Stenographischen Berichten* |
| ASS | *Archiv für Sozialwissenschaft und Sozialpolitik* |
| BB | *British Business* |
| BCB | *Barge Canal Bulletin* |
| BDL | *Bulletin of the Department of Labor* |
| BHR | *Business History Review* |
| BJ | *Baustatistisches Jahrbuch* |
| BRM | *Bradshaw's Railway Manual, Shareholders' Guide and Official Directory* |
| BSG | *Bradshaw's Shareholders' Guide, Railway Manual and Directory* |
| BTJ | *Board of Trade Journal* |
| BW | *Business Week* |
| CBP | *County Business Patterns* |
| CC | *Capital and Class* |
| CCI | *Census of Construction Industries* |
| CE | *Civil Engineering* |
| CEN | *Chemical and Engineering News* |
| ChE | *Chemical Engineering* |
| CHJ | *Ceylon Historical Journal* |
| CILJ | *Cornell International Law Journal* |
| CM | *Construction Methods* |
| CollW | *Collected Works* |
| CoM | *Census of Manufactures* |
| ContR | *Contemporary Review* |
| CR | *Congressional Record* |
| CRev | *Construction Review* |
| CW | *Chemical Week* |
| DBB | *Dictionary of Business Biography* |
| DH | *Diplomatic History* |
| DNB | *Dictionary of National Biography* |
| EC | *Engineering-Contracting* |
| EHR | *Economic History Review* |

| | |
|---|---|
| EN | *Engineering News* |
| EngHR | *English Historical Review* |
| ENR | *Engineering News-Record* |
| ER | *Engineering Record* |
| ERev | *Edinburgh Review* |
| FA | *Foreign Affairs* |
| FAZ | *Frankfurter Allgemeine Zeitung* |
| FD | *Finance and Development* |
| FEER | *Far Eastern Economic Review* |
| FR | *Fortnightly Review* |
| FT | *Financial Times* |
| FW | *Financial World* |
| GC | *Le Génie Civil* |
| GG | *Geschichte und Gesellschaft* |
| GW | *Gesammelte Werke* |
| HB | *Handelsblatt* |
| HBR | *Harvard Business Review* |
| HES | *Histoire, Économie et Sociéte* |
| HM | *Historia Mexicana* |
| HS | *Handwörterbuch der Staatswissenschaften* |
| IC | *International Construction* |
| IDCH | *International Directory of Company Histories* |
| IJURR | *International Journal of Urban and Regional Research* |
| ILR | *International Labour Review* |
| ILRR | *Industrial and Labor Relations Review* |
| IWPDC | *International Water Power and Dam Construction* |
| JAH | *Journal of African History* |
| JBE | *Journal of Business Ethics* |
| JCL | *Journal of Corporation Law* |
| JEEH | *Journal of European Economic History* |
| JEH | *Journal of Economic History* |
| JEI | *Journal of Economic Issues* |
| JG | *Jahrbuch für Geschichte* |
| JLAS | *Journal of Latin American Studies* |
| JSAH | *Journal of the Society of Architectural Historians* |
| JSE | *Journal of Structural Engineering* |
| JTH | *Journal of Transport History* |
| LCP | *Law and Contemporary Problems* |
| LD | *Literary Digest* |
| LS | *Legislative Series* |
| MAI | *Moody's Analysis of Investments* |
| MDB | *Monatshefte der Deutschen Bundesbank* |
| ME | *Mechanical Engineering* |
| MEJ | *Middle East Journal* |
| MES | *Middle Eastern Studies* |
| MIM | *Moody's Industrial Manual* |
| MIntM | *Moody's International Manual* |
| MLR | *Monthly Labor Review* |
| MMCS | *Moody's Manual of Corporate Securities* |
| MMI | *Moody's Manual of Investments: American and Foreign: Industrial Securities* |
| MMRCS | *Moody's Manual of Railroads and Corporation Securities* |
| MPICE | *Minutes of the Proceedings of the Institution of Civil Engineers* |
| MR | *Monthly Review* |
| MSC | *Merit Shop Contractor* |

| | |
|---|---|
| *NAR* | *North American Review* |
| *NCAB* | *National Cyclopædia of American Biography* |
| *NDB* | *Neue Deutsche Biographie* |
| *NIER* | *National Institute Economic Review* |
| *NLRB* | *Decisions and Orders of the National Labor Relations Board* |
| *NPMM* | *Nash's Pall Mall Magazine* |
| *NR* | *New Republic* |
| *NYT* | *New York Times* |
| *NZ* | *Die Neue Zeit* |
| *NZILR* | *New Zealand Industrial Law Reports* |
| *NZJIR* | *New Zealand Journal of Industrial Relations* |
| *NZLJ* | *New Zealand Law Journal* |
| *NZZ* | *Neue Zürcher Zeitung* |
| *OB* | *Official Bulletin* |
| *OGJ* | *Oil and Gas Journal* |
| *PASCE* | *Proceedings of the American Society of Civil Engineers* |
| *PBE* | *Production of the Built Environment: Proceedings of the Bartlett International Summer School* |
| *PD* | *Parliamentary Debates (Hansard)* |
| *PFR* | *Poor's Financial Records* |
| *PFV* | *Poor's Fiscal Volume* |
| *PG* | *Professional Geographer* |
| *PHR* | *Pacific Historical Review* |
| *PIV* | *Poor's Industrial Volume* |
| *PK* | *Probleme des Klassenkampfs* |
| *PP* | *Parliamentary Papers* |
| *PRWET* | *Pacific Research and World Empire Telegram* |
| *PSQ* | *Political Science Quarterly* |
| *RA* | *Railway Age* |
| *SA* | *Scientific American* |
| *SAUS* | *Statistical Abstract of the United States* |
| *SB* | *Schweizerische Bauzeitung* |
| *SBVR* | *Stenographische Berichte über die Verhandlungen des Reichstags* |
| *SCB* | *Survey of Current Business* |
| *SCSH* | *Smith College Studies in History* |
| *SEER* | *Slavonic and East European Review* |
| *SEP* | *Saturday Evening Post* |
| *SJ* | *Statistisches Jahrbuch* |
| *SJPE* | *Scottish Journal of Political Economy* |
| *SM* | *Successful Methods: A Magazine of Construction Service* |
| *TASCE* | *Transactions of the American Society of Civil Engineers* |
| *TC* | *Technology and Culture* |
| *TI* | *Trade and Industry* |
| *TR* | *Technology Review* |
| *UMS* | *University of Missouri Studies* |
| *WA* | *Weltwirtschaftliches Archiv* |
| *WD* | *World Development* |
| *WLR* | *Wisconsin Law Review* |
| *WP* | *Water Power* |
| *WPJ* | *World Policy Journal* |
| *WPost* | *Washington Post* |
| *WS* | *Wirtschaft und Statistik* |
| *WSJ* | *Wall Street Journal* |
| *YCS* | *Yearbook of Construction Statistics* |
| *ZB* | *Zeitschrift für Bauwesen* |

# PART I

# THEORETICAL FRAMEWORK

The profitable effect of capital, directed to a given object in the hope of profit, is...a main element of the subject on which the modern Engineer has to exert his skill and judgment. It may, indeed, be termed...as much a part of the whole, to be dealt with by practical science, as the method of construction, or the choice of materials. ...

The practical science of our day, as enlisted in the service of monied enterprise, must indeed confess itself at fault, if, by any defect of its own, that enterprise were defrauded of its fair reward. ... For it is obvious that, when the employment of science by wealth is mainly actuated by the stimulus of gain, the spur being withdrawn, the occupation must cease. [C]apital seeks its harvest elsewhere.... [T]he financial result of their joint operation is not their least important feature...and the appreciation of this side of the question really concerns the Engineer no less than the Statesman, or the Capitalist.

Joseph Locke, "Address of the President," in
17 *Minutes of the Proceedings of the
Institution of Civil Engineers* 128, 151 (1858)

# 1

# The Paradox of International Construction: A New World Market Within "The New International Division of Labor"

The so exceedingly favorable situation of the construction industry is explained by the fact that the construction industry does not work for the world market, but rather exclusively for the local market; it does not have foreign competition to fear and it is not threatened by the stamp "Made in Germany."[1]

Unlike manufacturing processes of production, in which the final products are in motion while the instruments of production are stationary, in construction the relationship is reversed: the products become fixed while the ambulatory fixed capital and the hypermobile construction worker, "who must be prepared to be a nomad," are moved or find their way to new sites.[2] As early as the 1850s and 1860s, British railway construction contractors were shipping "the vast mass of dead weight" of machines and materials as well as workers around the world to Canada, India, Argentina, and Australia.[3] Tens of thousands of Chinese coolies were pressed into service on railroads in Africa, South America, and North America in the nineteenth century.[4] By the 1880s, the huge excavation and dredging machinery that Ferdinand de Lesseps' Compagnie Universelle du Canal Interocéanique sent to the Isthmus of Panama, some of which had been used to dig the Suez Canal two decades earlier, "was computed by engineers as capable of performing the labor of half a million men."[5] The even more advanced labor-saving equipment, such as steam shovels and derricks, sent by the U.S. Isthmian Canal Commission shortly after the turn of the century to Panama, was then dispatched by congressional order in 1915 to Alaska for use in railway and dock construction.[6] At the beginning of the twentieth century, British and U.S. bridge-

---

[1]Michael von Tugan-Baranowsky, *Studien zur Theorie und Geschichte der Handelskrisen in England* 414 (1901).

[2]International Labour Organisation, Building, Civil Engineering & Public Works Committee, 7th Sess., Report II: *Technological Changes in the Construction Industry and Their Socio-Economic Consequences* 8 (1964). See also *idem*, 6th Sess., Report II: *International Migration of Labour in the Construction Industry* (1959); Gertrude Bancroft & Stuart Garfinkle, "Job Mobility in 1961," 86 *MLR* 897, 904 (1963). The developer of Levittowns described his process as "'a reversal of the Detroit assembly line...: In the case of our houses, it was the workers who moved, doing the same jobs at different locations.'" Richard Pérez-Peña, "William Levitt, 86, Suburb Maker, Dies," *NYT*, Jan. 29, 1994, at 11, col. 1.

[3]*Report from the Select Committee on East India (Railways)* v (14 *PP* 1857-58); see also chapter 4 below. In the 1840s, the American engineer, George Washington Whistler, whom Tsar Nicholas I invited to Russia to direct construction of the railway from St. Petersburg to Moscow, took a steam excavator, pile driver, and engine along on the ship. J. Allhands, *Tools of the Earth Mover: Yesterday and Today Preserved in Pictures* 180 (1951); Albert Parry, *Whistler's Father* (1939).

[4]See Persia Campbell, *Chinese Coolie Emigration to Countries Within the British Empire* (1923); Pierre Berton, *The Impossible Railway: The Building of the Canadian Pacific* 373-81 (1972 [1970]).

[5]David Wells, *Recent Economic Changes* 50 (1890); Allhands, *Tools of the Earth Mover* at 224.

[6]Joseph Bishop, *The Panama Gateway* 330, 335-41, 447-49 (1913); Ira Bennett, *History of the Panama*

building firms were also sending thousands of tons of pre-assembled bridge sections to Africa.[7]    And at the end of twentieth century, multinational construction firms still ship their own equipment from project to project around the world while importing workers from great distances.[8]

Yet despite this built-in "technical-economic peculiarity"[9] of mobility, it has long been a commonplace that the domestic construction industry is both sheltered from international competition and prevented from exporting.[10]   Hence the paradox of international construction.   On the one hand, the shape of the industry seems to be determined by local factors, primarily sites, labor, raw materials and, at least to some degree, heavy equipment.   On the other hand, the larger, more profitable firms in the industry operate on a global scale.   Does this mean that the portable factors of construction, such as financing, engineering design, site management, and know-how are scarce or less prone to competition, that they outweigh local factors as a source of project profitability?

Associated with and reinforcing this view has been the similarly exceptionalist thesis that the construction industry, as the paradigm of perfect competition prevailing among numerous small firms, could not fruitfully be analyzed as subject to the structural restraints of capital accumulation that apply to capital-intensive oligopolized manufacturing industries. Moreover, according to the received wisdom, before the post-World War II period, "construction companies rarely operated outside their own country."[11]

Developments in the last quarter of the twentieth century have eroded the plausibility of these images of an economically and technologically aberrant construction industry.[12]   In particular the windfall of petrodollar-generated large-scale involvement of multinational firms in Middle Eastern construction projects in the mid-1970s—as late as 1970, the major study of the prospects for construction exports prepared by the U.S. Department of Commerce did not even mention Saudi Arabia among attractive Near Eastern markets—finally forced observers to acknowledge that the industry had been catapulted beyond what they had regarded as desultory overseas forays superadded to traditional national domestic patterns.[13]   Yet they continued to ignore the significance and to some extent even the existence of that prehistory.

Historically, two trends in transnational construction projects have been observed.   One has been associated with extraction, which has led to building projects at the sites of raw materials, such as mines and oil wells, as well as to

---

*Canal: Its Construction and Builders* 365-71 (1915); Ulrich Keller, *The Building of the Panama Canal in Historical Photographs*, photographs no. 5-10 (1983); S. Res. 169, 63d Cong., 1st Sess., 49 *CR* 3651 (1913); S. Doc. No. 258: *Panama Canal Equipment*, 63d Cong., 2d Sess. (1914); Act of Mar. 12, 1914, ch. 37, 38 Stat. 305, 306; Harold Williamson & Kenneth Myers, *Designed for Digging: The First 75 Years of Bucyrus-Erie Company* 92-99 (1955); Edwin Fitch, *The Alaskan Railroad* 53 (1967).

[7]See e.g. "The Zambesi River Bridge, Victoria Falls, Rhodesia," 52 *ER* 346-47. (1905).

[8]*Facts About Bechtel* 11 [no pagination] (n.d. [ca. 1968]); see also chapters 8-10 below.

[9]P. Podshivalenko et al., *Ekonomika stroitel'stva: Uchebnik* 10 (1962).

[10]See e.g., Herbert Robinson, *The Economics of Building* 4, 12 (1939); *National Interests in an Age of Global Technology* 31 (Thomas Lee & Proctor Reid ed., 1991).

[11]E. Stallworthy & O. Kharbanda, *International Construction* 11 (1986).

[12]For examples of exceptionalist theses, see Colin Clark, *The Conditions of Economic Progress* 381-82 (3d ed. 1957 [1940]); Peter Cassimatis, "The Performance of the Construction Industry" 40-67 (Diss., New School for Social Research, 1967); idem, *Economics of the Construction Industry* 57-59 (Nat. Indus. Conf. Bd., Studies in Business Economics, No. 111, 1969); Alain Lipietz, "Building and the Crisis of Fordism: The Case of France," 6 *PBE* 1-13, 1-16 (1984). H. Wiedmann, *Hochtief: Aktiengesellschaft für Hoch- und Tiefbauten vorm. Gebr. Helfmann* 7-15, 27 (1931), offers a comprehensive catalog of peculiarities of the construction industry but nevertheless stresses that the significant capital investment embodied in machinery and the technical-scientific administrative apparatus requires constant full utilization.

[13]U.S. National Export Expansion Council, *Report of the Industry Committee on Engineering and Construction Services* 88-90 (1970).

constructing an infrastructure to service those sites, ranging from rail lines, canals, pipelines, and telegraph and telephone lines to electrical or other power sources. The other involves local production and economic development ventures. Construction of this type is designed to be integrative at various levels: of infrastructure, national productive capacity, and capital accumulation. Construction projects, in terms of what is built and how it is built, have the potential for fostering or inhibiting overall national economic growth. If, for instance, construction projects develop a local economy in highly specialized ways and through foreign control of the construction itself, it may be more vulnerable to outside influence than a more self-sustaining economy.

In short, this potential for inhibiting economic development in the petroleum-producing countries and other dependently industrializing societies through specialization is bound up with broader questions about the formation of the so-called new international division of labor, which has permitted a worldwide dispersion of production locations.[14] Here history has repeated itself. For this new-new international division of labor has a precursor in the new division of labor that emerged in the nineteenth century. Late-twentieth-century multinational construction firms also find their forerunners in the nineteenth-century English, French, and German railway construction and civil engineering firms that were integrated into a world market that they helped forge. By means of the international projection of European construction-engineering they contributed crucially to the imposition of a dependent political-economic role on colonized regions by making possible the extraction and expedition of mineral and agricultural resources back to Europe.

Projects reminiscent of the nineteenth-century international division of labor still abound. Bechtel Corporation, for example, completed in the 1970s a technically challenging assignment for a U.S. firm, Freeport Minerals, by building a pipeline in a spectacularly inaccessible part of the Indonesian province of West Irian in order to ''open'' a thirty-three million ton copper deposit ''to international markets.'' Because the central government in Jakarta devoted almost none of the proceeds to developing the local economy, ''a minor civil war'' erupted among the local population.[15]

Typically, however, First World construction firms operating in the Third World[16] in the late twentieth century have become the agents of a more complex process. Rooted in the availability in the Third World of an inexhaustible supply of state-disciplined cheap labor, a fragmentation of industrial processes amenable to the employment of unskilled workers, and the development of more efficient and cheaper transportation and communication technologies, the rise of dependent and yet competitive industries in a number of countries outside Europe, North America, and Japan has required the construction of industrial and extractive facilities and infrastructure that mimic those of their First World progenitors.[17] In those

---

[14]For a not entirely persuasive effort to conceptualize the differences between the positions of the wealthy OPEC countries and other underdeveloped countries, see Jacqueline Ismael, *Kuwait: Social Change in Historical Perspective* 115-16, 154-60 (1982).

[15]*Compressed Air*, Nov. 1975, at 10-121 (Westlaw-Dialog); "Papuan Power," *Economist*, Jan. 1978, at 60 (Nexis). On the extraordinarily profitable mine operations, see Freeport-McMoRan, *1992 Annual Report* 1, 10-15, 48-49 (1993).

[16]No term has yet emerged to replace this obsolete one. See Nigel Harris, *The End of the Third World: Newly Industrializing Countries and the Decline of an Ideology* (1986). "Third World" is used here throughout interchangeably with "underdeveloped," "developing," and "peripheral" although they too are hopelessly ideologically freighted.

[17]Folker Fröbel, Jürgen Heinrichs, & Otto Kreye, *Die neue internationale Arbeitsteilung* 30 (1977); *idem, Umbruch in der Weltwirtschaft* 438-79 (1986); Brian O'Reilly, "Your New Global Work Force," *Fortune*, Dec. 14, 1992, at 52. For a critical evaluation the New International Division of Labor approach emphasizing the limited scope and depth of industrialization in most of the Third World and its concentration in a few Newly Industrializing Countries, see Roger Southall, "Introduction," in *Trade*

countries, such as South Korea, Taiwan, and Brazil, in which the intense development of autochthonous world-market-oriented industrial capital has initiated a process of de-peripherilization,[18] the role of international construction firms has become contested as domestic firms have begun to acquire the capital, engineering knowledge, and technology to carry out their own complex projects.

This book pursues three interrelated objectives. First, it uses the development of a world market to show how the construction industry more closely resembles other industries with respect to the structural imperatives and constraints of capital accumulation and concentration than has traditionally been recognized. Building on the journalistic and trade literature on the recent internationalization of construction, this is the first scholarly work to emphasize the growth of the general world market as a factor in forcing the construction industries of the advanced economies into a world construction market.

Second, by focusing on the concrete role that construction firms—which form "the nation's primary capital goods industry"[19]—play in producing and implanting other industries' fixed capital across national boundaries, this book emphasizes the crucial but neglected historically changing role that multinational construction firms have played as creators of the physical skeleton of the international economy and as agents of the incorporation of the economic periphery into internationalized capital circuits. Examination of the micro-histories, beginning with the 1830s, of individual companies and the construction industries of Western Europe, the United States, and Japan, brings to light the pioneering contributions that multinational construction firms have made to the projection of metropolitan political-economic power to Africa, Asia, and Latin America. Despite the vast literatures on world systems, multinational firms, and the effect of "development" on the environment, this is the first work to place the internationalization process in the context of the construction industry's contribution to the creation of a world market for commodities and capital.

More than any other group of entrepreneurs, construction engineering firms have historically understood the transnational interests of capital as their personal opportunities for enterprise. In their role as designers and managers of transnational construction projects, they have been crucial to the expansion and shaping of capitalism—in the development of global industries and international divisions of labor. Their imagination of projects that could and could not feasibly be completed in economically undeveloped territories has been a leading determinant of capital decisions at the metropolitan cores. Understanding the secondary role of engineering in capital-allocation decisions helps explain why Third World industrial capacities do not readily transform Third World economies into less dependent competitors—why, for example, metropolitan oil companies charged construction firms with building oil wells, pipelines, and ports rather than local refineries in the Third World.

And third, although scholars have written case studies of the impact of individual construction projects on the environment, this book provides a comprehensive historical view of the physical transformation and reconstruction of

---

Unions and the New Industrialization of the Third World 1, 4-20 (Roger Southall ed., 1988); James Petras & Dennis Engbarth, "Third World Industrialization and Trade Union Struggles," in id. at 81-99.

[18]Stephen Haggard, *Paths from the Periphery: The Politics of Growth in the Newly Industrializing Countries* (1990); Scott McMurray & James McGregor, "Asia Targets Chemicals for the Next Assault on Western Industry," *WSJ*, Aug. 4, 1993, at A1, col. 6. For a skeptical view of the long-term prospects of industrialization in the Third World, see Elmar Altvater, *Sachzwang Weltmarkt: Verschuldungskrise, blockierte Industrialisierung und ökologische Gefährdung: Der Fall Brasilien* (1987).

[19]U.S. Bureau of Labor Statistics, *Construction During Five Decades* iii (Bull. No. 1146, 1954). See also Simon Kuznets, *Capital in the American Economy: Its Formation and Financing*, tab. 14 at 146-50 (1961).

the Third World's second nature wrought by the transfer of First World construction-engineering technology in the service of world-market-oriented natural resource exploitation. The monopolies that First World manufacturing and construction firms have held on the underlying technologies of the built environment in large part explain the peculiarities of the development and structure of the world construction market.

The remainder of the theoretical framework sketched in part I begins with an examination of the applicability to construction of the distinction, common to other industries, between exports and direct investment abroad. Of particular salience here is the role played by exports of prefabricated buildings and structures as physical analogs to that of manufactured commodities. An analysis of the micro- and macro-political-economic bases of construction firms' decisions to build beyond national boundaries forms the concluding section of chapter 2.

Part II explores the history of the course of transnational construction activities of European and U.S. firms prior to World War II. The rise of large British railway construction firms in the 1830s and 1840s is explained by reference to the separation of engineering from contracting and the use of labor subcontracting as the most profitable form of managing the labor force (chapter 3). In the nineteenth and early twentieth century these British firms built railroads and other infrastructure designed to facilitate the incorporation of the primary commodities of Africa, Asia, and Latin America into Britain's circuits of capital (chapter 4). The role of the state in the nineteenth century in Britain and, secondarily in other European countries, in transforming the colonies into unequal participants in the world market then provides the background for the overseas expansion of European construction firms (chapter 5). The counterpart competitive processes in the German and French colonial empires and elsewhere are evaluated in chapter 6. The emergence of internationally oriented U.S. construction firms in response to the rise of U.S. imperialist aspirations at the end of the nineteenth century and to the country's new role as a capital exporter during World War I forms the focus of chapter 7.

Part III is devoted to the evolution of a world market for construction. Chapter 8 accounts for the post-World War II ascendancy of U.S. multinational construction firms. Worldwide exploitation of petroleum resources beginning in the 1930s and far-flung military construction performed by U.S. firms during World War II furnished the latter with the technology, capital, and private economic and state networks to occupy a privileged international position in the postwar years. The absolute political-economic and military dominance of the United States as a whole during the early postwar period and the massive preemptive demands that reconstruction in Europe and Japan made on the capacities of each domestic construction industry initially left U.S. construction firms without significant international competition. Chapter 9 then reconstructs the erosion of the dominant U.S. position since the Vietnam War against the background of the OPEC building boom. The unprecedented volume of transnational construction made possible by the enormous revenues flowing to the Middle Eastern OPEC states in the mid-1970s created a world market for construction by broadening and deepening the participation of producers and consuming firms and states. In responding to this expanded demand for specialized engineering technology, construction firms from advanced capitalist countries unwittingly helped institutionalize new pressures on their capital investment that initiated a profound process of internationalization. Although U.S. firms in particular profited immensely from this integration into the world market, it eventually deprived them of the hegemony that their manufacturing counterparts had lost earlier in the postwar period.

After delineating the unparalleled international mobilization of construction labor occasioned by the huge increase in Middle Eastern building, which has enabled multinational firms to engage in worldwide sourcing for a factor of production theretofore kept immobile by transportation costs and legal restrictions (chapter 10), this book presents the available quantitative indicators of the internationalization of construction firms in the United States and in the entire world during the postwar period (chapter 11). The concluding analyses are devoted to the collapse of the OPEC boom in the early 1980s, which compelled multinational firms to seek means to counteract the decline in profitability associated with their overaccumulation of capital. The most salient strategies are the competitive interpenetration of First World markets (chapter 12) and the dependent industrialization of the Third World with its concomitant consequences for the global environment (chapter 13).

# 2

# A Taxonomy and Etiology of International Construction Activities

You see a child, a little thing perhaps of six years old, leading and guiding at its will a team of magnificent horses. This sight forces upon the mind a feeling of satisfaction at the immense preponderance of the human intellectual power, as shown in this child, over the brute force of these powerful creatures. Such has been the sway of capital, often very ignorantly, childishly we may say, applied in ordering the construction of railways. Schemes recklessly promoted, or at any rate promoted without any view to the general good, have been efficiently carried out by the docile contractor, whom, by the way, I am rather ashamed to compare for the moment, except for faithfulness and docility, to the horse.[1]

### Exports of Prefabricated Structures

[I]t was not the absence of stone and clay and timber and metal ores in Australia and South Africa and the West Indies which created the large market for prefabricated houses, warehouses, theatres and churches in these places in the nineteenth century. It was the absence of an infrastructure and population sufficient to meet locally the immediate needs of colonialism, combined with the existence of the metropolis and the economic viability of making and transporting prefabricated structures in the industrial age.[2]

Within the framework of world industrial markets, it is customary to distinguish between the export of commodities and the export of or investment in productive facilities for production beyond the producing firm's national boundaries. The limited scope of direct construction exports is said to result from the industry's "most important peculiarity"—its extraordinary dependence on physical location, that is, on particular geographic sites.[3] This argument is eminently plausible when applied to certain massive civil engineering projects. The construction of a highway through the Brazilian jungle, of a railroad in Turkey, or of a subway in Mexico City must perforce take place on-site: "Transportation of the product is impossible."[4] Even when such objects as bridges or tunnels are prefabricated and exported, on-site processes of excavation, assembly, and erection are still necessary.[5]

---

[1]Arthur Helps, *Life and Labours of Mr. Brassey: 1805-1870*, at 338 (1872).

[2]W. McGhie, "The Industrialisation of the Production of Building Elements and Components," in [4] *PBE, 1982: Labour in Building and Construction* 3-21, 3-33 (1983).

[3]G. Levin and I. Osmakov, "Reserven der Bauproduktion," in Autorenkollektiv, *Intensivierung und ökonomische Reserven* 285, 289 (Gerhard Krupp tr., 1972) [*Intensifikatsiia i rezervy ekonomiki* (1970)].

[4]Helen Rainbird & Gerd Syben, "Introduction," in *Restructuring a Traditional Industry: Construction Employment and Skills in Europe* 1, 5 (Helen Rainbird & Gerd Syben ed., 1991).

[5]See "Prefabricated Bridge Takes a Long Ride," *ENR*, Sept. 14, 1967, at 20 (exported by Dorman,

        Viewed in this light, the issue of exports does not differ from the issue
raised by location-dependence within a national market: to the extent that
prefabrication methods become economical, the traditional location-dependence of
certain types of structures diminishes.[6] The outstanding nineteenth-century example of domestic shipments of prefabricated housing units in the United States
was the so-called balloon frame wooden house.[7] The international export of
prefabricated buildings and other structures from Victorian Britain also attained
remarkable dimensions and sophistication.
        Prefabricated housing was sent to Australia and Africa as early as the late
eighteenth century. In 1819 houses were sent from Boston to Hawaii. By the
1830s, the Manning "Portable Colonial Cottage for Emigrants," which could be
assembled in a few hours, was being produced and shipped to the Antipodes in
large numbers. In addition to mass-producing thousands of huts for soldiers during
the Crimean War, British manufacturers such as William Fairbairn, Sons, & Co.
and E. T. Bellhouse & Co. also produced and exported to Turkey, India, Hong
Kong, Uruguay, South Africa, and elsewhere a variety of elaborate prefabricated
structures including an iron house for a corn mill and a woollen factory.[8] As early
as 1807 a firm shipped the components of an iron bridge weighing fifty tons to
Jamaica. The transaction then became common during the ensuing decades. By
the 1840s a 130-foot lighthouse was constructed, erected, dismantled, and shipped
to Barbados. This type of prefabrication also spread.[9] Within a few years British
firms were exporting houses and warehouses to Africa and the West Indies. The
British firm of Henry Grissell, for example, exported a prefabricated iron building
to Mauritius.[10]
        Soon large iron residential, governmental, commercial, railway, and
industrial buildings as well as hotels, churches, hospitals, and mining facilities were
being prefabricated and exported for reassembly all over the world. In the 1850s,
a British firm manufactured the entire Buenos Aires gas works, transporting 2,000
tons of building elements in ten ships. Another firm exported a lighthouse to the
United States in 1851 for the federal government, while Grissell sent a fifty-ton
lighthouse to the Falkland Islands in 1853. During the gold rush California became
one of the largest markets for prefabricated houses. Producers on the east coast of
the United States, forced to ship their products around South America to San
Francisco, faced competition from Hong Kong, New Zealand, and Australia as well
as from England and Belgium for the sale of thousands of houses, which three or
four workers reputedly could assemble in three or four days.[11]

---

Long from England to Zambia to avoid labor and logistical problems); "Danish Specialty: Prefabricated
Tunnels," *ENR*, Mar. 28, 1968, at 30 (exported to and installed in Belgium by Christiani & Nielsen).

    [6]See H. Brede et al., *Ökonomische und politische Determinanten der Wohnungsversorgung* 29 (1975).
See also The Battelle Memorial Institute, *The State of the Art of Prefabrication in the Construction Industry*
(1967); U.N. Economic & Social Council, Committee on Housing, Building & Planning, Fifth Session,
*Industrialization of Building* 86-87 (1967).

    [7]See Horace Greeley et al., *The Great Industries of the United States* 40-41 (1872); Siegfried Giedion,
*Space, Time and Architecture* 345-51 (1959 [1941]); "The Prefabricated House," *AF*, Dec. 1942, at 49,
50; Carl Condit, *American Building* 43-45 (1968); Bob Reckman, "Carpentry: The Craft and Trade," in
*Case Studies in the Labor Process* 73, 80-82 (Andrew Zimbalist ed., 1979); William Cronon, *Nature's
Metropolis: Chicago and the Great West* 178-79 (1991).

    [8]2 *MPICE* 125-26 (1843) (Fairbairn's exports to Turkey).

    [9]See Peter Paterson, "An Account of the Cast-Iron Lighthouse Tower in Gibb's Hall, in the Bermudas,"
in 2 *MPICE* 182-85 (1843).

    [10]Henry Grissell (1817-1883), was a civil engineer who also built bridges in Egypt and waterworks in
Vienna and Leipzig, and promoted engineering works in Russia carried out by English capital. See the
obituary in 73 *MPICE* 376-78 (1883).

    [11]See generally Gilbert Herbert, *Pioneers of Prefabrication: The British Contribution in the Nineteenth
Century* (1978); "Cast-Iron Lighthouse for the Falkland Islands," 11 *Builder* 573 (1853); Henry-Russell
Hitchcock, 1 *Early Victorian Architecture* 516-17 (1972 [1954]); Charles Peterson, "Prefabs in the

Nor were the British the only major nonresidential construction exporters in the nineteenth century. Among their competitors was Gustave Eiffel, whose firm, Eiffel & Co., exported prefabricated churches throughout the world.[12] The dismantling, overseas transport, and reassembly of entire factories was also practiced in the nineteenth century, as witnessed by a steel-pipe plant that was moved from the United States to Russia and a sugar mill transported from Florida to the west coast of Mexico in the 1890s.[13]

The definitive separation in the colonies of the mass of the European settler population from the means of production and the concomitant rise of capitalist relations of production, however, reduced the need for imports of prefabricated buildings. The emergence of transitional economies in white settler territories, in which wage labor had not yet become second nature because ownership of the means of production, in particular, of land, had not yet become a categorical class distinction, made problematic large-scale enterprises that required considerable fixed capital.[14] As Henry George explained the consequences for the labor market of one version of this frontier hypothesis to the U.S. Congress in the 1880s:

> [L]and reform properly carried out would result in making wage-workers independent; that is, instead of men competing with each other for the privilege of working, most employments would be competing for men to work at them, because, the land being free, there would be a constant opening there and the present conditions would be reversed, so that instead of the workingmen seeking employment the employers would seek workers; and whoever seeks is a slave.[15]

But as state land and immigration policies promoted the proletarianization of the colonial population and thus increased "the availability of labor—always the controlling factor of local production of houses and the inverse key to prefabrication"—capitalistically organized construction operations could be inaugurated.[16] When, for example, "Melbourne was in course of erection, stores, shops, houses, hotels, and offices were immediately and urgently required, ...it was only by the constant supply of competition which immigration furnished that labour...was kept at such a price as to be at all accessible."[17] Once the labor question was resolved in favor of capital, as newly colonized or settled regions such as Australia and California developed, they were able to dispense with extraordinary injections of advanced technology in the form of prefabricated construction imports.

The so-called scramble for African colonies in the last quarter of the nineteenth century reignited demand for prefabricated housing by the European colonizers. At the request of the governor of German East Africa, for example, a German firm in Altona shipped framework houses to Dar es Salaam to provide

---

California Gold Rush, 1849," 24 *JSAH* 318-23 (1965).

[12]"Alexandre Gustave Eiffel: A Towering Engineering Genius," *ME*, Feb. 1992, at 58, 61.

[13]John McKay, *Pioneers for Profit: Foreign Entrepreneurship and Russian Industrialization 1885-1913*, at 184 (1970); J. Sitterson, *Sugar Country: The Cane Sugar Industry in the South, 1753-1950*, at 363 (1953).

[14]This noncapitalist interlude associated with gold rushes disturbed Engels at mid-century when he still believed in the imminence of an economically determined revolution: "California and Australia are two cases, which were not provided for in the 'Manifesto': Creation of large new markets out of nothing. They still have to go in [to our theory]." Letter from Engels to Marx, 24 Aug. 1852, in Karl Marx [&] Friedrich Engels, 28 *Werke* 117, 118 (1963).

[15]U.S. Senate, 1 *Report of the Committee of the Senate upon the Relations Between Labor and Capital* 800-801 (1885). See also Karl Marx, 1 *Das Kapital: Kritik der politischen Ökonomie* 745-56 (1867 [reprint 1959]).

[16]Herbert, *Pioneers of Prefabrication* at 22.

[17]"The Demand for Labour in Melbourne," 1 *Engineer* 345 (1856).

shelter for the new arrivals until the colonial government could organize its own.[18] The 1880s also witnessed the first exports of cabins and labor camps from Germany. In the aftermath of the devastation of World War I, U.S. firms exported demountable houses to France; and in the 1920s, Swedish firms began exporting houses.[19]   Again during and after World War II international—and especially U.S.—exports of prefabricated military facilities and housing increased strikingly.[20]   By 1949, Swedish firms alone had exported $45 million dollars worth of prefabricated houses, chiefly to Persian Gulf oil centers and Israel.[21]   An English firm exported prefabricated aluminum housing to the British West Indies and Portuguese East Africa, while German firms found a ready market in Australia and New Zealand for prefabricated wooden houses.[22]   The Korean War provided a further spike of demand for exports of prefabricated shelters.  By the 1960s, Japan was also exporting prefabricated houses.[23]

Physical exports of elements of the built environment resumed in the second half of the twentieth century on a much higher technological plateau.  Thus in spite of the often unique properties of many large commercial buildings and industrial plants, new construction techniques and transportation facilities have made exports possible that would have been impossible earlier in the century.  In 1930, for example, it was a relatively simple process for the Stalingrad Tractor Plant, Europe's largest, to be built in the United States, dismantled, shipped to the Soviet Union, and reassembled by Americans and Germans under the supervision of the Austin Company.[24]   A half-century later, however, a 6,500-ton prefabricated hydroelectric plant could be built in France, shipped across the Atlantic Ocean to New Orleans, and then floated 1,600 miles up the Mississippi and Ohio rivers to an Army Corps of Engineers lock and dam in Ohio.[25]   The Japanese firm that built a polyethylene plant in a shipyard for turnkey delivery on an ocean-going barge to Argentina offers shipment to any location accessible by deep water.[26] Japanese firms also built a nine-story hotel on a barge.  Designed especially for developing countries in which construction is hampered by shortages of land and skilled workers, the floating hotel can be delivered to any coastal area in the world.[27]

International exports of modern prefabricated houses have also resumed. Manufacturers of prefabricated houses have located markets even in advanced capitalist countries.  In Sweden, for example, where prefabrication technology dominates housing production, firms have been increasingly successful in shipping their products to Europe, Japan, and the United States.  Direct construction exports

---

[18]Friedrich Gurlitt, "Die ersten Baujahre in Deutsch-Ostafrika," 55 *ZB* 57, 75 (1905).

[19]Burnham Kelly, *The Prefabrication of Houses* 9-12 (1951); "French Housing Contract Awarded to New York Firm," 83 *ENR* 393 (1919) (2000 houses by MacArthur Bros.).

[20]See e.g., "Army Engineers Package and Ship Hospitals to Southwest Pacific," 134 *ENR* 719 (1945); "British Cancel Orders for Houses Designed and Prefabricated in the U.S.," 135 *ENR* 355 (1945); "Sell Prefabricated Homes to France," *id.* at 557; 136 *ENR* 385 (1946) (from Sweden to Denmark).

[21]*ENR*, Sept. 8, 1949, at 31.

[22]140 *ENR* 596 (1948); "German Prefabs for Antipodes," *ENR*, Jan. 25, 1951, at 50.  The export of prefabricated housing from Britain to Australia was curbed by the imposition of a high import duty in the early 1950s.  *ENR*, Aug. 21, 1952, at 54.

[23]"Defense Needs Prod Prefabs Upward," *ENR*, Jan. 25, 1951, at 25; "Japan Will Export Prefab Houses," *ENR*, Aug. 29, 1963, at 42.

[24]Anthony Sutton, *Western Technology and Soviet Economic Development 1930-1945*, at 185-86 (1930).

[25]"Low-Head Hydro Finds Ohio Home," *ENR*, Jan. 8, 1981, at 22; "Prefab Powerplant Floats into Place," *ENR*, Sept. 10, 1981, at 14.

[26]E. Stallworthy & O. Kharbanda, *International Construction* 32-34 (1986).  See also Suzanne Shelley, "Making Inroads with Modular Construction," *ChE*, Aug. 1990, at 30 (Nexis).

[27]"World's First Floating Hotel," *IC*, Nov. 1983, at 5.

from the United States, on the other hand, have been limited during the post-World War II period although federal legislation mandating that new housing for U.S. troops stationed in Europe be manufactured in the United States by U.S. firms may provide an impetus for such transatlantic shipments.[28]

### International Production

> [T]he extension of railway communications into wild and uncivilised countries, demands from the Engineers, Agents, and Contractors...the exercise of more than ordinary observation, self-discipline, and energy. ... It becomes...the wise policy of all foreign Railway Companies, and of all Contractors...to exercise the greatest strictness...in ascertaining that the agents sent out from this country...are...possessed of gentlemanly feelings and habits...converting the Railway Engineer into a pioneer of civilisation and a missionary of science.[29]

In contrast to the causes of direct foreign investment in manufacturing industries, which have long been the object of controversy,[30] the reasons underlying expansion beyond national boundaries in construction are relatively straightforward. In close analogy to the situation of the extractive industries—for which international construction firms also build facilities and infrastructure—those reasons are bound up with the search for sites of production.[31] Firms may be impelled to diversify geographically by the relative saturation of a domestic market that no longer allows realized profits to be reinvested (or the existing fixed capital to be utilized adequately). Firms also "increasingly spread[] their projects around the globe to even out business cycles" and make themselves "less vulnerable to fluctuations in domestic construction."[32] As a leading promoter of international trade and capital export observed during World War I: "'[T]he foreign field offers to the American contractor the same advantage which export trade offers the manufacturer—the stabilization of his business by diversification of his outlets. It spreads his risk, and he is more certain of normal business than if all activities are confined to one country.'"[33] Finally, other countries may offer projects and profits of a magnitude not currently available on the national construction market.[34]

So long as the security of domestic capital investment was so much greater than that of investment outside the protective reach of the national state that it

---

[28]See e.g. Kelly, *Prefabrication of Houses* at 365-66; "Danish Blues," *Building*, Dec. 17, 1976, at 32; U.S., International Trade Administration, *Foreign Builders Target the United States: Implications and Trends* 8-10 (Nat. Tech. Infor. Serv. PB88172457, 1988); U.S. Bureau of the Census, *Historical Statistics of the United States, Colonial Times to 1970*, pt. 1 (1975), ser. F 668-723 at 272-83; U.S. Bureau of Labor Statistics, *The Structure of the U.S. Economy in 1980 and 1985*, at 382-87 (Bull. No. 1831, 1975); U.S. Bureau of the Census, *SAUS: 1975*, tab. 1363 at 813 (96th ed. 1975); Military Construction Authorization Act, 1984, Pub. L. No. 98-115, § 803, 97 Stat. 757, 784-85 (1983); "Prefab Housing: Military Push in Europe Gives U.S. Firms a Boost," *ENR*, Aug. 30, 1984, at 22.

[29]John Brunton, "Description of the Line and Works of the Scinde Railway," 22 *MPICE* 451, 473 (1863).

[30]See e.g., John Dunning, *Explaining International Production* (1988).

[31]Klaus Busch, *Die multinationalen Konzerne* 245-49 (1974); John Dunning, *Multinational Enterprises and the Global Economy* 57 (1993).

[32] Gerald Parkinson & Ken Fouhy, "Riding the E&C Wave," *ChE*, Sept. 1991, at 30 (Nexis); "One Firm's Formula for Success: Diversification," *ENR*, Apr. 11, 1957, at 34, 40 (referring to Utah Construction Co.).

[33]"Will Help American Contractors in Handling Work in Foreign Fields," 73 *ER* 93, 94 (1916) (quoting Williard Straight, vice-president, American International Corp.).

[34]Roland Neo, *International Construction Contracting: A Critical Investigation into Certain Aspects of Financing, Capital Planning and Cash Flow Effects* 78-81 (1976); "The Top International Contractors," *ENR*, July 16, 1981, at 68, 73; Chester Lucas, *International Construction Business Management* 2 (1986).

more than compensated for potentially higher rates of profit abroad, internationalization of production was impeded. The extension of European nation-states' power to the conquered colonies in the nineteenth century then created the requisite degree of security. Since that time the salient question in the construction industry has been not so much why firms seek cross-border orders, but rather how they can compete with local firms. Historically, the answer lay chiefly in the peculiar configuration of international construction markets, which were largely confined to the less developed countries. Western European and U.S. construction firms, responding in part to a demand for infrastructure in those countries generated by European and U.S. industrial capital, competed with one another outside of their own domestic markets. Not until the late twentieth century has the more complicated phenomenon—which appeared much earlier in manufacturing—of the interpenetration of advanced capitalist construction markets arisen as a consequence of world construction market depression. In particular the evanescent OPEC building boom forced the European and U.S. multinational firms that had accumulated enormous capital in the Middle East to invade certain sectors of one another's domestic construction markets in order to continue to valorize that capital.[35]

The microeconomic possibility of the existence of profitable international production operations is rooted in the structure of monopolistic competition. As Charles Kindleberger, a leading contemporary theorist and historian of international economics, has pointed out, such overseas direct investment makes no sense unless the invading firms

> possess some advantage which they can transfer from one country to another but which cannot be acquired by local firms. With perfect international markets for technology, management, labor skills, components, and other material input, the market abroad will be served by a local firm.
> Put the matter another way: in a world of perfect competition for goods and factors, direct investment cannot exist. In these conditions, domestic firms would have an advantage over foreign firms in the proximity of their operations, so that no firm could survive in foreign operation. For direct investment to thrive there must be some imperfection in markets for goods or factors, including among the latter technology, or some interference in competition by government or by firms, which separates markets.[36]

Kindleberger groups the monopolistic advantages that can induce overseas direct investment under the headings of goods markets, factor markets, and economies of scale. Departures from perfect competition in goods markets include such strategies as product differentiation and special marketing skills. Departures from perfect competition in factor markets run the gamut from patents and discriminatory capital access to "differences in skills of managers organized into firms rather than hired in competitive markets."[37]

Since the types of construction that have traditionally been performed abroad almost exclusively both are one-of-a-kind and enter as inputs into other firms' production processes, they tend not to be subject to the marketing strategies that promote the sale of mass-produced fungible consumer products. Economies of scale and privileged access to labor and embodied and liquid forms of capital therefore constitute the principal bases for internationalizing construction.

Kindleberger himself rejects the notion that foreign investors could derive any competitive advantage from discriminatory access to labor "other than

---

[35]See chapter 12 below.

[36]Charles Kindleberger, *American Investment Abroad: Six Lectures on Direct Investment* 12-13 (1971 [1969]).

[37]*Id.* at 14.

management and technical staff.''[38] Both nineteenth-century railway building in Europe and the colonial areas and contemporary construction in thinly populated Third World countries belie this argument. Privileged access to and exportation of navvies and skilled workers from Britain then and of workers from the so-called labor-surplus countries of Asia today have formed a crucial element in the ability of firms from advanced capitalist countries to undertake construction abroad.[39]

Privileged access to the most efficient means of production, the cheapest and strongest building materials, and to engineering knowledge that may not have been proprietary but that had nevertheless not yet been appropriated by a critical mass of engineers in the periphery played a significant part in the international construction activities of European and, to a lesser extent, of U.S. construction firms in the nineteenth century. In the hydrocarbon era, in contrast, proprietary engineering technology has assumed greater importance than during the railway age.[40]

Many specialists in construction economics have contended that the fact that firms build one-of-a-kind products is inconsistent with economies of scale and hence concentration in construction. This thesis was not even accurate in the nineteenth century, when oligopoly prevailed, and a "handful of bankers and contractors controlled nearly all railway building in the world, outside the U.S.A., between 1840 and 1870, and a large share of transport developments in the half-century after.''[41] At the beginning of the twentieth century, one of the leading U.S. construction-engineering journals spoke admiringly of "[t]he monopoly of large and difficult work, which the more powerful firms deservedly possess....''[42] And by mid-century, one large U.S. firm explained its post-World War II attachment to the world market by reference to the fact that because international projects called for "more than the ordinary amount of knowledge, know-how and construction ability...only larger contractors are equipped to handle" them.[43] In effect, the scale of the projects themselves created functionally equivalent barriers to entry—as it still does.[44]

Since even the greatest mid-Victorian entrepreneurial contractors such as Thomas Brassey and Morton Peto lacked training as engineers, a question arises as to the basis of their role as international carriers of engineering technology.[45] This question poses itself with even greater force at the end of the nineteenth and beginning of the twentieth century with respect to a contractor such as George Pauling, who, "with no capital but his brains and magnificent physique," excelled chiefly at physically assaulting those who got in his way. Yet he is credited with having built a number of railways in South Africa and all of Rhodesia's.[46]

The civil engineering knowledge and technology required to build

---

[38]*Id.* at 16.

[39]See chapters 4-6, 9, and 10 below.

[40]See chapters 4, 5, 9, and 10 below. For an example of embodied technology conferring a competitive advantage in railway construction in the 1860s, see Robert Middlemas, *The Master Builders: Thomas Brassey; Sir John Aird; Lord Cowdray; Sir John Norton-Griffiths* 96 (1963).

[41]Middlemas, *Master Builders* at 307.

[42]"When Contract Work is Advisable," 53 *ER* 468 (1906) (editorial).

[43]"One Firm's Formula for Success: Diversification" at 40 (Utah Construction Co.).

[44]See chapter 12 below.

[45]Revealing light was shed on the diffusion of the requisite engineering knowledge by a British colonel in the Bengal Engineers, who stated in the 1850s that although his military engineers could construct the bridges, embankments, and viaducts for railways, they would have to go to England for experience for building stations and engine-sheds. *Report from the Select Committee on East India (Railways)*, Q. 3454 at 243 (14 *PP* 1857-58 [161]).

[46]*Times*, Feb. 13, 1919, at 14, col. 2 (obituary) (quotation); *The Chronicles of a Contractor: Being the Autobiography of the Late George Pauling* 60-61 (David Bucahn ed., 1926).

technically challenging mountain routes for many non-European railroads generally exceeded the capacities of formal and informal colonial societies in the nineteenth and early twentieth centuries.[47] This gap widened when it came to boring long tunnels through rock[48] or erecting bridges such as the spectacular 135-meter high, two-hinged spandrel-braced steel arch Victoria Falls Bridge, the world's highest railway bridge when constructed cantilever-wise over the Zambezi at the turn of the century.[49] In the 1850s, for example, when the Brazilian government sought to build the country's first railway linking Rio de Janeiro with regions beyond the coastal escarpment, the British contractor "was given the freedom to build the road as he saw fit, since the Brazilians frankly admitted that they did not know the first thing about the special problems involved in crossing the *serra*."[50]

Even the Japanese Meiji state, which consciously sought to avoid dependence on foreign capital, not only borrowed almost £1 million in London in 1870 to finance construction of its first railway, from Yokohama to Tokyo, and mortgaged the loan with railway receipts and customs duties, but also employed English engineers (in part to train Japanese engineers) to build all of its initial lines.[51]  Significantly, however, after internal political opposition to this concession erupted, the Japanese government decided to carry out the work itself rather than to engage foreign contractors.  The English engineers were therefore required to follow the terms dictated by the government.[52]  The Japanese learned much from this experience and soon established their own engineering schools—initially staffed by Westerners.[53]  Contrary to the foreign engineers' advice, Japan proceeded to use its own contractors for future rail construction.[54]

---

[47]See e.g., F. Baltzer, *Kolonial- und Kleinbahnen*, pt. 2: *Bauliche Ausgestaltung von Bahn und Fahrzeug* 36-37 (1983 [1920]). For a detailed technical description of the engineering aspects of one colonial railway project followed by a discussion by the leading engineers of the day, see William Ridley, "The Grand River Viaduct, Mauritius Railways," in 25 *MPICE* 237 (1866).

[48]On the compressed-air boring machinery that made possible tunneling through rock in the Alps in the 1850s and 1860s, see "The Seven-Mile Tunnel Through the Alps," 8 *Builder* 231 (1850); "Passage of the Alps—Railways in Italy," 11 *Builder* 354-55 (1853); "An Account of the Tunnel Through Mont Cenis," 20 *Builder* 381 (1862); "The Tunnel Through the Alps," 21 *Builder* 666-68 (1863); Helps, *Life and Labours of Mr. Brassey* at 178-80. Yet at the same time an Australian firm built a tunnel in New Zealand through "basaltic rocks of the hardest description, against which the machinery employed at Mt. Cenis would be powerless." "The Lyttleton Tunnel, Canterbury, New Zealand," 21 *Builder* 811 (1863).

[49]See "The Victoria Falls Bridge," 99 *Engineer* 339 (1905); George Hobson, "The Victoria Falls Bridge," 170 *MPICE* 1 (1907); G. Hobson, "The Great Zambezi Bridge," in 2 *The Story of the Cape to Cairo Railway and River Route, from 1887 to 1922: The Main Line as It Exists To-Day from the Cape to the Nile Delta* 43-59 (n.d. [1922]); F. Baltzer, *Die Kolonialbahnen mit besonderer Berücksichtigung Afrikas* 139-43 (1916). For an overview of the engineering design of mid-Victorian railway tunnels and bridges, see G. Drysdale Dempsey, *The Practical Railway Engineer* 103-249 (1855).

[50]Richard Graham, *Britain and the Onset of Modernization in Brazil 1850-1914*, at 53 (1968). See also Stephen Haber, *Industry and Underdevelopment: The Industrialization of Mexico, 1890-1940*, at 30 (1989).

[51]See *Times*, Apr. 5, 1870, at 12, col. 1; "Railways in Japan," 29 *Engineer* 194 (1870); *Times*, Mar. 14, 1876, at 10, col. 4 (the line was sold for £600,000 to a Japanese corporation); J. Rein, *The Industries of Japan* 513 (1889); E. Herbert Norman, *Japan's Emergence as a Modern State: Political and Economic Problems of the Meiji Period* 114-17, 121-22 (1940); W. Macpherson, *The Economic Development of Japan c. 1868-1941*, at 37 (1987). See also Richard Brunton, "The Japan Lights," 47 *MPICE* 1 (1877) (when Britain, France, and the United States demanded the erection of lighthouses in the treaty ports, Japan acquiesced, but lacking the technology, let foreigners build them).

[52]Kōtsū hakubutsukan, *Tetsudo no nihon: Tokaido shin kansen kaitsū shuppan* 5-11 (1964); Masaho Noda et al., *Nihon no tetsudo: seiritsu to tenkai* 7-27 (1986).

[53]See e.g., "Engineering Education in Japan," 21 *Engineering* 152 (1876); "The Imperial College of Engineering, Tokei, Japan," 24 *Engineering* 74 (1877).

[54]See "The Railways of Japan," 24 *Engineer* 179, 180 (1877); "The Construction of Railways in Japan," 25 *Engineer* 379 (1878) (racist account); William Potter, "Railway Work in Japan," 56 *MPICE* 2, 14 (1879); W. Cargill, *id.* at 17-20 (discussion contribution). Where necessary, the Japanese continued to permit Western and especially English firms to transplant new technology to Japan, after which indigenous contractors took control. See e.g., John Turner, "The Construction of the Yokohama Water-Works," 100 *MPICE* 277 (1890).

Shortly after the turn of the century, the Chinese financed, engineered, and built their own railway, demonstrating that foreign-built lines in the territorial concession areas were more politically imposed than technologically required. The fact that the Chinese even built their line more cheaply than the foreigners, in part by dispensing with the "middlemen or compradors" used by Western firms,[55] inspired the leading U.S. construction-engineering journal to engage in an unwonted polemic against "this occidental, or perhaps Caucasian condescension," which refused to grasp that Western-trained engineers were all brothers under the skin—"that off on the other side of the globe yellow men in queer costumes are working out the same problems as are we, and apparently are doing it equally as [sic] well."[56]

Despite the technological gap between metropoles and periphery in the nineteenth century, Latin American engineers in a number of cases also built—or prepared the plans for, or approved the plans of, European or U.S. contractors for—several technically demanding railways in the Andes.[57] While some South American states continued to rely on European or U.S. firms,[58] others, in order to avoid bond issues, promotion expenses, and contractors' profits, built their own, co-opting a few foreign engineers.[59] By the 1930s, the formation of a critical mass of native engineers prompted the Mexican government to stop hiring foreign engineers and Mexican engineers to petitition the legislature to exclude U.S. engineers altogether.[60]

Another way of posing the question articulated by Kindleberger is as follows: If the labor, scientific knowledge, technology, means of production, and the money capital to buy them all can be purchased on the world if not the local market, why did or do less developed countries permit, invite, or prefer advanced capitalist conquistadors to produce their built environment rather than assemble the requisite organizations themselves? This question is particularly pertinent for the mid-nineteenth century when even the largest British international railway contractors "were not multinational corporations, []or even a limited company, but a loose partnership with a variety of other partners and agents, constantly dissolving and reforming in new guises."[61]

The question becomes more pointed still with regard to the spectacular mountain railway construction in South America in the 1860s and 1870s by the American, Henry Meiggs, who had fled San Francisco after committing forgeries, without an organization, training or experience as an engineer or building

---

[55]See J. Dobbins, "The Imperial Peking-Kalgan Railway and Its Extension," 64 *EN* 191, 192 (1910).

[56]64 *EN* 207 (editorial).

[57]See A. Currie, *The Grand Trunk Railway of Canada* 28 (1957); Brian Fawcett, *Railways of the Andes* 44 (1963); Daniel Headrick, *Tentacles of Progress: Technology Transfer in the Age of Imperialism, 1850-1940*, at 69-70 (1988); Wolfgang Schivelbusch, *Geschichte der Eisenbahnreise: Zur Industrialisierung von Raum und Zeit im 19. Jahrhundert* 90-92 (1977); Watt Stewart, *Henry Meiggs: Yankee Pizarro* 49, 87-89, 104-108, 110-11 (1968 [1946]); Rory Miller, "Transferring Techniques: Railway Building and Management on the West Coast of South America," in Rory Miller & Henry Finch, *Technology Transfer and Economic Development in Latin America, 1850-1930*, at 1, 10-13 (1986) (on Chilean engineers). For nontechnical accounts of the relevant engineering technolgies in the nineteenth century, see L. Vernon-Harcourt, *Achievements in Engineering During the Last Half Century* (1892); Archibald Williams, *How It Is Done; or, Victories of the Engineer* (1908); Richard Kirby & Philip Laurson, *The Early Years of Modern Civil Engineering* (1932).

[58]See e.g., G. Sawyer, "The Transandean Railway from Arica, Chile, to La Paz, Bolivia," 70 *EN* 1059 (1913) (built by the firm of Sir John Jackson [Chile] Ltd.).

[59]See e.g., "Railway Construction in Ecuador Just South of the Equator," 71 *EN* 1053, 1054 (1914).

[60]See "Mexico to Stop Hiring Foreign Engineers," 117 *ENR* 875 (1936); "Mexicans Move to Exclude American Engineers," 119 *ENR* 533 (1937).

[61]R. Joby, *The Railway Builders: Lives and Works of the Victorian Railway Contractors* 73 (1983). On why Britain's largest international builders—Brassey and Peto—rejected legal forms that would have limited their liability, see Middlemas, *Master Builders* at 98.

contractor.  In performing the contracts that the governments of Chile and Peru had awarded him, Meiggs was constrained to purchase all the factors of production in the relevant markets, which were generally located outside the country of performance.    If the state financed all of Meiggs's operations itself by hypothecating state revenues and guano sales in Europe in any event, what did Meiggs offer that Peruvians lacked?  In Meiggs's own case they appear merely to have been wanting the ingenuity to devise the system of pyramiding bribes that Meiggs developed to "manage[] the men who managed Peru."[62]

The point made by the story of this one particular buccaneer is larger than its sordid context.  In contrasting Victorian railway engineers and contractors, the social historian Asa Briggs inadvertently focuses on the latter's international raison d'être:

> [C]ontractors had to make their terms with governing classes in the cities, in Parliament, and in distant and difficult countries like Egypt and Mexico. A local contractor would have to learn how to handle the Mayor: an international contractor had to learn to handle Prince Couza or Porfirio Diaz. The engineer's skills came to depend more and more on the possession of expert knowledge, even though there was often long and bitter disagreement between...experts about answers to particular problems: the contractor's skills were more varied, requiring a combination of judgement and imagination. ... The skills could only be learnt through experience.... Four of the skills implied different kinds of judge-ment—first financial manipulation; second, knowledge of bricks and mortar, iron and steel; third, ability to handle a heterogeneous and often foreign labour force; and fourth, political capacity, measured not only by the winning of contracts but by the orderly and profitable completion of them.[63]

In short, the early international construction contractors were the archetypical Schumpeterian innovating entrepreneurs who

> revolutionize[d] the pattern of production.... To undertake such new things is difficult and constitutes a distinct economic function, first, because they lie outside of the routine tasks which everybody understands and, secondly, because the environment resists in many ways.... To act with confidence beyond the range of familiar beacons and to overcome that resistance requires aptitudes that are present in only a small fraction of the population and that define the entrepreneurial function....[which] does not consist in...inventing anything.... It consists in getting things done.[64]

The enormous competitive advantage of being a pioneer who has succeeded "in getting things done" cannot be neglected in this context.   Where an enormously expensive infrastructure project such as a nineteenth-century railway or a twentieth-century hydroelectric dam or nuclear power plant involves obvious long-term multifaceted fundamental transformations of the natural, physical, and social-economic environments that are also perceived as capable of unleashing catastrophic damage,[65] the first firms to perform successfully are able to erect a reputational barrier to competition for orders from risk-averse purchasers eager to avoid the kind of "public, spectacular, visible" failure that would "reflect badly on the prestige of the country and its regime."[66]

---

[62]Stewart, *Henry Meiggs* at 110-15, 119, 158-64, 96, 263-70, 44-55 (quotation at 47).

[63]Asa Briggs, "Foreword," in Middlemas, *Master Builders* at 13, 15.

[64]Joseph Schumpeter, *Capitalism, Socialism and Democracy* 132 (1966 [1942]).

[65]See e.g., *Dams in Africa: An Interdisciplinary Study of Man-Made Lakes in Africa* (Neville Rubin & William Warren ed., 1968); 1 Edward Goldsmith & Nicholas Hildyard, *The Social and Environmental Effects of Large Dams: Overview* (1984).

[66]J.E. Goldthorpe, *The Sociology of the Third World: Disparity and Involvement* 151 (1975). Successful performance by a leading construction firm emphatically does not mean that it adopted a holistic ecological

This particular aspect of entrepreneurial innovation is well illustrated by the career of the overtowering figure of nineteenth-century British international railway constructors. In 1834, for example, when Brassey completed his first successful railway contract:

> The construction of railways...was...altogether a novelty, not only to him, but to all persons engaged in it. [I]t required new modes of operation, and the creation of skilled labour of a new kind; also the management of larger bodies of men than hitherto had been brought together for public works, and a more rapid movement of these *armies* of labouring men....[67]

Because George Stephenson, Britain's leading railway engineer, recognized that he could rely on Brassey's organizational talents, Brassey's career was launched. The experience and reputation thus gained then inspired Joseph Locke, the engineer in charge of the first British overseas railway project, to select Brassey to build the line in France over untested French contractors submitting untrustworthy bids.[68] Once such organizations had acquired extensive practical knowledge of the potential sources of miscalculation on bidding, it became difficult for invaders to underbid them without disastrous consequences for the safety of the finished product or the neophytes' finances.[69]

The oligopolistic structure of the world construction market in the twentieth century has often thrown into relief not so much the question as to why and how First World multinational firms compete with local Third World firms, but rather the fact that many of their projects would not be built at all in the absence of such penetration. For the nineteenth century, when contractors' organizations were much more primitive, the situation was much less clear cut; perhaps at most such projects would have been built but with some delay.[70]

Analysis of international oligopolistic competition is complicated by firms' linkages to and differential intervention by the various national states. Kindleberger has proposed a tripartite classification of firms operating outside the political borders of their head offices: the national firm with foreign operations, the multinational corporation, and the international corporation. The national firm, which is "[f]irst and foremost...a citizen of a particular country,...must earn a higher return on foreign than on home investment because the former is risky, the latter risk-free." The multinational firm, which "seeks to be a good citizen of each country where it has operations," accepts varying rates of profit. The international corporation, in contrast, which "has no country to which it owes more loyalty than any other,...equalizes the return on its invested capital in every country, after adjusting for risk which is free of the myopia that says home investment is automatically risk-free and all foreign investments are risky." Perceiving a tendency toward ultimate evolution into the international corporation, Kindleberger suggests that the latter "can develop as a monopolist or as an instrument of national goals, or it can operate in the cosmopolitan interest to spread

---

approach that anticipated and avoided numerous adverse environmental impacts, but simply that the narrow reductionist economic-technological goal, for example, of producing cheap electric power, was achieved without the short-term self-destruction of this particular element of the built environment. See Barry Commoner, "Summary of the Conference: On the Meaning of Ecological Failures in International Development," in *The Careless Technology: Ecology and International Development* xxi-xxix (M. Farvar & John Milton ed., 1972); Gilbert White, "Organizing Scientific Investigations to Deal with Environmental Impacts," in *id.* at 914-26.

[67]Helps, *Life and Labours of Mr. Brassey* at 27.

[68]Joseph Locke, "Address of the President," 17 *MPICE* 128, 143 (1858).

[69]Helps, *Life and Labours of Mr. Brassey* at 25-30, 58.

[70]See Stewart, *Henry Meiggs* at 345 (railways would have been built but later without Meiggs); Middlemas, *Master Builders* at 21, 45, 88 (infrastructure would have been built a decade later).

technology, reallocate capital, and enlarge competition."[71]

From Brassey to Bechtel, global construction firms have always performed all three of these roles because as individual capitals seeking the greatest possible self-valorization they are also creators and agents of the world market. By incorporating new regions, products, and producers into the system of universal production for exchange and universal appropriation of nature, they demonstrate "the great civilizing influence of capital."[72]   But the tendency of capital, including construction capital, to reproduce on an expanded scale of accumulation is common to all national capitals; consequently, they all seek to overcome their national overproduction crises through the world market, which in turn cyclically both counteracts and globalizes those national crises.[73]  Individual capitalist and individual national advantage-seeking is inextricably bound up with the aforementioned civilizing influence: that linkage is the form in which the invisible hand operates on the world market.

Like large-scale manufacturing capital, which was driven to export its commodities and to invest abroad, Brassey and other large nineteenth-century contractors were "compelled...to continuous activity" outside of Britain and then outside of Europe in order to amortize their fixed capital: "There was in fact no choice for him but to go on."[74]  In the most intense crises, such as that of 1866, which bankrupted Brassey's sometime partner, Peto, such capital had to be liquidated.[75]  The quasi-monopoly that Brassey or Peto had forged in the non-European periphery offered an escape to "secure profits" from a domestic market competitively ruined by the presence of many small contractors "who were content with profits on a scale too narrow to satisfy him or the enormous overheads of his organization."[76]

Just as the nineteenth-century railway builders acted as agents both of the world market and of British capital in general by internationalizing in order both to amortize their capital and to maintain their accumulatable profit, so, too, late-twentieth-century construction firms have willy-nilly become bearers of internationalizing forces.  Such world market forces, in turn, both favor the aggregate national capitals and states of which these firms are still constitutent components and promote the accumulation of new capitals in the erstwhile periphery, while creating the possibilities of crises on a global scale.[77]

These tensions created by the anarchy of private production for profit that is enmeshed in a universal social system are mirrored in the career trajectories of several pioneering British contractors, the results of whose activities on the programmatic level "were as much random as planned: there was no...great conspiracy to subject countries to 'economic imperialism'...."[78]  Yet in examining the details, their biographer inadvertently conceptualizes the systemic impact of the world market:

> Brassey became a determining figure in the economy of whole states; enticing

[71]Kindleberger, *American Business Abroad* at 180, 182, 183, 184.

[72]Karl Marx, *Grundrisse der Kritik der politischen Ökonomie (Rohentwurf) 1857-1858,* at 313 (1953).

[73]See Karl Marx, 3 *Das Kapital: Kritik der politischen Ökonomie,* in Karl Marx [&] Friedrich Engels, 25 *Werke* 247-50 (1964 [1894]); [Klaus] Busch, [Wolfgang] Schöller, [& Frank] Seelow, *Weltmarkt und Weltwährungskrise* 14 (1971).

[74]Middlemas, *Master Builders* at 59.

[75]See "Messrs Peto, Betts, and Co.," *Economist,* June 16, 1866, at 698-99; Middlemas, *Master Builders* at 29-32, 105-10. Hedley Smyth, *Property Companies and the Construction Industry in Britain* 70-77 (1985), fails to grasp this connection for the nineteenth or the twentieth century.

[76]Middlemas, *Master Builders* at 91. On Brassey's organization, see *id.* at 42.

[77]See chapters 12-13 below.

[78]Middlemas, *Master Builders* at 24.

them by the initial and enormous capital outlay to acquire a huge national debt and in the end to the necessity of creating national industries—forcing them to specialize in order to trade with the West and to make the railways pay: an economic determinant of far greater importance than he himself saw...; almost a random consequence....[79]

Consequently, these international infrastructuralists could no more escape the web of the world market than the raw-materials-producing countries in which they operated:

> In underdeveloped countries enormous tracts of land or controlling blocks of shares were to be part of the price paid, and the contractor's return could not...be in cash, but in increased land values, in the profits of colonization, in the growth of ports and of trade which increased the value of their holdings;...they had to be colonizers and gamble on the future needs of a world market....[80]

Late-twentieth-century policy-oriented discussions of the role of such multinational enterprises tend to avoid the linkages between national rates of profit and the dynamics of the world market. Instead, implicitly denying the assumption that a "business firm's behavior is determined by" requirements of profit maximization, "not by its nationality,"[81] national industrial policy advocates have formulated a dichotomized view of transnational firms. Over against the "pure multinational" or so-called denationalized firm—Kindleberger's "international" corporation—which seeks to maximize its own net earnings and hence "owes its allegiance to no particular country," these policymakers set the "national multinational." The latter type of firm "is pledged to promote the welfare of its home country's citizens." As "agents of their national economies," the national multinationals' "foreign investments are...geared to increasing the real wages" of their national working class.[82]

In light of the fact that even purely national firms do not categorically evince such quasi-eleemosynary behavior, it is unclear what mechanisms might be supposed to trigger this supra-class transmogrification of the firm once it has become drawn into the world market.[83] Although, again, from Brassey to Bechtel, construction firms have profitably served avowedly national goals in projecting the economic power of individual and collective capitalist customers and the political-economic and military power of their nation-state customers, these commercial engagements have always taken place within frameworks constrained by antagonistic national class and international politics.[84]

---

[79]*Id.* at 80.

[80]*Id.* at 80, 81. On such a concession in connection with the railway that Brassey and Wheelwright built in Argentina in the 1860s, see *id.* at 100-101.

[81]Stephen Hymer, "Direct Foreign Investment and the National Economic Interest," in *idem, The Multinational Corporation: A Radical Approach* 173 (1979 [1966]).

[82]Robert Reich, *The New American Frontier* 260-61, 263 (1983). On the possibility of internationally induced denationalization, see Ernest Mandel, *Der Spätkapitalismus* 306-307 (1973 [1972]).

[83]See e.g. Peter Drucker, *The New Society: The Anatomy of Industrial Order* (1962 [1949]). For evidence that Japanese firms have begun to be forced to abandon the role that Reich ascribes to them, see Andrew Pollack, "Japan's Companies Moving Production to Sites Overseas," *NYT*, Aug. 29, 1993, sect. 1, at 1, col. 3 (nat. ed.).

[84]See chapters 4-9, 12 below.

# PART II

# CONSTRUCTING THE WORLD MARKET: THE HISTORICAL COURSE TO WORLD WAR II

In its [the Suez Canal's] formation history has repeated itself, and the relics of the ancient canal (now hardly to be traced) attest how surely Nature heals the wounds made on her surface, and how she is ever working to efface the signs of labour and skill....

"The Suez Canal," 8 *Engineering* 353 (1869) (editorial)

# 3

# The Rise of Large British Railway Construction Firms

It has been said with some truth that the civil engineer never makes anything but an income. Railways, harbours, docks, are almost invariably made by contractors.[1]

## The Separation of Construction Contracting from Engineering

It is not easy to say at what historical period the contractor came into existence.... [I]t seems to have been discovered automatically that the world got on best with a division of labour, the engineer to design and the contractor to make.[2]

During the early railway era, when the leading British railway engineers such as George Stephenson (1781-1848),[3] his son, Robert Stephenson (1803-1859),[4] his one-time apprentice Joseph Locke (1805-1860),[5] Charles Vignoles (1793-1875),[6] Isambard Kingdom Brunel (1806-1859),[7] and John Hawkshaw (1811-91),[8] virtually monopolized the design and execution of the undertakings in Britain, construction contracting was not yet clearly separated from the tasks of the pioneering engineers.[9] The rapid proliferation of rail lines, however, soon exceeded the engineers' capacity to oversee all aspects of the business on behalf of the railway owners. The increase in the size of the operations that the new contractors were able to bring under their control in the 1830s and 1840s relieved the engineers, in their capacity as employees or consultants of the railway companies, of part of their far-flung tasks.

Nor was this process of the separation of the two functions in these early stages spontaneous or unwanted. Locke, for example, whom *The Times* eulogized as "the remaining chief of the engineering world" after the deaths of Brunel and

---

[1]"English Engineers and American Bridges," 87 *Engineer* 391 (1899) (editorial).

[2]"Engineers and Contractors," 113 *Engineer* 98 (1912) (editorial).

[3]See John Rowland, *George Stephenson: Creator of Britain's Railways* (1954).

[4]19 *MPICE* 176-82 (1860) (obituary).

[5]See 20 *MPICE* 141-48 (1861) (obituary).

[6]20 *Engineering* 400 (1875).

[7]See 19 *MPICE* 169-73 (1860) (obituary); Peter Hay, *Brunel: His Achievements in the Transport Revolution* (1973); *The Works of Isambard Kingdom Brunel: An Engineering Appreciation* (Alfred Pugsley ed. 1976); Adrian Vaughan, *Isambard Kingdom Brunel: Engineering Knight-Errant* (1991).

[8]107 *MPICE* 321-35 (1891) (obituary).

[9]See James Brand, "Working Methods of Engineering Contractors," 89 *Engineer* 262 (1900).

Stephenson,[10]

> hoped that the time would come when the contractor would see almost as quickly
> as himself, or at least after very simple explanation, the nature and cost of the
> works which he had to construct; and that the fair remuneration which had
> accrued from the skilful carrying out of short, would soon enable him to
> undertake much longer lengths. He had been very patient and painstaking with
> a number of small capitalists. He relied upon soon having to do with a few larger
> ones.[11]

This deepening of the division of labor presupposed that the large
contractors had appropriated the technological advances embodied in the new
engineering principles. This transfer process took place by means of the quasi-
apprenticeships that the contractors (such as Edward Betts) served under the
engineers (such as George Stephenson), who supervised the overall railway
construction process.[12]  A doubtless somewhat glorified version of the transition
from an engineer-driven system to one in which the contractor was at the very least
a co-equal if not the dominant element was offered by the Institution of Civil
Engineers in its obituarial appreciation of the largest railway construction
contractor, Brassey:

> The early contractors were...men of strong natural abilities, insight into cost and
> method of executing work amounting to instinct, low tastes, violent habits, and
> grasping tenacity of purpose.  A contract being once made, it seemed to be
> regarded as natural that the contractor should set his wits to work to make the
> most of it.  This was done, on the one hand, by grinding his labourers under the
> pressure of the truck system..., and on the other hand by "scamping" his work.
> Under the three grades of engineers ordinarily engaged ranked an array of
> inspectors.  These were men set to watch that the requisitions were not eluded....
> Very frequently these men began by displaying extreme severity, greatly to the
> cost of the contractor.  As a rule, vexatiously minute inspectors were open to
> bribes.  ...  This matter once arranged, the less scrupulous contractors and sub-
> contractors often drove a roaring trade....  Against this system of scamping and
> bribery Mr. Brassey was one of the first to make a stand.  ...  It was his plan...to
> "smother the engineer."   This smothering, however, consisted only in
> extinguishing all just causes of complaint.  To do his work fairly and faithfully,
> to render inspection superfluous, and thus to annihilate the power of the
> inspectors, was...one main element of Mr. Brassey's extraordinary success.[13]

Missing from this version is the strategy that railway company engineers
devised to suppress scamping.  Because small contractors gave no bond or security,
the companies were frequently compelled to pay them or an equally incompetent
successor to complete work.  In order to avoid this problem, engineers such as
Locke required contractors to deposit with the railway directors 10 per cent of the
capital at stake, which they forfeited if they violated their contractual
obligations.[14]   Once the capital-less contractor was eliminated, the transition to
large contracting organizations linked to solid financing intermediaries was
irreversible.

To be sure, even the pioneering British engineers were autodidacts, who
shared the typical merits and defects of the self-taught.  This British laissez-faire
model of the engineering foundations of the industrial revolution stood in sharp
contrast with contemporaneous developments in France.  French civil engineering,

---

[10]*Times*, Sept. 21, 1860, at 10, col. 1.

[11]Joseph Devey, *The Life of Joseph Locke* 145-46 (1862).

[12]"Edward Ladd Betts," 13 *Engineering* 187 (1872) (obituary).

[13]33 *MPICE* 246, 248-49 (1872).

[14]Devey, *Life of Joseph Locke* at 121-22.

institutionally grounded since the eighteenth century in the state Corps des Ponts et Chaussées (1716) and the École des Ponts et Chaussées (1775), attained a theoretical orientation that insured it international scientific-technical preeminence until the mid-nineteenth century.  In contrast, the British engineers' practical, empirical, and inductive approach was based on apprenticeship, free enterprise, and private cost and profit considerations rather than on the French model of formal engineering education and construction projects (including railways), planned, built, and financed by the central government.[15]  The establishment of the Army Corps of Engineers and of a civil engineering curriculum at the U.S. Military Academy at West Point in the first quarter of the nineteenth century positioned engineering in the United States somewhere between the British and French models.[16]

The elder Stephenson best personified the British empirical tradition.  The overtowering figure in the formative years of the railway based on his crucial contributions to the development of the locomotive steam engine, he nevertheless lacked the capacity for detail to survey, organize, and execute a great railway project.  But unlike other engineers, who were still thinking in terms of local and regional networks, Stephenson pursued a national perspective, within the framework of which he was able to propose a route that accommodated the requisite engineering necessities, traffic, and local resources that the new line could exploit.  Of particular relevance to the contractors' tasks, Stephenson, Locke, and other engineers surveyed possible routes with a view to calculating and prescribing the gradients and curvature of the road as a function of friction, gravitational force, and the use of the locomotive's power in order to decide whether to trade off steep gradients for short cuts or additional trackage for long levels.  The engineers also recommended the kind of materials to be used for the tracks and roadbed.[17]  These engineering considerations were shaped with reference to the costs of construction of tunnels and bridges, additional fuel, and the constant expenses in engine power and wear and tear of the rolling stock.[18]

The know-how that Brassey, Peto, Betts, Thomas Jackson,[19] George Wythes,[20] and other contractors acquired from engineers in this manner then enabled them to build lines even in Western Europe—albeit always in association with an engineer.[21]  In time, both empirically oriented engineers and experienced contractors even came to nurture a contempt for the theoretically trained continental engineers whom foreign governments assigned as superintendants of the projects but who were "perfectly ignorant of all railway practice."[22]  In turn, professionally educated civil engineers regarded Stephenson as an impostor, who

---

[15]See Arthur Dunham, "How the First French Railways Were Built," 1 *JEH* 12, 13, 18-19 (1941); Hans Straub, *A History of Civil Engineering: An Outline from Ancient to Modern Times* 171-73 (E. Rockwell tr., 1952 [1949]); Frederick Artz, *The Development of Technical Education in France 1500-1850*, at 81-84, 86, 110-11, 162-63, 244-45, 266-68 (1966); D.S.L. Cardwell, *Turning Points in Western Technology: A Study of Technology, Science and History* 122-27 (1972); John Weiss, *The Making of Technological Man: The Social Origins of French Engineering Education* 6-12, 222-25 (1982).

[16]See Leonard White, *The Jeffersonians: A Study in Administrative History 1801-1829*, at 251-65 (1965 [1951]); Daniel Calhoun, *The American Civil Engineer: Origins and Conflict* 37-50 (1960).

[17]See Devey, *Life of Joseph Locke* at 137-43; Calhoun, *American Civil Engineer* at 58-60.

[18]G. Drysdale Dempsey, *Practical Railway Engineer* 2-55 (1855).  At the time, Locke prevailed against Stephenson in his view that the cost of additional fuel and motive power required by steeper gradients was less than the sum needed to pay the interest on the additional capital required by longer and more easily graded routes.  L. Rolt, *Great Engineers* 125 (1962).

[19]On Jackson (1808-1885), see *Times*, Jan. 13, 1885, at 6, col. 5.

[20]Wythes (1811-1883) built railways in Europe, the Orient, and North America.  See the obituaries in *Times*, Mar. 7, 1883, at 7, col. 5; 74 *MPICE* 294-97 (1883).

[21]John Hawkshaw was one of the key railway engineers operating overseas during this period for private contractors and British colonial governments.

[22]John Valentine, "Description of the Line and Works of the Railway from Lisbon to Santarem," in 21 *MPICE* 1, 23 (1859) (discussion contribution of George Bidder).

had never acquired the technical qualifications of the profession.[23]   The large
staffs of scientific and commercial personnel that, for example, Brassey's and
Peto's organizations maintained, the origins of which can also be traced back to the
eighteenth-century canal building organizations,[24] eventually promoted a re-
consolidation of engineering and construction functions in twentieth-century
multinational construction-engineering firms.[25]   Even in the late nineteenth
century, many British contractors were also engineers while some of the most able
construction-engineers were contractors.[26]

## Subcontracting as Profit-Maximizing Labor Force Management

> We must get more money out of business...than we put in...and the only way to
> do this is to turn labor into capital by means of existing capital.[27]

In order to capture what was both novel and indispensable about the great
railway contractors, it is necessary to focus on their capacity to organize
unprecedentedly large projects—especially the recruitment and supervision of huge
labor forces.  Of Brassey, after all, it has been said that "in the management and
control of large labour forces he was a genius without rival."[28]   The large
contractors who emerged in the 1830s have been seen as successors to those who
undertook civil engineering projects in the later eighteenth and early nineteenth
centuries under the supervision of such engineers as James Brindley (1716-1772)
and Thomas Telford (1757-1834).[29]

Indeed the term "contractor," in the sense of one who undertakes work by
contract in the building trades, arose in the eighteenth century.[30]   In its generic
sense the term has become misleading in its unique application to construction
since "[e]very manufacturer is a contractor—nothing more, nothing less.  The
primary difference is that the manufacturer has a fixed plant, whereas the
contractor moves his plant from place to place."[31]   It remains to explore whether
this connotation of a contractually stipulated price-cost structure rather than of a
capital investment requiring valorization captures a significant aspect of the
economics of the construction industry or merely garnishes an ideological pose.
In any event, the Victorian railway contractors' adoption of subcontracting as a
management method as it had previously evolved in road and above all in canal
building—the workers on which, *navigators* or *navvies*, formed a personal and

---

[23]See e.g. Samuel Smiles, *The Life of George Stephenson and of His Son Robert Stephenson* 281-95,
353-61, 368-74 (1868); L. Rolt, *The Railway Revolution: George and Robert Stephenson* 227, 250-56, 280,
296 (1962 [1960]); Michael Robbins, *George and Robert Stephenson* 27-28 (1966); S. Checkland, *The Rise
of Industrial Society in England 1815-1885*, at 85 (1971 [1964]); Arthur Helps, *Life and Labours of Mr.
Brassey: 1805-1870*, at 225-28 (1872); Leland Jenks, *The Migration of British Capital to 1875*, at 134-35
(1963 [1927]); Robert Middlemas, *The Master Builders* 34, 121, 166, 262, 310 (1963).

[24]See W.H.G. Armytage, *A Social History of Engineering* 129 (4th ed. 1976 [1961]).

[25]For the claim that at least in some fields engineers assumed contractors' functions, see Per Jensen,
"Work and Qualifications of Civil Engineers in Relation to the Development of the Labour Process in the
Construction Industry," in [4] *PBE, 1982: Labour in Building and Construction* 1-23, 1-24 (1983).

[26]See e.g., "Contractors and Engineers," 50 *Engineer* 425 (1880) (editorial); "The Liege Contractors'
Congress," 52 *Engineer* 117 (1881) (editorial).

[27]Maurice Parsons, "The Philosophy of Engineering," 77 *TASCE* 38, 48 (1914).

[28]Rolt, *Railway Revolution* at 214.

[29]See L. Rolt, *Thomas Telford* (1962 [1958]).  Telford acted as engineer for the king of Sweden on the
Gotha Canal beginning in 1808, an enterprise that required the shipment from England in 1819 of 48-ton
iron lock gates. *Id.* at 93-109.  See generally, Samuel Smiles, 1-2 *Lives of the Engineers* (1861).

[30]2 *Oxford English Dictionary* 915 (1961 [1933]).

[31]"What the Great English Engineer, Telford, Said About Day Labor as Compared with Contract
Work," 31 *EC* 345, 346 (1909) (editorial).

linguistic link with railway construction—has crystallized out as the key defining characteristic of the new railway contractors.[32]

The connection between mobilization and control of large bodies of workers on the one hand and subcontracting on the other was in fact crucial. Perhaps the most valuable material on this subject emerged from the evidence presented to two parliamentary inquiries held in 1846 on railways and the abusive conditions of railway laborers near the peak of the second railway mania in Britain when more than a quarter-million workers were constructing new rail networks.[33] Not only did the largest contractors and most influential engineers testify, but Brassey's railway construction operations in France were discussed in detail.

The contractor Peto, whom the engineer Brunel called "probably the largest in the world at present, or that has ever carried on work of this decription,"[34] testified to the Select Committee on Railway Labourers that he had 9,000 men in his employment, 3,700 of whom he employed directly. By 1854, when Peto himself had become a member of Parliament and his field of operations had reached across the oceans, his worldwide employment figures reached 30,000, making him "one of the largest employers of labour in the kingdom."[35] As to unions among his men, he had "never heard anything of the kind at all."[36] Perhaps in mitigation of such deprivation, Peto felt it his "duty to provide them with scriptural instruction." Whether his scriptural readers in their reports to Peto focused on his men's spiritual or other concerns, Peto did not testify. Instead, he stressed that he furnished bibles gratis to all his literate workers in complete derogation of the aforementioned distinction between those in his direct and indirect employ.[37]

In response to a question as to whether he exercised any control over those whom he did not employ directly, Peto stated that:

> The parties to whom I let the work are entirely under my own control; many of them have been gangers under me on previous works, who have saved enough money to buy horses and railway wagons and plant. I let them the earth-work, principally by the lump, instead of employing men directly under myself.[38]

This testimony seemed to suggest that his gangers were petty capitalists who had worked their way up and out of the proletariat.

Yet his and others' testimony was not easily reconcilable on this point. The parliamentary committee also heard that the ganger, who was himself a laborer and the lowest form of subcontractor with twelve to fourteen men below him, was selected for "his power to keep his men in order." Part of their income the gangers took out of their supervisees' pockets by various wage payment and truck strategems.[39] In many instances gangers merely received wages and some

---

[32]See Sidney Pollard, *The Genesis of Modern Management: A Study of the Industrial Revolution in Great Britain* 60-62, 106-10 (1968 [1965]); W. Cunningham, *The Growth of English Industry and Commerce in Modern Times: The Mercantile System* 532-35 (1925); Paul Mantoux, *The Industrial Revolution in the Eighteenth Century* 112-32 (1961 [1928])); Terry Coleman, *The Railway Navvies: A History of the Men Who Made the Railways* 56-65 (1970 [1965]); Charles Hadfield, *British Canals: An Illustrated History* 33-47 (1974 [1950]); *idem, The Canal Age* 50-60 (1981).

[33]See R. Lewis, "Edwin Chadwick and the Railway Labourers," 3 *EHR* (2d ser.) 107 (1950); Phyllis Deane and W.A. Cole, *British Economic Growth 1688-1959: Trends and Structure* 231-32 (1969 [1962]).

[34]*Report from the Select Committee on Railway Labourers* Q. 2060 at 134 (13 *PP* 1846 [530]).

[35]*Id.,* QQ. 1228, 1230 at 72; 130 *PD* (3d ser.) 761 (1854); William Galt, *Railway Reform: Its Importance and Practicability* 352 (1865) (quotation).

[36]*Report from the Select Committee on Railway Labourers,* Q. 1302 at 77.

[37]*Id.,* QQ. 1302, 1348-73 at 77, 80-81.

[38]*Id.,* Q. 1232 at 72.

[39]*Id.,* QQ. 596 (quotation), 225, 229, 603-35, 768-69 at 38, 14, 38-39, 46.

compensation for finding horses, or, as chiefs of butty-gangs, received the money from the contractor and shared it among the workers.[40] Three-quarters of a century later, a U.S. engineer was at least frank enough to admit that the use of the term "contractor" to describe the "penniless" Nicaraguan miners employed "to drive the bore at so much a foot" in building a hydroelectric plant owned by a U.S. company was "misleading." Since the company provided all the materials and equipment and the "contractor" was too impoverished to provide a bond, the contract could not be enforced by the company let alone the workers.[41]

Curiously, whatever efficiencies Peto's organization purportedly derived from this system of delegation were dissipated and perhaps even outweighed by the elaborate hierarchy of supervision which Peto devised and which had no other purpose than to curb his straw bosses' irrepressible kleptomania. Peto's chief agent, who supervised the work in its entirety, had under him subagents, who were in charge of eight or nine miles of track; under these in turn were timekeepers, whose job it was to account for the time of every worker on two miles of track. "The work is then let to gangers, who employ the men." Based on the timekeepers' report of the amounts payable to each worker, Peto testified, the accounts were made up and

> in convenient change, and in a sealed bag, is handed over to the ganger the amount necessary to pay all his men; and it is then the duty of the time-keeper to see that these men are paid the money paid in bulk by me, and that these men have the money in accordance with the amount of time so returned by him to the sub-agent.[42]

Baffled by these arrangements, the committee members asked Peto why he needed the gangers or, alternatively, why he exercised such supervision since he had, after all, let the work to others. Peto's not entirely enlightening responses were that "we cannot have a control without" gangers and that he otherwise would not have the satisfaction of knowing that the workers had been paid properly by his frankenstein, the ganger, who was however "quite safe in my hands"—despite the fact that "[v]ery often" he had had to dismiss gangers for violating his regulations.[43] When Peto let two or three miles in bulk, he engaged in no bargaining with his gangers or ex-gangers: he merely gave them take-it-or-leave-it prices. "If he is a good man, I do not pay the money perhaps every week, but every month, if I know he has plenty of capital; but if not a strong-backed man, as we call it, he has it every fortnight or every week."[44]

In this regard Peto's methods resembled Brassey's, whose "organization of supervisors, inspectors, and sub-inspectors, by which this industrial kingdom was regulated, made the labour of this vast community proceed as methodically as the machinery of a clock."[45] Brassey's subcontractors "did not exactly contract with him, but he appointed them their work, telling them what price he should give for it." Moreover, Brassey furnished "all the materials, and all the plant."[46] As labor-only subcontractors, who supplied 100 to 300 workers, it is unclear how gangers could curtail Brassey's losses when work was delayed or reduce the amount of variable capital that Peto had to advance since he appeared to finance

---

[40]*Id.*, QQ. 2793-99 at 183.

[41]H. Thackwell, "Tunnel Building in Nicaraguan Jungles," 86 *ENR* 821, 822 (1921).

[42]*Report from the Select Committee on Railway Labourers*, Q. 1245 at 73.

[43]*Id.*, QQ. 1248-50, 1276 at 73, 75.

[44]*Id.*, QQ. 1264, 1266 at 74.

[45]Devey, *Life of Joseph Locke* at 150-51.

[46]Helps, *Life and Labours of Mr. Brassey* at 45, 47.

the entire payroll.[47]     Yet Peto insisted that without subletting parts of the construction "a very much larger capital" would be required, indeed, that "it would be almost impracticable, and that in any event it offered advantages that he did "not desire to forego"—or to elucidate.[48] Nor was Peto's account made any more comprehensible by Brunel's testimony that Peto had such "an immense capital" that he could afford the most advanced systems of accounting and superintendence.[49]

These lump-of-labor English gangers, who were also widely used by British contractors overseas,[50] had to be supervised as if they were employees[51] Peto's confused testimony notwithstanding: "I do not exercise any superintendance over him beyond the time-keeper; but then, over him is an agent whose duty it is to watch the progress of the work, to make a weekly report to the principal agent, and to make a report to me also."[52] Peto's attachment to his middlemen is the more puzzling not only for his clear understanding that under labor-protective legislation "the petty contractors, and others under them...would be the difficult people to keep in check thoroughly," but also by virtue of his suggestion that both the railway company and the principal contractor be made responsible for the gangers' failure to pay in cash.[53]

When gangers absconded with his payroll, Peto asserted that he held the navvies harmless—provided that they could convince him that they had not colluded with the ganger.[54] Peto evinced a decided preference to act as his own magistrate in such nonpayment matters, a course of action in which his navvies, like all poor workers in England, were constrained to acquiesce.[55] Like their contemporary native counterparts in India whose wages were pilfered by middlemen, they may have had a cause of action, but the fact that the expenses of litigation would have exceeded the recovery effectively precluded suits in both countries.[56] The middleman system operated in a particularly rapacious manner in the 1850s in India, where it left native construction workers on British railways with only enough "to keep body and soul together."[57]

The only coherent raison d'être for the subcontracting system was offered by Brunel, who testified that all grades of subcontractors,

---

[47]*Report from the Select Committee on Railway Enactments*, Q. 857 at 54 (14 *PP* 1846 [590]); John Francis, *A History of the English Railway: Its Social Relations and Revelations 1820-1845*, I, 271; II, 75-84 (1968 [1851]); Helps, *Life and Labours of Mr. Brassey* at 45-51, 78, 160; Middlemas, *The Master Builders* at 22, 35, 42, 44, 73.

[48]*Report from the Select Committee on Railway Labourers*, Q. 1338 at 79.

[49]*Id.*, Q. 2083 at 137.

[50]See e.g., Valentine, "Description of the Line and Works" at 21. A half-century later the same system was described for the construction of railways supervised by English engineers in China. "These gangers are really contractors for labour of the class to which they themselves belong...." The major difference was that they were paid monthly and "do not require an advance every week, affording...an example to British navvies." Edward Rigby & William Leitch, "Railway Construction in North China," 160 *MPICE* 271, 308 (1905). At the turn of the century, Pauling "sub-contracted to Chinese navvies" railway work he was performing in Borneo. For Pauling's otherwise incredible account, see *Chronicles of a Contractor: Being the Autobiography of the Late George Pauling* 181-85 (David Buchan ed., 1926).

[51]The contractor Thomas Jackson agreed with his questioner that his subcontracts were worded so as to "leave the control of the manner in which the work is conducted in his [Jackson's] hands...." *Report from the Select Committee on Railway Labourers*, Q. 1912 at 124. On the issue of firms' decisions regarding control over employees and non-employees, see Marc Linder & Larry Zacharias, "Opening Coase's Other Black Box: Why Workers Submit to Vertical Integration into Firms," 18 *JCL* 371 (1993).

[52]*Report from the Select Committee on Railway Labourers*, Q. 1266 at 74-75.

[53]*Id.*, QQ. 1338-43 at 79.

[54]*Id.*, QQ. 1333-35 at 79.

[55]*Id.*, QQ. 1277-78 at 75.

[56]*Report from the Select Committee on East India (Railways)*, Q. 1140 at 74 (14 *PP* 1857-58 [161]).

[57]*Id.*, QQ. 1135 and 1140 at 74.

including the lower ones also, are necessary for the protection of such contractors as Mr. Peto and others; but for the competition of the small contractors, I do not think the public would have the advantage of these large contractors, and large capitalists disposed to execute works at low prices. We have contractors very much below Mr. Peto in point of capital...and the way that class of contractors get their work cheap is by subletting the different portions of the work to gangs of excavators and small bricklayers, who have their working bricklayers under them; and the consequence is, therefore, that on these works a very small class of contractors is employed, because the ganger or sub-contractor under the principal contractor is in fact the very contractor for the work, running his risk of the price at which he has taken it being sufficient or not. That leads frequently, certainly, to defaulters, and to distress among the men...; but I do not see, in the first place, that it is possible to prevent it; I do not believe it is at all desirable to prevent it, because but for the fact that we can get works executed at moderate prices, we certainly should not get large capitalists, who would very soon have a monopoly of all these works, to execute works at low prices. The price at which railways are constructed, compared with those at which large government works were constructed 30 years ago, is a strong instance of that; in those days there was a monopoly by the large contractors.[58]

Once Brunel had committed to the system of subcontracting with penny capitalists, it was consistent for him to maintain that if the state prevented the ganger from cheating workers, "the instant the ganger found that the work did not pay him, he could go away and leave the company to pay."[59] But:

If a contractor has taken work at a lower price than he can execute it at, and the contractor fails, the money is not forthcoming; and unless you go back upon the [railway] company...it would be impossible to pay the men. If you did that you would destroy the whole system of contract throughout England; on these large works...you would not have any means of executing those.... [B]ut if you made the company liable for everything, and if they require sufficient security to meet such liabilities, the contractors would directly raise the prices at which they took the work. There are no doubt great difficulties in all this; but the system of free competition for contracts is that which enables us to execute works in England so extensively over the country at a moderate price, and I should fear to destroy this.[60]

Brunel, as an engineer allied with railway owners and viewing construction from the perspective of maximizing the profitability of their (and his own) investments—like the Stephensons, he "died rich"—did nothing less than sketch a system in which such profitability hinged on making workers share fully in all risks.[61] Thus the worker was to suffer not only the wage laborer's normal risk of unemployment and the capitalist's normal risk of not realizing the value of the commodity he has already produced, but even the risk of not realizing the value of a commodity (labor power) that he had already sold and thus of remaining uncompensated for work already performed. This transparently biased in-dividualistic conceptualization of labor was and remained common in the profession. As George Stephenson's nephew explained to the Institution of Civil Engineers in his presidential address three decades after Brunel's parliamentary testimony: "The effect of recent combinations of workmen has been to deny the

---

[58] *Report from the Select Committee on Railway Labourers*, Q. 2063 at 134-35.

[59] *Id.*, Q. 2075 at 136.

[60] *Id.*, QQ. 2087-88 at 137-38.

[61] "Robert Stephenson," 8 *Engineer* 379, 380 (1859) (obituary by the French engineer, Flachat). Engineers sometimes invested in the railways the construction of which they supervised. Vignoles, for example, was the largest shareholder in a Brazilian railway—a circumstance, however, that did not prevent the other shareholders from losing their confidence in him when they suspected that he was ordering the performance of unnecessary construction. "Mr Vignolles [sic] and the Bahia and San Francisco Railway," 22 *Engineer* 340 (1866).

just right of employers to regard either wages or labour as a commodity."[62]

Brunel in effect pleaded for maintenance of an elaborate pyramid of nonresponsibility, which rested quite fittingly on the image of a "man who is working piece-rate at the bottom of a mine [and] is thrown entirely upon his own resources." Any change that made the master liable for accidents that befell those occupying the lower rungs would "inevitably alter the present position of things, by which every department, from highest to lowest, is sublet to men, who are free agents, and seek to execute the work in the cheapest way. Some risks, I admit, are run in consequence; but I do not think that the results of those risks are at all to be compared with the advantage attained in our manufactures generally by that system...."[63]

This brutally frank language of one of the leading mid-nineteenth-century constructional engineers exposes striking structural-functional parallels between hierarchical construction subcontracting on the one hand and its direct late-twentieth-century descendant in the building industry in Britain and elsewhere—labor-only subcontracting or the Lump.[64] Such subcontracting systems are also homologous with the mid-Victorian agricultural gang system and its descendant—the migrant farm labor contracting system in the United States.[65] None of these systems was in any sense physically required by the process of production in construction or agriculture; neither system was in any sense physically more efficient or productive than centrally organized production. Indeed, the Brassey-Peto regime represented precisely such centralization. The only advantage offered to agricultural employers by, and the sole raison d'être of, farm labor contractors is "reducing labor costs by violating labor laws."[66] Common to all of these systems is that the employer, by dealing with a labor contractor, became "an accessory before the fact to his robbing somebody else."[67]

In an era of pervasive state intervention into the employment relationship, such schemes as labor-only subcontracting or farm labor contracting are restorationist devices designed to eject workers from the realm of labor-protective legislation by creating the fiction of self-employment. What is intriguing about the nineteenth-century variant is that even prior to the emergence, and thus in the absence, of state intervention such as minimum wage laws, railway construction subcontractors could fulfill a homologous role by enabling those above them—railway owners and/or large contractors—to get the work done more cheaply and/or to expand their profits by shifting the risk of underpayment or nonpayment to the laborers. And like farm labor contractors today, gangers were financial straw men, whose own impecuniosity rendered legal recourse senseless: "[T]here is often a defeat of justice, where wages are found due because the employers of the men are only lodgers, having no goods, and the magistrates can only proceed against their goods, by distress and sale...."[68]

Even when construction workers were able to secure legal representation, the results were typically disappointing. The construction of the Crystal Palace at mid-

---

[62]George Robert Stephenson, "Address of the President," 44 *MPICE* 2, 11 (1876).

[63]*Report from the Select Committee on Railway Labourers*, Q. 2124 at 141.

[64]See e.g., Michael Ball, "The Housing Production Process and the Crisis of Production," in [4] *PBE 1982: Labour in Building and Construction* 2-18 (1983); Ellen Leopold, "The Costs of Accidents in the British Construction Industry," in *id.*, 1-28, 1-34-1-35.

[65]See Marc Linder, *Migrant Workers and Minimum Wages: Regulating the Exploitation of Agricultural Labor in the United States* (1992).

[66]Philip Martin, *Seasonal Workers in American Agriculture: Background and Issues* 38 (National Commission for Employment Policy, Research Rep. RR-85-04, 1985).

[67]Gradus, "A Treatise on Building by Contract," 14 *Builder* 296, 297 (1856).

[68]*Report from the Select Committee on Railway Labourers* at viii.

century presented one such opportunity, as workers filed 200 wage payment actions against the contractors. When painters sued the large firm of Fox & Henderson, for example, the firm denied liability on the ground that the subcontractor was the employer. The plaintiffs admitted that the alleged subcontractor had hired them, but stated that they had every reason to believe that he was merely the firm's foreman especially since they were paid by the firm. When the judge, who considered subcontractors "a positive evil," asked why the firm paid the wages of those not in its employ, its representative could point merely to custom. The judge, conceding that he could not imagine that Fox even knew of the dispute, then asked the firm's representative why the dispute should not be referred to Fox; the representative rejected this approach as "a bad precedent." The judge then urged the plaintiffs to sue the subcontractor, in whose favor he eventually ruled.[69]

The wage-theft associated with so-called subcontracting flourished among, but did not expire with, the Victorian railway constructors.[70] International construction firms have repeatedly shown a penchant for contractual designation of their work forces as subcontractors. An internationally prominent U.S. firm building highways in Colombia in the 1930s, for example, simply converted its day laborers into sub-contractors, lending them tools and charging for other items.[71] Then again a Danish consortium that built extensive railway systems in Turkey in the 1920s and 1930s was required by the Turkish government to entrust the actual building to local contractors. Because these local contractors lacked experience in railway construction and were "almost without resources...technically, commercially and financially...in effect...all the local contractors had to do was to supply the labour...." The local contractors, in turn, divided the excavation or construction sections into piecework subcontracts. The Danish firms "tolerate[d] the system in spite of its drawbacks, on condition that the contractors take responsibility for the wages of the sub-contractors' men. This was absolutely necessary on account of dishonesty among the sub-contractors." Although it was never explained how contractors with "slender resources at their disposal" could be relied on to compensate for dishonest subcontractors, the salient point was the "cheap labour" of the "well behaved" Turkish peasants with which "machines cannot compete...."[72]

---

[69]Collins & Baker v. Fox & Henderson (Brompton County Ct.), as reported in 9 *Builder* 422, 470 (1851).

[70]Coleman, *Railway Navvies* at 64-65.

[71]Albert Mittag, "Constructing Highways in Colombia," 5 *CE* 361, 362 (1935) (R.W. Hebard & Co.)

[72]"Railway Construction in Asia Minor," 133 *Engineering* 120, 122, 123 (1932).

# 4

# The Internationalization of British Railway Constructors

So long as capital accumulates in this country, it must be expended in some productive way at home or abroad. Judiciously planned public works are always productive and the men who find the means will appoint the agents for carrying out their works, and those agents will always be their own countrymen, so long as they are competent. ... Be sure of this, that while we remain the greatest capitalists of the world, and the chief iron-producers of the world, the world at large will be glad to come to us for our capital, our material, and our scientific skill.[1]

The complex of macro- and microeconomic causes inducing firms to transfer their production across political boundaries is neatly represented in the first major modern paradigm of international construction—British railway building in the mid-nineteenth century. This early phase of the internationalization of construction arose under the specific conditions of uneven development between Great Britain and Western Europe. Later, "a new...international division of labor" between the industrialized nations and the societies that they transformed into their "outlying agricultural...establishments" while dominating their domestic markets generated even more elaborate projects.[2]

The focus in this chapter is on the free-lance constructors and their profit-driven projects in Europe and the overseas white-settler colonies. The next chapter examines the transformation that the burgeoning international railway construction industry underwent as firms became subordinated to the political-economic and military goals of their national states in the exploitation colonies.

### Brassey and Peto

The chief essential of trade is the means of transit. ... It is the great mission of England to supply that want, and increase the amount of profitable employment for her constantly increasing capital.[3]

As the railway construction mania in Britain subsided toward the end of the 1840s—it was not until the *Gründerjahre* following the Franco-Prussian War that Germany surpassed Britain in kilometers of line open—"railway building became

---

[1]"Address of Mr. James Brunlees, President," 72 *MPICE* 2, 21 (1883).

[2]Karl Marx, 1 *Das Kapital: Kritik der politischen Ökonomie* 442 (1867 [reprint, 1959]); John Stuart Mill, *Principles of Political Economy*, Bk. III, ch. 25, § 5 at 685 (W. Ashley ed. 1926 [1848]). See generally Ernest Mandel, *Der Spätkapitalismus* 47-48 (1973 [1972]).

[3]"Railways in China," 18 *Engineer* 283 (1864) (editorial).

a service which Great Britain could dump abroad when her financial and constructing plant could not be kept employed at home."[4] But whereas French capital and the French state, for example, soon overcame "this technical and financial colonization on the part of England,"[5] and became in the latter half of the nineteenth century the dominant force in building and financing European railways, the formal and informal colonies did not.[6]

To the extent that capitalist production in Europe and North America presupposed the mass production of commodities and the mass valorization of capital, those economies could become reliant on distant sources and markets only because faster and cheaper means of transportation and communication made them accessible and accommodated the constant hurling of masses of capital and labor from one sphere of production to another that the new world market increasingly demanded.[7] "British industry was linked to sources of food and raw materials by the world's largest fleet of deep-sea vessels. Further increases in supplies necessitated the improvement of communications at the other end, which by 1850 could only be provided by rail in the absence of a navigable river."[8]

British overseas construction activities therefore had to precede large-scale direct investments overseas by British manufacturing firms: "It was under the auspices of Brassey and Peto and Wheelwright that the full effects of the industrial transformation of Great Britain were transported abroad. And in the middle of the nineteenth century they were the active agents in the migration of much British capital upon the Continent and elsewhere."[9] Although their projects promoted the export of English capital goods associated with the overseas construction, their shifting cosmopolitan alliances with European contractors and financiers eventually helped expand the world market beyond British domination.[10]

In order to appreciate the crucial role that the railway constructors Thomas Brassey (1805-70), Samuel Morton Peto (1809-89), and Edward Betts (1815-72) occupied in globally radiating capitalism, it is first necessary to situate their position within Britain.[11] In contrast with Brassey's modest origins, Peto inherited a large building business from his uncle, Henry Peto. After successful completion

---

[4]Leland Jenks, *The Migration of British Capital to 1875*, at 133-34 (1927) (quotation); Henry Lewin, *The Railway Mania and Its Aftermath 1845-1852* (1936); B. Mitchell, *European Historical Statistics 1750-1970*, at 581-88 (1975).

[5]L. Girard, "Transport," in 6 *The Cambridge Economic History of Europe: The Industrial Revolutions and After: Incomes, Population and Technological Change (I)* 212, 239 (H. Habakkuk & M. Postan ed., 1965).

[6]See Arthur Helps, *Life and Labours of Mr. Brassey: 1805-1870*, at 80-81 (1872); C. Hobson, *The Export of Capital* 119-20 (1963 [1914]); W.O. Henderson, *Britain and Industrial Europe 1750-1870: Studies in British Influence on the Industrial Revolution in Western Europe* 64-75 (2d ed. 1965 [1954]); Rondo Cameron, *France and the Economic Development of Europe 1800-1914*, at 204-325 (1961). On the displacement of English by Danish subcontractors on the Danish railways, see Helps, *Life and Labours of Mr. Brassey* at 222.

[7]See Karl Marx, *Grundrisse der Kritik der politischen Ökonomie (Rohentwurf) 1857-1858*, at 423 (1953); *idem*, 1 *Das Kapital* at 370; Werner Sombart, 3 *Der moderne Kapitalismus: Das Wirtschaftsleben im Zeitalter des Hochkapitalismus* 285-95 (1927).

[8]R. Joby, *The Railway Builders: Lives and Works of the Victorian Railway Contractors* 73 (1983).

[9]Jenks, *Migration* at 138. William Wheelwright (1798-1873) was an American entrepreneur, who, after developing shipping and mining businesses in South America, built the first rail line in 1850 to make mines in Chile accessible; later he collaborated with Brassey on the construction of railways in Argentina. See J. Albérdi, *The Life and Industrial Labors of William Wheelwright in South America* (1877); Charles Walker, *Thomas Brassey: Railway Builder* 126-27 (1969). For a literary caricature of the Victorian railway contractor melding Peto and Brassey, see the character Roger Scatcherd in Anthony Trollope, *Doctor Thorne* (1858).

[10]Jenks, *Migration of British Capital* at 173-78; George Hallgarten, 1 *Der Imperialismus vor 1914: Die soziologischen Grundlagen der Aussenpolitik europäischer Grossmächte vor dem Ersten Weltkrieg* 62-63 (2d ed. 1963 [1951]).

[11]For the obituaries, see *Times*, Dec. 10, 1870, at 12, col. 1; 33 *MPICE* 246 (1872); 36 *id.* 285 (1873); *Times*, Nov. 15, 1889, at 10, col. 2; 99 *MPICE* 400 (1890).

of a number of projects including the new Houses of Parliament, Morton Peto and his cousin and co-inheritor, Thomas Grissell, dissolved their partnership in 1846 because the latter wished to avoid the risks associated with their railway construction undertakings in Britain. That same year Peto formed a partnership which was to last a quarter-century with Betts, who had married Peto's sister. While Peto was occupied with negotiating contracts and financing, Betts was in charge of carrying out the work.[12]

By 1847 Brassey and Peto & Betts employed almost two per cent of the British labor force, used a tenth of the iron produced for domestic consumption, and were the largest customers of British industry. At their peak they were the largest single employer in Britain, with a cash flow reputedly larger than that of the then-world's-largest company, the London and North Western Railway. They managed as much as a third of all British railroad construction. Brassey alone accounted for one-twentieth of the worldwide rail network. At his peak, Brassey employed as many as 80,000-100,000 (all non-union) workers worldwide through his system of pyramidal subcontracts.[13]

> Brassey became...a European power. He ruled over a little kingdom; but, unlike other subjects, his wees were kept by him, not taxed. They attended him to France, to Belgium, to Italy, to Spain...ready to follow their liege lord in his grand leadership of developing the resources and strengthening the pacific intercourse of nations. ... He is...the very Ashuerus of contractors.[14]

The capital that these constructors accumulated "during the British Railway Mania became available for recirculation elsewhere."[15] Their contemporary, Karl Marx, characterized these firms' accumulated capital as the product of the double exploitation of their construction workers "as industrial soldiers and as renters" of the unhygienic wooden huts of, as a parliamentary committee put it, "a most wretched description" that the contractors provided them.[16]

When, in 1841, the directors of the London and Southampton Railway, of which Brassey had built a segment, decided to gain control of the carrying trade along the Le Havre-Rouen-Paris route by building a railway, they and their engineer, Locke, provided Brassey, who had been contracting for only a few years, with his first project outside Britain.[17] In the absence of adequate French manufacturing facilities, Brassey soon co-financed the construction in France of factories to produce the requisite rails and rolling stock. That French railway construction was more profitable than similar projects in Britain[18] helps explain why by 1848 Brassey and his partners had participated in the construction of three-quarters of the French trackage. Brassey and Peto & Betts, separately and in partnership, in the 1840s, 1850s, and 1860s shifted their operations to other parts of Western Europe—France, Belgium, Piedmont, Switzerland, Austria, Spain,

---

[12][Henry Peto], *Sir Morton Peto: A Memorial Sketch* 6-19, 51 (1893).

[13]See chapter 3 above. As a member of Parliament, Peto was frequently referred to as one of Britain's largest employers of labor. See e.g., 168 *PD* (3d ser.) 1147 (1862) (statement of Mr. Seeley). Middlemas claims, without documentation, that the difference between Brassey's labor force of 100,000 and the 45,000 of the largest early-twentieth-century British international builder, Weetman Pearson, was "entirely the result of increased mechanization." Robert Middlemas, *The Master Builders* 173 n.2 (1963). On the London & North Western as the world's largest joint-stock corporation, see Lewin, *Railway Mania* at 427.

[14]Devey, *Life of Joseph Locke* at 151.

[15]Middlemas, *Master Builders* at 51, 57; Joby, *The Railway Builders* at 58.

[16]Marx, 1 *Das Kapital* at 652-53; *Report from the Select Committee on Railway Labourers* vi (13 *PP* 1846 [530]).

[17]On the financial origins and structure of this first British-built railway in France, see Devey, *Life of Joseph Locke* at 157-58; *Memoirs of Sir Edward Blount* 51-58 (Stuart Reid ed., 1902). On Brassey's partner in this project, William Mackenzie, see the obituary in 11 *MPICE* 102-105 (1852).

[18]See Locke, "Address of the President," 17 *MPICE* 128, 129-39 (1858).

Portugal, Denmark, and Norway. Brassey's operations accounted for almost one-tenth of the total length of continental European tracks laid between 1840 and 1860.[19]

By the latter half of the 1850s, French, German, and Belgian companies had begun building railways throughout Europe. The Pereire brothers, for example, through their Crédit Mobilier, which rested on stock speculation, constructed railways in Spain and Russia, although the Russian government strove to build its system as domestic enterprises aided by Western European and American engineers.[20] In some instances English firms complained of being ousted by French firms, whereas on other lines the Crédit Mobilier employed English engineers and contractors or at least bought English rolling stock.[21]    And Baron Maurice Hirsch's organization, supported by the German and Austrian governments, which were interested in trade routes to the East outside the control of Britain and France, built long sections of the railways in the European part of the Ottoman Empire between 1869 and 1872.[22]

In the aftermath of the world economic crisis at the end of the 1850s, British capital turned away from what the depression had turned into unprofitable investments in Western Europe and the United States and toward new capitalist settlements and peripheral areas. Once capitalist industrialization had forged ahead in Western Europe, its agents sought to take hold of its raw materials base: "It was only by putting steam to the task of persuading farm produce to seek a market that equilibrium could be maintained, and...profits.  The effects of the Industrial Revolution were thus communicated to countries in which railways needed to be operated as well as built by aliens."[23]

Systemic needs meshed here with the contractors' pursuit of profit. Driven by the goal of escaping from the aforementioned Continental competition which had undermined the British building firms' quasi-monopoly profits, Brassey, Peto & Betts, and others, aiding and in turn abetted by British investment capital, undertook the proto-imperialist construction of railroads in Eastern Europe, Russia, Algeria, India, Canada, Australia, and South America in the search for higher profits.[24]    By migrating to such "frontiers of economic civilization," they "helped to push these frontiers farther back."[25]  Where, as in yet undeveloped areas such as Argentina in the 1860s, Brassey and his partners, who also became major investors in the railroads they were building, were in part paid in land

[19]Helps, *Life and Labours of Mr. Brassey* at 52-71, 161-277; *Sir Morton Peto*; 3 *HS* 573, 578 (J. Conrad et al. ed., 2d ed. 1900) (s.v. "Eisenbahnstatistik"); Jenks, *Migration*, at 136-52, 168, 196, 419-20; Hobson, *Export of Capital* at 119-20; Middlemas, *Master Builders* at 33-45, 61-69; Girard, "Transport" at 236; Walker, *Thomas Brassey* at 34-173; 9 *DNB* 972, 973 (1968) (s.v. "Peto"). His obituary stated that between 1848 and 1861 Brassey built or participated in the building of 2,374 miles of railway for £27,998,224. *Times*, Dec. 10, 1870, at 12, col. 1.

[20]See e.g. Cameron, *France and the Economic Development of Europe* at 248-52, 276-83; J. Westwood, *A History of Russian Railways* 29-45 (1964); William Blackwell, *The Beginnings of Russian Industrialization 1800-1860*, at 270-302 (1968); G. Kurgan-van Hentenryk, *Rail, finance et politique: Les Entreprises Philippart (1865-1890)*, at 114-48 (1982); D. Platt, *Foreign Finance in Continental Europe and the United States, 1815-1870: Quantities, Origins, Functions and Distribution* 46-54 (1984). See also Karl Marx, "The French Crédit Mobilier," in Karl Marx & Frederick Engels, 15 *CollW* 8 (1986 [1856]); "Crédit Mobilier," *id.* at 270 (1857).

[21]"Annual Report Session 1858-59," in 18 *MPICE* 165, 166-68 (1859) (contractor Thomas Jackson and engineer John Hawkshaw built Riga & Dunaburg line); "Annual Report Session 1859-60," in 19 *MPICE* 133, 148 (1860).

[22]Kurt Grunwald, *Türkenhirsch: A Study of Baron Maurice Hirsch Entrepreneur and Philanthropist* 28-62 (1966).

[23]Jenks, *The Migration of British Capital* at 195-96.

[24]Hans Rosenberg, *Die Weltwirtschaftskrise 1857-1859*, at 151-52 (1974 [1934]); Middlemas, *Master Builders* at 79; J. Jensen & Gerhard Rosegger, "British Railway Builders Along the Lower Danube, 1856-1869," 46 *SEER* 105 (1968).

[25]Girard, "Transport" at 241.

running along the line, they became colonizers as well.[26]

The same economic logic of capital accumulation that compelled these contractors to operate overseas caused them to build "contractors' lines" by accepting the railroad companies' securities in lieu of cash or even assuming the initiative of financing, constructing, and at times operating both domestic and foreign railways, looking for buyers only afterwards.[27] Thus from 1852 to 1866, the implacable financial weight of the contractors' growing fixed capital caused a reversal of "the original relation between the contractor and the promoters and proprietors." A contemporary of Brassey and Peto explained this point with all imaginable clarity:

> So long as he remains in business, he cannot for any considerable period permit his capital to lie idle, for his plant is so enormous that were it long to remain idle, it would eat away very much of the profits of even his most successful ventures. Hundreds of earth-waggons and horses, scores of miles of rails and sleepers for "temporary way," several locomotive and several stationary engines, tools of countless numbers and endless variety—these in addition to enormous accumulations of timber, brick, stone, rails, and a host of other materials, all vociferously call for more employment. And although the mere "hands"—the Titanic navvies—...involve no eating of capital when the work is done, the contractor must have a very large staff of scientific, commercial, and skilled *employés*, whom he must keep in permanent employ, else the whole work of superior organization and drill would have to be re-undertaken when every new enterprise was undertaken. This, of course, would be as impossible as it would be...costly, and hence it is that contractors are constantly pressing forward new undertakings; being willing frequently, so long as they can only secure employment for their brains, capital, and staff, to accept in very large proportion shares of new enterprises in part repayment of their services and expenditures.[28]

In the next stage, the largest contractors made the transition from passive risk-takers to promoters of new railway lines, contributing more to the financing than "the private capitalists."[29] To that end they "use[d] parliamentary influence to have them legalized, and employ[ed] their private influence among their own circles of connections and dependents to have sufficient shares taken up to induce Parliament to pass bills." Ultimately, then, the contractors' own "insatiate and...*inevitable*, craving for contracts...precipitated many enterprises prematurely...."[30] This speculative railway investment mania, which became international at mid-century, eventually resulted in the crash of 1866, which bankrupted many contractors, including Peto, and their finance companies.[31]

These British contractors also created a civil engineer corps during the Crimean War. Shipping all the required materials and navvies from Britain, Peto and Brassey built the Balaklava Railway to the trenches, the first military railroad,

---

[26]Helps, *Life and Labours of Mr. Brassey* at 246; H.S. Ferns, *Britain and Argentina in the Nineteenth Century* 337 (1960).

[27] *BSG for 1855: A Hand-Book for Companies and Shareholders* 332-33, 339 (1855) (detailing the financial involvement of Peto and Brassey as directors of the Norwegian Grand Trunk Railway and of Peto, Betts, and Brassey in the Royal Danish Railway); Helps, *Life and Labours of Mr. Brassey* at 167-69, 177; Harold Pollins, "Railway Contractors and the Finance of Railway Development in Britain—I," 3 *JTH* 41 (1957); Harold Pollins, "Railway Contractors and the Finance of Railway Development in Britain—II," 3 *JTH* 103 (1957); Middlemas, *Master Builders* at 70-92.

[28]William Galt, *Railway Reform: Its Importance and Practicability* 350, 349 (1865). For a virtually identical passage, see Anon., "Railway Morality and Railway Policy," *ERev*, Oct. 1854, at 420, 434-35.

[29]Platt, *Foreign Finance in Continental Europe and the United States* at 182.

[30]Galt, *Railway Reform* at 349-50. Betts' obituary fondly recalled that, as chairman of the Eastern Counties Railway Company, Betts in the early 1850s had crushed an engine-drivers' strike. 36 *MPICE* at 286-87.

[31]P. Cottrell, "Railway Finance and the Crisis of 1866: Contractors' Bills of Exchange, and the Finance Companies," 3 *JTH* (n.s.) 20 (1975).

in 1855. The British government conferred a baronetcy on Peto for this project ("Taking Sebastopol by Contract"),[32] which he purported to have carried on without profit although the claim was later disputed.[33] Peto became a prominent Liberal member of Parliament from 1847 to 1855 and 1859 to 1868. There he vigorously advocated antitruck legislation requiring wage payments in money, calling attention to his employment practices with regard to his own employees—an exception to the regime of laissez-faire that, to be sure, even Lord Palmerston was constrained to accept as necessary.[34]

## Overreaching Overseas

> Englishmen are interested in gaining rapid means of transit to almost every part of the known world.... India and Australia...we have every interest in communicating with directly. The constantly developing products of those plains of plenty and those mines of wealth are becoming so important that we ought...to reduce the time inevitably lost going to and fro; and as time represents money, why should we lose the interest upon gold, and silver, and precious stones, and costly fabrics, and expensive spices, and silks, and teas, and light goods of untold value, by going a roundabout way to those lands...?[35]

Such was Brassey's and Peto's worldwide renown that in the 1860s the legislature in New South Wales offered a resolution inviting Peto "or some other eminent contractor" to prepare estimates for a new railway.[36] To be sure, Peto soon disillusioned the government by "not proceeding at the rapid rate that was anticipated from the engagement of so eminent a firm."[37] The fact, however, that overseas Brassey's "profits were, of course, enormous,"[38] created difficulties for his organization in undeveloped countries where fledging local contractors were ostensibly able to build more cheaply.

Thus as early as 1848, when the East Indian Railway Company asked Brassey and other leading British contractors to submit bids, because "no English contractors would send or go out except on the certainty of very large profits," they refused on the ground that overly exacting government supervision would lead to penny-wise and pound-foolish economizing.[39] The colonial government's refusal to accommodate them was reflected in the rhetorical question posed ten

---

[32]"Taking Sebastopol by Contract," 12 *Builder* 634 (1854).

[33]See *Sir Morton Peto* at 33; "Balaklava Railway," 12 *Engineer* 392 (1861) (Peto responding to election campaign charge that he had overcharged the government for the rails); Michael Robbins, "The Balaklava Railway," 1 *JTH* 28 (1953); David Brooke, *The Railway Navvy: 'That Despicable Race of Men'* 123-31 (1984). After the war Peto & Betts used the rails to build the Smyrna-Aidin railway in Turkey. Jenks, *Migration of British Capital* at 404 n.11.

[34]*Dod's Parliamentary Companion: New Parliament* 268 (33d ed. 1865); 130 *PD* (3d ser.) 761 (1854). Palmerston, using a revealing code, conceded that "from the artifical arrangements of society, cases will arise in which some of the parties are more or less dependent on the others, and unable therefore to take proper care of their own interests and concerns. ... It is perfectly notorious that at times when the masters had a pull on the men, in consequence of the state of trade, they compelled them, on pain of dismissal, to accept things which were given them at prices far beyond their value, and for which they had no use whatever... as part of their wages." *Id.* at 767. Peto and other contractors testified in favor of payment in cash in *Report from the Select Committee on Railway Labourers.*

[35]"From London to Calcutta," 1 *Engineer* 243 (1866) (letter from W.H. Villers Sankey, civil engineer).

[36]*BSG for 1864*, at 362 (1864).

[37]"Railways in New South Wales," 11 *Engineer* 3 (1861).

[38]4 *Encyclopaedia Britannica* 435 (11th ed. 1910) (s.v. "Brassey"). According to Brassey's contemporary biographer, "He laid out about seventy-eight millions of other people's money, and upon that outlay retained about two millions and a-half. The rest of his fortune consisted of accumulations." Helps, *Life and Labours of Mr. Brassey* at 158. See also *DNB* at 974.

[39]*Report from the Select Committee on East India (Railways)* Q. 3993 at 281 (quote); Q. 3565 at 251 (14 *PP* 1857-58 [161]) (testimony of Macdonald Stephenson, director of the East India[n Railway] Co.).

years later by the chairman of the parliamentary committee investigating the railways in India: "I presume, that the Government had a certain jealousy or fear that the profits of these contractors would be too large...?"[40] Under Governor-General Dalhousie, the colonial government began in 1853 to promote construction on a guarantee basis, which became very expensive for the Indian taxpayer.[41] Nevertheless, when, in the aftermath of the parliamentary inquiry, Brassey's organization finally did undertake construction of the Eastern Bengal Railway, the impact of inflation on the contractually fixed price schedules meant that Brassey's "'usual good fortune did not attend him....'"[42]

Similarly, Peto's and Brassey's profit-maximizing overreaching and blatant deployment of political and international banking influence in securing the contract in the 1850s to build the Grand Trunk Railway in Canada raised doubts about the periphery's alleged need to rely on the center's building firms. Even Canadians conceded that they lacked the capital to build what was then the world's longest railway line "and could not borrow in London on terms half as favorable as could the English promoters—especially if the latter blocked their efforts."[43] Yet the reputations of Brassey and Peto, which had already been tarnished by their failure to mobilize the capital to build railways in New Brunswick and Nova Scotia in 1852-53, suffered further when their methods and antiquated plant, developed in relatively low-wage countries, turned out not to be adapted to North American needs for labor-saving machinery. Dispute therefore erupted over whether Canadian firms possessed the experience and capacity to execute such work.[44]

The Grand Trunk, which was designed to enable its owners to control the U.S. midwestern grain trade from the Great Lakes to the Atlantic, was one of the "'contractors' roads,'" on which the builders were required to spend large sums before they began construction. "What wonder," then, that Peto and Brassey "should drive a somewhat hard bargain with the company of their own creating, should protect themselves by a rather one-sided contract against the loss of their previous expenditure, and...should include a profit which in ordinary risks would be deemed too exorbitant."[45] The political ill will that Brassey and Peto's practices—for example, increasing the line's trackage merely in order to increase their profit—engendered in tandem with their organization's inferior construction, which was in part intended to economize on their costs so that they would not suffer losses as a result of being paid in watered-down stock that was selling for less than its par value, put an end to their construction activities in Canada.[46]

Brassey reputedly suffered a loss on the Grand Trunk, which was neither his first nor last. "In the disaster of 1866 Mr. Brassey was probably the largest individual sufferer," losing more than £1 million.[47] Although he was forced to go hat in hand to his banker, Glyn, for a mere £30,000, by 1869 he was "richer" than ever before, and his business flourished until his death in 1870, after which

---

[40]*Id.* Q. 3567 at 251 (Chairman Henry George Liddell).

[41]See Jenks, *Migration of British Capital* at 206-30.

[42]Helps, *Life and Labours of Mr. Brassey* at 273 (reproducing account of Charles Henfrey).

[43]Oscar Skelton, *The Life and Times of Sir Alexander Tilloch Galt* 90 (1920).

[44]Oscar Skelton, *The Railway Builders: A Chronicle of Overland Highways* 66-70 (1920); Skelton, *Life and Times of Sir Alexander Tilloch Galt* at 105.

[45]"Railways of Canada—No. I," 25 *Engineering* 175, 175-76 (1878).

[46]See Anthony Trollope, *North America* 61-62 (1951 [1862]); Helps, *Life and Labours of Mr. Brassey* at 183-213; H.A. Lovett, *Canada and the Grand Trunk 1829-1924*, at 25-62 (n.d. [1924]); A. Currie, *The Grand Trunk Railway of Canada* 3-70 (1957); Middlemas, *Master Builders* at 61-69. Brassey's firms performed a limited amount of work on the Northern Railway about 1860. See Currie, *Grand Trunk* at 265.

[47]"The Late Mr. Thomas Brassey," 10 *Engineering* 443 (1870). The engineer for the construction of the Bilbao Railway in Spain in 1858 stated that Brassey lost £200,000 on the fixed-sum contract. Olinthus Vignoles, *Life of Charles Blacker Vignoles: Soldier and Civil Engineer* 374 (1889).

his contracts gradually ran out. Toward the end of his career he confided to one of his financier associates that "the net profit which he had made, after deducting losses, was about 3 per cent. upon all he had done."[48] In light of the fact that by 1865 Brassey had in hand contracts amounting to £60 million, the contemporaneous claim becomes plausible that "[p]robably never in the history of the world has any one class of traders or manufacturers...so rapidly risen from such small beginnings to the possession of great wealth as the leading contractors of the world...."[49]

Peto & Betts, in contrast, whom their bankers, Baring and Glyn, the chief mobilizers of capital for Canada in the mid-nineteenth century, had continued to finance on the Grand Trunk, despite their knowledge of the shoddy work, because their bankruptcy would probably have made completion of the work impossible and provoked even more disfavor,[50] failed during the crash of 1866, which was itself the culmination of a contractor-centered international railway speculation. Peto & Betts's last contract, for the London, Chatham, & Dover Railway, which, like the Grand Trunk, required them to be paid in shares in lieu of cash, drew them into the failure of the leading British bill-brokers, Overend, Gurney, whose suspension in May 1866 triggered the panic and crash. Peto had, the *Economist* noted in a financial obituary, "engaged in operations beyond the force even of his great capital, and in consequence he borrowed at rates of interest so high as to be injurious to his credit as well as destructive of his profit. Still the immense mass of his business was good, and some of it doubtless stupendously profitable."[51]

The international economic crisis of 1866 not only terminated Peto's business and parliamentary career,[52] but also "put an end to the ascendancy of the Contractor." Not for another two decades would British contractors reemerge as international leaders. This account suggests that occasionally local competitors in the periphery could convince the public that the imperial entrepreneur was wearing no clothes. Such consciousness evolved early in Canada, where faster and cheaper North American firms had ousted British railway contractors by the 1860s. Even Brassey had to learn to accept the limits of effective control in conducting operations at a distance of 3,000 miles in an undeveloped country.[53]

## Mobilizing Free and Unfree Labor Abroad

England may remain the heart or vital centre, but the fever heat cannot be absorbed within herself, it must be subdued by an extent of circulation; the "geometrical progression of science" cannot go on without a corresponding extension of territory.[54]

---

[48]*Memoirs of Sir Edward Blount* at 96-97, 99; *Times*, Dec. 10, 1870, at 12, col. 1.

[49]Galt, *Railway Reform* at 350, 349.

[50]Philip Ziegler, *The Sixth Great Power: A History of One of the Greatest of All Banking Families, the House of Barings, 1769-1929*, at 223-27 (1988); Currie, *Grand Trunk* at 66-69.

[51]"Sir Morton Peto at Bristol," *The Times*, Oct. 25, 1866, at 7, col. 3; *Sir Morton Peto* at 47; P. Cottrell, "Sir Samuel Morton Peto," in 4 *DBB* 644, 649 (David Jeremy ed., 1985); "Messrs Peto, Betts, and Co.," *Economist*, June 16, 1866 at 698-99. In 1865 Peto & Betts agreed to take as part payment for building the Holland-Westphalia Railway all the preferred stock. "Holland-Westphalia Railway," 1 *Engineering* 187 (1866).

[52]Between 1866 and 1872 Peto unsuccessfully sought contracts in Budapest and Russia and completed two minor railway projects in Britain. He also resigned his seat in Parliament, living on until 1889. *Times*, June 16, 1866, at 12, col. 4; *Sir Morton Peto* at 47-50, 113; Karl Marx, *Das Kapital: Kritik der politischen Ökonomie*, I: *Der Produktionsprocess des Kapitals* 226 n.40 (2d ed. 1872). Such was Peto's decline that a leading construction-engineering journal found it necessary to characterize him in an obituary as "a contractor very well known in his day." "The Late Sir Morton Peto," 48 *Engineering* 634 (1889).

[53]Jenks, *Migration of British Capital* at 198-206, 240-62 (quotation at 262); Helps, *Life and Labours of Mr. Brassey* at 145; Middlemas, *Master Builders* at 29-32, 68-69; Joby, *The Railway Builders* at 77-78.

[54]"Emigration," 1 *Builder* 177 (1843) (editorial).

The logistics of transporting the embodied technology of the capitalist world to the colonies were in themselves considerable. Thus when Brassey's firm undertook the construction of a railway in New South Wales in 1859, all the manufactured equipment and materials—including equipment, rails, ironwork, and rolling stock—had to be shipped to Australia from Britain.[55] Some of the raw materials that entered into the production of this capital may have previously been shipped from the colonies to Britain,[56] but as Rosa Luxemburg also noted: "English capital that flowed to Argentina into railway construction may previously have been Indian opium that was realized in China."[57]

In the tow of this international circuit of productive capital in its commodity form followed the requisite embodied labor power, thousands of British navvies. Or as Locke, the first British railway engineer to build a line overseas, described his and Brassey's first project in France in his presidential address to the British Institution of Civil Engineers: "Amongst the 'appliances' carried there by these gentlemen, there were none more striking, or important, than the 'navvies'... [f]ollowing in the wake of their masters...."[58] The British railway construction firms were preeminent agents and organizers of the overseas migration of tens of thousands of British navvies whom they employed abroad and for whose families they in many instances paid travel advances. British firms organized such transports even to other capitalist countries. Thus Brassey sent 5,000 British navvies to France in the 1840s because he considered them superior to French workers; in the 1850s he sent 3,000 more to Canada to build the Grand Trunk because his recruiters failed to find sufficient laborers in French Canada, and another 2,000 to Australia. During the American Civil War, 5,000 laborers from England were among the 15,000 imported to build the Atlantic & Great Western Railway.[59] Overseas, by employing local peasants as navvies, Brassey was instrumental in transforming them into an industrial "proletariat."[60]

Brassey's international comparative experience taught him that low wages were not the absolute precondition of high profits even in a labor-intensive industry. Testifying before Parliament in 1846, Brassey noted that although he paid English and Irish navvies, who constituted a third of his work force in France, about 30 per cent more than the French workers, their labor was worth the difference.[61] More generally, he concluded, based more on primitive ergonomics than on transformations in cultural consciousness, that the higher productivity of well-paid and well-fed British workers made them at least as cheap as low-paid coolies: "With regard to unskilled labour men seem to be like machines: the work given out bears some relation to the food consumed."[62]

---

[55]Helps, *Life and Labours of Mr. Brassey* at 236.

[56]Gilbert Herbert, *Pioneers of Prefabrication: The British Conbtribution in the Nineteenth Century* 25-26 (1978). On the circuit of productive capital, see Karl Marx, *Das Kapital: Kritik der politischen Ökonomie*, II: *Der Zirkulationsprozeß des Kapitals*, in Karl Marx [&] Friedrich Engels, 24 *Werke* 69-87 (1963 [1885]).

[57]Rosa Luxemburg, *Die Akkumulation des Kapitals: Ein Beitrag zur ökonomischen Erklärung des Imperialismus*, in *idem*, 6 *GW* 344 (1923 [1913]).

[58]Locke, "Address of the President" at 143.

[59]See *Report from the Select Committee on Railway Labourers*, Q. 377 at 23; Terry Coleman, *The Railway Navvies* 176-91 (1967 [1965]); Earl Brassey, *Work and Wages: The Reward of Labour and the Cost of Work* 9 (1916 [1872]); Helps, *Life and Labours of Mr. Brassey* at 74-96, 238-39; J. Clapham, *An Economic History of Modern Britain: The Early Railway Age 1820-1850*, at 406-12 (1926); *idem, An Economic History of Modern Britain: Free Trade and Steel 1850-1886*, at 235-38 (1932); Currie, *Grand Trunk* at 29; Middlemas, *Master Builders* at 39, 64, 94; Emerson Fite, *Social and Industrial Conditions in the North During the Civil War* 54-55 (1910).

[60]Middlemas, *Master Builders* at 309.

[61]*Report from the Select Committee on Railway Enactments*, QQ. 854-61, 893 at 54, 56 (14 *PP* 1846 [590]).

[62]Helps, *Life and Labours of Mr. Brassey* at 364 (reprinting letter from John Hawkshaw, one of

Such insight was not new—even in the midst of the mercantilist period's apotheosis of low wages some authors had argued that English workers' higher wages were associated with higher productivity and a higher standard of living.[63] Yet Brassey, "by making a virtue out of" the necessity of paying higher wages than those prevailing in agriculture in areas where "he was competing for labour anyway in a difficult market," was able to enhance his reputation.[64] For Marx, this profitable use of English workers to build railways in less capitalistic regions (including Eastern Europe and Asia) alongside indigenous workers—except, of course, where hot weather allegedly precluded work by Europeans[65]—merely confirmed the theoretical point that higher wages were paired with a higher rate of exploitation because capitalist production enforced a higher intensity and productivity of labor which English workers must have internalized and taken with them overseas.[66]

By the same token, international contractors were not above using slave and other forms of unfree labor. By the 1850s, the British, threatening imprisonment of the recalcitrant, exploited compulsory labor on "almost all the works that have been hitherto executed in India."[67] That the American Meiggs, universally held to have been unscrupulous, bought entire cargoes of Chinese coolies to build railways in Peru in the 1860s and 1870s is hardly surprising: much of Peru's labor at the time was performed by 90,000 coolies, and the guano exports that ultimately financed railway construction were also based on the slave, convict, and quasi-slave coolie labor that dug the bird manure off the coast of Peru for immediate shipment to Europe and the United States.[68]

Even Brassey resorted to slaves in 1862 in building the Rio de Janeiro drainage system.[69] Nor was he the only British constructor to succumb to the temptation on Brazilian infrastructure projects. In spite of the prohibition on the use of slaves on public works projects and the British government's insistence that railway companies formed in Britain not use slaves in Brazil, firms continued both to purchase and to hire slaves.[70]

Once slaves became less accessible, British engineers and contractors, for whom the massive existence of wage labor in Western Europe had become self-

---

Brassey's engineers, to Helps, Dec. 11, 1871). Brassey's views on this subject were systematized by his son, who was a member of Parliament. See Thomas Brassey, *Foreign Work and English Wages* 118-50, 157-96 (1879); *idem, Work and Wages* at iv, vi. U.S. firms reinvented this wheel in the post-World War II period by rediscovering that where Third World workers were malnourished, "productivity can be increased substantially by feeding the work force three times a day. The accompanying boost in production...can far offset the cost of this food." "Beating the Odds When Building Abroad," *ENR*, Mar. 27, 1958, at 31, 32.

[63]See [Daniel Defoe], *A Plan of the English Commerce* 32-39 (especially at 37) (2d ed. 1967 [1730]); Eli Heckscher, 2 *Merkantilismen: Ett led i den ekonomiska politikens historia* 149-53 (1931).

[64]Middlemas, *Master Builders* at 55. For an overview of the wage rates paid by Brassey at various times in various places, see Helps, *Life and Labours of Mr. Brassey* at 370-73.

[65]*Report from the Select Committee on Eurphrates Valley Railway* QQ. 34-35 at 4 (9 *PP* 1872).

[66]Karl Marx, 1 *Das Kapital*, in Karl Marx [&] Friedrich Engels, 23 *Werke*, 584-87 (1962).

[67]*Report from the Select Committee on East India (Railways)*, QQ. 1128, 1133-40 at 74 (testimony of George Sibley, civil engineer). But see *id*. Q. 3381 at 238 Col. William Baker, Bengal Engineers, denying use of forced labor).

[68]Watt Stewart, *Henry Meiggs: Yankee Pizzaro* 112, 160-64 (1968 [1946]); *idem, Chinese Bondage in Peru: A History of the Chinese Coolie in Peru, 1849-1874*, at 95-98 (1951); Jonathan Levin, *The Export Economies: Their Pattern of Development in Historical Perspective* 85-90, 99-108 (1960); Shane Hunt, "Growth and Guano in Nineteenth-Century Peru," in *The Latin American Economies: Growth and the Export Sector, 1880-1930*, at 255, 286-87 (1985); Richard Wines, *Fertilizer in America: From Waste Recycling to Resource Exploitation* 43-45 (1985).

[69]Charles Walker, *Thomas Brassey: Railway Builder* 115, 152 (1969).

[70]Edward Webb, "On the Means of Communication in the Empire of Brazil," 19 *MPICE* 240, 248, 251 (1860).

explanatory, began to complain in the 1850s of the practical difficulties inherent in forging a proletariat out of self-sufficient producers in the periphery.[71] Vignoles, the engineer for the construction of the Bahia & San Francisco Railway, was frustrated by the fact that "where the slightest labour suffices to procure food from the fertile and abundant lands, and where there are few wants, it is difficult to get the ignorant to work...."[72]  Another engineer observed that "as they can maintain themselves, in their simple way of living, without work, they must first be persuaded, not only that it is to their advantage to work, but to leave their homes and families and to walk 200 or 300 miles to obtain employment."[73]  The non-work with which the proffered fossorial employment had to compete was described by a British engineer in these terms: "The poor native Brazilian is not inclined to work hard; necessity does not compel him to do more than...plant[] a few banana trees, clear[] a small patch of ground for the mandioca root, or for the cultivation of black beans and rice...."[74]  Motivating such precapitalist producers "require[d] more tact, temper, and discretion, than [we]re ordinarily to be found in an English ganger, or foreman, to keep them on the work."[75]  Only for the fortunate construction firm operating in tropical paradises such as Ceylon did "famine," resulting from the failure of the staple (rice) crop, "c[o]me to the rescue, and d[o] that which no inducement of high pay had been able to do, viz., prevent the coolies from the coffee estates returning as usual to India when the coffee season was over."[76]

An eminent engineer, George Bidder,[77] listening to a disquisition on the virtues of slave labor before the Institution of Civil Engineers, insisted on Brassey's insight that such labor, despite its cheapness, was less valuable than higher-priced free labor: "in scarcely any country in the world, could the same amount of work be done at so small a cost, as in England."[78]  The theoretical point seemed to be lost on those whom British capital sent out to produce the transportation foundations of the world market in areas in which primitive accumulation had not yet created the classical doubly free proletariat—free of non-economic compulsion and of subsistence property.[79]  Six decades later, the British contractor Sir John Norton-Griffiths, motivated by "labour troubles" and a labor shortage, was still using forced labor for railway construction in Kenya.[80]

British constructors were not alone in their use of various forms of unfree labor abroad.  The most notorious nineteenth-century example of the use of forced labor on an international construction project—the Suez Canal—sparked an Anglo-French debate over whether either country's capitalists had sufficiently clean hands to justify attacking their competitors' practices.  The Egyptian government, which contractually specified that four-fifths of the canal laborers be Egyptian in order to diminish the possibility of foreign occupation, furnished Lesseps' company with

---

[71]Capitalists seemed equally impatient of precapitalist nature in Brazil: "A large proportion of the empire of Brazil is uncultivated forest, notwithstanding the European value of the furniture and dye woods growing so abundantly in a state of nature.  Railways will change all that by conveying the timber to market, clearing the land...." "The San Paulo (Brazilian) Railway," 22 *Engineer* 332 (1866).

[72]"Railway Labour in Brazil," 8 *Engineer* 329 (1859).

[73]William Peniston, "Public Works in Pernambuco, in the Empire of Brazil," in 22 *MPICE* 385, 399 (1863).  On the labor supply in Brazil at the time of emancipation, see Celso Furtado, *Formação econômica do Brasil* 117-41 (12th ed. 1974).

[74]Webb, "On the Means of Communication in the Empire of Brazil" at 244.

[75]Peniston, "Public Works in Pernambuco" at 399.

[76]"The Ceylon Railway," 22 *Engineer* 419 (1866).

[77]See 57 *MPICE* 294-309 (1879) (obituary of Bidder).

[78]Webb, "On the Means of Communication in the Empire of Brazil" at 262 (discussion contribution).

[79]Marx, 1 *Das Kapital* at 132, 700.

[80]Middlemas, *Master Builders* at 288-89.

20,000-25,000 corvée laborers. With equal contingents en route to and from the canal 60,000 workers were withdrawn from the agricultural labor force at any time.[81]

When British opponents of the Suez Canal fastened on Lesseps' use of the corvée as a pretext for opposing continued construction of the Canal, Lesseps forcefully reminded them that the British too had used forced labor to build the Cairo-Suez railway. Indeed in the 1850s the Egyptian viceroy, Abbas Pasha, had placed fellahs at the disposal of Robert Stephenson, who directed construction of that line.[82] The viceroy's urgent need for fellahs on his newly acquired cotton lands during the boom created by the U.S. Civil War finally impelled him to accept Napoleon III's arbitration, which required Egypt to pay the Suez Company 38 million francs in compensation. The termination of corvée labor in 1864 and the failure of the Scottish contractor, William Alton, to perform satisfactorily, afforded the French contractor Couvreux and especially the firm of Borel-Lavalley et Cie. a strong impetus both to invent their own and to order from French factories large steam-driven dredging labor-saving machinery—the very symbols of European industrialization that propelled projects such as the Suez Canal.[83]

Despite the availability of such labor-saving equipment in certain sub-branches of construction, by the turn of the century, contingents of various national proletariats were criss-crossing the globe to build railroads for other countries' capital in colonial areas. Chinese and Indian coolies were ubiquitous.[84] Italian laborers, too, were found with increasing frequency far from Europe. Much more unusual was the West-East transshipment of laborers from Barbados to the Belgian Congo in the 1890s to build the private line from Matadi to Léopoldville.[85] Together with British capital's own navvies, these multinational labor forces, recruited and retained by various means of economic and extra-economic compulsion, laid the foundation for metropolitan incorporation of the colonies into the world market.

---

[81]Voisin Bey, 1 *Le Canal de Suez: Histoire administratif et actes constitutifs de la Compagnie*, pt. I: *Période des études et de la construction 1854 à 1869*, at 205 (1902).

[82]Lionel Wiener, *L'Égypte et ses chemins de fer* 71, 641-44 (1932).

[83]"The Suez Canal Works," 18 *Engineer* 312 (1864); "The Suez Canal," *id.* at 315 (editorial); J. Clerk, "Suez Canal," 5 *FR* (n.s.) 80, 97-100 (1869); J. Nourse, *The Maritime Canal of Suez* 32 (1869); Percy Fitzgerald, 1 *The Great Canal at Suez: Its Political, Engineering, and Financial History* 200-212, 328 (1876); Voisin Bey, 1 *Le Canal de Suez* at 213, 219, 227 (reproducing Napoleon's arbitral decision); Voisin Bey, 5 *Le Canal de Suez*, II: *Description des travaux de premier établissement*, pt. II: *Exécution des travaux* (1904) (on Borel-Lavalley); Charles Hallberg, *The Suez Canal: Its History and Diplomatic Importance* 187-88, 201-202, 206-207, 213 (1931); David Landes, *Bankers and Pashas: International Finance and Economic Imperialism in Egypt* 179-81 (1979 [1958]); Herbert Bonin, *Suez: Du Canal à la finance (1858-1987)*, at 22-23 (1987). The original decree issued by Viceroy Mohammed-Said Pasha in 1856 on native workers provided for the use of laborers under the age of twelve at one-third of the adult rate. Reproduced in Fitzgerald, *The Great Canal at Suez* 307-308.

[84]Most of the 22,000 workers who built the railway in Uganda at the turn of the century, for example, were brought from India. "The Uganda Railway," 48 *ER* 326 (1903).

[85]*Die Eisenbahnen Afrikas: Grundlagen und Gesichtspunkte für eine koloniale Eisenbahnpolitik in Afrika*, in *SBVR*, 12th Legis. Per., 1st Sess., 241 *ASB*, Doc. No. 262, at 1596 (1907). On Italian workers in German South West Africa, see chapter 6 below.

# 5

# The Metropolitan State and the World Market

[I]n the Railway Age, the development of foreign and colonial railway systems abroad out of British capital, when British materials, British savings, and British engineering enterprise were opening up the world for the supply of food and raw materials, was greatly in the interest of this country as well as of the world.[1]

The construction of railroads seems to be a simple, natural, democratic, cultural, civilizing undertaking.... In fact capitalist threads, by means of thousands of networks connecting these enterprises with private property in the means of production in general, have converted this construction into an instrument of oppression of a *billion* people (colonies plus semi-colonies), that is, more than half of the population of the earth in the dependent countries....[2]

In mid-Victorian England it was clear that "[i]f there is one phenomenon more than another apparent in the mercantile history of the country, it is the constant advance of its commerce over the means of transit...."[3] Accommodating the circulation of commodities to their production became the province of civil engineering. As delineated by the British Institution of Civil Engineers on the eve of the railway age in its 1828 charter, the relatively new branch of civil engineering encompassed the

art of directing the great sources of power in nature for the use and convenience of man, as the means of production and of traffic in states both for external and internal trade, as applied in the construction of roads, bridges, aqueducts, canals, river navigation and docks, for internal intercourse and exchange, and in the construction of ports, harbours, moles, breakwaters and lighthouses...and in the drainage of cities and towns.[4]

These transnational projects creating the general conditions of production were generated by a crucial historical stage in the revolution of world communication and transportation systems that achieved an unprecedented advance in connecting theretofore remote regions. They not only increased the speed, regularity, mass, and certainty of world trade and helped perfect international lending, but also accelerated the disintegration of precapitalist economies everywhere—even if they initially transformed the Third World into de-industrialized exclaves of European capital rather than into capitalist economies in

---

[1]*Britain's Industrial Future: Being the Report of the Liberal Industrial Inquiry* 110 (1928).

[2]V.I. Lenin, *Imperializm, kak vysshaia stadiia kapitalizma*, in *idem*, 27 *Polnoe sobranie sochinenii* 299, 304-305 (1962 [1917]).

[3]Joseph Devey, *The Life of Joseph Locke* 50 (1862).

[4]*Charter, By-Laws and Regulations, and List of Members of the Institution of Civil Engineers* 9 (1881).

their own right.[5] In the year 1800, several decades before this revolution had taken place, the German philosopher Fichte observed that no matter how unfavorable their trade balances might be with one another, all European states participated in Europe's "collective spoils" from the rest of the world, which resulted from trade "without adequate equivalent."[6] Construction firms played a critical role in transforming the basis of and intensifying competition for such world-market-mediated profits.

### Linking Colonial Mines and Fields to the Metropolis

I know that the English millocracy intend to endow India with railways with the exclusive view of extracting at diminished expenses the Cotton and other raw materials for their manufactures. But when you have once introduced machinery into the locomotion of a country, which possesses iron and coals, you are unable to withhold it from its fabrication. You cannot maintain a net of railways over an immense country without introducing all those industrial processes necessary to meet the immediate and current wants of railway locomotion, out of which there must grow the application of machinery to these branches of industry not immediately connected with railways.[7]

"Railroadization" gave the most powerful impetus to the international economic cyclical upswing during the quarter-century after the revolutions of 1848.[8] But the period also witnessed the construction of canals and dams, such as those built by British and French firms in India and Egypt, largely to promote production of cotton for British textile firms.[9] Egypt will serve as an illustration here.

When the American Civil War caused Lancashire manufactures to be famished for cotton, Egypt, "[n]ormally a producer of a surplus of grain and cereals for export,...subordinated all other agriculture to the production of cotton; as a consequence the country was dependent upon the outside world for food for man and beast, and in the interior...there was much suffering if not actual famine conditions." After the Civil War and the resumption of cotton exports from the South, Lancashire cotton capitalists again pushed for increased production of Egyptian cotton because they feared that the expansion of U.S. cotton manufacturing would deprive them of U.S. cotton. Dissatisfied with the transformation of Egypt "from a more or less self-sufficient agricultural region to a one-crop country," the British manufacturers urged their government to insure that the proper irrigation works be undertaken in Egypt to meet their needs.[10] After

---

[5]See Paul Baran, *The Political Economy of Growth* 194 (1968 [1957]); Christel Neusüß, *Imperialismus und Weltmarktbewegung des Kapitals* 161 (1972); Paul Bairoch, "International Industrialization Levels from 1750 to 1980," 11 *JEEH* 269, 277, tab. 4 at 281 (1982).

[6]Johann Fichte, *Der geschlossene Handelsstaat*, in *idem*, 3 *Sämmtliche Werke* 392-93 (1845 [1800]).

[7]Karl Marx, "The Future Results of British Rule in India," in Karl Marx [&] Friedrich Engels, I:12 *Gesamtausgabe (MEGA)* 248, 251 (1984 [1853]).

[8]See Hans Rosenberg, *Die Weltwirtschaftskrise 1857-1859*, at 44-45 (1974 [1934]); N. Kondratieff, "Die langen Wellen der Konjunktur," 56 *ASS* 573, 578 (1926); Joseph Schumpeter, 1 *Business Cycles: A Theoretical, Historical, and Statistical Analysis of the Capitalist Process* 303-51 (1939).

[9]Rosenberg, *Die Weltwirtschaftskrise 1857-1859* at 154; Robert Middlemas, *The Master Builders: Thomas Brassey; Sir John Aird; Lord Cowdray; Sir John Norton-Griffiths* 82-89, 141-55 (1963); Daniel Headrick, *The Tentacles of Progress: Technology Transfer in the Age of Imperialism, 1850-1940*, at 176-204 (1988); Romesh Dutt, *The Economic History of India in the Victorian Age* 166-73 (1904); Robert Collins, *The Waters of the Nile: Hydropolitics and the Jonglei Canal, 1900-1988*, at 105 (1990). For an exuberant account of the transportation revolution, see E. Hobsbawm, *The Age of Capital 1848-1875*, at 64-87 (1977 [1975]).

[10]Edward Earle, "Egyptian Cotton and the American Civil War," 41 *PSQ* 520, 521, 541-45 (1926); E[dward]. Owen, *Cotton and the Egyptian Economy 1820-1914: A Study in Trade and Development* 89-179

Britain's occupation of Egypt in 1882, "as the economy moved beyond subsistence and into production for world markets, it lost its tolerance for poor agricultural performance and its capacity to absorb bad years."[11] At this juncture, the British Empire's engineers began to devote themselves to devising the requisite irrigation systems for expanding the scope and yields of cotton cultivation. This endeavor culminated in the construction of the Aswan Dam by John Aird & Sons, which was completed in 1902.[12] Because, from the perspective of metropolitan capital, Egypt was "an essentially cotton country," projects such as the turn-of-the-century Aswan Dam could be characterized as having "made Egypt."[13]

As one of the foundations of the modern world market,[14] the mid-nineteenth-century transportation revolution also insured that the newly incorporated precapitalist economies became subject to the cyclical rhythms of world depression and crisis emanating from Europe and the United States—the first of which promptly broke out in 1857.[15] This forcible incorporation of largely self-sufficient communities into the world market was synonymous with increasing dependence on world market prices and, given the decline in self-provisioning, the threat of famine for indigenous producers.[16] The British, however, urged the new inductees to examine the advantages. After all, if the African producer would just agree to sell them his cotton so that they could manufacture calico to sell him, "we may lay up our slave squadron, as we shall have removed the great cause of slavery, and the effect must cease. Let the free African have a market for his home-produced cotton, and the motive will be gone for transporting him to grow slave cotton."[17]

The railways that the British colonial rulers, urged on by British manufacturers desirous of importing cotton by way of Bombay, began building at mid-century in India also exemplify the hierarchically internationalizing role of the new means of transportation.[18] "Being constructed primarily from the point of view of the British economy, with the aim of facilitating military security and secondly of getting the raw produce out cheaply and British goods in..., [railways] served to strengthen the complementary colonial relationship and further subordinate the Indian to the British economy."[19]

Perhaps the most extreme mid-nineteenth-century example of railroadization in the service of metropole-oriented colonial monoculture was Mauritius. One of the island way stations that Britain so assiduously assembled to protect the empire's

(1969).

[11]John Waterbury, *Hydropolitics of the Nile Valley* 39 (1979).

[12]See Owen, *Cotton and the Egyptian Economy* at 187, 212-15, 336-37; Maurice Fitzmaurice, "The Nile Reservoir Assuan," 152 *MPICE* 71 (1903).

[13]C. Burge, "The Nile Irrigation Question," 58 *ER* 65 (1908); Hanbury Brown, "Land Values in Egypt," 114 *Engineer* 456 (1912).

[14]In a note to the third volume of *Capital*, Engels confirmed that after the crisis of 1867, the "colossal expansion of the means of communication and transport—ocean steamers, railways, electrical telegraphs, Suez Canal—have for the first time really created the world market." Karl Marx, 3 *Das Kapital,* in Karl Marx [&] Friedrich Engels, 25 *Werke* 506 n.8 (1964 [1894]).

[15]Michael von Tugan-Baranowsky, *Studien zur Theorie und Geschichte der Handelskrisen in England* 124 (1901); Rosenberg, *Die Weltwirtschaftskrise 1857-1859* at 132-34.

[16]Francesca Schinzinger, *Die Kolonien und das Deutsche Reich: Die wirtschaftliche Bedeutung der deutschen Besitzungen in Übersee* 58 (1984).

[17]"Mr Consul Campbell on African Cotton," 6 *Engineer* 122, 123 (1858).

[18]*Report from the Select Committee on the Growth of Cotton in India* viii-ix, Q. 1199 at 109-10, Q. 3461 at 289 (9 *PP* 1847-48 [1]); Amba Prasad, *Indian Railways: A Study in Public Utility Administration* 46 (1960).

[19]Gunnar Myrdal, 1 *Asian Drama* 456-57 (1968). See also Prasad, *Indian Railways* at 46-47; Daniel Headrick, *The Tools of Empire: Technology and European Imperialism in the Nineteenth Century* 180-91 (1981); idem, *The Tentacles of Progress* at 49-96.

sea route to the east before the opening of the Suez Canal,[20] Mauritius, with the exception of sugar cane, "raises scarcely anything required for its consumption, but exports nearly its whole product, and imports all articles required for food and for its other necessities. Everything grown in the country is sent to Port Louis for exportation...."[21]   In such remote and artifically settled monocultures lacking a resource base for industrialization, Marx's contention that British capital was unleashing forces in India that would eventually undermine its own rule was less applicable.

In general the colonial powers in Africa and Asia—especially Britain and France—pursued the same strategy of building railways to transport minerals and agricultural products to ports for export and to conquer and control native populations.[22]   Even if Cecil Rhodes's fabled Cape-to-Cairo Railway had ever been completed, it would still have suffered from the defect that the gauges of the connecting lines were incompatible.[23]   The sections of the route that Rhodes and his constructor, George Pauling, did build were, nevertheless, "largely responsible for the maintenance of British supremacy" in South Africa and Rhodesia.[24]   The European powers built roads and railways—as the United States, when it too was seeking access to colonial resources after World War II, was fond of pointing out—"with only one idea in mind: to tap the resources of particular areas, and bring out produce from farms or mines to the seacoast for shipment to Europe."[25] They therefore left a deeply sunk infrastructural investment that made it that much more difficult for the post-colonial states to integrate interior regions and promote more balanced national development.[26]

Metropolitan hegemony was so profoundly embedded in colonial policy that, when imperial engineers during the depression of the 1930s began mooting "The Respective Merits of Roads and Railways for Colonial Development," their narrow focus remained the colonies' capacity as markets for Britain's manufactures.[27] Consequently, in the twentieth century as in the nineteenth, "[t]he essential transportation problem" throughout the colonial world "was that raw materials and commodities produced in the interior had to find their way to a port for shipment

---

[20]"Works in the Mauritius," 7 *Engineer* 132 (1859) (on building docks for mailboats to Australia); W. Baker Brown, 4 *History of the Corps of Royal Engineers* 143 (1952).

[21]James Mosse, "The Mauritius Railways—Midland Line," in 28 *MPICE* 232, 233 (1868-69).

[22]See e.g. Virginia Thompson & Richard Adloff, "French Economic Policy in Tropical Africa," in 4 *Colonialism in Africa 1870-1960: The Economics of Colonialism* 127, 148 (L. Gann ed., 1988 [1975]); Jan Hagedorn, "Economic Initiative and African Cash Farming: Pre-Colonial Origins and Early Colonial Developments," in *id.* at 283, 294-96.

[23]*Die Eisenbahnen Afrikas: Grundlagen und Gesichtspunkte für eine koloniale Eisenbahnpolitik in Afrika* in *SBVR*, 12th Legis. Per., 1st Sess., 241 *ASB*, Doc. No. 262, at 1672, 1740-41 (1907). See generally Lois Raphael, *The Cape-to-Cairo Dream: A Study in British Imperialism* (1936).

[24]"The Katanga Railway," 126 *Engineer* 501, 502 (1918). Long sections of the Cape-to-Cairo Railway in South Africa and Rhodesia were built by George Pauling's Pauling and Co. Ltd., which between 1894 and 1910 built about 2,500 miles. *Id.*; "The Rhodesia Railways, Limited," 52 *ER* 226 (1905); *The Chronicles of a Contractor: Being the Autobiography of the Late George Pauling* 129-34, 204 (David Buchan ed., 1926).

[25]Frederick Brewster, "Colonial Powers Discuss African Transport Integration," *ENR*, Mar. 22, 1951, at 36.

[26]See Middlemas, *Master Builders* at 255-57; Headrick, *The Tools of Empire* at 192-203; Winthrop Wright, *British-Owned Railways in Argentina: Their Effect on Economic Nationalism, 1854-1918,* at 5 (1974); Eduardo Galeano, *Las venas abiertas de América Latina* 310-11 (4th ed. 1973 [1971]); W. Woytinsky & E. Woytinsky, *World Commerce and Governments* 354-56 (1955). Colonial railway policy resembled that pursued by the antebellum southern planter class and its northern trading partners in the United States. See Jonathan Wiener, *Social Origins of the New South: Alabama, 1860-1885,* at 140-41, 184-85 (1981 [1978]).

[27]John Spiller, "The Respective Merits of Roads and Railways for Colonial Development," 237 *MPICE* 546 (1935).

overseas...."[28] As late as World War II, representatives of U.S. capital were still repeating the nineteenth-century African colonialists' argument justifying the construction exclusively of railways of penetration—namely, that it would be wasteful to interconnect the countries of Central America by roads or waterways because they produced, exported, and imported the same goods for, to, and from the United States and Europe, and had therefore no need for mutual intercourse.[29] And even when, at the end of the twentieth century, such links have been established, multinational Brazilian construction firms still complain of the precarious transportation between Brazil and its main markets in Latin America: "It is cheaper to transport something from the United States or Europe to them than from Brazil. There are no railways, roads, shipping lines, or accessible air transportation."[30]

Even in the formally independent "financial colonies" of South America such as Argentina,[31] the British and French capital that financed the railways insured that they "were built to serve external trade rather than (as in white-settled North America and Europe) to open up and unify the South American continent."[32] From the time of capitalist pioneers like William Wheelwright in the 1850s into the twentieth century, the Andean and other South American railways, for example, ultimately accomplished little other than making it possible to exploit mineral resources for export.[33] Thus at the turn of the century Peru was still being instructed that the first step in becoming a "progressive" nation was "extending its railway system, following upon the recent movement among capitalists, British and American, towards the opening up of the country's great mining resources."[34]

In Porfirian Mexico, railroads were designed to transport raw materials to the U.S. border in derogation of agricultural production for local consumption and peasant land ownership; they "served other centers of population only as an afterthought."[35] Although the Mexican rail network, unlike that in the rest of Latin America, did run through sections of the country that did not specialize in export production, the railroads nevertheless played a major role in transforming Mexico from a backward into an underdeveloped economy by promoting dependence—even for basic foods—on external flows of capital and technology. A leading U.S. railway journal editorialized that "Mexico is not and never can be, an agricultural country in the sense that our country is. [S]uch a country rarely

---

[28]Spiller, "The Respective Merits of Roads and Railways for Colonial Development" at 617 (correspondence contribution by Fred Lavis).

[29]See Fred Lavis, 106 *ENR* 661 (1931) (letter) (president, International Railways of Central America); *idem*, "The Part of Inland Waterways in Latin American Transportation," 131 *ENR* 277 (1943). For the original colonialist version, see e.g., M. Bourrat, "Rapport fait au nom de la commission du budget chargée d'examiner le projet de loi portant fixation du budget général de l'exercice 1905 (chemins de fer colonies)," in 66 *ACDDP*, Annéxes No. 1959 & 1960, at 1867, 1868-69 (Session ordinaire de 1904, pt. 2, July 4-13, 1904, 1905).

[30]Josmar Verillo, "Brazil," in *The Global Construction Industry: Strategies for Entry, Growth and Survival* 180, 197 (W. Strassmann & Jill Wells ed., 1988).

[31]L. Knowles, *The Economic Development of the British Overseas Empire* 39 n.1 (1924).

[32]William Woodruff, "The Emergence of an International Economy 1700-1914," in 4 *The Fontana Economic History of Europe: The Emergence of Industrial Societies Part Two* 656, 692-93 (1973); L. Girard, "Transport," in 6 *The Cambridge Economic History of Europe: The Industrial Revolutions and After: Incomes, Population and Technolgical Change (I)* 212, 256-57 (H. Habakkuk & M. Postan ed., 1965).

[33]See Watt Stewart, *Henry Meiggs: Yankee Pizarro* 345 (1968 [1946]); Brian Fawcett, *Railways of the Andes* 31 (1963); Middlemas, *Master Builders* at 99, 263-65; Heraclio Bonilla, *Guano y burguesía en el Perú* 61 (1974).

[34]C. Enock, "Railway Development in Peru," 53 *EN* 463 (1905).

[35]Steven Sanderson, *The Politics of Trade in Latin American Development* 20 (1992) (quotation); William French, "In the Path of Progress: Railroads and Moral Reform in Porfirian Mexico," in *Railway Imperialism* 85, 87 (Clarence Davis & Kenneth Wilburn, Jr., ed., 1991).

produces enough for home consumption, if there is any other employment for labor."[36] The direct beneficiaries of such railroads were, in addition to their foreign owners, the foreign owners of the mines, the products of which they transported, and the foreign suppliers of railroad inputs.[37] As *Railway Age*, commenting on the first train to cross the Rio Grande in 1881, phrased it: "The capitalists who have been bold and enterprising enough to undertake the great work of opening Mexico to modern civilization certainly ought to be well rewarded...."[38]

In Honduras and Guatemala rail lines were dedicated exclusively to transporting bananas from plantations to ports for export with few positive externalities. More generally, then, throughout Latin America, "railroad networks—and regions—succeeded or failed as the international demand for the commodity they carried."[39] Exemplary in this sense was the most important railway undertaken in Brazil in the 1860s. Built by a British firm, it played a key role in developing that country's world market-oriented coffee monoculture by making possible cultivation farther inland and then serving "as a funnel...gathering the agricultural products of a vast region and pouring them into the British ships gathered in the harbor."[40]

British (and French) capital pursued a similar policy in the European periphery. For example, when British steel firms discovered that the hematite ore that Britain lacked was to be found in Spain, British capital built a railway in the vicinity of Bilbao in the 1870s to transport the ore.[41] Because the railways in Spain "merely formed the connexion between foreign-owned mines and foreign-owned ships," they were "an alien implantation for which Spain provided merely the subsoil, both as track-bed and as cargo."[42] The investment required to open up these sources in such exclaves consisted in part of the export of machinery and raw materials, which was "financed and organised in the same way as investment at home and from an economic point of view it is home investment, though geographically located overseas."[43] Because the colonial and imperialist contractors built the facilitating infrastructure "in the way and at the time they did they bound countries to certain types of development."[44] In the case of Spain, into the twentieth century "the transport of Spanish commodities between Spanish centres remained prohibitively expensive while foreign goods could be deposited in Spanish ports at overwhelmingly competitive prices."[45]

In furnishing communications in and with the newly conquered nations, private constructors proved to be worthy successors to the construction-engineering organizations accompanying the Roman armies, which had carried out imperial building projects such as roads, harbors, waterways, and fortifications in the conquered provinces almost two thousand years earlier.[46] Toward the end of the

---

[36]"Going to Mexico," 7 *RA* 212 (1882).

[37]See John Coatsworth, *Growth Against Development: The Economic Impact of Railroads in Porfirian Mexico* 122, 145, 181 (1981).

[38]6 *RA* 449-50 (1881) (editorial).

[39]Sanderson, *Politics of Trade in Latin American Development* at 21.

[40]Richard Graham, *Britain and the Onset of Modernization in Brazil 1850-1914*, at 51, 60-61 (1968).

[41]Edward Woods, "Address of Mr. Edward Woods, President," 87 *MPICE* 1, 16-18 (1886).

[42]Clive Treblicock, *The Industrialisation of the Continental Powers 1780-1914*, at 363, 352 (1981).

[43]Joan Robinson, *The Accumulation of Capital* 370 (3d ed. 1971 [1956]).

[44]Middlemas, *Master Builders* at 25.

[45]Treblicock, *Industrialisation of the Continental Powers* at 350.

[46]See E. De Renty, 1 *Les Chemins de fer coloniaux en Afrique: Chemins de fer des colonies allemandes, italiennes et portugaises* 2 (1903); Curt Merckel, *Die Ingenieurtechnik im Alterthum* 226-63 (1969 [1899]); Raymond Chevallier, *Les Voies romaines* 68-69, 89-115 (1972).

nineteenth century, as colonial empires became more formalized, the construction-engineering industry even proudly proclaimed its Roman lineage. Under the heading, "Engineering Burmah into Tranquility," a leading British trade journal in 1888 proffered as first among the "engineering methods of suppression" the building of railways. Just as "[t]he Romans of old pacified conquered countries by running roads through them," the British should have learned from the recent experiences of their army and Corps of Royal Engineers in Afghanistan that pacifying Burma by locomotive rather than the sword would both be cheaper and open new markets.[47] Even American engineers approved of this transvaluation: "Like the proconsuls of ancient Rome, who were always on the look-out for new means of communication to obtain supplies for their armies and to transport their legions with rapidity from place to place, the governors of the English colonies were intent on opening up highways for trade, commerce, and inter-urban communication generally."[48]

### Colonial Planning

The same British state that failed to plan the country's domestic railways also refrained, in the initial period of diffusion of railroads in the non-European periphery, from establishing an imperial masterplan to guide the pioneering railway contractors in selecting profitable overseas routes. The principal exception was dictated by direct British rule in India.[49] Under Governor-General James Ramsay, the 10th Earl of Dalhousie, who in the mid-1840s had lacked the power as the head of the Railway Department of the Board of Trade to implement an overall railway policy in Great Britain itself,[50] the government formulated and effectuated a comprehensive policy. In his influential minute of 20 April 1853, which also focused on the military advantages of a railway system, Dalhousie was attentive to the fact that "England is calling aloud for the cotton which India does already produce in some degree, and would produce sufficient in quality, and plentiful in quantity, if only there were provided the fitting means of conveyance for it from the distant plains, to the several ports adopted for its shipment."[51] The government then planned a trunk system to facilitate British policies of expansion and annexation, especially in the aftermath of the Sepoy Mutiny in 1857, all at the expense of the Indian taxpayers.[52]

Dalhousie's conception of an overall transportation and communications system did not, however, extend to railway construction by the state. If for no other reason, he contended that the government did not have enough engineers at its disposal to undertake such projects on its own account.[53] He did, to be sure, acquiesce in state construction of canals because they "produc[ed] no immediate

---

[47]"Engineering Burmah into Tranquility," 45 *Engineering* 439-40 (1888) (editorial). On the "stupendous...engineering difficulties" that the Royal Engineers encountered in building the mountain line in the 1880s, see Whitworth Porter, 2 *History of the Corps of Royal Engineers* 328-33 (1951 [1889]); on the British military campaigns in the late 1870s in Afghanistan without benefit of railways, see R. Ensor, *England 1870-1914*, at 62-63, 69-70 (1936).

[48]Charles Prelini, "The Erie Canal.—No. I," 90 *Engineering* 1 (1910).

[49]For an overview of railway construction in the British Empire toward the end of the century, see Woods, "Address" at 22-53.

[50]See J. Clapham, 1 *Economic History of Modern Britain: The Early Railway Age 1820-1850*, at 417-24 (1926).

[51]"Minute by the Most Noble the Governor-general; dated the 20th April 1853," in *Railways (India)*, ¶¶ 5, 6 at 113, 114, 115 (76 *PP* 1852-53 [481]). See generally Suresh Ghosh, *Dalhousie in India, 1848-56: A Study of his Social Policy as Governor-General* 57-92 (1975).

[52]Middlemas, *Master Builders* at 82-89.

[53]"Minute...dated the 20th April 1853," ¶ 71 at 133.

return'' and would therefore not be built otherwise.  This policy was consonant with the position that Adam Smith had articulated three-quarters of a century earlier: The sovereign bore the duty of erecting public works, such as roads, bridges, canals, and harbors, which facilitate ''Commerce in general'' but the profit from which ''could never repay the expence to any individual or small number of individuals'' and could therefore not induce the latter to build them.[54]

Railways, on the other hand, appeared to Dalhousie to fall outside the ambit of traditional public works:

> I hold that the creation of great public works, which, although they serve important purposes of State, are mainly intended to be used in those multifarious operations which the enterprise, the trade, and the interests of the community, for ever keep in motion, is not part of the proper business of a Government.  [T]he conduct of an enterprise which is undertaken mainly for commercial purposes, and which private parties are willing to engage for, does not fall within the proper functions of any Government.[55]

In fact, however, the only intelligible distinction that Dalhousie even implicitly identified between canals and railways was that capital was available for investment only in the latter, thus making state intervention unnecessary.  If this distinction could be sustained for India, its validity was merely phenomenological rather than categorical, as witnessed by the massive and in part very profitable private investment in canals in Britain in the last quarter of the eighteenth and the first quarter of the nineteenth century.[56]

The scope of those elements of ''infrastructure'' that must be built collectively because they are not profitable for capital is subject to a historical process of contraction and expansion.[57]  Writing (for himself) at the same time as Dalhousie was acting, and taking the English path of railway construction as the model, Marx argued that ''[t]he highest development of capital'' was the production of such general conditions of the societal process of production not from state taxes, but from ''capital as capital'' because it indicated, on the one hand, the degree to which capital had subsumed under it all conditions of societal production, and, on the other, the extent to which societally productive wealth had been capitalized and all needs were satisfied in the form of exchange.[58]

Marx's model did not, however, underlie Dalhousie's conception, which provided for a state financial guarantee system for the builders.  Marx's analysis did, however, fit the dilemma of agency regarding the creation of the general conditions of production in a profit-driven society as perceived by those most directly affected—construction-engineering firms.  The British trade journal *Engineering* editorially conceptualized the contradictions of self-valorization of infrastructural capital in what has become the familiar framework of public goods:

> How many more times than their cost the roads, bridges, canals, railways, harbours, docks, drainage, and other engineering works of the kingdom have added to the public wealth can hardly be estimated.... It is the complaint of

[54]Adam Smith, *An Inquiry into the Nature and Causes of the Wealth of Nations* 681-82 (Edwin Cannan ed., 1937 [1776]).

[55]''Minute...dated the 20th April 1853,'' ¶ 72 at 133.

[56]Clapham, *An Economic History of Modern Britain: The Early Railway Age* at 75-85.

[57]See Rolf Knieper, ''Staat und Nationalstaat: Thesen gegen eine fragwürdige Identität,'' 23 *Prokla*, No. 90, at 65, 68 (1993).

[58]Karl Marx, *Grundrisse der Kritik der politischen Ökonomie (Rohentwurf) 1857-1858,* at 431 (1953). For a discussion of Marx's approach, see Dieter Läpple, *Staat und allgemeine Produktionsbedingungen: Grundlagen zur Kritik der Infrastrukturtheorien* 61-67, 97-162 (1973). Although Marx wrote extensively on India for newspapers and referred to Dalhousie frequently, he does not appear to have commented on this particular aspect of Dalhousie's railway policies.

capital that in but few cases can it, when employed in conferring this dividend upon non-investors, obtain more than a tithe, if as much, for itself. No one doubts that it is justifiable, upon every consideration of commercial policy, to embark a thousands pounds of capital in any undertaking which will...effect a saving of from 50*l*. to 100*l*. yearly in any process of production or transport. But it does not follow that A is to embark his thousand pounds to secure this saving to B, who embarks nothing, and who will give nothing to A in return. Nor even, were the State to carry out all works of public advantage...would the case be greatly different.... And this would not be a benefit...of public safety, public order, or other good constituting the common weal, but distinct commercial benefit, of which A, favourably placed to receive it, might enjoy a large share, while B, out of the way, but bearing his full burden of taxation, would go altogether without.

It is to speculative enterprise, however, the enterprise that is reasonably, not rashly speculative, that engineers must look for employment.[59]

Viewed from a different perspective, this contradiction reflects the lack of identity between the systemic need of the capital invested in the construction and operation of railways to self-expand on the one hand and a national developmental policy on the other. As a high-ranking British colonial railway official observed: "Large profits made by railway companies must, as a rule, be considered as taken from the general community for the benefit of the few, and may work incalculable mischief by checking the development of trade."[60] The colonies offered specific contexts for the resolution of this contradiction.

Thus the governor-general of Mauritius, which by 1840 had become the chief sugar producer in the empire at a time of rapidly rising British consumption, proposed in 1857 that a railroad be built to connect the scattered sugar estates to the port of Port Louis. The colonial government acted in response to representations by the Mauritian planters, who could not satisfy the increasing demand for sugar by depending on schooners, whose dampness subjected the sugar to depreciation, or on expensive mule and horse cart road transport. Not only did no private company finance construction, but despite the planters' promise to contribute land gratis, "when the time arrived for the fulfilment of this patriotic arrangement, their feelings of liberality had completely vanished."[61] Thus from 1862 to 1865 a partnership under Brassey and George Wythes performed the work for a state-owned system financed by the colony's reserve fund and £1 million of colonial debentures.[62]

In an unusual contribution to the public policy debate about colonial railways within the British Institution of Civil Engineers, in effect a convocation of imperial railway engineers, the surveyor general of Mauritius questioned the need for the rail system in general. Observing that large parts of the island had not benefited at all from the rail line, Colonel Morrison argued that for one-fourth of the cost, the inhabitants could have built a road system covering the entire

---

[59]"Capital and Engineering," 7 *Engineering* 409 (1869) (editorial).

[60]Guilford Molesworth, "Address," 159 *MPICE* 5, 19 (1905). A leading British journal agreed that it was wise for the Brazilian state to take over the construction of a railway on its own account because, although the direct return did not generate significant interest on the invested capital, "the indirect benefits" for the country as a whole justified the undertaking. "Bahia and San Francisco Railway," 19 *Engineering* 300 (1875) (editorial).

[61]Mosse, "The Mauritius Railways" at 276 (discussion contribution by Col. Morrison, surveyor general of Mauritius). See also E. De Renty, 2 *Les Chemins de fer coloniaux en Afrique: Chemins de fer dans les colonies anglaises et au Congo Belge* 140-44 (1904).

[62]Helps, *Life and Labours of Mr. Brassey* at 165; Arthur Jessop, *A History of the Mauritius Government Railways 1864 to 1964*, at 1-2 (1964); P. J. Barnwell & A. Toussaint, *A Short History of Mauritius* 176 (1949); Moses Nwulia, *The History of Slavery in Mauritius and the Seychelles, 1810-1875*, at 188-89 (1981); John Addison & K. Hazareesingh, *A New History of Mauritius* 50, 53 (1984).

island.[63] The counterargument by the colonial government's consulting engineer, John Hawkshaw, arguably the leading international railway engineer, that the benefits generated by a railway for a country exceed those accruing merely to the proprietors,[64] while surely correct, failed to confront the broader issue of the overall rationality of such colonial monoculture transportation systems.[65] In 1865, when the new lines began operating, sugar accounted literally for 99.9 per cent of the colony's exports.[66] Three years later the governor reported that annual appropriations for interest and the sinking fund of the railway debt would exceed net receipts of the railway by £40,000-50,000 for many years to come.[67]

Colonial Ceylon offered yet another illustration of the contradictions generated by metropolitan state-supported infrastructure on behalf of world market monoculture. In the 1860s, British coffee planters in Ceylon also successfully urged construction, by private contractors, of a railway line designed primarily to connect their highland plantations with the port of Colombo.[68] During the middle third of the century, the Kandyan Highlands, which had been largely self-sufficient economically, were incorporated into the world economy in accordance with the needs of the British economy: coffee came to account for two-thirds of Ceylon's exports as it turned into a net food importer.[69] For the indigenous population, however, the railroad "was not a necessity" because the existing road "was sufficient to meet their simple trading needs."[70]

In one of the most remarkable critiques of the narrow world-market orientation of metropolitan transport policy ever penned for publication by a British colonial official, William Morris, an administrator who had lived for more than thirty years in Ceylon, observed in a letter to *The Engineer* that although the Colombo-Kandy railway was designed for the European planters and "the indigenous inhabitants of Ceylon...derive no advantage" from it:

> still by an apparent anomaly, whilst the coffee lands of the Europeans on the hills are all exempt from the land tax, the lands of the natives are subject to a tax to the Government of one-tenth their produce in grain. Not only is this so, but when providing a guarantee, as security to the shareholders for the interest on the sums to be expended on the Kandy Railroad, the Government, in addition to imposing an export duty on coffee for this specific purpose...have mortgaged the entire revenues of Ceylon as a guarantee; that is to say, to ensure a railroad for the exclusive benefit of the coffee estates, not the produce of those estates alone has been rendered liable to the charge, but the great bulk of the revenue levied off the lands of the natives, in remote regions utterly unaffected by the railroad, have been hypothecated for the same purpose; and thus the taxes on the cultivation of rice in the lowlands, on the distillation of arrack, and on the manufacture of

[63]Mosse, "The Mauritius Railways" at 278-79 (discussion contribution by Morrison).

[64]*Id.* at 266 (discussion contribution by Hawkshaw).

[65]For the parallel history of railways in the French Indian Ocean sugar-producing colony of Réunion, see F. Baltzer, *Die Kolonialbahnen mit besonderer Berücksichtigung Afrikas* 228-30 (1916).

[66]*Reports Showing the Present State of Her Majesty's Colonial Possessions for the Year 1865: Pt. I—West Indies and Mauritius* 109 (58 *PP* 1867 [3812]).

[67]*Reports Showing the Present State of Her Majesty's Colonial Possessions for the Year 1868: Part III,* at 34 (C. 151, 59 *PP* 1870).

[68]*Ceylon Railway* (45 *PP* 1860 [111]); *Papers Relating to the Affairs of the Ceylon Railway* 4 (C. 289, 47 *PP* 1871 [605]); James Mosse, "Ceylon Government Railways," 63 *MPICE* 63 (1881); University of Ceylon, 3 *History of Ceylon* 307-308 (K. De Silva ed., 1973). Brassey bid on this project, but the contract was awarded to William Faviell (1822-1902), who had built the first railway in Western India in 1853 and later built a line in the Cape Colony. *Reports of Her Majesty's Colonial Possessions for the Year 1862: Part II,* at 143 (40 *PP* 1864 [3309-I]); 150 *MPICE* 463 (1902) (obituary).

[69] *Reports Showing the Present State of Her Majesty's Colonial Possessions for the Year 1867, Part III: Eastern Colonies* 11 (43 *PP* 1868-69 [4090-I]); Asoka Bandarage, *Colonialism in Sri Lanka: The Political Economy of the Kandyan Highlands, 1833-1886,* at 66-82, 276-79 (1983).

[70]Indrani Munasinghe, "The Colombo-Kandy Railway," 25 *CHJ* 239, 244 (Nos. 1-4, 1978).

cocoa-nut oil and the consumption of salt by the natives at all parts of the coast, as well as the duty on every article imported for their use, are to be given as security for the formation of a railroad to the coffee estates of Europeans in a single district of the hills.[71]

In vain, Morris, who suggested that coffee monocropping might exhaust the highland soil anyway, urged construction of a comprehensive line which, in combination with restoration of ancient irrigation systems, would have promoted the cultivation of a variety of crops by the native population.[72] Not only was Morris's proposal ignored, but two decades later *The Engineer* was still editorializing in favor of an extension of the coffee railroad, this time to improve the transport of manure to the coffee plantations in an effort to stave off soil depreciation.[73] But the plea came too late: within a few years tea replaced coffee as Ceylon's next world-market monoculture export.[74] In the first decade of the twentieth century, forty years after he had been director-general of the railways and director of public works in Ceylon, Guilford Molesworth confirmed Morris's critique. In his presidential address to the Institution of Civil Engineers, he agreed both that railways had done little "for the general development of the country and that the same line proposed by Morris "would be of inestimable value...in the development of a country, which, once fertile and prosperous, has now lapsed into uninhabited jungle."[75]

If in the 1850s—when native Indian contractors were already performing well—the British colonial government in India lacked enough experienced engineers to build railways on its own, by the 1870s it was able to rely on the departmental system of construction, under which the Department of Public Works, employing a thousand civil and Royal Engineers, built for its own account more cheaply than Brassey could.[76] More importantly, even the governor-general had come to acknowledge that the contradiction between the profitability of railway construction capital as guaranteed by public revenue and "satisfactory progress" had to be resolved in favor of state intervention. In his crucial minute of 9 January 1869, Sir John Lawrence rejected the state guarantee system as "placing the State in so false a financial relation to the constructors of railways" in which "[t]he whole profit goes to the companies, and the whole loss to the Government."[77] Anticipating the charge of promoting state socialism, he observed that:

> It is often objected to the prosecution of public works by the Government, that it is not proper for the Government to interfere with private enterprise (which is said to be the proper agency by which works like railways should be carried out), and that the Government should not take advantage of its position to prevent the investment of capital by private persons in large public works. Now, the Government of India has for several years been striving to induce capitalists to undertake the construction of railways in India at their own risk...with a minimum

[71]"Ceylon Railroads," 10 *Engineer* 172 (1860) (letter from William Morris).

[72]*Id.* at 172-73. Morris was an official of the Eastern Province, which would have benefited from his proposal.

[73]"Railways in Ceylon," 46 *Engineer* 80 (1878) (editorial).

[74]Bandarage, *Colonialism in Sri Lanka* at 84-86.

[75]Guilford Molesworth, "Address" at 17-18, 36.

[76]See *Report from the Select Committee on East India (Railways)* QQ. 3388-89 at 238, QQ. 3673-76 at 259 (14 *PP* 1857-58); "Civil Engineers in India," 6 *Engineering* 441 (1868); "Engineering Progress in India," 15 *Engineering* 253 (1873) (college for civil engineers staffed by Westerners); "The Indian Public Works Department," 37 *Engineering* 385 (1884) (1000 engineers by 1877); H. Jagtiani, *The Rôle of the State in the Provision of Railways* 124-27 (1924); Knowles, *Economic Development of the British Overseas Empire* at 337-42; Prasad, *Indian Railways* at 46-69; Middlemas, *Master Builders* at 82-89.

[77]"Minute by His Excellency Sir John Lawrence, Governor General, dated 9th January 1869: Railway Extension in India," in *East India (Railways)* ¶¶ 9-10 at 20, 22 (47 *PP* 1868-69 [129]).

of Government interference.  But the attempt has entirely failed, and it has become obvious that no capital can be obtained for such undertakings otherwise than under a guarantee of interest, fully equal to that which the Government would have to pay if it borrowed directly on its own account.  It is an abuse of language to describe, as an interference with private enterprise, what is only a refusal to support private speculation and to guarantee them from all possible loss by the credit of the State, or to allege that the investment of capital by private persons is hindered by the Government executing works, when private persons refuse to do so at their own risk.[78]

By eliminating the contractors, the state inaugurated the "departmental system," under which "the whole of the direct profits can be added to the public revenues...."[79]

Toward the end of the nineteenth century, British colonial administrations elsewhere also became much more interventionist on behalf of colonial capital in contradistinction to the narrower interest of railway constructors and investors.  In British Malaya in the mid-1880s, the government began building railway lines by the departmental system in order to link the tin mines to ports.  A decade later a similar development got underway in Nigeria and Uganda, where, as the Empire Cotton-Growing Committee later observed, cotton and transport developed in tandem.[80]  This shift was in large part associated with the social imperialist movement, which became policy when Joseph Chamberlain took over the colonial office in 1895 and pushed the construction of railways in Africa in order to increase the yield of the colonies for Britain.[81]

A similar process played itself out in the Dutch East Indies.  There, too, "planters knew better than to invest money in" railways when the Dutch colonial administration could do it for them.[82]  Thus by the 1870s and 1880s, the Dutch government began building railways both to pacify the indigenous population and to link coal fields.[83]

By the turn of the century, and especially in Africa, the colonial military and economic purposes of railways coalesced.[84]  As the leading French civil engineering journal observed:

> The creation of the first railways, in Africa, was imposed at first by the necessities of conquest: transport and supply of troops.  As soon as it was possible to broach the question of the valorizing [mise en valeur] of the conquered territories...it was a matter...for each colony to drain the products of the hinterlands toward its ports....[85]

This military-industrial integration of colonial railways was pithily captured in

---

[78]*Id.*, ¶ 11 at 22.

[79]*Id.* at 23.

[80]*Report to the Board of Trade of the Empire Cotton Growing Committee* 30-33, 38-39 (Cmd. 523, 16 *PP* 1920 [16]); Knowles, *The Economic Development of the British Overseas Empire* at 133-35, 480, 494, 501-503; A.M. O'Connor, *Railways and Development in Uganda* 6-7 (1965).

[81]Baker Brown, 4 *History of the Corps of Royal Engineers* 85; Ensor, *England 1870-1914*, at 224-26; Bernard Semmel, *Imperialism and Social Reform: English Social-Imperial Thought 1895-1914*, at 74-88 (1968 [1960]).

[82]J. Furnivall & A.C.D. De Graeff, *Netherlands India: A Study of Plural Economy* 204 (1939).

[83]See A. Kuntze, "The State Railway on the West Coast of Sumatra," 105 *MPICE* 370 (1891); "State Railways in Western Sumatra," 59 *Engineering* 495 (1895); G. Allen & Audrey Donnithorne, *Western Enterprise in Indonesia and Malaya: A Study in Economic Development* 226-27 (1957).

[84]Almost three decades before the first railways were built in colonial sub-Saharan Africa, a leading British construction-engineering journal urged that "the more valuable its produce is proved to be to this country...the more promising a field it appears to open up for the triumph of steam." "African Railroads and Agriculture," 2 *Engineer* 473 (1856).

[85]"Les Chemins de fer africains," 46 *GC* 424 (1905).

Cecil Rhodes's memorable phrase that "[i]n the colonies the railway is cheaper than the cannon and reaches farther."[86] With alacrity the French and German colonialists expressly emulated the British policy of using railways to pacify occupied territories as soon as possible.[87] For them it was clear that "the suppression of unruly tribes, the military conquest and subjection of the area to be opened up" was part and parcel of the purpose of colonial railways, which was "to utilize the human labor power in the interior of the country to provide households in Europe with...cocoa, tobacco, coffee, cotton, oil, etc., which every worker needs today."[88]

Several systems were available for building railroads in the colonies. At one extreme, firms could be authorized to build and operate lines as private enterprises. Some of the sections of Rhodes's mineral exploitation-driven Cape-to-Cairo system built by George Pauling fit this description.[89] The more typical system involved state guarantees, subventions, and land and mineral concessions. The leading French firm, Société de Construction des Batignolles, built the railway in the French colony of Senegal under this regime in the 1880s.[90] The state could also build railroads either by accepting bids from, or entering into agreements with, contractors, whom it then supervised through a consulting engineer.[91] The railways in the British colonies of Sierra Leone and the Gold Coast were built in this way under the supervision of William Shelford's consulting-engineering firm at the turn of the century.[92]

Finally, in the departmental system, the colonial government became its own construction organization.[93] In the French colonies in Africa, the departmental system was largely run by military engineers of the Génie Corps, which built, for example, the railways in Guinea and Madagascar at the turn of the century.[94] Britain also used its Corps of Royal Engineers to build military railways in the Sudan.[95] In the early 1880s, the Royal Engineers performed well in contrast with the failure of Lucas & Aird, "an English contractor of world-wide experience," to complete the Suakin-Berber line.[96] The Corps also built the railway to Khartoum in the late 1890s to support the army's conquest of the Sudan, although a U.S. firm, Pencoyd Iron Works, caused a sensation by underbidding all the British bridge builders for one of the bridges on the route.[97] Even under the departmental system, colonial governments still contracted out some work such as

---

[86]Baltzer, *Die Kolonialbahnen* at 15.

[87]Bourrat, "Rapport" at 1867.

[88]Baltzer, *Kolonialbahnen* at 17-19.

[89]See Raphael, *The Cape-to-Cairo Dream* at 199-202; Norman Pollock, *Nyasaland and Northern Rhodesia: Corridor to the North* 361-94 (1971); *Chronicles of a Contractor* at 204.

[90]E. de Renty, 3 *Les Chemins de fer coloniaux en Afrique: Chemins de fer dans les colonies françaises* 8-9 (1905).

[91]For Pauling's scathing view of government engineers in his pre-Rhodes days, see *Chronicles of a Contractor* at 56-61.

[92]"The Sierra Leone Government Railway," 52 *ER* 498 (1905); 163 *MPICE* 384-86 (1906).

[93]See Hans Meyer, *Die Eisenbahnen im tropischen Afrika: Eine Kolonialwirtschaftliche Studie* 21-32, 173-77, 184-85 (1902); Bourrat, "Rapport" at 1882-83.

[94]See *Papers Relating to the Construction of Railways in Sierra Leone, Lagos, and the Gold Coast* 26-32 (Cd. 2325, 56 *PP* 1905 [361]); De Renty, 3 *Les Chemins de fer* at 93-125, 257-307; Bourrat, "Rapport," at 1923; Baltzer, *Kolonialbahnen* at 208, 225-26. For an overview of the systems used in Africa, see *Eisenbahnen in Afrika* at 1564-1635.

[95]For an early proposal to develop the corps of military engineers in India, see "Military Engineering," 16 *Builder* 29 (1858).

[96]"The Suakim-Berber Railway," 39 *Engineering* 579 (1885) (editorial); Porter, 2 *History of the Corps of Royal Engineers* at 81-82, 163; Baker Brown, 4 *History of the Corps of Royal Engineers* 7 (quotation).

[97]Charles Watson, 3 *History of the Corps of Royal Engineers* 63-70 (1954 [1914]); F. Baltzer, *Die Kolonialbahnen mit besonderer Berücksichtigung Afrikas* 105-107 (1916); chapter 7 below.

large permanent bridges and harbors, which required special plant and specialized personnel.[98]

The colonial governments moved further away from the pure capitalist model not merely because no Brassey or Peto was willing to mobilize or risk his own capital—at least where those governments offered some kind of guarantee system.[99] Rather, the reason that British colonies such as Sierra Leone, Lagos, the Gold Coast, Ceylon, Uganda, and Kowloon as well as the French colonies of Guinea and the Ivory Coast[100] preferred not to authorize the passing of these public works into "domain of works undertaken by capital itself"[101] was that by becoming or employing their own constructional engineers, they eliminated the need for a "middle man in the shape of a contractor" and his profit.[102] Experience under the guarantee system with what today would be called private contractors' cost overruns frequently caused colonial governments to abandon that system. The French colonial government in Dahomey, for example, discovering that the concessions it had made to a private firm (Borelli) were untenable, took over construction itself in 1904.[103] These governments' wish to appropriate or save that profit may, to be sure, have corroborated Marx's point that one of the prerequisites of pure capitalist undertaking in this area is that the share capital involved be satisfied with interest rather than profit.[104]

This tendency to constrain the scope and profits of railway constructors in the colonies overlapped with the rise in the 1890s in Britain itself of a trend among local governments to carry on public works by means of so-called direct labor. Just as the British used the departmental system in the Chinese concession Kowloon to "break the rings" of a few large Chinese construction firms that kept prices high,[105] the direct labor system was designed to curb the corruption associated with contractors and rings in the metropole. As a "progressive" governmental measure, it was also promoted by the labor and "municipal socialism" movements, particularly in the London County Council.[106]

---

[98]*Private Enterprise in British Tropical Africa* at 8, 12 (Cmd. 2016, 8 *PP* 1924 [195]).

[99]See Frederic Shelford, "Some Features of the West African Government Railways," 189 *MPICE* 1, 22 (1912) (discussion contribution by George Denton to the effect that the government built the Lagos line because no one would do it under contract without exorbitant sums).

[100]See *Papers Relating to the Construction of Railways in Sierra Leone, Lagos, and the Gold Coast* at 8, 10, 30-34; *Papers Respecting Proposed Railway from Mombasa to Lake Victoria Nyanza* (C.-6560, 16 *PP* 1892 [27]); De Renty, 3 *Les Chemins de fer* at 127-65; Bourrat, "Rapport" at 1880-82; *Die Eisenbahnen Afrikas* at 1579-82; K.M. de Silva, *A History of Sri Lanka* 284-85 (1981).

[101]Marx, *Grundrisse* at 429-30.

[102]*Private Enterprise in British Tropical Africa* at 8; *Papers Relating to the Construction of Railways in Sierra Leone, Lagos, and the Gold Coast* at 29-30; *Correspondence Relating to Railway Construction in Niger* (Cd. 2787, 78 *PP* 1906 [21]); *Report on the Construction and Working of the Mombasa-Victoria (Uganda) Railway and Steamboat Services on Lake Victoria, 1903-1904* (Cd. 2332, 13 *PP* 1905 [317]). The engineer who was the spiritual progenitor of the Aswan Dam estimated that "[i]f the dam could have been built by departmental agency, in the way in which such works are built in India," it would have cost only three-fifths of its cost under the private contractors Aird & Sons. W. Willcocks, 2 *Egyptian Irrigation* 744-45 (3d ed. 1913).

[103]De Renty, 3 *Les Chemins de fer coloniaux en Afrique* at 167-210. Early and unsystematic efforts at government construction of railways in German East and South West Africa that were expensive and time-consuming purportedly led to government subsidized private construction of railways. Baltzer, *Kolonialbahnen* at 295-96, 214.

[104]Marx, *Grundrisse* at 428. An American engineer formulated this view at the turn of the century: "It is felt more and more that the only fair way to fix the compensation of the various factors contributing to the creation of public benefits outside the range of competition is to induce the capitalists to furnish their contribution, not by promising them the net earnings which they might get by...charging what the traffic will bear, but by promising the smallest rate of interest for which capital is obtainable in the open market." Joseph Mayer, "Canals Between the Lakes and New York," 26 *PASCE* 972, 975 (1900).

[105]Graves Eves, "The Canton-Kowloon Railway: British Section," 192 *MPICE* 190, 191 (1913).

[106]See Caroline Bedale, Michael Paddon, & Peter Carter, "Direct Labour: A Form of Socialised Production in the Construction Industry," in 1 *PBE* 175 (1980); Linda Clarke, "The Importance of a

Predictably, curtailment of even a small sphere of capitalist production prompted vigorous attacks by the construction industry on this "little mad orgie of socialism."[107]

Colonial states in the tropics often built their own railways because "private capital would not undertake the risks...not being able to calculate what the cost would be" in unexplored and unsurveyed regions. The areas in which governments planned railways chiefly to move troops in order to maintain control were frequently countries where the very same "disturbed condition hindered" the investment of private capital in railways. Where colonial administrations in Africa had earlier relied on English consulting engineers to let small sections of a line to local contractors, the latter engaged in a bidding war for labor, which not only increased the wage costs that were passed through to the government, but also "produced bad work on the part of the native. He knew if he did not please one man he could walk over to another, who would be glad to get him." Dissatisfied with these consequences of the transition from slave to free labor, colonial administrators fashioned a system intended to fuse the best of both worlds. They established their own construction-engineering staffs, which "obtained the labour through the chiefs, [and] the labourers obeyed the officials they knew who could...enforce discipline.... There was no counter bidding for labour with the consequent demoralization."[108] At the turn of the century, for example, after a private firm employed Italian, Indian, Chinese, and Malaysia workers to build a railway in Madagascar, the French colonial government took over the construction, shifting instead to compulsory native labor.[109]

The departmental system became more and more widespread in the British crown colonies during the latter half of the nineteenth century not (only) because "the mode of production based on capital" there had not yet developed to its "highest stage," in which "the real community constituted itself in the form of capital."[110] Given the colonies' status as exclaves of English capital, that stage need only have been reached in England itself, where individual capitals already felt the limits of the means of transportation and communications in and to and from the colonies. In fact, however, even colonial settlers in Africa felt those limits because they viewed the considerable amount of indigenous labor devoted to human porterage of their commodities as a drain on the scarce labor available for production.[111]

Indeed, colonial governments in Africa promoted railway construction as a means of forging a wage labor force. Thus in 1905, the governor of German East Africa, Count Goetzen, submitted a memorandum in which he characterized construction of a railway in that colony both as made an urgent necessity by the "labor question" and as solving that problem. The crisis that threatened the colony was the lack of labor for the coastal plantations, which could be alleviated either by making labor in the interior accessible or by "rigorously tightening the tax screw." Failure to do one or the other would bring plantations to a halt, a stoppage that would destroy one of the advantages "that a colony is designed to yield for its mother country." Construction of a railway line to the interior

---

Historical Approach: Changes in the Construction Industry," in *id.* at 30, 34; "The Works of the London County Council," 62 *Engineering* 647 (1896) (editorial). Colonial Secretary Joseph Chamberlain, who was responsible for inaugurating railway building in the African colonies, had advocated municipal socialism as mayor of Birmingham. Semmel, *Imperialism and Social Reform* at 81-82.

[107]"The London County Council and Contractors," 61 *Engineering* 349, 350 (1896) (editorial).

[108]Knowles, *The Economic Development of the British Overseas Empire* at 148-50.

[109]*Die Eisenbahnen Afrikas* at 1625-26.

[110]Marx, *Grundrisse* at 428, 430.

[111]Leroy Vail, "The Making of an Imperial Slum: Nyasaland and Its Railways, 1895-1935," 16 *JAH* 89, 90-91 (1975).

"would immediately solve the labor question for the plantations" by providing access to the large population of the interior and by freeing 40,000 to 60,000 porters for production.[112]   In South West Africa, a new railway line was promoted on the ground that it would make available for the diamond mines workers from Ovamboland, who could be employed at one-third the wages being paid to the workers from the Cape Colony. This railway was also applauded as securing for the mine owners an additional quarter-million work days annually by making the ten-day march from Ovamboland unnecessary.[113]

Colonial officials praised as a third by-product of railway construction that African workers who had been successfully recruited to build the lines would be more likely after that experience to become wage workers on the plantations.[114] The declaration of the Brussels Conference of 1890 that the construction of railways to the interior of Africa would be an efficacious means of combating the slave trade "en vue de substituer des moyens économiques et accélérés du transport au portage actuel par l'homme"[115] thus becomes intelligible against the background of the manifest advantages accruing to colonial capital.

## The Decline of the Independent Colonial Railway Constructors

By the beginning of the twentieth century, then, the British free-lance contractor, guided by his own judgment as to the profitability of particular projects, was no longer the dominant figure. On the one hand, his entrepreneurial discretion became circumscribed by the changes in the financial system after the crisis of 1866, which conferred greater power on banks, and by increasing competition from European and even U.S. contracting firms.[116]   On the other hand, by the last quarter of the nineteenth century, when British global economic superiority began to be eroded by French and especially German and U.S. firms, the new competition generated a second wave of colonial expansion designed to open up new sources of raw materials and markets or to preserve privileged access to already existing ones.[117]   The need to control such supplies and markets "through railway penetration was increasingly viewed as part of a British counter-offensive to the challenge of world-wide competition."[118]

State-formulated imperialist political-military considerations supervened as the colonial powers in Asia and Africa became increasingly enmeshed in military hostilities; Britain and France began systematically to interconnect their colonies through rail links.[119]   Where, as in Siam or China, for example, informal

[112]Gouverneur Graf Goetzen, "Denkschrift, betreffend den Bau von Eisenbahnen in Deutsch-Ostafrika," in *Die Eisenbahnen Afrikas: Grundlagen und Gesichtspunkte für eine koloniale Eisenbahnpolitik in Afrika,* in *SBVR* (12th Legis. Per., 1st Sess.), 241 ASB, Doc. No. 262, at 1563, 1719, 1721, 1723 (1907).

[113]Baltzer, *Kolonialbahnen* at 93-94.

[114]See Schinzinger, *Die Kolonien und das Deutsche Reich* at 64.

[115]*General Act of the Brussels Conference, 1889-90,* art. 1, ¶ 3 at 2 (Cd. 6048, 50 *PP* 1890 [1]).

[116]Middlemas, *Master Builders* at 117-18.

[117]The origin of this analytic tradition is associated with J. Hobson, *Imperialism: A Study* 71-81 (1967 [1902]), from whom it then passed to Lenin.   On the debate over whether a sea change in imperialist practice took place in the late nineteenth century, see *The Robinson and Gallagher Controversy* (Wm. Louis ed., 1976).

[118]R. Dumett, "Joseph Chamberlain, Imperial Finance and Railway Policy in British West Africa in the Late Nineteenth Century," 90 *EngHR* 287, 297 (1975).

[119]See Guillaume Depping, "Le Transsaharien," 17 *GC* 105-107 (1890); "The Railways of Africa," 42 *EN* 206 (1899); J. Clapham, *An Economic History of Modern Britain: Free Trade and Steel 1850-1886,* at 213 (1932); idem, *An Economic History of Modern Britain: The Early Railway Age* at 421-23; Rosa Luxemburg, "Riesenwerke des Kapitalismus," in idem, 1:1 *GW* 286-88 (1970 [1898]); Middlemas, *Master Builders* at 24-25, 76, 82-89, 94-95.

imperialism prevailed, construction firms relied heavily on their respective national governments to apply the appropriate doses of pressure to insure that they received profitable contracts.[120]

> Whether it was the U.S.A. penetrating Mexico and Latin America, Britain dominating India on railways designed for military use, or Germany seeking colonial power along the Berlin-Baghdad route,...it ceased to be a matter of indifference who built a railway or won a concession of land beside it. Brassey leased or was given nearly 30,000 square miles of the Argentine in payment for one of the easiest railways he ever built; but fifty years later the whole diplomatic resources of Washington were used to prevent Cowdray extending his oil empire to control the sources of Columbia.[121]

French rule in Indochina presented a somewhat aberrant evolution. Driven primarily by colonial military and political considerations, the government believed "that railways, merely by their passage through a country, would create wealth. ... No one foresaw that there was little to transport. Natives, in most parts of the colony, raised only enough for their wants and did not exchange the surplus, if any, because adjacent districts produced the same things."[122] Although the purpose of colonial railways was not to create internal linkages but to transport the extracted surplus to metropole, "[t]he poverty of human and material resources in Indochina meant that there were no obvious accumulations of local capital or extensive markets to capture."[123] By the mid-1880s even the leading French civil engineering journal recognized that it would be more rational to postpone construction of railways until local agriculture developed products other than rice.[124] In spite of this advice, the French colonial state proceeded with construction of politically dictated lines that ran through deserted areas while neglecting the most developed regions. Predictably, graft and the government's financial guarantees meant that the ventures were profitable only for the French contractors and engineers—and certainly not for the tens of thousands of Chinese coolies who died building them.[125] Among these French construction firms was Société de Construction des Batignolles, one of the most experienced colonial railway builders, which built the line from Indochina to Yunnan in China in the years before World War I.[126]

Foreign railway construction in China also deviated from the British free-lance and colonial models. This development peculiar to China was a function of the absence of direct colonial rule.[127] Two decades before the wave of concessions that China was compelled to grant to the Great Powers in the wake of the Sino-Japanese War in the mid-1890s, a more orthodox beginning had taken place. In 1875-76, the British trading firm Jardine, Matheson financed a 10-mile rail line

---

[120]See e.g., David Holm, "Thailand's Railways and Informal Imperialism," in *Railway Imperialism* at 121-35.

[121]Middlemas, *Master Builders* at 308. On the pressure exerted by the U.S. government on Colombia, see J. Spender, *Weetman Pearson First Viscount Cowdray 1856-1927,* at 209-10 (1930).

[122]Virginia Thompson, *French Indo-China* 206 (1968 [1937]).

[123]Martin Murray, *The Development of Capitalism in Colonial Indochina (1870-1940),* at 167 (1980).

[124]R. Gentilini, "Les Voies de communication en Cochinchine," 9 *GC* 177-82, 199-203, 225-29, especially at 229 (1886).

[125]Thompson, *French Indo-China* at 207-11; Murray, *Development of Capitalism in Colonial Indochina* at 166-77.

[126]"The French Yunnan Railway," 95 *Engineering* 6, 8 (1913); Joelle Deniot, *Usine et cooperation ouvrière: Métiers-syndicalisation conflits aux Batignolles* 5-7 (1983).

[127]Years before British capital introduced railways into China, a journal anticipated the problem of expropriation associated with enterprise in noncolonized areas by threatening that "it is more than likely that reparation would be exacted in a manner which would forever establish English influence in the East." "Railways in China," 17 *Engineer* 341 (1864) (editorial).

between the ports of Woosung and Shanghai both as a profit-making enterprise and as a kind of demonstration in the hope that it would galvanize the same enthusiasm for railroads in China that the Japanese were contemporaneously showing.[128] One of the British contractors, John Dixon, boasted that the introduction of railways heralded "the opening of vast markets for the absorption of our manufactures."[129]   The day in 1875 that Dixon dispatched "the first lot of navvies" to China would, *The Engineer* assured its readers, "be long remembered."[130]

Even as the inauguration of this weapon of capitalist penetration was being celebrated in *The Times*,[131] a prescient anti-imperialist raised a dissenting voice in its columns.  Outlining the objections of China's governing classes, Robert Douglas observed:

> The fate of India is a nightmare which is contantly haunting them, and to avoid a similar absorption is the ruling motive of their policy.  Seen from this standpoint, the appearance of English engineers measuring out the length and breadth of the land, hollowing out mountains, and spanning rivers would seem to them to be but a foreshadowing of the arrival of English Governors and Viceroys, and the completion of a network of railways worked and partly or entirely owned by Englishmen would in their eyes be equivalent to handing over the destinies of the Empire to the hated foreigner.[132]

Steam-driven transportation would enter China's program, Douglas predicted, "when native engineers shall be found equal to the task of constructing lines and locomotives, and when Chinese capital shall out of its abundance supply the necessary dollars for the undertaking."[133]   To which Dixon, the contractor, laconically replied: if British capital waited until the Chinese had the capital and engineers to build railways, "we better give up at once."[134]

When the Chinese government bought up and dismantled the Woosung-Shanghai railway a year after it went into operation and packed off the materials and rolling stock to Formosa, foreigners' apprehension increased.[135]   The reason for British impatience with these precapitalist rhythms was manifest: "Here is a country extending over nearly a million and a-half square miles, with mineral and agricultural resources capable of infinite expansion and as yet practically untapped, with a population of nearly four hundred millions, who would be only too willing to purchase our productions and sell us their own, if communication with them were only rendered convenient and cheap."  A quarter-century after the dismantling, *The Engineer* was still editorializing that "really it seemed almost to justify the suggestion that China should be coerced into progress for her own good."[136]

By the turn of the century, Japan, Russia, and the Western capitalist powers had embarked on precisely such a program.[137]   The rivalry for concessions among

---

[128]"Modern China from an Engineer's Point of View: No. I—Railways and Railway Projects," 85 *Engineer* 251 (1898); "Railways in China," 90 *Engineer* 32 (1900) (editorial).

[129]*Times*, Oct. 15, 1877, at 6, col. 4 (letter to editor).

[130]"Navvies for China," 40 *Engineer* 270 (1875).

[131]*Times*, Oct. 5, 1876, at 5, col. 6; Oct. 12, 1876, at 7, col. 5; Oct. 18, 1876, at 6, col. 4.

[132]*Times*, Oct. 24, 1876, at 5, col. 5 (letter to editor).

[133]*Id.*

[134]*Times*, Oct. 26, 1876, at 3, col. 5 (letter to editor).

[135]See Richard Rapier, "Brief Account of the Woosung Railway," 59 *MPICE* 274-77 (1880); Percy Kent, *Railway Enterprise in China: An Account of Its Origins and Development* 9-15 (1907).

[136]"Chinese Railway Progress," 89 *Engineer* 594 (1900) (editorial).

[137]See generally Clarence Davis, "Railway Imperialism in China, 1895-1939," in *Railway Imperialism*

the Great Powers coincided with the emergence of intense Chinese government interest in railways as an element of national development. China's predicament lay in the fact that "China wants railways, but she does not want their construction to be the means of introducing foreign yoke.... [S]he has but to look at the swindling in connection with American railroad construction to know what capitalists from that quarter would do."[138] China was, however, unable to avoid this political trap despite the fact that by 1908, under the supervision of Chinese engineers educated abroad, China was building its own railway and would soon be able to dispense with foreign firms.[139]

When a foreign power entered into a construction agreement with the Chinese government,[140] it "secured a new sphere of interest and tremendous profits for its national investors," primarily banks and industrial exporters, in the first instance by "extend[ing] a usurious loan to the Chinese railway administration at almost no risk, since repayment was guaranteed by a lien on government revenues. Then the money so loaned would be promptly returned to the foreigners' pockets as payment for the construction costs charged by the foreign country's railroad contractors."[141] In their franker pronouncements, British industrial interests conceded that whereas "there is a considerable case for the concession railway...for a continually increasing market for the products of the concessionaires," "[t]he very natural objection to the concession agreement from the Chinese point of view is that they have no share in the probable profits, which have amounted from 10 per cent. to 20 per cent. on some of the Government railways, after paying interest on the foreign loans."[142] But from a metropolitan perspective that identified "industrial development" per se with "the introduction of unlimited foreign capital,"[143] such considerations weighed little especially in light of the fact that the capitalist powers also pursued railway building so vigorously in China because it was a source of enormous profit for manufacturers of steel, locomotives, and other materials and equipment.[144]

Japanese railway contractors, though faced with no foreign competition in their building operations in Korea and Formosa during the period of Japanese colonial expansion, were much more creatures of the state than free-lance entrepreneurs. From the turn of the century on, they worked almost exclusively for the Japanese army, navy or colonial governments. That pattern persisted even as late as the 1930s, when they constructed hydroelectric facilities and mines in occupied Manchuria.[145]

---

155-73 (Clarence Davis & Kenneth Wilburn, Jr. ed., 1991).

[138]"Railway Construction in China," 15 *EN* 347 (1886) (reprinted from *Herapath's Journal*).

[139]See e.g. E-tu Zen Sun, *Chinese Railways and British Interests 1898-1911* (1971 [1954]); 59 *EN* 257 (1908) (letter from Roger Toll).

[140]See Wáng Jing-chūn, *Railway Loan Agreements of China* (1922).

[141]Frederic Wakeman, Jr., *The Fall of Imperial China* 238 (1977 [1975]); Baltzer, *Kolonialbahnen* at 283-84. For a concise description of the concession system, see "Railway Concessions and Contracts in China," 115 *Engineer* 458 (1913); "Railways in China: Shantung Railway," 118 *Engineer* 6 (1914). For a wartime British anti-German perspective, see "The German Railway Record in China," 103 *Engineering* 515 (1917). For an example of European railway construction heavily reliant on Chinese "contractors," see John Schrecker, *Imperialism and Chinese Nationalism: Germany in Shantung* 105-106 (1971). On Japanese railway construction in China using Chinese and Korean laborers, see J. Dobbins, "Rebuilt Antung-Mukden Ry., China," 68 *EN* 809 (1912).

[142]"British Engineering Enterprise and Chinese Railways," 106 *Engineering* 92, 93 (1918).

[143]"British Engineering Enterprises in China," 106 *Engineering* 220 (1918).

[144]See e.g., "American Competition in China," 65 *Engineer* 698-99 (1898); Mi Rucheng, "Deutscher Eisenbahnbau in China, 1870-1938," in *Von der Kolonialpolitik zur Kooperation: Studien zur Geschichte der deutsch-chinesischen Beziehungen* 101-39 (Kuo Heng-yü ed., 1986).

[145]Yasuyuki Hippo & Saburo Tamura, "Japan," in *The Global Construction Industry* at 59, 60.

## The Case of the Not-So-Ideal Aggregate Capitalist: Palmerston's Obstinate Opposition to the Suez Canal

Lord Palmerston last week did not hesitate to give a very decided opinion as to the Suez Canal question; and if an opinion of his lordship is sufficient to prevent the carrying out of this scheme, it is, of course, shelved for this century at all events.[146]

No mechanistic one-to-one correspondence ever obtained between the abstract systemic mandate of the "bourgeois period of history...to create the material basis of the new world—universal intercourse founded upon the mutual dependency of mankind" and the requisite means of transportation on the one hand and the actions of capitalists and states on the other.[147] Even if "the capitalist mode of production is a historical means of developing the material productive force and creating the world market corresponding to it," the world market cannot guarantee that its human agents will always make rational decisions optimally designed to comply with its imperious demands of developing the means of transportation and communication so as to reduce the time and costs of circulation of capital in the world market.[148]

A prime example of such globally irrational decisionmaking is the stubborn opposition by the British state to the building of the Suez Canal, which, in the event, benefited British capital most by opening India, China, and eventually Australia to steamship traffic and reducing the circulation time of commodity shipments from a year to three months. In large part this revitalized supremacy of British shipping was based on the Suez Canal's promotion of iron and steel-hulled steamships driven by the new compound engines—which economized on the consumption of coal, thus freeing space for cargo—in which British technology surpassed that of U.S. shipbuilders.[149] The increased size of the new ships, in turn, made most harbors and ports obsolete; especially in the colonial regions, "[t]he whole export trade of a country may be hung up if it has to be squeezed through a neck too narrow to accommodate more than a small amount at a time...."[150] Thus by the turn of the century, a steady demand for expanded port facilities made a British firm, S. Pearson & Son, the world's leading contractor for the requisite dredging work.[151]

Yet in spite of all these manifest benefits to British capital, and contrary to dogmatic left-academic belief in the quasi-self-executing character of economic imperatives,[152] the British state engaged in international intrigues with the Ottoman Empire and Egypt for more than two decades in an unsuccessful effort to frustrate construction of the Suez Canal.[153] That Prime Minister Palmerston, one of the great landowners in Ireland and leader of the Whigs before industrialists

---

[146]"The Suez Canal," 4 *Engineer* 45 (1857) (editorial).

[147]Marx, "The Future Results of British Rule in India" at 252.

[148]Marx, 3 *Das Kapital* at 260; *idem*, 2 *Das Kapital*, in Karl Marx [&] Friedrich Engels, 24 Werke 254 (1963 [1885]).

[149]See Marx, 3 *Das Kapital* at 81 (chapter written by Engels); Knowles, *Economic Development of the British Overseas Empire* at 17-18, 316-17; Max Fletcher, "The Suez Canal and World Shipping, 1869-1914," 18 *JEH* 556-73 (1958); Thomas Marston, *Britain's Imperial Role in the Red Sea Area 1800-1878*, at 385 (1961).

[150]Knowles, *The Economic Development of the British Overseas Empire* at 147.

[151]Middlemas, *Master Builders* at 179.

[152]For one such historically inaccurate account of British capital and the Suez Canal, see Elizabeth Petras, *Jamaican Labor Migration: White Capital and Black Labor, 1850-1930*, at 55-61 (1988).

[153]Palmerston, who was the leading force shaping Britain's foreign policy from 1830 until his death in 1865, stated in 1857 that Britain had been working against the canal for fifteen years. 146 *PD* (3d ser.) 1043-44 (1857).

gained control of that party,[154] failed to function adequately as what Engels later called the personified fictitious or ideal aggregate English (let alone world) capitalist, insuring the average interest of aggregate capital as the real average existence of the individual capitals, is unsurprising.[155]   Marx, given his bottomless contempt for Palmerston, should not have been surprised by the latter's deficiencies as an ideal aggregate capitalist although he does not appear to have commented on Palmerston's policy with regard to the Suez Canal.[156]

As foreign minister in 1847, recognizing that the canal would necessarily be advantageous to England as the world's greatest commercial country and sea power, Viscount Palmerston did not oppose its construction.[157]   Ten years later, however, Prime Minister Palmerston, obsessed for Great Power political reasons with the canal's alleged disintegrative impact on the Ottoman Empire,[158] claimed that the Suez Canal was yet another "bubble scheme" "palmed upon gullible capitalists," and expressed surprise that its promoter, Ferdinand de Lesseps, was speculating on the "credulity of English capitalists" vis-à-vis a scheme hostile to British interests.[159]   Palmerston's parliamentary debate in 1857 with his rival, Gladstone, who would eventually replace him as the head of an industrialists' party, was revealing.  Gladstone told Parliament that although he was not qualified to judge "whether the Suez Canal would be advantageous to this country...no man...could look at the map of the globe, and deny that a canal through the Isthmus of Suez...would be a great stroke for the benefit of mankind.[160] Palmerston, in contrast, boasted that when Lesseps came "preaching all over England in order to induce English capitalists to give him those means which he is unable to obtain from the rest of the world," he, Palmerston, had taken the proper "course in explaining to British capitalists that in affording money for the construction of such a work they would be aiding a scheme which was fraught with injury to the interests of England itself."[161]   After listening to such rhetoric during a private audience with Palmerston, Lesseps observed to a correspondent that he had to ask himself whether he was dealing with "un maniaque ou un homme d'État."[162]

Palmerston's cabinet in the mid-1850s unanimously opposed his position, suggesting instead that the canal be placed under international control.[163] Palmerston's response—"that it would be best for the French and English Governments to leave this scheme as a commercial and engineering question to be settled by the...money markets of Europe"[164]—was, in the light of his elaborately

---

[154]See E. Steele, *Palmerston and Liberalism, 1855-1865*, at 134, 214, 228, 320 (1991).

[155]Friedrich Engels, *Herrn Eugen Dührings Umwälzung der Wissenschaft*, in Karl Marx [&] Friedrich Engels, 20 *Werke* 260 (1968 [1878]) (on the "Staat der Kapitalisten, der ideelle Gesamtkapitalist"); Elmar Altvater, "Zu einigen Problemen des Staatsinterventionismus," *PK*, No. 3, May 1972, at 1, 5-8.

[156]See e.g., Karl Marx, "Lord Palmerston," in Karl Marx [&] Friedrich Engels, I:12 *Gesamtausgabe (MEGA)* 357 (1984 [1853]); *idem*, "The English Election," in Karl Marx [&] Frederick Engels, 15 *CollW* 226 (1985 [1857]); *idem*, "The Defeat of Cobden, Bright and Gibson," in *id.* at 238.

[157]Leland Jenks, *The Migration of British Capital to 1875*, at 302 (1963 [1927]) (citing unpublished Foreign Office record).

[158]See Herbert Bell, 2 *Lord Palmerston* 355-61 (1936).

[159]146 *PD* (3d ser.) 1044, 1706 (1857).

[160]147 *PD* (3d ser.) 1667 (1857).

[161]147 *PD* (3d ser.) 1682 (1857).

[162]Ferdinand de Lesseps, *Lettres, Journal et Documents pour servir à l'histoire du Canal de Suez (1854-1855-1856)*, at 377 (1875) (letter of Apr. 7, 1856 to A.M. Barthélemy Saint-Hilaire).

[163]See 1 *George Douglas Eighth Duke of Argyll (1823-1900)*, at 568 (Dowager Duchess of Argyll ed., 1906) (Argyll was Lord privy seal in that cabinet).

[164]Letter from Palmerston to [Foreign Secretary] Earl Russell, Dec. 8, 1861, printed in Evelyn Ashley, 2 *The Life of Henry John Temple Viscount Palmerston: 1846-1865*, at 325, 328 (2d ed. 1876).

orchestrated diplomatic campaign against the canal, disingenuous. Indeed, in 1858, when the Radical John Roebuck proposed a resolution in the House of Commons to the effect that England's power and influence not be used to induce the sultan to withhold his consent from the project, Palmerston, who was temporarily out of office, led the forces that rejected the proposal.[165]

Although a large majority of businessmen opposed Palmerston's policy,[166] he succeeded in ensuring that no one in England subscribed to any of the Suez company's shares.[167] The City appreciated the manifest benefits of shortened transportation links to India. To "the rich and thrusting middle classes...the canal meant only one thing: business."[168] The *Daily News*, the leading organ of advanced Liberalism, criticized Palmerston's view as "a senile piece of nonsense on his lordship's part...."[169] Roebuck told members of Parliament that "anything more puerile, he had almost said anile" than Palmerston's course of action was inconceivable.[170] Although in 1855 *The Times* reported that construction of the Suez Canal was not possible and that the canal itself would not reduce shipping times, it soon experienced a conversion.[171] Four years later it asked editorially "what could have persuaded...the mistress of India and the most commercial State on the face of the globe...to oppose a work by which it would be the greatest gainer?"[172] And in the age of free trade, when political opposition to the Suez Canal seemed "retrogressive,"[173] the leading free trade organ, *The Economist*, denounced Palmerston's "selfish policy [as] owing either to some very mistaken theory, or some very awkward management on the part of the Government."[174]

That English capital was in general little impressed by a French military threat was underscored by its contemporary backing of the Paris, Nantes, and Cherbourg Railway. In the mid-1850s, the leading English railway contractor, Brassey, together with the railway engineer Locke and considerable English labor, built the line, which was vital to the French military. "The cry raised by many...English newspapers, that Cherbourg was originally planned and designedly executed as a menace to England, did not hinder Englishmen from embarking their purses and their muscles in making this naval stronghold effective by connecting it with the leading lines of railway communication in France...."[175]

Palmerston's failure to "foresee the great advantages to be derived by British commerce from this great work"[176] was compounded by a false analysis of the Suez Canal's political-economic impact on Britain's control over its empire, in particular over India, and on its command of the sea route around the Cape of Good Hope. His real, anti-French, animus, as he revealed in a private letter to the editor of *The Times*, in response to the aforementioned editorial, was France's

[165] 150 *PD* (3d ser.) 1361-1401 (1858) (the vote was 62 to 290). According to de Lesseps, Palmerston told him in 1855 that the canal would deprive England of its advantage by being open to all ships. Ferdinand de Lesseps, 1 *Recollections of Forty Years* 269-71 (C. Pitman tr., 1887).

[166] 231 *PD* (3d ser.) 855 (1876).

[167] Ferdinand de Lesseps, 2 *Recollections of Forty Years* 121 (C. Pitman tr., 1887).

[168] Charles Beatty, *Ferdinand de Lesseps: A Biographical Study* 153 (1956). See also Jenks, *Migration of British Capital* at 304.

[169] *Daily News*, Sept. 10, 1857, quoted in Lesseps, 2 *Recollections of Forty Years* at 78.

[170] 150 *PD* (3d ser.) 1366 (1858).

[171] "The Projected Canal Across the Isthmus of Suez, *Times*, Oct. 25, 1855, at 6, col. 5.

[172] *Times*, Dec. 16, 1859, at 8, col. 2.

[173] "Isthmus of Suez Canal," 6 *Engineer* 277, 278 (1858).

[174] "England's Suez Policy," *Economist*, Dec. 17, 1859, at 1398. See also "The Political Objection to the Suez Canal," *id.*, Dec. 24, 1859, at 1426.

[175] Devey, *Life of Joseph Locke* at 234.

[176] 20 *Encyclopaedia Britannica* 645, 648 (11th ed. 1911) (s.v. "Palmerston").

alleged object of establishing "a French colony in the heart of Egypt," which would simultaneously enable the French military "to seize the canal...and steam away through the canal to India, sweep our commerce, take our colonies...long before our reinforcements...could arrive by long long sea voyage" around Africa.[177] Palmerston's opposition was bolstered by the equally erroneous and/or self-interested high engineering authority of Robert Stephenson. One of the leading British railway engineers and a member of Parliament, Stephenson opined that construction of the canal was impracticable. Lesseps charged that his testimony was suborned because he had also built a competing railway in Egypt, the owners of which desperately wanted to thwart construction of the Suez Canal.[178] Stephenson, ever attentive to his reputation among the investing class, responded that he did not want to be viewed as even "tacitly allowing capitalists to throw away their money on...an unwise and unremunerative speculation."[179]

In 1869 Britain was confronted with the accomplished fact of a canal built by a private French company and under French control. With the aid of a loan from the London Rothschilds while Parliament was not in session, the new British ideal aggregate capitalist, Prime Minister Disraeli, who had equivocated on Suez as Chancellor of the Exchequer in the Earl of Derby's cabinet in 1858, overcame the Victorian state's alleged distaste for interferences with markets and bought half the shares in the Suez Canal in 1875 on the cheap from the bankrupt Egyptian Ismail Pasha.[180] Thus in the best of all possible English capitalist worlds, "the Suez Canal was built by French enterprise at Egyptian expense for British advantage."[181]

Nor was the British ideal capitalist alone in its misreading of the commands of the world market. In its lack of interest in, or condemnation of, the Suez Canal, Dutch capital, in particular as organized in the Amsterdam Chamber of Commerce, also misapprehended the canal's importance for exploiting the Dutch colonial possessions in the East Indies.[182]

---

[177]Letter from Lord Palmerston to John Delane, Dec. 16, 1859, printed in Arthur Dasent, *John Thadeus Delane Editor of "The Times": His Life and Correspondence* 326-28 (1908). By the mid-twentieth century, a French biographer of Lesseps characterized Palmerston's position as incredible. George Edgar-Bonnet, *Ferdinand de Lesseps: Le Diplomate, Le Créateur de Suez* 261 (1951). For a not very cogent defense of Palmerston's position, see Donald Southgate, *'The Most English Minister...': The Policies and Politics of Palmerston* 539-40 (1966).

[178]See 146 *PD* (3d ser.) 1706-1707 (1857); 150 *PD* (3d ser.) 1371-73 (1858) (Stephenson's statements); Michael Robbins, *George and Robert Stephenson* 56-57 (1966). On Robert Stephenson and the building of the railway from Alexandria to Cairo to Suez, see 5 *Engineer* 364 (1858); Charles Hallberg, *The Suez Canal: Its History and Diplomatic Importance* 101-109 (1931); Lionel Wiener, *L'Égypte et ses chemins de fer* 64-82 (1932). See also "Annual Report Session 1859-60," 19 *MPICE* 133, 142 (1860). For belated recognition that Stephenson got the engineering wrong, see "The Suez Canal," 16 *Engineer* 67 (1863).

[179]"The Isthmus of Suez," 6 *Engineer* 94, 95 (1858) (printing letter from Stephenson to *Austria Gazette*).

[180]See 149 *PD* (3d ser.) 850 (1858); 150 *PD* (3d ser.) 1391-96 (1858); 227 *PD* (3d ser.) 266-67 (1876); Hallberg, *The Suez Canal* at 101-212, 229-53; Percy Fitzgerald, 2 *The Great Canal at Suez: Its Political, Engineering, and Financial History* 269-303, 314-15 (1876); Jenks, *Migration of British Capital* at 320-25.

[181]Rondo Cameron, *France and the Economic Development of Europe 1800-1914: Conquests of Peace and Seeds of War* 472 (1961). See also Beatty, *Ferdinand de Lesseps* at 273: "Never more feminine, Britannia had a sudden craving for an article which had been in the world's shop window for years...but had never seemed likely to suit her, and now she wanted no one else to have it." For a concise account of British opposition to the Suez Canal, see Halford Hoskins, *British Routes to India* 343-72 (1966 [1928]).

[182]See Ernst Baasch, *Holländische Wirtschaftsgeschichte* 524-25 (1927).

# 6

# Non-British Competition

When competition of all against all replaced the domination of the world market by a single Power, conceptions of international economic morality necessarily became chaotic.[1]

## A Comparative Historiographical Interlude

British firms by no means monopolized the construction of colonial or imperialist infrastructure projects in the nineteenth century, although their preeminence and cosmopolitan character was demonstrated by the fact that even the French government selected Peto & Betts to build the first railway in colonial Algeria in 1859-1860, a short section between Algiers and Blida, which primarily served military purposes.[2] At the beginning of the twentieth century, too, as a function of the virtual ubiquity of British capital, British construction firms were selected to build railways associated with British-dominated mining operations in the Belgian and Portuguese African colonies.[3]

Nevertheless, French and German construction firms competed with British firms for international railway, bridge, harbor, and canal building orders. Gustave Eiffel's French construction-engineering firm, for example, built bridges between 1867 and 1889 in Portugal, Russia, Greece, Egypt, Indochina, and South America.[4] More suggestive of the state of international industrial competition was the railway and bridge construction that integrated French and German steel firms performed as adjuncts to their manufacturing operations. Thus beginning in the 1850s, the French firm Schneider built railway bridges in Italy, Portugal, and Spain; later it carried out this type of work in Africa and South America as well.[5] Similarly, Krupp secured the concession to build a railway in Venezuela in the 1890s, which

---

[1]Edward Carr, *The Twenty Years' Crisis, 1919-1939: An Introduction to the Study of International Relations* 82 (1964 [1939]).

[2]See "Algerian Railways," 7 *Engineer* 337 (1859); *Times*, Apr. 9, 1860, at 7, col. 2; *BRM for 1864*, at 359 (16th ed. 1864); [Henry Peto], *Sir Morton Peto: A Memorial Sketch* 23 (1893); Charles-André Julien, *Histoire de l'Algérie contemporaine: La Conquête et les débuts de la colonisation (1827-1871)*, at 421-22 (1964). By 1874, however, the French firm Batignolles began building railways in Algeria and then in Tunisia in particular in connection with the exploitation of phosphates and ore. Société de Construction des Batignolles, *L'Oeuvre d'un siècle 1846-1946*, at 47-48 (1952).

[3]See F. Baltzer, *Die Kolonialbahnen mit besonderer Berücksichtigung Afrikas* 240-41, 245, 254, 256, 264-65 (1916); *The Chronicles of a Contractor: Being the Autobiography of the Late George Pauling* 131-34, 142, 214-16 (David Bucahn ed., 1926) (Pauling & Co.).

[4]"Alexandre Gustave Eiffel"; John Ellis, "Gustave Eiffel: A Biographical Sketch," 112 *JSE* 1404-12 (1986).

[5]"Messrs. Schneider and Co.'s Works at Creusot: Ship and Bridge-Building Department, Chalon-sur-Saône," 66 *Engineering* 417, 476-77, 511-13 (1898).

was characterized as "without doubt one of the greatest monuments of German enterprise abroad...probably the greatest."[6]

The most outstanding example of an integrated construction firm closely linked to its nation-state's foreign policy was the French firm, La Société de Construction des Batignolles. A forward-integrated producer of locomotives and steel, Batignolles built so many railways in the French colonies in Africa that it shaped their overall evolution and prided itself on its "contribution à la mise en valeur de l'Empire Colonial Français."[7] Founded in 1846 as Ernest Goüin et Cie with financial support from the Rothschilds and others, the firm quickly expanded from locomotives to metal bridges, shipbuilding, and finally in 1862 to railway construction in Spain, Italy, and elsewhere. After the Franco-Prussian War, the re-named Société de Construction des Batignolles, in seeking to diversify its markets, decided to focus on central Europe in order to counter German influence in the Balkans as part of the French government's overall political-financial strategy on behalf of French capital. By 1885, railway construction was no longer a matter of finding markets for Batignolles as a locomotive manufacturer, but for a firm that had become so diversified that it had outgrown domestic expansion and required the world market for large-scale projects. During the next three decades, in addition to railways and ports in Romania, Greece, Bulgaria, and the eastern Mediterranean, Batignolles also built a bridge in Russia as part of the anti-German alliance.[8]

Although the independent international constructors had declined since Brassey's day, the large British firms retained more of the character of those pioneers than their European counterparts. In spite of the considerable volume of domestic and colonial harbor and industrial works that he carried on behalf of the British government, the most outstanding example of such entrepreneurial autonomy was Weetman Pearson, who, like many prominent British contractors, was a member of the House of Commons.[9] Between 1895 and 1907 Pearson's firm built the Grand Canal to drain Mexico City—for which he specially ordered in England the largest dredgers ever built—Veracruz harbor, and the Tehuantepec Railway linking the Atlantic and Pacific Oceans in Mexico. The railway marked a turning point in Pearson's operations: for the first time he invested his own capital, becoming the Mexican government's partner. The line was almost immediately made obsolete as an interoceanic route by the opening of the Panama Canal—but not before Pearson made a profit on it.[10]

These projects in the Western Hemisphere catapulted Pearson into the front ranks of Britain's large imperial contractors along with Lucas & Aird and Sir John Jackson Ltd. The international intensity of Pearson's operations can be gauged by the fact that of the 66 projects valued at £42.5 million that his firm undertook during the three decades between 1884 (when Pearson moved his headquarters to London and began operating nationally) and World War I, 31, accounting for 62 per cent of the value of his firm's contracts, were located outside of the United Kingdom.[11] During the 1890s about half of Pearson's volume was performed in

[6]"The Great Venezuela Railway," 57 *Engineering* 392 (1894). The Große Venezuela Eisenbahngesellschaft (Berlin & Hamburg) performed the construction.

[7]Société de Construction des Batignolles, *L'Oeuvre* at 77 (quotation); Baltzer, *Kolonialbahnen* at 181, 188, 202; *Chronicles of a Contractor* at 171; Lionel Wiener, *Les Chemins de fer coloniaux de l'Afrique* 21-22 (1930).

[8]Société de Construction des Batignolles, *L'Oeuvre* at 23-47, 55-64.

[9]Brassey was the chief exception although his sons became members of Parliament. For a typical contemporary celebration of Pearson, see T. O'Connor, "Lord Cowdray: A Study in Personality," 51 *NPMM* 353 (1913).

[10]82 *Engineer* 365 (1896); J. Spender, *Weetman Pearson First Viscount Cowdray 1856-1927,* at 84-123 (1930); Edward Glick, "The Tehuantepec Railroad: Mexico's White Elephant," 22 *PHR* 373 (1953).

[11]Calculated according to Spender, *Weetman Pearson* at 287-90. These figures include projects that

Mexico alone.[12]

Pearson's position was immeasurably enriched by oil holdings in Mexico, which he in large part owed to the more than one million acres in drilling concessions granted him by President Porfirio Diaz and part of which he sold to Royal Dutch Shell at the end of World War I.[13] Diaz's preference for Pearson was in part grounded in his desire to use a British firm to counterbalance U.S. influence in Mexico.[14] As he did elsewhere in Latin America, Pearson, vertically integrating forwards, built for his own account some of the Mexican gasworks, electrical light and power plants, and tramways that were in his control by World War I.[15] These operations not only led one historian to speculate that Pearson "probably garnered larger profits from Mexico than any other man, either during or since the Spanish Conquest," but prompted the U.S. government in 1913 to induce the government in Colombia to put an end to Pearson's efforts to gain control over the oil resources in that country as well.[16] By the time of his death in 1927, Pearson (who had been Lord Cowdray since 1910) had reorganized his enterprise, leading to the termination of the construction firm and a shift to oil, airlines, financial services, and publishing.[17]

Unlike such relatively independent British constructors, German construction firms were rarely more than mere agents of German industrial and especially finance capital, which played a historically unique role in facilitating industrial capital accumulation in the pre-World War I era.[18] The political-economically most influential German international constructional undertaking during that period epitomized the gap between the positions of British and German capital. By the 1880s, German capital, which had until then been excluded from forging a colonial empire, fixed its attention on the exploitability of the peasants and raw materials of Anatolia and the availability of export markets in the Near East. Under the leadership of the Deutsche Bank, which was just beginning to fulfill its historic role of "providing strongholds for German foreign trade in the distant world,"[19] heavy industry and the military persuaded the Ottoman sultan, whose principal activities consisted in levying troops and taxes, that construction of a railway from Constantinople to Baghdad and the Persian Gulf would also shore up his fragile semi-colonial regime.[20] Yet the German construction firm—the largest at the

---

extended through the war.

[12]*Id.*; David Jeremy, "Weetman Dickinson Pearson," in 4 *DBB* 582, 583-84 (David Jeremy ed., 1985).

[13]Spender, *Weetman Pearson* at 149-204; Robert Middlemas, *The Master Builders: Thomas Brassey; Sir John Aird; Lord Cowdray; Sir John Norton-Griffiths* 184-97, 209-30 (1963); Daniel Yergin, *The Prize: The Epic Quest for Oil, Money, and Power* 229-32 (1992); Jonathan Brown, *Oil and Revolution in Mexico* 47-70, 143-70 (1993).

[14]Cathryn Thorup, "La competencia económica británica y norteamericana en México (1887-1910): El caso de Weetman Pearson," 31 *HM* 599, 626-40 (1982).

[15]William Fuller, "Dam Building and Bullet Dodging in Mexico," 67 *EN* 1002 (1912) (construction of dam for power plant in Chihuahua); Middlemas, *Master Builders* at 220.

[16]J. Fred Rippy, *British Investments in Latin America, 1822-1949: A Case Study in the Operation of Private Enterprise in Retarded Regions* 102 (1959) (quotation); J. Fred Rippy, *The Capitalists and Columbia* 106-13 (1931); Spender, *Weetman Pearson* at 209-10.

[17]Pearson, for example, took over Lazard Frères. Spender, *Weetman Pearson* at 248-49. Desmond Young, *Member for Mexico: A Biography of Weetman Pearson, First Viscount Cowdray* (1966), is shamelessly derivative of Spender's biography.

[18]See generally Hans Mottek, Walter Becker, & Alfred Schröter, 3 *Wirtschaftsgeschichte Deutschlands: Von der Zeit der Bismarckschen Reichsgründung 1871 bis zur Niederlage des faschistischen deutschen Imperialismus 1945*, at 99-105 (1974); Willfried Spohn, *Weltmarktkonkurrenz und Industrialisierung Deutschlands 1870-1914: Eine Untersuchung zur nationalen und internationalen Geschichte der kapitalistischen Produktionsweise* 273-308 (1977).

[19]Fritz Seidenzahl, *100 Jahre Deutsche Bank 1870-1970*, at 116 (1970).

[20]See Edward Earle, *Turkey, the Great Powers, and the Bagdad Railway: A Study in Imperialism* (1923); Lothar Rathmann, *Berlin-Bagdad: Die imperialistische Nahostpolitik des kaiserlichen Deutschlands* 23-33

beginning and end of the twentieth century—that built the Turkish railways occupies no niche in popular consciousness.

These divergent structures are also reflected in English and German historiography. Economic and even social historians of the internationalizing impact of British capital generally pay considerable attention to the role of the English railway contractors abroad and have produced several monographs and semi-popular books devoted exclusively to them.[21] Historians of Bismarckian and Wilhelmine Germany, however, even East German historians, who were otherwise disinclined to permit any aspect of German imperialism to escape their scathing scrutiny, either ignore the contribution of German railway construction firms to the building of the "infamous Baghdad Railway" or mention it only cursorily.[22] Pre-World War I German oriental imperialism may have celebrated its romantic pioneers, but contemporary public opinion paid even less attention to commercial builders than to the bankers and armaments manufacturers who drove the economic apparatus of penetrating Turkey.[23]

Consequently, the following appreciation by Eric Hobsbawm, the leading English Marxist social historian of the nineteenth century, of the feats of British contractors in creating the material prerequisites for a world market, though penned in the tradition of Marx and Engels' account of the world-historical achievements of a bourgeoisie that drives permanent global revolution,[24] finds no counterpart in the German literature:

> Neither can we fail to be moved by the hard men in top hats who organised and presided over these vast transformations of the human landscape—materials and spiritual.    Thomas Brassey...was merely the most celebrated of these entrepreneurs, the list of his overseas enterprises an equivalent of the battle honours and campaign medals of generals in less enlightened days....''[25]

With this type of quasi-romanticized history can be contrasted the much more sober account presented by Rosa Luxemburg on the eve of World War I, in which she focused on the consequences for the precapitalist producers of the formerly remote regions of the particular societal content of the technological

---

(1962); Fritz Klein, *Deutschland von 1897/98 bis 1917*, at 72-76 (3d ed. 1972); Kurt Steinhaus, *Soziologie der türkischen Revolution: Zum Problem der Entfaltung der bürgerlichen Gesellschaft in sozioökonomisch schwach entwickelten Ländern* 48-49 (1969).

[21]See e.g. Asa Briggs, *The Making of Modern England 1783-1867*, at 399 (1965 [1959]); S. Checkland, *The Rise of Industrial Society in England 1815-1885* 137-38 (1971 [1964]); Peter Mathias, *The First Industrial Nation: An Economic History of Britain 1700-1914*, at 325 (1969).

[22]Mottek, Becker, & Schröter, 3 *Wirtschaftsgeschichte Deutschlands* at 105. See also William Dawson, *The Evolution of Modern Germany* 345-47 (n.d. [1908]); Hermann Schmidt, *Das Eisenbahnwesen in der asiatischen Türkei* 48 (1914); C. Mühlmann, "Die deutschen Bahnunternehmungen in der asiatischen Türkei 1888-1914," 24 *WA* 121\*-137\*, 365\*-399\* (1926); E. Brünner, *De Bagdadspoorveg: Bidrage tot de kennis omtrent het optreden der mogenheden in Turkije 1888-1908*, at 27 (1957); Hans-Ulrich Wehler, *Bismarck und der Imperialismus* 228-29 (1976 [1969]); Martin Kitchen, *The Political Economy of Germany 1815-1914*, at 227, 229, 255, 262-63, 268, 277 (1978); Johann Menzenreiter, *Die Bagdadbahn: Als Beispiel für die Entstehung des Finanzimperialismus in Europa (1872-1903)*, at 59-61 (1982); John Wolf, *The Diplomatic History of the Bagdad Railroad* in 11:2 *UMS* 14 (Apr. 1, 1936) (mistakenly referring to "Holzermann"). An antisemitic Nazi-era monograph is part of the same genre. Reinhard Hüber, *Die Bagdadbahn* 29-30, 35 (1943). Even Jürgen Kuczynski, the East German economic statistician who found nothing too trivial to include in his monumental 40-volume *History of the Condition of Workers Under Capitalism* if only it reflected poorly on capitalists or capitalism, took Holzmann to task only for its failure to condemn Nazism in its company history. Jürgen Kuczynski, 17 *Die Geschichte der Lage der Arbeiter unter dem Kapitalismus: Zur westdeutschen Historiographie—Schöne Literatur und Gesellschaft im 20. Jahrhundert und andere Studien* 9-11 (1966).

[23]George Hallgarten, 2 *Der Imperialismus vor 1914: Die soziologischen Grundlagen der Aussenpolitik europäischer Grossmächte vor dem Ersten Weltkrieg* 176-77 (2d ed. 1963 [1951]).

[24]Karl Marx & Friedrich Engels, *Manifest der kommunistischen Partei*, in Marx [&] Engels, 4 *Werke* 459, 463-68 (1959 [1848]).

[25]E. Hobsbawm, *The Age of Capital 1848-1875*, at 72-73 (1977 [1975]).

advances in transportation that made possible the violent incorporation of those areas into the world market. To be sure, Luxemburg's analysis cannot be separated from her environmentally naive notion, typical of German Social Democratic theory and practice in general, that the pernicious products of the capitalist mode of production could undergo an immediate transvaluation after a socialist revolution.[26]

Thus in 1898 Luxemburg observed that although such gigantic undertakings as the Panama Canal were "children of naked commercial and bellicose interests," they would nevertheless "outlast their creator—the capitalist economy" and "show what colossal forces of production slumber in the womb of our society and what an upswing progress and culture will experience once they have gotten rid of the fetters of capitalist interest."[27] How a socialist Panama Canal would differ from the one built by "the Yankees" she did not reveal to the proletarian readers of the *Sächsische Arbeiter-Zeitung* in Dresden. But the quasi-eschatological implications were clear: canals and railways, by mobilizing colonial armies, tended to foment conflicts between the European powers; by promoting trade and capitalist development, they also accelerated the collapse of capitalism. Consequently, "[t]he great means of transportation ultimately can have only a destructive impact on the bourgeois world and everything it creates. But for general cultural progress they are of enormous and lasting value."[28]

Luxemburg's analysis of the functions of late nineteenth-century and early twentieth-century railway and canal building for the global accumulation of capital formed a part of her attempted proof that the incorporation of precapitalist societies into the world market serves to stave off realization crises—until the absorption of all such societies leads to the ultimate collapse of capitalism. The fruitfulness of her concrete dissection of such projects as the Suez Canal or the Baghdad Railway does not, however, hinge on the soundness or plausibility of that larger theory.[29]

Her account ran along the following lines.[30] The imperialist phase of capital accumulation or the phase of world market competition of capital included the industrialization and capitalist emancipation of the previous hinterlands of capital. Among its chief methods of operation were foreign loans and railways. The development of the world railway network approximately mirrored the geographic penetration of capital: it grew most quickly in the 1840s in Europe, in the 1850s in the United States, in the 1860s in Asia, in the 1870s and 1880s in Australia, and in the 1890s in Africa.[31]

In the international sphere, the realization of surplus value required only the

---

[26]See the critique by Walter Benjamin, "Geschichtsphilosophische Thesen," in *idem, Illuminationen* 268, 273-74 (1961).

[27]Rosa Luxemburg, "Wasserkonstruktionen in Nordamerika," in *idem* 1:1 *GW* 282, 283 (1970 [1898]).

[28]Rosa Luxemburg, "Riesenwerke des Kapitalismus," in *idem,* 1:1 *GW* 286, 287-88 (1970 [1898]).

[29]For critiques, see *Zamechanie V.I. Lenina na knigu R. Luksemburg "Nakoplenie kapitala,"* in 22 *Leninskii Sbornik* (1933 [1913]); Henryk Grossmann, *Das Akkumulations- und Zusammenbruchsgesetz des kapitalistischen Systems (zugleich eine Krisentheorie)* (1929); Paul Sweezy, *The Theory of Capitalist Development: Principles of Marxian Political Economy* 202-207 (1968 [1942]); Tony Cliff, *Rosa Luxemburg* 73-91 (1969 [1959]).

[30]Rosa Luxemburg, *Die Akkumulation des Kapitals: Ein Beitrag zur ökonomischen Erklärung des Imperialismus,* in *idem,* 6 *GW* 336-60 (1923 [1913]).

[31]*Id.* at 336-37. The diffusion of railways depended in part on the nature of the commodities to be exchanged on the world market. In British colonies such as Australia, New Zealand, and South Africa, railways failed to foster inland penetration significantly before 1870 because the economies depended on livestock with a walking capacity, whereas India and Canada, for example, exported jute, indigo, tea, rice, cotton, timber, and grain, most of which were exposed to competition from European and U.S. producers, whom they could undersell only if they managed to reduce transport costs from the interior. Only when Australia, New Zealand, and South Africa began to center their export economies on wheat, dairy products, and gold and diamonds, did inland penetration by railways become vital. See L. Knowles, *The Economic Development of the British Overseas Empire* 13 (1924).

general diffusion of commodity production, whereas its capitalization required the progressive ousting of simple commodity production by capital production. The utilization of international capital for the expansion of the world railway network mirrored this shift. Railway building and loans from the 1830s to the 1860s "served chiefly the ousting of the natural economy and the diffusion of the commodity economy. ... On the other hand railway construction in Asia for about the last twenty years as well as in Africa serves almost exclusively imperialist policy, the economic monopolization and subjugation of the hinterlands." German railway undertakings in the Near East and German and English railways in Africa exemplified the latter phenomenon.[32]

Luxemburg took as her crisis-theoretical point of departure the fact that even if the capital, means of production, and labor power were all available in England, the lack of demand for railways and canals there explained why all these inputs were sent to noncapitalist areas.[33] The question then became: Who ultimately paid for the external loans that financed the construction of this infrastructure in the precapitalist countries and who realized the surplus value of the enterprises founded with them? In order to provide concrete answers, Luxemburg examined the cases of Egypt and Turkey. Her analysis emphasized aspects that those who celebrate world progress through world trade have tended to ignore.[34]

For the construction of the Suez Canal the Egyptian government obligated itself to provide gratis 20,000 fellahs and 40 per cent of the total share capital of Lesseps' company, which eventually became a public debt that the peasantry paid through taxes and special tributes. At the time of the American Civil War, when England was suffering from a shortage of cotton, the Egyptian viceroy confiscated land for cotton plantations on which he also used fellahs and thus came to require the fellahs whom he had assigned to the Compagnie Universelle du Canal Maritime de Suez. In a not entirely other-regarding speech, one member of the British Parliament observed that the withdrawal of 70,000 to 80,000 men from their regular village labors "must seriously interfere with the production of the most advantageous occupation for labor—for instance the production of cotton."[35] The viceroy Ismail extracted from the same fellahs the 38 million francs that Egypt was required to pay, pursuant to Napoleon III's arbitration, to indemnify the Suez Company for withdrawing their labor. The fellahs made the entire operation profitable for the viceroy and European capital by virtue of the land that was expropriated from them, their forced labor, and the money that was extracted from them through taxation and in part in kind.[36] Even though the limits of forced labor power for capital production became evident, the unlimited command over the mass and duration of the exploitation more than compensated for them. This process, Luxemburg argued, also brought about the destruction of the peasant economy. As in China and Morocco, so too in Egypt: militarism as the executor of capital accumulation lurked behind the international loans, railway construction, waterworks, and similar civilizing works.[37]

---

[32]Luxemburg, *Akkumulation* at 338.

[33]*Id.* at 344-45.

[34]But see Jenks, *Migration of British Capital* at 294-325.

[35]168 *PD* (3d ser.) 1148 (1862) (Layard, M.P.). The larger number of workers took into account the contingents who were continuously on their way to and from the canal. This speech was marked by self-interest inasmuch as British cotton manufacturers were vitally interested in buying Egyptian cotton and British governments were using the corvée as a basis for attacking French construction of the Suez Canal.

[36]In Egypt in the 1860s and 1870s, "revenue collection became a system of tribute rather than of taxation. If the docile peasants could not pay, their possessions were confiscated." Herbert Feis, *Europe the World's Banker 1870-1914*, at 383 (1965 [1930]).

[37]Luxemburg, *Akkumulation* at 345-54. The Suez Canal also caused Egypt to become a backwater of world commerce as it lost its position in the transit trade. Rondo Cameron, *France and the Economic Development of Europe 1800-1914: Conquests of Peace and Seeds of War* 481 (1961).

The international circulation of surplus value, according to Luxemburg, passed through different circuits in the case of the Baghdad Railway in Asiatic Turkey. Here the Turkish government gave the German railway company a state guarantee in the form of a per-kilometer sum for which it mortgaged the tithes of the provinces along the route.[38] German capital thus built the railways and pressed new surplus value out of the Asians who worked on it. This surplus value together with that embodied in the German-exported means of production used in the process (raw materials and machinery) from Germany, however, had to be realized. This realization was in part effected through the commodity trade spurred by the railway itself. A brisk trade was in fact immediately triggered by railway construction in theretofore natural economies: German exports to Turkey quadrupled between 1896 and 1911.[39]

To the extent that the Anatolian natural economy was not commodified quickly enough, the state used compulsion to transform the in-kind income of the population into money for the purpose of realizing the invested capital together with its surplus value. Grain as a simple consumption product of the primitive peasant economy flowed from the fields directly as a commodity to the tax farmer, who then transformed it into money for the state. Thus the grain executed the accumulation of European capital before it even became a commodity. This metamorphosis took place in its brutal and naked form directly between European capital and the Asiatic peasant economy while the Turkish state was reduced to its role as political apparatus for squeezing the peasant economy on behalf of capital. The result, concluded Luxemburg, was on the one hand capital accumulation and a sphere of interest as a pretext for further political and economic expansion of German capital and, on the other, railways and commodity commerce on the basis of the disintegration, ruin, and bleeding of the peasant economy and the growing financial and political dependence of the state on European capital.[40]

## The German Baghdad Railway

How does the microhistory of the German firm that built the Turkish railway fit into a global account such as Luxemburg's? At the end of the 1880s Germany could not yet boast of a single construction firm that could have independently carried out such a major railway project in a distant and industrially weakly developed country. Nevertheless, with financial support mobilized by the Deutsche Bank, which continued to be represented on its board of directors and to control it financially throughout the twentieth century, Philipp Holzmann & Cie. was launched onto an international career in the service of German industrial capital and the German state, transforming it from "Germany's largest German construction enterprise into a world firm."[41] Until its co-optation into the

---

[38]On the tithes, see Edwin Pears, "The Bagdad Railway," 94 *ContR* 570, 577 (1908); Karl Helfferich, 3 *Georg von Siemens: Ein Lebensbild aus Deutschlands großer Zeit* 34, 71, 74 (1923). The British trade press agreed that "[t]o the Turkish Government the guarantee system is working in a manner little less than disastrous." "Railways in Asiatic Turkey," 81 *Engineer* 558 (1896). On similar privileges extended to German and English road builders earlier in the century, see "Road Contracts in Turkey," 26 *Engineer* 67 (1868).

[39]German investment in Turkey also rose from 40 million marks in 1880 to 600 million marks by World War I. Feis, *Europe the World's Banker* at 319.

[40]Luxemburg, *Akkumulation* at 353-60.

[41]Hans Meyer-Heinrich, "Die Entwicklung des Gesamtunternehmens und die Wandlung seiner Organisation," in *Philipp Holzmann Aktiengesellschaft im Wandel von Hundert Jahren 1849-1949*, at 9, 132 (Hans Meyer-Heinrich ed., n.d. [1949]). On influential bankers associated with the Deutsche Bank who sat on Holzmann's board of directors before World War I, see Hallgarten, 2 *Der Imperialismus vor 1914* at 176. In 1993, two members of the Deutsche Bank's board of management were members of Holzmann's supervisory board. Philipp Holzmann Aktiengesellschaft, *Geschäftsbericht 1992*, at 4 (1993). On the

Ottoman enterprise, Holzmann's cross-border activities had been limited to a few projects in countries bordering on Germany. Thus from 1876 to 1881 Holzmann built the municipal sewerage system in Linz, Austria; in the late 1870s and early 1880s it built bridges in Basel and Zurich; in 1882 it built the Amsterdam railway station; and from 1888 to 1890 it built its first railroad outside of Germany—a short narrow-gauge railway in Switzerland.[42]

Precisely because Germany in the 1880s still lacked "enterprises that were organized for carrying out large railway construction under difficult foreign conditions," Georg von Siemens, the director of the Deutsche Bank and the organizational force behind German capital's drive into Turkey, wanted to co-opt an experienced English or French firm. When his negotiations with Weetman Pearson's firm failed to bear fruit, he entered into an agreement with Count Georges Vitali, director of a large French railway construction firm, under which Vitali built the first section of the Anatolian Railway and ordered most of the materials from German firms.[43] Siemens may have been willing to cooperate with Vitali or Pearson because he wanted to induce economic and financial circles in France or England to influence their governments to make decisions favorable to the Deutsche Bank.[44]

Vitali, whose firms, Vitali, Charles, Picard et Cie. and Régie Générale des Chemins de Fer, had since the 1860s built railways in Italy, the Netherlands, and European Turkey,[45] was constrained to fulfill a wish to which Siemens attached great importance: "In connection with the execution of the first railway line assumed by German capital, Siemens wanted to train a German construction firm for construction tasks of this kind; he therefore made it a condition that the construction firm Phillip Holzmann & Co., which was closely connected with the Deutsche Bank, be given a share of the construction."[46] To that end Holzmann and Vitali's Régie Générale formed the Gesellschaft für den Bau der Anatolischen Bahnen. Between 1889 and 1892 it built the section from Ismid to Angora, employing largely Italian and Croatian masons and stonecutters and Turkish laborers. Under the guidance of Vitali's firm, Holzmann was able to gain the experience it needed to build the Konia and Baghdad lines. For the section Eskischehir-Konia, which was begun in 1894, the technical supervision was exclusively Holzmann's. All the construction material was purchased from German industry.[47]

Holzmann's in-house company history described these origins of Germany's imperialist thrust into the Near East in the following euphemistic terms:

---

Deutsche Bank's continuing control, see Jörn Janssen, "Unternehmenspolitik der Großkonzerne verantwortlich für Baukostenexplosion," 25 *WSI Mitteilungen* 392 (1972).

[42]See Meyer-Heinrich, "Die Entwicklung des Gesamtunternehmens" at 9, 132, 137, 46, 48, 53, 40, 62; 9 *NDB* 577 (1972) (s.v. "Holzmann, Philipp").

[43]Helfferich, 3 *Georg von Siemens* at 40 (quotation), 45-47. For a not entirely trustworthy account by George Pauling, who was apparently unaware of Holzmann's existence, of the collapse of the negotiations with Pearson, see *Chronicles of a Contractor* at 101-102.

[44]Helmut Mejcher, "Die Bagdadbahn als Instrument deutschen wirtschaftlichen Einflusses im Osmanischen Reich," 1 *GG* 447, 458 (1975).

[45]Cameron, *France and the Economic Development of Europe* at 295, 299, 322.

[46]Helfferich, 3 *Georg von Siemens* at 47. The in-house centennial history of the Deutsche Bank, which devotes two tendentious chapters to the bank's financing of the Turkish railroads, never mentions Holzmann. Seidenzahl, *100 Jahre Deutsche Bank* at 63-81, 141-61.

[47]Prof. Dr. Forchheimer, "Die Eisenbahn von Ismid nach Angora," 41 *ZB* 359, 377-78 (1891); "A Great Turkish Railway Enterprise—A Fifteen Hundred Mile Line," 16 *RA* 528 (1891); Helfferich, 3 *Georg von Siemens* at 47; Kurt Zander, "Das Eisenbahnwesen der Türkei mit Berücksichtigung der wirtschaftlichen Entwicklungsmöglichkeiten der Bagdadbahn," in *Das Türkische Reich* 48, 58 (Josef Hellauer ed., 1918). On the French firm owned by Count Philipp Vitali and his son Count Georges Vitali, see "Les Chemins de fer en Asie," 13 *GC* 110 (1888); Ch. Cotard, "Inauguration de la voie ferrée de Lefké à Bilédjik (Ligne d'Anatolie)," 19 *GC* 103-105 (1891).

A favorable opportunity for extensive activity abroad presented itself to the firm Philipp Holzmann & Cie. in Turkey when the government there resolved to link its largely still quite independent border provinces more closely with the capital of the Empire by means of an efficient traffic route and thereby at the same time to usher in together with a strengthening of its power a successful economic utilization of the country.[48]

From the end of the 1880s, when the Internationale Baugesellschaft, a firm with which Holzmann was associated, undertook the construction of the first sections of the Anatolian Railway, until World War I, Holzmann stood at the center of the construction of the Baghdad Railway, which, when finally completed (by others) in 1940, ran from the Straits of Bosporus to the Persian Gulf.[49]

Germany's challenge to Britain's hegemony in the Middle East and especially in India led to initial British resistance to the plan for the railway, which necessitated complicated arrangements for financing its construction. British commercial interests perceived the German transportation scheme as cutting off the existing British Aidin and Cassaba lines from extensions to the south and southeast and conflicting with Britain's paramountcy in the Persian Gulf.[50] Moreover, the use of the Turkish state's customs duties to finance the railway restricted British textile exports to Turkey.[51] When speculation arose that Germany would seek a coaling station along the Persian Gulf near the terminus of the Baghdad Railway, British concern about preserving its regional hegemony intensified.[52] The railway further exacerbated imperialist rivalries because it was also an integral part of the Deutsche Bank's acquisition of one-quarter ownership of the Turkish Petroleum Company, which the British seized during World War I.[53]

The economic, political, military, and diplomatic conflicts, contradictions, and alliances that converged in the financing, construction, and ultimate uses of the Turkish railway system were extraordinarily complex.[54] The Baghdad Railway thus became, as the leading U.S. construction-engineering journal observed, a striking illustration of "the conflicting interests of European countries in developing their foreign commerce and in supporting their colonial possessions."[55] Even before the most violent form of resolution of imperialist conflicts, World War I, of which the Baghdad Railway was a "prominent side issue," thwarted the German project and halted construction,[56] the progress of the railway had been severely impeded by the war between Turkey and Italy over

---

[48]Otto Richter, "Die Anatolische Bahn und die Bagdadbahn," in *Philipp Holzmann Aktiengesellschaft* at 249, 250.

[49]On Régie Générale's demand in 1903 that the Deutsche Bank assign Holzmann's lead role to a French firm, see Heinz Lemke, "Das Scheitern der Verhandlungen über die offizielle Beteiligung Frankreichs am Bagdadbahnunternehmen 1903," 29 *JG* 227, 236 (1984). Three years later the Deutsche Bank considered reassigning the construction to a French firm in order to retain the good will of the French capital market. Hallgarten, 2 *Der Imperialismus vor 1914* at 45-46.

[50]"Railways Extension in Asiatic Turkey," 78 *Engineer* 366 (1894) (editorial); "The German Bagdad Railway," 88 *Engineer* 597 (1899) (editorial).

[51]Hallgarten, 2 *Der Imperialismus vor 1914* at 46-47.

[52]"Railways in Asia Minor," 89 *Engineer* 335 (1900) (editorial); "The Bagdad Railway," 82 *Engineer* 359 (1906).

[53]See "Mineral Resources of Asiatic Turkey," 100 *Engineering* 372 (1915); Yergin, *Prize* at 185-90; Heinz Lemke, "Die Erdölinteressen der Deutschen Bank in Mesopotamien in den Jahren 1903-1911," 24 *JG* 41 (1981).

[54]See e.g., Hallgarten, 1 *Der Imperialismus vor 1914* at 595-610; 2 *id.* at 44-51, 159-64, 173-78.

[55]"A European-Asiatic Railway Problem," 86 *ENR* 411 (1921) (editorial).

[56]"The Bagdad Railway—An International Problem," 86 *ENR* 423 (1921). See also Morris Jastrow, *The War and the Bagdad Railway: The Story of Asia Minor and Its Relation to the Present Conflict* (1918 [1917]); Maybelle Chapman, *Great Britain and the Bagdad Railway 1888-1914*, in 31 *SCSH* (1948) Fritz Fischer, *Krieg der Illusionen: Die deutsche Politik von 1911 bis 1914*, at 424-43 (1969).

Tripoli, which had led to the expulsion of the large contingent of Italian construction workers.[57] Unsurprisingly, in the 1920s and 1930s, when the revolutionary Kemalist state initiated an expansion of the transport system oriented for the first time toward planned national development, it selected two Danish engineering-contracting firms in order to avoid once again giving the Great Powers "too much of a footing in the country."[58]

Against the background of this classic example of construction capital's self-interested collaboration with German finance capital and imperialism, it is instructive to note the continuity in Holzmann's appreciation of its historical role. In 1974, at the ceremony celebrating the firm's 125th anniversary, the honorary chairman of its supervisory board chose to focus his address on Holzmann's role in building the Baghdad Railway. At the time, Hermann J. Abs had been a member of the firm's supervisory board since 1938 and its chairman for thirty years. Two decades later he was still its honorary chairman.[59] As chairman of the Deutsche Bank and as chairman or member of the supervisory board of an extraordinary number of large German firms, Abs "was the most powerful private individual in Germany's economic scene" since Nazi rule.[60] In a 1974 retrospect (that Holzmann disseminates for public relations purposes) of the cooperation between the Deutsche Bank and Holzmann in "opening" Turkey as a source of raw materials and foodstuffs as well as a market for German industry, Abs, who had been convicted in absentia as a war criminal for his financial plundering in Yugoslavia during the Nazi period,[61] assured his listeners that it was no exaggeration to characterize their work as "development aid."[62]

### Railway Construction in the German African Colonies

[I]t is not railways, roads, and power stations that give rise to industrial capitalism: it is the emergence of industrial capitalism that leads to the building of railways,...roads,...and power stations.[63]

German construction firms also occupied key positions in laying the groundwork for the exploitation of Germany's formal colonies. Within the framework of Bismarck's social-imperialist policy, Germany quickly seized a colonial empire in the 1880s in South West, East, and West Africa before it, unlike Britain and France, had commercially penetrated these territories.[64] Driven by the search for markets and more profitable investments, which in turn was triggered by the overproduction, depression, shift from free trade to high tariffs, and need to divert attention from internal class struggle that characterized European

---

[57]Richter, "Die Anatolische Bahn und die Bagdadbahn" at 249-64.

[58]123 *Engineering* 673 (1927); Steinhaus, *Soziologie der türkischen Revolution* at 124-26.

[59]Wilfried Guth, in *1849-1974 H[olzmann]: Ansprachen beim Festakt anläßlich des 125jährigen Bestehens der Firma Philipp Holzmann* 5 (1974) (untitled address); Philipp Holzmann Aktiengesellschaft, *Geschäftsbericht 1992* at 4.

[60]Ferdinand Protzman, "H. J. Abs, 92, a German Banker with Key Role in Postwar Growth," *NYT*, Feb. 8, 1994, at B10, col. 4 (nat. ed.).

[61]See Kurt Pritzkoleit, *Männer-Mächte-Monopole: Hinter den Türen der westdeutschen Wirtschaft* 34-43 (1958 [1953]); *idem, Bosse Banken Börsen: Herren über Geld und Wirtschaft* 129-30, 136-40, 200-210 (1954); Eberhard Czichon, *Der Bankier und die Macht: Hermann Josef Abs in der deutschen Politik* 126-30, 150-51, 244 (1970); Tom Bower, *Blind Eye to Murder: Britain, America and the Purging of Nazi Germany—A Pledge Betrayed* 17-31, 408-409 (1983 [1981]).

[62]Hermann Abs, in *1849-1974 H[olzmann]* at 13, 15, 22.

[63]Paul Baran, *The Political Economy of Growth* 193 (1968 [1957]).

[64]See Fritz Müller, *Deutschland-Zanzibar-Ostafrika: Geschichte einer Kolonialeroberung 1884-1890*, at 62-63 (1959).

capitalism in the last quarter of the nineteenth century,[65] German colonialism in Africa soon attained a stage of development that required significant improvement of the transportation system. In conformity with Germany's status as a colonial latecomer, German advocates of African railways emphasized the need to secure privileged access to colonial production of certain raw materials, such as rubber, sisal, and especially cotton, not to participate in, but rather to reduce Germany industry's dependence on, a world market perceived as dominated by foreign and hostile monopolies.[66] In particular, they pointed to the cotton famine during the American Civil War that attended England's reliance on cotton imports from the United States as a weighty reason for seeking to circumvent the world market.[67]

In the German Reichstag debates in 1904 and 1905 devoted to the issue of state loans and guarantees for the construction of these colonial railways, both left-wing and revisionist members of the Social Democratic Party, which opposed the reactionary form of German colonial conquests if not of all colonialism,[68] attacked state subventions of such private undertakings. Thus while the leftist Georg Ledebour argued that if the railways were profitable, the cotton capitalists should pay for them since they would be the beneficiaries, the revisionist Albert Südekum characterized the entire legislative plan as "a large capitalist maneuver" designed to shift the risk to the state.[69]

The initiatives were, however, enacted despite the Social Democrats' opposition. Under the leadership of the newly appointed director of Germany's colonial office, State Secretary Bernhard Dernburg, who had been director of one of the largest German banks, the Darmstädter Bank, Germany "made the transition from the system of monopoly colonial capitalism to rational, industrial capitalism in the colonies."[70] During his tenure from 1906 to 1910, Dernburg not only mobilized private capital from German banks and large enterprises for the construction of colonial railways, but also induced the Reichstag to authorize the expenditure of hundreds of millions of marks to guarantee private loans or build railways.[71]

The first German line, from Swakopmund to Windhuk, had been built by military commandos of the railway brigade in South West Africa beginning in 1897 when ox-wagon transport was interrupted by cattle plague.[72] In 1904 the Hereros and Hottentots, impelled by the German occupiers' life-threatening theft of their grazing land, organized a rebellion against the colonial regime. The following year the German parliament authorized and financed construction by the Deutsche

---

[65]See generally Hans-Ulrich Wehler, *Bismarck und der Imperialismus* (1976 [1969]).

[66]See e.g., Bernhard Dernburg, *Zielpunkte des deutschen Kolonialwesens: Zwei Vorträge* 49 (1907).

[67]See e.g., 4 *SBVR*, 11th Legis., 1st Sess. 3136B (June 14, 1904); Francesca Schinzinger, *Die Kolonien und das Deutsche Reich: Die wirtschaftliche Bedeutung der deutschen Besitzungen in Übersee* 58, 65 (1984).

[68]See Hans-Holger Paul, *Marx, Engels und die Imperialismustheorie der II. Internationale* 92-103 (1978); Helmut Stoecker & Peter Sebald, "Enemies of the Colonial Idea," in *Germans in the Tropics: Essays in German Colonial History* 59-72 (Arthur Knoll & Lewis Gann ed., 1991).

[69]8 *SBVR*, 11th Legis., 1st Sess. 5943B-C (May 11, 1905); 4 *SBVR*, 11th Legis., 1st Sess. 3152C (June 15, 1904).

[70]Hallgarten, 2 *Imperialismus vor 1914* at 43 n.1. See also *id.* at 73-76; Mary Townsend, *The Rise and Fall of Germany's Colonial Empire 1884-1918*, at 246-64 (1930). Promotion of rationalized capitalism was apparently consistent with racism—even on the part of a German Jew. Dernburg conceded that the population of Togo and Cameroon was "morally very inferior," but emphasized that these West African colonies had the same "human material" that produced cotton in the United States. Dernburg, *Zielpunkte des deutschen Kolonialwesens* at 34.

[71]Klein, *Deutschland von 1897/98 bis 1917* at 180-81; L. Gann, "Economic Development in Germany's African Empire, 1884-1914," in 4 *Colonialism in Africa, 1870-1960: The Economics of Colonialism* at 213, 239; L. Gann & Peter Duignan, *The Rulers of German Africa 1884-1914*, at 53-55, 185-88 (1977).

[72]See Baltzer, *Die Kolonialbahnen* at 78-80; 1 *Deutsches Kolonial-Lexikon* 537 (Heinrich Schnee ed., 1920); "Die Eisenbahnen Afrikas" at 1601; Gann, "Economic Development in Germany's African Empire, 1884-1914" at 213, 241.

Kolonial-Eisenbahn-Bau- und Betriebs-Gesellschaft of a southern line to help suppress the uprising.[73]

At the same time the Berlin firm of Arthur Koppel and Company, a forward-integrated manufacturer of rails and railways cars, which also maintained production facilities and offices in Europe and the United States (at Pittsburgh and Chicago),[74] built the Otavi Railway in South West Africa at German government expense to connect a copper mine to the coast. When the Herero rebellion led to a shortage of labor in a thinly populated area, the firm then imported more than a thousand Italian workers. Their market-conforming behavior, however, proved "disappointing" to the firm,[75] which was unaccustomed to the experience of isolated workers' taking advantage of a tight labor market. Turning the tables on their employers, "feeling secure from the competition of other workers, they exploited their situation" by demanding higher wages, performing less work, striking, and even suing.[76] Trumping the untoward consequences of a free labor market, the colonial government then obliged Koppel by furnishing 2,000 Hereros from concentration camps.[77]

Although many of the later railroads in Africa also served military-strategic purposes, they were, like colonial railways everywhere, largely designed to transport agricultural and mineral raw materials from the interior to ports for export. The monocultural focus of such railways was pushed to such an extreme in Togo that they were called the "coconut," "cocoa," and "cotton line."[78] Most of these lines in Togo and Cameroon were built by firms managed by Friedrich Lenz (1846-1930). A self-taught engineer and the leading builder of light and branch railways in Germany from the 1880s to World War I, he formed Lenz & Co. GmbH in 1892. In addition to Lenz himself and S. Bleichröder, one of Germany's leading banks, Friedrich Krupp's firm, which had long sold the rails for laying on Lenz's railways, also financially participated in the founding of Lenz & Co.

The principal financial force behind Lenz, however, was one of Germany's most influential banks, the Berliner Handels-Gesellschaft, which was controlled by Carl Fürstenberg, formerly an associate of the powerful private banking house Bleichröder. The Berliner Handels-Gesellschaft, which was a pioneer in industrial financing, had corporate interlocks with such internationally leading firms as Walther Rathenau's Allgemeine Elektrizitäts-Gesellschaft. Fürstenberg, who had maintained close business relations with Dernburg before the latter became state secretary in the Colonial Department of the Foreign Office, possessed wide-ranging financial interests in the German colonies as well as in railways throughout the world.[79] Dernburg furthered the colonial interests of Fürstenberg and the Berliner Handels-Gesellschaft by his conscious promotion of railway building in the African colonies as the mainstay of German capital export.[80]

---

[73]Baltzer, *Die Kolonialbahnen* at 86-89; Klein, *Deutschland 1897/98 bis 1917* at 179-80; Horst Drechsler, *Südwestafrika unter deutscher Herrschaft* (1966).

[74]29 *EC* 314 (1908) (obituary).

[75]"The Otavi Railway in South Africa: The Longest 24-Inch Gage Railway in the World," 58 *EN* 378 (1907).

[76]F. Baltzer, 2 *Kolonial- und Kleinbahnen: Bauliche Ausgestaltung von Bahn und Fahrzeug* 32 (1983 [1920]). See generally 6 *SBVR*, 11th Legis. 1st Sess. (1903/1905) 4131-43 (Jan. 31, 1905).

[77]Lionel Wiener, *Les Chemins de fer coloniaux de l'Afrique* 410 (1930).

[78]See e.g., August Full, *Fünfzig Jahre Togo* 198 (1935); Arthur Knoll, *Togo Under Imperial Germany 1884-1914: A Case Study in Colonial Rule* 130 (1978).

[79]See Carl Fürstenberg, *Die Lebensgeschichte eines deutschen Bankiers, 1870-1914*, at 130-31, 270, 307, 429-31, 465-71 (Hans Fürstenberg ed., 1931); Pritzkoleit, *Bosse Banken Börsen* at 202-11; Volker Wellhöne, *Großbanken und Großindustrie im Kaiserreich* 114-16, 135-40 (1989).

[80]Dieter Schulte, "Die Monopolpolitik des Reichskolonialamts in der 'Ära Dernburg' 1906-1910: Zu

In the first decade of the twentieth century, Lenz, through the subsidiaries Aktiengesellschaft für Verkehrswesen and Deutsche Kolonial-Eisenbahn-Bau und Betriebs-Gesellschaft, directed the building of almost 1,800 kilometers of lines in the German colonies, many of which the latter firm also operated (in addition to operating railroads built by others). These railways, which were ultimately financed by the German government and proved very profitable for Fürstenberg-Lenz, included the Usambara line in East Africa, the Banana (Lomé-Palime) and Cotton (Lomé-Atakpame) lines in Togo, the northern and middle lines in Cameroon, and three railways in the southern part of South West Africa. Two other German firms, the Maschinenbaugesellschaft Nuremberg and the Vereinigte Maschinenfabrik Augsburg, joined in the construction of a railroad in Togo.[81] Beginning in 1908, the German colonial regime there made forced labor available for railway construction. Among these unfree workers the mortality rate was "terrific."[82]

By the mid-1890s the ubiquitous Deutsche Bank, together with the German East Africa Society, having recognized that the resources of the colonies could not be adequately exploited without the construction of a railway network, began developing plans for a railway from Dar es Salaam. Not until 1904, however, when the Deutsche Bank finally convinced the government to provide financial guarantees, could Holzmann, the sole construction firm member of the East African Railway Syndicate, initiate construction. In 1911 the German parliament provided an additional 52 million marks to Holzmann for the extension of the line.[83]

The only point of contention that did arise between the colonial government and Holzmann focused on the "labor question." Competition among the government itself, the army, planters, and Holzmann for native workers apparently did not have the theoretically expected consequence of improving the terms of employment. When the colonial government therefore appointed worker commissioners to protect native workers against "exploitation by unconscientious planters and entrepreneurs," Holzmann did not consider this a step toward solution of "the labor question." In order to mobilize a labor force of 20,000 for the project in the face of an alleged scarcity of indigenous labor, the Deutsche Bank sought and received the approval of the colonial government to import several thousand Chinese coolies. Ultimately, however, Holzmann decided not to consummate this transaction because experts "feared an unpleasant influence of Chinese customs and habits on the Negroes."[84]

Discovering that local workers performed excellently as helpers to European craftsmen, Holzmann undertook the work on the Dar es Salaam railway in 1905, the completion of which facilitated the development of commercial cotton growing in East Africa.[85] Holzmann then directed its efforts to the Tanganyika Railway,

---

frühen Formen des Fuktionsmechanismus zwischen Monopolkapital und Staat," 24 *JG* 7, 19-23 (1981); Helmuth Stoecker, "The German Empire in Africa Before 1914: General Questions," in *German Imperialism in Africa: From the Beginnings until the Second World War* 185, 195-203 (Helmuth Stoecker ed., Bernd Zöllner tr., 1986). Dernburg also aided the Berliner Handels-Gesellschaft (and other banks) by issuing a decree awarding one of its creatures monopoly rights to the newly discovered diamond fields in South West Africa.

[81]1 *SBVR*, 11th Legis. Per., 2d Sess. 105D (1905-1906); "Die Eisenbahnen Afrikas" at 1584-86; 1 *Deutsches Kolonial-Lexikon* at 531, 536; Harry Rudin, *Germany in the Cameroons 1884-1914: A Case Study in Modern Imperialism* 238-42 (1938); Erich Lübbert, *AGVI 1901-1931*, at 9-11, 15-16, 19-20, 33-48 (1963); Knoll, *Togo Under Imperial Germany* at 130-31; Schinzinger, *Die Kolonien und das Deutsche Reich* at 68, 79-82; 14 *NDB* 222-23 (1985) (s.v. "Lenz").

[82]Robert Kuczynski, *The Cameroons and Togoland: A Demographic Study* 394-95 (1930).

[83]See 4 *SBVR*, 11th Legis., 1st Sess. 3153B (June 15, 1904); Baltzer, *Die Kolonialbahnen* at 45, 52; Schinzinger, *Die Kolonien und das Deutsche Reich* at 71.

[84]Ferdinand Grages, "Bau der Mittellandbahn Daressalam-Kigoma in Ostafrika," in *Philipp Holzmann Aktiengesellschaft* at 283, 287, 288.

[85]See *Report to the Board of Trade of the Empire Cotton Growing Committee* 33 (Cmd. 523, 16 *PP*

which it worked on from 1908 until World War I, employing at the peak of operations more than 15,000 African workers  When Holzmann's own engineers blew it up during World War I to deny it to British troops, they brought to its logical conclusion the European powers' African transportation policy of "deliberately cho[osing] a different gauge to discourage trade with other territories."[86]

### International Competition in Other Civil Engineering Infrastructural Projects

In spite of this considerable French and German competition, British firms

enjoyed the advantage of experience of pioneering work in these fields in the British Isles and of a virtual monopoly of the market represented by the colonies. Their access to the London money market made it possible for them to offer facilities for the financing of the work which they were carrying out.... British engineers, supervisory staff, plant and materials were used; ...and the works, when completed, were largely operated by British companies or the nominees of the British banks which had financed them.[87]

Moreover, the sizable British portfolio investment in overseas railway and canal bonds favored construction of those projects by British firms,[88] just as the international loans that financed other infrastructural projects often provided that construction firms and suppliers of the lending nation perform the work.[89]

The construction of the complex infrastructure of modern cities, such as gas and water pipe systems, reservoirs, sewerage, and, later, underground railways, also emerged as a significant impulse towards international expansion of building firms. Beginning in the 1850s, John Aird, an self-taught engineer who had created his own firm after working for a gas company laying mains in Britain, cashed in on the growing need throughout Europe for gas lighting and water systems for the self-preservation of the transformed urban agglomerations.  The pioneering scale of the pumping stations, reservoirs, and filtration plants in England enabled Aird to specialize at a time when the Brasseys of Britain were fully occupied with railway construction: "With his special knowledge and experience, he saw an almost untouched market on the Continent."  In quick succession he built waterworks in Rotterdam, Amsterdam, Copenhagen, Berlin, Hamburg, and Moscow. Although his dominant position was eroded after the crisis of 1857, his like-named son (1833-1911) extended the firm's activities to gas and waterworks in Warsaw, Palermo, Calcutta, Ottawa, Singapore, Argentina, and Brazil.  By the

---

1920 [16]).

[86]W.S. Woytinsky & E.S. Woytinsky, *World Commerce and Government* 356 (1955).  See generally Meyer-Heinrich, "Die Entwicklung des Gesamtunternehmens" at 130, 131; Grages, "Bau der Mittellandbahn Daressalam-Kigoma in Ostafrika" at 283-95; Baltzer, 2 *Kolonial- und Kleinbahnen* at 30; John Day, *Railways of Northern Africa* 13-18 (1964).

[87]J. Colclough, *The Construction Industry of Great Britain* 139 (1965).

[88]See 2 *Cambridge History of the British Empire: The Growth of the New Empire 1783-1870*, at 788-802 (J. Rose ed., 1968 [1940]); "The Railways of Mexico," 50 *Engineer* 256 (1890) (British owned railways in Mexico built by British firms such as Bowes-Scott, Read, Campbell & Co.). On British investment in Latin American railways, see U.S. Bureau of Foreign and Domestic Commerce, *Railways of Central America and the West Indies* (Trade Promotion Ser. No. 5, 1925) (written by W. Long); *idem, Railways of South America*, pt. I: *Argentina* (Trade Promotion Ser. No. 32, 1926) (written by George Brady); *idem, Railways of South America*, pt. II (1927) (written by W. Long); *idem, Railways of South America*, pt. III: *Chile* (Trade Promotion Ser. No. 93, 1930).  D. Platt, *Foreign Finance in Continental Europe and the United States, 1815-1870: Quantities, Origins, Functions and Distribution* 182 (1984), argues, without hard evidence, that the converse was not true—namely, that British investors did not necessarily finance railways built by British contractors.

[89]See Nikolai Bucharin, *Imperialismus und Weltwirtschaft* 106-107 (1969 [1929]).

turn of the century, when Aird's firm completed the £2 million Aswan Dam in Egypt, Lucas & Aird was, together with S. Pearson & Son and Sir John Jackson, Ltd., one of the three largest English international construction firms.[90]

Other British contractors also built water- and gasworks in Europe and Latin America, while Charles Fox (a civil and consulting engineer who built railways in France, Switzerland, Germany, and Denmark), George Wythes (who was Brassey's partner on railways in Spain, India, Mauritius, and Argentina), and William Cubitt also successfully competed for waterworks contracts abroad.[91] In preparation for its construction work, the Manchester firm of Bellhouse & Company shipped all of the requisite iron work to Buenos Aires in the 1850s to build the gasworks there.[92]

In its restructuring of European-Asian trade routes, and by favoring the larger metal-hull steamships, the Suez Canal set off a worldwide boom in dock and harbor construction from Valparaiso to Singapore. This type of overseas project enabled the firm of Sir John Jackson (1851-1919), who carried out considerable works for the British Admiralty and domestically combated "the absurd pretension of the present-day trades unionism,"[93] to become one of the world's largest construction firms by the end of the century. Soon Jackson, Pearson, Holzmann, and others were engaged in worldwide competitive bidding against one another.[94] Cross-border European projects were exemplified by the harbor works performed by the French firm of Couvreux and Hersent at Antwerp in the 1870s and 1880s.[95] Overseas, British and European (and later U.S.) construction firms, often using mechanical navvies and specialized steam dredgers capable of crossing the Atlantic, undertook dredging, excavating, and building operations on all continents well into the post-World War I period.[96] Couvreux and Hersent, for example, rebuilt the harbor at Montevideo at the beginning of the twentieth century, while Batignolles built the sewage and water systems in Santiago and the port in Recife.[97]

One of the more remarkable phenomena of pre-World War II international construction was the extensive European and overseas business conducted by a firm from one of Europe's smallest countries. The Danish firm Christiani & Nielsen was founded in 1904 to build bridges, marine works, and other reinforced concrete structures according to methods that it had invented. It was not only immediately active in neighboring Sweden, where it eventually built hundreds of bridges, but

[90]"Sir John Aird," 111 *Engineer* 38 (1911) (obituary); Middlemas, *Master Builders* at 121-26 (quotation at 124).

[91]"Annual Report Session 1859-60," in 19 *MPICE* 133, 151, 153; 21 *MPICE* 554, 557 (Cubitt built Berlin water-works); Helps, *Life and Labours of Mr. Brassey* at 161-66; 39 *MPICE* 264-66 (1875); 7 *DNB* 533 (1968) (s.v. "Charles Fox"); Jenks, *Migration of British Capital* at 185-86.

[92]"Buenos Ayres Gas-Works," 13 *Builder* 595 (1855); "The Gas Company of Buenos Ayres," 14 *Builder* 629 (1856).

[93]"The Institution of Junior Engineers," 72 *Engineering* 695 (1901) (speech by Jackson). "Although the workmen in his employ numbered at times as many as 5,000 he never had labor difficulties of any great duration." "The Late Sir John Jackson," 108 *Engineering* 831 (1919).

[94]105 *Engineer* 4 (1908) (projects performed by Pearson and Jackson); "The Valparaiso Port Works," 121 *Engineer* 190 (1916) (Pearson outbid Holzmann and Jackson); David Jeremy, "Sir John Jackson," 3 *DBB* 462-67 (David Jeremy ed., 1985). Jackson continued to expand Singapore for the British Admiralty in the 1930s. "Singapore Dock and Harbour," 165 *Engineer* 197 (1938).

[95]*Nouvelles Installations maritimes du Port d'Anvers: Notice explicative dex travaux projétés et des moyens d'éxécution proposés par MM. A. Couvreux & H. Hersent* (1880).

[96]During the 1890s the British engineer and contractor Walker performed £7 million worth of dock and port works in Buenos Aires for the Argentinian government. 85 *Engineer* 249 (1898). See also Middlemas, *Master Builders* at 113, 134, 157, 175, 199, 231, 244, 266, 287; George Edgar-Bonnet, *Ferdinand de Lesseps: Le Diplomate, Le Créateur de Suez* 462 (1951) (Dussaud brothers built ports at Algiers).

[97]"The Argentine Centenary II.—Engineering Development," 89 *Engineering* 654-55 (1910); Sociéte de Construction des Batignolles, *L'Oeuvre* at 67-68.

before World War I had already opened branch offices in Germany, Britain, and Russia. In Hamburg, for example, it introduced reinforced concrete quay walls in 1911, which then became the dominant type of harbor construction in northern Germany.[98]

Harbor works were only one of many kinds of infrastructure projects enjoying a worldwide boom. "The last decade of the nineteenth century saw the beginning of a world-wide boom in the building of electric light and power plants, electric railways, and telephone systems, in which Americans took an important part." In building such infrastructure in Europe, Latin America, and Asia, U.S. construction firms were subordinate to the manufacturers of the electrical equipment such as Westinghouse, General Electric, and Western Electric.[99] This relationship at times mirrored that between railway builders and the manufacturers that produced the rails and rolling stock such as Krupp.[100]

In regions of overlapping or contested colonial control such as Latin America, the pre-World War period witnessed "fierce" competitive struggles among European and U.S. firms over the construction of such infrastructure projects. Driven by the military and economic functions of railroads in consolidating rival colonial powers in Asia and Africa and the worldwide installation of electric power systems, the process of internationalization left its imprint on major European construction firms. On the eve of World War I, one of the largest French construction companies, La Société Générale d'Entreprises, which specialized in electrification, performed half of its business overseas.[101] Even at the peak of German involvement in Turkey, French companies such as Vitali's Régie Générale, La Sociéte de Construction des Batignolles, and Hersent held numerous contracts there for roads, ports, docks, tramways, irrigation, lighting and power plants. Société Générale d'Entreprise dans l'Empire Ottoman employed 10,000 workers by the beginning of World War I.[102] When a German-owned electric company in Chile was confiscated after World War I, Weetman Pearson's firm used the proceeds from its sale of oil wells in Mexico to buy that enterprise and to forward-integrate by building its own hydroelectric plants.[103]

Between 1895 and the end of World War I, the largest German firm, Holzmann, performed 36 per cent of its total of one billion marks worth of construction abroad. The fact that Holzmann shipped almost all its building materials such as cement, iron, and wood as well as machines and equipment to overseas building sites from Germany also increased that country's exports. Although the Baghdad and East African railways, to be sure, accounted for the vast bulk of this overseas business, Holzmann during this period also worked on such geographically diverse projects as the expansion of the harbors at Tangier, St.

---

[98]Christiani & Nielsen, *75 Years of Civil Engineering 1904-1979*, at 7, 37, 42, 44, 98-99 (Leif Nilsen ed., 1979).

[99]Cleona Lewis, *America's Stake in International Investments* 324-25 (1938).

[100]On the building of the Caracas-Valencia line by the Große Venezuela Eisenbahngesellschaft under a concession granted Krupp and financed by the Diskontogesellschaft, see "The Great Venezuela Railway," 57 *Engineering* 392 (1894); Hallgarten, 1 *Der Imperialismus vor 1914* at 561-62; Raymond Poidevin, *Les Relations économiques et financières entre la France et l'Allemagne de 1898 a 1914*, at 623-26 (1969); Nikita Harwich Vallenilla, "El modelo economico del liberalismo amarillo: Historia de un fracaso, 1888-1908," in *Politica y economia en Venezuela 1810-1976*, at 203, 222-25 (Alfredo Boulton ed., 1976).

[101]See Werner Sombart, 1 *Der moderne Kapitalismus* 521-22 (1902); Alfred Sohn-Rethel, *Ökonomie und Klassenstruktur des deutschen Faschismus* 57-58 (1973); Daniel Headrick, *The Tentacles of Progress: Technology Transfer in the Age of Imperialism, 1850-1914*, at 145-70 (1988) (on Hong Kong, Calcutta, and Dakar); Dominique Barjot, "L'Analyse comptable: Un Instrument pour l'histoire des enterprises. La Société Générale d'Entreprises (1908-1945)," 1 *HÉS*, No. 1, 1982, at 145, 149.

[102]Feis, *Europe the World's Banker* at 321 & n.10; Jacques Thobie, *Intérêts et impérialisme français dans l'empire ottoman (1895-1914)*, at 392-402 (1977).

[103]Middlemas, *Master Builders* at 244-45.

Petersburg, and Reval.[104]

German firms also carried on considerable construction work within Europe during this period. The Actiengesellschaft für Hoch- und Tiefbauten, which had been founded as Helfmann Brothers in 1875, gained its first international contract in 1899. This large turnkey project for the construction of reinforced concrete grain silos at the port of Genoa permitted the Italian city to compete with Marseille as a port of entry for overseas grain. Between 1907 and 1912 the firm also built a railway station in Basel for 10 million marks, one of its largest single prewar contracts.[105] More extensive still were the European industrial and commercial projects of Wayss & Freytag, a firm formed in 1890 as a merger of two firms specializing in and developing their own ferro-concrete construction methods. Early on the firm built plants for heavy industry in neighboring Belgium, Luxemburg, and France. Following its construction of a spinning mill in Finland in 1902, Wayss & Freytag developed a considerable business in European Russia, including a department store and a hotel in St. Petersburg which it also operated until World War I. In addition to earthquake-proof apartment houses in Italy and Mediterranean harbor works, the firm also built silos in Argentina in 1909, leading to the establishment of a branch there.[106] Two other German firms, Grün & Bilfinger and Julius Berger, also performed considerable harbor, excavation, and road work in the German colonies in East, West, and South West Africa in the years before World War I.[107]

Not surprisingly, British-built urban infrastructure tended to be found in British-built colonial cities.[108] Yet even in countries dominated by British capital, French and German firms succeeded in asserting themselves. At the turn of the century, for example, French entrepreneurs built the water supply system in Valparaiso, Chile and a German firm built the electric tramway in Cairo, while in Argentina, beginning in 1906 the Deutsch-Überseeische Elektricitäts-Gesellschaft, which was an industry leader in South America formed by the Allgemeine Electricitäts-Gesellschaft and the Deutsche Bank, contracted with Philipp Holzmann & Cie. to build its electrical plant in Buenos Aires—a project that required the importation from Germany of all the materials and equipment. Ultimately German firms monopolized the lighting and power industry in Buenos Aires.[109]

World War I marked a caesura in the internationalization of construction.

[104]Hugo Ritter, "Holzmann in Marokko und Ägypten," in *Philipp Holzmann Aktiengesellschaft* at 299; Meyer-Heinrich, "Einleitung" in *id.* at 247; Meyer-Heinrich, "Die Entwicklung des Gesamtunternehmens" at 129, 131; for inconsistent data suggesting an alternative share of 30 per cent, see *id.* at 91, 128.

[105]H. Weidmann, *Hochtief: Aktiengesellschaft für Hich- und Tiefbauten vorm. Gebr. Helfmann* 51 (1931); *Hochtief 1875-1975*, at 157, 161 (n.d. [1975]); Heiner Radzio, *Die Aufgabe heisst Bauen: 110 Jahre Hochtief* 16, 20 (1985); "De l'importation des céréales dans les ports de Marseille et de Gênes," 38 *GC* 332 (1901).

[106]Wayss & Freytag, *100 Jahre Wayss & Freytag 1875-1975* [no pagination] (n.d. [1975]); Hermann Bay, "Emil Mörsch: Erinnerungen an einen großen Lehrmeister des Stahlbetonbaus und technischen Mentors der Wayss & Freytag AG," in *Herausragende Ingenieurleistungen in der Bautechnik: Schriftenreihe der VDI-Gesellschaft Bautechnik*, No. 3 (1985).

[107]"Bilfinger & Berger Bau A.G.," in 1 *IDCH* 560 (Thomas Derdak ed., 1988). These firms merged in 1975 into Bilfinger & Berger Bau Aktiengesellschaft.

[108]The same was true of French colonial cities. See e.g. 82 *Engineer* 417 (1896) (French firm builds electric tramway in Algiers).

[109]See R. Joby, *The Railway Builders: Lives and Works of the Victorian Railway Contractors* 17 (1983); A. Marquand, "Travaux d'adduction d'eau potable à Valparaiso (Chile)," 32 *GC* 309 (1898); "The Cairo Electric Tramway," 87 *Engineer* 438 (1899); "A New Electrical Generating Station at Buenos Ayres," 108 *Engineer* 263 (1909); 72 *EN* 792-93 (1914) (letter of M. Lorenth, Stone & Webster Engineering Corp.); "German Overseas Electric Enterprise," 100 *Engineering* 10 (1915); "Electric Power Supply at Buenos Aires," 105 *Engineering* 4 (1918); Walter Kossmann, "Holzmann in Argentinien und Uruguay," in *Philipp Holzmann Aktiengesellschaft* at 303; Seidenzahl, *100 Jahre Deutsche Bank* at 116-40; Ian Forbes, "German Informal Imperialism in South America Before 1914," 31 *EHR* (2d ser.) 384, 394 (1978); Andrés Regalsky, "Foreign Capital, Local Interests and Railway Development in Argentina: French Investments in Railways, 1900-1914," 21 *JLAS* 425 (1989).

It not only interrupted many private ventures by withdrawing capital for armaments and blocking access to belligerents, but also destroyed an immense volume of infrastructure and private buildings in Europe and the Near East. The war also forged a matrix of new conditions of national competition. The British construction-engineering industry, hard pressed by German and American firms before 1914, uttered a collective "Thank Heaven" that the war had made it impossible for the British government to "sell[] the prestige of the British engineering industry" by letting contracts to foreign firms that allegedly took work at a loss precisely in order to invade the British market.[110] In South America, "antagonistic opposition" by the "vested interests" of British and U.S. firms persuaded governments to abandon German firms.[111]

Even during the early months of World War I, the British construction-engineering industry began looking forward to a postwar restoration of British supremacy. In the Near East, for example, and especially in Turkey, where German firms "had practically ousted British engineering," "German competition will be compulsorily eliminated...." With France prostrate, British and U.S. "[c]ontractors will be at a premium, and they will have the time of their lives...carrying on the enormous number of contracts" for reconstructing the Middle East.[112]

Yet German firms returned to the world market after the war. Launched by the aforementioned public port and canal projects for the Argentinian state, Holzmann, drawing as always on the financial support of the Deutsche Bank, had founded the Compañia General de Obras Publicas (Geopé) in 1913. During the following three decades, until the Peronist government seized Geopé in 1945, it carried out a great volume of construction in Argentina (and Uruguay) in the areas of public waterworks, dams, roads, subways, hydroelectric and other power plants, public and private commercial buildings, and production facilities (including a rayon factory for DuPont). By 1930, Geopé had become the largest construction firm in South America, employing more than 5,000 persons.[113] Holzmann also founded companies in Chile (1915), Peru (1925), and Brazil (1927), where the governments, supported by international loans, organized civil works projects to build bridges, roads, ports, waterworks, power plants, and buildings. Much of the work, especially in Peru, was spawned by the building of the Pan-American Highway. By the 1920s, Holzmann, like the British firms, had to bid in competition against U.S. firms in Latin America.[114] Wayss & Freytag also reentered the South American market, creating subsidiaries in Argentina, Brazil, and Uruguay, which operated until their expropriation during World War II.[115] The Danish firm Christiani & Nielsen also established a subsidiary in Brazil in 1922, five years after it had built a paper mill there, where it then embarked on a career of almost continuous construction of marine works.[116]

During the period between the two world wars international construction also resumed in Asia, Africa, and Europe. In the aftermath of World War I,

---

[110]"The War and the British Engineer," 118 *Engineer* 203, 204 (1914).

[111]120 *Engineer* 314 (1915) (the German firm of Orenstern & Köppel was constrained to abandon building a railway in Ecuador).

[112]"Engineering Prospects in Turkey," 119 *Engineer* 371 (1915).

[113]Kossmann, "Holzmann in Argentinien und Uruguay" at 303-21; Bernhard Bahr, "Finanzierungsprobleme bei der Durchführung südamerikanischer Bauten," in *Philipp Holzmann Aktiengesellschaft* at 347, 350.

[114]Heinrich Schloemann, "Holzmann in Brasilien," in *Philipp Holzmann Aktiengesellschaft* at 322-28; Norbert Mayrock, "Holzmann in Perú," in *id.* at 329-35; Karl Kellermann, "Holzmann in Chile," in *id.* at 335-46; Middlemas, *Master Builders* at 297-98 (misspelling "Ulen" as "Ulan").

[115]Wayss & Freytag, *100 Jahre Wayss & Freytag* [no pagination].

[116]Christiani & Nielsen, *75 Years* at 58, 60.

German construction firms such as Hochtief, Holzmann, and Wayss & Freytag were at first heavily committed to extensive port, canal, and dam projects in France carried out within the framework of the Versailles reparations agreements.[117] Hochtief became involved in reparations construction as a result of the firm's takeover by Hugo Stinnes in 1921, who had created Europe's largest industrial empire during the early years of the Weimar Republic. Stinnes had acquired Hochtief at least in part to use it for work on the French Mosel Canal and as a very lucrative conduit for directing business to other industrial firms he owned. Hochtief was not, however, confined to such reparations projects. Beginning in the 1920s it not only built a part of the Trans-Iranian Railway but joined a consortium building infrastructure in the Soviet Union.[118] Julius Berger, too, became active in the Soviet Union, taking up the reconstruction of the Petrograd harbor facilities in 1922.[119]

Soon Holzmann was also at work on ports at Suez and in the Azores, railways in Turkey and Iran, and commercial and industrial buildings in Yugoslavia and Greece. Berger began its involvement in the Trans-Iranian Railway in 1923, while Grün & Bilfinger carried out highway, tunnel, and dam projects in Uruguay, Argentina, and Brazil in the 1920s.[120] By 1925 Wayss & Freytag employed one-third of its 7,400 employees abroad.[121] In the 1930s its international orders increased as it used compressed air methods to carry out harbor works in Riga, Dublin, Amsterdam, and Rotterdam.[122] A multinational consortium consisting of Batignolles, Schneider, Hersent, and Belgian and Danish firms built the Polish deep-water port at Gdynia in the 1920s and 1930s, which the Polish government wanted in order not to be dependent on the port at Danzig, which was under international control.[123]

With the gradual exhaustion of large discrete public works projects in the advanced industrial countries and the spread of the requisite construction technology, competition for the remaining projects in the underdeveloped areas intensified. In the wake of the world depression of the 1930s, these rivalries assumed national political forms as English, French, German, Scandinavian, and U.S. firms individually and jointly competed for railway, irrigation, bridge, port, highway, and building contracts in Turkey, Iran, Iraq, India, China, and other countries.[124] As with the Baghdad Railway and other nineteenth-century railroads, in Iran and elsewhere the chief purpose of the railway was ultimately to intensify the government's military, political, and economic control, which even beforehand was strong enough to force "those least able to afford it" to pay for the construction through regressive taxes.[125] In spite of the availability of this

---

[117]Weidmann, *Hochtief* at 50; Meyer-Heinrich, "Die Entwicklung des Gesamtunternehmens" at 234-37; Ritter, "Holzmann im Marokko und Ägypten" at 299; Wayss & Freytag, *100 Jahre Wayss & Freytag* [no pagination].

[118]See Richard Lewinsohn (Morus), *Die Umschichtung der europäischen Vermögen* 98-99 (1926); Radzio, *Die Aufgabe heisst Bauen* at 20-23; Charles Maier, *Recasting Bourgeois Europe: Stabilization in France, Germany, and Italy in the Decade After World War I*, at 62, 209-12 (1975); *Hochtief 1875-1975* at 165, 169.

[119]Anthony Sutton, *Western Technology and Soviet Economic Development 1917 to 1930*, at 252-53 (1968).

[120]"Bilfinger & Berger" at 560.

[121]Weidmann, *Hochtief* at 27.

[122]Wayss & Freytag, *100 Jahre Wayss & Freytag* [no pagination].

[123]Sociéte de Construction des Batignolles, *L'Oeuvre* at 74-75.

[124]Hellmuth Cuno, "Hochbauten in der Türkei," in *Philipp Holzmann Aktiengesellschaft* at 265-69; Otto Richter & Karl Leeger, "Andere Arbeiten in Kleinasien," in *id.* at 270-73; Karl Leeger, "Holzmann in Iran (Persien)," in *id.* at 273-79; *idem*, "Holzmann im Irak, in Indien und China," in *id.*, at 279-81; Sohn-Rethel, *Ökonomie und Klassenstruktur des deutschen Faschismus* at 57-58.

[125]Nikki Keddie, *Roots of Revolution: An Interpretive History of Modern Iran* 99-100 (1981). On the

mechanism of internal redistribution, external bank financing remained crucial.[126] Its critical importance in international construction was underscored by Holzmann's gradual retrenchment in Asia as a result of its loss of Deutsche Bank support after World War I.[127]

International orders "secured the survival" of some European construction firms during the Great Depression, many of which participated in the massive industrial and infrastructure works of the Soviet First and Second Five-Year Plan.[128] Thus the 50 million mark contract that Hochtief gained for building a fifteen-kilometer section of the Albert Canal in Belgium between 1930 and 1934, which was in part financed by German reparations and designed to cheapen freight transport for the Belgian steel industry, was approximately twice the firm's normal annual turnover. During the 1930s Hochtief also built a large paper factory for a German firm in Finland,[129] while the Swedish Johnson Construction Company built a 750-kilometer road in Rumania.[130] An English firm, Balfour, Beatty, & Company built Bermuda's first railway during this period.[131] Christiani & Nielsen, in addition to expanding its operations to Thailand, Mexico, South Africa, and Venezuela, where it built piers, concrete roads, and a railroad, also pioneered the construction of a submerged, concrete reinforced tunnel at Rotterdam.[132] Other cross-border construction continued through the depression, notably major bridge-building projects in Denmark carried out by German and English firms.[133] One of these firms, Dorman, Long, and its venerable competitor, Cleveland Bridge and Engineering Company, were also building bridges all over the world in the interwar period—in Siam, India, Rhodesia, and even Portuguese East Africa.[134] At the onset of World War II, Dorman, celebrating its fiftieth anniversary, claimed to be "the largest constructional engineering group in Europe."[135]

---

construction of the Trans-Iranian Railway in the 1920s and 1930s by German, U.S. (Ulen and J.G. White), English (Stewart & McDonnell and Costain), French (Batignolles), and Scandinavian (Kampmann, Kierulff, and Saxild) firms, see "Interests Here Share in Persian Contract," *NYT*, July 12, 1928, at 32, col. 2; "The Trans-Iranian Railway," 164 *Engineer* 675 (1937); "Iran Builds a Railroad," 121 *ENR* 793 (1938).

[126]See e.g. "Agree on Turkish Loan," *NYT*, Apr. 6, 1927, at 44, col. 1 (Turkish government accepts $20 million loan for railway construction in Anatolia by Ulen).

[127]Cuno, "Hochbauten in der Türkei" at 269.

[128]See Sutton, *Western Technology and Soviet Economic Development, 1917 to 1930; idem, Western Technology and Soviet Economic Development, 1930 to 1945* (1971).

[129]A. Delmer, 1 *Le Canal Albert* 221, 330 (1939); "The Albert Canal," 148 *Engineering* 431, 433 (1939); Radzio, *Die Aufgabe heisst Bauen* at 25-26; *Hochtief 1875-1975* at 169. Dyckerhoff also participated. DYWIDAG, *Dyckerhoff & Widmann AG 125 Years* 3 (n.d. [1990]). "The Albert Canal," 159 *Engineer* 557 (1935), mentioned many firms but not any German firms.

[130]Stephen Drewer, "Scandinavia," in *The Global Construction Industry* at 160, 161.

[131]"First Railway in Bermuda Nearing Completion," 107 *ENR* 366-67 (1931). Balfour also secured a contract to carry out a flood control project on the Euphrates in Iraq as World War II began. 167 *Engineer* 757 (1939).

[132]Christiani & Nielsen, *75 Years* at 11-12, 85, 87, 89.

[133]See Anker Engelund, "Danes Introduce New Caisson Practice at Little Belt Bridge," 114 *ENR* 841 (1935) (Grün & Bilfinger, Fried. Krupp, and Louis Eilers active from 1928 to 1935); "Start to be Made on New Danish Bridge," 110 *ENR* 541 (1933); "Longest Bridge in Europe Nears Completion," 117 *ENR* 206 (1936) (Dorman, Long).

[134]See "Civil Engineering in Siam," 106 *ENR* 928 (1931); "Steel Arch of 1,100-ft Span to be Built in Africa," 112 *ENR* 522 (1934); "Long Rail Bridge Completed Over Zambesi River in Africa," 113 *ENR* 725 (1934); "The Zambesi Bridge," 158 *Engineer* 403 (1934); "Rhodesian Suspension Span Contract Let," 119 *ENR* 441 (1937); "Long Cantilever in India," 126 *ENR* 538 (1941).

[135]167 *Engineer* 650 (1939).

## Penetrating the U.S. Market

In the United States, in contrast, European firms never performed any significant volume of construction work.[136] British contractors, for example, did not follow in the wake of heavy portfolio investment by British capital, which formed the principal market for U.S. railway securities.[137] There were a few exceptions. One was George Wythes' involvement as contractor for the Detroit and Milwaukee Railroad in the latter half of the 1850s at the behest of a connecting Canadian railway, which itself performed some of the construction work in Michigan.[138] More prominent was the Civil War-era Atlantic & Great Western Railway, the failure of which contributed to that of Peto, who had promoted it.[139] But generally the massive construction of railroads in the United States gave rise to large-scale domestic construction firms operating with subcontractors—as they had in Britain—and the mass recruitment of laborers from Europe and China,[140] while U.S. railway engineering gradually deviated from the English models.[141]

Shortly before and after the turn of the century, however, two of Europe's biggest international construction firms engaged in a variety of very large-scale civil engineering projects in New York. The first of these unusual instances of construction work performed by a European firm in the United States before World War I, which for that very reason prompted "world-wide surprise" and considerable contemporary reporting, was the execution by Pearson's firm of tunneling in New York City.[142] After an American contractor had failed to complete the tunnel under the Hudson River, the English engineers hired by the English capitalists who financed the project contracted with S. Pearson & Son. From 1889 to 1892 it carried out the work by adopting technology (the Greathead shield) that had been developed in Britain to tunnel under the Thames. Pearson too was compelled to abandon the Hudson tunnel when its own technology failed, leading at one point to an annual death rate of 25 per cent among the sandhogs; once the technical causes of this slaughter had been eliminated, however, the English bondholders foreclosed their mortgage.[143]

---

[136]In 1940, the Danish firm of Christiani & Nielsen, which operated all over the world, moved its headquarters for all projects outside the Axis countries to New York, yet never performed any construction work in the United States. "Rudolph Christiani Honored on Firm's 50th Anniversary," *ENR*, Feb. 25, 1954, at 48.

[137]See Feis, *Europe the World's Banker* at 24-28; Lewis, *America's Stake in International Investments* at 36-41; Leland Jenks, "Britain and American Railway Development," 11 *JEH* 375-88 (1951); Peter Buckley & Brian Roberts, *European Direct Investment in the U.S.A. Before World War I*, at 69-70 (1982). For a dissenting view on the significance of international financing of U.S. railways, see Platt, *Foreign Finance in Continental Europe and the United States* at 154-63.

[138]A. Currie, *The Grand Trunk Railroad of Canada* 171-92 (1957).

[139]Jenks, *Migration* at 255-62; Edward Hungerford, *Men of Erie: A Study of Human Effort* 180-99 (1946); Dorothy Adler, *British Investment in American Railways, 1834-1898*, at 94-120 (1970).

[140]See Frederick Cleveland & Fred Powell, *Railroad Finance* 57-72 (1912) (discussing also formation of "inside" construction companies by railroads); Alfred Chandler, Jr., *The Visible Hand: The Managerial Revolution in American Business* 93-94 (1978 [1977]). On the successive waves of Irish, Italian, Swedish, Hungarian, and Chinese workers, see "Nationalalities in Railroad Labor," 12 *EN* 150 (1884); *Testimony Taken by the United States Pacific Railway Commission*, S. Exec. Doc. No. 51, 50th Cong., 1st Sess, VI, 3139-40, 3486 (1887); Robert Riegel, *The Story of the Western Railroads* 229-42 (1926); Paul Gates, *The Illinois Central Railroad and Its Colonization Work* 89, 94-98 (1934); George Taylor, *The Transportation Revolution, 1815-1860*, at 347 (1968 [1951]).

[141]See Caroline MacGill et al., *History of Transportation in the United States Before 1860*, at 310, 313 (1917); Daniel Calhoun, *The American Civil Engineer: Origins and Conflict* 68-78 (1960).

[142]"Viscount Cowdray," 143 *Engineer* 499 (1927).

[143]See "Getting English Capital," *NYT*, Mar. 15, 1889, at 6, col. 1; "Under the Hudson River," *NYT*, Dec. 18, 1889, at 10. col. 3; "Under the North River," *NYT*, June 4, 1891, at 3, col. 5; Charles Prelini, "The New York Subaqueous Tunnels.—No. II," 83 *Engineering* 367 (1907); Spender, *Weetman Pearson* at 52-58; Brian Cudahy, *Rails Under the Mighty Hudson* 9 (1975). On the shield that Greathead developed in combination with compressed air, see James Greathead, "The City and South London Railway; with

By the beginning of the new century there were "more subaqueous tunnels in the course of construction in New York and its vicinity than in the rest of the world together."[144]    In 1903 Pearson secured the contract for four tunnels under the East River for the Pennsylvania Railroad Company, which were characterized at the time as the greatest engineering undertaking in the history of the country.[145]    At the conclusion of this project in 1908, at the peak of its worldwide activities, the firm was said to have been involved in $200 million worth of construction.[146]

The largest German construction firm, Holzmann, also became active in New York State in two of the largest civil engineering projects underway at the beginning of the century in the United States, which also attracted thousands of "alien laborers" trapped in the abusive padrone system.[147]  Although it is unclear whether Holzmann was seeking to conceal its penetration of the U.S. market, its formation of Empire Engineering Corporation in 1903 for building significant waterworks prompted no public comment.[148]    The U.S. press, while mentioning the formation of Kerbaugh Construction—the firm with which Holzmann collaborated—for the special purpose of building the Kensico Dam, does not appear to have been aware of Holzmann's involvement.  Kerbaugh Empire Company, which was founded in 1911, owned all the capital stock of H.S. Kerbaugh, Inc. and Empire Engineering.  The long-time representative of the Deutsche Bank in the United States, the banker Edward Dean Adams, was a director of Kerbaugh Empire until 1914.  When Adams left the board, he was replaced by Otto Riese, the director of Holzmann's foreign department, who remained on the board until 1917, the year the United States declared war on Germany.[149]    Even the voluminous reported intercorporate, personal injury, and contract litigation that Empire Engineering's business spawned failed to mention Holzmann's involvement.[150]

Holzmann's projects included multimillion-dollar contracts for sections of the New York State Barge Canal—on which Pearson's firm managed to secure only one contract, having bid too high on at least eight contracts for other sections[151]—and dredging in the port of Buffalo.[152]  The barge canal, for which

Some Remarks upon Subaqueous Tunneling by Shield and Compressed Air," 123 *MPICE* 39, 55-70 (1896); 127 *MPICE* 365-69 (1897) (obituary).

[144]Charles Prelini, "The New York Subaqueous Tunnels.—No. I," 83 *Engineering* 297 (1907).

[145]"The Tunnel Work of the Pennsylvania Railroad Under the East River," 56 *EN* 43-46 (1906); Charles Prelini, "The New York Subaqueous Tunnels.—No. V," 83 *Engineering* 667 (1907); Alfred Noble, "The New York Tunnel Extension of the Pennsylvania Railroad: The East River Division," 35 *TASCE* 888 (1909); James Brace, Frances Mason, & S. Woodard, "The New York Tunnel Extension of the Pennsylvania Railroad: The East River Division," 35 *TASCE* 1045 (1909); Spender, *Weetman Pearson* at 75-83.

[146]"Viscount Cowdray Dies Suddenly," *NYT*, May 2, 1927, at 14, col. 1.

[147]Lillian Wald & Frances Kellor, "The Construction Camps of the People," 23 *Survey* 449 (Jan. 1, 1910).

[148]*Philipp Holzmann Aktiengesellschaft* at 130; *NYT*, Apr. 16, 1911, at 12, col. 5; Alfred Flinn, "The New Kensico Dam," 67 *EN* 772, 773 (1912).

[149]14 *MMRCS: Part 2*, at 4394 (1913). 15 *MMRCS: Industrial and Public Utility Section* 1598 (1914); 18 *MMRCS: Industrial Section* 977 (1917); *Philipp Holzmann Aktiengesellschaft* at 128; Seidenzahl, *100 Jahre Deutsche Bank* at 93, 246. On the origin of Kerbaugh Empire, see Rodgers v. H.S. Kerbaugh, Inc., 161 N.Y.S. 1016, 1018 (Sup. Ct., App. Div. 1916).

[150]See e.g. Shannahan v. Empire Engineering Corp., 98 N.E. 9 (N.Y. 1912) (Hudson dredging); Huntley v. Empire Engineering Corp., 211 F. 959 (2d Cir. 1914) (Barge Canal); Empire Engineering Corp. v. Mack, 111 N.E. 475 (N.Y. 1916) (Barge Canal). But see Rodgers v. H.S. Kerbaugh, Inc., 190 N.Y.S. 245 (Sup. Ct. 1921) (mentioning that Deutscher [sic] Bank made large advances to Empire and Kerbaugh for work on Kensico Dam).

[151]S. Pearson & Son, Inc. received in excess of $1 million for dredging the Mohawk river channel between 1909 and 1915. 2 *BCB* 267-68, 296 (1909); 6 *BCB* 199, map (between 208 & 209) (1913); 8 *BCB* 294, 299 (1915); 11 *BCB* 40-41 (1918); 12 *BCB* 4 (1919). See also Spender, *Weetman Pearson* at 289; S. Pearson & Son, Inc. v. State, 182 NYS 481 (Ct. Cl. 1920). Among the well-known U.S. firms that

a referendum in 1903 had authorized the expenditure of $101 million, was designed to modernize and restructure the Erie Canal in order to facilitate freight traffic from the Great Lakes to the port of New York in competition with the railroads.[153] But for the simultaneous construction of the Panama Canal, which overshadowed it in popular consciousness if not in magnitude, the 400-mile Barge Canal would have gained greater recognition as the enormous engineering project it was.[154] By successfully bidding on ten separate dredging and excavating contracts totaling six to seven million dollars, Empire Engineering, which performed its excavation work on sections of the canal between Rochester and Buffalo between 1905 and September 1914, conducted one of the largest operations on the project.[155] Holzmann's Empire Engineering also worked on one part of the New York City Catskill water supply system—the Kensico Dam in 1911-1912—which was one of the world's largest masonry dams and "the greatest municipal water-supply system ever undertaken."[156]

World War I ultimately put an end to German construction activity in the United States for many years.[157] Nor did construction firms from countries not at war with the United States find it easier to gain access to the U.S. market. Not until 1935, for example, did the British firm Taylor Woodrow found a housing and development company on Long Island, N.Y.[158] The war did, however, create new forms of internationalism in the construction industry as firms in the warring nations such as Holzmann and Pearson and Norton-Griffiths vied to build and destroy behind enemy lines.[159] 1914 also witnessed another precedent: when the U.S. War Department awarded a contract to a Chinese firm to build a hospital in Hawaii, it marked the first time that the U.S. government had ever let "such a contract" to a foreign firm.[160]

---

underbid Pearson were James Stewart and Foundation. See 2 *BCB* 271 (1909); 3 *BCB* 199, 265, 398-99, 509 (1910); 4 *BCB* 25, 28-29 (1911); 5 *BCB* 229-31 (1912).

[152]1 *BCB* 204-205, 252, 295-96 (1908); "Reject Canal Sub-Contract," *NYT*, Mar. 20, 1909, at 1, col. 3; Emile Low, "Economic Analysis of Excavation Methods on a Typical Section of New York State Barge Canal Work," 39 *EC* 583, 584 (1913). Emile Low, "A German Excavator on the New York Barge Canal," 53 *ER* 503 (1906), alluded to Empire Engineering's use of German machinery without mentioning that it was itself a German company.

[153]State of New York, *Report of the Commission on Barge Canal Operation* (1913). On the political machinations of the competing railroads designed to thwart the construction of a ship canal, which would have created a direct route virtually from the point of production to overseas ports, see Joseph Mayer, "Canals Between the Lakes and New York," 26 *PASCE* 972 (1900); Charles Prelini, "The Erie Canal.—No. II," 90 *Engineering* 76, 77 (1910); Harold Moulton, *Waterways Versus Railways* 417-38 (1912).

[154]See "Our Two Great Canal Projects," 93 *SA* 314 (1905); Day Willes, "The Enlargement of the Erie Canal," 95 *SA* 45 (1906); "The New York State Barge Canal," 99 *SA* 220 (1908); "Comparison of Excavation on the Barge and Panama Canals," 1 *BCB* 3-4 (1908); "Magnitude of Work on New York State Barge Canal," 101 *SA* 54 (1909); Noble Whitford, "New York State Barge Canal," 108 *SA* 377 (1913); Ray Yates, "New York State Barge Canal," 111 *SA* 492 (1914). On the sale of dredging and excavation equipment for the canal, see Harold Williamson & Kenneth Myers, *Designed for Digging: The First 75 Years of Bucyrus-Erie Company* 89-90 (1955).

[155]6 *BCB* 16-18, map (between 208 & 209) (1913); 7 *BCB* 374, 389 (1914); 11 *BCB* 40-42 (1918); 12 *BCB* 4-8, 16-17 (1919).

[156]Wilson Smith, "Excavation and Foundation Work for the Kensico Dam," 71 *EN* 763 (1914); Alfred Flinn, "Architecture of Kensico Dam," 74 *EN* 433 (1915); "The Kensico Dam," 121 *Engineer* 4 (1916). See Lazarus White, *The Catskill Water Supply of New York City: History, Location, Sub-Surface Investigations and Construction* 522-41 (1913).

[157]Empire Engineering, which by 1918 changed its address from Manhattan to Buffalo, apparently continued to perform small amounts of work through 1918. Since the Holzmann representative left the board of directors in 1917, it is plausible that Holzmann severed its connections with Empire Engineering when the United States and Germany entered into war against each other. See 11 *BCB* 77, 120, 126 (1918).

[158]"Taylor Woodrow," in 1 *IDCH* 590 (Thomas Derdak ed., 1988).

[159]See Meyer-Heinrich, "Die Entwicklung des Gesamtunternehmens" at 106; Middlemas, *Master Builders* at 233, 274-75.

[160]72 *EN* 470 (1914).

# 7

# The Imperialist Origins of the International Operations of U.S. Construction Firms

Statistics of exports from the United States to foreign countries fail to reveal the full indebtedness of American trade to American engineers and contractors. In Mexico and in South Africa, in Siam and in the Altai region, in Australia and in Peru, in Brazil and in China, the American mining engineer, railway builder, dredging contractor, the builder of bridges have left an indelible impress....[1]

## Competing with European Firms

Whereas British construction firms internationalized their operations in advance of their industrial counterparts, the sequence was reversed in the United States. This lag was largely a function of the enormous demand for railway and infrastructure construction in the United States throughout the nineteenth century, which made external expansion unnecessary for contractors. Moreover, the major colonial powers—Britain, France, and Germany—made penetration of their "captive" colonial markets by U.S. firms difficult.

One of the first profit-making construction projects undertaken by U.S. entrepreneurs was the Panama Railroad. Undertaken in 1849 by William Aspinwall,[2] a merchant and shipper with interests on the Pacific Coast, and New York capitalists in time to cash in on the Forty-Niners' desire to reach California as quickly as possible, it established the stratified recruitment pattern, adopted later on a larger scale in excavating the Panama Canal, of relying on the United States as a source of engineers and skilled workers, while absorbing the unskilled from Europe and especially from the West Indies as the mainstay of its 7,000-man work force. The West Indian laborers ultimately proved to be cheaper than the thousand imported Chinese coolies, hundreds of whom allegedly committed suicide for lack of opium.[3]

U.S. construction contractors in the latter half of the nineteenth century built a number of single-use industrial railroads for U.S. producing firms designed to transport raw materials, such as hardwoods or manganese ore in Cuba.[4] Phenomena typical of the periphery's increasing dependence on the metropoles commonly underlay such projects. Thus, for example, the government of Peru,

---

[1] J. Wolfe, "Engineering Construction Work Under Foreign Laws," 89 *ENR* 559 (1922).

[2] *NYT*, Jan. 19, 1875, at 8, col. 3 (obituary).

[3] Tracy Robinson, *Fifty Years at Panama 1861-1911*, at 2-21 (2d ed. 1911 [1907]); Miles DuVal, *And the Mountains Will Move: The Story of the Building of the Panama Canal* 19 (1968 [1947]); Joseph Schott, *Rails Across Panama: The Story of the Building of the Panama Railroad 1847-1855*, at 176-81 (1967); Elizabeth Petras, *Jamaican Labor Migration: White Capital and Black Labor, 1850-1930*, at 59-81 (1988).

[4] "Railway Work in Cuba," 33 *EN* 242 (1895).

seriously weakened as a result of its defeat by Chile in the saltpeter war, was constrained to enter into an agreement with Grace Bros. & Co., co-owned by William Grace, then-mayor of New York City, to settle its foreign debt. In exchange for a 66-year lease on two state-owned railroads, part of the annual guano output, and ownership of silver mines, Grace agreed to build a $10 million extension of the Oroya Railroad, begun by Meiggs in 1870, to reach "the grand objective, the famous silver mines of Cerro del Pasco, said to be the richest silver deposit in the world."[5]    In addition to building railroads in Chile, Colombia, Guatemala, Costa Rica, and Jamaica,[6] U.S. firms also initiated but failed to complete a number of lines in Latin America during this period.  Collins Brothers of Philadelphia, for example, began building the Madeira & Mamoré Railway in Brazil in 1878, but abandoned it when a quarter of its U.S. employees fell victim to sickness and accidents.[7]

Once construction of Canadian canals and railways was underway by the mid-nineteenth century, the propinquity of the lines to the U.S. border, the interconnections of U.S. and Canadian routes, and the desire of U.S. firms both to use southern Ontario as a short-cut and to control a share of Canadian commerce all led to the participation of U.S. contractors in the building of the Welland Canal and Canadian railways such as the Grand Trunk and Great Western in the 1850s.[8] Later, U.S. firms routinely carried out related projects in Canada in addition to erecting numerous large commercial buildings.[9]   Henry J. Kaiser, for example, began his construction business paving roads in British Columbia in 1914.[10]

By 1880, *Engineering News*, a recently founded construction-engineering journal, heralded America's belated entry into imperialist competition: "The months now passing are the first flush times in which American capital is enlisted abroad."[11]    That year marked the onset of railway construction in Mexico as the "Boston capitalists who are pushing the Atchison, Topeka, & Santa Fe Rail Road system" built a line through Sonora in order to find an alternative route to the Pacific Coast in competition with the Huntington railroad interests.[12]  Construction of lines connecting the mining and agricultural regions of Mexico to the Southwest of the United States formed part of the *Porfirista* project of building capitalism with foreign capital.[13]   Because the vast majority of Mexican railroads had been

---

[5]13 *EN* 111, 361 (1885); 1 *IDCH* 547 (Thomas Derdak ed., 1988).  On the later history of the railway and the silver mines, see Cleona Lewis, *America's Stake in International Investments* 237-38 (1938).

[6]William Curtis, "Railway Construction in Central and South America," 29 *EN* 616 (1893); William Curtis, "The Railroads of Central America," 10 *RA* 698 (1885); "Guatemala Northern Railway," 36 *EN* 14 (1896); 78 *Engineer* 549 (1894) (James P. MacDonald of Knoxville, Tennessee secured contract to build line in Jamaica).

[7]The line was not finished until 1912. A. Hess, "Notes on a Costly Brazilian Railway Line," 68 *EN* 578 (1912).

[8]See G.P. de T. Glazebrook, *A History of Transportation in Canada* 173 (1938); G. Stevens, 1 *Canadian National Railways: Sixty Years of Trial and Error (1836-1896)*, at 98-100 (1960) (Ferrell & Von Voorhis, and Farewell & Co., owned by Samuel Zimmerman, built the Great Western from 1851 to 1853); A. Currie, *The Grand Trunk Railway of Canada* 163 (1957).

[9]See e.g., W. Ruegnitz, "Building Bridge Substructures on the Canadian Trunk Ry.," 72 *EN* 710 (1914) (Bates & Rogers Construction Co., Chicago); George A. Fuller Company, *George A. Fuller Company: General Contractors 1882-1937*, at 60, 74, 82, 268, 276, 278, 280, 283, 285-86, 292-93, 303, 307-309, 313, 315, 317 (1937).

[10]Kaiser Industries Corporation, *The Kaiser Story* 7-8 (1968); Mark Foster, *Henry J. Kaiser: Builder in the Modern American West* 26-30 (1989).

[11]"Mexican Railway Projects," 7 *EN* 321, 322 (1880).

[12]7*EN* 255 (1880) (quotation); "The Mexican Railroads," 8 *EN* 88 (1881); Fred Powell, *Railroads of Mexico* 123-25 (1921); Lewis, *America's Stake* at 314-21; David Pletcher, *Rails, Mines, and Progress: Seven American Promoters in Mexico, 1867-1911* (1958). For an overview of U.S. economic penetration of Latin America during this period, see Myra Wilkins, *The Emergence of Multinational Enterprise: American Business Abroad* 113-34, 149-72, 173-95 (1970).

[13]See Sergio de la Peña, *La formación del capitalismo en México* 163-86 (1977 [1975]); Steven

financed by U.S capital, the accompanying increase in exports meant that increasingly "Mexico enters the world through the United States" rather than through Europe.[14]

By the turn of the century, U.S. capital investment in Mexico was estimated at a half-billion dollars, 70 per cent of which was directed to railways.[15] The other leading U.S. construction-engineering journal, *Engineering Record*, reported that "[a]ll railroad construction in Mexico is carried on under the direction of Americans...."[16] This U.S.-oriented railway network, four-fifths of the stock of which was concentrated in a few American hands, transformed the character of economic relations between the two countries. The new dependence expressed itself in the fact that, by 1910, the United States accounted for almost three-fifths of Mexican imports and three-quarters of its exports, which were largely minerals, timber, and agricultural commodities.[17] The Mexican Southern Railway, for example, which was being promoted by ex-President Ulysses Grant—a vanguard of American imperialism in Mexico in the early 1880s—was to pass through Oaxaca, "full of valuable timber, with miles and miles undisturbed by the woodman's axe."[18] Grant's assurance to Mexicans that such railways "would, in a brief time, make Mexico a rich and populous republic" remained unfulfilled.[19]

By the early 1880s, U.S. firms were building bridges in such remote locations as Brazil and Australia, shipping all the ironwork and erecting gear and crews from New York.[20] As the gap in iron prices between the United States and Britain narrowed by the mid-1880s, U.S. bridge-building firms began ousting British firms in Latin America and even in the British colonies.[21] By underbidding British and German competitors to secure the contract to build the largest bridge in the Southern Hemisphere in 1886, the technically challenging Hawkesbury Bridge in New South Wales, the Union Bridge Company of New York gave the European construction-engineering industry pause.[22] Before the end of the century, the Phoenix Bridge Company of Pennsylvania erected numerous railway bridges in China, Korea, and Japan, while the Pennsylvania Steel Company, underbidding all its British competitors, built one in Burma.[23]

---

Sanderson, *Agrarian Populism and the Mexican State: The Struggle for Land in Sonora* 31-35 (1981). For an example of further railway construction by U.S. firms in Mexico, see "Construction Work on the Mexican Central Railway," 48 *EN* 215 (1902) (Bell & Semmers).

[14]W. Nevin, "The Railway Situation in Mexico," 14 *EN* 86, 87 (1885) (author was secretary of the Mexican National R.R. Co.). See also "American Trade with Mexico," 7 *RA* 654 (1882) (editorial); "Mexican-American Commerce—A Great Opportunity," 14 *RA* 804 (1889) (editorial).

[15]47 *ER* 248 (1903).

[16]"Railroad Construction in Mexico," 53 *ER* 264-45 (1906).

[17]John Hart, *Revolutionary Mexico: The Coming and Process of the Mexican Revolution* 133-34 (1987).

[18]"Mexican Railways," 6 *RA* 520 (1881) (editorial).

[19]"Mexico's Opportunity," 6 *RA* 30 (1881) (editorial). On Grant and the Mexican Southern Railway, see Pletcher, *Rails, Mines, and Progress* at 157-81; William Hesseltine, *Ulysses S. Grant: Politician* 439, 444-45 (1935); William McFeeley, *Grant: A Biography* 486-92 (1981).

[20]"American Bridge Building in the Antipodes," 9 *EN* 15 (1882) (Edgemoor Iron Comp., Wilmington, Del.);"American Contracting in Brazil, *id.* at 241; Walter Cook, "Erection of the Nairne Viaducts, near Adelaide, South Australia," 112 *MPICE* 185 (1903).

[21]"The Verrugas Viaduct," 51 *Engineering* 460 (1891) (erection gang sent from United States to build bridge on Oroya Railway in Peru); "American Bridges in English Colonies," 14 *EN* 345 (1885).

[22]See "The Hawkesbury Bridge," 58 *Engineer* 363 (editorial); "Hawkesbury Bridge, New South Wales," 15 *EN* 79 (1886); Charles Burge, "The Hawkesbury Bridge, New South Wales," 101 *MPICE* 2 (1890).

[23]"American Bridges in Japan," 40 *ER* 700 (1899); 39 *ER* 563 (1898-99); "American Bridge-Building," 68 *Engineering* 308 (1899); *id.* at 307 (letter to editor); 39 *SB* 80-81 (1900); A. Holley & Lenox Smith, "American Iron and Steel Works: No. XXXVIII.—The Works of the Phoenix Iron Company," 29 *Engineering* 103 (1880).

In 1899 a furor erupted—a British engineer chided the complaining businessmen: "This whining is un-English"[24]—when the British War Ministry awarded a contract to Pencoyd Iron Works in Pennsylvania, which had already performed work in the Netherlands and Japan, to erect the bridge over the Atbara river in the Sudan for the railway that British and Indian military engineer troops, dervish prisoners of war, and indigenous fellahs subject to the corvée were building between Wadi Halfa and Khartoum. By completing the work much more quickly than could its British competitors, the U.S. firm (and the erecting gang it sent out from the United States) contributed to Britain's military reconquest of the Sudan.[25]

In dedicating the bridge, the British commander-in-chief of the Egyptian army, Lord Kitchener, himself once a Royal Engineer, addressed the deep-seated trend that he saw as underlying this incident. The British firms' inability to supply such a large undertaking so rapidly "demonstrates that the relations between labor and capital in our country are not such as to give sufficient confidence to capitalists to induce them to run the risk of establishing great up-to-date workshops with the plant necessary to enable Great Britain to maintain her proud position as the first constructing nation of the world."[26] A U.S. construction-engineering journal argued that although it was true that U.S. workers' wages were three times higher than their British counterparts' while their productivity was four to five times greater, U.S. structural steel firms' chief advantages lay in the attention that they devoted to standardization, specialization, and organization as well as their permanent revolutionizing of the means of production.[27]

In seeking to explain why British civil engineers suddenly preferred to do business with U.S. bridge builders, a leading British engineering trade journal concluded that British firms had not thoroughly integrated the three elements of engineering, steel manufacture, and erection:

> It has been said that bridges are built by the mile in the States and cut off by the yard as wanted. This is not strictly true; but it is true that a great deal of work is done ready cut-and-tried in the offices of the best firm, and that they are always in a position to submit designs for any bridge....[28]

Another such turn-of-the-century incident even triggered a parliamentary flap.[29] The American Bridge Company was incorporated in 1899 to bring under the House of Morgan's unitary control twenty-five of the largest bridge-building firms (including Pencoyd Iron Works), which, however, as finished-steel companies, depended on other producers for most of their crude steel. The new amalgamation, which accounted for nine-tenths of bridge tonnage erected in the

---

[24]92 *Engineer* 128 (1901) (letter to editor from John Graham). "Probably no bridge contract ever gave rise to so much controversy...." "The Atbara Bridge," 109 *Engineer* 247 (1910).

[25]"American Plans Accepted," *NYT*, Mar. 22, 1899, at 1, col. 4; 41 *EN* 232 (1899) (editorial); C. Wennas, "Erecting the Bridge in the Heart of the Sudan," 40 *ER* 526 (1899); Hans Meyer, *Die Eisenbahnen im tropischen Afrika: Eine kolonialwirtschaftliche Studie* 153-55 (1902); E. de Renty, *Les Chemins de fer coloniaux en Afrique: Chemins de fer dans les colonies anglaises et au Congo Belge* 197 (1904); Victor Clark, 3 *History of Manufactures in the United States: 1893-1928*, at 120 (1929).

[26]"Lord Kitchner's Dedicatory Address," 40 *ER* 528 (1899).

[27]"American Shop Practice in Bridge Construction," 46 *ER* 97 (1902) (editorial). On the policy of continuous obsolescence at the leading U.S. steel works, Carnegie Steel, and a comparison with the policy in Britain, see Harold Livesay, *Andrew Carnegie and the Rise of Big Business* 116-17 (1975).

[28]"The Atbara Bridge," 87 *Engineer* 543 (1899) (editorial). The journal also reprinted an article from the *Philadelphia Record* explaining that in the preceding three years the U.S. steel industry had invested in the most modern equipment. "The Secret of Our Manufacturers' Success in Foreign Markets," *id.* at 453.

[29]88 *PD* (4th ser.) 500, 687-88 (1900).

United States,[30] submitted the lowest bid (£135,000) to build thirty bridges on the British railway in Uganda, which required it to ship 6,000 tons of steel from New York to Mombassa.[31] The company also sent to this location, "so remote from a skilled labor market," an erection gang consisting of a superintendent, seventeen skilled erectors, and a cook. The U.S. workers were paid twice their normal wages, which enabled some of them to buy "comfortable homes" on their return.[32]

Under these Americans, literally, worked 150 Hindu riveters and carpenters and 150 African laborers, whose wages were less than a quarter of the Hindus'. Their vulnerable position proved too much of a temptation to American Bridge, a leader of the anti-union open-shop movement in the first decade of the twentieth century.[33] Discovering a scope of freedom that cantankerous unions and occasionally enforced statutes precluded in the United States, the company's U.S. foremen found it "necessary almost to go back to old slave days" in their treatment of African workers. "They could be punished in no way except by the whip or by fining them," one of the firm's engineers boasted to the engineering profession: the most effective procedure was to "act as police, judge, and executioner yourself." Hand in hand with this atavistic attitude went American Bridge's disavowal of Brassey's approach to international labor: the company appreciated the "exceedingly cheap labor even if one good white man is equal to three or more Indians."[34]

The enormous volume of bridgebuilding in the United States enabled the industry to attain a very high degree of development. The absorption of American Bridge by J. P. Morgan's newly formed U.S. Steel Corporation in 1901 strengthened this trend.[35] Structural steel work designed by specialists and fabricated in "monster works" dedicated exclusively to it enabled U.S. firms to reduce the manufacture and erection of bridges to such simple terms that export prices "in almost inaccessible parts of the world" were not significantly higher than those of bridges erected in the United States.[36] The British Institution of Civil Engineers heard a paper in 1902 by an engineer who had studied the Pencoyd plants in an attempt to understand the emergence of such strong U.S. competition. Among the salient differences, Henry Bridges Molesworth observed fewer union limitations on output, 24-hour a day operations, and greater scientific knowledge in the drawing room. At the U.S. Steel plant, moreover, "[e]ven comparatively new machinery, if superseded by anything better, is ruthlessly relegated to the scrapheap."[37]

---

[30]"The Organization of the American Bridge Company," 42 *ER* 17 (1900); Luke Grant, *The National Erectors' Association and the International Association of Bridge and Structural Iron Workers* 16-17 (1971 [1915]); Clark, 3 *History of Manufactures in the United States* at 121; Lewis Corey, *The House of Morgan: A Social Biography of the Masters of Money* 248-50 (1930); William Hogan, 1 *Economic History of the Iron and Steel Industry of the United States* 272-75 (1971); Kenneth Warren, *The American Steel Industry 1850-1970: A Geographical Interpretation* 176-78 (1973); Naomi Lamoreaux, *The Great Merger Movement in American Business, 1895-1904*, at 83-84 (1988 [1985]).

[31]"The Bridge Contracts for the Uganda Railway," 71 *Engineering* 215 (1901) (including table with all the bids); A. Lueder, "Experience in the Erection of American Viaducts on the Uganda Railway," 51 *EN* 345, 347 (1904).

[32]"American Bridge Building in Equatorial Africa," 50 *ER* 276-78, 310-11 (1904).

[33]See Grant, *The National Erectors' Association*; David Brody, *Steelworkers in America: The Nonunion Era* 50-79 (1969 [1960]); Philip Foner, 5 *History of the Labor Movement in the United States: The AFL in the Progressive Era, 1910-1915*, at 7-8 (1980).

[34]Lueder, "Experience in the Erection of American Viaducts" at 346.

[35]Horace Wilgus, *A Study of the United States Steel Corporation in Its Industrial and Legal Aspects* 44 (1973 [1901]); Arundel Cotter, *The Authentic History of the United States Steel Corporation* 21-22 (1916).

[36]"The Export Business in Steel Bridges," 50 *ER* 265 (1904) (editorial); Clark, 3 *History of Manufactures in the United States* at 120.

[37]Henry Molesworth, "American Workshop Methods in Steel Construction," 148 *MPICE* 58, 59, 72

In 1902, U.S. Steel Corporation sought a new construction-related vehicle for expanding its exports.  Its partner in this endeavor was George A. Fuller Company, which, when capitalized at $20 million the previous year, had become the largest construction firm ever organized in the United States.[38]  The two firms, high-ranking executives of each of which owned stock in the other, formed a trust, the U.S. Realty and Construction Company, in order to "'enter foreign fields, with the view of introducing steel construction in cities like London, Paris and Berlin.'" Although financial problems thwarted these plans, Fuller became the largest building firm in the United States with a virtual stranglehold on the construction of tall buildings in New York City, and in the 1920s succeeded in introducing steel-skeleton buildings in Japan.[39]

The beginning of the new century witnessed yet another unmistakable manifestation of the emerging dominance of U.S. industrial capital.  When the Westinghouse Electrical Manufacturing Company built the largest electrical machinery and engine factory complex in Britain near Manchester, *The Times* correspondent announced the appearance of a "new order," in which "British capital, British enterprise, and British engineering skill" would no longer hold sway.[40]  If the means of production housed in these $7 million facilities were not emblematic enough of the coming sea change, a U.S. firm also managed the quite uncommon feat of wresting away from British firms the contract for constructing the nine substantial buildings.[41]  The St. Louis firm of James Stewart and Company, founded in 1845 and thus one of the oldest construction firms in the United States, had specialized in grain elevator construction; it later incorporated in New Jersey in 1913, moving its headquarters to New York.[42]  In penetrating the English market, Stewart "pushed forward to completion with a rapidity probably never before attained in the construction of substantial steel and brick buildings."[43]  To the astonishment and disbelief of English employers, Stewart enforced a much faster pace of work, requiring the British workers, members of the Bricklayers' Union, to conform to the alleged U.S. norm of 1,500 to 2,500 bricks in nine and one-half hours as opposed to the customary 330 to 700 per day.[44]  Just a quarter-century earlier the economist Alfred Marshall had cited the Bricklayers as a union whose strength in large part derived from being unrestricted by foreign competition.[45]  Stewart achieved this output both by threatening to employ nonunion workers and by paying an hourly wage 15 per cent above the union rate.  To sustain this level of output, Stewart described for *The Times* how, on another English project, the erection of a chimney at the Mersey Tunnel Power

(1902).

[38]"Great Building Concern Organized," *NYT*, Mar. 30, 1901, at 1, col. 4.

[39]John Moody, *The Truth About Trusts* 327-35 (1904) (quoting U.S. Realty statement at 328); Ray Stannard Baker, "The Trust's New Tool—The Labor Boss," 22 *McClure's* 30, 38-39 (Nov. 1903); 4 *MMCS* 1679 (1903); Paul Starrett, *Changing the Skyline: An Autobiography* 115-16, 130, 205-19 (1938).

[40]"The British Westinghouse Electrical Works," *Times*, Feb. 25, 1902, at 13, col. 6.

[41]47 *EN* 60 (1902); A. Sartorius Freiherr von Waltershausen, *Das volkswirtschaftliche System der Kapitalanlage im Auslande* 174 (1907).

[42]See "Members of the Merchants' Exchange of St. Louis, January 1st, 1904," at 27 in Geo. Morgan, *Annual Statement of the Trade and Commerce of St. Louis for the Year 1903* (1904); 14:2 *MMRCS* 4671 (1913); 13 *MAI: Industrial Investments* 1248 (1922); "The 'Old Timers'—And How They Stayed Alive in Contracting," *ENR*, Apr. 30, 1959, at 30.

[43]"The Works of the British Westinghouse Electrical Manufacturing Company—No. I," 73 *Engineering* 397 (1902).

[44]A contemporaneous National Association of Manufacturers publication claimed that bricklayers in closed shops in the United States were laying 800 to 1,000 bricks in eight hours compared with 3,000 a few years earlier.  Walter Drew, *Closed Shop Unionism* 10 (n.d. [1910]).

[45]Alfred Marshall, "Fragments on Trade Unions," in 2 *The Early Economic Writings of Alfred Marshall, 1867-1890*, at 346 (J. Whitaker ed., 1975 [ca. 1874-75]).

Station at Birkenhead, he had used such innovations as double platform lifts that permitted quick transportation of the bricks up to the bricklayers while the other lift was descending.[46]

Although one member of the British Institution of Civil Engineers sought consolation in the fact that Americans were not always successful in competing for work in Britain,[47] soon U.S. firms specializing in the export of structural steelwork were building bridges all over the world.[48] Thus when the British Cleveland Bridge and Engineering Company built the world's highest railway bridge at Victoria Falls in 1904, the achievement prompted a national commercial sigh of relief: "It is a source of congratulation in these times, when we hear so much about the foreigner taking contracts that used to be secured by British firms."[49] The British constructional steel manufacturing and erection industry was, moreover, hardly at the point of collapse. Its largest firms, such as Dorman, Long & Co., Ltd., which was integrated backward (into mines) and forward, remained internationally dominant for decades.[50] Yet by the end of the nineteenth century, even Dorman, Long conceded that it was subject to severe competition from German and U.S. steel manufacturers.[51]

## The Spanish-American War and the Construction of the Panama Canal

The United States had since the early 1880s sought a role among the Great Powers in East Asia and the Pacific Basin. In Korea, for example, "a rich but backward region far from the restraints of 'civilization,'" U.S. entrepreneurs began "playing for big stakes" as they joined their rivals in "grabbing all the resources of the country they could lay their hands on...."[52] After U.S. financiers gained control of the richest gold mines in Asia in the 1890s, the U.S. firm of Collbran & Bostwick built the first steam railway, electric railway, waterworks, and office building in Korea.[53]

The advent of so-called insular imperialism, that is, the assembly of a network of naval, coaling, and cable stations through the acquisition of Guam, Hawaii, the Philippines, and Wake positioned the United States to penetrate the Chinese market.[54] Yet U.S. capital initially failed in its efforts to move beyond

---

[46]*Times*, Mar. 10, 1902, at 7, col. 6 (J.C. Stewart, building manager, letter to editor).

[47]148 *MPICE* 105-106 (1902) (correspondence contribution by Malcolm Blair).

[48]See e.g. "The Quebec Bridge," 41 *ER* 391 (1900) (Phoenix Bridge Co.); "The Rio Grande Bridge of the Pacific Railway of Costa Rica," 46 *ER* 390-94 (1902); "Rio Grande Bridge of the Pacific Railway of Costa Rica," 74 *Engineering* 537 (1902); (Milliken Bros.); "The Tula and the Chone River Bridges, Mexico," 50 *ER* 362 (1904) (American Bridge and Phoenix Bridge).

[49]"The Victoria Falls Bridge," 99 *Engineer* 339 (1905) (editorial).

[50]13 *MAI: Industrial Investments* 454 (1922); Jonathan Boswell, "Sir Arthur John Dorman," in 2 *DBB* 136-39 (David Jeremy ed., 1984). Founded in 1876, Dorman continued building bridges overseas long after it weakened as a steel producer in the late 1920s. 137 *Engineer* 238 (1914) (Sydney); "Sydney Harbour Bridge," 153 *Engineer* 304 (1932); "Bangkok Bridge," 154 *Engineer* 248 (1932); "A New Zambesi Bridge," 163 *Engineer* 717 (1937); "Bridge Improves Portuguese Transport," *ENR*, Mar. 6, 1949, at 59; *ENR*, Sept. 4, 1952, at 223, 225 (New Zealand). For a description of its manufacturing facilities, see "Northeast Coast Institution of Engineers and Shipbuilders," 91 *Engineer* 578 (1901); "The Works of Messrs. Dorman, Long, & Co., Limited, Middlesex," 86 *Engineering* 408 (1908). In the 1920s Dorman and Pearson entered into a partnership in collieries. J. Spender, *Weetman Pearson First Viscount Cowdray 1856-1927*, at 242-44 (1930).

[51]84 *Engineer* 585 (1897).

[52]Howard Beale, *Theodore Roosevelt and the Rise of America to World Power* 274 (1967 [1956]).

[53]See Fred Harrington, *God, Mammon, and the Japanese: Dr. Horace N. Allen and Korean-American Relations, 1884-1905*, at 144-45, 182-201 (1944); 45 *ER* 592 (1902). Harry Collbran, who emigrated to the United States from Britain in 1881 and built railways in the West, began work in Korea in 1896. 7 *Who's Who in America* 425-26 (1912-1913); *NYT*, Feb. 16, 1925, at 19, col. 4 (obituary).

[54]Thomas McCormick, *China Market: America's Quest for Informal Empire 1893-1901*, at 106-107

trade with, to large-scale investment in, China. Whereas entrepreneurs from the European Great Powers and Japan recognized that it was necessary to take a long-term view of railway construction as "the chief means of internal development in China, opening the way for greater investment of foreign capital and creating a large market for manufactured goods,"[55] U.S. financial consortia in the 1890s and 1900s lost several opportunities for building railways because "American capital was not yet competitive enough to accept the more marginal terms that European capital would risk."[56]

The establishment of a formal U.S. colonial empire in the wake of the Spanish-American War, however, soon prompted U.S. construction-engineering firms to take advantage of the coalescing imperialist global financial, military, and political apparatus to challenge British, French, and German competitors.[57] As the leading industry trade journal, *Engineering News*, editorialized at the conclusion of the Spanish-American War:

> The course of recent events appears to indicate that within a few years the great empire of China may offer a new field to the American engineer and merchant, and that the overthrow of Spanish misrule and medievalism in the West Indies and the "Far East" will also lead to possibilities of rapid development of American interests in these smaller fields. Development in such cases means, first of all, the introduction or extension of the railway. While the American engineer in his own country has shown his ability to build light and inexpensive railways for development purposes...he has so far had but little opportunity to exercise this ability in other countries, with the exception of Mexico. It is true that he has built railways in the West Indies, in Central and South America, and in the Hawaiian Islands, and is building one in Korea, but most of these have been short lines, built to accommodate an existing traffic from mines, or along established routes of travel, rather than to serve as lines of general development.[58]

Almost immediately *Engineering News* began carrying announcements, circulated by the U.S. diplomatic corps, of opportunities to build railways in Latin America. Thus in 1900 the U.S. consul in Para, Brazil, reported that the governments of Brazil and Bolivia were offering subsidies for the construction of railways that would "open up a new and important market for American goods and open up rubber belts and cattle lands, now inaccessible." Interested contractors were asked to contact the consul.[59] Characterizing the railways in Central America as a "Peace Agent," *Engineering Record* proclaimed that "[t]he United States is necessarily obliged to exercise a sort of protection over the countries in question...in order to guide the development of their resources...."[60]

Symbolically the U.S. government itself inaugurated overseas activities in the new century as the Army Corps of Engineers began building fortifications in the recently acquired Philippines and Cuba.[61] The U.S. government insured that

---

(1967).

[55]Charles Vevier, *The United States and China 1906-1913: A Study of Finance and Diplomacy* 99-100 (1955).

[56]McCormick, *China Market* at 70-76, 87-89 (quotation at 75); Beale, *Theodore Roosevelt* at 181-91, 219.

[57]See generally William Williams, *The Contours of American History* 345-89 (1966 [1961]); *idem, The Roots of Modern American Empire: A Study of the Growth and Shaping of Social Consciousness in a Marketplace Society* (1970 [1969]); Philip Foner, 1-2 *The Spanish-Cuban-American War and the Birth of American Imperialism 1895-1902* (1972).

[58]"Pioneer Railway Construction in New Countries," 40 *EN* 200 (1898).

[59]43 *EN* 33 (1900).

[60]"The Railroad as Peace Agent," 57 *ER* 57 (1908) (editorial).

[61]See e.g. *Report of the Chief of Engineers U.S. Army, 1908*, pt. I, at 16 (1908).

the infrastructural projects in the Philippines, which were designed to move that country's economy toward dependence on the United States, also benefited U.S. construction firms. Thus during the first decade of the twentieth century, American Bridge erected a highway bridge, J. G. White & Company built a railway, and Atlantic, Gulf & Pacific Company undertook $4 million worth of harbor development in the Philippines.[62]

In order to facilitate exploitation of Cuba's natural resources, especially its iron ore and sugar, which U.S. firms had been mining and processing since the 1880s, the U.S.-owned Cuba Company built a major railroad across Cuba during the U.S. military occupation. More than half of the 10,000 construction laborers were imported from Spain in large part because they were "more docile" than U.S. workers.[63] The U.S. Army's handling of a large contract for paving and sewerage in Havana was severely criticized as providing excessive profits to Michael Dady, a private contractor, who also happened to be a high officer in the Republican Party in Brooklyn.[64] It was in occupied Cuba that the newly incorporated Snare & Triest Company began its overseas work. Founded in 1902 by Frederick Snare, a former vice president of Pencoyd Iron Works, it immediately secured a contract to build a pier at Matanzas "at a time when few American companies dared venture outside the boundaries of the United States." During the next half-century, Snare, which went on to build manufacturing plants, mills, bridges, power plants, ports, and terminals throughout Latin America, "obtained a larger proportion of the heavy construction contracts [in Cuba] than any of its competitors." In particular, it performed most of the construction work for the American & Foreign Power Company, a dominating entity in Cuba, as well as nickel production plants for Freeport Sulphur Company.[65]

U.S. firms operating in Latin America had no compunctions about using state force to disrupt the untoward workings of a free labor market. In the course of building the Guayaquil & Quito Railway in the first decade of the twentieth century, James P. McDonald Company of New York entered into an agreement with the Jamaican government for a supply of 3,500 Jamaican laborers who were to be paid 50 to 60 cents for a 10-hour day. When the company took umbrage at the workers' desertion for the local sugar plantations, the Ecuadorian government "came to the rescue" by criminalizing the employment of Jamaicans by anyone other than the railway contractors.[66]

The largest empire-building project carried out by the United States was the construction of the Panama Canal during the decade preceding World War I, "which called together the largest number of men that were ever employed at one time on any modern or medieval peaceful enterprise."[67] Unlike the private capital that built virtually all other international infrastructure projects of the period "for what could be made out of it," the U.S. government did "not stand in the

---

[62]H. Stevens, "Some Road Building in the Philippines," 50 *ER* 535 (1904); "The Philippine Railway System," 57 *ER* 114-15 (1908); "San Francisco Bridge Co.,"5:4 *AB* 1, 3-4 (1959); Glenn May, *Social Engineering in the Philippines: The Aims, Execution, and Impact of American Colonial Policy, 1900-1913*, at 135, 138, 162-65 (1980).

[63]Victor Clark, "Labor Conditions in Cuba," 7 *BDL* 663, 686 (quotation), 730 (1902); Walter Vaughan, *The Life and Work of Sir William Van Horne* 276-96 (1920); Russell Fitzgibbon, *Cuba and the United States 1900-1935*, at 52-56 (1935); James Hitchman, *Leonard Wood and Cuban Independence 1898-1902*, at 69-71 (1971); Hugh Thomas, *Cuba or the Pursuit of Freedom* 464-66 (1971); Josef Opatrný, *Antecedentes históricos de la formación de la nación cubana* 210-24 (1986); Mark Reutter, *Sparrows Point: Making Steel—The Rise and Ruin of American Industrial Might* 72-86 (1989 [1988]).

[64]See "Engineering Work in the City of Havana," 45 *EN* 90 (1901); *id.* at 8 (editorial); 46 *EN* 357, 377 (1901); Herman Hagedorn, 1 *Leonard Wood: A Biography* 279-80, 331-32 (1931).

[65]"The Frederick Snare Corporation," 5:8 *AB* 1, 2 (1959).

[66]"Construction Difficulties on the Guayaquil & Quito Railway," 50 *ER* 477 (1904).

[67]William Sibert & John Stevens, *The Construction of the Panama Canal* 110 (1915).

position of a private corporation with reference to" the Panama Canal.[68]   It occupied its state-entrepreneurial role most prominently in engineering the "secession" of Panama from Colombia, which reduced the cost of building the canal considerably by creating a compliant client state.[69]

Originally considered in the mid-nineteenth century as a means of opening the American West and as a tool in contesting British claims to Central America, when finally built, the Panama Canal was motivated by military and national and international economic considerations.  The canal's military character has even been used to explain its origins as a public enterprise.[70]   As naval operations in the Cuban theater of the Spanish-American War showed, the canal would enable the U.S. Navy to transfer its fleets between the East and West Coasts much more expeditiously in order to administer the budding American empire.[71]   "The extension of our territory to include the Hawaiian Islands and...the Philippines has made this connection most desirable for the proper exercise of governmental functions wherever they are to be discharged."[72]   Indeed, the Isthmian Canal has been interpreted as underlying the Spanish-American War itself: control of Cuba and Puerto Rico made it possible to ward off any European efforts to interfere with U.S. domination of the new canal.[73]

The Panama Canal also assisted U.S. intercoastal trade: "The costs of transportation had for a long time restricted the volume of trade between the eastern and western sections of the country, but the canal has made possible the greatest freedom of interchange of commodities produced in both sections."[74]   Perhaps even more importantly, the canal would facilitate U.S. capital penetration of South America, which at the turn of the century still consisted of British "commercial annexes."[75]   The Panama Canal served to satisfy the economic necessities of securing raw materials from Asia and the Pacific coast of South America and competing with European capital for the export of manufactured commodities to those same regions.  High transportation costs were seen as particularly damaging to U.S. interests on the west coast of South America, to which the United States accounted for only one-tenth of exports.  The cheapening of freight made possible by the new canal would induce the building of railways, without which a successful mining industry, which was dependent on heavy and expensive equipment, was not possible.  But once "the railroads thoroughly open up the Andean Plateau to the American capitalist and mining engineer...the return to capital...promises to be liberal."[76]   Although U.S. manufacturers of many products were already producing at lower cost than their European competitors, the Suez Canal had brought the latter closer to Asian markets than Atlantic and Gulf port exporters.  Together with Suez, the Panama Canal thus effectively shifted the

[68]Peter Hains, "The Labor Problem on the Panama Canal," 179 *NAR* 42, 49 (1904) (brigadier general and member of Isthmian Commission).

[69]See Rippy, *The Capitalists and Colombia* 91-102 (1931); David McCullough, *The Path Between the Seas: The Creation of the Panama Canal 1870-1914*, at 361-402 (1977).

[70]Merle Fainsod & Lincoln Gordon, *Government and the American Economy* 663 (rev. ed., 1948 [1941]).

[71]See e.g. Harry Knapp, "The Navy and the Panama Canal," in *History of the Panama Canal: Its Construction and Builders* 255-65 (Ira Bennett ed., 1915).

[72]*Report of the Isthmian Canal Commission, 1899-1901*, at 43 (S. Doc. No. 222, 58th Cong., 2d Sess. 1904).

[73]See Samuel Bemis, *The Latin American Policy of the United States: An Historical Interpretation* 123-66 (1971 [1943]).

[74]Emory Johnson et al., 1 *History of Domestic and Foreign Commerce of the United States* 363 (1915).

[75]W. Stead, *The Americanization of the World: The Trend of the Twentieth Century* 217, 221 (1902 [1901]).

[76]Emory Johnson, "Report on the Industrial and Commercial Value of the Canal," in *Report of the Isthmian Canal Commission, 1899-1901*, at 515, 582, 589, 580.

hub of international sea routes back to the Northern Hemisphere.[77]

The U.S. version of an Isthmian Canal got underway a quarter-century after French capital had failed. The private Compagnie Universelle du Canal Interocéanique, directed by Ferdinand de Lesseps, who had also been the guiding entrepreneurial force behind the Suez Canal, initiated construction of a sea-level canal in 1880.[78] Although mortality at Panama under the French regime did not approach the 120,000 deaths that Herodotus had assigned to an unsuccessful attempt by an oriental despotic regime to build a Suez Canal 2,500 years earlier,[79] the deaths of perhaps as many as 30,000 West Indian, European, and U.S. workers did considerably exceed the 10,000 Chinese, Chileans, and Peruvians who had died building the Oroya Railway in the Peruvian Andes in the 1870s under Henry Meiggs, who "was not sufficiently careful of the health of his workmen."[80]

The majority of Panama Canal laborers were recruited from Jamaica, Martinique, and Colombia. So plentiful was the supply that *Engineering News* alerted its readers that from Jamaica "it would seem that negroes may be had ad libitum (a wink for contractors in Southern climes)."[81] Although Lesseps's Canal Company furnished the laborers and housing and often the machinery as well, "all but a fraction of the labor force worked for the contractors."[82] This apparent fractionation of the work force was magnified when the French prime contractor, Couvreux, Hersent et Compagnie, withdrew in 1882 in favor of a multitude of subcontractors. Couvreux had also built the Suez Canal, introducing there the first excavating machines, which it then developed further in projects at Vienna and Antwerp in the 1860s and 1870s.[83] Among the dredging and excavation companies receiving the bulk of the contracts at Panama were several Dutch, French, Swiss, Swedish, English, and Colombian firms.[84] In particular the San Francisco firm of Huerne, Slaven, & Company, later known as the American Contracting and Dredging Company, which had the world's largest excavation equipment specially built for its sections of the canal, secured huge profits—"[t]he profits of these dredges at Panama have been fabulously great; so great that we do not like to put them on record in cold print"—before the entire undertaking collapsed.[85]

---

[77]See Emory Johnson, "The Isthmian Canal in Its Economic Aspects," *AAAPSS*, Jan. 1902, at 1, 3-7; Lincoln Hutchinson, *The Panama Canal and International Trade Competition* (1915); Arnold Henry, *The Panama Canal and the Intercoastal Trade* (1929); William Woodruff, "The Emergence of an International Economy," in *The Fontana Economic History of Europe: The Emergence of Industrial Societies Part Two*, at 697-98 (1973).

[78]Possibly anticipating the emergence of an American Palmerston, one of the leading British construction-engineering journals cautioned de Lesseps that even if he could show the United States "that the canal would be a paying concern when once completed, and if all the world were under one master this might be sufficient to get the capital to do it with...[nevertheless] there are many masters, and their interests are not exactly the same." "The Panama Canal," 48 *Engineer* 150 (1879) (editorial).

[79]Herodotus, *Historiae*, 2.158; James Breasted, *A History of Egypt* 487-88 (1964 [1905]). See also Karl Marx, 1 *Das Kapital: Kritik der politischen Ökonomie* 315-16 (1867).

[80]Watt Stewart, *Henry Meiggs: American Pizarro* 173-77 (1968 [1946]); Ian Cameron, *The Impossible Dream* 47, 68-69, 98 (1971) (estimating 22,000 to 30,000 deaths); Joseph Bishop, *The Panama Gateway* 97 (1913) (16,500 deaths); Gerstle Mack, *The Land Divided: A History of the Panama Canal* 347 (1944) (5,000 deaths). See also Petras, *Jamaican Labor Migration* at 85-125.

[81]9 *EN* 167 (1882).

[82]McCullough, *The Path Between the Seas* at 159. According to Charles Jameson, "Notes on the Panama Canal," 16 *EN* 202 (1886), 60 per cent of the workers were "negroes" from Jamaica and Martinique and 20 per cent from Colombia.

[83]"Les Travaux du canal de Panama," 4 *GC* 1, 3 (1883); "The Panama Canal Finances and Contracts," 10 *EN* 365 (1883); Max de Nansouty, "Travaux du Canal de Panama: Les Excavateurs," 13 *GC* 131-35 (1888); McCullough, *The Path Between the Seas* at 170, 148-51.

[84]"The Panama Canal," 13 *EN* 168 (1885) (listing the firms and the value of their contracts).

[85]See "Nicaragua and Panama," 20 *EN* 31, 32 (1888) (editorial) (quotation); "The 'Hercules Dredgers' for the Panama Canal," 10 *EN* 49 (1883); S, "Canal de Panama: Dragues du type américain 'l'Hercules,'" 4 *GC* 381 (1884); "The Panama Canal," 15 *EN* 88 (1886) (explaining how contracts permitted contractors

Despite the use of the most advanced dredging and excavation machinery ever deployed,[86] the mistaken choice of a sea-level rather than a lock canal and financial failures in the 1880s ultimately led to termination of the French project, thus enabling the U.S. government to undertake and complete the monumental work. Against the background of the scandals surrounding the French project, *Engineering News* applauded the intervention of the state: "We have escaped the danger this great work might be turned over to a syndicate of capitalists to handle as they pleased, which means in such a manner as would yield them the largest profit on the sale of securities and the work of construction."[87] To be sure, the journal was also constrained to acknowledge that there were in any event no contractors large enough to bid for the whole contract and to give sufficient financial guarantees.[88]

The U.S. governmental construction organization deployed even more powerful excavation machinery than had the French—including steam shovels, unloaders, spreaders, and trackshifters. They all contributed to the creation of Lake Gatun, which inundated twenty-five villages and dispossessed thousands of meagerly indemnified inhabitants.[89] This unprecedented capital-intensity notwithstanding, the project at its peak in 1913 still absorbed the labor of 45,000 workers. The West Indies furnished the largest contingent. Indeed, virtually the whole adult male population of Barbados deemed physically acceptable by the U.S. recruiters worked at some point in Panama.[90] The suggestion that Blacks from the U.S. South be employed was rejected by southern congressmen, who objected to the untoward consequences that such a drain would have on their employing constituents' source of cheap labor.[91]

In mustering the possible sources of labor, canal construction supervisors substituted racist-genetic rhetoric for Marx's political-economic and cultural account of the differential intensity and productivity of labor between workers from advanced capitalist and not-yet capitalized societies.[92] Avoiding direct comparison, they argued, for example, that West Indians were

> constitutionally incapable of the performance of what would be considered a day's work in the United States. The best that railroad contractors have ever been able to get out of colored day laborers in the tropics is one third of what the average white man will accomplish in the Temperate Zone....[93]

European observers parroted these sentiments. Thus Eugen Tincauzer, a

---

to profit even if they abandoned work on reaching rock); William Williams, "Plant and Material of the Panama Canal," 19 *TASCE* 273, 274 (1888) (contractors made "the largest amount of money in the shortest possible time"); *Report of the Isthmian Canal Commission, 1899-1901*, at 202-206; Robinson, *Fifty Years at Panama* at 150-57 (on Henry and Moses Slaven); Cameron, *Impossible Dream* at 57, 82; McCullough, *Path Between the Seas* at 148, 156-58.

[86]See e.g., Nathan Appleton, "What the Slaven Dredges are Doing at Panama," 19 *EN* 490 (1888); "Travaux du Canal de Panama: Excavateur de MM. Weyher et Richemond," 8 *GC* 151 (1886).

[87]51 *EN* 468 (1904) (editorial).

[88]"Shall the Panama Canal Be Built by Contract," 55 *EN* 297 (1906).

[89]66 *EN* 723 (1911); McCullough, *Path Between the Seas* at 489, 587. For an accounting of the compensation, see *ARICC for the Fiscal Year Ending June 30, 1911*, at 490-92 (1911); *ARICC for the Fiscal Year Ending June 30, 1912*, at 524-25 (1912); *ARICC for the Fiscal Year Ending June 30, 1913*, at 518-20 (1913).

[90]See *ARICC for the Fiscal Year Ended June 30, 1913*, at 383; Bishop, *The Panama Gateway* at 335-41, 447-49; Mack, *The Land Divided* at 540; McCullough, *Path Between the Seas* at 475-76, 496-98; Michael Conniff, *Black Labor on a White Canal: Panama, 1904-1981*, at 24-44 (1981).

[91]McCullough, *Path Between the Seas* at 473-74.

[92]See chapter 4 above.

[93]W[alter]. Pepperman, *Who Built the Panama Canal?* 159-60 (1915) (author was Chief of Office of Administration of the Second Isthmian Commission).

Prussian state engineer who was one of the non-American members of a board of consulting engineers appointed by President Theodore Roosevelt to advise the Isthmian Canal Commission, justified the racial wage differential on the ground that "so long as the Negro still has a dollar in his pocket he won't work"; higher wages would therefore only lead to greater absenteeism.[94] An English engineer combined paternalistic contempt for the "naturally lazy" West Indian workers with patronizing contempt for their upstart masters: "The American foremen and overseers...are under the fallacious impression that showers of abuse, or acts of violence, will command obedience and stimulate the energy of their gang. They quite fail to understand that under two centuries of British rule the West Indian negro has been subjected to kindness and strict justice, under protection of unbiassed law courts."[95]

To be sure, by the end of the project, these very supervisors acknowledged that West Indian workers had become as productive as their European counterparts—if only because the latter's output deteriorated as a result of their prolonged stay. As measured by the rigid racially segmented division of labor and wage structure, which placed all white Americans among the higher-paid skilled and all nonwhite non-U.S. citizens among the low-paid unskilled workers, this refusal to accommodate prejudice to experience proved to be a valuable cost-cutting device.[96] By the same token, employment of Spanish workers also helped to reduce state expenditures on the Panama Canal because while "worth relatively three times as much" as West Indians, they were paid only twice as much.[97]

### World War I and the U.S. Breakthrough to Capital Exporting Status

England's pioneers in all cases were the engineers and their co-workers, the contractors. ... We now have the material basis, surplus funds, for foreign expansion.[98]

The eruption of European capitalist rivalries in World War I coincided with and overshadowed the opening of the Panama Canal.[99] A turning point in many respects, the war (which enabled U.S. Army Engineers to carry out building projects in Europe for the first time),[100] definitively shifted the focal point of world capital accumulation to the United States. "With all the other industrial countries of the world busy destroying one another"[101] and withdrawing their capital from their far-flung enterprises, especially in Latin America, internationally oriented American capitalists decided to seize the unique but long-awaited opportunity to project U.S. capital overseas.[102] In November 1915 a group led by Frank Vanderlip, the president of National City Bank, and including the most important industrial and financial capitals in the United States founded (and capitalized at $50 million) the American International Corporation. *The New York Times* immediately hailed it as "by far the most ambitious attempt that has ever

[94]Eugen Tincauzer, "Der Bau des Panamakanals," 61 *ZB* 611, 619 (1911).

[95]A. Thompson, "The Labour Problem of the Panama Canal," 83 *Engineering* 589, 590 (1907).

[96]Bishop, *The Panama Gateway* at 302; Petras, *Jamaican Labor Migration* at 127-203.

[97]Sibert & Stevens, *Construction of the Panama Canal* at 117-18.

[98]Charles Stone, "Engineer's Relation to Foreign Expansion," 75 *ER* 5, 6 (1917).

[99]McCullough, *Path Between the Seas* at 609, 611.

[100]See e.g. Robert Tomlin, Jr., "American Road-Building Work in French War Zone Organized," 80 *EN* 198 (1918); "What the American Army Engineers Did in the War," 82 *ENR* 953 (1919).

[101]"Commercial and Engineering Possibilities in South America," 72 *EN* 407 (1914) (editorial).

[102]See generally Harry Scheiber, "World War I as Entrepreneurial Opportunity: Willard Straight and the American International Corporation," 84 *PSQ* 486 (1969).

been made to put the United States among the ranking nations in world commerce and finance."[103] Promoters and directors included representatives of the House of Morgan, Standard Oil, Chase Bank, National City Bank, Anaconda, Armour, McCormick, International Nickel, General Electric, American Telephone & Telegraph, and Grace.[104]

American International was established, inter alia, to promote the construction of infrastructure abroad. Until that time, the United States had "'figured little in construction work in South America, Russia, or the East. That was because we ourselves were borrowers of capital.'"[105] The two major exceptions were Stone & Webster Engineering Corporation and J. G. White Engineering Corporation. Before embarking on overseas projects, both firms had gained significant experience financing electric light and power companies in the United States. Stone & Webster, which began as consulting engineers in 1889, soon branched out into construction. During the depression that began in 1893, bankers planning to buy up unprofitable electric utilities co-opted Stone & Webster, which had already been managing and supervising public utilities. The firm's capacity for raising capital for utilities secured it an advantageous position in obtaining contracts for construction. At first Stone & Webster marketed clients' securities for a service commission; later it evolved into an underwriter and investment banker.[106] This domestic financial strength enabled Stone & Webster to work in a similar manner overseas.[107]

Operating on a much smaller scale, J. G. White & Co., Inc., which started out in electric power construction engineering, also combined management of utilities with investment securities dealing and bond distribution.[108] By 1913, J. G. White Engineering already maintained offices in London, Para (Brazil), Buenos Aires, and Santiago for its work in designing and constructing hydroelectric and electric light and power projects, and electric railways.[109]

World War I quickly transformed the configuration of international capital flows. As the president of American International, Charles Stone, an owner of Stone & Webster, explained to U.S. construction firms, with the growth in U.S. manufacturing exports, "surplus capital" would have to seek "employment abroad...in world-development work."

> The development of a country is essentially an engineering task—the building of railroads, of ports, of municipal works, of public utilities. England's mechanical and engineering superiority in the early part of the last century, combined with her wealth, fitted her admirably for such development work. Great firms sprang up that carried British engineering genius to every part of the world—and where England's engineers went and invested English gold, English trade followed.

---

[103]"Raise $50,000,000 for World Trade," *NYT*, Nov. 23, 1915, at 1, col. 1. See also 72 *ER* 745 (1915) (editorial) ("the greatest single step taken by American business to cope with the problems of international trade"); Harold Cleveland & Thomas Huertas, *Citibank 1812-1970*, at 91-94 (1985).

[104]"See $500,000,000 Gain in Venture in World Trade," *NYT*, Nov. 24, 1915, at 1, col. 1. Harold Faulkner, *The Decline of Laissez Faire 1897-1917*, at 85 (1951), referred to American International as a Morgan subsidiary.

[105]"Raise $50,000,000 for World Trade" at 6, col. 6.

[106]*Electric-Power Industry: Control of Power Industries*, S. Doc. No. 213, 69th Cong., 2d Sess. 177-87 (1927); J. Chamberlain, "From Edison to the Atomic Age: Stone & Webster Rolls Along," *ENR*, May 21, 1953, at 59.

[107]See *MMI: Public Utility Securities* 1628 (1929).

[108]*Electric-Power Industry* at xxxv, 217-22; 12 *MAI*, Pt. 2: *Public Utility Investments* 1001 (1926).

[109]14 *MMRCS*, pt. 2, at xx (1913) (advertisement). White had also secured a $20 million contract in 1914 to control flooding in China. "To Stop Chinese Floods," *NYT*, Feb. 4, 1914, at 3, col. 3. In describing White's waterworks project in Ecuador during World War I, a British trade journal referred to J. G. White & Co. Ltd., London, without even noting that it was a U.S. firm. "New Water Supply for Guayaquil," 122 *Engineer* 407 (1916).

[T]o-day such great firms as S. Pearson & Son, Ltd...., engineers and contractors both, continue to serve as the pioneers for English trade expansion, for trade follows investment, and these firms build English investment money into public works, utility systems and industries.

Powerful German engineering and construction companies, such as Philip [sic] Holzmann Aktiengesellschaft, have developed, too, and their work forms the basis of greater German trade.[110]

One obstacle to the propulsion of U.S. construction capital onto the world market was peculiar to the mode of financing public works in Europe and South America. In Latin America such projects were "let only to contractors who are prepared to accept payment in bonds that do not have a ready market.... Only one American firm, Wm. R. Grace & Company, ever carried out this system on the large scale and with the financial resources that European houses have found profitable."[111] In Brazil, for example, most railway construction in the beginning of the twentieth century was financed by French, German, and English bankers who held Brazilian government bonds and had an understanding that their representatives would be given the contracts for the construction. Consequently, "[t]he success of American contracting firms will...depend...upon their ability to interest American capital in the Brazilian field in other lines" such as founding a bank.[112]

John Aird's work on the Aswan Dam at the turn of the century furnished another example of the kind of financing that had become necessary in international construction yet remained inaccessible to U.S. firms. Aird's contract provided that the £2 million were to be paid in sixty semi-annual installments not to begin until the work was completed. The Egyptian government issued bonds payable over thirty years, which the wealthy British financier Ernest Cassel, who was heavily invested in Egypt, took over, thus permitting the contractor to be paid in cash on the usual monthly certificates.[113]

Overcoming these kinds of financial obstacles was the avowed purpose of American International. By enabling construction firms to dispose of the bonds taken in payment for their work, American International was designed to make it possible for them to compete on the world market.[114] Within months of its establishment, in "one of largest contracts ever placed with an American firm" in South America, American International provided the financing for Ulen Construction Company to build waterworks and sewerage systems in several cities in Uruguay.[115]

Several of American International's founders had long cultivated an intense interest in investment in and trade with China.[116] A subsidiary of American

---

[110]Stone, "Engineer's Relation to Foreign Expansion" at 6.

[111]"The Banking Opportunities in Contracting Opportunities," 59 *ER* 365-66 (1909). Through its London representative, Grace Bros. & Co. Ltd., Grace built the Transandine Railway. "The Construction of the Transandine Railway," 59 *ER* 704 (1909).

[112]"Contracts for Public Works in Brazil," 59 *ER* 40 (Current News Supplement, Feb. 13, 1909). For an example of the complicated financing of the Arica-La Paz Railway, which was built by the British firms of Jackson and Griffiths, see Percy Martin, "Arica-La Paz Railway," 112 *Engineer* 452 (1911); "The Arica-La Paz Railway," 107 *Engineer* 444 (1909).

[113]Maurice Fitzmaurice, "The Nile Reservoir, Assuan," 152 *MPICE* 71, 77 (1903); *DNB 1912-1921*, at 97, 98 (1927) (s.v. "Cassel").

[114]"Will Help American Contractors in Handling Work in Foreign Fields," 73 *ER* 93 (1916) (interview with Willard Straight, vice president of American International). On American International's later development (it was merged with Adams Express in 1969), see Cleveland & Huertas, *Citibank* at 368 n.25.

[115]"American $5,500,000 Contract for Work in Uruguay," 75 *EN* 868 (1916); "International Corporation Will Finance Uruguay Work," 73 *ER* 496 (1916).

[116]Faulkner, *Decline of Laissez Faire* at 83-85; George Mazuzan, "'Our New Gold Goes Adventuring': The American International Corporation in China," 43 *PHR* 212 (1974).

International, Siems-Carey Canal and Railway Company, promptly secured a contract to rebuild the world's oldest and longest canal, the Grand Canal in China. Although this project eventually came to nought, the British engineering-construction industry quickly noticed that its U.S. competitors had begun to use credit to overcome what it had theretofore been its greatest competitive obstacle—insistence on immediate payment in dollars.[117]

In the aftermath of the devastation of World War I, governments in Europe, especially France, after initial resistance, awarded some contracts to U.S. firms for reconstruction.[118] To the ultimate disappointment of U.S. contractors, however, domestic firms performed the vast majority of the work.[119] Elsewhere in Europe, however, U.S. firms did gain a foothold. The Foundation Company, for example, which was founded in 1902 and maintained branch offices or performed work in Peru, Chile, Bolivia, Argentina, and Colombia, incorporated a separate entity, Foundation Company (Foreign), in 1925 to carry on projects in the rest of the world including France, Spain, Italy, and Japan.[120] It built the library of the university in Louvain, Belgium, in addition to performing drainage work in Greece and subway excavation in England. Other companies built grain elevators in Bulgaria and government buildings in Turkey.[121]

In a move of greater long-term significance, U.S. industrial companies operating overseas began to entrust non-infrastructure projects to U.S. building firms.[122] Thus in 1920 Standard Oil contracted with the Austin Company of Cleveland to build several standard factory units for distribution centers in Turkey, Bulgaria, and Greece.[123] Austin, which had been incorporated in 1904, pioneered the standardized steel-frame factory building in the United States in the course of constructing a large number of electric lamp factories in the years before World War I. In addition to exporting prefabricated structures to Europe and South Africa, Austin also undertook the reconstruction of Belgian glass plants destroyed during World War I.[124] A decade later U.S. Corn Products Refining Company selected H. K. Ferguson to build its factory in Korea.[125] By the late 1920s, with the onset of Stalin's gargantuan accelerated industrialization program, U.S. construction-engineering firms such as Badger, Lummus, Foster-Wheeler, J. G.

---

[117]"Americans to Rebuild Grand Canal of China," 81 *EN* 1049 (1918); Mazuzan, "'Our New Gold Goes Adventuring'" at 230-31; "The Question of American Competition," 122 *Engineer* 13 (1916) (editorial); "International Engineering Interests in China," 107 *Engineering* 827-29 (1919); Roberta Dayer, *Bankers and Diplomats in China 1917-1925: The Anglo-American Relationship* 43-49 (1981).

[118]See "Are We Wanted in France and Belgium?" 82 *ENR* 2 (1919) (editorial); "Are American Engineers and Contractors Wanted in France," *id.* at 31; "$200,000,000 French Contract to American Firm," *id.* at 1231 (Vulcan Steel Products Co. co-opted MacArthur Bros. and McClintic-Marshall Co. to perform construction work with French workers).

[119]See "French Reconstruction Not for United States Engineers and Contractors," 84 *ENR* 59 (59); E. Mehren, "American Contractors and Labor Conditions in France," 85 *ENR* 340 (1920).

[120]*MMI: American & Foreign: Industrial Securities* 2635-36 (1932); *PIV 1937*, at 1942 (1937). It declared bankruptcy in 1963. "Foundation Co., 4 Units File Under Chapter 11 of the Bankruptcy Act," *WSJ*, Nov. 13, 1963, at 4, col. 2; *MIM 1964*, at 2739 (1964).

[121]"Foreign Work Being Done by New York Contractors," 88 *ENR* 672 (1922); "Foreign Contracts Awarded to American Contractors," 93 *ENR* 650 (1924); "Foreign Contracts Awarded to American Concerns," 95 *ENR* 897 (1925).

[122]The plant that Ford built in Argentina in 1919 was designed by Albert Kahn, the leading U.S. industrial design firm, but construction itself was supervised by a Ford employee, R.R. Brown, although it is unclear whether the work was done by force account. Myra Wilkins & Frank Hill, *American Business Abroad: Ford on Six Continents* 93-94 (1964).

[123]"Lets Contracts for Buildings in the Levant," 84 *ENR* 299 (1920) (Standard Oil's own erecting force was also involved).

[124]Martin Greif, *The New Industrial Landscape: The Story of the Austin Company* 25, 57-59, 74, 95, 149-50 (1978).

[125]Wells Thompson, "Modern Factory Built in Korea," 1 *CE* 1275 (1931). Morrison-Knudsen acquired Ferguson in 1950. *MMI* 1254-55 (1952).

White, and Kellogg began competing with European and especially German firms for contracts to build roads, hydroelectric dams (including Dnieprostroi), and industrial facilities in the Soviet Union; during the 1930s, Soviet industrialization provided crucial demand for Western firms and employment for thousands of unemployed engineers and construction workers seeking refuge from the worldwide depression.[126] The best known of these projects were the construction by Austin (and Ford Motor) of an automobile factory at Nizhni Novgorod and McKee Corporation's construction of the world's largest steel complex at Magnito-gorsk.[127]

U.S. construction firms even managed to penetrate the Japanese construction market. Using technology developed in the United States, Stone & Webster, for example, built a hydroelectric plant in Japan in 1920.[128] In the same year the Japanese government invited the George A. Fuller Company to organize a branch in Japan to build and to instruct Japanese contractors and engineers in U.S. methods. The George A. Fuller Company of the Orient, Ltd. began work on four steel-frame office buildings, including two in Tokyo for the Japan Steamship Company and the Japan Oil Company. Importing the machinery and materials from the United States, the firm employed a skeletal staff of U.S. skilled workers and supervisors together with Japanese laborers.[129] No sooner had these buildings been erected than the monumental earthquake of 1923 put them to a severe test, which they passed structurally.[130] The early 1920s also saw Mitsui hire James B. Stewart & Company to build a bank and other office buildings in Tokyo, while Foundation was awarded a contract for $82 million to build an underground electric railway in Tokyo, and Westinghouse built railway electrification facilities.[131] Other U.S. firms built bridges in Japan in the 1920s.[132]

While the U.S. Navy Civil Engineer Corps was occupied with a far flung empire extending from Haiti to Guam and the Army Engineers were building roads in Cuba,[133] U.S. construction firms began to profit from the infrastructural

[126]See e.g., "American Firm Gets Big Road Contract in Russia," 103 *ENR* 74 (1929) (C.F. Seabrook Co. involved in $150 million 10,000 mile six-year project); "American Firm to Build Russian Industrial Plants," *id.* at 825 (MacDonald Engineering Co. to build cement factories, grain elevators, and flour mills); "More Than 600 Americans Are Now Working for the Soviets," *BW*, July 16, 1930, at 25; Peter Filene, *Americans and the Soviet Experiment, 1917-1933*, at 221-27 (1967); Anthony Sutton, *Western Technology and Soviet Economic Development 1917 to 1930*, at 39, 202-205 (1968); *idem, Western Technology and Soviet Economic Development 1930 to 1945*, at 82, 87, 127-28, 249-52, 270, 345 (1971); Edward Carr & R. Davies, 1 *Foundations of a Planned Economy 1926-1929*, at 950-68 (1974 [1969]); Joan Wilson, *Ideology and Economics: U.S. Relations with the Soviet Union, 1918-1933*, at 67-69 (1974); Gilbert Ziebura, *Weltwirtschaft und Weltpolitik 1922/24-1931: Zwischen Rekonstruktion und Zusammenbruch* 155, 157 (1984). On the industrialization program, see Akademiia Nauk SSSR, *Postroenie fundamenta sotsialisticheskoi ekonomiki v SSSR 1926-1932 gg.* (1960).

[127]"To Build Auto Plant for Russia," *NYT*, Nov. 4, 1929, at 45, col. 2; "Soviet Rejects Town Plan," *id.*, Apr. 11, 1930, at 14, col. 6; Allan Austin, "Communism Builds Its City of Utopia," *id.*, Aug. 9, 1931, § V, at 10; Frank Southard, *American Industry in Europe* 203-206 (1931); Allan Nevins & Frank Hill, *Ford: Expansion and Challenge 1915-1933*, at 677-84 (1957); Wilkins & Hill, *American Business Abroad* at 208-27; Sutton, *Western Technology and Soviet Economic Development 1917 to 1930*, at 246-49; *idem, Western Technology and Soviet Economic Development 1930 to 1945*, at 74-77; Greif, *The New Industrial Landscape* at 97-102.

[128]"U.S. Firm to Build Hydro-Electric Plant in Japan," 84 *ENR* 299 (1920).

[129]"U.S. Contractor to Erect Office Buildings in Tokio," 84 *ENR* 597-98 (1920); "Constructing Modern Office Buildings in Japan," 89 *ENR* 476-78 (1922).

[130]"Structural Lessons Learned from Survey of Steel-Frame Buildings After Japan's Earthquake," 91 *ENR* 728 (1923). In the aftermath of the earthquake, the Japanese-American Engineers' and Contractors' Corp. was organized to participate in the reconstruction. "Organize Big Company to Reconstruct Tokyo," 92 *ENR* 135 (1924).

[131]"Foreign Projects Awarded to American Contractors," 93 *ENR* 650 (1924).

[132]"Tokyo Builds Two New Bridges," 7 *SM*, July 1925, at 12-13; 8 *id.*, Aug. 1926, at 45.

[133]See e.g., P. Searles, "Difficulties of Construction Work on the Island of Guam," 97 *ENR* 106 (1926); "Activities of Navy Civil Engineering Corps Tabulated for Fiscal Year," 101 *ENR* 586 (1928); "The Great

projects in South America that U.S. finance capital was making possible.[134] Vanderlip, the chairman of American International, promoted bank credit for Latin America as a means of ousting European capital.[135] In 1920, Foundation secured a $50 million contract for construction of waterworks and sewerage systems in Peru. The 1920s also saw R. W. Hebard & Company of New York build highways in Colombia and Panama and a railway and roads in El Salvador, while Turner Construction Company performed worked for the Standard Oil Company of New Jersey in Cuba, Winston Bros. Company built a railway in Colombia, and Simmons Construction Corporation of Charlotte, North Carolina secured a large road contract in Costa Rica.[136] Raymond International, a firm that had secured contracts in Canada, Mexico, Chile, and Argentina beginning in 1907, owed its strong market position to its having patented the cast-in-place concrete pile—that is, driving hollow steel shells to the required depth and then filling them with concrete to avoid the damage otherwise associated with pile driving. By the 1920s it was performing port and other work throughout Latin America as well as in the Philippines, Sumatra, China, and Japan, where it built an electric station at Yokohama.[137]

Other firms performed road work in Peru as well as a variety of work in Canada and the Caribbean.[138] They built warehouses, docks, piers, and yacht clubs in Cuba, hotels in Nassau owned by U.S. companies, the U.S. embassy in Brazil, and modern steel office buildings in Buenos Aires.[139] In Mexico, too, U.S. firms continued to build railways (for the Southern Pacific) and pave roads during the 1920s, although even the largest U.S. firms were often underbid by Mexican competitors.[140]

In addition to such activities performed by construction firms, U.S. multinational firms engaged in the private corporate counterpart to the departmental system of railway construction adopted by colonial governments. In South America, mining and power companies carried on major construction projects by force account, while the Firestone Rubber Company built a power dam and its own highways on its huge rubber plantations in Liberia and from it to the coast.[141]

During the international "obesely lucrative...orgy of lending" after

---

Road Improvements in Cuba," 57 *ER* 240 (1908).

[134]See 90 *ENR* 805 (1923).

[135]Carlos Marichal, *A Century of Debt Crises in Latin America: From Independence to the Great Depression, 1820-1930*, at 180-81 (1989).

[136]"Colombian Highway to the Sea Awarded to New York Contractors," 97 *ENR* 727 (1926); John Caton, "Building the 'Road-to-the-Sea' in Colombia," 101 *ENR* 950 (1928); R. Hardman, "Highway Construction in Panama," 91 *ENR* 594 (1923); "Central American Railway of 185 Miles Put Under Contract," 93 *ENR* 972 (1924); "Large Highway Contract Awarded by Costa Rica,"101 *ENR* 748 (1928); "Winston Bros. Company—1875-1950," 1:1 *AB* 1, 4 (Sept. 1952); "Turner Construction Company," 2:6 *AB* 1, 3 (1954).

[137]"Raymond Pushes Back World Frontiers," *ENR*, May 29, 1952, at 62, 64; Leon Weaver, "Raymond Concrete Pile Company," 4:6 *AB* 1, 4-5 (1957).

[138]See 11 *CM*, Jan. 1929, at 52-53; "Peru Increases Mileage of Modern Roads," 7 *SM*, Apr. 1925, at 4-6; Aberthaw Construction Company, *Aberthaw Construction Company: A Quarter Century of Fulfilment* 9, 17-22 (1919); Mira Wilkins, *The Maturing of Multinational Enterprise: American Business Abroad from 1914 to 1970*, at 135 (1974).

[139]"Foreign Work Being Done by New York Contractors," 88 *ENR* 672, 1083 (1922); "Foreign Work Being Done by New York Contractors," 89 *ENR* 634 (1922); "N.Y. Firm Gets $35,000,000 South American Contract," 92 *ENR* 952 (1924) (George E. Nolan Co.).

[140]"Foreign Contracts Awarded to American Contractors," 93 *ENR* 650 (1924); "Foreign Contracts Awarded to American Concerns," 95 *ENR* 897 (1925); "Large Contract for Highways Reported Let in Mexico,"110 *ENR* 510 (1933) (Warren Brothers and Foundation submitted higher bids).

[141]See e.g., C. Newton, "The Hydro-Electric Development of the Braden Copper Co.," 69 *EN* 1041 (1913) (in Chile); George Bayles, "Constructing a 98-Kilometer Water Conduit in Chile," 83 *ENR* 593 (1919) (for a U.S. copper mine); "American Engineers Build Power Dam in Liberia," 132 *ENR* 336 (1944); A. Carter, "American Roadbuilding in Liberia," 123 *ENR* 479 (1939).

1925,[142] large U.S. construction firms, in association with U.S. banks, further implemented the program outlined by American International in financing overseas public works projects. As originally foreseen: "In some cases the projects may have to be suggested, and the people of the country educated up to an appreciation of the expediency of undertaking them."[143] Although the construction firms "charged exorbitant prices and reaped enormous profits," the crash and depression at the end of the decade revealed the risks inherent in this internationalizing strategy.[144] Ulen & Co., which was founded in 1922 by American International, Stone & Webster, and Ulen Contracting Company to carry out work in South America,[145] proceeded in this manner to manage the building of tramways, gas and waterworks, and ports in Athens, Warsaw, and Latin America. It derived its profits primarily from fees and bonds.[146] Bolivian government bonds financed Ulen's construction of a state-owned railway in the 1920s.[147] Chile secured $200 million in loans from U.S. banks for infrastructure projects such as waterworks, railways, and ports, which Ulen, Foundation, and Warren Brothers Company carried out.[148] The riskiness of Third World operations during the Great Depression was demonstrated by the fact that Ulen declared bankruptcy between 1939 and 1941.[149]

Warren Brothers, the largest highway construction firm in the United States, was another internationally oriented U.S. building firm during this period that was originally launched on a patent—for paving material—in 1900 after several decades in the coal tar and oil business. Warren, which both manufactured "bitulithic" pavement and owned several foreign subsidiaries including ones in Argentina, Chile, Guatemala, Europe, and Australia, performed road and paving work throughout Latin America. During the late 1920s and 1930s, it also did paving in Spain and Poland.[150]

In 1927, Warren secured a contract for $75 million to pave 481 miles of the 700-mile Central Highway in Cuba, assertedly the longest paved road ever put under contract until that time. The remaining 211 miles were awarded to the Compañía Cubana de Contratistas, which gave the Cuban president, General Gerardo Machado, and his friends "a magnificent opportunity...to enrich themselves."[151] The highway, which the firm advertised as *The Largest Highway Contract in History*, was touted as enabling American tourists to indulge their

---

[142]Bemis, *The Latin American Policy of the United States* at 333. For a breakdown of the almost $2 billion of dollar bonds issued by Latin American governments, see *id.* at 336, 341. See generally Charles Kindleberger, *The World in Depression 1929-1939,* at 58-82 (1975 [1973]); Derek Aldcroft, *From Versailles to Wall Street: 1919-1929,* at 187-217, 239-67 (1981 [1977]); Barbara Stallings, *Banker to the Third World: United States Portfolio Investment in Latin America, 1900-1986,* at 60-75 (1987).

[143]"South American Fields Begin to Materialize," 73 *ER* 407 (1916) (editorial).

[144]Marichal, *Century of Debt Crises in Latin America* at 190.

[145]"Ulen & Co. Formed," *NYT,* Feb. 16, 1922, at 21, col. 6; *PFV 1938,* at 2864-66.

[146]*PIV 1937,* at 2064 (1937); *Sale of Foreign Bonds or Securities in the United States: Hearings Before the Senate Committee on Finance,* 72d Cong., 1st Sess. 739, 2098, 2102 (1931-32); Lewis, *America's Stake* at 371-72; Wilkins, *Maturing of Multinational Enterprise* at 135-36.

[147]"Bolivian State Railway Being Built by Americans," 89 *ENR* 352-53 (1922).

[148]"Chile Has $200,000,000 Fund for City and State Public Works," 103 *ENR* 803 (1929).

[149]*PFR: 1941 Industrial Manual* 2823-24 (1941).

[150]J. Allhands, "Warren Brothers Company," 2:7 *AB* 1-6 (1954); Herbert Warren 3rd, "The Warren Story: A History of Warren Brothers Company and Its Founders" (1969 [1965]); "Reflections: 1900-1975," *The Spreader,* Fall 1975, at 2, 7, 10.

[151]Gonzalo de Quesada y Miranda, 1 *¡En Cuba Libre! Historia documentada y anecdótica del Machadato: 1925-1931,* at 79 (1938) (quotation); Warren Brothers Company, *Historical Review of the Warren Brothers Company Contract with the Government of Cuba for Construction of a Part of the Cuban Central Highway* 1-5 (n.d. [1936]); Raymond Buell et al., *Problems of the New Cuba: Report of the Commission on Cuban Affairs* 382-83 (1935); Hugh Thomas, *Cuba or The Pursuit of Freedom* 581-82 (1971) (incorrectly referring to "the little-known Warren Bros.").

pastime of "driving through the country in their own cars" which they were wont to ship ahead.[152]

On its section Warren Brothers employed 5,000 workers. Unlike the standard pattern for overseas construction projects, the contract negotiated by the Cuban government limited the role of foreign workers: three-quarters of the workers were required to be Cuban. Warren reported that only a small number of skilled Americans worked on the highway. In order to take advantage of Henry Kaiser's highway equipment, Warren also sublet a $20 million section to Kaiser Paving Company, of which it was majority owner and with which it had both competed and cooperated on projects in Canada. Kaiser had, until this time, been well known in the West, but had not been "even remotely in the 'big time.'" The Central Highway—Kaiser Paving's share of which was triple the firm's total volume of business during its previous 14-year existence—became a "turning point" for Kaiser: it was his last large road project before advancing to more complex types of heavy construction. The year after Kaiser's firm completed its section of the highway, it included Warren in the company that Kaiser and Warren Bechtel formed to participate in building Boulder Dam.[153]

The *Carretera Central* was recognized at the time as an extravagant public works program "which would have been a luxury in the wealthiest country"; on a per capita basis, its cost would have been the equivalent of a $3.5 billion highway in the United States.[154] Although the highway was persiflaged at the time as being ballyhooed into "Pharaonic" proportions,[155] later socialist and anti-socialist authors agree that the incorporation of several rich agricultural zones into the national market depended on the completion of the highway.[156]

Because the Cuban government had manifestly overextended itself in light of its reduced revenues in the latter half of the 1920s, a question arises as to why Warren Brothers, which protested to the U.S. government in 1929 when rumors of impending action against the dictator Machado were circulating,[157] and the Chase National Bank, which was closely aligned with Machado, employed his son-in-law as manager of its Cuban branch,[158] and financed construction through a complicated series of loan transactions, entered into this deal. U.S. firms saw a guarantee of security in Cuba in the neocolonialist financial, trade, customs, and military control that the United States had assembled there.[159] These controls included the "right to intervene" that the United States had arrogated to itself and imposed on Cuba in the form of the Platt Amendment, the large accumulation of U.S. investments, and Machado's probusiness attitude.[160] After Machado's

---

[152]Hamilton Wright, "Havana-Matanzas Highway Opening Celebrated Today," *Havana Post*, May 20, 1929, reprinted in Warren Brothers Company, *The Largest Highway Contract in History* 21 (n.d. [ca. 1929-30]).

[153]E. Ruiz Williams, "Cuba Begins New Central Highway 700 Miles Long," 98 *ENR* 558 (1927); "New Cuban Highway Begun," *NYT*, Dec. 28, 1927, at 34, col. 2; Horace Ash, "Progress on Central Highway of Cuba During 1927," 100 *ENR* 22, 23 (1928); Kaiser Industries Corp., *Kaiser Story* at 13, 15 (quotations); Mark Foster, "Giant of the West: Henry J. Kaiser and Regional Industrialization, 1930-1950," 59 *BHR* 1,3 (Spring 1989); Foster, *Henry J. Kaiser* at 39-42; chapter 8 below.

[154]Buell et al., *Problems of the New Cuba* at 369, 372. See also Hudson Strode, *The Pageant of Cuba* 275 (1936 [1934]).

[155]Quesada, *¡En Cuba Libre!* at 71-83.

[156]See Julio Le Riverend, *Historia económica de Cuba* 625-26 (4th ed. 1985 [1974]); Cuban Economic Research Project, *A Study on Cuba* 193 (1965).

[157]See Robert Smith, *The United States and Cuba: Business and Diplomacy, 1917-1960*, at 118-19 (1960).

[158]Quesada, *¡En Cuba Libre!* at 79.

[159]Marichal, *A Century of Debt Crises in Latin America* at 174, 179, 189, 191.

[160]Act of Mar. 2, 1901, ch. 803, § III, 31 Stat. 895, 897; Jules Bergman, *The United States and Cuba: Hegemony and Dependent Development, 1880-1934*, at 40-41 (1977); Buell et al., *Problems of the New*

terroristic rule led to his ouster in 1933,[161] a successor government suspended payments, causing Warren Brothers to file for bankruptcy, from which the firm emerged in 1942 after having settled with the Cuban government.[162]

Major integrated U.S. bridgebuilders such as John A. Roebling & Sons and American Bridge carried on work throughout Latin America in the 1930s.[163] Frederick Snare Corporation built a deep-water port at Cartagena, Colombia, while Ulen constructed a dam in Chile.[164] And once the United States began co-financing the Pan-American Highway in the 1930s,[165] U.S. road and bridge builders secured significant contracts in Latin America supervised by the U.S. Bureau of Public Roads.[166]

By the time of World War II, then, U.S. construction firms had developed a considerable volume of overseas operations. This new international orientation was symbolized by the creation in 1928 of what was "perhaps the largest construction firm in the world." United Engineers and Constructors, Inc., the result of the merger of Public Service Production Company (Newark), United Gas Improvement Contracting Company (Philadelphia), Day & Zimmerman Engineering & Construction Company (Philadelphia), and Dwight P. Robinson & Company (New York), was expressly "formed to operate in any part of the world" in every type of construction-engineering.[167] The firm's construction of the Buenos Aires subway in 1931 was merely one among its many overseas projects.[168]

In spite of the macro-political-economic importance of this whole range of intensified internationalization in the wake of World War I, overseas projects nevertheless accounted for "but a small percentage of the average annual volume" of aggregate U.S. construction.[169] By the same token, however, these projects also expanded export markets for U.S. producers of steam shovels, grading equipment, steel rails, pipes, and rolling stock.[170] Among the most proleptic of

---

*Cuba* at 383-87, 390-91, 395.

[161]For a characterization of Machado's dictatorship and of the political forces that led to his expulsion, see Jürgen Hell, *Kurze Geschichte des kubanischen Volkes* 220-76 (1976).

[162]See *Sale of Foreign Bonds or Securities in the United States* at 739-42, 2039-43, 2097-98; Fitzgibbon, *Cuba and the United States* at 238-43; Warren Brothers Company, *Historical Review of the Warren Brothers Company Contract* (most detailed albeit biased account); Buell et al., *Problems of the New Cuba* at 388-96; "Warren Brothers' Reorganization Planned Pending an Adjustment of Debt by Cuba," *NYT*, Feb. 2, 1937, at 31, col. 6; *PIV 1937* at 2066; Lewis, *America's Stake* at 378-79, 382-87; In re Warren Bros. Co., 43 F. Supp. 173 (D. Mass. 1942); "Reflections" at 10.

[163]See e.g., Charles Jones, "The San Rafael Bridge in San Domingo," 112 *ENR* 249 (1934); "Plan Unique Over South American River," 129 *ENR* 605 (1942); "Open Largest Central American Suspension Bridge," *id.* at 74. Roebling did not perform work outside the United States until the 1930s. Hamilton Schuyler, *The Roeblings: A Century of Engineers, Bridge-Builders and Industrialists* (1931).

[164]13 *MAI: Industrial Investments* 562 (1922); R. Cady, "New Deep-Water Port at Cartagena, Colombia," 115 *ENR* 710 (1935); "Will Build Dam in Chile," *NYT*, Jan. 1, 1930, at 52, col. 8.

[165]Act of June 19, 1934, ch. 648, 48 Stat. 1021, 1042.

[166]See e.g., Conde McCullough, "Bridging the Rio Chiriqui on the Pan American Highway," 117 *ENR* 757 (1936).

[167]"Large Construction Firms Form Huge Single Organization," 100 *ENR* 126 (1928). See also "Companies Merge to Build Utilities," *NYT*, Jan. 17, 1928, at 37, col. 2.

[168]"Buenos Aires Subway 4.6 Miles Long Built in Twenty Months," 106 *ENR* 923 (1931); "Gain by United Engineers," *NYT*, Feb. 5, 1930, at 30, col. 2.

[169]H. Bookholtz & C. Judkins, *The Construction Industry* 50 (Bureau of Foreign & Domestic Commerce, Market Research Ser. No. 10.1, 1936). The Census of Construction reported that the value of work done by U.S. contractors in outlying possessions and foreign countries in 1929 amounted to only $24 million—compared with a domestic volume of $1 billion. As a result of the way the data were collected, however, "the foreign business here reported is only fragmentary and does not in any sense represent the total amount of business done by American contractors abroad." U.S. Bureau of the Census, *Fifteenth Census of the United States: 1930: Construction Industry* 62, tab. 4 at 85-87 (1933).

[170]Lewis, *America's Stake* at 379.

these projects for the course of internationalization was the construction in the 1920s and 1930s by the M.W. Kellogg Company of twenty newly introduced high-pressure thermal cracking process units for the production of motor gasoline in eleven Latin American, European, and Asian countries.[171]

---

[171]National Research Council, *Building for Tomorrow: Global Enterprise and the U.S. Construction Industry* 19 (1988).

# PART III

# AN EMERGING WORLD MARKET FOR CONSTRUCTION: THE POST-WORLD WAR II PERIOD

Trading capital is not very patriotic, but follows the laws of profit and loss without any regard to political speculation.

Joseph Devey, *The Life of Joseph Locke* 234-35 (1862)

# 8

# The Post-World War II Ascendancy of U.S. Multinational Construction Firms

Now...that we are in a new era, when we have an exportable surplus of finished products, our turn has come to cultivate the buyers of other lands. In this process engineering is the handmaiden of commerce.[1]

## Depression-Era Government-Financed Infrastructure Projects as a Source of Accumulation Enabling Western Firms to Internationalize

Steve [Bechtel] can walk with governments, but he infinitely prefers to walk and talk with the oil men, the chemical men, the industrialists who represent his own type of rugged individualism in the American tradition. As long as some projects are too big and complex for private purses, or are tied in with national defense, Steve Bechtel will build for the government, but the business firms that operate for business motives are his choice.[2]

The course of internationalization of U.S. construction firms was decisively transformed during the depression of the 1930s and World War II. Whereas firms had previously had to rely on demand from private firms or foreign governments, World War II military orders introduced a new contingent of companies to construction abroad. During the decade before the federal government offered these opportunities, however, it had provided a small group of western firms with the requisite capital and experience with complex construction projects in the form of gigantic hydroelectric and irrigation projects.

The trajectories of several of the world's best known multinational construction firms, founded between the turn of the century and World War I, illustrate this development. Brown & Root, for example, began as an earth-moving company in 1919, but did not move "into the big time" until it built the Marshall Ford Dam in Texas for the federal government during the late 1930s, after which "the rise of [its] fortunes was swift."[3] The project marked the beginning of Brown & Root's long-term symbiotic relationship with Lyndon Johnson to which it in no small part owes its prosperity and prominence. Its pioneer role in the late 1930s and early 1940s in building the first commercial offshore drilling platforms in the Gulf of Mexico helped secure it a dominating position beginning in the 1950s in the North Sea, Persian Gulf, Venezuela, and Peru.[4]

---

[1]"Closer Relations with Latin-America Through Engineering," 89 *ENR* 422, 423 (1922) (editorial).

[2]Neill Wilson & Frank Taylor, *The Earth Changers* 293 (1957). Although Wilson and Taylor claimed to have written "an unsponsored, independent review" rather than a "'company book,'" their completely uncritical chatty boosterism does offer some informative material, especially for the post-World War II period, based on "the valued cooperation of those chiefly involved...." *Id.* at 7.

[3]"Roadbuilders with a Flair for Other Jobs," *BW*, May 25, 1957, at 90, 98; "The Brown & Root Story," 3:7 *AB* 1, 2 (1954).

[4]See Robert Caro, *The Years of Lyndon Johnson: The Path to Power* 458-68, 469-75, 742-53 (1982);

After several years of building railroads as a railway employee and supervisor in the West, Warren A. Bechtel (1872-1933) began subcontracting in 1906. His Oakland-based firm, which he did not incorporate until 1925, then built railroad lines, train sheds, and terminals for the Southern Pacfic, Western Pacific, Northwestern Pacific, Union Pacific, and Santa Fe roads, and dams in the West.[5]

Bechtel's genesis resembled that of several other western builders of a similar vintage—Utah Construction Company, Morrison-Knudsen, and Henry J. Kaiser—which frequently collaborated with one another on projects.[6] Harry Morrison (1885-1971) worked for a Chicago firm building a dam and then for the U.S. Reclamation Service in the Northwest for several years in positions ranging from axman to construction supervisor before he and another Reclamation Service employee, Morris Knudsen, formed a partnership in Idaho in 1912, which built canals, dams, railways, and roads in the West.[7] In 1914 Kaiser (1882-1967) began his street, road, and highway paving operations in British Columbia and the Pacific Northwest. In the period between World War I and the depression, government-funded road building, performed in large part by private contractors, became an increasingly significant and capital-intensive sector of construction. Although Kaiser Paving Company gained some prominence in the West as one of the pioneers in mechanizing road construction during this period, the firm had not yet reached the front ranks of the industry.[8]

Utah Construction was an older and larger organization.[9] Indeed, Bechtel had begun subcontracting irrigation and railroad projects under Utah Construction, "one of the great railroad construction firms of the West," as early as 1910.[10] The association became a turning-point for Bechtel's firm. By 1915, "the tidy sum" that Bechtel received as subcontractor under Utah inspired him to confide that he had "'never expected to have that much money in a lifetime.'"[11] By 1930, Utah's president, William Wattis, was "one of the wealthiest men in the West."[12] He and his brother Edmund had completed several railroad construction projects in the Northwest before forming Utah Construction in 1900. During the next thirty years Utah built thousands of miles of railroad track in addition to many major dams (including Hetch Hetchy, American Falls, and Guernsey), bridges, and irrigation projects, becoming "the largest building organization in the West" with "a virtual monopoly on all major western contracts...."[13]

idem, *The Years of Lyndon Johnson: Means of Ascent* 180 (1990); [Brown & Root], *Brownbuilder: The First 50 Years* 1-6 (1969); *Brownbuilder*, No. 1, 1992, at 11.

[5]Robert Ingram, *A Builder and His Family: 1898-1948*, at 1-25 (1961 [1949]); 24 *NCAB* 224 (1967 [1935]) (s.v. "Bechtel"). The dearth of monographic literature still makes it necessary to rely heavily on semi-official company histories as source material. See H. Larson, *Guide to Business History* 266 (1948).

[6]"The Earth Movers I: Beginning the Epic of the Six Companies of the West," *Fortune*, Aug. 1943, at 99.

[7]*NCAB*, Current Vol. G 1943-46, at 225 (1946) (s.v. "Morrison, Harry"); "The Earth Mover," *Time*, May 3, 1954, at 86, 91; Robert Brown, Jr., "The Story of M-K," 3:4 *AB* 1-4 (1954); Wilson & Taylor, *Earth Changers* at 37-44; J. Bonny, *Morrison-Knudsen Company, Inc.: "Fifty Years of Construction Progress"* 18-19 (1962).

[8]John Grier, "Construction," in President's Conference on Unemployment, 1 *Recent Economic Changes in the United States* 219, 244-48 (1929); Thomas Cochran & William Miller, *The Age of Enterprise: A Social History of Industrial America* 298 (rev. ed., 1961 [1942]); John Hicks, *Republican Ascendancy, 1921-1933*, at 9 (1963 [1960]); Frank Taylor, "Builder No. 1," *SEP*, June 7, 1941, at 9; R. LeTourneau, *Mover of Men and Mountains* 136-63 (1967 [1960]); Kaiser Industries Corporation, *The Kaiser Story* 5-13 (1968).

[9]Sidney Hyman, *Marriner S. Eccles: Private Entrepreneur and Public Servant* 36-37 (1976).

[10]"The Earth Movers I" at 102.

[11]Ingram, *A Builder and His Family* at 8-13 (quotations at 8, 13).

[12]Joseph Stevens, *Hoover Dam: An American Adventure* 3 (1988).

[13]25 *NCAB* 294 (1967 [1936]) (s.v. "Wattis") (quotation); Wilson & Taylor, *Earth Changers* at 23-25; Stevens, *Hoover Dam* at 36, 39 (quotation).

By 1931, in spite of being the largest contractors in the West, these firms were "by industrial standards...far from rich."[14] Moreover, with the exception of Kaiser, they had also been only marginally or not at all involved in international projects before World War II. Kaiser's subcontract under Warren Brothers for the Central Highway in Cuba had expanded its capacities considerably by 1930. Utah's only cross-border activity had been laying tracks for the Southern Pacific into Mexico in 1923, whereas Bechtel and Morrison-Knudsen had conducted strictly domestic operations.[15] A number of East Coast construction companies such as Warren, Ulen, Fuller, and Raymond were not only internationally oriented but also significantly larger.[16] Morrison-Knudsen's business volume, for example, did not reach a million dollars until 1923.[17]

Thus when the owners of the western firms met in 1931 to discuss submission of a bid on the enormous Boulder (Hoover) Dam project, they could not "scrape together" the $8 million in working capital that the surety companies demanded to underwrite the construction. To be sure, *Fortune* exaggerated in 1943 when it asserted that within "a few short years" these firms had been transformed "from...just a roving band of unknown contractors" into "tycoons" with "practically unlimited" credit."[18] Far from being still "all but unknown" even in northern California,[19] Warren Bechtel had already been national president of the Associated General Contractors of America (AGCA), the largest membership association of construction firms in the United States.[20]

After Congress authorized the Boulder Canyon Project in 1928,[21] President Hoover's Secretary of the Interior, Ray Lyman Wilbur, had to decide whether to build the dam directly with government employees and equipment or to enter into contracts with low-bidding construction firms.[22] Since the turn of the century, the federal government had developed considerable experience in building huge infrastructure projects by force account. In addition to the Panama Canal, construction of which was overseen by the Isthmian Canal Commission,[23] the U.S. Reclamation Service built many large canals and dams in the West such as Arrowrock. Although contractors such as Utah and Morrison-Knudsen had also built a number of dams for the government, "[f]ew private firms were capable of building structures of such unprecedented size and sophistication...."[24] By the

[14]"The Earth Movers I" at 99.

[15]"'Damn Big Dam,'" *Time*, Mar. 23, 1931, at 14, 15; "One Firm's Formula for Success: Diversification," *ENR*, Apr. 11, 1957, at 34, 38; Wilson & Taylor, *Earth Changers* at 25; chapter 7 above.

[16]In 1931, these four firms' total assets were $27 million, $18 million, $13 million, and $5 million respectively. *MMI* 2789, 688, 2947, 461 (1932). Morrison-Knudsen's total assets were still only $4 million in 1939 (the first year for which *Moody's* published data about it) and $19 million at the height of World War II in 1943. *MMI* 1643 (1941); *MMI* 1368 (1945). Utah Construction's total assets increased from $7 million in 1931 to $13 million in 1943. *MMI* 1096 (1932); *MMI* 1933 (1945). Bechtel and Kaiser, as individually owned firms, were not listed in *Moody's*.

[17]Ernie Hood, "Putting a New Face on Old Afghanistan Is One of Morrison-Knudsen's Projects," *ENR*, Feb. 21, 1952, at 45, 48.

[18]"The Earth Movers III: Despite Henry Kaiser's Ventures into Industrial Realms, They Decide to Stay As They Are—'Contractors Looking for Business,'" *Fortune*, Oct. 1943, at 139, 144-93. Utah Construction borrowed its $1 million share from Crocker First National Bank. Marriner Eccles, *Beckoning Frontiers: Public and Personal Recollections* 63 (Sidney Hyman ed., 1951).

[19]Marc Reisner, *Cadillac Desert: The American West and Its Disappearing Water* 131 (1987 [1986]).

[20]Ingram, *A Builder and His Family* at 38.

[21]Boulder Canyon Project Act, ch. 42, 45 Stat. 1057 (1928).

[22]It is unclear what *Fortune* meant in characterizing government supervision of private contractors as a compromise between government and private construction. "The Dam," *Fortune*, Sept., 1933, at 74, 82.

[23]See chapter 7 above.

[24]Michael Robinson, *Water for the West: The Bureau of Reclamation 1902-1977*, at 20 (quotation), 22 (1979); *History of Public Works in the United States 1776-1976*, at 318, 321 (Ellis Armstrong ed., 1976);

mid-1920s, with the restoration of "normalcy," the newly created Bureau of Reclamation moved toward contracting out work previously executed by the government.[25]

Nevertheless, during the 1920s, the AGCA—of which Warren Bechtel was national president in 1928, followed four years later by Kaiser—was engaged in a constant battle with the U.S. Army Corps of Engineers, allegedly the world's largest owner of construction equipment. The AGCA accused the Corps of Engineers of interfering with private enterprise and driving contractors out of business.[26] In the 1930s, the AGCA also denounced the Tennessee Valley Authority (TVA), which built its own dams and adopted advanced labor-relations policies with its employees, and the Works Progress Administration for "push[ing] the general contractors completely out of the public works picture...."[27]

By and large the federal government did not itself build the great hydroelectric projects in the West during the Depression. In particular for Hoover's administration, "keeping the Government out of any business that would yield a profit" was axiomatic.[28] Thus, instead of entrusting construction to the Bureau of Reclamation or other government agency, Wilbur "farmed out Boulder Dam," which at the time was the largest civil contract into which the federal government had ever entered, to low-bidding nonunion firms.[29] Those low bidders were Bechtel, Kaiser, Morrison-Knudsen, Utah, and several other contractors, which formed Six Companies, Inc., the joint venture that built Boulder Dam between 1931 and 1936.[30]

Against the background of unprecedented unemployment, the dam's remote location, and government support for the companies, the dam workers during the first summer unsuccessfully struck over demands for better working and living conditions and five dollars for a day's work in "[t]emperatures of 140 degrees in the shade."[31] Relying on armed force, "Six Companies, in concert with the federal officials running the project reservation, cracked down hard on labor organizers." Having suppressed the strike in 1931 aimed at the collective sale of labor power, the firms were able to "use the almost unlimited supply of cheap labor...drawn from the huge pool of unemployed men loitering in Las Vegas" to impose take-it-or-leave-it conditions.[32] In the absence of federal or state labor-protective intervention[33]—the labor provision of the contract between the

---

"'Damn Big Dam,'" *Time*, Mar. 23, 1931, at 14, 15 (Utah built American Falls, Gibson, and Guernsey dams). According to a former director of the Reclamation Service, the government often chose to accept the risk itself rather than trusting in a low-bidding contractor to build deep foundations for dams in inaccessible places or tunnels where conditions were difficult to foresee. F. Newell, "Federal Land Reclamation: A National Problem: 1. Origin, Problems and Achievements of Federal Land Reclamation," 91 *ENR* 666, 671 (1923).

[25]Stevens, *Hoover Dam* at 37-38; Robinson, *Water for the West* at 44.

[26]In the nineteenth century, when members of the Corps of Engineers were frequently detailed to private entities such as railroads, construction firms were less ungrateful. Forest Hill, *Roads, Rails and Waterways: The Army Engineers and Early Transportation* (1957).

[27]Booth Mooney, *Builders for Progress: The Story of the Associated General Contractors of America* 40, 48, 54, 74-76, 78 (1965); Marguerite Owen, *The Tennessee Valley Authority* 236 (1973); "Tennessee Valley Authority Adopts Labor Relations Policy," 115 *ENR* 511 (1935).

[28]Charles Beard & Mary Beard, *America at Midpassage* 42 (1939).

[29]Judson King, "Open Shop at Boulder Dam," 67 *NR* 147 (1931) (quotation); William Warne, *The Bureau of Reclamation* 29 (1973).

[30]See George Pettitt, *So Boulder Dam Was Built* (1935). The entity actually consisted of eight companies, the other four being MacDonald & Kahn, J.F. Shea, Pacific Bridge, and General Construction.

[31]See "Early Resumption of Dam Predicted," *NYT*, Aug. 12, 1931, at 14, col. 5; "1400 Men Laid Off at Hoover Dam After Demand for $5 Wage," 107 *ENR* 271 (1931); Elwood Mead, "The Construction of Boulder Dam," *LD*, Nov. 4, 1933, at 14 (Commissioner, U.S. Bureau of Reclamation).

[32]Stevens, *Hoover Dam* at 99, 71 (quotations), 65-79.

[33]On the companies' successful contestation of state safety law jurisdiction over the project, see Six

government and Six Companies was confined to a prohibition on the employment of "Mongolian labor"[34]—"each man must depend upon his own individual initiative in dealing with the contractors...."[35] Consequently, as Edmund Wilson, on location at the time, observed, "the companies automatically resort[ed] to that systematic skimping, petty swindling and barefaced indifference to the fate of their employees which is necessary to provide stockholders and officers with profits...."[36]

Chief among the Six Companies' chiseling methods was the venerable institution of payment in scrip redeemable only at the company store. The employees could expect no intervention by the Hoover administration because it "saw nothing wrong with the contractors' turning a profit on the dam job whenever and wherever they could." It was only two years later that Roosevelt's Secretary of the Interior ordered an end to this additional source of profits.[37] Like Peto and other British railway contractors ninety years earlier, Six Companies also extracted profit by means of housing their captive labor force; over the four-year period the rate of return on this capital investment may have been as high as 641 per cent. As a result of monopsony on the labor market and monopoly on consumer markets, the partners "were earning multimillion-dollar profits at a time when other construction firms were begging for work or going out of business."[38]

In spite of this unexpected financial success, the companies aspired to reduce wage rates and speed up the pace of work still further even if higher accident and mortality rates resulted. If sued by injured workers, Six Companies was not above jury-fixing. The employers also held labor costs to a minimum by refusing to include the travel time between the camp and dam site as part of the working day.[39] Little wonder that aggrieved workers spoke of "the organized greed of the 'Six Companies' which has the tacit endorsement or acquiescence of the Federal Government."[40]

Although continuous efforts by police and company officials "to purge the Hoover Dam employment rolls of union organizers" enabled the employers to atomize the work force, the unavailability of the New Deal federal government as a strike breaker weakened Six Companies' position somewhat. Thus in 1935, when workers shut the project down for two weeks in a strike directed at longer shifts and "a company-police system which the union maintained was used to subdue and terrorize men who 'have the temerity to complain against the atrocious conditions prevalent,'" they were not completely unsuccessful.[41]

That same year, the Department of Justice finally charged Six Companies with 70,000 individual violations of the federal public works eight-hour law, which at five dollars per violation exposed the firms to a liability of $350,000. Protests by Kaiser and Elwood Mead, the Commissioner of the Bureau of Reclamation, however, led to a settlement reducing the fine to $100,000. Although this sum was "hardly an excessive fine since the Six Companies reportedly made eighteen

---

Companies, Inc. v. Stinson, 58 F.2d 649 (D. Nev. 1932); Six Companies v. Stinson, 2 F. Supp. 689 (D. Nev. 1933).

[34]U.S. Bureau of Reclamation, *Boulder Canyon Project Final Reports*, Pt. I: *Introduction*, Bull. 1: *General History and Description of Project* 85-86 (1948).

[35]King, "Open Shop at Boulder Dam" at 147.

[36]Edmund Wilson, "Hoover Dam," 68 *NR* 66 (1931).

[37]Stevens, *Hoover Dam* at 150, 175 (quotation); *NYT*, May 11, 1933, at 6, col. 5.

[38]Stevens, *Hoover Dam* at 169 (quotation), 129, 285 n.23.

[39]*Id.* at 289 n.15, 99, 167, 164, 60, 206-14, 70.

[40]Victor Castle, "Well, I Quit My Job at the Dam," 133 *Nation* 207, 208 (1931).

[41]Stevens, *Hoover Dam* 234 (quotation), 234-41; 44 *MLR* 660, 661 (1935) (quoting from the *Bulletin of Metal Trades Department*, Aug. 1935). By the time Bonneville Dam was built in the mid-1930s, Kaiser conducted an all-union operation. Kaiser Industries Corp., *Kaiser Story* at 60.

million dollars," by law it inured not to the benefit of the workers, but to that of the United States.[42]

Whereas the TVA was able to "eliminate middleman costs for managerial services" by executing its projects by means of its own organization,[43] Hoover Dam proved to be "a gold mine for Six Companies," netting the firms more than $10 million in after-tax profits on a $49 million contract.[44] This contribution from "the inexhaustible springs of the national treasury," a like sum from two other depression-era public works in the West, Bonneville and Grand Coulee dams, and additional amounts for building the San Francisco-Oakland Bay Bridge and other infrastructure projects (including the third set of locks for the Panama Canal) enabled four of the joint venturers, Bechtel, Morrison-Knudsen, Kaiser, and Utah, to accumulate sufficient capital to launch joint and separate international military-industrial careers.[45] Moreover, by building such hydroelectric and irrigation projects, these firms were instrumental in industrializing the West—making possible, for example, the mass production of aluminum—and thus opening up expansive opportunities for others' and their own capital. In particular, they were able to realize Kaiser's vision of ending the "longstanding eastern domination of the construction industry and precipitate a major shift of economic power from the Atlantic Coast to the Pacific."[46]

Although the data on the growth of the firms' assets demonstrate that it is an exaggeration to claim that the Bechtels and Morrison-Knudsens became "instant giants after cutting their teeth on Hoover Dam,"[47] the project did signal an end to the relative anonymity of construction firms. Marriner Eccles, "the moving power" of Utah Construction whose family owned a substantial share of the company, relinquished his position as president to become chairman of the board on leave when he became special assistant to the Secretary of the Treasury and then governor of the Federal Reserve Board while his firm was still building the dam.[48] In particular Kaiser

> brought about a fundamental change of style in the way heavy construction companies presented themselves to the public. Previously, contractors tended to believe that the noise of their rivets, trip hammers and concrete mixers would bespeak their virtues. Kaiser, a fertile-minded publicist, generated a steady flow of news stories, information kits, progress reports and special "briefings" which built a national and international reputation for the Six Companies.[49]

---

[42]40 U.S.C. §§ 321, 324 (1934); "Boulder Dam Payroll Impounded by Federal Court," 114 *ENR* 362 (1935); "Six Companies Inc. Protests Payroll Seizure in Telegram to Ickes," 114 *ENR* 400 (1935); James Kluger, *Turning Water with a Shovel: The Career of Elwood Mead* 147, 195 (1992) (quotation).

[43]Gordon Clapp, *The TVA: An Approach to the Development of a Region* 30 (1955).

[44]"Complete Unit Prices for Hoover Dam," 106 *ENR* 505 (1931); "The Earth Movers I" at 214.

[45]"The Earth Movers I" at 99 (quotation); "The Earth Movers II: They Turn to Shipbuilding and Change the Face of the West," *Fortune*, Sept. 1943, at 119, 120-21; Ingram, *A Builder and His Family* at 28-29, 31-41; Kaiser Industries Corp., *Kaiser Story* at 23; Peter Wiley & Robert Gottlieb, *Empires in the Sun: The Rise of the New American West* 15-23, 31-38 (1982); Mark Foster, *Henry J. Kaiser: Builder in the Modern American West* 46-64 (1989).

[46]See U.S. Bureau of Reclamation, *The Story of Boulder Dam* (Conservation Bull. No. 9, 1941); Donald Worster, *Rivers of Empire: Water, Aridity, and the Growth of the American West* 210-12, 269-71 (1992 [1985]); Reisner, *Cadillac Desert* at 151-70; Stevens, *Hoover Dam* at 42 (quotation).

[47]Reisner, *Cadillac Desert* at 153.

[48]*MMI* 1096 (1932); "Marriner Stoddard Eccles," *Fortune*, Feb., 1935, at 62, 64 (quotation); *NCAB: Current Volume E* (1937-38), at 434-35 (1938) (s.v. "Eccles"); Eccles, *Beckoning Frontiers* at 45-46, 63, 175; Arthur Schlesinger, Jr., *The Age of Roosevelt: The Politics of Upheaval* 237-41 (1960); Hyman, *Marriner S. Eccles* at 160.

[49]Hyman, *Marriner S. Eccles* at 76.

# World War II: Laying the Foundation of U.S. Hegemony

> Allied with international bankers, sometimes with the aid of manufacturers and producers of equipment and materials...these builders focussed their attentions mainly on Central and South America.... Until the shadows of World War II began to gather, this was a small and select fraternity, whose activities caused scarcely a ripple in the main current of construction which was concerned with building...America.[50]

A major breakthrough toward the creation of a world construction market occurred shortly before and during World War II in conjunction with the exploitation of petroleum resources in Venezuela and the Middle East. On the basis of the leading role played by the U.S. domestic oil industry, U.S. construction firms had already acquired the expertise and capital equipment necessary for building wells, pipelines, and refineries. Since U.S. oil companies were also preeminent internationally, U.S. contractors were able to gain favored access to overseas projects.[51]

The early history of several of the world's largest multinational construction firms reflects this oil-based internationalization. Fluor Corporation, which was founded in 1912, began building refineries in California in 1922 for Richfield Oil. Having abandoned general contracting by the mid-1920s, Fluor expanded its operations beyond California by 1930, but did not receive a major overseas contract until 1947 when Aramco awarded it one to expand its facilities in Saudi Arabia. "This experience in the Middle East would lead Fluor into prominent positions in a variety of markets around the world."[52]

Bechtel, alone and in partnership with others including Kaiser, had been building pipelines in the West and Midwest since 1929 for Standard Oil of California and Pacific Gas and Electric—two of the principal supporters of the Industrial Association, an organization of large construction industry users and banks, which from 1921 to 1936 imposed an open-shop on the strongly unionized San Franciso building trades[53]—and other large gas and oil firms.[54] Having "decided that there was more money in designing refineries than in building pipelines,"[55] Bechtel formed a new entity in 1937 together with John A. McCone—future head of the Atomic Energy Commission and the Central Intelligence Agency—whose Consolidated Steel Co. had sold steel to Six Companies for Boulder Dam. "[S]elf-contained," the newly formed Bechtel-McCone-Parsons Corporation "was able to design, engineer, procure equipment and materials, and build the complex processing structures of petroleum refining and industrial chemistry."[56] This venture marked the beginning of Bechtel's shift away from low-technology heavy construction toward construction-engineering.[57]

After building such plants and pipelines for Standard Oil of California, Hercules Powder, and other industrial firms in the United States in the 1930s, the new firm "prepared to gear up for service on a global scale" by building a

---

[50]"U.S. Construction Overseas," *ENR*, July 30, 1953, at 28, 29.

[51]See e.g., Harvey O'Connor, *The Empire of Oil* (1955); Ingram, *A Builder and His Family* at 41-87.

[52][Fluor Corp.], *Heritage* [no pagination] (n.d. [ca. 1989]); "Emphasis on Sales Makes Fluor the Largest Construction Firm," *ENR*, July 15, 1976, at 24.

[53]William Haber, *Industrial Relations in the Building Industry* 409-41, 575 n.39 (1930); Michael Kazin, *Barons of Labor: The San Francisco Building Trades and Union Power in the Progressive Era* 256-76 (1989).

[54]Ingram, *A Builder and His Family* at 26-28; Foster, *Henry J. Kaiser* at 39.

[55]"The Earth Movers I" at 106.

[56]Ingram, *A Builder and His Family* at 42.

[57]Robert Ingram, *The Bechtel Story: Seventy Years of Accomplishment in Engineering and Construction* 12 (1968).

pipeline for the Standard Oil Company of Venezuela and docks for the Venezuelan government in 1940 in a joint venture with Raymond, whose harbor projects had already provided it with extensive international experience. During World War II, Bechtel began building petroleum refineries for Shell, Caltex, and Aramco in Curacao, Bahrain, and Saudi Arabia respectively as well as the large Canol military pipeline and refinery project in northwestern Canada and a section of the world's biggest pipeline in the United States.[58]

The Bechtels' self-portrayal in their in-house company history as "getting their resources ready for the country's service"[59] at the outset of World War II indirectly called attention to the other contest in which the United States was engaged—that with Britain over control of petroleum resources in the Middle East, especially in Saudi Arabia.[60] The role of private firms in the construction of oil facilities as well as of the U.S. Air Force base at Dhahran—which was its largest between Germany and Japan and occupied a strategic position for international communication lines—was crucial to implanting U.S. economic and military hegemony in that region over British imperial objections.[61] The restructuring of the internationally oriented U.S. construction industry, in turn, signaled the rise of petroleum industry-related firms such as Bechtel, which quickly surpassed Warren Brothers and other companies that had pioneered overseas before World War II, but then became confined largely to roadbuilding and other infrastructure projects in Latin America.[62]

Of World War II military construction projects valued at $2.4 billion, U.S. firms performed half in countries of the British Commonwealth. They carried on a further tenth in Latin America especially in connection with building, under the auspices of the U.S. Army Corps of Engineers, the Pan American or Inter-American Highway, which was designed to protect the Panama Canal. The participation by Morrison-Knudsen in the U.S. Navy's billion-dollar Pacific Naval Air Bases (PNAB) program during World War II, which increased its revenues tenfold, was perhaps the foremost example of this military route to internationalization.[63] But its Six Companies partners, Bechtel and Utah, were

---

[58]Ingram, *A Builder and His Family* at 42, 45-47, 72-75, 81; "Earth Movers I" at 102; "Earth Movers III" at 144; Edward Cleary, "Building the World's Biggest Oil Line," 129 *ENR* 915, 920 (1942) (Texas to New York).

[59]Ingram, *A Builder and His Family* at 47.

[60]See "Oil Projects Announced for the Middle East Area," 132 *ENR* 165 (1944); Herbert Feis, *Three International Episodes: Seen from E.A.* 93-190 (1966 [1946]); E. Varga, *Osnovnye voprosy ekonomiki i politiki imperializma (posle vtoroi mirovoi voiny)* 258-73 (1953); Gabriel Kolko, *The Politics of War: The World and United States Foreign Policy, 1943-1945,* at 294-313 (1970 [1968]); Joyce Kolko & Gabriel Kolko, *The Limits of Power: The World and U.S. Foreign Policy, 1945-1954,* at 69-73, 413-20 (1972); Fred Halliday, *Arabia Without Sultans* 50-51 (1974); Aron Miller, *Search for Security: Saudi Arabian Oil and American Foreign Policy, 1939-1949* (1980); Michael Stoff, *Oil, War, and American Security: The Search for a National Policy on Foreign Oil, 1941-1947* (1980); Wm. Roger Louis, *The British Empire in the Middle East 1945-1951: Arab Nationalism, the United States and Postwar Imperialism* 173-93 (1984); David Painter, *Oil and the American Century: The Political Economy of U.S. Foreign Oil Policy, 1941-1954* (1986).

[61]James Gormly, "Keeping the Door Open in Saudi Arabia: The United States and the Dhahran Airfield, 1945-46," 4 *DH* 189, 195 (1980). For an overview of Bechtel's activities in the Middle East, see Bechtel Corp., *The Arab Lands: An Age of Change* 19-31 & unpaginated (n.d. [ca. 1979]).

[62]See e.g., "Big Bolivian Highway Goes to American Firm," 135 *ENR* 88 (1945) (Warren); "Big South American Road Programs Will Aid International Communication," *id.* at 687 (J.A. Jones); "South America's Biggest Water Supply Job," 136 *ENR* 297 (1946) (U.S. firms using U.S. equipment operators in Caracas). By 1963, when *ENR* published its first listing of the 400 largest U.S. construction firms, the value of Bechtel's overseas contracts was five times greater than Warren Brothers'. "The 400 Largest Contractors," ENR, Aug. 6, 1964, at 69, 72. By 1969, when Bechtel was ranked first, Warren's new awards (in Canada and Spain) were less than one-tenth of Bechtel's. "Overseas Contracting: Big But Could Be Bigger," *ENR,* Nov. 5, 1970, at 80-81.

[63]"The Earth Mover," *Time,* May 3, 1954, at 86, 92; Morrison Knudsen Corporation, "History, 1912-1993," at 2 (n.d. [1993]).

also heavily involved in the Philippines and Samoa. Three other construction firms, Turner, Raymond, and Dillingham, also secured significant PNAB contracts.[64] Morrison-Knudsen, which even before the end of the war had carried out projects in Canada, Mexico, Panama, Venezuela, and Brazil, soon became one of the largest U.S. construction firms both domestically and internationally.[65]

By furnishing the larger U.S. construction firms the opportunity to execute these military projects all over the world as well as others such as the Alaskan-Canadian Highway, the state enabled them to obtain the technology, accumulate the capital, and establish the governmental and private economic contacts necessary to "go global."[66] Thus alone in 1946-47, businesses purchased construction machinery from government surplus assets stocks valued at $271 million—a sum almost equal to the capital assets less reserves of construction corporations in 1944.[67] These advantages did not accrue to the largest firms exclusively as a result of their wartime construction activities. "As quasi-industrialists," Bechtel, Kaiser, and other Six Companies entities also built and operated the world's largest cement plant and became the world's largest shipbuilders. Bechtel-McCone also built and operated the federal government's huge airplane-modification center in Alabama.[68]

Germany's largest construction firm, Philipp Holzmann, also did its "duty...in good faith for our fatherland" during World War II, as it had during World War I and during the Nazi militarization of the economy in the 1930s. The company furnished employees and equipment, which became the core of its *Firmeneinsätze* in the Eastern and Western European countries occupied by the Nazi troops. Even after the defeat of the Nazis, Holzmann officials found no more damning circumlocution for their military construction achievements than "soulless mass output."[69] Hochtief, Wayss & Freytag, Berger, and Bilfinger & Grün, too, contributed their share to building Nazi fortifications, such as the West Wall in preparation for the war and along the French coast, as well as airports and naval installations and other military projects in Nazi-occupied Europe.[70] Unlike their U.S. competitors, however, these German firms, which had long been operating internationally, neither required nor were able to use a world war to expand their

---

[64]"The Earth Movers I" at 101; "The Earth Movers III" at 144; Ingram, *A Builder and His Family* at 60-65.

[65]*MMI* 1368 (1945). Because the data published by *Moody's* during this period excluded Morrison-Knudsen's revenue from foreign subsidiaries, it is difficult to quantify the degree of internationalization.

[66]"U.S. Contractors Go Global," *BW*, Apr. 14, 1956, at 139, 140; Henry Durham, "Road Construction in Paraguay," 126 *ENR* 876 (1941) (R.E. Hebard Co.); "Americans to Build War Facilities in Middle East," 127 *ENR* 776 (1941); "Pan American Highway Construction Award Made to Civilian Contractors," 129 *ENR* 340 (1942); W. Bober, "The Construction Industry After the War," 20 *HBR* 427-36 (1942); *Seventy Years, The Foley Saga* (n.d.); "The Earth Movers," *Fortune*, Aug. 1943, 99-107; *id.*, Sept. 1943, at 119-22, 219-26; *id.*, Oct. 1943, at 139-44, 193-99; A. Carter, "Building the Inter-American Highway. Part I—History, Survey, Access, and Housing," 131 *ENR* 209-22 (1943); Harold Richardson, "Alcan—America's Glory Road. Part III: Construction Tactics," 130 *ENR* 63, 70 (1943); "Army Reports on Pan American Highway," 13 *CE* 515 (1943); E. James, "Development of the Inter-American Highway," 14 *CE* 5 (1944); "Inter-American Highway Work Cost Four Times Original Estimate," 135 *ENR* 71 (1945); "U.S. Forces Build Airfields in Arabia," *id.* at 641; "Construction Industry Logs the War Years and Appraises Its Future," 136 *ENR* 192-93 (1946); Van Renssaler Sill, *American Miracle: The Story of War Construction Around the World* (1947).

[67]U.S. Bureau of Economic Analysis, *Fixed Nonresidential Business Capital in the United States, 1925-73*, at 481 (1974) (valued at original acquisition prices).

[68]"The Earth Movers III" at 142 (quotation), 139; "The Earth Movers II" at 220, 222, 225-26; Ingram, *A Builder and His Family* at 49-59, 75-76.

[69]Hans Meyer-Heinrich, "Die Entwicklung des Gesamtunternehmens," in *Philipp Holzmann Aktiengesellschaft im Wandel von Hundert Jahren 1849-1949*, at 231-32, 106, 209-28 (Hans Meyer-Heinrich ed., n.d. [1949]).

[70]Heiner Radzio, *Die Aufgabe heisst Bauen: 110 Jahre Hochtief* 26-27 (1985); "Bilfinger & Grün" at 561; Wayss & Freytag, *100 Jahre Wayss & Freytag 1875-1975* [no pagination] (n.d. [1975]).

markets. Military defeat also compelled the second albeit temporary loss of those markets within a quarter-century.

### From World War II Until the End of the Keynesian Expansion: The American Quarter-Century

Since the war the American construction industry has taken on a new dimension.... This is an entirely new phenomenon, marking a sharp departure from the situation prewar. Then the industry's foreign legion numbered not more than a dozen firms whose activities were largely confined to Latin America. [I]n the end it is the willingness of American capital to go abroad that will make the export of U.S. construction a thriving business.[71]

In the aftermath of the war, "aggressively profit-motivated private sector design and construction firms" soon displaced the U.S. military engineering units in constructing bases abroad as a "'military' component to the Marshall Plan...." As early as 1943, Bechtel and other large U.S. construction firms, which as "quasi-industrialists...were spreading themselves all over the world," clearly saw "Europe and South America and Asia as needing old factories rebuilt and new ones engineered." While many other industries, economists, and politicians feared a recurrence of depression, the Bechtels were "'not worried about any postwar letdown. For us the postwar is the period when we really come into our own.'"[72] In general, then, as most of the developed capitalist economies lay in ruins, overseas "dozens of U.S....contracting firms...[we]re moving energetically and with purpose."[73]

In the aftermath of destruction in Europe left behind by World War II, "the American construction industry developed into a world power."[74] As the reconstruction of Europe began, firms in the more developed industrial countries there had the technical capability to perform the vast bulk of the work on their own. Outside of U.S. military installations, U.S. firms were therefore largely confined to projects requiring the most advanced technology. M.W. Kellogg, Badger (Stone & Webster), Foster Wheeler, and Lummus opened offices to build, often for their U.S. corporate customers, refineries and fertilizer and petrochemical plants—to which they could easily transfer their experience in building refineries—based on the recently developed technologies that they monopolized. These firms, for example, "built the British oil refining industry from nothing to over 20 million tons capacity" because domestic firms lacked the ability.[75] In less-developed European countries such as Greece, where the U.S. military projected its power, U.S. firms exerted much greater influence.[76]

In the Western Hemisphere, Bechtel, Morrison-Knudsen, and Stone & Webster also opened offices in Canada by the early 1950s, which reflected their

---

[71]"The Export of U.S. Construction," *ENR*, July 30, 1953, at 156 (editorial).

[72]National Research Council, *Building for Tomorrow: Global Enterprise and the U.S. Construction Industry* 26 (1988); "The Earth Movers III," *Fortune*, Oct. 1943, at 142, 144, 199; Douglass North, *Growth and Welfare in the American Past: A New Economic History* 181 (1966). See also "The Earth Mover," *Time*, May 3, 1954, at 86, 92-93; .

[73]"World Construction Report," 140 *ENR* 131 (Feb. 19, 1948).

[74]"U.S. Construction Overseas" at 30-31.

[75]"U.S. Construction Overseas" at 57-72 (quotation at 57); Philip Fleming, "Impoverished Europe Faces Slow Comeback," 136 *ENR* 203-208 (1946); "Intake Caisson Lowered into Thames," *ENR*, Apr. 10, 1952, at 59 (Lummus builds refinery for Vacuum Oil Co. in England); Peter Spitz, *Petrochemicals: The Rise of an Industry* 303, 518 (1988); M.W. Kellogg, "The M.W. Kellogg Company" [no pagination (at 3)]; "Foster Wheeler Corporation," in 6 *IDCH* 145 (Paula Kepos ed., 1992). See also *ENR*, Feb. 19, 1953, at 200 (Foster Wheeler builds refinery for Standard-Vacuum Oil in South Africa).

[76]"U.S. Construction Overseas" at 66.

involvement in the development of that country's natural resources.[77] Morrison-Knudsen, for example, in the late 1940s and early 1950s built a hydroelectric facility for the Aluminum Company of Canada designed to reduce the cost of smelting the aluminum oxide reduced from bauxite in Jamaica.[78] Supported by U.S. Export-Import Bank loans and enjoying "an impressive preferred position," U.S. firms undertook a large volume of infrastructure construction throughout Latin America. Dams, hydroelectric projects, and roads together with mining facilities formed the bulk of this work. Although Morrison-Knudsen was the most intensively involved, Bechtel, Kaiser, Stone & Webster, Ebasco, Raymond, Snare, Utah, Jones, and American Bridge also performed many of these projects.[79] In a country such as Venezuela, in which the state channeled large and rapidly rising petroleum revenues into civil engineering projects designed to transform the state itself into an adequate agent of macrosocietal capital accumulation, a number of domestic construction firms emerged that were technically and financially capable of carrying out such less advanced work as roads. Where local firms secured politically privileged access to these contracts, U.S. firms focused on the technologically more demanding projects.[80]

U.S. funding funneled through the Mutual Security Agency provided privileged access for U.S. firms in Pakistan, Iran, Turkey, and other Asian and Middle Eastern countries. Again, Morrison-Knudsen was in the forefront of this dam and highway construction.[81] Morrison-Knudsen also bought some of the government-owned equipment it had used during the war in the Pacific from surplus stocks to transport to Afghanistan, where, beginning in 1946, Morrison-Knudsen Afghanistan Inc., financed by $40 million from the Export-Import Bank and additional funds from other U.S. government agencies, built dams, canals, and roads designed to ward off Soviet "penetration." Under the name Morrison-Knudsen International Company, Inc., it performed several million dollars worth of work in China before the revolution in 1949.[82]

In the Philippines, the U.S. government created privileged access for U.S. capital by means of the Philippine Trade Act of 1946, which created equality between U.S. and Filipino firms with regard to the exploitation and development of natural resources and public utilities.[83] Only in Africa was the domination of the colonial powers so tight during the early postwar years that U.S. firms managed to secure contracts only under the aegis of the U.S. Air Force to build airbases in North Africa. The ubiquitous Morrison-Knudsen excelled here too. And during the Korean War the same firm formed two joint ventures to handle major infrastructure projects—Atlas Constructors with four other U.S. firms, and Société Anonyme Batignolles-Morrison Knudsen with the venerable French colonial

---

[77]"U.S. Firms Open Canadian Offices," *ENR*, Jan. 8, 1953, at 56, 60; Ingram, *Bechtel Story* at 19-20.

[78]Wilson & Taylor, *Earth Changers* at 192-206.

[79]"U.S. Construction Overseas" at 33-50 (quotation at 33); "Latin America Pushes Construction Jobs," 136 *ENR* 209-16 (1946); "Builders Beat Waves and Weather on Pipeline Under Venezuelan Gulf," *ENR*, Apr. 28, 1949, at 49; "American Firm to Rebuild Venezuelan National Ry," *ENR*, Feb. 15, 1951, at 68 (Morrison-Knudsen).

[80]Ana Brumlik, "State Intervention and the Barriers to Accumulation of Capital in Construction, with Special Reference to the Labour Process: Venezuela, 1945-58," [4] *PBE, 1982: Labour in Building and Construction* 3-37, 3-42 (1983).

[81]See e.g. *ENR*, Mar. 3, 1949, at 33 (Ceylon); "American Engineering Firms in Asia," *ENR*, Jan. 19, 1950, at 54; "U.S. Construction Overseas" at 85-97; Bonny, *Morrison-Knudsen Company, Inc.* at 13-14.

[82]*MMI* 1982 (1947); *MMI* 800 (1948); Hood, "Putting a New Face on Old Afghanistan is One of Morrison-Knudsen's Projects" at 46; Wilson & Taylor, *Earth Changers* at 124-38 (quotation at 124). On British construction firms' late entry into Afghanistan, see "British Construction Work Overseas 1966-67," 193 *BTJ* 916, 918 (1967).

[83]Philippine Trade Act of 1946, ch. 244, § 341, 60 Stat. 141, 151; "Opportunities in the Philippines Are Open for U.S. Contractors," 17 *CE* 284 (1947).

railway builder.[84]

With as many as "400,000 local men on its payrolls," Morrison-Knudsen, in addition to building airfields for countries such as Turkey that had entered into military alliances with the United States, was occupied with the construction of tunnels for copper and zinc mines in Peru and for roads in Venezuela, highways in Columbia, hydroelectric facilities in Brazil, dams in Afghanistan, Turkey, and Iran, as well as other infrastructure projects in Iraq, Sumatra, and Mexico.[85] A firm which grossed "a whopping" $87 million dollars at the height of World War II construction, by 1951 Morrison-Knudsen executed $300 million worth of construction—30 per cent of it overseas.[86]

Although postwar foreign policy proved irreconcilable with Henry Wallace's grandiose projections of U.S. participation in the building of TVAs on the Danube, Ob, Ganges, and Paraná, during the late 1940s and 1950s internationally oriented U.S. construction firms did become vanguard elements in laying the military-industrial foundations of the burgeoning Pax Americana.[87] Thus, on the one hand, they built airbases for $700 million in the remote Atlantic areas—Greenland, Iceland, Newfoundland, the Azores, and Bermuda—bereft of local labor.[88] When, on the other hand, shrinking U.S. oil reserves led to increased exploitation of petroleum reserves in the Middle East, U.S. construction firms, following in the tow of U.S. oil companies, became indispensable links in the "oil supply of the free world."[89] The vast increase in demand for petroleum products generated by the Korean War, for example, consolidated Fluor's position as an international petrochemical plant constructor.[90]

By the late 1940s, Bechtel had become "the largest engineer-constructor of oil transportation and processing facilities in the Middle East."[91] Between 1944 and 1948, Bechtel built refineries, pipelines, and infrastructure for Aramco at Dhahran totalling $200 million. By the mid-1950s, Bechtel, together with Morrison-Knudsen, Stone & Webster/Badger, and the British firm Wimpey, had already participated in the construction of the Trans-Arabian pipeline (originally requested by the U.S. Navy in order to supply the Sixth Fleet in the Mediterranean), an Iraqi-Syrian pipeline, refineries in Bahrain and Aden (for Anglo-Iranian Oil Company, whose refinery in Iran had been nationalized), a mining project in Venezuela, pipelines and refineries in Canada, and power plants in South Korea (supported by U.S. foreign aid funds).[92] Bechtel was grossing $250 million annually—half of which stemmed from international projects—compared with only $20 million twenty years earlier.[93] Bechtel's former partner, Parsons, who had formed his own company in 1944, performed his

---

[84]*MMI* 1114 (1951); "Combine for Overseas," *ENR*, Feb. 1, 1951, at 24; *id.*, May 3, 1951, at 56; "U.S. Construction Overseas" at 75.

[85]"The Earth Mover" at 86, 87; "Big Contractor's Best Year," *ENR*, Apr. 12, 1956, at 115; Bonny, *Morrison-Knudsen Co.* at 13-14; "Morrison-Knudsen Corp., "Partial Listing of Countries with Multiple MK Projects"; *idem*, "MK's Major Projects" at 2 (n.d. [ca. 1993]).

[86]Hood, "Putting a New Face on Old Afghanistan is One of Morrison-Knudsen's Projects" at 45, 47-48; "The Earth Mover" at 92.

[87]H. Wallace, "The Way to Abundance," *NR*, Mar. 27, 1944, at 414.

[88]"U.S. Construction Overseas" at 55.

[89]*ENR*, May 8, 1952, at 68.

[90]"Fluor Corporation," in 1 *IDCH* 569, 570 (Thomas Derdak ed., 1988).

[91]Ingram, *Bechtel Story* at 19.

[92]138 *ENR* 544 (1947); "Near East Pipeline Adds 300,000 bl a Day to the Oil Supply of the Free World," *ENR*, May 8, 1949, at 68 (Bechtel and Wimpey build Iraq-Syria pipeline); Ingram, *A Builder and His Family* at 93-100; Wilson & Taylor, *Earth Changers* at 155-76; Halliday, *Arabia Without Sultans* at 51.

[93]Robert Sheehan, "Steve Bechtel: Born to Build," *Fortune*, Nov. 1955, at 142.

first overseas construction project in 1952—a petroleum refinery in Turkey.[94]

By the mid-1950s, U.S. and European oil companies—directly through refinery construction and indirectly through the ancillary pipelines, shipping terminals, and power stations—accounted for half of postwar overseas construction available to U.S. firms.[95] The modern internationalization of the construction industry was clearly underway. That the leading international petroleum industry construction firms occupied a key position between "leading American and British oil interests...and the respective governments" of the Middle East was organizationally reflected in the fact that in 1950 Bechtel's owner and Warren Bechtel's son, Stephen Bechtel, joined, and in 1958 succeeded the president of Standard Oil of New Jersey as the chairman of, the Business Advisory Council, whose "impressive roster of the captains of industry and finance" advised the Secretary of Commerce on "'the business interests of the country.'"[96] The first member of the board of directors of J. P. Morgan & Co. from the West Coast, Bechtel "long had substantial investments in other enterprises" such as oil and utilities, which represented two-thirds of the family's resources. Although Bechtel, unlike Kaiser, was not interested in owning the plants that his firm built, his investments closely tracked the industries for which Bechtel produced the fixed capital. Thus of the more than $1 billion in construction that Bechtel completed during the first half of the 1950s, refineries, pipelines, and power plants accounted for almost four-fifths.[97] In 1957 *Fortune* ranked Bechtel as one of the richest Americans, with wealth estimated at between $100 million and $200 million.[98]

By the mid-1950s, when "US contractors dominated the scene worldwide, being responsible for more than 90 per cent of the large-scale construction work,"[99] leading firms had diversified into mining and power projects as well as geographically. Apprehensive that the next world war might exhaust the Mesabi and other Lake Superior iron ore ranges, U.S. steel manufacturers began exploring the periphery for relatively accessible reserves. In the early 1950s, Bechtel, together with Morrison-Knudsen, Raymond, and other firms, built the United States Steel Corporation's Orinoco iron ore facility in Venezuela. The largest of its kind in South America, it yielded ore competitively priced with that mined in the United States. During the same period, Utah Construction carried out its own iron ore project in Peru on a speculative basis.[100] In spite of this incipient global scope, Bechtel, which was performing approximately half of its total construction volume abroad (in South America, the Middle East, Korea, the Philippines, Europe, and Canada), still did not consider itself "fully international."[101]

Raymond International, whose overseas involvement antedated World War I but which was also the leading contractor for PNAB construction in World War II, employed more than half of its work force abroad by 1952.[102] As the world's largest builder of foundations, in the 1950s it became one of the three or four leading U.S. firms operating abroad. International projects accounted for almost

[94]"The Parsons Story," at 6 (mimeo, n.d. [ca. 1970]).

[95]"U.S. Contractors Go Global" at 140.

[96]Robert Engler, *The Politics of Oil: A Study of Private Power and Democratic Directions* 314-16 (1967 [1961]); Ingram, *Bechtel Story* at 112.

[97]Sheehan, "Steve Bechtel" at 145, 148, 150.

[98]Richard Smith, "The Fifty-Million-Dollar Man," *Fortune*, Nov. 1957, at 176, 177. The owners of Brown & Root, George and Herman Brown, were placed in the $75 million to $100 million category.

[99]Stallworthy & Kharbanda, *International Construction* at 17 (citing no source for 1956).

[100]W. Wanamaker, "Vast and Varied Engineering Works Develop Venezuelan Iron-Ore Deposit," 23 *CE* 807 (1953); "Moving a Mountain from Venezuela to the U.S.," *ENR*, Jan. 28, 1954, at 52-55; Ingram, *Bechtel Story* at 49-50; Wilson & Taylor, *Earth Changers* at 107-12, 177-88.

[101]Ingram, *Bechtel Story* at 26-28, 61-64; Sheehan, "Steve Bechtel" at 142.

[102]"Raymond Pushes Back World Frontiers," *ENR*, May 29, 1952, at 62, 66.

half of its volume, fluctuating between 13 per cent in 1951 and 64 percent in 1958.[103]   By the mid-1950s, Morrison-Knudsen was performing more than one-third of its quarter-billion-dollar annual construction overseas.[104]   Kaiser's vertically integrated international operations remained unique, building, for example, the automobile concern's own plant in Argentina in addition to other firms' industrial plants such as the Tata Iron Works in India.[105]

The post-World War II military wing of an internationalizing construction industry was most clearly embodied in Brown & Root, whose "first big overseas assigment" began in 1946 with the reconstruction of Guam and was followed by construction of NATO air bases in France and U.S. Navy and Air Force bases in Spain.   Within a period of several years, then, "Uncle Sam...[w]as...a good customer" in the amount of more than $200 million.[106]   Morrison-Knudsen, too, became heavily committed to military construction, in particular by building the Distant Early Warning Line across northern Canada.[107]   "In 1955 alone, the Corps of Engineers committed...around $1.5 billion—about 30% of it abroad, with most of the jobs going to U.S. contractors."[108]   The pattern of military and civilian construction, destruction, and reconstruction of Korea again furnished U.S. construction firms with profitable projects—but also with future competitors in the form of the participating South Korean firms, which, at the end of the domestic construction boom, shifted into overseas markets in order to keep their expanded capital profitable.[109]

Beginning in 1962, Brown & Root, Morrison-Knudsen, and Raymond joined in "one of the greatest construction programs of all time"—building bridges, airports, seaports, highways, bases, power plants, and hospitals in support of U.S. military intervention in Vietnam.   Under the aegis of Morrison-Knudsen, profit-making firms were for the first time given a major share of construction in a war zone.   Employing a work force of more than 52,000 by 1966, these firms, together J. A. Jones, became the ninth largest military contractor that year (receiving $550 million), a position to which no construction firm had ever attained before.[110]   Brown & Root has remained a mainstay of the U.S. military.   With the subsequent

---

[103] Joseph Wilkinson, "Raymond International, Inc. Goes Up on the Big Board," *ENR*, June 16, 1960, at 44, 46.

[104] "U.S. Contractors Go Global" at 139.

[105] Wright Price, "Auto Manufacturing Plant Built in Argentina," 27 *CE* 88 (1957); "Victory in the Making," *Newsweek*, Aug. 26, 1957, at 80 (Tata); "Kaiser's Big Business All Began in Building," *ENR*, Jan. 17, 1963, at 62; Kaiser Industries Corp., *Kaiser Story* at 47-48; Foster, *Henry J. Kaiser* at 169-76, 250-51.   Kaiser sold its holdings in Industrias Kaiser Argentina, the largest automobile manufacturer in Latin America, to Renault in 1967.

[106] "Roadbuilders with a Flair for Other Jobs," *BW*, May 25, 1957, at 90, 97 (quotation); "Navy Lists $134 Million Construction for National Defense Installations," 140 *ENR* 460-61 (1948); "Navy Pushes Guam Dam in Race Against Rainy Season," *ENR*, Sept. 2, 1950, at 47; Brown & Root, "The First 50 Years" at 4; "Spanish Base and Its Builders," *ENR*, Oct. 20, 1955, at 24 (Brown & Root, Raymond, and Walsh);

[107] "Army Awards Pacific, Alaska Contracts," 137 *ENR* 1 (1946); "Aftermath in Morocco—Good Airbases," *ENR*, Aug. 27, 1953, at 30-41; V. Smith, "African Airbases—A Job Well Done," *ENR*, Aug. 11, 1955, at 34-42; Morrison Knudsen Corp., "Partial Listing of Countries with Multiple MK Projects" 2 (n.d. [1992]); *idem, History* at 2-3.

[108] "U.S. Contractors Go Global" at 140.

[109] National Research Council, *Building for Tomorrow* at 26; "Hyundai Looks Further Afield," *IC*, Mar. 1984, at 26; Shanmugam Visvanathan, "International Construction Industry" at 150 (M.A. thesis, University of Texas at Austin, 1990).

[110] "Builders Pave Way for S.E. Asian Action," *ENR*, June 7, 1962, at 20; "Construction-South Vietnam: Work Increases as War Expands," *ENR*, May 13, 1965, at 25; "Jack Bonny's Tub: Keeping Top Contractor Up Top," *ENR*, Aug. 19, 1965, at 44; "Construction Escalation in Vietnam," *ENR*, Feb. 3, 1966, at 11; "Construction's Man of the Year," *ENR*, Feb. 17, 1966, at 99; "Vietnam: On Schedule but Slowing," *ENR*, Aug. 11, 1966, at 61; "Who Needs It?" *ENR*, Dec. 15, 1966, at 242 (editorial); Robert Ploger, *Vietnam Studies: U.S. Army Engineers 1965-1970*, at 27-31 (U.S. Dept. of the Army, 1974).

advent of the New World Order, Brown & Root entered into an umbrella contract with the Army Corps of Engineers "to support unexpected operations around the world" should the military "be called to go into other countries."[111]

This type of long-term faithful and profitable commitment to the "home" nation-state may provide the most determinate way of "[i]dentifying the nationality" of multinational enterprises.[112] These entrepreneurial counterparts to the Roman legions have, not so much in spite of, but precisely through their transnationality, demonstrated as much loyalty to their state as the nineteenth-century colonial railway constructors did to theirs.

The principal internationalizing impulses during the 1950s and 1960s largely stemmed from the international economic boom, which called forth in industries in which U.S. manufacturers were dominant an enlarged demand for relatively sophisticated types of construction—such as nuclear power plants, petroleum refineries, and chemical plants—which only a limited number of firms possessed the technical knowledge and capital to perform. A further push towards internationalization occurred in the second half of the 1950s, when "oil processing capacity, especially in the United States, temporarily outran the demand, and the obvious result was a big reduction in refinery construction projects." Acting as a conjunctural buffer, foreign operations "took up part of the slack."[113]

By 1967, Bechtel, a leading constructor of all these facilities, had become the largest U.S. construction firm by having increased its volume 20 per cent annually during the preceding decade.[114] The "spectacular progress" in the production of synthetic materials based on oil and gas-derived organic chemicals in tandem with increasing plant size meant that by the mid-1960s, refineries and oil and gas plants accounted for one-fifth of total annual world investment in manufacturing. Whereas before World War II chemical firms typically designed their own plants and acquired the hardware directly from producers, by the 1960s three-fourths of major new plants were engineered and constructed by a small group of specialist firms. This transformation, which accompanied the shift from coal to oil and gas derivatives as well as from batch to flow production techniques, meant that chemical plants, like refineries before them, began to be conceived as "an integrated system, rather than as a conglomeration of separate vessels and pumps."[115]

By the beginning of the twentieth century the U.S. chemical industry had gained a historically crucial "path-dependent" advantage over its European competitors by virtue of its ability to effect an early shift to a petrochemical base as a result of its access to a domestic petroluem industry. Just as much of the know-how was transferred from U.S. petroleum refiners to U.S. chemical processors, a number of the construction firms that had been innovators in oil refinery construction, made the switch to chemical plants. In time the division of labor intensified, giving rise to chemical engineering, "the application of mechanical engineering to production activities involving chemical processing," in order to develop techniques for producing laboratory research results on a commercial basis.[116] The specialized chemical construction engineering firms

---

[111]"Brown & Root Drafted for Duty in Somalia," *ENR*, Jan. 4, 1993, at 12.

[112]John Dunning, *Multinational Enterprises and the Global Economy* 10-11 (1993).

[113]Ingram, *Bechtel Story* at 79, 78, and chapters 5-7.

[114]"Simple Formula to the No. 1 Spot," *ENR*, May 11, 1967, at 33.

[115]OECD, *The Petrochemical Industry: Trends in Production and Investment to 1985*, at 7 (1979); C. Freeman, "Chemical Process Plant: Innovation and the World Market," *NIER*, No. 45, Aug. 1968, at 29, 30.

[116]Ralph Landau & Nathan Rosenberg, "Innovation in the Chemical Processing Industries," in *Technology & Economics: Papers Commemorating Ralph Landau's Service to the National Academy of Engineering* 107, 110, 114 (1991).

performed a crucial role in the creation of a world chemical and petrochemical market:

> Once a major new process technology was developed, or the scaling up of a given production process was carried out, SEFs [specialized engineering firms] could reproduce that new technology, or larger scale production process, for many clients. Such economies could not be accumulated by the chemical manufacturers themselves, precisely because they could produce that technology only for their own, limited internal needs, whereas SEFs had a much more extensive experience with designing that particular plant many times for different clients. Moreover, as they worked for many different clients, they accumulated useful information related to the operation of plants under a variety of conditions.[117]

Drawing on U.S. domestic industrial leadership in these sectors and acting as important transmission belts of technology and uncodified know-how in their own right, U.S. construction-engineering firms were able to achieve a dominant position in this burgeoning world market. From 1960 to 1966, for example, U.S. firms accounted for almost two-thirds of the value of world export contracts for chemical, oil, and gas plants. Whereas U.S. firms secured more than one-third of the contracts (by value) of all plants in Western Europe during this period, non-U.S. firms accounted for less than one per cent of the contract value for plants in the United States. U.S. firms gained more than 85 per cent of all contracts awarded to foreign firms in the Western Hemisphere and more than 70 per cent in Western Europe, which in turn accounted for 44 per cent of U.S. firms' foreign contracts (by value). Western European firms achieved their greatest successes building petrochemical plants in the Soviet Union and Eastern Europe, where U.S. firms did not compete for political reasons, and infrastructural projects in their respective nation-state's (former) colonial empires.[118]

The worldwide demand for plastics triggered such an increase in demand for ethylene that by the 1950s Stone & Webster was "engineering ethylene plants worldwide for most every major oil company." Many of these plants it built in Japan. Indeed, Stone & Webster had made such advances in developing the relevant processes that Esso decided to rely on it (and other U.S. firms such as Lummus, Braun, and Kellogg) instead of its own engineering division to build its olefin units. Kellogg, in association with the chemical industry, achieved similar successes in engineering proprietary processes for large-scale ammonia plants, of which it had built half of the world total by 1967—a field which it continued to dominate.[119]

---

[117]*Id.* at 117-18.

[118]Freeman, "Chemical Process Plant," tab. 2-4 at 33-35. The British firm John Brown Ltd., for example, built several chemical and petrochemical facilities in the Soviet Union in the 1960s and 1970s. "British Construction Work Overseas 1963-64," 187 *BTJ* 593, 595 (1964); "British Construction Work Overseas, 1965-1966," 191 *BTJ* 874 (1966); "British Construction Work Overseas 1971/72," 9 *TI* 294, 295 (1972).

[119]William Allen, Jr., *Stone & Webster: A Century of Service* 18 (1989); Spitz, *Petrochemicals* at 378, 430-35 444-45; Freeman, "Chemical Process Plant" at 39, 48; M.W. Kellogg, "The M.W. Kellogg Company" [no pagination (at 4)].

# 9

# The Emergence of a World Construction Market and the Relative Decline of U.S. Firms

"We used to make 30% to 40% on a foreign job in the old days," said a U.S. construction man. "Now we make only 15% to 20% at the most." He smiled when he said it.[1]

## The Resurgence of European and Japanese Competition

During the early postwar period European and Japanese construction firms remained preoccupied with domestic reconstruction projects. Yet by early 1954, the U.S. construction industry's principal press organ, *Engineering News-Record* (*ENR*), was concerned enough to ask "Who forms our competition overseas?" In an unprecedented listing of "foreign firms with far flung construction operations in other lands," *ENR* cautioned that U.S. firms' operations were "being matched" by European competitors' "return to a pre-war pattern." It singled out German firms' renewal of contacts in South America and the Middle East, especially Turkey.[2] A year earlier the journal had editorially prepared U.S. firms for the filling of the immediate postwar international vacuum by observing that some opportunities would inevitably disappear when the U.S. overseas military expansion that had fueled them eventually slowed down. Even in 1953, *ENR* admonished the trade that once the protective shield of the U.S. war machine was removed, international competition would intensify especially since some European engineering-contracting firms had been "our equals or betters all along."[3]

In spite of *ENR*'s claim that by the mid-1950s the "international operations of foreign construction firms represent[ed] a return to a pre-war pattern,"[4] the patterns of postwar competition were not identical with those that had prevailed earlier in the century. In part the new configurations were bound up with the fact that the once-dominant British firms lacked "the capital resources to speculate in overseas constructional work."[5] Venerable international operators such as Cleveland Bridge and Dorman, Long continued to build bridges in Turkey, Iraq, Zambia, Brazil, and elsewhere separately and jointly until Trafalgar House acquired Cleveland Bridge in 1970 and Dorman in 1982.[6] And other British firms

---

[1]"U.S. Contractors Go Global," *BW*, Apr. 14, 1956, at 139, 142.

[2]"Who Forms Our Competition Overseas?" *ENR*, Mar. 11, 1954, at 52.

[3]"The Export of U.S. Construction," *ENR*, July 30, 1953, at 156.

[4]"Who Forms Our Competition Overseas?" at 52.

[5]J. Colclough, *The Construction Industry in Great Britain* 140 (1965).

[6]"Overseas Constructional Work by British Contractors in 1956-57," 173 *BTJ* 554, 555 (1957); "British Construction Work Overseas 1967-68," 195 *BTJ* 980, 981 (1968); "British Construction Work Overseas 1969-70: New Record," 199 *BTJ* 838, 842 (1970); 2 *MIntM* 1991, at 4259 (1991); Trafalgar House Public Limited Company, "Background Information" at 5 (July 1993).

continued building in British Commonwealth countries—ranging from copper mines in Africa, to apartment houses in Canada, and a high school in the Bahamas. Indeed, in the mid-1950s, Commonwealth markets, in which British firms "have special advantages," still accounted for more than 70 per cent of the work that they performed and new contracts that they obtained.[7]

Supported by British annual expenditures of £150 million on overseas development, however, British companies also expanded to new areas to carry on new types of construction. By 1960, six firms already accounted for half of total British overseas construction, several even performing more work abroad than in Britain.[8] Moreover, firms that before World War II had never or only marginally operated outside the United Kingdom became increasingly dependent on the world market. Indeed, unlike the largest U.S. firms, four of Britain's five largest construction firms—Wimpey, Costain, Taylor Woodrow, and Laing—first became large-scale enterprises during the interwar period by undertaking domestic speculative housebuilding.[9] The histories of representative firms illustrate this internationalization process.

From its founding in 1880 until the 1930s, George Wimpey had specialized in road construction and private housebuilding. Rechristened Wimpey 680 General Construction Company, Royal Engineers, the firm received so much work building military airfields in Britain during World War II that it "became almost embarrassing."[10] When a high-ranking official in the Air Ministry with considerable knowledge of desert road and airfield construction became a Wimpey director in 1946, the firm began orienting itself toward the Middle East. After having created contacts with the Anglo-Iranian Oil Company, which was majority-owned by the British government, by performing civil engineering work on the oil company's refinery in Britain in 1947, Wimpey secured its first overseas contract to build the infrastructure for oilfields in Kuwait. The next year another large British oil company afforded it the same kind of opportunity in Borneo. Wimpey then became junior partner to Bechtel in building a pipeline from Iraq to Syria and carrying out the harbor and housing work for the very large British refinery at Aden. Wimpey significantly enhanced its international capacities by finally acquiring the expertise to perform mechanical and electrical construction for oil refineries, which Anglo-Iranian hired it to do at a British facility in 1950, although it continued to specialize in more conventional infrastructure for oil-related projects in the Middle East, New Guinea, and the West Indies. Like other Western companies, Wimpey also built its share of World Bank-financed hydroelectric dams in South America. During the early postwar period, Wimpey also engaged in considerable traditional construction in British Commonwealth countries such as a skyscraper in Hong Kong and a university in Ghana. An unusual deviation from the standard international process was the firm's diversification into speculative housebuilding in Canada in the mid-1950s.[11]

Another large British firm, Costain, which was founded in 1865, had not performed any major overseas projects until it participated in the building of the Trans-Iranian Railway in 1935; during World War II it then established offices in

---

[7] "Overseas Constructional Work by British Firms in 1955-56 Amounted to £87 Million," 171 *BTJ* 636 (1956); "British Construction Work Overseas in 1959-60 Valued at £124m," 179 *BTJ* 513 (quotation), 516 (1960); "British Construction Work Overseas 1971/72" at 296, 298.

[8] "British Construction Work Overseas in 1959-60 Valued at £124 m" at 514, 516.

[9] Michael Ball, *Housing Policy and Economic Power: The Political Economy of Owner Occupation* 34 (1983).

[10] Valerie White, *Wimpey: The First Hundred Years* 1-20 (1980) (quotation at 20).

[11] White, *Wimpey* at 28-38. Wimpey's inferior international position vis-à-vis Bechtel was reflected on the anecdotal level by an incident in 1952 when Bechtel reserved rooms at the Waldorf Astoria Hotel in New York for several Wimpey officials who, because of currency restrictions, could barely pay the bill.

Turkey, Nigeria, and Rhodesia. Yet from the 1950s on, impelled to intensify its internationalization by a decline in domestic construction, Costain was doing at least two-fifths of its work abroad. A focal point of its projects was British colonial Africa, where Costain built, for example, roads in Nigeria and parts of Zambia University.[12] Taylor Woodrow was constrained to undertake industrial and commercial projects in British East and West Africa, Afghanistan, Pakistan, and Guyana for the opposite reason: it "had grown so large that it needed to expand overseas."[13] John Laing, another large speculative housebuilding firm during the interwar years and wartime airfield builder that had never engaged in international operations since its founding in 1848, initially pursued a traditional Commonwealth path when it opened a branch in South Africa in 1947 to perform building, civil engineering, and housebuilding, soon followed by road and housebuilding in Rhodesia, Zambia, and Canada. By 1951, it had expanded beyond the Commonwealth into Libya and Syria to build a power plant and harbor works. In the 1960s it established large operations in Spain and the Middle East.[14]

The quantitative evolution of postwar British international construction is presented in table 9.1. In the decade from 1955, when the British Ministry of Works first began surveying contractors, to 1965, the value of work performed by British firms overseas more than doubled—from £70 million to £160 million.[15] Thus by the late 1950s, they were annually putting in place in excess of $300 million worth of construction abroad. In addition to performing projects throughout the British Commonwealth, they recorded notable gains in Iran and Brazil, where U.S. firms were also active.[16]

By 1950, despite foreign exchange restrictions and the intensive reconstruction requirements in West Germany, Philipp Holzmann had already received orders from Turkey, Iraq, Greece, and Pakistan. The same year the German firm Julius Berger also resumed overseas irrigation work in Egypt and the Sudan.[17] In the 1950s, Hochtief and Holzmann built roads, harbors, dams, tunnels, pipelines, copper refineries, and nuclear power plants in Turkey, Iraq, Peru, Egypt, India, Chile, Paraguay, Sierra Leone, Portuguese Africa, and elsewhere.[18] During the 1950s, German firms' overseas orders averaged

---

[12]Costain Group PLC, "Company Milestones" (Sept. 30, 1992); Hedley Smyth, *Property Companies and the Construction Industry in Britain* 125-26, 128 (1985); "British Construction Work Overseas, 1965-1966" at 875.

[13]"British Construction Work Overseas 1966-67," 193 *BTJ* 916-18 (1967); "Taylor Woodrow," in 1 *IDCH* 590 (Thomas Derdak ed., 1988) (quotation).

[14]"British Construction Work Overseas 1967-68" at 980-81; Roy Coad, *Laing: The Biography of Sir John W. Laing, C.B.E. (1879-1978)*, at 19, 81, 97-116, 152-60, 184-85 (1992 [1979]).

[15]"How Overseas Constructional Work Helps Export Drive," 169 *BTJ* 937 (1955). The annual data refer to the twelve months ending March 31. Unlike the survey data collected by *ENR*, the British data encompass the value of work done, of new contracts obtained, and of work outstanding. The data on the value of work done show greater continuity than those on contracts obtained. A third of a century later it remains true that "even the United States with their extensive statistical services do not regularly collect statistics similar to those collected here." "British Construction Work Overseas in 1959-60" at 513. The table stops with 1982 because the data ceased to be "directly comparable" when the U.K. Department of Environment changed its questionnaire "at the request of the Export Group for the Constructional Industries." "Building Up—to £3.8 bn," 12 *BB* 456, 457 (1983).

[16]"British Contractors Boost Overseas Business," *ENR*, Nov. 19, 1959, at 188; "British Firm Gets Contract for Large Brazilian Dam," *ENR*, June 26, 1958, at 52 (Wimpey).

[17]Kurt Hecker, in *1849-1974 H[olzmann]: Ansprachen beim Festakt anläßlich des 125jährigen Bestehens der Firma Philipp Holzmann* 1, 3 (1974) (untitled address); Philipp Holzmann Aktiengesellschaft, *Das umfassende Leistungsangebot der Holzmann-Gruppe* 38 (1992); "Bilfinger & Berger Bau A.G.," in 1 *IDCH* 560, 561 (Thomas Derdak ed., 1988).

[18]See e.g., *Samsun Harbour in Turkey: A Joint Enterprise of the Companies Rar-Insaat Türk, Philipp Holzmann, Hochtief* (n.d. [1961]); "Building Iraqi Dam Has an International Operation," *IC*, Oct. 1962, at 2; "South-East Asia's Largest Pipeline," *id.*, Dec. 1962, at 20; "Germany's Hochtief Builds High and Deep Everywhere," *ENR*, Nov. 3, 1966, at 40; "Tunnel Under the Nile," *IC*, Nov. 1968, at 17; "Peruvian Harbour Development," *id.*, July 1969, at 8; C. Tupholme, "Cabora Bassa," *id.*, Apr. 1970, at 24;

**Table 9.1**
**British Construction Firms' Overseas Contracts, 1955-82**

| Year | New Contracts (£ million) | Index (1955=100) | Work Done (£ million) | Index (1955=100) |
|------|------|------|------|------|
| 1955 | 72 | 100 | 70 | 100 |
| 1956 | 109 | 151 | 87 | 124 |
| 1957 | 102 | 142 | 102 | 146 |
| 1958 | 119 | 165 | 114 | 163 |
| 1959 | 114 | 158 | 120 | 171 |
| 1960 | 131 | 182 | 124 | 177 |
| 1961 | 98 | 136 | 135 | 193 |
| 1962 | 122 | 169 | 113 | 161 |
| 1963 | 147 | 204 | 111 | 159 |
| 1964 | 118 | 164 | 123 | 176 |
| 1965 | 198 | 275 | 160 | 229 |
| 1966 | 190 | 264 | 169 | 241 |
| 1967 | 170 | 236 | 172 | 246 |
| 1968 | 232 | 322 | 182 | 260 |
| 1969 | 234 | 325 | 204 | 291 |
| 1970 | 341 | 474 | 220 | 314 |
| 1971 | 311 | 432 | 274 | 391 |
| 1972 | 300 | 417 | 320 | 457 |
| 1973 | 346 | 481 | 317 | 453 |
| 1974 | 554 | 769 | 362 | 517 |
| 1975 | 1084 | 1506 | 457 | 653 |
| 1976 | 1280 | 1778 | 857 | 1224 |
| 1977 | 1588 | 2206 | 1250 | 1786 |
| 1978 | 1676 | 2328 | 1597 | 2281 |
| 1979 | 1385 | 1924 | 1678 | 2397 |
| 1980 | 1385 | 1924 | 1384 | 1977 |
| 1981 | 1366 | 1897 | 1271 | 1816 |
| 1982 | 1870 | 2597 | 1478 | 2111 |

*Source*: 171 *BTJ* 636 (1956); 173 *BTJ* 554 (1957); 175 *BTJ* 515 (1958); 179 *BTJ* 514 (1960); 183 *BTJ* 549 (1962); 187 *BTJ* 593 (1964); 191 *BTJ* 877 (1966); 195 *BTJ* 980 (1968); 199 *BTJ* 838 (1970); 9 *TI* 294 (1972); 17 *TI* 97 (1974); 33 *TI* 128 (1978); 37 *TI* 359 (1979); 9 *BB* 257 (1982)

somewhat more than 200 million marks annually. By the first half of the 1960s, in part as a result of the integration of the firms into their government's foreign development aid programs in Africa and Asia, annual orders rose to 331 million marks; orders rose again by more than double to 777 million marks during the latter half of the decade.[19]

The new postwar political-economic constellation of forces required French firms to reorient themselves geographically. For Batignolles, for example, it was no longer possible to profit from the "privileged situation" which it had enjoyed for sixty years in central and eastern Europe. Although the firm was able to build ports, airports, and factories in French colonial Africa, it quickly recognized that large projects would require it to associate with other firms.[20] French firms, in addition to maintaining a stranglehold on markets in the former and remaining French colonies, especially those in Africa, were competitive enough to invade such long-time U.S. strongholds as Cuba.[21] And several Italian firms, impelled by the decline in construction of domestic hydroelectric plants once the postwar reconstruction had been completed, began using the expertise that they had accumulated in the Alps to build dams in Third World countries in the late 1950s.[22] In particular Impresit (Imprese Italiane all' Estero), founded by Fiat in 1929 to promote Italian overseas enterprise, separately and as the Impregilo consortium with Girola and Lodigiano, built the Kariba Dam in Rhodesia and the Volta River Dam in Ghana in the 1950s and 1960s.[23]

The Danish firm Christiani & Nielsen, which had been internationally oriented almost since its formation in 1904, resumed its overseas participation almost immediately after the war. Indeed, its subsidiary in Brazil had been building there almost continuously since World War I. In the late 1940s the company constructed an important pier in Rio de Janeiro as well as the world's largest football stadium. In a joint venture with British firms, it began work on the Owen Falls hydroelectric project in 1949; the next year it constructed an airfield in Burma.[24]

No Japanese construction firm, however, was awarded an overseas contract—except for projects carried out within the framework of war reparation and economic cooperation programs such as hydroelectric projects, tunnels, and hotels in Burma, South Vietnam, Indonesia and the Philippines—until 1961. Japanese firms were still merely "on the verge of entering the world market."[25] Only with the end of the domestic building boom in the mid-1960s, did large

---

"Cabora-Bassa, World's Greatest Hydro-Electric Scheme," *id.*, Jan. 1975, at 2.

[19]Karin Behring, Erich Gluch, & Volker Rußig, *Entwicklungstendenzen im deutschen Auslandsbau*, tab. 2.1 at 25 (1982); Hauptverband der Deutschen Bauindustrie, *BJ 1975* at 51; Erich Gluch & Jürgen Riedel, "The Federal Republic of Germany," in *The Global Construction Industry: Strategies for Entry, Growth and Survival* 120-23 (W. Strassmann & Jill Wells ed., 1988).

[20]Société de Construction des Batignolles, *L'Oeuvre d'un siècle 1846-1946*, at 86, 87 (1952).

[21]27 *CE* 899 (1957) (Sociéte des Grandes Travaux de Marseille builds tunnel in Havana).

[22]"Italy," *IC*, Sept. 1973, at 55, 65-66 (foreign contract awards peaked in 1968 at £308 million, declining to only £35 million by 1971); Aldo Norsa, "Italy," in *The Global Construction Industry* at 86, 89-90.

[23]See James Moxon, *Volta: Man's Greatest Lake* 117-19 (1969); H. Olivier, *Great Dams in Southern Africa* 98 (n.d. [1976]); "Impreglio Power Push Dominates World Market," *ENR*, June 17, 1982, at 74; Norsa, "Italy" at 89, 96.

[24]Christiani & Nielsen, *75 Years of Civil Engineering 1904-1979*, at 22, 58, 60, 69, 87 (Leif Nilsen ed., 1979).

[25]"Japanese Builders Eye the World Market," *ENR*, May 4, 1961, at 40 (mentioning however a steel mill that a Japanese firm began building in Brazil in 1958). See also "Japanese Push to Enter Australian Construction," *ENR*, Apr. 17, 1958, at 92; "Kajima, the Versatile Giant of Japanese Construction," *ENR*, Apr. 14, 1966, at 44; Yasuyuki Hippo & Saburo Tamura, "Japan," in *The Global Construction Industry* at 59, 61-62.

Japanese firms feel pressure to enter the world market.[26]  By the early 1970s, Japanese firms, which had just begun to expand their international scope beyond Asia, were still only marginally active overseas.[27]

As a result of this lagged re-internationalization of non-U.S. construction firms, by 1956, when European firms were just beginning to compete with U.S. firms, the latter were estimated to have an annual overseas volume of $750 million to $1 billion, while British, German, and Italian firms combined accounted for about $660 million.[28]  The situation was little changed a decade later: "In the late 1960s most international construction was still American."[29]

Even in retrospect, some European firms appeared uncomfortable in explaining what had propelled them overseas.  Hochtief, which as late as the 1960s accounted for more than half of all construction work performed by West German firms abroad,[30] could articulate no more plausible motivation than "that human personality can be developed and liberated by work in a distant clime under unusual conditions, by a flight from the secure conditions of employment at home and from the dangers of a society where greater perfectionism was ever being sought, and by confrontation with people who had other aims in life and practiced other cultures."  Only as an afterthought did the in-house company history add that it was also "felt that...money could be made abroad even if at considerable risk."[31]

By the 1960s, the largest construction firms in Britain and Germany were already clearly integrated into the world market.  In 1968, overseas projects accounted for one-seventh of the turnover of Britain's largest firm, George Wimpey; the international shares for John Laing and Taylor Woodrow, were similar, while Costain's hovered at two-fifths.[32]  That pattern still embraced quasi-monopoly colonial markets.  Hochtief, for example, complained that although Germany and France contributed equal amounts to a special European Common Market fund for the development of former colonies, German construction firms were almost completely excluded from the former French colonies in Africa. Nevertheless, by 1965 Hochtief had done $300 million worth of overseas work since the end of World World War II, and international projects accounted for one-quarter of its total annual income.[33]  From 1960 to 1969, the aggregate annual value of West German firms' new orders from abroad rose almost eight-fold to 1.5 billion marks, which was, however, still only one-twelfth of the U.S. volume.[34]

Once non-U.S. firms became integrated into the world market, they were most competitive in the traditional building and civil engineering infrastructural

---

[26]"Japan Scrambles for Overseas Work," *ENR*, Apr. 29, 1965, at 77; "Japan Flexes Its Muscle Abroad," *ENR*, Dec. 11, 1969, at 36.

[27]Basil Caplan, "The Japanese Construction Industry: Part 1: Construction Activity," *IC*, June 1969, at 54, 60; "Japan," *id.*, June 1974, at 34, 51 (in 1971 overseas contracts awarded to Japanese firms amounted to only £70 million); Fumio Hasegawa, *Built by Japan: Competitive Strategies of the Japanese Construction Industry* 82 (1988); Peter Rimmer, "Japanese Construction Contractors and the Australian States: Another Round of Interstate Rivalry," 12 *IJURR* 404, 408 (1988).

[28]"Competition Tightens Overseas," *ENR*, Nov. 14, 1957, at 25. According to another estimate, U.S. firms carried out £250 million of work overseas in 1956 compared with about £90 by British firms. "Overseas Construction Work by British Contractors in 1956-57" at 554.

[29]W. Strassmann, "The United States" in *The Global Construction Industry*, at 22, 23.

[30]Heiner Radzio, *Die Aufgabe heisst Bauen: 110 Jahre Hochtief* 32 (1985).

[31]*Hochtief 1875-1975*, at 4 (n.d. [ca. 1975]).

[32]Basil Caplan, "The U.K. Construction Industry: Part 1: Construction Activity," *IC*, Oct. 1969, at 49, 54, 59.

[33]"Germany's Hochtief" at 43, 49.

[34]*BJ 1975* at 51.

projects that required limited transfers of advanced technology.[35] Yet as early as 1962, U.S. firms acknowledged that the U.S. share of international construction volume was declining, and by 1970 warnings were issued that non-U.S. firms were closing the technology gap, leading to lower profits abroad for U.S. firms.[36] And during the Vietnam War, European firms saw U.S. companies' preoccupation with military construction in South East Asia and the concomitant reduction of U.S. government financing for construction elsewhere in the Third World as lessening the U.S. companies' competitiveness.[37]

Despite the large strides taken towards the creation of an international construction market, the industry was still characterized by a lower degree of integration and competition than that prevailing in numerous manufacturing industries. This difference was expressed most clearly in the relative lack of direct competition or transnational acquisitions among American, Western European, and Japanese construction firms in one another's domestic markets. When Taylor Woodrow, for example, undertook a £2 million office building project in Paris in the mid-1960s, it was the first of its kind since World War II.[38] Costain's construction of a food depot in Belgium at the same time was the first contract awarded by a Belgian company to a British firm for a project in Belgium.[39] Not only was there no "European construction market" in the 1960s,[40] but some authorities asserted that building standards and methods varied so greatly from country to country "that general building must inevitably remain outside the field of international enterprise."[41] Foreign holdings as a share of West German construction corporations' stock were as late as 1970 only one-third of the average for all West German industry (7.6 per cent and 21.7 per cent respectively).[42]

At the beginning of the 1970s, the United Nations reported that:

> Overseas contracting has grown significantly in the postwar period, and although the international market is still dominated by United States contractors (1 to 1.5 billion dollars of overseas construction a year), firms from France and the United Kingdom ($400 million each)...Italy ($300 million), the Federal Republic of Germany ($100 million) and Japan ($100 million) are increasingly active. Most of this work consists of civil engineering projects in developing countries. For western Europe as a whole overseas construction is estimated at between 1 and 3 per cent of gross construction output....[43]

Thus by 1972, British construction firms did £320 million of work overseas—twice the amount performed in 1965 (table 9.1). Yet of the total value of new foreign contracts that they obtained from 1968 to 1982, all of Europe accounted for only 2 to 17 per cent, while the European Economic Community countries accounted

---

[35]Strassmann, "The United States" at 34

[36]Gerald O'Connor, "Foreign Competition in Overseas Construction," *CE*, Feb. 1962, at 56 (official of Raymond International, also claiming without evidence that U.S. firms' overseas volume was declining absolutely); "Foreign Competitors Winning Race for Overseas Work," *ENR*, Nov. 5, 1970, at 85.

[37]"Germany's Hochtief" at 49.

[38]"British Construction Work Overseas, 1965-1966," 191 *BTJ* 874 (1966).

[39]"British Construction Work Overseas 1966-67" at 916.

[40]Götz Hohenstein, "Konzentration in der Bauwirtschaft," *FAZ*, May 11, 1963, at 5, col. 5 (business section).

[41]Colclough, *The Construction Industry of Great Britain* at 142.

[42]See "Ausländische Beteiligungen an Unternehmen in der Bundesrepublik," 24 *MDB* 28, 36-38 (Jan. 1972). See also Hohenstein, "Konzentration in der Bauwirtschaft."

[43]U.N., Secretariat of the Economic Commission for Europe, *Economic Survey of Europe in 1971*, pt. I: *The European Economy from the 1950s to the 1970s*, at 62 (1972). See also Roland Neo, *International Construction Contracting: A Critical Investigation into Certain Aspects of Financing, Capital Planning and Cash Flow Effects*, tab. 2.1 at 38, 59-60 (1975) (U.S. firms accounted for two-thirds of world market excluding projects undertaken by socialist countries [without accurate source for U.S.]).

for only 0.5 per cent to 3 per cent.[44]

Similarly, only three per cent of the foreign contract value awarded to West German contractors in 1974 derived from European countries—one per cent from within the EEC and even less from North America; 95 per cent was issued for work in African and Asian (including Middle Eastern) countries.[45] Among those firms performing intra-European construction, Christiani & Nielsen occupied a leading position based on its specialized expertise. It built bridges, marine terminals, submerged tunnels, and motorways in West Germany, Britain, Belgium, and Portugal.[46]

As late as 1973, European and Japanese construction firms faced such obstacles to overcoming U.S. industrial firms' preference for U.S. construction firms that the United States and Canada accounted for only a twentieth of the world's export markets for construction firms.[47] That in the 1960s one of Britain's largest firms, Taylor Woodrow, acquired a 49 per cent interest in a medium-size regional construction company in the United States constituted a minor exception.[48] Although U.S. firms did perform industrial, refinery, and pipeline construction in Western Europe in the 1960s and 1970s, they complained of politically inspired obstacles. The U.S. National Export Expansion Council charged that access to these markets was hampered by the fact that countries such as France and Italy maintained government-subsidized constructors, effectively excluding U.S. firms.[49]

Sheltered national construction markets in the advanced capitalist countries of Western Europe have nevertheless not been the product of domestic monopoly in the same way in which historically national manufacturing monopolies, in reacting to intensified world market competition, generated protective tariffs.[50] Other reasons adduced to account for lagging interpenetration among construction firms in EEC countries were heterogeneous building standards and construction methods; moreover, in order to avoid the risks of alien labor relations and legal systems, firms wishing to exploit patents or industrialized building methods were said to prefer licensing arrangements to establishing subsidiaries.[51]

A much different structure of competition evolved in the less developed countries where indigenous construction firms only gradually began to develop the capacity to execute the work on technologically more complex projects.[52] For

---

[44]Calculated according to data in *FT*, July 28, 1976, at 20; and *id.*, Nov. 15, 1976, at 25; "British Construction Work Overseas 1973/74," 17 *TI* 96, 97 (1974); "Going Up—British Building Business Overseas," 37 *TI* 358, 359 (1979); "Building Up: The Work of UK Construction Firms Overseas," 9 *BB* 256, 257 (1982); Smith, *Property Companies and the Construction Industry in Britain*, tab. 7.1 at 202.

[45]*BJ 1975* at 51. See also *WSJ*, Apr. 25, 1975, at 21; Neo, *International Construction Contracting* at 42-43, 54 (70 per cent of Western European contractors' foreign work in 1972 took place in developing countries [without a source]).

[46]Christiani & Nielsen, *75 Years* at 37-38, 44, 50, 92, 97.

[47]Kenneth Brooks, "The U.S. Engineering-Construction Industry: Is It Ready for a Building Boom?" *CW*, Mar. 21, 1973, at 33, 38.

[48]"World Competition Grows Sharper," *ENR*, Nov. 1, 1962, at 61; Caplan, "The U.K. Construction Industry" at 59. The company, Blitman Construction Corp. of New York, ranked 119th in contracts awarded in 1968. "Top 400," *ENR*, Apr. 10, 1969, at 70, 76.

[49]See "The 400," *ENR*, Apr. 10, 1969, at 70; "The 400," *ENR*, Apr. 9, 1970, at 42; National Export Expansion Council, *Report of the Industry Committee on Engineering and Construction Services* 47 (1970).

[50]See e.g., Rudolf Hilferding, *Das Finanzkapital: Eine Studie über die jüngste Entwicklung des Kapitalismus* 406-20 (1968 [1910]).

[51]Colclough, *Construction Industry in Great Britain* at 142.

[52]See Derek Miles & Richard Neale, *Building for Tomorrow: International Experience in Construction Industry Development* 63 (ILO, 1991) ("most...international projects undertaken by Singapore firms were residential and commercial buildings"); A. Zahlan, *The Arab Construction Industry* (1984); Peter Cassimatis, *Construction and Economic Development* (NTIS, 1975); Edward Jaycox & Clifford Hardy, "Domestic Construction Industries in Developing Countries," *FD*, Mar. 1975, 21-24, 46; E. Howenstine,

U.S. construction firms, even prior to the Middle Eastern construction boom, the impoverished rather than the enriched nations constituted the chief overseas market. From 1960 to 1968, three-fifths of U.S. constructors' repatriated profits stemmed from Third World countries and only one-fourth from Western Europe. In 1968 for example, Iran, where the shah displayed a penchant for spectacularly gigantic projects of comparatively little economic value, alone accounted for one-tenth of U.S. construction companies' repatriated profits. In contrast, approximately three-quarters to four-fifths of U.S. foreign direct investment in manufacturing were located in Western Europe and Canada during the 1960s.[53]

The prospect of numerous large and very profitable projects in the Third World drove U.S., Western European, and Japanese construction firms into a phase of intense competition, which led in turn to the intercession of individual national governments to create the best possible conditions for "their" firms.[54] This "growing importance of political and financial expertise to big engineering outfits that operate on a global scale" is most clearly reflected in the recruitment by Bechtel of such former high-ranking government officials as the Secretary of Labor and Secretary of the Treasury, George Shultz (who also joined the board of directors at J. P. Morgan & Co.), the Secretary of Health, Education, and Welfare, Caspar Weinberger, the CIA director, Richard Helms, and the president of the U.S. Export-Import Bank (which provides loans for many of the Third World projects for which Bechtel competes), John Moore.[55]

Despite the reemergence of Shultz and Weinberger as Secretary of State and Secretary of Defense respectively in the Reagan Administration, one specialist in international construction has asserted, without evidence, that a "coherent government-military-industrial complex for exploiting the rest of the world is not their...ideology. [T]hese former (and future) businessmen in government believe in sink-or-swim market place individualism. Heading a government agency to them is simply heading a different sort of enterprise that has adversarial relations with other enterprises."[56] Yet detailed studies suggest that such state-firm personnel interpenetration has directly and significantly benefited Bechtel.[57]

A final type of international construction that multinational firms perceived as constricting rather than expanding their world market was the more than 3,000 projects that the Soviet Union carried out in the Third World during the postwar period. The best known of these was the mammoth Aswan High Dam in Egypt in

---

"Social Considerations in Promoting Construction Work in Developing Countries," *CRev*, June 1972, at 4; Charles Cockburn, *Construction in Overseas Development* (1970); W. Strassmann, "Construction Productivity and Employment in Developing Counties," 101 *ILR* 503-18 (1970); *idem*, "The Construction Sector in Economic Development," 18 *SJPE* 391-409 (1970); U.N. Industrial Development Organization, *UNIDO Monographs on Industrial Development, Industrialization of Developing Countries: Problems and Prospects*, No. 2: *Construction Industry* (1969).

[53]National Export Expansion Council, *Report* at 58 and Exhibit 3-2 at 61 (citing unpublished data furnished by the U.S. Bureau of Economic Analysis); U.S. Bureau of the Census, *Historical Statistics of the United States Colonial Times to 1970*, pt. 2, ser. U 41-46 at 870-71 (1975); Bahman Nirumand, *Persien, Modell eines Entwicklungslandes oder die Diktatur der Freien Welt* 51 (1967); Nikki Keddie, *Roots of Revolution: An Interpretive History of Modern Iran* 176-77 (1981).

[54]See National Export Expansion Council, *Report*; "Problems of Overseas Construction," *CRev.*, Oct. 1966, at 9; "Eximbank's New Policies Will Aid Construction Firms," *CRev.*, Aug. 1970, at 9; "Foreign Competitors Winning Race for Overseas Work," *ENR*, Nov. 5, 1970, at 85; "Export Promotion Cuts Draw Builder Concern," *id.*, Feb, 20, 1975, at 77; "Foreign Competition," *id.*, May 29, 1975, at 10.

[55]"Where George Shultz Fits in at Bechtel," *BW*, May 18, 1974, at 76; *NZZ*, July 10, 1974, at 14; "Room at the Top for Ex-Cabinet Men," *BW*, Sept. 1, 1975, at 19-20; "Bechtel: A Builder Moves into Financing and Operations," *id.*, Oct. 22, 1979, at 119-20; Victor Zonana, "Megabuilder Bechtel Tries to Stay on Top by Being Aggressive," *WSJ*, Oct. 16, 1984, at 1, col. 6.

[56]Strassmann, "The United States" at 47.

[57]See Laton McCartney, *Friends in High Places: The Bechtel Story* 152-228 (1988). For Strassmann's partial defense of Bechtel in rebuttal, see his review of McCartney's book, 23 *JEI* 275 (1989); see also the more sympathetic review by C. Pursell, in 30 *TC* 702 (1989).

the late 1950s and 1960s, on which a work force of more than 33,000 labored.[58] The prominence of the Tanzanian-Zambian railway built by the People's Republic of China in the late 1960s and early 1970s and other large development projects overshadowed the hundreds of infrastructure projects that China carried out on a commercial basis in Asia and Africa and even in Kuwait. Eastern European state entities set up in developing countries in conjunction with projects financed by Eastern European countries also performed a considerable volume of capital construction.[59] The significant volume of construction performed within the socialist countries in the form of international labor collectives represented another unique facet of internationalization.[60]

The fact that Soviet bloc states had all of their societies' resources at their command and could operate "with an indifference to profits...which no private investor can match" enabled them to engage in international development projects with a "resounding advantage over the United States."[61] Even in the mid-1950s, U.S. firms complained about losing contracts—especially for dams and hydroelectric plants—to "Communist" state-owned enterprises that worked at a loss.[62] The U.S. government's response to such political competition brought to consciousness the contradictory consequences for U.S. multinational capital of U.S. foreign policy.

This contradiction was most blatantly exemplified by the withdrawal of U.S. aid for the Aswan Dam, and U.S. pressure on the American president of the World Bank, Eugene Black, a Wall Street banker, to attach "patronizing" conditions to its loan for construction of the dam in retaliation for Egypt's closer relationship with the Soviet Union at the height of the Cold War during the Eisenhower administration.[63] On the one hand, the construction industry, eager for more of the profitable projects in the Third World that U.S. foreign aid made possible,[64] called for using construction as "an arm of our foreign policy to a far greater extent than it has been in the past."[65] On the other hand, it was acutely aware that precisely such ideological militance generated political criteria so rigid that U.S. firms would lose business to the Soviet Union: "[T]here's the problem of neutralism. Most of the weak and newly independent nations want to stay neutral. Moscow has actively supported those desires. The U.S. has been more anxious to enlist the underdeveloped nations as military allies."[66]

A specific instance of Cold War competition will illustrate the attitude that

---

[58]Waldo Bowman, "Construction Begins on Aswan Dam—Russian Style," *ENR*, Feb. 23, 1961, at 32-38; "Aswan's First Stage Completed," *ENR*, May 21, 1964, at 55; National Research Council, *Building for Tomorrow: Global Enterprise and the U.S. Construction Industry* 46-47 (1988); Tom Little, *High Dam at Aswan* (1965); Marshall Goldman, *Soviet Foreign Aid* 61-72 (1967). For a critical view of the environmental and economic impact of the Aswan Dam, see John Waterbury, *Hydropolitics of the Nile Valley* 116-53 (1979); Edward Goldsmith & Nicholas Hildyard, 1 *The Social and Environmental Effects of Large Dams: Overview* 250-57 (1984).

[59]"Vielgestaltige chinesische Entwicklungshilfe," *NZZ*, Sept. 30, 1974, at 9; Martin Bailey, "Freedom Railroad," *MR*, Apr. 1976, at 32; "China—the Sleeping Giant," *IC*, June 1983, at 30, 31; "Bulgaria Special," *IC*, Aug. 1984, at 58; Yu Fai Law, *Chinese Foreign Aid* 181, 221-22 (1984); Carl McMillen, *Multinationals from the Second World: Growth of Foreign Investment by Soviet and East European Enterprises* 99, 149 (1987).

[60]L. Vasil'ev, *Mezhdunarodnye trudovye kollektivy stroitelei stran-chlenov SEV: praktika i perspektivy razvitii* (1987).

[61]Raymond Vernon, "The American Corporation in Underdeveloped Areas," in *The Corporation in Modern Society* 237, 241 (Edward Mason ed. 1966 [1959]).

[62]"U.S. Contractors Go Global" at 139.

[63]Waterbury, *Hydropolitics of the Nile Valley* at 102-109 (quotation at 105); Edward Mason & Robert Asher, *The World Bank Since Bretton Woods* 627-42 (1973).

[64]"What Foreign Aid Means to You," *ENR*, June 9, 1960, at 19.

[65]"Aswan to Baghdad and Beyond," *ENR*, July 31, 1958, at 92 (editorial).

[66]"Foreign Aid: New Look Needed?" *ENR*, July 31, 1958, at 21, 22.

the multinational firms adopted toward the changed circumstances in the Third World that their noncommercial rivals from the Second World had helped trigger. After the military coup in Iraq in 1958 disposed of the British-installed monarchy, U.S. construction firms such as Morrison-Knudsen and J. A. Jones felt threatened by "stiff future competition from Iron Curtain countries" that had theretofore been barred from participation in the most extensive construction program yet undertaken in an underdeveloped country.[67] They had, moreover, little understanding for the new regime's criticism of projects that benefited the few rather than the masses—especially a regime that "squeeze[d]" foreign firms by introducing the eight-hour day, overtime pay, social security taxes, and making dismissal more difficult.[68]

## "Reclaiming Petrodollars by Exploiting the...$500-billion Mideast Construction Market"[69]

By the 1970s, important internationalizing impulses also derived from three other sources situated outside North America, Western Europe, and Japan: First, the mounting worldwide search for and exploitation and processing of petroleum and mineral resources at sites outside the Middle East (such as Australia, Malaysia, Nigeria, Indonesia, and Singapore) for export to the advanced capitalist economies; second, the incipient industrialization of certain Third World countries such as Brazil, Taiwan, and Hong Kong; and third, the construction of various large industrial complexes in the Soviet Union, which for political reasons benefited European firms such as those from Finland more than U.S. firms.[70]

All these projects, however, were overshadowed by the paroxysm of construction activity in the Middle East. The enormous increase in revenue that began flowing to the members of the Organization of Petroleum Exporting Countries (OPEC) in 1973 enabled them to implement unprecedented industrial development programs based on the strategy of securing an increased share of total world production of refined petroleum products and petrochemicals.[71] Oil revenues also financed monumental construction schemes running the gamut from such infrastructure projects as highways, harbors, airports, and desalination projects to housing, hospitals, schools, and a camel race track grandstand for the ruler of Dubai.[72] In Saudi Arabia, the largest OPEC producer, oil-related government revenues rose 11-fold from 1972-73 to 1977-78 and 27-fold to the peak year of 1981-82—from 12 billion to 324 billion Saudi riyals.[73] The increase in value

---

[67]"Construction's Stake in Iraq," *ENR*, July 24, 1958, at 23, 24; Waldo Bowman, "Iraq's Operation Bootstrap—Part One: A Modern Mesopotamia is Molded," *ENR*, Dec. 12, 1957, at 34.

[68]"How U.S. Firms Will Make Out in Iraq," *ENR*, Jan. 29, 1959, at 44 (mentioning a Frank Lloyd Wright opera house); "Iraq Squeezes Western Builders," *id.* at 42, 44.

[69]"U.S. 'Arrogance' Costs Firms Billions in Lost Jobs," *ENR*, Nov. 29, 1979, at 26, 28.

[70]See e.g., "Singapore Refiners in Midst of Huge Construction Campaign," *OGJ*, July 20, 1992, at 23 (Nexis); "The Top 250 International Contractors: Instability Slows Growth Abroad," *ENR*, July 22, 1991, at 30 (Hong Kong and Taiwan "are on huge infrastructure spending sprees"); [Brown & Root], *Brownbuilder*, No. 1, 1992, at 15; "Nixon Uses Credit to Push Soviet Trade," *BW*, June 1, 1974, at 24; "But Chemico's Four-Plant Contract is Biggest Ever With USSR," *ENR*, June 27, 1974, at 9; Rimmer, "Japanese Construction Contractors and the Australian States"; Visvanathan, "International Construction Industry" at 81-85.

[71]See Faribarz Ghadar, "The Impact of the New OPEC Downstream Operations on Oil Industry Structure," in *Petroleum Resources and Development: Economic, Legal and Policy Issues for Developing Countries* 232-45 (Kameel Khan ed. 1988).

[72]"Building Up to £3.8bn," 12 *BB* 456, 458 (1983).

[73]Calculated according to data in Kingdom of Saudi Arabia, Central Dept. of Statistics, *Statistical Year Book*, tab. 10-2 at 381 (14th Issue, 1978); *id.*, tab. 10-2 at 522 (19th Issue, 1983); *id.*, tab. 10-2 at 554 (24th Issue, 1988). During this period the exchange rate rose from about 4.15 to 3.415 riyals to the U.S. dollar.

added in Saudi construction during this period almost exactly mirrored the rise in government revenues, increasing from 1973 to 1981 from 1.8 to 50.3 billion riyals.[74] The other major OPEC producers registered similar increases. In Iran and Iraq, for example, government oil and gas revenues rose eight-fold and ten-fold respectively alone from 1972 to 1974.[75]

In order to build so-called downstream facilities such as refineries, petrochemical complexes, and gas-gathering and processing plants, OPEC states had to rely on the few multinational, and especially U.S., engineering and construction firms competent to carry out these very large and technologically complex projects.[76] The largest construction firms in the United States, Western Europe, and Japan have therefore ranked high among the capital-goods-producing beneficiaries of the recapture of petrodollars. But industrially advanced building on such a gargantuan scale simultaneously created a secondary international redistribution of profits in the form of a proportionately expanded demand for capital goods from the advanced capitalist oil-consuming nations.[77] "In most cases, the value of this industrial equipment [to be installed] can be three or four times that of the engineering and construction services."[78]

The scope of these ancillary exports, which are even more profitable than the construction operations themselves, can be measured by the fact that in 1975 two-thirds of the value of large U.S. construction firms' overseas contracts went to materials, equipment, and machinery, of which in turn 44 per cent were procured in the United States.[79] In the same year, "the total that U.S. builders spent on domestic equipment and services for export to foreign construction sites came to about $9.6 billion. That pushed heavy construction past the defense industry as the top industrial bulwark of America's balance of trade."[80] Middle Eastern expenditures on construction machinery quickly rose to per capita levels approaching those in the United States.[81]

These massive construction programs initiated by the Middle Eastern oil-exploiting nations in the mid-1970s afforded an immense impetus to the

---

After 1978, the data for taxes include non-oil company income taxes, but these are relatively minuscule and for the sake of comparability have been used for all years. The other rubric of oil-related revenue is "Royalties from Oil," which is decidedly smaller. In contrast to the English translation, the Arabic text incorrectly uses "intāj al-zait" ("oil production" or "output"). Telephone interview with Dr. Hilali, Saudi Arabian embassy, Washington, D.C. (Feb. 2, 1993) (confirming the error).

[74]Calculated according to data in U.N., *YCS 1973-1980*, at 158 (1982); *id., 1984*, at 179 (1986). For descriptions of infrastructure projects and the construction industry in Saudi Arabia, see Ali Johany, Michel Berne, & J. Mixon, Jr., *The Saudi Arabian Economy* 131-40 (1986); Hossein Askari, *Saudi Arabia's Economy: Oil and the Search for Economic Development* 67-85 (1990).

[75]Calculated according to data in Statistical Centre of Iran, *Statistical Yearbook of Iran 1352 (March, 1973-March, 1974)*, at 461 (1976); Republic of Iraq, Central Statistical Organization, *Annual Abstract of Statistics 1976*, at 256 (n.d.). For an overview of the oil revenues and construction programs throughout the Middle Eastern oil producing nations, see Jim Antoniou, *Construction in the Middle East* 7-25, 31-53 (Economist Intelligence Unit Special Report No. 55, 1978).

[76]See U.S. International Trade Administration, *Current Developments in U.S. International Service Industries* 55-56, 61-62 (1980). On the strategy in Iran, see Jahangir Amuzegar, *Iran: An Economic Profile* 66-77 (1977); Abolghassem Atighetchi, *Industriepolitik als Versuch der Überwindung ökonomischer Unterentwicklung im Iran* (1983).

[77]See Ernest Mandel, *The Second Slump: A Marxist Analysis of Recession in the Seventies* 34-46, 129-32 (1978).

[78]National Export Expansion Council, *Report* at 33.

[79]National Export Expansion Council, *Report* at 36; U.S. International Trade Administration, *Current Developments in U.S. International Service Industries* at 57. These data are consistent with domestic U.S. data showing that value added in the industrial and nonresidential building sectors account for a little less than one-third of the output. *SAUS: 1992*, tab. 1201 at 705.

[80]"Where the Constructors Strike it Rich," *BW*, Aug. 23, 1976, at 46, 48-49.

[81]See Winfred Richter, "Middle East Construction: Potentials and Prospects," *IC*, Sept. 1975, at 80.

internationalization of construction.[82] In 1975, as the OPEC building bubble expanded, the value of Middle East contracts amounted to 10 per cent of the total construction volume and one-third of the overseas volume credited to the 400 largest U.S. construction firms.[83] This sea change was captured by the vast shift in the geographic distribution of international profits: in 1970 U.S. construction firms derived 22 per cent of their overseas net receipts from Western Europe and 25 per cent from OPEC members; by 1978 the corresponding figures were 7 per cent and 61 per cent.[84]

Internationally oriented British firms' dependence on the Middle East became even more pronounced. From 1972-73 to 1976-77, their new overseas contract awards more than quadrupled, from £346 million to £1,588 million (table 9.1), while the share accounted for by Middle Eastern countries rose from 22 per cent to 55 per cent. The United Arab Emirates alone accounted for almost half of the Middle East total.[85] Despite the ongoing extraordinary reliance of French multinational construction firms on markets in the former French colonial Africa, they too witnessed a tripling of their international construction work between 1973 and 1976.[86] French firms, such as Bouygues, that had been largely domestic builders finally became enmeshed in the world market through huge contracts in Iran, Saudia Arabia, and Iraq.[87]

In the Middle East, a politically mediated benefit accrued to U.S. firms, which, as the U.S. National Academy of Engineering acknowledges, "[t]o some degree ha[ve] enjoyed...a relationship with Saudi Arabia" similar to that of the British and French construction industries with their respective countries' former colonies.[88] In particular, non-U.S. construction firms were frustrated by the fact that their prime competitors could rely on a military superpower's expeditionary Army Corps of Engineers, which "'has all its fingers in the pie....'"[89] During the Cold War, under the dual banners of rolling back communism and spreading American free enterprise, Congress had authorized the Army Corps of Engineers to provide (reimbursable) services to friendly foreign countries. In addition to considerable military construction in many regions, in some of which the larger projects are initially set aside for exclusive bidding by U.S. firms,[90] the Army Corps of Engineers managed or performed multi-billion dollar civil construction projects in Saudi Arabia from the 1960s to the 1980s. Pursuant to the Foreign Assistance Act of 1961, 1963, and 1964—in which Congress celebrated "the vital

---

[82]See Walter McQuade, "The Arabian Building Boom is Making Construction History," *Fortune*, Sept. 1976, at 112-15, 186-90. See also "Building a New Middle East," *BW*, May 26, 1975, at 38-54; "Where the Constructors Strike it Rich"; "Middle Eastern Construction," *FT*, July 28, 1976, at 13-28; "'Mekka' für die Baubranche," *HB*, Aug. 2, 1974, at 19; "Baubranche sucht neue Ertragsquellen," *id.*, Aug. 16-17, 1974, at 15; Shawn Tully, "France's Master Builder is on the March," *Fortune*, May 2, 1983, at 210.

[83]"Foreign Contracts Account for One Third of '75 Volume," *ENR*, Apr. 15, 1976, at 62.

[84]Calculated according to data in Anthony DiLullo, "Service Transactions in the U.S. International Accounts, 1970-80," *SCB*, Nov. 1981, at 29, tab. 8 at 40. By 1980 the shares had become about one-eighth and two-fifths respectively.

[85]Calculated according to data in "Building Big Business Overseas," 33 *TI* 126-28 (1978); "Going Up—British Building Business Overseas," 37 *TI* 358, 359, 362 (1979).

[86]By 1978, 22 per cent of French firms' international work was performed in the Middle Eastern oil producing countries compared with 45 per cent in Africa. Behring, Gluch, & Rußig, *Entwicklungstendenzen im deutschen Auslandsbau* at 52-53.

[87]Elisabeth Campagnac & Vincent Nouzille, *Citizen Bouygues ou l'histoire secrète d'un grand patron* 93-138 (1988).

[88]National Research Council, *Building for Tomorrow* at 16. For charges that the Saudi national oil company even rigs bidding in favor of U.S. firms, see John Egan, "Rigged Bids," *FW*, July 24, 1990, at 56 (Nexis).

[89]"The Top International Contractors," *ENR*, July 19, 1984, at 78 (quoting complaint of West German firm speculating about the impact of "Persian Gulf hostilities" on military construction in Saudi Arabia).

[90]See "U.S. Firms Lose Job for Lack of Bidders," *ENR*, Apr. 4, 1985, at 79.

role of free enterprise''—which directed the U.S. Agency for International Development to encourage the use of "engineering and professional services of United States firms,'' the Army Corps of Engineers contracted with private U.S. firms on capital projects financed under the statute.[91]

Although the Army Corps of Engineers accorded an absolute monopoly to U.S. architect-engineering-design firms, ironically, by the end of the 1970s, only one-quarter of the actual construction work, which the Saudi payors insisted be contracted to the lowest bidder, had been performed by U.S. firms (most prominently by Morrison-Knudsen).[92]  Even where U.S. construction firms were not low bidders on projects in Saudi Arabia managed by the Army Corps of Engineers, however, "specifications generally specify American material and equipment.... So there is a great amount of money that comes back into the United States...."[93]  In contrast, neither the British Royal Engineers, which began building railways in the African colonies in the late nineteenth century and carried out a large volume of reconstruction work after World War II, nor the French Génie Corps nor the Corps des ponts et chaussées, which were particularly active in colonial railway construction and beginning in the mid-nineteenth century in the construction of ports and water systems in North Africa, has had the same international commercial impact as its U.S. counterpart in the post-World War II period.[94]

The OPEC construction programs also projected the defeated national capitals of World War II (Germany, Italy, and Japan) back onto the world market. Bereft of ties to the infrastructure forged by former or current military power, West German firms, for example, "without the ready-made foreign markets of former colonial powers such as Britain and France,'' were reported by *Business Week* to "have traditionally stayed at home.'' Stymied at first in seeking to overcome "the depression in their domestic market'' by obtaining projects in the Middle East at the outset of the OPEC-financed boom, once it expanded beyond the capacities of the traditional internationalist American, British, and French firms, the new entrants quickly became incorporated into the developing world market.[95]  West German firms, for example, specializing in harbors, hospitals, and airports, experienced an 18-fold increase in the value of foreign construction contracts in the short span between 1970 and 1976—from 700 million marks to more than 12 billion marks.[96]

---

[91]Foreign Assistance Act of 1961, Pub. L. No. 87-195, §§ 601, 607, 75 Stat. 424, 438, 441 (1961); Foreign Assistance Act of 1963, Pub. L. No. 88-205, § 301(a)(3), 77 Stat. 379, 385 (1963); Foreign Assistance Act of 1964, Pub. L. No. 88-633, § 301(b), 78 Stat. 1009, 1012 (1964) (codified as amended at 22 U.S.C. §§ 2351, 2357(a) (1990); *Activities of the United States Army Corps of Engineers in Saudi Arabia: Hearing Before the Subcomm. on Europe and the Middle East of the House Comm. on Foreign Affairs*, 96th Cong., 1st Sess. (1979); *The History of the US Army Corps of Engineers* 109-12 (n.d. [1986]).

[92]*Activities of the United States Army Corps of Engineers in Saudi Arabia* at 3-4, 31-32, 40, 43. Complaint about this distribution was reflected in the American trade press. See "U.S. 'Arrogance' Costs Firms Billions in Lost Jobs," *ENR*, Nov. 29, 1979, at 26-27, 37. *WSJ*, Feb. 27, 1978, at 6, col. 1-2, also reported that U.S. firms' share of Saudi construction, which "had once been an American preserve," had sunk to 15 per cent. The figures presented there showing U.S. firms' ranking twelfth in Mideast construction contracts in the late 1970s were either inaccurate or represented an anomalous situation superseded throughout the 1980s and into the 1990s by clear U.S. dominance in the region. See chapter 11 below.

[93]*Activities of the United States Corps of Engineers in Saudi Arabia* at 44.

[94]See W. Baker Brown, 4 *History of the Corps of Royal Engineers* 85, 92, 101, 110-13, 122-23 (1952); 7 *History of the Corps of Royal Engineers: Campaigns in Mesopotamia and East Africa, and the Inter-War Period, 1919-38*, at 245-48 (H. Pritchard ed., 1952); R.P. Pakenham-Walsh, 9 *History of the Corps of Royal Engineers: 1938-1948*, at 545-79 (1958) A. Brunot & R. Coquand, *Le Corps des ponts et chaussées* 513-19, 599-603 (1982); chap. 5 above.

[95]*BW*, Nov. 9, 1974, at 64. See also Behring, Gluch, & Rußig, *Entwicklungstendenzen im deutschen Auslandsbau* at 53, 61; National Research Council, *Building for Tomorrow* at 17.

[96]Behring, Gluch, & Rußig, *Entwicklungstendenzen im deutschen Auslandsbau* 28, tab. 2.1 at 25. These

Between 1973 and 1976, as Italian firms' overseas awards rose sixfold, the share accounted for by oil-producing countries (including Nigeria and Venezuela) jumped from 12 per cent to 69 per cent. Italian construction companies, several of which are owned by the state-controlled Ente Nazionale Idrocarburi (Snamprogetti) and Istituto per la Ricostruzione Industriale (Italimpianti) and specialize in oil and steel-related projects, recorded such strong gains in the 1970s that they contributed to a surplus in Italy's balance of payments. Overseas construction has accounted for as much as 15 per cent of total Italian construction and 15 per cent of total national exports of goods and services.[97]

Japanese construction firms had been operating overseas—primarily in Asia—on a commercial basis for only a few years at the time of the onset of the OPEC boom. Despite their lack of experience in the Middle East and the sharp competition from Korean firms, they succeeded in virtually doubling their orders annually from 1972 to 1976. By the latter half of the decade, Japanese firms were taking more than half of their international orders from the Middle East. Their particular reliance on projects in Iraq exposed some firms to significant losses as a result of the war with Iran beginning in 1980. A strategic diversification process then ensued, leading Japanese firms back to their traditional markets in Southeast Asia and, when these faltered in the early 1980s, on to new markets in Australia and the United States.[98]

Finally, the petroleum-funded Middle East building spree created an absolutely unprecedented phenomenon: a (former) Third World country, South Korea, joined the export market, capturing a significant share of the Middle Eastern construction market between 1976 and 1985. Originally drawn into the world market as contractors to the U.S. Army Corps of Engineers for military projects in Korea, Vietnam, Guam, and Saudi Arabia, South Korean firms found that their patron's expulsion from South Vietnam in 1975 had left them "with no jobs, idle equipment and unemployed workers." Coincidentally, the advent of the Middle East boom rescued their fixed capital investment.[99]

Korean firms were able to underbid Western firms by 20 to 30 per cent by using a "regimented workforce (backed with army approval and full government support)." They secured orders for many labor-intensive projects largely on the basis both of the much lower wages that they paid their own national manual workers, managers, and supervisors and of credit extended by the largest U.S. banks.[100] Their successful strategy, which was made possible by the absence of a large supply of cheap labor on site, stemmed from their greater facility at transferring cheap labor from their domestic labor market to the Middle East than the First World firms initially showed in recruiting workers from third-party Third World countries. When the focus of the international construction market shifted from the population-poor Middle East to sites where cheap labor was more

figures are understated because they exclude contracts executed by affiliates of German firms abroad. Erich Gluch & Jürgen Riedel, "The Federal Republic of Germany," in *The Global Construction Industry* at 121. For examples of some of the larger West German projects in the Middle East, see Philipp Holzmann Aktiengesellschaft, *Hafen Damman Saudi Arabien* (n.d. [ca. 1976]); *idem, Medizinisches Zentrum in Riyadh Saudi-Arabien: Schlüsselfertige Planung und Ausführung* (1980); *idem, Ausbau des Trinkwasser-Systems der libyschen Hauptstadt Tripolis* (1984).

[97]Behring, Gluch, & Rußig, *Entwicklungstendenzen im deutschen Auslandsbau* at 54-56; Bruno Amoroso & Ole Olsen, *Lo Stato imprenditore* 308-15 (1978); "Italy's World Builders," *Economist*, Nov. 11, 1978, at 80; Norsa, "Italy" at 91.

[98]Hippo & Saburo, "Japan" at 59, 62-65.

[99]Dae Chang, "The Republic of Korea," in *The Global Construction Industry* at 141, 42-43.

[100]Antoniou, *Construction in the Middle East* at 62 (quotation); "South Korea Faces Slackening Growth," *NYT*, Jan. 25, 1976, sect. 3, at 70; "Korean Contractors Invade the Mideast," *BW*, May 29, 1978, at 34; Youssef Ibrahim, "How Koreans Built Saudi Success," *NYT*, June 19, 1978, at D5, col. 1; Chang, "The Republic of Korea," tab. 7.1 at 142.

plentiful, Korean firms lost much of their competitive advantage. As the world market demanded more capital- and technology-intensive projects, Korean firms, despite efforts to move into these more sophisticated types of construction, were displaced by traditional competitors. Undercapitalized to begin with, Korean firms' "ridiculously low bids in the Middle East" led to mass insolvencies and mergers as many of them were forced to siphon all their profits into interest payments.[101]

---

[101]Chang, "The Republic of Korea" at 148, 150-51 (quotation), 158; chapter 10 below.

# 10

# The World Construction Market Constructs Its Own World Labor Market

> Society, the united individuals, may possess the surplus time to build the road, but only united. ... Insofar as the uniting of their powers increases their productive power, it is by no means clear that they possess numerically the labor power all taken together—if they do not work together.... Hence the forcible rounding up of the people in Egypt,...India, etc. for compulsory construction and public compulsory works. Capital effects the same union in another way, through its manner of exchange with free labor.[1]

Technological progress in transportation and communication has imparted a different character to the "annihilation of space by time"[2] in the late twentieth century than that which prevailed in the mid-nineteenth century when British railway builders had to ship capital and labor halfway round the world. Nevertheless, even in an age when billions of dollars of capital in its money form can be electronically flashed from New York, Frankfurt, or Tokyo to Jakarta, Riyadh, or São Paulo almost instantaneously, the physical movement of less abstract forms of capital remains a formidably capital-intensive and arduous process. The assembly of all the dead and living labor required for the recreation of the built environment in less industrialized societies is a particularly mammoth logistical undertaking. The construction of an industrial city in Saudi Arabia, a copper or gold mining complex in New Guinea or the Peruvian Andes, or a hydroelectric dam in Mozambique has been likened to the invasion of Normandy: "Tons of supplies are shipped in, prefabricated dwellings are hauled over jungle roads, and helicopters ferry the amenities and personnel."[3]

The purchase, lease, and timely shipment of huge quantities of raw materials and machinery as well as the industrial plant and equipment to be installed to areas such as the Middle East—where "the only materials not imported are sand, gravel, and gasoline"[4]—is a complex task of coordination.[5] The daily purchase orders of Fluor in the mid-1970s, for example, included five tons of structural steel, $2.5 million of process equipment, and $1.5 million of piping and valves. Fifteen years later, Bechtel was procuring $4 billion annually in materials and equipment.[6] In

---

[1]Karl Marx, *Grundrisse der Kritik der politischen Ökonomie (Rohentwurf) 1857-58*, at 427 (1953).

[2]*Id.* at 423.

[3]Michael Kolbenschlag, "Bechtel's Biggest Job—Constructing Its Own Future," *Forbes*, Dec. 7, 1981, at 138, 141.

[4]Shawn Tully, "France's Master Builder Is on the March," *Fortune*, May 2, 1983, at 210, 216.

[5]For a good overall description, see Walter McQuade, "The Arabian Building Boom is Making Construction History," *Fortune*, Sept. 1976, at 112.

[6]"Where the Constructors Strike it Rich," *BW*, Aug. 23, 1976, at 46, 56; *1991 Bechtel Report to Employees* at 31 (n.d.).

extreme cases, the firms' "engineers dream up their own exotic machinery"—such as "the building of the world's largest air-cushioned amphibious barges to carry 250-ton modules" to a liquefied-natural-gas plant on an island in the Persian Gulf.[7]    These exports of productive capital generated by the international construction industry constitute a significant source of demand for the products of First World heavy industry such as steel and machinery. Unsurprisingly, an inverse relationship exists between a "host" country's GNP and its volume of construction machinery imports.[8]

This ongoing worldwide transshipment of construction capital in its productive form is promoted by competitive bidding practices.    Although multinational companies generally calculate their bids by assuming that their capital equipment will be used up and thus completely amortized on one project, frequently they can continue to use it on subsequent projects. Firms therefore have a competitive incentive to submit their next round of bids without making any financial provision for their already written-off capital equipment (especially for the more sophisticated kinds) in order to lower their bids.[9]

## International Migrancy

> In the present day labour can with the utmost ease be transferred from place to place—exported, shipped, or sent by rail like any other commodity.[10]

This physical mobilization of capital has brought in its wake an unprecedented and multilayered system of recruitment, mobilization, provisioning, housing, and control of the requisite multinational, multiracial, multilingual unaccompanied male labor force.[11]    In camps specially built and segregated to avoid "the constant threat of conflict" international construction firms may be "feeding and servicing" upwards of fifteen thousand workers.    And although the labor force of any single one of these projects may be eclipsed by the 20,000

[7]Dan Cordtz, "Bechtel Thrives on Billion-Dollar Jobs," *Fortune*, Jan. 1975, at 90, 142.

[8]National Export Expansion Council, *Report of the Industry Committee on Engineering and Construction Services* 112 (1970).

[9]Erich Gluch & Jürgen Riedel, "The Federal Republic of Germany," in *The Global Construction Industry: Strategies for Entry, Growth and Survival* 120, 136 (W. Strassmann & Jill Wells ed., 1988).

[10]"The Importation of Foreign Labour," 44 *Engineer* 299, 300 (1877) (editorial).

[11]See J. Birks & C. Sinclair, *International Migration and Development in the Arab Region* 110-11 (1980); Sooyong Kim, "Contract Migration in the Republic of Korea" at 45 (ILO, International Migration for Employment Working Paper 4, 1982).    Scattered exceptions exist to be sure.    Under U.S. rule, female laborers figured prominently on road-building projects in the Philippines.    "Philippine Road Building," 75 *EN* 112 (1916).    One-tenth of the workers employed by Kaiser in the construction of a steel mill in India in the 1950s were local women.    "Beating the Odds When Building Abroad," *ENR*, Mar. 27, 1958, at 31, 32.    U.S. military contractors also employed many Vietnamese women in Vietnam.    "Vietnamization: Roads, Bases and Skills," *ENR*, Jan. 15, 1970, at 25.    In general, however, the international construction industry lags behind developments even in the United States, where fifteen years after the U.S. Department of Labor promulgated hiring goals for women, only 1.9 per cent of construction workers are female—compared with 1.2 per cent in 1970. See Georgia Dullea, "Women Fight for More Construction Jobs, Less Harassment," *NYT*, Aug. 23, 1977, at 30, col. 1; "U.S. Rules Will Push More Women's Jobs in Construction," *WSJ*, Apr. 10, 1978, at 3, col. 4; "Women in Construction Still Waiting for Respect," *NYT*, Sept. 29, 1992, at B12, col. 1 (nat. ed.).    In the Soviet Union women, who accounted for 30 per cent of all construction workers, while female construction workers constituted six per cent of all female workers, "perform a man's work and get a man's pay." Waldo Bowman, "Construction Today in the U.S.S.R.," *ENR*, Aug. 30, 1962, at 38, 39 (quotation); Svetlana Turchaninova, "Trends in Women's Employment in the USSR," 112 *ILR* 253, 256 (1975); Norton Dodge, *Women in the Soviet Economy* 178-79 (1966). Women's share of construction employment was, except for transportation, nevertheless the lowest of any industry in the Soviet Union. Tsentral'noe Statisticheskoe Upravlenie pri Sovete Ministrov SSSR, *Narodnoe khoziaistvo SSSR v 1974 g.: Statisticheskii ezhegodnik* 559 (1975). In the other former Comecon countries women formed between one-sixteenth and one-seventh of all construction workers. Institut für die Wirtschaft des sozialistischen Weltsystems an der Akademie der Wissenschaften der UdSSR, 3 *Sozialistisches Weltwirtschaftssystem: Arbeitsteilung und Standortverteilung der Produktion* 101 (1968).

corvée laborers pressed into service to build the Suez Canal in the 1860s, or the 45,000 workers recruited from almost 100 countries who worked on the Panama Canal in 1913,[12] at any one time a large multinational firm may be overseeing the work of more than a half-million workers around the world.[13]

Multinational firms have met some of their labor requirements during the post-World War II period by resurrecting the nineteenth-century practice of dispatching (often unemployed) First World construction workers to the Third World. Thus in mid-1976, 10,000 British construction workers found employment in the Middle East in part to avoid the building depression in Britain.[14] The prominence of Italian construction firms in Third World markets in the 1970s and 1980s was in part a function of the willingness of tens of thousands of Italian construction workers, who may have accounted for as many as a quarter of those employed abroad by these firms, to "accept[] working and environmental conditions that would be refused by Americans or most other Europeans."[15]

U.S. construction firms began sending tens of thousands of skilled and unskilled workers to their overseas projects in the early post-World War II period. Many of these sites were U.S. military bases. This stream of recruitment expanded through the 1950s and reached its absolute peak during the massive involvement of civilian construction firms and workers in building military facilities in Vietnam in the second half of the 1960s. The petroleum boom during the 1970s and early 1980s created a second, albeit lower, peak demand for U.S. workers especially in the Middle East, but also in other oil-producing countries such as Indonesia and Venezuela.[16]

Multinational construction firms' employment of First World construction workers in the Third World was checked to some extent when "host" governments in the 1950s began inserting clauses into their contracts requiring companies to hire and train local workers.[17] By the mid-1950s, U.S. construction firms had also begun to reduce the number of U.S. personnel employed abroad as one means of staving off competition by European firms that paid lower wages and salaries.[18] Later, international construction firms, driven by competitive cost-cutting, initiated even greater restraints on the hiring of First World workers as they increasingly

---

[12]John Marlowe, *The Making of the Suez Canal* 152-57 (1964); *Annual Report of the Isthmian Canal Commission and the Panama Canal for the Fiscal Year Ended June 30, 1914*, at 293 (1914); Gerstle Mack, *The Land Divided: A History of the Panama Canal* 533-51 (1944); Ian Cameron, *The Impossible Dream* 142-43, 153-59 (1971).

[13]See Robert Ingram, *The Bechtel Story: Seventy Years of Accomplishment in Engineering and Construction* 61-62 (1968); "Where the Constructors Strike it Rich" at 56; E. Stallworthy & O. Kharbanda, *International Construction* xv (1986).

[14]James Buxton, "Manpower: An Army Moves in," *FT*, July 28, 1976, at 15, col. 1.

[15]"Italy's World Builders," *Economist*, Nov. 11, 1978, at 80, 81 (quotation); Karin Behring, Erich Gluch, & Volker Rußig, *Entwicklungstendenzen im deutschen Auslandsbau* 56 n.3 (1982) (estimating the share of Italian workers in the absence of data); Aldo Norsa, "Italy," in *The Global Construction Industry* at 87, 91.

[16]"Combine for Overseas," *ENR*, Feb. 1, 1951, at 24; "Labor Sought for Offshore Work by Joint Ventures," *id.*, Mar. 22, 1951, at 16. Much of the information in this paragraph was furnished by the president of the Overseas Craftsman's Association, an organization that has referred U.S. construction workers overseas since the end of World War II. Telephone interview with Gary Koontz, Cypress, California (July 21, 1993).

[17]Telephone interview with Gary Koontz (July 21, 1993). There are several earlier isolated instances of such contractual requirements in Latin America. Thus the Chilean government stipulated that three-quarters of the staff employed by Sir John Jackson, Ltd. on railway construction be local workers. "The Arica-La Paz Railway," 62 *ER* 16 (1910). And when John Roebling & Sons built a bridge in the Domincan Republic in the 1930s, the government required the firm to employ only native workers with the exception of one resident engineer. Allegedly the firm recruited the bridge workers from the peasantry. Charles Jones, "The San Rafael Bridge in San Domingo," 112 *ENR* 249, 253 (1934). On similar provisions in effect on the Cuban Central Highway project in the 1920s and 1930s, see chapter 7 above.

[18]"Competition Tightens Overseas," *ENR*, Nov. 14, 1957, at 25, 27.

came to rely on the "host" country or third countries such as South Korea, Thailand, Pakistan, India, Yemen, the Philippines, Turkey, Portugal, Egypt, and Sri Lanka for the hundreds of thousands of manual laborers whom they employ overseas while continuing to send engineers and managers from the First World to world market sites. Thus French construction firms employed 90,000 workers abroad in 1978 of whom only 17,000 were sent from France. In performing construction services abroad, U.S. firms were estimated to have employed 162,000 workers in 1982; only one-seventh of them, however, were American citizens working outside the United States.[19] Intensified competition finally led multinational firms to hire cheaper Third World engineers as well for overseas projects.[20] Consequently, by the early 1990s, perhaps only one-fifth as many U.S. construction workers were working overseas as at the height of the Vietnam-era military construction.[21]

The character and function of this international movement of so-called contract laborers have changed little in the century since socialists began attacking it as "the capitalistically organized importation of sweated labor." Already in the nineteenth century advances in transportation and communication made it feasible for employers in Western Europe and the United States to recruit workers from less industrialized regions whose lower standard of living created a reference point that pressed down on the value of labor power of their competitors in the advanced capitalist countries. Then, too, capitalists preferred such workers on large construction projects such as railroads, canals, and ports in order to suppress the wage increases associated with sudden spikes in demand in the labor market. In order to seize upon the full culturally internalized significance of the importees' precapitalist standard of living, recruiters obligated workers to the terms of employment while they were still in their home countries and thus without insight into the cost of living at the remote location. And if, after arrival at the construction site, the workers' experience with their new working and living conditions impelled them to demand a wage increase, their employers could fire them, leaving them unable to find other employment and without the means to travel home. If this threat did not suffice to dampen their rebellious spirits, the state could intervene by punishing them for breach of contract or deporting them.[22]

All of these characteristics have been reproduced by multinational construction firms operating in the Middle East and elsewhere. If the "Yankee Pizarro" Henry Meiggs could make his fortune by buying cargoes of Chinese coolies to build railways in the Andes in the 1860s and 1870s, and John "Empire Jack" Norton-Griffiths made his on the Angolan railway in 1905 with "shipment[s]" of Hindu coolies, Senegalese, and Cape Verde Islanders,[23] a century later multinational construction firms are achieving the same end with workers from other Asian countries.

Against the background of this venerable history, it is not surprising that the prediction by the trade press in the late 1970s that "cheap labor mainly on a subcontract basis" could create only a "short-lived" success[24] did not resonate with multinational firms. Instead, they promptly resolved to enhance their

---

[19]Behring, Gluch, & Rußig, *Entwicklungstendenzen im deutschen Auslandsbau* at 53 (data exclude overseas subsidiaries); Strassmann, "The United States," in *Global Construction Industry*, tab. 2.2 at 26 (the data exclude work performed by the Corps of Engineers).

[20]Gluch & Riedel, *The Federal Republic of Germany* at 125, 134-35.

[21]Telephone interview with Gary Koontz (July 21, 1993).

[22]Otto Bauer, "Proletarische Wanderungen," 26:1 *NZ* 476, 482-84 (1907).

[23]Robert Middlemas, *The Master Builders: Thomas Brassey; Sir John Aird; Lord Cowdray; Sir John Norton-Griffiths* 256 (1963).

[24]"Non-U.S. Firms Grab Big Share of Global Market," *ENR*, Dec. 6, 1979, at 26, 36.

competitiveness by increasing their use of low-cost labor from the Third World. Thus the largest U.S. construction firm in 1975, Fluor, trained several thousand Javanese workers for a project in Indonesia and planned to "ship" them to a new site in Saudi Arabia, where it had been experiencing difficulty in recruiting 30,000 workers for a huge gas program. The training and transportation costs were more than offset by monthly wages of fifty dollars.[25] Nor is this type of transshipment peculiar to U.S. firms. For example, when the Swedish firm Skanska completed projects in Saudia Arabia in the 1970s, it sent its Thai workers on to the next sites in Algeria although that country offered "a reasonable supply of local labour."[26]

The specific model of the international division between mental and manual or supervisory and executory labor on construction projects in the periphery organized by metropolitan capital[27] was strictly implemented, for example, during the construction of the Panama Canal, for which (in part for racist reasons) all the skilled workers and no unskilled laborers were recruited from the United States.[28] The model was linguistically captured in Ghana shortly after World War II when the large British firm of George Wimpey Ltd. built a university: "It was not long before any white man of the works-foreman category became a 'wimpey.'"[29]

The model was reestablished by the U.S. military and U.S. construction firms, which recruited large numbers of low-wage third-country nationals, principally Filipinos, in the 1950s and 1960s to perform construction work in Korea, Vietnam, Thailand, and Guam especially during the Korean and Indochina wars.[30] This racial-geographic division of labor still flourishes. The common law of international construction projects prescribes, for example, that no U.S. workers ever take orders from Asian foremen. It also recreates a national wage hierarchy ranging from Filipinos to Sri Lankans.[31]

When, for example, a major British firm built one of the largest industrial projects ever undertaken, an aluminum smelter project in Dubai in the late 1970s, 500 Europeans supervised 3,500 Third World nationals. Seen from a different perspective, the system is also illustrated by the practice of one of the world's most diversified multinational construction firms, Bechtel, which in the early 1980s performed half of its work outside the United States but employed four-fifths of its workforce in the United States, where it concentrated its engineering and design activities.[32]

The fact that First World construction firms operating in the Third World have had access to this worldwide labor sourcing meant that no nation's firms

[25]*ENR*, Nov. 19, 1987, at 11; "Where the Constructors Strike it Rich" at 56; Jim Antoniou, *Construction in the Middle East* 70-71 (1978).

[26]Stephen Drewer, "Scandinavia," in *The Global Construction Industry* at 160, 174.

[27]This model was not universally applied in Latin America even in the pre-World War II period. Thus Pearson is said to have employed Mexican engineers and workers on his many turn-of-the-century projects in Mexico. See J. Spender, *Weetman Pearson First Viscount Cowdray 1856-1927*, at 100 (1930).

[28]See Velma Newton, *The Silver Men: West Indian Labour Migration to Panama 1850-1914*, at 36-47 (1984); Cameron, *The Impossible Dream* at 142.

[29]James Moxon, *Volta: Man's Greatest Lake* 28 (1969).

[30]See *Foreign Assistance and Related Agencies Appropriations for 1964: Hearings Before the Senate Committee on Appropriations*, 88th Cong., 1st Sess. 216-30 (1963) (statement and testimony of George Fischer, Exec. Sec'y, Overseas Craftsman's Ass'n, Inc.); L. Lazo, V. Teodosio, & P. Sto. Thomas, "Contract Migration Policies in the Philippines" at 12 (ILO, International Migration for Employment Working Paper 3, 1982); John Smart, "Saudi Demand for Filipino Workers: Labor Migration Issues in the Middle East," 9 *APCF*, Aug. 1982, at 1, 2.

[31]Telephone interview with Gary Koontz (July 21, 1993).

[32]P. Marsh, "The Dubai Aluminium Smelter Project," in *Management of International Construction Projects: Proceedings of a Conference Organized by The Institution of Civil Engineers* 155 (1985); *U.S. International Competitiveness: The Construction Industry: Hearing Before the Subcomm. on International Policy & Trade of the House Comm. on Foreign Affairs*, 98th Cong., 1st Sess. 11 (1985) (testimony of Michael Stephenson, vice president, Bechtel National, Inc.).

could compete primarily on the basis of a cheap captive labor force. The one exception was South Korean companies. At least through the 1970s, virtually all Korean construction workers in the Middle East worked for Korean firms, which, in turn, employed almost exclusively Korean workers. With labor costs preeminent in international construction projects, South Korean construction firms, by employing manual workers at wages only one-quarter of those paid to workers from Western capitalist countries, were, at least on labor-intensive projects, ultimately able not only to break through the oligopoly maintained by First World firms, but to become, for a time during the early 1980s, the leading contractors in Saudi Arabia. The Korean firms' meteoric rise was reflected in their construction exports, which jumped a hundred-fold from $83 million in 1972 to $8 billion in 1978. By 1983, 162,000 South Korean construction workers were employed abroad, 150,000 of them in the Middle East.[33] Importing their own nationals enabled Korean firms to "impose their own standards of discipline without difficulty" especially when the entire workforce was employed under the terms of a standard labor contract, designed by the South Korean government, that entitles employers to dismiss workers who instigate a slowdown or work at another construction site.[34]

South Korean firms were, however, themselves soon overtaken by others from Turkey, the Philippines, Thailand, India, Pakistan, and Bangladesh, which "as an element of their national economic planning...have invested in export construction capability as a means of raising export income."[35] By using the South Korean model of "price dumping via wage cuts," they "began to deprive Korean firms of their comparative advantage built around cheapo labor costs."[36] Consequently, South Korean construction firms too began hiring laborers from even lower-wage third countries such as Thailand, Pakistan, India, Bangladesh, and the Philippines. The Korean firms paid them only half of the wages that they offered Korean workers overseas, whose own low basic wage for an eight-hour day caused them to work overtime despite the consequences to their health of such long workdays in temperatures of 50° centigrade. The Third World workers' productivity was sufficiently close to the Koreans' that the Korean firms were able to achieve the desired cost reductions. But once the focus of Saudi construction projects shifted from labor-intensive infrastructure to technology-intensive industrial projects, even very low wage costs could not keep the Korean firms competitive. Because the Korean firms failed to diversify—in 1982, for example, more than 90 per cent of their new contracts (by value) was to be performed in the Middle East—their loss of the Middle Eastern market also signaled their decline on the world market altogether. This decline was clearly mirrored in the rankings of the 250 largest international contractors: the contingent of Korean firms, which had peaked at thirty in 1982, fell by 1989 to a mere four; likewise, their share of the value of Middle East contracts fell from more than one-fifth in 1982 to zero seven years later.[37] Stymied in the Middle East, some South Korean contractors have

---

[33]See Strassmann, "The United States" at 33; Kim, "Contract Migration in the Republic of Korea" at 1, 21; Chung In Moon, "Korean Contractors in Saudi Arabia: Their Rise and Fall," 40 *MEJ* 614, 616-18 (1986); OECD, *Globalisation of Industrial Activities: Four Case Studies: Auto Parts, Chemicals, Construction and Semiconductors* 107, 111 (1992).

[34]Mahlon Apgar, "Succeeding in Saudi Arabia," *HBR*, Jan.-Feb. 1977, at 14, 33; Kim, "Contract Migration in the Republic of Korea" at 27. Hedley Smyth, *Property Companies and the Construction Industry in Britain* 202 (1985), confuses or incorrectly lumps Japanese with South Korean construction firms.

[35]National Research Council, *Building for Tomorrow: Global Enterprise and the U.S. Construction Industry* 17 (1988). On Brazil "as the South Korea of the Western Hemisphere," see Maurice Samuelson, "How Brazil Won Angolan Dam Deal," *FT*, Nov. 22, 1984, § I at 4 (Nexis); "Brazil Pushes Foreign Work," *ENR*, Dec. 17, 1981, at 43.

[36]Moon, "Korean Contractors in Saudi Arabia" at 630.

[37]"Cut Backs Clip Korea's Wings" at 30; Dae Chang, "The Republic of Korea," in *The Global*

resorted to shipping even lower-wage Chinese workers to the United States (that is, to the Northern Mariana Islands).[38]

Reliance on third-country migrant workers is overwhelming in the Arab oil-producing states in which the local population either is too sparse in relation to the grandiose construction plans or has acquired ''a privileged and parasitic position'' inconsistent with the performance of manual labor. Thus in 1975-76, non-nationals—two-fifths of whom worked in construction—comprised six-sevenths of all construction workers in Bahrain, Kuwait, Libya, Oman, Qatar, Saudi Arabia, and the United Arab Emirates.[39]

Although the distribution of a portion of the oil revenues by the autocratic ruling families in the form of 'cake and circuses' to the citizen populations in countries such as Kuwait imparts a different character to the reasons for the unavailability of a local labor force,[40] the labor market consequences for late-twentieth-century multinational construction firms resemble those perceived by the U.S. Isthmian Canal Commission in casting about for labor at the turn of the century to build the Panama Canal:

> The native Isthmian will not work. He is naturally indolent...; has no ambition; his wants are few in number and easily satisfied. He can live for a few cents a day, and he prefers to take it easy, swinging in a hammock and smoking cigarettes. The native population is wholly unavailable.[41]

This lack of an indigenous proletariat cut off from easy escape into precapitalist livelihoods made the recruitment of an international migrant labor force both a necessity and a virtue. And even then its employers insisted that it be a class whose members had been educated in the permanence of their dependence on wages. For that very reason those in charge of building the Panama Canal were skeptical of the Chinese coolie because ''as soon as he gets a few dollars, he wants to keep a store,''[42] and dismayed that from ''the white man's point of view,'' the wants of West Indian workers were ''primitive, and their efforts to supply them hardly go beyond the aim of securing food enough to ward off starvation.''[43] Multinational construction firms' enhanced capacity for worldwide labor sourcing has dispensed them from the necessity of fashioning a world labor market in rigid conformity with precisely these characteristics. Indeed, unlike Brassey's mid-nineteenth-century pioneering operations in the periphery, the Mideast building boom not only did not give rise to an indigenous proletariat, but, to the extent that the Asian migrant workers on their return to their countries of origin invest their small savings in various penny-bourgeois spheres, the medium-term net international impact may be formal deproletarianization.[44]

Construction firms' worldwide sourcing of labor has added a new dimension to the real abstractions of capitalism that must be borne by workers.[45] By

---

*Construction Industry* at 141, 152; Kim, ''Contract Migration in the Republic of Korea'' at 34, 40-43; ''Top International Contractors,'' *ENR*, July 18, 1985, at 54, 55; Moon, ''Korean Contractors in Saudi Arabia'' at 630.

[38]Philip Shenon, ''Saipan Sweatshops Are No American Dream,'' *NYT*, July 18, 1993, at 1, col. 2, at 6, col. 6 (nat. ed.).

[39]Fred Halliday, *Arabia Without Sultans* 421 (1974); R. Shaw, ''Migration and Employment in the Arab World: Construction as a Key Policy Variable,'' 118 *ILR* 589, tab. 2 at 592 (1979).

[40]See e.g., Halliday, *Arabia Without Sultans* at 432-40.

[41]Peter Hains, ''The Labor Problem on the Panama Canal,'' 179 *NAR* 42, 50 (1904).

[42]*Id.* at 50.

[43]William Sibert & John Stevens, *Construction of the Panama Canal* 111 (1915).

[44]See Cyrus Mechkat, ''Production d'architecture, concentration du capital et migration du travail dans le golfe arabo-persique,'' in [4] *PBE: 1982, Labour in Building and Construction* 4-8, 4-36 (1983).

[45]See Marc Linder, *Reification and the Consciousness of the Critics of Political Economy: Studies in*

metaphorically analogizing workers and money and the labor market and foreign exchange market, John Dunning, one of the foremost specialists on multinational enterprises, inadvertently captures an aspect of this reification of human beings inherent in their transformation into a mere coordinate factor of production. Dunning called attention to one of the real abstractions of capitalism by characterizing international construction companies that transport unskilled workers across national borders as "performing an arbitrage function which the international labour market is apparently unable to do."[46] By the same token, however, if "[a]rbitrage is the mechanism which makes two markets, physically separate, a single market in the economic sense,"[47] constructors have performed that function only imperfectly. The enclave-exclave structure of the projects that multinational construction firms carry out in the Middle East with third-country Asian workers has meant that there is strictly speaking no labor market at all in the "host" country. Thus although the labor markets, for example, of Thailand and Kuwait have not become one economically, the firms have "been able to create new O[wnership] advantages."[48]

### Feckless International Labor Law

I am immensely struck by the character of American employees who are engaged not merely in superintending the work, but in doing all the jobs that need skill and intelligence. [M]en and machines do their task, the white men supervising matters and handling the machines, while the tens of thousands of black men do the rough manual labor where it is not worth while to have machines do it.[49]

The analysis that the International Labour Organisation (ILO) has made of the advantages of a world construction labor market accruing to countries such as Saudi Arabia applies also to the multinational building firms: "[B]y increasing the number of sources of its labour the labour importing country reduces the prospect of the formation of a union of emigrant workers or a cartel of labour exporting countries...."[50] Overcoming whatever competitive antagonisms otherwise divide them,[51] multinational construction firms and their state and private customers have reached a consensus that, in order to maintain the upper hand over atomized migrant workers who might seek to take advantage of the projects' tight deadlines and the lack of a local labor force willing to engage in hard physical labor, several counterforces are indispensable: enclave-like work camps building sites to segregate the labor force from the local population, rapid means of international transportation to expedite the shipment of replacements, and state-enforced violence.[52]

Thus in 1975 when 100 Pakistani workers "rioted over 'wages and living conditions' at a $400 million LNG plant that Bechtel [wa]s building on Das Island

---

*the Development of Marx' Theory of Value* 317-25 (1975).

[46]John Dunning, *Multinational Enterprises and the Global Economy* 351 (1993).

[47]Charles Kindleberger, *International Economics* 60 (3d ed. 1963 [1953]).

[48]Dunning, *Multinational Enterprises* at 351.

[49]Letter from President Theodore Roosevelt to Kermit Roosevelt, Nov. 20, 1906, in 5 *The Letters of Theodore Roosevelt* 496, 497-98 (Elting Morison ed., 1952).

[50]C. Stahl, "International Labour Migration and the Asean Countries" at 95 (ILO, International Migration for Employment Working Paper 13, 1982).

[51]For an example of such a dispute involving a project mentioned in the text paragraph, see Abu Dhabi Gas Liquefaction Co., Ltd. v. Eastern Bechtel Corp., in *FT*, June 29, 1982, sect. I, at 8 (Nexis).

[52]Ismail Serageldin et al., *Manpower and International Labor Migration in the Middle East and North Africa* 49-51 (1983).

in the Arabian Gulf... [t]hey were shipped home after apologies to the governments involved."[53] Two years later, when the "grueling" working conditions of some 4,000 Korean workers in Jubail, Saudi Arabia "caused some riots," they too were "rapidly quelled."[54] To discourage future such acts of ingratitude, a Saudi Security Forces firing squad is said to have summarily executed three workers at random. "Saudi authorities tell the story to new arrivals to frighten them into behaving...and the executions worked."[55] Nevertheless, the rebellion persuaded the *Economist* Intelligence Unit that "exploitation of cheap labour from the Far East may not be a simple solution." If Asian workers' "dissatisfaction" arises out of their awareness of "the major difference in wages and living standards between themselves, the local Arab population and Western expatriates,"[56] enforced ignorance may dampen expectations. The relative infrequency of such revolts may therefore be a function of the fact that spatially segregated exclave workers "are under the control of employers in respect of virtually every aspect of their daily lives in the camps."[57]

If, on the other hand, workers' protests are ignited not by comparisons with others' living and working conditions but rather with the promises that were made to them at the time and place of recruitment in Asia, then camp segregation cannot in itself blunt the insight. In fact, Asian workers recruited to the Gulf commonly do "find themselves at the mercy of someone who provides only the very minimum of facilities resulting in conditions no better than the ones he [sic] left behind." Desperation (for example, for early discharge from the South Korean army) and fraud are partial answers to the market-knows-best question as to why workers—including skilled U.S. building trades workers—would accept employment so far from home if the conditions leave them no better off.[58]

One of the coercively fraudulent employment practices that has prompted such rebellions has long been well-known to domestic and international migrants in a number of industries. Under so-called contract substitution, "Asians who have signed a contract before leaving home are confronted with a choice on arrival of either signing a fresh contract, providing for a substantial wage cut and reduced working conditions, or an order to leave the country immediately."[59] High unemployment in the Asian sending countries has also led to intense competition for jobs in the Middle East, which in turn has enabled recruiters to increase the fees they charge workers:

> The process of securing work abroad can put the prospective migrant heavily in debt.... Because...of the need to recover the huge initial investment made prior to departure..., migrant workers are in an extremely vulnerable situation on their arrival.... This pressure...means that migrant workers frequently work long hours under hazardous conditions and take unnecessary risks...for fear of losing their jobs or earnings.[60]

---

[53]"Where the Constructors Strike it Rich" at 56.

[54]Youssef Ibrahim, "How Koreans Built Saudi Success," *NYT*, June 19, 1978, at D5, col. 1-2.

[55]Said Aburish, *Pay-Off: Wheeling and Dealing in the Arab World* 78-79 (1985). Although Aburish dates this strike to 1981, he appears to be referring to the same one mentioned in the text.

[56]Antoniou, *Construction in the Middle East* at 73.

[57]Kim, "Contract Migration in the Republic of Korea" at 37.

[58]Antoniou, *Construction in the Middle East* at 68-69 (quotation), 72. On complaints by U.S. workers recruited to work on a large petrochemical project in the Virgin Islands, see Richard Korman, "The Other Side of Paradise," *ENR*, June 7, 1993, at 6.

[59]Thomas Land, "Migrant Labour Suffering from Mid-East Cut-Backs," *IC*, June 1984, at 4.

[60]ILO, Sectoral Activities Programme, Building, Civil Engineering and Public Works Committee, Eleventh Session, *Measures to Overcome Obstacles to the Observance in the Construction Industry of ILO Standards* 64 (1986).

As these practices demonstrate, construction firms' control over this international migrant labor force has been significantly augmented by the accommodating role of the labor-importing states' regulations: "The ability to control workers' movements has been central to the Saudis' importation of foreign labour": the workers' "passports are usually held by their employers...to stop them from moving to better jobs or leaving the country on short notice."[61] In the United Arab Emirates, the state has rendered such employer self-help unnecessary: since 1980 foreign employees who leave their work before the expiration of their contracts are statutorily prohibited from accepting, and other employers are prohibited from offering, employment for the period of a year.[62]

Such actions on the part of labor-importing states are complemented by those of the states in the Asian "labour catchment area," such as Pakistan, Bangladesh, Thailand, Sri Lanka, India, and the Philippines, which have organized the "manpower export business" in order to monitor and capture the workers' mandatory remittances as a major source of foreign exchange. Although the promotion of a hybrid private-state corporate labor export strategy might weaken the multinational firms' oligopsony, without the formation of a labor union as a countervailing force, such a strategy is calculated only to redistribute income from the construction employers to the Third World recruiting entities. By imposing and enforcing restrictions on the workers it sends to Middle East construction sites, the Philippines government, for example, deprives its own highly mobile citizens—in 1983 230,000 Filipinos were working in construction in the Middle East—of the freedom of movement that is a prerequisite of normally functioning labor markets.[63] South Korea has imposed similar restrictions on the mobility of its international construction labor force, also forbidding its nationals to form unions while engaged in "contract migration" in the Middle East.[64] And in the case of Pakistan, the standard overseas employment contract expressly requires employees solemnly to confirm: "I shall not strike or abet it in the Middle Eastern country. In case of such activity, the Employer may terminate my contract."[65]

Less easily classifiable are the thousands of workers sent abroad by Chinese firms, such as the China Civil Engineering Construction Corporation, since they began competing for overseas contracts in 1979. Although their crews work with large capitalist firms, such as Philipp Holzmann AG, the Chinese government contends that such international labor enterprises are designed to "'remedy the current pattern of...unequal international economic relations by...seeking the mini[m]um of profits.'"[66] In addition to the nominally cheap labor, which appeals even to other Third World (such as Brazilian) contractors who prefer Chinese workers to their own nationals, one of the virtues of "the Chinese-type contract" is that "any worker's complaint is directed to the Chinese government, not the

---

[61]Sara Marlowe, "Saudi Guest Workers Say Farewell," *FT*, Sept. 25, 1990, § I, at 2 (Nexis).

[62]United Arab Emirates, Federal Law to Regulate Employment Relationships, § 128 (No. 8, Apr. 20, 1980), reprinted in International Labour Organisation, *LS*, 1980—United Arab Emirates 1.

[63]Stahl, "International Labour Migration and the Asean Economies" at 17-18, 95-97; Catholic Institute for International Relations, *The Labour Trade: Filipino Migrant Workers Around the World* 80 (1987); Katherine Gibson & Julie Graham, "Situating Migrants in Theory: The Case of Filipino Migrant Contract Construction Workers," 29 *CC* 130 (Summer 1986); ILO, Sectoral Activities Programme, Building, Civil Engineering and Public Works Committee, Eleventh Session, *General Report* 131-32 (1987); ILO, Sectoral Activities Programme, *Recent Developments in Building, Civil Engineering and Public Works, Twelfth Session, Report I* at 29 (1992).

[64]Kim, "Contract Migration in the Republic of Korea" at 25; ILO, 1 *World Labour Report: Employment, Incomes, Social Protection, New Information Technology* 112 (1984).

[65]"Foreign Service Agreement," ¶ 33.e, reproduced in W. Böhning, *International Contract Migration in the Light of ILO Instruments, with Special Reference to Asian-Migrant-Sending Countries* 54, 56 (ILO, International Migration for Employment Working Paper 8, 1982).

[66]"China's Labour Pleases," *IC*, June 1983, at 31 (quoting Chen Muhua, Minister of Foreign Economic Relations); "Germans, Chinese in Iraq," *ENR*, Oct. 3, 1985, at 26.

contractor," thus sparing companies possible litigation costs.[67]

At the height of the Middle East construction boom, the ILO promulgated a Declaration of Principles Concerning Multinational Enterprises and Social Policy, stating both that the employees of such firms should have the right to organize and that governments offering special incentives to attract foreign investment should not include among them limitations on workers' freedom of association or freedom to engage in collective bargaining.[68] Yet in a region where labor unions are prohibited, labor "agitation" criminalized, "foreign workers deported for any form of protest," and labor codes either are so vague as to preclude enforcement or expressly exclude foreign workers, multinational firms have succeeded in freeing themselves of many of the labor market and legal limitations to which they are subject in their and their competitors' metropolitan domestic markets.[69] Migrant workers' contestation of such law-free international labor relations regimes has been made more difficult by the fact that both Saudi Arabia and the United States—the only such advanced capitalist country—have refused to ratify the ILO conventions guaranteeing workers freedom of association and the right to organize and to bargain collectively.[70]

Although ILO Convention No. 97 ("Concerning Migration for Employment") obligates each member state to afford to international migrant workers "treatment no less favorable than that which it applies to its own nationals" with regard to rights to union membership and collective bargaining, neither the United States nor any Middle Eastern oil-producing state has ratified it.[71] Even if Saudi Arabia, for example, had ratified this convention, the outcome for migrant construction workers there would be unchanged since the Saudi monarchy has deprived its own citizens of the rights in question by making it "illegal for any employee or employer to do any act that may bring pressure to bear on the freedom of the other or on the freedom of other employees or employers with the object of obtaining any interest or supporting any point of view which they adopt and which is inconsistent with the freedom of work...."[72]

---

[67]Josmar Verillo, "Brazil," in *The Global Construction Industry* at 180, 184-85, 190.

[68]"Tripartite Declaration of Principles concerning Multinational Enterprises and Social Policy," in International Labour Organisation, 66 *OB*, Ser. A, No. 1, ¶¶ 41, 45, at 49, 54 (1978). On the fecklessness of the ILO, see the vacuous remarks by the chief of its International Employment for Migration Branch, W. Böhning, "International Contract Migration in the Light of ILO Instruments," in *idem, Studies in International Labour Migration* 233, 244-45 (1984 [1982]).

[69]U.S. Bureau of Labor Statistics, *Labor Law and Practice in Saudi Arabia* 28 (Report No. 269, 1964); U.S. Bureau of Labor Statistics, *Labor Law and Practice in the Kingdom of Saudi Arabia* 57 (Report No. 407, 1972); Nazli Choucri, "Asians in the Arab World: Labor Migration and Public Policy," 22 *MES* 252, 266-67 (1986).

[70]Convention No. 87: Convention concerning Freedom of Association and Protection of the Right to Organise (1948); Convention No. 98: Convention concerning the Application of the Principles of the Right to Organise and to Bargain Collectively (1949), in International Labour Office, *International Labour Conventions and Recommendations: 1919-1981*, at 4, 7 (1982); International Labour Office, International Labour Conference, 75th Session, Report III (Part 5): *List of Ratifications of Conventions (as at 31 December 1987)*, at 59, 64-65 (1988); Edward Potter, *Freedom of Association, the Right to Organize and Collective Bargaining—The Impact on U.S. Law and Practice of Ratification of ILO Conventions No. 87 & No. 98*, at 109-12 (1984). New Zealand, which has a strong labor movement, has not ratified Convention 87 because its labor statute gives the government the authority to deregister unions in contravention of article 4 of Convention 87. See Gordon Anderson & Peter Brosnan, "Freedom of Association: New Zealand Law and ILO Convention 87," *NZLJ*, Sept. 1984, at 307; Gordon Anderson, "International Labour Standards and the Review of Industrial Law," 11 *NZJIR* 27 (1986).

[71]ILO Convention No. 97: Concerning Migration for Employment, art. 6, § 1 (1949); ILO, *List of Ratifications of Conventions* at 63. But see International Labour Office, *The Rights of Migrant Workers: A Guide to ILO Standards for the Use of Migrant Workers and Their Organisations* 6 (1986) ("The right of all workers in member States of the ILO to belong to trade unions is protected by...Convention...Nos. 87 and 98...and by the Constitution of the ILO, so that this basic right must be protected even in countries whose governments have not ratified the Conventions").

[72]Saudi Arabia, Labor Code, § 22 (Royal Decree No. M/21, Nov. 15, 1969), reprinted in International Labour Organisation, *LS*, 1969—Saudi Arabia 1. Violators can be sentenced to three years' imprisonment.

Such repressive bans on unions—to which the institutional memory of First World employers runneth not in their home markets[73]—have been adduced as one reason why, even during the period when U.S. firms employed in the Middle East significant numbers of U.S. construction workers who were members of building trades unions in the United States, these firms were always able to avoid collective agreements.[74]   The potential conflict between the Saudi Arabian statutory prohibition of collective bargaining and the U.S. National Labor Relations Act (NLRA), which makes it unlawful for employers "to interfere with, restrain, or coerce employees in the exercise of...the right to bargain collectively,''[75] does not appear ever to have been litigated before a U.S. tribunal.

In light of the enormous proliferation of multinational employment relationships in construction, manufacturing, mining, and other industries, this lack of protection for potentially vulnerable workers or even of clear legal guidelines may itself be an incentive for firms to operate in this legal no-man's land.   One doctrinal barrier to reaching this question is the threshold issue of the extraterritorial applicability of the NLRA to U.S. workers temporarily employed abroad by U.S. firms.[76]   Surprisingly, even this matter has only rarely been adjudicated.   The two clearest cases involved the International Brotherhood of Electrical Workers, which in the 1970s sought to represent employees of Radio Corporation of America (RCA) at a Distant Early Warning site in Greenland and telephone equipment installers of General Telephone and Electric (GTE) working in Iran.   In both instances the National Labor Relations Board (NLRB) merely asserted apodictically that employees employed outside the United States do not fall under the jurisdiction of the NLRA.[77]

The only legal precedent that the NLRB cited on either occasion was a decision by the U.S. Supreme Court that neither logically supports the claim that the NLRA has no extraterritorial application nor presents any socioeconomic arguments as to why extraterritoriality would not serve the purposes of the NLRA.[78]   In that earlier case, *Benz v. Compania Naviera Hidalgo, S.A.*, the Supreme Court merely held that the NLRA did not apply to picketing by a U.S. union of a ship that was owned by a foreign employer and operated entirely by foreign seamen under an agreement made abroad under the laws of a foreign country, while the ship was temporarily in a U.S. port.   In fact, the Supreme Court's explanatory observation that the NLRA "is concerned with industrial strife between American employers and employees" could, in connection with its emphasis of the fact that the conditions of work were prescribed by the British

---

*Id.* § 190.   On the origins of these bans as responses to strikes by Aramco workers in the 1950s, see Halliday, *Arabia Without Sultans* at 66-67.

[73]See Karen Orren, *Belated Feudalism: Labor, the Law, and Liberal Development in the United States* (1991).

[74]Telephone interviews with Bill Sheridan and Rick Swaak, National Foreign Trade Council, New York (Feb. 3 & 4, 1993); Joe Maloney, secretary-treasurer, Building & Construction Trades Dept., AFL-CIO, Washington, D.C. (Feb. 4, 1993); Gary Koontz (July 21, 1993) (stating that U.S. construction workers have never worked under union contracts outside the United States except pursuant to a requirement in a U.S. government contract).

[75]29 U.S.C. §§ 158, 157 (1991).

[76]On the applicability of U.S. labor laws in general to the employment abroad by U.S. multinational firms of U.S. nationals and non-U.S. nationals, see James Zimmerman, *Extraterritorial Employment Standards of the United States: The Regulation of the Overseas Workplace* (1992).

[77]RCA OMS, Inc. (Greenland) v. International Bhd. of Elec. Workers, 202 N.L.R.B. 228 (1973); GTE Automatic Electric Inc. v. International Bhd. of Elec. Workers, 226 N.L.R.B. 1222 (1976). But see Great Lakes Dredge & Dock Co. v. United Marine Division, 240 N.L.R.B. 197 (1979) (upholding jurisdiction over U.S. employer that refused to hire workers in the United States for dredging operations in Saudi Arabia because they were union members).

[78]See Gary Nothstein & Jeffrey Ayres, "The Multinational Corporation and the Extraterritorial Application of the Labor Management Relations Act," 10 *CILJ* 1, 24-25 (1976).

Maritime Board,[79] buttress the claim of workers, such as some of the aforementioned GTE employees, who worked under a union contract with the employer in the United States before being assigned to work overseas, that they and their U.S. employer can carve out a labor law exclave overseas where applicability of the law of the worksite-country would result in less favorable treatment of the workers.

The NLRB, however, decontextualizing phrases in the Supreme Court decision, has failed to come to grips with these substantive considerations. Commenting—in dictum—on the consequences of *Benz* for workers like the RCA employees, the NLRB quoted the Supreme Court's observation that "[t]he only American connection was that the controversy erupted while the ship was transiently in a United States port and American labor unions participated in its picketing."[80] From this statement the NLRB directly concluded that "although the employer and employees were American and the hiring occurred in America, the employees worked entirely in Greenland and any controversy would occur in Greenland, so that the single element in Benz that might have provided a basis for jurisdiction was lacking in RCA."[81] This conclusion, however, lacks textual anchorage because the Supreme Court never held that a U.S. territorial worksite is an absolute precondition for—let alone the only basis of—jurisdiction over purely U.S. parties. Rather, the Supreme Court merely held that in light "of the clear congressional purpose to apply the [NLRA] only to American workers and employers,"[82] the absence of U.S. parties to the underlying employment relationship was fatal to a claim of jurisdiction.

Despite this defective precedential foundation, the NLRB continues to deny jurisdiction over U.S. employees working overseas for a U.S. employer and the leading labor law treatise approves of that practice.[83] Only where a labor union's alleged unfair labor practice was at issue, have the courts and the Board recognized that *Benz* "did not restrict the scope of the NLRA to conduct which occurs within the geographic boundaries of the United States."[84] Confronted with this precedential monolith, U.S. construction unions, which perceive themselves as lacking the economic strength to enforce a collective bargaining agreement thousands of miles from the United States, have chosen not to contest the merely legal barriers to transnational organizing (except for their membership in Canada).[85] Such a predicament might not arise in countries such as Tunisia that permit key workers of the contractor's imported task force to benefit from the more favorable provision as between the host- and home-country law.[86] In other national legal systems, however, in which the extraterritoriality of labor laws is not an obstacle, application of international conflicts of labor law offers the possibility that First World employees could prevail against their employer's defense that it was merely obeying the law of the worksite.

Precedent for precisely such an outcome exists. The great expansion of international construction work performed by Finnish firms since the beginning of

[79]Benz v. Compania Naviera Hidalgo, S.A., 353 U.S. 138, 139, 143-44 (1957).

[80]*Benz* at 142.

[81]Freeport Transport, Inc. v. Carr, 220 N.L.R.B. 833, 834 (1975).

[82]Windward Shipping v. American Radio Ass'n, 415 U.S. 104, 110 (1974).

[83]NLRB General Counsel Advice Memorandum, Case No. 19-CC-1300, 1981 NLRB GCM Lexis 95; *The Developing Labor Law* 1581-82 (Patrick Hardin ed., 3d ed. 1992)

[84]Dowd v. International Longshoremen's Ass'n, 975 F.2d 779, 788 (11th Cir. 1992). See also International Longshoremen's Ass'n v. Coastal Stevedoring Co., 313 NLRB No. 53 (1993).

[85]Telephone interview with Bud Fisher, International Brotherhood of Electrical Workers, Washington, D.C. (Mar. 8, 1993).

[86]Ridha Ferchiou, "Tunisia," in *Global Construction Industry* at 199, 206.

the 1970s, making the industry one of the leading Finnish exporters, furnished the Finnish Labor Court with ample opportunity to adjudicate the issue. The industry-wide collective agreement between the Finnish Building Industry Federation and the Building Workers' Federation in force since 1972 provided that Finnish labor law would apply to the temporary employment overseas of Finnish workers employed by Finnish firms. It also specified that workers were to receive special cost of living allowances. A large multinational construction firm, Yleinen Insinööritoimisto (YIT), nevertheless sent employees to worksites in Saudi Arabia with contracts specifying that Saudi law would apply and failed to observe the aforementioned clause. The union then sued YIT in the Finnish Labor Court, alleging that the employer had also violated the Finnish Hours of Work Act as well as the hours provisions of the collective agreement. YIT defended, inter alia, on the ground that collective agreements were invalid in Saudi Arabia. The court, while conceding the force of this point, finessed it by ruling in 1979 and 1980 against the employer on the ground that terms derived from foreign collective agreements could and, under the Finnish Collective Agreements Act must, be included in individual contracts of employment.[87]

The presence of strong domestic construction unions and the enforcibility of much more stringent labor and immigration laws may account for the fact that First World firms generally do not import Third World (or even export their own domestic or other First World) workers for projects in other First World countries, although Scandinavian firms have relied on their own workers for projects in the Soviet Union.[88] One exception was the expansion of a New Zealand Refining Company refinery at Whangarei, one of the largest construction projects ever undertaken in New Zealand, by a joint venture between a U.S. firm, Badger, and a Japanese firm, Chiyoda, in 1982. The New Zealand Federation of Labour objected to the recruitment of boilermakers and riggers from the United Kingdom at a time of high unemployment especially because the employers allegedly both excluded certain local workers as troublemakers and violated their contractual responsibility to train New Zealand workers in order to maximize their employment on the project. This importation led to violent strikes, which the state ultimately quelled by enactment of an unprecedented statute. The Whangarei Refinery Expansion Project Disputes Act named eight scaffolders with whom it was unlawful for the workers to refuse to work, imposed fines for further unauthorized strikes, and deprived workers who refused to work under the terms of the statute of unemployment insurance benefits for four months.[89]

By the same token, however, metropolitan construction firms have a long history of importing workers from other capitalist countries in order to break strikes or otherwise to readjust temporarily unfavorable labor markets. One of the most infamous such incidents took place in London in 1877 when the firm building

---

[87]See Timo Esko, *The Law Applicable to International Labour Relations* 7, 13-14 (1982); *Työtuomioistuimen Vuosikirja,* TT 1979 No. 169 and TT 1980 No. 135; Felice Morgenstern, *International Conflicts of Labour Law: A Survey of the Law Applicable to the International Employment Relation* 104 (1984); A. Suviranta, *Labour Law and Industrial Relations in Finland* 55-56 (1987). In 1979 YIT was the 100th largest firm in terms of the value of international contracts awarded that year. "Non-U.S. Firms Grab Big Share of Global Market," *ENR,* Dec. 6, 1979, at 26, 29.

[88]Telephone interviews with Mark Nacu, Human Resources Dept., Bechtel Corp., San Francisco (Feb. 3, 1993); Joe Maloney, secretary-treasurer, Building & Construction Trades Dept., AFL-CIO, Washington, D.C. (Feb. 4, 1993); Terry Chamberlain, Associated General Contractors, Washington, D.C. (Feb. 8, 1993); Drewer, "Scandinavia" at 174.

[89]See Whangarei Refinery Expansion Project, Arbitration Court 162/82 and 198/82, [1982] NZILR 597, 605; Whangarei Refinery Expansion Project Disputes Act 1984, N.Z. Stat. 1984, No. 2, *repealed by* Labour Relations Act 1987, N.Z. Stat. 1987, No. 77, § 358; "Before the Wave Breaks," *Economist,* June 30, 1984, at 45; *OGJ,* July 2, 1984, at 42 (Nexis); *Report of the Committee of Inquiry into Industrial Relations on the Whangarei Refinery Expansion Project at Marsden Point* 95-127 (1985); Badger, "Construction Services" (n.d.).

the New Law Courts, Bull and Company, responded to a strike by masons over higher wages and fewer hours by importing strikebreakers from Germany, Italy, and even the United States. Although the majority of the U.S. workers promptly joined the union, the employer ultimately prevailed.[90]

In the early part of the twentieth century German construction firms imported thousands of Italian and Polish workers to perform heavy and unhealthful infrastructure labor in Germany. Italian migrants also built railways and performed other construction work in France, Austria, Switzerland, Turkey, and Tunisia.[91] Once again in the 1950s and 1960s construction firms in West Germany, France, Switzerland, and other Western European countries were able to keep down wage costs by importing hundreds of thousands of workers from Italy, Yugoslavia, Turkey, Spain, Portugal, and North Africa for work on domestic projects under conditions inferior to those of domestic workers. In West Germany, for example, foreign workers accounted for 28 per cent of total construction employment by 1972. That country's largest construction firm, Philipp Holzmann, based its profit-maximizing strategy in large part on the employment of a reserve army of such workers.[92] Then beginning in the 1970s, Rumanian, Polish, and Yugoslav construction firms were permitted to employ their nationals on construction sites in West Germany. The use of such project-tied workers from lower-wage countries is expected to increase once freedom of movement is established in the European Community.[93]

Third World states, however, have thus far unsuccessfully insisted on negotiating the issue of opening First World construction markets to Third World labor. They have sought to do so as a countermove to demands by First World states that the General Agreement on Tariffs and Trade (GATT) extend its rules to cover international trade in services in order to preserve access to markets in the Third World. Whereas large internationally oriented U.S. construction firms tend to favor inclusion as a means of forcing open markets, smaller firms operating in local markets have opposed GATT coverage for fear of increased competition from foreign firms operating in the United States.[94]

After the multinational firms prevailed in the shaping of U.S. GATT policy on this issue, the more industrialized developing countries such as Brazil, Egypt, India, and Venezuela resisted the advanced capitalist countries' proposals. Basing themselves on infant industry arguments and the ramifying developmental linkages emanating from the growth of a domestic construction industry, they feared that such liberalization would "tend to freeze the industrialized countries' existing lead in service industries."[95] In order to create a bargaining position, Third World

---

[90]*Times*, Oct. 23, 1877, at 9, col. 5; Oct. 24, 1877, at 9, col. 6; Oct. 30, 1877, at 4, col. 4; "The Importation of Foreign Labour," 44 *Engineer* 299 (1877); Sidney Webb & Beatrice Webb, *The History of Trade Unionism* 328-29 (new ed. 1902 [1894]).

[91]Otto Liebich, *Organisations- und Arbeitsverhältnisse im Baugewerbe: Eine volkswirtschaftliche Studie* 75 (1922); Robert Foerster, *The Italian Emigration of Our Time* 135, 139, 152, 157, 174-77, 191-93, 211, 214-15 (1924); Hans Meyer-Heinrich, "Die Entwicklung des Gesamtunternehmens und die Wandlung seiner Organisation," in *Philipp Holzmann im Wandel von Hundert Jahren 1849-1949*, at 9, 84 (Hans Meyer-Heinrich ed., n.d. [1949]).

[92]Hauptverband der Deutschen Bauindustrie, *BJ 1975*, at 56; Jörn Janssen, "Unternehmenspolitik der Großkonzerne verantwortlich für Baukostenexplosion," 25 *WSI Mitteilungen* 392, 394-95 (1972).

[93]See ILO, Building, Civil Engineering and Public Works Committee, Sixth Session, *The International Migration of Labour in the Construction Industry* 39, 73-75 (1959); ILO, *Meeting of Experts on Problems of Foreign Construction Workers Employed in European Countries* (1979); "Ostblock-Baufirmen verunsichern die deutsche Baubranche," *HB*, Feb. 1, 1974, at 18; "Auch Ostblock-Baufirmen spüren jetzt die Folgen der Flaute," *HB*, Aug. 21, 1974, at 5; Edith Gross, "Migration Within and Towards the European Community and Its Impact on the Construction Industry," 12 *PBE* (forthcoming 1993).

[94]See James Lee & David Walters, *International Trade in Construction, Design, and Engineering Services* 63-111 (1989).

[95]*ENR*, Oct. 10, 1985, at 7; U.N. Centre on Transnational Corporations, *Transnational Corporations in*

countries pressed the issue of labor mobility—India, South Korea,[96] and Mexico were planning to send their construction workers to the United States while Pakistan targeted the European labor market—by urging the inclusion of labor as a service under GATT rules. Despite multinational firms' extensive promotion of international labor mobility as a cost-cutting strategy overseas, they were not amused by the Third World countries' effort to take this approach to its logical conclusion. The U.S. trade representative for services characterized as not "salable" the Mexican suggestion of "'a quid pro quo where we would provide an open market for their people and they would provide an open market for our investment.'"[97]

*the Construction and Design Engineering Industry* 40, 44 (1989).

[96]Impressed by the fact that average wages for construction workers in Alaska were twice as high as the salaries of Korean managers involved in a project on which it had bid, a Korean firm planned to hire as many naturalized Korean-American workers as possible. "Koreans Crack U.S. Market," *ENR*, Dec. 5, 1985, at 46.

[97]"Construction Labor Looms as Spoiler in Trade Talks," *ENR*, Jan. 19, 1989, at 12; "GATT Negotiator Nixes Foreign Unskilled Labor," *ENR*, Feb. 23, 1989, at 16. For the U.S. position on regulating trade in construction services with the Third World, see *U.S. National Study on Trade in Services: A Submission by the United States Government to the General Agreement on Tariffs and Trade* 128-33 (n.d. [1984]).

# 11

# The Internationalization of the Construction Industry: Empirical Indicators

> The number of contracting firms which possess the equipment and financial responsibility to construct large projects is probably so small that conditions bordering on oligopoly exist....[1]

Because many multinational construction firms remain privately owned and controlled and are therefore not subject to the disclosure requirements imposed on public issue corporations, assembling the data relevant to trends in their internationalization is much more difficult than for most other industries. It is, however, possible to begin studying the empirical development of the world industrial construction market for U.S. firms and all firms since 1963 and 1978 respectively on the basis of two unique sets of data compiled by the annual surveys conducted by the leading trade publication, *Engineering News-Record* (*ENR*). The journal has become "the principal source of information...by tracking down major tenders world-wide."[2] The data for U.S. firms cover the 400 largest nonresidential construction firms, which, in turn, account for virtually all overseas construction awards to U.S. firms and for the bulk of U.S. domestic nonresidential work.[3] The counterpart set of data for all firms covers the world's 250 largest firms.

The largest of these firms have oligopolized the huge market for the construction of the technically complex building component of the fixed capital of their oligopolistic counterparts in the retailing, manufacturing, and especially

---

[1]Clarence Long, Jr., *Building Cycles and the Theory of Investment* 144 (1940).

[2]Moody's Investors Service & U.N. Centre on Transnational Corporations, *Directory of the World's Largest Service Companies* 191 (Series I—Dec. 1990). In 1958 *ENR* began publishing tabulations of the largest U.S. contractors, adjusting the methodology, comprehensiveness, and strictness over the following five years until it reached its current scope of 400 firms' domestic and international awards. During these early years the data it reported excluded international contracts; the impetus to include overseas contracts appears to have stemmed from the large internationally oriented firms themselves, which objected to the low rankings resulting from the exclusion. See "ENR Spotlights 62 Biggest Contractors," Jan. 2, 1958, at 21; "Top Contractors," Apr. 17, 1958, at 11; "77 Firms Join $25-Million Club," Apr. 30, 1959, at 21; "Some Views on 'Top Contractors,'" June 18, 1959, at 30; "The 67 Top Contractors of 1959," July 28, 1960, at 19; "88 Swept Into Favored Position," July 20, 1961, at 24; "ENR's Top-Contractor List for 1961," July 26, 1962, at 22; "81 Firms Make Top Contractor List," Aug. 29, 1963, at 17.

[3]See "The 400," *ENR*, Aug. 6, 1964, at 69; "The 400," *ENR*, Apr. 9, 1970, at 42. In 1963, these 400 firms accounted for 24 per cent of the value of all contract construction awards in the United States; if residential construction contracts, on which they by and large do not bid, are excluded, the share rises to 44 per cent. By the late 1970s, these figures had levelled off at about two-fifths and three-quarters respectively. Calculated according to data in U.S. Bureau of the Census, *Historical Statistics of the United States*, pt. 2, ser. N 78-89 at 624; *idem, SAUS: 1982-83*, tab. 1335 at 745 (103d ed. 1982). As explained below, the double-counting that inflates these data makes them valuable for the trends they indicate rather than for the absolute values. This caveat was underscored once *ENR* shifted to amplified double-counting by including the value of construction management contracts in 1980: at that point the contract awards began to exceed the actual value of construction put in place.

power-production industries as well as of the large-scale general conditions of production embodied in infrastructure.[4] Many of these firms were already well capitalized enough in the early 1960s to build offices and warehouses for their own investment.[5]

*ENR* obtains the underlying figures, which reflect the prospective value of contracts awarded—not the value of work performed—in a given year, by means of a questionnaire which it sends to about 2,000 U.S. firms.[6] For nonresponding non-U.S. firms, the journal attempts to estimate annual awards.[7] The resulting data suffer from a number of defects that make them unreliable as indicators of absolute dollar amounts.[8] In particular, *ENR* systematically overstates the aggregate volume of building activity by double-counting the sub-contracts already accounted for by main contract awarded to other large firms. Such a procedure also distorts firm rankings by understating the positions of those companies that focus on "pure construction using [their] own workforce."[9] *ENR* compounded the problem of double-counting in 1980 when it began including the value of most "construction management contracts."

Construction or project management, in which the managing firm's chief function "is to ride herd on other contractors and to make certain that the work is carried out on time, within budget" for costs plus a fixed fee, has modified the traditional system of general contractors as projects have grown more complex technically while the concomitant increase in capital costs has led to demands for shorter deadlines.[10] Although the diminished commitment of capital and risk associated with the shift from construction to management[11] does warrant analysis of "the changing ways construction's Top 400 do business," double-counting of the entire value of such projects introduced an additional source of overestimation.[12]

---

[4]For a breakdown of industrial and commercial construction by industry and firm for 1991, see "Top Owners," *ENR*, Nov. 23, 1992, at 22-38. On infrastructure, see generally Dieter Läpple, *Staat und allgemeine Produktionsbedingungen: Grundlagen zur Kritik der Infrastrukturtheorien* (1973).

[5]"The 400," *ENR*, Aug. 6, 1964, at 70. At the time it was reported that all available industrial land in Chicago was held by contractors. *Id.* at 71.

[6]Rob McManamy, "Bigger Firms Busted in Foreign Work," *ENR*, Apr. 14, 1988, at 66, 67.

[7]"Top International Contractors," *ENR*, July 16, 1981, at 92.

[8]*ENR* prefers the criterion of awards to construction put in place or annual revenues because "neither method would so definitively show the direction of the [worldwide construction] market nor would they allow for much mobility in a contractor's rank." "The 400," *ENR*, Apr. 10, 1975, at 50, 67. *ENR* has introduced a ranking of U.S. firms based on revenues, but the refusal by many of the largest firms to provide the data has thus far limited their usefulness. William Krizan, "Ranking Data Rankles Some," *ENR*, May 24, 1993, at 67.

[9]Basil Caplan, "Decade of Diversification Keeps M-K Ahead," *IC*, July 1983, at 26 (referring to Morrison-Knudsen).

[10]Dan Cordtz, "Bechtel Thrives on Billion-Dollar Jobs," *Fortune*, Jan. 1975, at 90, 146; J. Elton, "Management Contracting," in *Management of International Construction Projects: Proceedings of a Conference Organized by The Institution of Civil Engineers* 73 (1985) (author is employee of Bechtel Great Britain Ltd.).

[11]There are also at-risk variants of contract management as well as hybrid for-fee/at-risk variants. "The Top 100 CM Firms," *ENR*, June 21, 1993, at 31-32.

[12]*ENR* was vastly understating when it conceded that the innovation might "cause some rankings to appear inflated...." *ENR*, Apr. 16, 1981, at 9, 87. During the first three years of the new method of counting, this additional rubric inflated aggregate awards by $30-40 billion. Although *ENR* publishes data that would make it possible to eliminate all the construction management contract figures for the year 1980 and forward, such an across-the-board deletion would in itself distort the result because some large firms perform construction and construction management on the same project whereas others do not. "The ENR 400," *ENR*, Apr. 16, 1981, at 85. The magazine acknowledged this problem by conceding that "due to the difficulty in defining the terms of construction management, some ambiguity remains in the survey." *ENR*, Apr. 16, 1981, at 87. Because construction management occupies a significant but fluctuating share of business (which is generally higher for the larger firms and in overseas work), even some of the distribution data may be incomparable from 1980 forward. See "The Top 400 Contractors," *ENR*, Apr.

In spite of these upward biases, the *ENR* data are nevertheless useful for capturing trends over time and relative distributions among firms and countries.

## The Internationalization of the U.S. Construction Industry and the Creation of a Proto-World Market

A stage has been reached where we can truly say that the world is our market....[13]

The growth in the value of international contracts of U.S. firms, as shown in table 11.1 and figure 11.1, has been considerably greater than that of domestic contract value for the four hundred largest U.S. firms. While domestic contract awards of these largest firms increased 14-fold, from $11 billion in 1963 to $156 billion in 1992, the corresponding figures for international contracts rose from $900 million to $75 billion, or an increase of 83-fold. In other words, the overseas component grew about six times as rapidly. As a result, the international share of total contract value for the 400 largest firms rose from about one-fourteenth to almost one-third.

Because the relative weight of the world market rather than the size of the absolute increases is the focus of the analysis, the data in this and later tables have not been adjusted for inflation; the aforementioned methodological deficiencies in the *ENR* survey also render absolute data much less useful. In order to place the "real" expansion of the world market in perspective, however, the aforementioned growth rates can be relativized by application of a U.S. construction industry-specific price index. From 1963 to 1992 this index rose by about 370 per cent. Consequently, the inflation-adjusted increases in domestic and international contract value during this 29-year period were approximately three-fold and 18-fold respectively.[14]

This growth, however, has not been uniform because the evolution of international contracts has been much more spasmodic than the course of domestic contract awards. Overseas work, fueled by the contracts awarded by the U.S. military in Vietnam, quadrupled from 1963 to 1966, reaching a plateau that held until 1972. The two major beneficiaries were Raymond International and Morrison-Knudsen; Brown & Root and J.A. Jones were also major participants.[15] Contract awards then virtually doubled every year for the next three years, peaking

---

14, 1988, at 32-33. Ironically, two years before *ENR* introduced this double-counting, it disparaged the domestic macroeconomic importance of construction management arrangements because they had "little direct beneficial effect on the U.S. economy" in the form of exports of materials, installed machinery, and construction equipment. "U.S. 'Arrogance' Costs Firms Billions in Lost Jobs," *ENR*, Nov. 29, 1979, at 26. Bill Krizan, who is in charge of the *ENR* survey, confirmed its basic flaws. Telephone interview (Feb. 17, 1993). ENR also introduced the value of construction management contracts in its international survey beginning with 1980. "Top International Contracts," *ENR*, July 16, 1981, at 92.

[13]George Havas, "Foreign Work Has Special Problems," 28 *CE* 905, 907 (1958) (vice-president and chief engineer, Henry J. Kaiser Co.).

[14]The following types of construction sub-markets enter into the Bureau of the Census composite fixed-weight construction price index: residential and non-residential buildings, highways, roads, railroads, conservation and development, electric light and power, gas, pipelines, and water-supply facilities. U.S. Bureau of Economic Analysis, *Business Statistics, 1963-91*, at 33, 151 (27th ed., 1992); *SCB*, Feb. 1993, at S-7. The Bureau of Economic Analysis has published price indexes broken down for purchases of the aforementioned kinds of structures. By and large the choice of index does not substantially change the inflation adjustment. U.S. Bureau of Economic Analysis, 2 *National Income and Product Accounts of the United States: 1959-88*, tab. 7.7 at 281-82 (1992). All of these indexes refer to construction in the United States and are not necessarily applicable to construction activity in the rest of the world, where the rates of inflation may have been higher or lower.

[15]See Richard Tregaskis, *Southeast Asia: Building the Bases, The History of Construction in Southeast Asia* 29, 426-27 (U.S. Dept. of the Navy, n.d. [1975]); "Vietnam Construction 50% Done," *ENR*, Feb. 9, 1967, at 31-33; Edwin L. Jones, *J.A. Jones Construction Company* (1965).

**Table 11.1**
**The 400 Largest U.S. Construction Firms, 1963-92**

| Year | Σ Contract Value ($ billion) | Σ Domestic Contract Value ($ billion) | Index (1963= 100) | Σ Foreign Contract Value ($ billion) | Index (1963= 100) | Foreign/ Σ Contract Value (%) |
|---|---|---|---|---|---|---|
| 1963 | 12.1 | 11.2 | 100 | 0.9 | 100 | 7 |
| 1964 | 16.1 | 14.0 | 125 | 2.1 | 233 | 13 |
| 1965 | 19.0 | 16.0 | 143 | 3.0 | 333 | 16 |
| 1966 | 21.9 | 18.2 | 163 | 3.7 | 411 | 17 |
| 1967 | 24.4 | 20.7 | 185 | 3.7 | 411 | 15 |
| 1968 | 28.6 | 25.1 | 224 | 3.5 | 389 | 12 |
| 1969 | 33.4 | 28.9 | 258 | 4.5 | 500 | 13 |
| 1970 | 32.4 | 28.4 | 254 | 4.0 | 444 | 12 |
| 1971 | 36.0 | 31.1 | 278 | 4.9 | 544 | 14 |
| 1972 | 40.0 | 36.4 | 325 | 3.6 | 400 | 9 |
| 1973 | 55.0 | 48.9 | 437 | 6.1 | 678 | 11 |
| 1974 | 75.6 | 63.9 | 571 | 11.7 | 1300 | 15 |
| 1975 | 69.5 | 47.7 | 426 | 21.8 | 2422 | 31 |
| 1976 | 59.9 | 44.3 | 396 | 15.6 | 1733 | 26 |
| 1977 | 72.8 | 56.9 | 508 | 15.9 | 1767 | 22 |
| 1978 | 79.9 | 61.6 | 550 | 18.3 | 2033 | 23 |
| 1979 | 91.3 | 69.1 | 617 | 22.2 | 2467 | 24 |
| 1980 | 113.0 | 66.0 | 589 | 47* | 5222 | 41 |
| 1981 | 162.8 | 114.0 | 1018 | 48.8 | 5422 | 30 |
| 1982 | 128.5 | 83.2 | 743 | 45.3 | 5033 | 35 |
| 1983 | 118.1 | 88.3 | 788 | 29.8 | 3311 | 25 |
| 1984 | 131.1 | 100.2 | 895 | 30.9 | 3433 | 24 |
| 1985 | 136.1 | 107.1 | 956 | 29.0 | 3222 | 21 |
| 1986 | 125.4 | 102.6 | 916 | 22.8 | 2533 | 18 |
| 1987 | 109.0 | 90.7 | 810 | 18.3 | 2033 | 17 |
| 1988 | 154.3 | 128.2 | 1144 | 26.1 | 2900 | 17 |
| 1989 | 187.0 | 147.7 | 1319 | 39.3 | 4366 | 21 |
| 1990 | 204.5 | 157.2 | 1404 | 47.3 | 5256 | 23 |
| 1991 | 229.8 | 156.8 | 1400 | 73.0 | 8111 | 32 |
| 1992 | 230.4 | 155.6 | 1389 | 74.8 | 8311 | 32 |

Source: "The 400," ENR: Aug. 6, 1964, at 69; Aug. 12, 1965, at 78; May 19, 1966, at 32; Apr. 27, 1967, at 34; Apr. 11, 1968, at 62; Apr. 10, 1969, at 70; Apr. 9, 1970, at 42; Apr. 8, 1971, at 46; Apr. 6, 1972, at 42; Apr. 12, 1973, at 46; Apr. 11, 1974, at 46; Apr. 10, 1975, at 50; Apr. 15, 1976, at 62; Apr. 14, 1977, at 66; Apr. 13, 1978, at 54; Apr. 12, 1979, at 70; Apr. 17, 1980, at 74; Apr. 16, 1981, at 82; Apr. 22, 1982, at 76; Apr. 28, 1983, at 64; Apr. 19, 1984, at 64; Apr. 18, 1985, at 46; Apr. 17, 1986, at 58; Apr. 16, 1987, at 50; Apr. 14, 1988, at 32; May 25, 1989, at 38; May 24, 1990, at 38; May 27, 1991, at 34; May 25, 1992, at 54; May 24, 1993, at 36.
*Beginning in 1980 the data include construction management contracts.

**Figure 11.1**
**The 400 Largest U.S. Construction Firms, 1963-92**

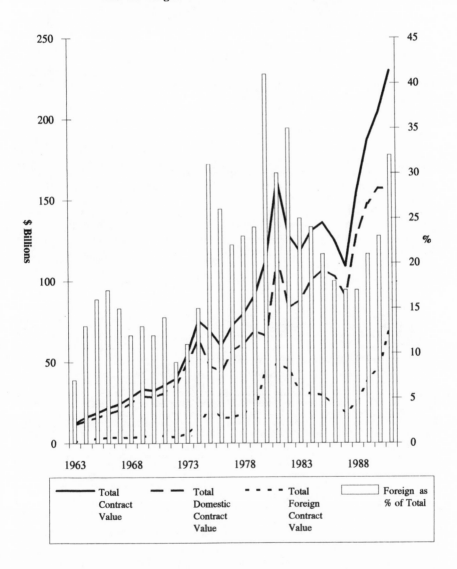

in 1975, when the Middle East OPEC countries suddenly became the source of one-tenth of all new business and one-third of all new foreign business.[16] In the latter half of the 1970s, contract values levelled off on a high plateau, again rising steeply from 1979 to 1980[17] and maintaining that unprecedented level for another two years, at the close of which Middle East contracts accounted for one-seventh of all new contracts signed by the 400 largest U.S. firms in the United States and abroad.[18] A precipitous decline then ensued, at the bottom of which in 1987 the value of new contracts was only three-eighths of the peak level of 1981. A quadrupling of contract value from 1987 to 1992 signaled the fourth—and heretofore longest—boom.

Domestic industrial construction, though also clearly cyclical, exhibited a much different pattern.[19] It increased, almost uninterruptedly, six-fold from 1963 to 1974, and then declined significantly for two years; it rose again in the latter half of the 1970s through 1981; after a sharp drop in 1982, it doubled again during the next eight years (despite a decline from 1985 to 1987).[20] The interaction between the convulsive fluctuations in overseas contracts and the steadier development in the national U.S. market produced cycles of international dependence ("intensity") bearing more of the former's imprint.[21] The international share thus more than doubled from one-fourteenth to one-sixth from 1963 to 1966, a level that was not exceeded for almost a decade, when it more than doubled in a single year (1975) to over three-tenths. Thereafter, the share fluctuated sharply, peaking at over two-fifths in 1980, and returning by 1991 to the level of 1975.

A different time series, collected by the U.S. Department of Commerce as part of the annual international balance of payments data, confirms the trend of U.S. construction firms' international undertakings.[22] Unlike the data in tables

---

[16]"The 400," *ENR*, Apr. 15, 1976, at 62. On the subsequent decline, see "A Saudi Slowdown Hits U.S. Builders," *BW*, Sept. 20, 1976, at 35-36.

[17]The doubling indicated in table 11.1 is an exaggeration resulting from the first-time inclusion of construction management contracts. If these are eliminated, the foreign contracts amounted to about $34 billion, which still represented a 50 per cent increase; similarly, foreign contracts as a share of all contracts rose to 30 (rather than the outlying 41) per cent. Calculated according to data in "The ENR 400," *ENR*, Apr. 16, 1981, at 81-88.

[18]"The Top 400 Contractors," *ENR*, Apr. 28, 1983, at 72.

[19]On the complicated connections between building cycles and general business cycles, see John Maurice Clark, *Strategic Factors in Business Cycles* 27-33 (1949 [1935]); W. Newman, *The Building Industry and Business Cycles* (5:4 *Studies in Business Administration*, 1935); Long, *Building Cycles*; Arthur Burns & Wesley Mitchell, *Measuring Business Cycles* 418-27 (1946); Alvin Hansen, *Business Cycles and National Income* 39-52 (1951); David Lapkin, "Building Construction and Business Cycles 1870-1938" (Ph.D diss., Columbia University, 1957). On the peculiarities of the cyclical movements in the construction and value self-destruction of industrial fixed capital, see David Harvey, *The Urban Experience* 73-83 (1989 [1985]).

[20]The sharp rise from 1980 to 1981 is, again, an artifact of *ENR*'s introduction of a new element of double counting (construction management contracts) and internal inconsistencies in *ENR*'s calculation of the data in 1980 and 1981. *ENR*'s estimate of the rise at 14 per cent approximates the 13 per cent increase that results from recalculating the domestic data without construction management figures (namely $79 billion for 1980 and $89.3 billion for 1981). "The Top 400 Contractors," *ENR*, Apr. 22, 1982, at 76.

[21]The coefficient of correlation between the foreign share and domestic contract value is 0.54; that between foreign share and foreign contract value is 0.81.

[22]Like—but for different reasons than—the *ENR* contract award data, these data, which are also in current dollars, are valuable as a trend indicator rather than for the absolute values. The U.S. Department of Commerce suspended publication and allegedly even tabulation of the data after 1960; it published retrospective data for the 1970s in 1981. Although the raw data may exist for the 1960s, the Department of Commerce officials in charge of them cannot locate them and insist that tabulation at this late date would be extremely time-consuming. Telephone conversations with Anthony DiLullo and John Sondheimer, Balance of Payments Division, U.S. Bureau of Economic Analysis (BEA) (Jan. 26 & 29, 1993). Yet the authors of the National Export Expansion Council, *Report of the Industry Committee on Engineering and Construction Services* 61 (1970), stated that the Department of Commerce had furnished them with data for the years 1960 to 1968. On the deficiencies of the data, see Obie Whichard, *U.S. International Trade and Investment in Services: Data Needs and Availability* 30-35 (U.S. BEA Staff Paper 41, 1984); *idem*, "U.S.

11.1, 11.3, and 11.4, which capture the gross value of contracts that may take years to perform and include considerable double-counting of subcontracts, the data in table 11.2 encompass a narrow category of income. By excluding the value of merchandise exports from the United States and all other outlays abroad (including wages), table 11.2 and figure 11.2 show the annual "net amount of funds remaining in the United States, or to United States account." This category of residual income, approximating repatriated profits, presumably lags behind the contract award data since it begins to flow only after performance.[23] After fluctuating around $100 million in the 1950s, overseas profits exhibited the same strong rise during the OPEC construction boom that was observed in table 11.1. From 1973 to the peak in 1982, profits rose by more than 400 per cent; both awards and profits declined by about two-thirds from peak to trough; and both series also reversed directions after 1987.[24]

The internationalization of the U.S. industrial construction and civil engineering industry has also witnessed the emergence of a group of firms that is particularly dependent on overseas construction. The ten largest firms—ranked annually according to new foreign contract volume—have, as shown in table 11.3 and figure 11.3, exhibited a remarkable dependence on overseas projects: their international intensity has risen as high as 73 per cent,[25] never falling below 30 per cent. This dependence also peaked during the Vietnam military construction boom and then again during the petrodollar building frenzy. From 1975 to 1992, the international share of the ten most internationally active firms averaged 54 per cent.

Precisely how extraordinary this intensity is can be gauged by a comparison with the largest U.S. industrial exporters. In 1991, for example, the average international intensity of these ten firms (55 per cent) was higher than the export

---

Sales of Services to Foreigners," *SCB*, Jan. 1987, at 22. A major definitional limitation is that they exclude all income deriving from construction services provided to the U.S. Department of Defense or on projects managed or supervised by the Army Corps of Engineers. U.S. BEA, Form BE-47: Annual Survey of Construction, Engineering, Architectural, and Mining Services Provided by U.S. Firms to Unaffiliated Foreign Persons, at [instruction page] 2 (rev. Sept. 1990). They therefore do not reflect the considerable services performed by U.S. firms as adjuncts to the U.S. military during the wars in Korea and Vietnam; they also exclude many projects overseen by the Corps of Engineers in the Middle East. Finally, the data include the income only of U.S. affiliates, excluding that of foreign affiliates. The BEA recently began publishing the latter data, which for the years 1986 through 1990 amounted to $106 million, $91 million, $88 million, $189 million, and $211 million, respectively. Anthony DiLullo & Obie Whichard, "U.S. International Sales and Purchases of Services," *SCB*, Sept. 1990, at 37, tab. 13.1-13.3 at 68-69); John Sondheimer & Sylvia Bargas, "U.S. Sales and Purchases of Private Services," *SCB*, Sept. 1992, at 82, tab. 12.1-12.2 at 129-30. For these five years, affiliates' (net?) sales amounted to between 11 and 30 per cent of parent companies' repatriated profits.

[23]U.S. Dept. of Commerce, Office of Business Economics, Form BE-47: Annual Survey of Construction, Engineering, Architectural, and Mining Services Provided by U.S. Firms to Unaffiliated Foreign Persons (Jan. 30, 1970) (reprinted in National Export Expansion Council, *Report* at 59). Since expenses may exceed receipts during the initial phase of a contract, this figure can be conceptualized as repatriated profits only over the whole life of a contract. Telephone interview with Daniel Thomas, U.S. BEA (Feb. 1, 1993). It has been independently estimated that more than three-quarters of the revenues accruing to U.S. firms for overseas projects remain abroad as local expenses. "Exporters Bring Big Bucks Home," *ENR*, Apr. 18, 1985, at 17.

[24]Because of the introduction of additional double-counting in the *ENR* data from 1980 forward, the two series are not strictly comparable for any period encompassing pre-1980 and post-1979 data. Some sense of the conceptual and methodological differences between the BEA and *ENR* data emerges from unpublished data that the BEA tabulated and furnished when confronted with the asymmetry between its published data for net exports and gross imports. In order to restore the symmetry, the BEA produced the figures for gross receipts for exports of construction services (of unaffiliated U.S. parents) for the years 1987 through 1991, which amounted to: $1,653,000,000, $1,533,000,000, $1,917,000,000, $2,647,000,000, and $2,624,000,000 respectively. Data provided by Sylvia Bargas, U.S. BEA (Feb. 2, 1993). They thus amount to less than one-twentieth of the value of overseas contracts awarded to the 400 largest U.S. firms.

[25]This extraordinary figure in 1982 resulted from an almost perfect overlap between the firms with the largest amount of new foreign contracts and new domestic contracts. See "The ENR 400," *ENR*, Apr. 28, 1983, at 69.

**Table 11.2**
**U.S. Construction Firms' Repatriated Profits, 1950-91**

| Year | Profits ($ million) | Index (1950= 100) | Year | Profits ($ million) | Index (1950= 100) |
|------|------|------|------|------|------|
| 1950 | 66 | 100 | 1971 | 347 | 526 |
| 1951 | 75 | 114 | 1972 | 392 | 594 |
| 1952 | 95 | 144 | 1973 | 384 | 582 |
| 1953 | 101 | 153 | 1974 | 520 | 788 |
| 1954 | 95 | 144 | 1975 | 855 | 1295 |
| 1955 | 99 | 150 | 1976 | 1234 | 1870 |
| 1956 | 129 | 195 | 1977 | 1241 | 1880 |
| 1957 | 144 | 218 | 1978 | 1262 | 1912 |
| 1958 | 140 | 212 | 1979 | 1004 | 1521 |
| 1959 | 124 | 188 | 1980 | 1563 | 2368 |
| 1960 | 141 | 214 | 1981 | 1881 | 2850 |
| 1961 | NA | | 1982 | 1945 | 2947 |
| 1962 | NA | | 1983 | 1464 | 2218 |
| 1963 | NA | | 1984 | 1276 | 1933 |
| 1964 | NA | | 1985 | 1176 | 1781 |
| 1965 | NA | | 1986 | 759 | 1150 |
| 1966 | NA | | 1987 | 668 | 1012 |
| 1967 | NA | | 1988 | 790 | 1197 |
| 1968 | 276 | 418 | 1989 | 939 | 1423 |
| 1969 | NA | | 1990 | 705 | 1068 |
| 1970 | 258 | 391 | 1991 | 1293 | 1959 |

Sources: **1950-1960**: U.S. Office of Business Economics, *Balance of Payments Statistical Supplement* tab. 36 at 144 (rev. ed. n.d. [ca. 1961]); **1961-1967, 1969**: Not available; **1968**: National Export Expansion Council, *Report of the Industry Committee on Engineering and Construction Services* 61 (1970); **1970-1980**: Anthony DiLullo, "Service Transactions in the U.S. International Accounts, 1970-80," *SCB*, Nov. 1981, at 29, tab. 7 at 39; **1981-1985**: Unpublished data, U.S. Bureau of Economic Analysis (Jan. 29, 1993); **1986-1991**: John Sondheimer & Sylvia Bargas, "U.S. International Sales and Purchases of Private Services," *SCB*, Sept. 1992, at 82, tab. 2 at 83.

**Figure 11.2**
**U.S Construction Firms' Repatriated Profits,1950-91**

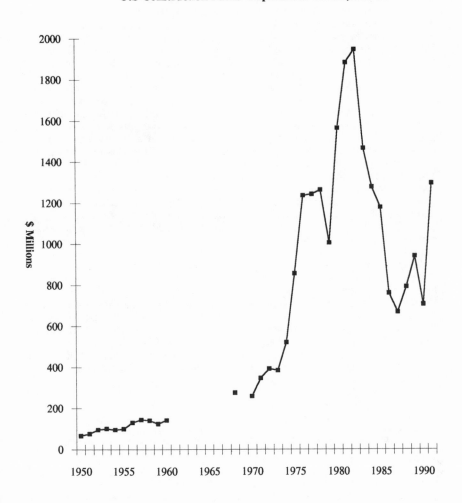

intensity of all the largest U.S. industrial exporters except Boeing (61 per cent).[26] Moreover, the international intensity of six of the ten firms—ranging from 63 per cent for Bechtel to 90 per cent for Foster Wheeler—exceeded Boeing's.[27] The concentration of international construction activity among these firms has also been extraordinary. The ten firms most dependent on the world market have accounted for between one-half and nine-tenths of all international contract value obtained by U.S. firms. This indicator of international intensity has, since the late 1970s, pointed toward a decided strengthening of the pull of the world market.

Internationalization has also manifested itself in an overlap between the largest firms ranked according to overseas contracts and the largest firms ranked according to total contracts. During the first half of the period under review, 1963 to 1977, the ten largest firms in terms of total contract value included on average 5.2 of the ten largest firms ranked according to foreign contracts; from 1978 to 1992, this infiltration increased to 7.4 firms.[28] Another way to illustrate the increasing importance of the world market is to compare the international intensity of these two groups of overlapping largest firms. From 1963 to 1977, the international intensity of the ten largest firms ranked according to all contracts averaged 24 per cent compared with 45 per cent for the largest firms ranked according to foreign contracts; for the second period, 1978 to 1992, the corresponding figures were 42 per cent and 54 per cent. In other words, as the degree of international intensity of the first group of large firms increased more quickly than that of the second group, both groups' world market dependence have begun to approximate each other. These indicators taken together, which reveal a majoritization of the group of largest firms by those operating outside the U.S. market, suggest that concentration and centralization of capital among U.S. construction firms is increasingly controlled by the world market. A long-term trend toward internationally reinforced oligopoly is thus unmistakable.

Despite year-to-year shifts in the composition of these ten largest firms, in part resulting from mergers and acquisitions within this group—Fluor bought Daniel International and Raymond International acquired Kaiser Engineers in 1977, Kellogg acquired Rust in 1980, and Brown & Root acquired C.F. Braun in 1989—they have maintained an extraordinary continuity over the thirty-year period.[29] Bechtel, Fluor Daniel, Foster Wheeler, Kellogg, Brown & Root, Lummus, and Parsons, all of which perform petrochemical-related construction, are the most prominent firms. Morrison-Knudsen, a firm whose emphasis on non-industrial heavy construction led to its gradual ouster from the largest and most lucrative overseas contracts since the 1950s and 1960s, when its government-financed dam, road, and airport civil engineering projects made it the largest international constructor, has in recent years shown a much diminished international intensity.[30]

---

[26]"Top 50 U.S. Exporters," *Fortune*, June 29, 1992, at 95 (calculated as a share of total sales). These two sets of data are not comparable to the extent that industrial exporters also produce outside of the United States. In fact, however, Boeing, which in addition to exhibiting the greatest export intensity is also the largest U.S. exporter in absolute terms, maintains no production facilities abroad. "U.S. Exporters Keep Rolling On," *Fortune*, June 14, 1993, at 130.

[27]Calculated according to "The Top 400 Contractors," *ENR*, May 25, 1992, at 58. The data are representative for recent years. See e.g., "Top 50 U.S. Exporters," *Fortune*, June 14, 1993, at 131.

[28]Calculated according to the data in the annual "Top 400" articles referenced in table 1.

[29]"Fluor Acquires 96% of Daniel," *ENR*, June 9, 1977, at 15; "Profit of Raymond International Said to Be Up in 2nd Period," *WSJ*, July 25, 1977, at 13, col. 3-5; "The 400," *ENR*, Apr. 17, 1980, at 75; "Kellogg Rust Plans to Stay on Top," *ENR*, June 9, 1983, at 26; UPI, Aug. 14, 1989 (Nexis). In 1993 Raytheon finally consolidated its two large construction subsidiaries, United Engineers & Constructors and Badger, into Raytheon Engineers & Constructors Inc. William Krizan, "Diversified Firms Are Chomping at Market," *ENR*, Apr. 5, 1993, at 34, 38.

[30]See e.g., "The Top Contractors," *ENR*, Apr. 17, 1958, at 11; "The 67 Top Contractors of 1959," *ENR*, July 28, 1960, at 19. See also chapter 8 above.

These same firms are for the most part also the largest domestic industrial construction firms. Foster Wheeler is the chief exception, whereas Morrison-Knudsen, Ebasco Services, Turner, and Rust International are the largest U.S. firms that in recent years have performed comparatively little work abroad.[31] This linkage between international and national markets becomes visible in the fact that the value of foreign contracts as a share of total contract awards among the ten largest firms overall has risen significantly over the whole period, currently approaching one-half.

Contrary to the recent claim that overseas and domestic concentration has been "about the same" among U.S. construction firms, the overseas concentration ratios, as recorded in table 11.3, have persistently exceeded domestic ones by a wide margin.[32] The gap is, again, in part accounted for by the fact that whereas a national concentration ratio is based on a fixed denominator—albeit one referring only to the 400 largest non-residential firms rather than to the whole universe of construction activity—the international market expands every time a foreign firm competes work away from an own-national firm. Because the vagaries of annual contract awards for a group of only four firms produce wide year-to-year swings, the excess of the international over the domestic ratios has ranged between 29 per cent and 309 per cent. Over the entire 29-year period between 1963 and 1992, however, the average overseas four-firm concentration ratio (48 per cent) has been 2.5 times greater than the domestic ratio (20 per cent).

## Comparative Firm-Size and Concentration in Construction and Manufacturing

Although even the domestic concentration ratio belies the picture-book image of construction as an industry characterized by perfect competition, the four-firm foreign concentration ratios—especially for the 1980s when they approached two-thirds—exceed the twenty-firm concentration ratios in most two-digit standard industrial classifications (SIC)-code industries of Fordist mass-production fungible goods, which averaged 18 per cent in 1987.[33] This comparability of concentration ratios is even more remarkable in light of the enormous size differences between the largest manufacturing and construction firms. A number of indicators document this gap.

In 1975 and 1976, in the midst of the Middle East boom, for example, when Fluor was the largest construction firm in the United States, its profits ranked only 283d and 254th respectively among the 500 largest publicly owned corporations. Its annual profit amounted to only one-twenty-fifth of that of General Motors and one-fiftieth of AT&T's.[34] Only one construction firm, according to the most recent (1987) economic census data, had more than $5 billion in assets compared with sixty-six such firms in manufacturing industries.[35]

Employment data corroborate these structural disparities. In 1987, the average manufacturing company employed seventy persons while its counterpart

---

[31]On Morrison-Knudsen's projects in Iran and Saudi Arabia in the 1970s, see "Morrison-Knudsen's Foray into Coal Mining," *BW*, June 20, 1977, at 51.

[32]W. Strassmann, "The United States," in *The Global Construction Industry: Strategies for Entry, Growth and Survival* 22, 28 (W. Strassman & Jill Wells ed., 1988).

[33]Although the two types of concentration ratios are not strictly comparable—because the manufacturing data include the entire universe of firms—tobacco, transportation equipment, and petroleum were the only industries in which the share of value of total shipments was considerably higher. U.S. Bureau of the Census, *1987 CoM: Concentration Ratios in Manufacturing*, tab. 3 at 6-4 (1992).

[34]"The Bottom-Line Directory," *FW*, July 15, 1976, at 13, 21; "The Bottom-Line Directory," *FW*, July 15, 1977, at 13, 27.

[35]U.S. Bureau of the Census, *1987 Enterprise Statistics: Large Companies*, tab. 4 at 30 (1990).

**Table 11.3**
**The 10 Largest U.S. Construction Firms, 1963-92**

| Year | Σ Contract Value of 10 Largest Firms ($ billion) | Σ Foreign Contract Value of 10 Largest Firms ($ billion) | Foreign Contract Value of 10 Largest Firms as Share of Their Σ Contract Value (%) | Foreign Contract Value of 10 Firms w/Highest Foreign Contract Value as Share of Σ Foreign Contract Value (%) | Foreign Contract Value of 10 Firms w/Highest Foreign Contract Value as Share of Their Σ Contract Value (%) | Share of Σ Foreign Contract Value of 4 Firms w/Highest Foreign Contract Value (%) | Share of Σ Domestic Contract Value of 4 Firms w/Highest Domestic Contract Value (%) |
|---|---|---|---|---|---|---|---|
| 1963 | 2.4 | 0.4 | 17 | 66 | 34 | 36 | 9 |
| 1964 | 4.1 | 1.3 | 32 | 71 | 39 | 45 | 11 |
| 1965 | 4.1 | 1.2 | 29 | 53 | 47 | 29 | 12 |
| 1966 | 4.9 | 1.8 | 37 | 57 | 46 | 31 | 10 |
| 1967 | 7.0 | 1.6 | 23 | 59 | 40 | 32 | 16 |
| 1968 | 7.9 | 1.5 | 19 | 66 | 37 | 31 | 16 |
| 1969 | 9.1 | 1.9 | 21 | 64 | 37 | 36 | 15 |
| 1970 | 8.4 | 1.7 | 20 | 63 | 43 | 35 | 14 |
| 1971 | 11.1 | 2.3 | 21 | 69 | 49 | 49 | 18 |
| 1972 | 12.9 | 1.2 | 9 | 50 | 30 | 31 | 24 |
| 1973 | 20.7 | 2.5 | 12 | 70 | 30 | 38 | 24 |
| 1974 | 32.0 | 4.8 | 15 | 64 | 36 | 38 | 25 |
| 1975 | 30.6 | 13.6 | 44 | 75 | 58 | 54 | 24 |
| 1976 | 21.8 | 8.2 | 38 | 66 | 58 | 49 | 19 |
| 1977 | 28.8 | 6.3 | 22 | 54 | 45 | 36 | 23 |
| 1978 | 28.9 | 11.6 | 40 | 74 | 54 | 55 | 18 |
| 1979 | 30.8 | 14.8 | 48 | 75 | 58 | 55 | 16 |
| 1980 | 62.9* | 33.9 | 54 | 77 | 69 | 52 | 29 |
| 1981 | 70.9 | 35.3 | 50 | 76 | 52 | 40 | 21 |
| 1982 | 48.3 | 32.5 | 67 | 75 | 73 | 40 | 14 |
| 1983 | 47.5 | 24.0 | 51 | 85 | 57 | 64 | 17 |
| 1984 | 54.6 | 26.3 | 48 | 86 | 49 | 61 | 19 |
| 1985 | 53.8 | 22.6 | 42 | 85 | 56 | 61 | 17 |
| 1986 | 46.7 | 17.3 | 37 | 86 | 53 | 62 | 17 |
| 1987 | 45.1 | 11.4 | 25 | 78 | 38 | 48 | 23 |
| 1988 | 63.5 | 21.7 | 34 | 90 | 45 | 65 | 20 |
| 1989 | 86.0 | 34.2 | 40 | 90 | 48 | 60 | 22 |
| 1990 | 93.4 | 38.3 | 41 | 86 | 45 | 52 | 23 |
| 1991 | 122.4 | 60.5 | 49 | 87 | 55 | 56 | 26 |
| 1992 | 123.9 | 59.8 | 48 | 84 | 53 | 56 | 27 |

*Source:* "The 400," *ENR*, 1964-1993 (see table 11.1)
*Beginning in 1980 the data include the value of construction management contracts.

**Figure 11.3**
**The 10 Largest U.S. Construction Firms, 1963-92**

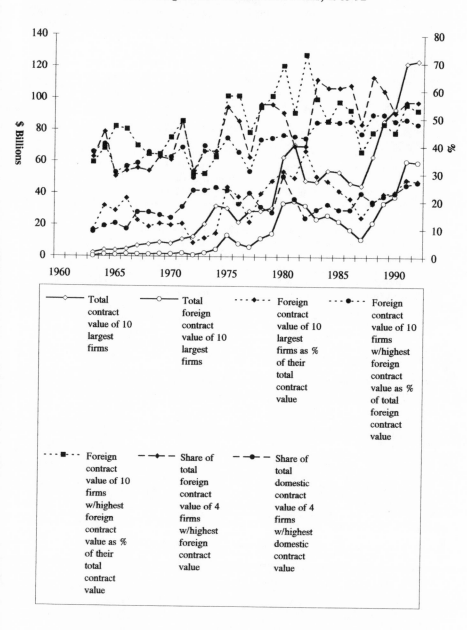

in construction employed ten.   Much more impressive than this seven-fold difference in mean size is the modal group: in manufacturing, companies with more than 10,000 employees employed far more persons than any other size group; in construction the modal group included companies employing between twenty and forty-nine employees.[36] The quinquennial economic censuses show the volume of employment in firms with more than 10,000 employees between 1967 and 1987. In 1967, when special tabulations also disclosed enterprises with more than 100,000 employees, fifteen manufacturing firms fell under this classification, whereas no construction firm employed as many as 25,000. The number of companies with more than 10,000 employees has varied from four to eleven in construction and from 267 to 314 in manufacturing. The share of total employment accounted for by these large entities has varied from 2 per cent (1967) to 7 per cent (1982) in construction and from 40 per cent (1987) to 45 per cent (1972, 1977, 1987) in manufacturing.

A more detailed examination of employment data, however, reveals indicia of oligopoly in construction too.   The wide gap between construction and manufacturing narrows considerably if instead of the entire construction industry, the reference point is confined to the subsector of heavy (excluding highway) construction, in which most of the internationally oriented firms compete. In 1982, eight of these firms employed 276,674 employees, accounting for more than 38 per cent of total employment in the subsector. This share amounted to 85 per cent of the manufacturing level.[37]

The greater detail of SICs available through the quinquennial Census of Construction Industries reveals even more surprising results. The group "heavy construction contractors, not elsewhere classified" (SIC 1629) includes firms building chemical complexes, petroleum refineries, nuclear and non-nuclear power plants, dams, harbors, subways, and missile facilities.[38]   These types of construction—in particular the chemical, petroleum, and power facilities, which form more than half of this subsector's receipts—are oligopolized by the largest international oriented firms.  Firms at the somewhat lower threshold of at least 1,000 employees accounted for 30, 41, 55, 58, and 33 per cent of all employees in this subsector in 1967, 1972, 1977, and 1982, and 1987 respectively.  In all of these years except 1967, this degree of employment concentration considerably exceeded that for the construction industry as a whole, which amounted to 6, 5, 8, 9, and 4 per cent respectively, and for manufacturing as a whole, which amounted to 33, 29, 28, 25, and 23 per cent respectively.[39]

---

[36]U.S. Bureau of the Census, *1987 Enterprise Statistics: Company Summary*, tab. 3 at 17-20 (1991). The employment data in this section exclude workers employed by U.S. firms outside the United States. *Id.*, App. D-1.

[37]Calculated according to the following publications of the U.S. Bureau of the Census: 1 *1967 Enterprise Statistics: General Report on Industrial Organizations*, tab. 2-3 at 123-24 (1972); 1 *1972 Enterprise Statistics: General Report on Industrial Organizations*, tab. 5 at 144, 148 (1977); 1 *1977 Enterprise Statistics: General Report on Industrial Organizations*, tab. 3 at 148, 150, 152 (1981); 1 *1982 Enterprise Statistics: General Report on Industrial Organizations*, tab. 3 at 96, 97, 99 (1986); *1987 Enterprise Statistics: Large Companies*, tab. 3 at 29; *1987 Enterprise Statistics: Company Summary*, tab. 2 at 13-14, tab. 3 at 17, 19. The share of total employment accounted for by heavy (excluding highway) construction firms with more than 10,000 employees has fluctuated wildly—from 13 per cent in 1972 and 1987 to 31 per cent in 1977. In 1987 the category encompassed heavy (except building) construction.

[38]For more detailed description, see U.S. Office of Management and Budget, *Standard Industrial Classification Manual 1987*, at 59-60 (1987).

[39]U.S. Bureau of the Census, 1 *CCI, 1967: Industry Statistics and Special Reports*, tab. 3 at 4-5 (1971); *idem*, 1 *CCI, 1972: Industry and Special Statistics* 9-8 (1976); *idem*, 1 *CCI, 1977: Industry and Area Statistics*, tab. 3 at 9-7 (1981); *idem*, *CCI, 1982: Industry Series: Heavy Construction Contractors, N.E.C.*, tab. 5 at 9-8, tab. 7 at 9-9 (1984); *idem*, *CCI, 1987: Industry Series: Heavy Construction Contractors, Not Elsewhere Classified*, 9-2, 9-3, tab. 5 at 9-8 (1990); *idem*, *SAUS* 1975, tab. 1260 at 736; *idem*, *SAUS 1982-83*, tab. 1387 at 779; *idem*, *1982 CoM: Subject Series: General Summary*, pt. 2: *Industry Statistics by Employment Size of Establishment*, tab. 1 at 1-3 (1985); *idem*, *1987 CoM: Subject Series: General Summary: Industry Product Class, and Geographic Area Statistics*, tab. 4 at 1-99 (1991).

This relationship is replicated in the annual *County Business Patterns* (*CBP*) surveys based in part on Social Security reports. From 1974, when the *CBP* first began publishing size distribution data for establishments with more than 1,000 employees, through 1986, the share of employment accounted for by such establishments in "heavy construction except highway" (SIC 162) exceeded the corresponding share in manufacturing every year. The share of such construction establishments fluctuated between a low of 30 per cent (1986) and a high of 39 per cent (1983); the more stable manufacturing shares varied between 26 and 29 per cent.[40]

Similar patterns in size-distribution obtain between manufacturing and construction firms in other advanced capitalist economies. In Britain, for example, the concentration of employment in the construction industry has exceeded that in the United States. Already by 1954, British establishments with more than 1,000 employees accounted for one-sixth of all construction employees compared with a peak level of one-twelfth; U.S. firms did not reach this level until 1982.[41] In 1973, British firms employing more than 1,200 operatives accounted for 19 per cent of total construction employment and half of employment in building and civil engineering. By contrast, British manufacturing firms employing 1,000 or more workers accounted for about one-third of total manufacturing employment.[42] In West Germany, too, comparative size differences between manufacturing and construction firms similar to those in the United States can be observed. In 1974, for example, the average manufacturing establishment was only four times larger than its counterpart in construction because official data exclude many categories of special trade contractors, which tend to be very small.[43] In both Britain and West Germany, too, even the largest construction firms have ranked far down on the list of the largest industrial companies.[44]

Construction enterprises in the former socialist countries exhibited a vastly different size structure. Whereas the average construction firm size in the United States, Western Europe, and Japan ranged between five and fifteen employees in the 1950s and 1960s, the corresponding figure for Eastern Europe was almost three orders of magnitude greater.[45] In the former German Democratic Republic, for example, construction enterprises with more than 500 employees accounted for more than three-fifths and those with more than 5,000 employees for almost one-fifth of all construction workers in 1973. In the Federal Republic of Germany, the corresponding figure for firms with more than 500 employees was only one-tenth.[46]

---

[40]In 1981, 1982, 1984, and 1987, the Bureau of the Census withheld data on the largest establishments in this construction classification to avoid identifying them although ostensibly they were no more easily identifiable than in other years. For unexplained reasons, from 1986 to 1988, the share of employment accounted for by these firms dropped from 30 per cent to 17 per cent as their total employment plummeted from 143,606 to 78,988. By 1990, the gap between this subsector (22 per cent) and manufacturing (23 per cent) had almost been closed. Calculated according to the data in tab. 1b in the U.S. Summary volume of U.S. Bureau of the Census, *CBP*, 1974 through 1990 (1977-1993).

[41]Marian Bowley, *The British Building Industry* 245 (1966).

[42]Great Britain, Department of the Environment, *Private Contractors' Construction Census 1973*, tab. 14 at 14 (1975); Great Britain, Central Statistical Office, *AAS 1975*, tab. 161 at 162 (No. 112, 1975). The data for manufacturing refer to 1972.

[43]Statistisches Bundesamt, *SJ 1976 für die Bundesrepublik Deutschland*, tab. 14.8 at 240-41, tab. 14.21 at 264 (1976).

[44]See J. Colclough, *The Construction Industry of Great Britain* 145-47 (1965); Götz Hohenstein, "Konzentration in der Bauwirtschaft," FAZ, May 11, 1963, at 5, col. 3 (business section).

[45]United Nations, *Industrialization of Building* tab. 2,1 at 74 (1967).

[46]Calculated according to data in *SJ der DDR 1974*, at 158 (1974); *WS*, Feb. 1974, at 113, 115. For similar data for Poland, see Witold Bień, *Ekonomika przedsiebiorstwa budowlanego* 30 (1969). See also Kang Chao, *The Construction Industry in Communist China* 19-20 (1968).

## Global Internationalization and the Relative Decline of U.S. Firms

"The whole world is our market-place."[47]

The growing incorporation of non-U.S. construction firms into the world market emerges from the parallel set of international data that *ENR* has collected since 1978. These data are subject to the same methodological caveats already noted above. In addition, market concentration ratios are slippery constructs in the international construction industry primarily because the boundaries of the world market are themselves constantly in flux.[48] A recent study concluded that only one-twentieth of the $1.4 trillion of construction performed in the world "was undertaken in a fully competitive international market." The other 95 per cent was either carried on by small-scale builders using traditional methods or subject to political restrictions. Thus demarcated, the international construction market was, however, dominated by thirty firms.[49] That pre-industrial methods have remained so massively invulnerable to the technological advances embodied in the multinational firms underlines just how inchoate and fragile this world market is.

Market shares in international construction are usually calculated by defining as the universe (denominator) the value of all contracts for work performed in one country by firms not "of" that country. Thus when a U.S. firm obtains a contract to perform work in France, the world market expands by the amount of that contract; the value of the projects in France being performed by French firms, however, does not appear as part of the world market. Thus *ENR's* characterization of the Middle East "the hub of the world market, accounting for 31% of all foreign work" can only mean that the journal does not consider the projects performed by U.S. firms in the United States a part of the world market.[50] Applying this framework to manufacturing would mean, for example, that the sales of Japanese automobiles in the United States would be compared only with sales of other non-U.S. firms in the United States, whereas sales of U.S. automobiles in the United States would be excluded from the world market. Such a conceptualization is artificial and misleading to the extent that the potential U.S. buyer of an automobile produced in the United States could just as well buy one imported from Europe or Japan. To the extent that multinational construction firms have not yet begun to compete in certain traditional market sectors, this conceptual distortion is mitigated somewhat in the construction industry. Yet at the very least, the impact of the world market should be measured by including those subsectors in which non-own-national firms bid or otherwise exert an influence on price, the development of technology, methods of production, or managerial practices.

The trend in the aggregate data shown in table 11.4 and figure 11.4 is strikingly dominated by the worldwide depression in the mid-1980s. This sharp decline was largely a function of the steep loss in oil revenues in the OPEC countries, which had been the pillar of internationalization. Despite the renewed strengthening of the world construction market since 1987, once inflation is taken into account, no real increase has been recorded since the previous peak of 1981.[51]

---

[47]"NCA Members Ply the World and Find Jobs on Every Continent," *ENR*, Dec. 5, 1974, at 14 (quoting William McKay, president, National Constructors Association).

[48]For a general methodological discussion of concentration ratios, see F. Scherer, *Industrial Market Structure and Economic Performance* 56-64 (2d ed. 1980).

[49]National Research Council, *Building for Tomorrow: Global Enterprise and the U.S. Construction Industry* 11, 15-16 (1988) (data for mid-1980s).

[50]"The 400," *ENR*, Apr. 16, 1981, at 82, 115.

[51]On deflated figures, see "Introduction," in *Global Construction Industry* at 6-7. The 13 per cent increase in total international contract value can be compared to the 34 per cent increase in the Bureau of the Census composite fixed-weight price index for construction in the United States between 1981 and 1991.

This flatness is also reflected in the relative decline in the importance of international orders among the 250 largest firms during the 1980s. Whereas overseas projects had accounted for more than half of their new contract value at the height of the boom in the early 1980s, at the bottom of the trough in 1987 the share declined to a quarter before rising again to three-tenths by 1992. Among the ten largest firms a much smaller decline occurred so that in the early 1990s they still relied on the international sector as heavily as the larger group had a decade earlier.

This global trend is mirrored in the profitability indicators of one of the largest public-issue U.S. firms, which is also among the most heavily dependent on overseas projects. Foster Wheeler Corporation's revenues ($1.7 billion), net earnings ($64 million), and rate of return on net assets (23 per cent) all peaked in 1981 and bottomed out in 1987 or 1988 ($1.1 billion, $3 million, and 0.7 per cent respectively). When revenues finally surpassed the 1981 level in 1991 ($2.0 billion), net earnings ($43 million) and the rate of return (8 per cent) remained far below peak levels of a decade earlier.[52]

The representation of U.S. firms among the 200-250 largest international construction companies declined from a high of three-tenths in 1978 to a low of one-seventh a decade later; by 1992, however, the U.S. share reached a new high, approaching one-third. Among the fifty largest international firms, U.S. firms' representation also rose from 26 per cent in 1978 to 28 per cent in 1992.[53] This stability contrasts with the trend in the manufacturing sector, in which U.S. industrial firms declined as a share of the world's fifty largest industrial corporations from 48 per cent in 1974 and 42 per cent in 1978 to 30 per cent in 1992.[54]

The U.S. construction firms' share of the total international market as measured by annual contract value, however, exhibited no decline at all. With an (unweighted) average of 35 per cent, that share never fell below one-quarter, increasing by the early 1990s to one-half. U.S. firms' statistical preeminence in the Middle East was never seriously threatened during these years: their share of contract value, which never fell below 30 per cent, rose to 60 per cent by 1992. Only in 1988 did Italian construction firms come within one percentage point of the U.S. firms. From 1989 to 1992, U.S. firms were the market leaders in virtually every geographic region (Japanese firms barely surpassing U.S. firms in Asia in 1990).

The global breadth of this dominant position has in large part been a function of the U.S. firms' preeminence among the largest oligopolists. The ten firms with the largest volume of international contracts accounted for an (unweighted) average of 37 per cent of the world construction market during the whole period from 1978 to 1992. This concentration attained its highest degree in 1992, reaching one-half. In fact, the largest-firm concentration ratio for construction compares favorably with that in many international industries.[55] The

---

[52]Foster Wheeler Corporation, *Annual Report 1990* at 21; Foster Wheeler Corporation, *Annual Report 1991*, at 17.

[53]Where data are given without a source in this section, they are taken from *ENR*'s annual "The Top International Contractors" article referenced in table 11.4.

[54]In 1992, U.S. firms accounted for 157 (31 per cent) of the 500 and sixty-four (32 percent) of the 200 largest industrial corporations. "The Fifty Largest Industrial Companies in the World," *Fortune*, Aug. 1974, at 184, 185; "The Fifty Largest Industrial Companies in the World," *Fortune*, Aug. 13, 1979, at 208; "The Global 500: The World's Largest Industrial Corporations," *Fortune*, July 27, 1992, at 176-82. Unlike the construction firms surveyed by *ENR*, the industrial firms are not defined by *Fortune* by reference to their exports or international production although they are by and large also leading firms on the world market.

[55]John Dunning, *Multinational Enterprises and the Global Economy*, tab. 2.19 at 45 (1993), compiled concentration ratios (defined as sales for the three largest firms as a percentage of the twenty largest) for construction (1983) and the main international industries (1982) showing an intermediate position for construction. In fact, however, the only industries with higher concentration ratios were calculated on the

**Table 11.4**
**The 250 Largest International Construction Firms, 1978-92**

| Year | Total Inter- national Contract Value | Inter- national Con- tract Value as Share of Total Con- tract Value | U.S. Firms as Share of All Firms | U.S. Firms' Share of Total Inter- national Contract Value | 10 Largest Firms' Share of Total Inter- nation- al Con- tract Value | Inter- national Share of 10 Largest Firms' Total Con- tract Value | U.S. Firms as Share of 10 Largest Firms | U.S. Firms' Share of 10 Largest Firms' Inter- national Contract Value |
|------|------|------|------|------|------|------|------|------|
| | ($ bill.) | (%) | (%) | (%) | (%) | (%) | (%) | (%) |
| 1978 | 52 | 50 | 30 | 32 | 38 | 72 | 50 | 58 |
| 1979 | 67 | 54 | 23 | 32 | 36 | 79 | 40 | 51 |
| 1980 | 110 | 51 | 19 | 44 | 37 | 73 | 70 | 82 |
| 1981 | 135 | 57 | 19 | 35 | 30 | 63 | 70 | 72 |
| 1982 | 123 | 57 | 18 | 36 | 30 | 77 | 60 | 66 |
| 1983 | 94 | 46 | 17 | 31 | 34 | 67 | 50 | 65 |
| 1984 | 80 | 42 | 16 | 38 | 38 | 68 | 60 | 75 |
| 1985 | 82 | 39 | 17 | 35 | 37 | 65 | 70 | 68 |
| 1986 | 74 | 32 | 17 | 31 | 34 | 58 | 50 | 63 |
| 1987 | 74 | 26 | 16 | 24 | 28 | 43 | 40 | 42 |
| 1988 | 94 | 27 | 14 | 28 | 36 | 58 | 50 | 58 |
| 1989 | 113 | 28 | 17 | 34 | 41 | 58 | 60 | 67 |
| 1990 | 120 | 26 | 25 | 36 | 38 | 48 | 60 | 68 |
| 1991 | 152 | 26 | 26 | 46 | 47 | 55 | 70 | 77 |
| 1992 | 147 | 30 | 32 | 49 | 50 | 53 | 70 | 78 |

*Source*: "The Top International Contractors," *ENR*: Dec. 6, 1979, at 26; July 17, 1980, at 42; July 16, 1981, at 68; July 15, 1982, at 77; July 21, 1983, at 50; July 19, 1984, at 54; July 18, 1985, at 34; July 17, 1986, at 38; July 16, 1987, at 26; July 7, 1988, at 38; July 13, 1989, at 42; July 5, 1990, at 24; July 22, 1991, at 30; Aug. 24, 1992, at 34; Aug. 23, 1993, at 28.

*Coverage*: Firm size is measured by the value of contracts to be performed outside the country in which the firm is located. The data set included only 200 firms in 1978 and 1979 and 225 in 1991 and 1992. The bottom 50 firms' foreign contract value is so small that it does not affect comparability. Beginning in 1980 the data include the value of construction management contracts.

**Figure 11.4**
**The 250 Largest International Construction Firms,**
**1978-92**

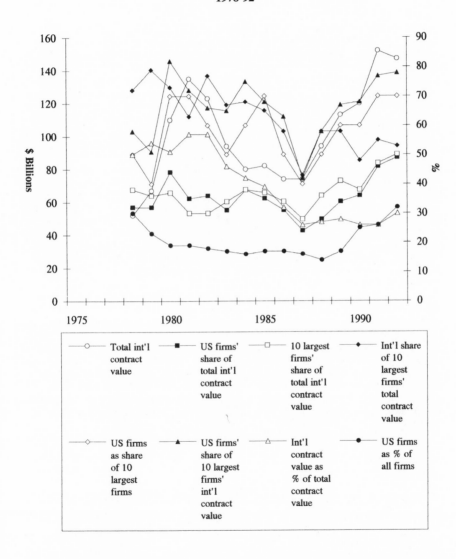

U.S. contingent among the ten largest multinational construction firms, in turn, accounted for 66 per cent of the value of that whole group's contracts during the fifteen years.

By the same token, European, and especially the numerous Italian, construction firms, facing smaller domestic markets, became considerably more reliant on the world market than U.S. firms. During the first half of the 1980s, 80 to 90 per cent of the internationally oriented Italian firms' new contract volume was to be performed outside Italy. The German, French, and British firms, which were approximately equal in number, secured about half of their new orders from abroad, while the U.S. firms derived about two-fifths of their work from overseas. During the depression of the 1980s these shares all declined.[56]

Only the Japanese firms, the largest of which such as Shimizu, have, based on their domestic construction, also ranked as the largest in the world in some years, remained relatively independent of the world market. Just as the Japanese construction market itself has until recently remained relatively impervious to non-Japanese competitors, so too the large Japanese firms have relied overwhelmingly on that market.[57] Their world market dependence, which had reached 27 per cent in 1982, fell to 7 per cent by 1992. The Japanese firms are such outliers that if they are eliminated from the *ENR* listings, the international intensity of the remaining firms increases dramatically—in 1992, for example, from 30 per cent to 42 per cent.

The collapse of the Middle East petrodollar boom is clearly reflected in the relative decline of the Middle East construction market: from the peak in 1982 to the trough seven years later, its share of a stagnant world market dropped from 42 per cent to 16 per cent. During the same period, the world market shares accounted for by contracts to be performed in Europe and the United States rose from one-tenth to one-quarter and from one-twenty-fifth to one-seventh respectively. Since 1987, Europe, the United States, and Canada have thus accounted for approximately two-fifths of world market demand. Consequently, intra-First World international construction activities have become the fastest growing component of the world market.

The amount of employment accounted for by foreign direct investment in construction in the United States almost quintupled from 1977 to 1981 (from 12,525 to 57,802 workers); the value of contracts awarded to non-U.S. firms in the U.S. rose approximately five-fold between 1983 and 1989.[58] Conversely, by the latter half of the 1980s, Europe surpassed the Middle East (and all other regions) as the largest market for U.S. construction firms, while the latter in turn became by far the largest international builders in Europe. Thus Europe accounted for approximately one-third (by value) of U.S. international firms' contracts while U.S. firms secured well over two-fifths of all new contract value in Europe. In contrast, the Middle East's share of U.S. firms' contract value fell from 43 per cent in 1983 to 20 per cent in 1989.[59]

The basis of this competitive interpenetration among First World firms,

basis of much smaller denominators, which skew the comparison.

[56]For a listing of the export shares of Europe's largest construction firms at the end of the 1980s, see Patricia Hillebrandt, "La Diversification des entreprises de construction en Europe," in *Les Grandes groupes de la construction: De nouveaux acteurs urbains?* 49, 55 (Elisabeth Campagnac ed., 1992).

[57]On the large Japanese firms Kajima, Kumagai Gumi, Obayashi, and Shimizu, see *Directory of the World's Largest Service Companies* at 217-20, 224-31, 236-39.

[58]"Foreigners Step Up U.S. Invasion" at 12-13; "The Top 250 International Contractors," *ENR*, July 5, 1990, at 24, 27; U.S. International Trade Administration, *Foreign Builders Target the United States: Implications and Trends*, tab. 3 at 33 (1988).

[59]"The Top 400 Contractors," *ENR*, May 24, 1990, at 81; "The Top 400 Contractors," *ENR*, May 27, 1991, at 72.

which follows the pattern set in the 1960s when Western European and Japanese industrial firms began to compete with U.S. firms by directly investing in plants in their competitors' national markets, is the fact that their domestic construction markets are by far the world's largest.[60]   In 1984, the twelve largest national construction markets (in $ billion) were: the U.S. (327); Soviet Union (317); Japan (200); West Germany (71); France (55); Italy (53); Poland (51); U.K. (43); Canada (30); Saudi Arabia (26); China (24); Brazil (21).[61]

The international data in table 11.4 seem to suggest that the preeminence of U.S. firms remains unimpaired. Yet such persistent competitive supremacy would be at odds with the postwar course of other industries, in which European and Japanese firms have successfully contested U.S. competition.   Qualitative commentaries are also inconsistent with the conclusion that the train of economic-historical logic is experiencing a delay.

The dominant rankings of U.S. firms may in part merely reflect the fact that these companies respond more completely to a U.S. trade journal's survey than do non-U.S. firms. More importantly, the *ENR* data may be biased in favor of U.S. firms because of the latter's specialization in design-engineering and managing large and technically complex projects: although the whole value of contract may "run through their books," most of it is channeled back to the foreign firms that subcontract to do the actual construction (with Third World labor). The continued preeminence of U.S. firms in the *ENR* listings may also be an artifact of the inclusion of the value of the very expensive installed equipment in turnkey refinery, power, and production plants, which skews the international shares in favor of U.S. firms, which excel in this submarket.[62]   In 1992, for example, petroleum-related projects alone accounted for almost three-fifths of the value of international contracts awarded to U.S. firms.   Industrial process projects accounted for an additional ten per cent.   Petroleum and petrochemical construction, in turn, accounted for more than two-fifths of the value of all new international contracts in 1992.[63]

Uncritical neglect of the methodological defects of their own survey has led the editors of *ENR* to vacillate in their appraisal of U.S. firms' competitive position.   1987 marked the first time that a non-U.S. (British) firm secured the largest volume of foreign contracts and another country (Italy) produced more top-ranked firms than the United States.   Although the former event has thus far remained unique while the latter recurred only the next year—after which the number of U.S. firms increased sharply while Italian firms declined rapidly—*ENR* editorialized that "[t]he sun appears to be setting on U.S. contractors abroad." Within four years, however, *ENR* had tacitly retracted its prediction as to the decline of the U.S. industry "as the dominant force in the international market"[64] by recording that "U.S. firms dominated the world construction market by

---

[60]OECD, *Globalisation of Industrial Activities: Four Case Studies: Auto Parts, Chemicals, Construction and Semiconductors* 105 (1992). On the concept of the interpenetration of capital, see Ernest Mandel, *Die EWG und die Konkurrenz Europa-Amerika* (1968).

[61]Patrick MacAuley, "World-Wide Value of New Construction Put in Place," *CRev*, Sept.-Oct. 1986, tab. 1 at 2, tab. 4 at 4-6.

[62]Telephone interview with Bill Krizan, *ENR* (New York, Feb. 17, 1993); Gary Hunt, Morrison Knudsen (Boise, Idaho, Feb. 18, 1993); "The 400," *ENR*, Aug. 6, 1964, at 69, 70; "Introduction," in *The Global Construction Industry* at 1, 6-9.   Although Karin Behring, Erich Gluch, & Volker Rußig, *Entwicklungstendenzen im deutschen Auslandsbau* 61 (1982), state that these sorts of operations do not fall under the German classification of *Bauhauptgewerbe* (construction industry), presumably the homogeneous *ENR* data would not be affected by this distinction.

[63]Rob McManamy & Mary Powers, "Firms Go Along for the Ride as More Clients Begin to Travel," *ENR*, May 24, 1993, at 74, 79; Peter Reina & Gary Tulacz, "International Contracts Dip Slightly in 1992," *ENR*, Aug. 23, 1993, at 28, 30.

[64]*ENR*, July 7, 1988, at 82.

capturing'' almost half the contract awards reported to the magazine.[65]

Whereas some non-American specialists date the competitive decline of U.S. firms as far back as 1970,[66] *Forbes* was still celebrating U.S. multinational constructors at the beginning of the 1980s: "If the U.S. is no longer the leader in manufacturing technology, it remains the leader in engineering technology on these grand scales. As the leader in the field, Bechtel ranks with IBM, Boeing, Caterpillar, AT&T and a handful of other world-class U.S. corporations."[67] Although at the time it was unclear how unflattering the comparison with IBM would become, at congressional hearings in 1985, a Bechtel vice-president bemoaned the fact that since the mid-1970s the U.S. construction industry had seen its international market share drop from 75 to 30 per cent.[68] In the expectation that the forging of a world market for construction would create the conditions under which the international erosion of U.S. manufacturing dominance of the last two decades would be reproduced, observers promptly began declaring that "[t]he US has ceased to be the leader in the field."[69]

---

[65]"The Top International Contractors: Firms Set Sail for Hot Markets," *ENR*, Aug. 24, 1992, at 34.

[66]E. Stallworthy & O. Kharbanda, *International Construction* 12 (1986). Without any data or sources, these authors also claim that by the end of the 1970s, U.S. firms, which now ranked fifth after Japan, South Korea, West Germany, and Italy in terms of volume of overseas business, had been "largely squeezed out of the lucrative Middle East business...." This assertion directly conflicts with the *ENR* data.

[67]Michael Kolbenschlag, "Bechtel's Biggest Job—Constructing Its Own Future," *Forbes*, Dec. 7, 1981, at 138, 142.

[68]*U.S. International Competitiveness: The Construction Industry: Hearings Before the Subcomm. on International Policy and Trade of the House Comm. on Foreign Affairs*, 98th Cong., 1st Sess. 11 (1985) (testimony of Michael Stephenson). In the crucial Middle East market the share declined from 45 to 20 per cent. The witness did not mention the data source.

[69]Jimmie Hize, *Construction Contracts* 262 (1993).

# 12

# Bringing the World Market Home: Depression-Induced Intra-First World Interpenetration

Bechtel is facing a competitive world as intimidating as the rain forests...it tamed to build its projects.[1]

The intense decade-long impulses toward internationalization emanating from the construction boom in the oil-exporting countries may have been a unique historical phenomenon, which came to an end with the onset of the world depression and the decline in oil prices at the beginning of the 1980s.[2] Thus from the peak in 1981-82 through 1988-89, Saudi government revenues from petroleum fell by 78 per cent.[3] The contraction of the Middle Eastern construction market was similarly dramatic: the value of new contracts decreased by 75 per cent, from $51 billion to $13 billion, from 1982 to 1987.[4] By 1993, OPEC countries' oil revenues were lower, in terms of the purchasing power of the dollar, than they had been before the price increases of 1973.[5]

Even apart from the issue of the Persian Gulf countries' financial capacity to sustain their peak levels of construction, the attainment of "'a certain degree of saturation for large infrastructure projects'" has reduced the demand for projects to be built by First World firms.[6] As one large Belgian construction firm put it: "'We've built just about everything there...and now they have an airport every 50 kilometers with 10 flights a day and 15 to 20 harbor ports that are half empty.'"[7] To be sure, wars such as those between Iraq and Iran and Iraq and Kuwait produce a desaturation that reignites solvent demand for the reconstruction of petrochemical facilities and infrastructure. Thus before the Iraqi invasion of Kuwait, Bechtel had been building near Baghdad a $2 billion petrochemical complex "that could help in the manufacture of chemical weapons. Only seven months later...Kuwait awarded Bechtel a potentially rich contract to help manage reconstruction of the

---

[1]Peter Behr, "Bechtel Bridging Financing Gap," *WPost*, Oct. 21, 1984, at K1 (Nexis).

[2]See Victor Zonana, "Builders' Megaprojects Fade with the Dreams of Oil-Rich Countries," *WSJ*, June 27, 1983, at 1, col. 6; Terry Povey, "Tougher Times for the Mega-Project," *FT*, Dec. 18, 1986, Survey sect. at 36 (Nexis).

[3]Calculated according to data in Saudi Arabia, Central Dept. of Statistics, *Statistical Year Book*, tab. 10-2 at 522 (1983); *id.*, tab. 10-2 at 554 (1988). The amounts were 324 billion and 71 billion riyals respectively.

[4]"The Top International Contractors," *ENR*, July 21, 1983, at 59; "The Top 250 International Contractors," *ENR*, July 7, 1988, at 40.

[5]Youssef Ibrahim, "Oil Prices, Plunging, May Not Have Hit Bottom," *NYT*, Sept. 13, 1993, at C1, col. 3, 6 (nat. ed.).

[6]"The Top International Contractors," *ENR*, July 17, 1980, at 42, 43 (quoting large West German construction firm).

[7]"The Top International Contractors," *ENR*, July 16, 1981, at 68, 73.

oil facilities devastated by Iraq.''[8]

The world construction market has been further constricted by the implementation of national economic plans in some Third World countries. Conceived in analogy to earlier programs of import substitution for First World manufactured products, they have promoted domestic construction industries, thus narrowing the scope of the international demand for construction services.[9] "As countries develop, international contractors find it progressively more difficult to compete with domestic firms, as these become stronger, first in building construction, and at later stages in tasks of increasing complexity, such as roads, airstrips, canals, small dams.... In the more advanced developing countries foreign contractors now supply only highly specialized services...."[10] The obverse side of world market-dependent Third World growth strategies has also severely limited the scope of very profitable undertakings for multinational firms. The increasingly large shares of national income required to service the enormous international debt incurred in unsuccessfully implementing those strategies have reduced the solvent demand for additional large projects.[11]

### Cost-Cutting in the Metropoles: Flexibility and Antiunionism

> Since...the world market does not exist outside the national spaces of reproduction, but rather as form of motion of capital in them, the contradictions...and crises necessarily reproduce themselves at the national level....[12]

This drastic contraction in the world market during the 1980s, which compressed "the individual business cycles" of the industrial sub-markets of geographically diversified firms into "the same cycle," markedly altered multinational firms' profit-maximizing strategies, depriving them of one kind of "flexibility" and imposing another.[13] Thus in the 1970s, Bechtel's huge staff of engineers and other professionally trained employees was said to be its "most valuable...asset," which permitted the firm the flexibility to assign 500 engineers to a new project immediately without interfering with ongoing projects.[14] Within a few years, however, worldwide depression induced Bechtel to administer an object lesson to those very engineers concerning their own flexibility in the labor market: "When a world-wide slump started hammering it in the mid-1980s...Bechtel discharged 22,000 of its 44,000 professionals, generally with little or no severance pay. By so doing...it avoided losses...."[15] Bechtel also reduced

---

[8]G. Zachary & Susan Faludi, "Bechtel, Hurt by Slide in Heavy Construction, Re-Engineers Itself," *WSJ*, May 28, 1991, A1, at col. 6, at A16, col. 1. See also "Iran and Iraq Bracing for Contractor Invasion," *BW*, Aug. 4, 1988, at 14; "Top International Constructors," *ENR*, July 18, 1985, at 54.

[9]National Research Council, *Building for Tomorrow: Global Enterprise and the U.S. Construction Industry* 17-18 (1988). On import substitution strategies, see Wolfgang Schoeller, *Weltmarkt und Reproduktion des Kapitals* 224-34 (1976); Celso Furtado, *Formação econômica do Brasil* 186-222 (12th ed. 1974); Raúl Prebisch, *Transformación y desarrollo: La gran tarea de la América Latina* 115-18 (1970).

[10]The World Bank, *The Construction Industry: Issues and Strategies in Developing Countries* 30 (1986 [1984]). See also "Introduction," in *The Global Construction Industry: Strategies for Entry, Growth and Survival* 1, 4-5 (W. Strassmann & Jill Wells ed., 1988).

[11]See generally Elmar Altvater, *Sachzwang Weltmarkt: Verschuldungskrise, blockierte Industrialisierung und ökologische Gefährdung: Der Fall Brasilien* (1987).

[12]Altvater, *Sachzwang Weltmarkt* at 79.

[13]"Bechtel: Fending Off the Recession by Hitting the 'Small Time,'" *BW*, Mar. 7, 1983, at 54, 58.

[14]Dan Cordtz, "Bechtel Thrives on Billion-Dollar Jobs," *Fortune*, Jan. 1975, at 90, 142.

[15]Zachary & Faludi, "Bechtel, Hurt by Slide, in Heavy Construction, Re-Engineers Itself" at 1, col. 1. See also Philip Kohn, "Engineering Firms Adopt a Survival Strategy," *ChE*, Oct. 18, 1982, at 45 (Nexis); "Shrinking Bechtel Matches Work," *ENR*, Aug. 1, 1985, at 66.

the total number of its technical and manual employees from 102,000 in 1980 to 30,900 in 1991.[16] Although Bechtel's extraordinary world market dependence caused it to implement especially drastic mass dismissals, other multinational firms such as Brown & Root, Fluor, and Holzmann also discharged up to half their employees during the depression of the 1980s.[17]

The new flexibility, at least with regard to international projects, entails passing risk on to others by entering into subcontracts with smaller entities and hiring engineers from the Third World at much lower cost on a project-by-project basis.[18] Multinational firms have also been forced to cope with the loss of overseas markets by having recourse to much smaller domestic projects, as large domestic firms have traditionally done during depressions.[19] At the height of U.S. international hegemony, "20th century pyramid-builders" such as Bechtel, Fluor, and Morrison Knudsen "would barely consider projects with price tags below a billion dollars."[20] In the meantime, however, Bechtel, for example, has been compelled to take contracts as small as $90,000 in order to valorize the capital it accumulated overseas; yet it is precisely that enormous "overhead" that causes it to make "little money on many small contracts."[21] It is a multidimensionally telling commentary that prison construction has become one of the markets with "strong potential" for the world's largest industrial builders such as Bechtel, Fluor, and Holzmann.[22]

Multinational firms driven back into the U.S. market by world market depression have discovered that they can reduce their labor costs by "hiring more non-union workers"[23] just as they sought out non-U.S. projects in the beginning of the 1970s to offset lagging domestic demand. Achievement of this cost-cutting goal has impelled even the largest unionized firms to join the so-called open-shop or merit-shop movement, which had been decimating union ranks since the early 1970s.[24]

---

[16]Michael Kolbenschlag, "Bechtel's Biggest Job—Constructing its Own Future," *Forbes*, Dec. 7, 1981, at 138; *1991 Bechtel Report to Employees* 5 (n.d.). Since the value of the contracts secured by Bechtel almost doubled during this period, Bechtel may have achieved this extraordinary reduction in part through increased reliance on contract management services and by converting employees into alleged independent contractors.

[17]Moody's Investors Service & U.N. Centre on Transnational Corporations, *Directory of the World's Largest Service Companies* 203, 208, 233 (Series I—1990).

[18]Behr, "Bechtel Bridging Financing Gap"; Herbert Northrup & Margot Malin, *Personnel Policies for Engineers and Scientists: An Analysis of Major Corporate Practices* 212, 259 (1986 [1985]); telephone interview with Gary Hunt, Morrison Knudsen Co. (Boise, Idaho, Feb. 18, 1993).

[19]Zachary & Faludi, "Bechtel, Hurt by Slide in Heavy Construction, Re-Engineers Itself"; "The Shrinking World of U.S. Engineering Contractors," *BW*, Sept. 24, 1984, at 84; "Bechtel: A Builder Moves Into Financing and Operations," *BW*, Oct. 22, 1979, at 119; Peter Cassimatis, "The Performance of the Construction Industry, 1946-1965," at 161, 295-96 (Ph.D. diss., New School for Social Research, 1967).

[20]Thomas Hayes, "Big Builders Learn to Think Small," *NYT*, July 28, 1985, sect. 3, at 1, col. 5 (Nexis).

[21]Zachary & Faludi, "Bechtel," at A16, col. 1-2.

[22]"The Top 400 Contractors," *ENR*, May 25, 1989, at 38-39 (quoting official of Fluor Daniel). See also Hayes, "Big Builders Learn to Think Small" (Bechtel builds county jail); "Florida Seeks Jail Developers," *ENR*, Sept. 14, 1989, at 53 (joint venture of Becon Construction Co., the non-union subsidiary of Bechtel, and Wackenhut Services Inc.); Zonana, "Megabuilder Bechtel"; Zachary & Faludi, "Bechtel," at A16, col. 1-2; "Tougher Times in Prisons: Fierce Competition for Work Helps Correction Agencies Stretch Prison Dollars," *ENR*, June 15, 1992, at 28; Philipp Holzmann Aktiengesellschaft, *Geschäftsbericht 1992*, at 33 (1993) (Holzmann's U.S. subsidiary Jones received orders for building penal facilities in the South).

[23]Hayes, "Big Builders Learn to Think Small."

[24]Bill Paul, "Nonunion Contractors Winning Sizable Share of Construction Work," *WSJ*, July 7, 1972, at 1, col. 6; "Open Shops Build Up in Construction," *BW*, Aug. 1, 1972, at 14; "Nonunion Firms Get an Increasing Share of Construction Work," *WSJ*, Dec. 18, 1975, at 1, col. 6; Herbert Northrup & Howard Foster, *Open Shop Construction* (1975); John Trimmer, "ABC: Profile of Philosophy," *MSC*, Jan. 1976, at 15; "Open-Shop Construction Picks Up Momentum," *BW*, Dec. 12, 1977, at 108; Gilbert Burck, "A

In the mid-1970s, the internationally oriented petrochemical and industrial process plant construction firms were, with the exception of Brown & Root—whose owners have a long antiunion history including the successful promotion of antilabor legislation in Texas[25]—members of the National Constructors Association (NCA). The most significant construction employers organization to emerge from World War II, the NCA was founded in 1947 by twenty-one of the largest firms engaged in oil refinery and steel and chemical plant building "to head off potential chaos threatened by the end of wage stabilization after World War II" through local and national collective bargaining.[26] The perceived need "to improve field labor relations" that gave rise to the NCA coincided with the establishment of labor-relations departments by the national construction firms, which had been necessitated by the increasingly large size of the projects built during and after the war.[27]

By 1974 the NCA's forty-two members accounted for eight of the ten largest nonresidential construction firms and 45 per cent of the value of all domestic and 67 per cent of that of all overseas contracts awarded to the 400 largest U.S. firms. Conversely, more than two-fifths of NCA members' total construction volume derived from international projects.[28] This heavy reliance on world market projects associated with cheap labor may in part explain these firms' initially relatively open attitude towards construction unions within the United States. Given the small number of firms competing in this subsector and the relatively inelastic demand for their products by U.S. domestic industrial consumers, which were often primarily interested in early completion dates made possible by the absence of strikes, the NCA firms' competitive focus on the uniformity of wages among members rather than on the absolute wage level was strategic. This hypothesis is supported by the fact that the president of the AFL-CIO Building and Construction Trades Department, Robert Georgine, "expressed a willingness to view the subject of government support of multinational construction firms with an open mind."[29]

As antiunion firms expanded the scope of their operations from housebuilding in rural areas and the South and Southwest to industrial building in the North, however, NCA members' position towards unions hardened. Whereas in 1965 seven NCA members accounted for 69 per cent of the total domestic contracts awarded to *ENR*'s ten largest firms, by 1975 this share had declined to 41 per cent. The "open shop" share rose during this period from one-seventh to three-fifths.[30] As early as 1973, the NCA, which at that time operated "100% union" within the United States, implicitly threatened that unless unions were

---

Time of Reckoning for the Building Unions," *Fortune*, June 4, 1979, at 82; Clinton Bourdon & Raymond Levitt, *Union and Open-Shop Construction: Compensation, Work Practices, and Labor Markets* (1980); Herbert Northrup, *Open Shop Construction Revisited* (1984); Steven Allen, "Declining Unionization in Construction: The Facts and the Reasons," 41 *ILRR* 343 (1988).

[25]"Roadbuilders with a Flair for Other Jobs," *BW*, May 25, 1957, at 90, 106.

[26]"NCA Increases the Pressure to Cut the Fat Out of Labor Costs," *ENR*, Mar. 1, 1973, at 18. See also John Dunlop & Arthur Hill, *The Wage Adjustment Board: Wartime Stabilization in the Building and Construction Industry* 43, 47 (1950).

[27]*To Amend the National Labor Relations Act, 1947, with respect to the Building and Construction Industry: Hearings Before the Subcomm. on Labor and Labor-Management Relations of the Senate Comm. on Labor and Public Welfare*, 82d Cong., 1st Sess. 126, 126, 128 (1951) (NCA folder submitted in evidence by its vice-president, J. O'Donnell) (quotation); *A Company of Uncommon Enterprise: The Story of the Dravo Corporation 1891-1966*, at 91 (1974); Daniel Mills, "Factors Determining Patterns of Employment and Unemployment in the Construction Industry of the United States," at 21 (Ph.D. diss., Harvard University, 1967).

[28]"NCA Increases the Pressure to Cut the Fat Out of Labor Costs" at 18; "NCA Members Ply the World and Find Jobs on Every Continent," *ENR*, Dec. 5, 1974, at 14; *ENR*, Nov. 27, 1975, at 22-23.

[29]"Construction to Prove Export Aid Need," *ENR*, May 29, 1975, at 9-10.

[30]"National Constructors Seek New Industrial Labor Pact," *ENR*, Oct. 21, 1976, at 15.

amenable to productivity increases that rendered their members wages competitive with the lower wages of the nonunion sector, the NCA itself might be "going open shop."[31]

Beginning in the late 1960s, industrial capitalist construction consumers launched a multipronged attack against the labor unions with which NCA negotiated and whose members were employees of NCA firms. The favored medium for this campaign was *Fortune*, which in 1968 declared the building trades unions "[t]he most powerful oligopoly in the American economy," which, counter-intuitive though it might have seemed at the height of the Vietnam War, was "the single most important direct contribution to the current wage-price spiral." The following year *Fortune* editorially urged that "something drastic must be done to bring this conglomeration of monopolies back to economic reality before it wrecks us all." The macroeconomic catastrophe that the magazine feared was that the "exorbitant" wage increases gained through construction unions' "murderous bargaining power" would spread to industrial unions. The editors blamed the construction firms themselves for failing to unite in resistance, and endorsed efforts by industrial construction users to intervene.[32]

The most infamous instance of alleged building trades union greed in the late 1960s was made possible by General Motors' rush order for construction of a plant for producing Vegas in Lordstown, Ohio. Because Ford had already begun production of its small automobiles, GM feared that delays might permanently endanger its share of this increasingly important submarket; GM was therefore willing to accept higher construction costs in order to expedite its entry into that market.[33] The wage increases associated with the sudden absorption of a large number of skilled workers and the extraordinary volume of planned overtime provided the occasion for *Fortune* to publish two pages of pictures of individual workers with captions detailing their purportedly outrageous $10 to $14 hourly wages.[34] Although the magazine censured GM for its role in this development, it was encouraged by the fact that GM had decided to "join...other major corporations whose aim is to support a tough stand by the contractors' associations at the bargaining table." These firms would "monitor all settlements in the construction industry and may chastise any company that forces a contractor to capitulate to the extreme demands of the building trades' unions."[35]

In order to dispel any sympathies that often lead "Americans as consumers...sentimentally [to] take sides with the workers against the bosses," *Fortune* asserted that "[i]n construction...the real conflict is not between labor and capital, but between labor and consumers, with the employers serving as a medium for passing labor's exactions on to the public at large."[36] This ideological claim, which is favored when business conditions permit such shifting so that wage increases can be decried as the sole cause of higher consumer prices, loses its propagandistic value when the shifting becomes cyclically impossible and the ensuing profit squeeze in fact appears as a conflict between construction firms and

---

[31]"NCA Increases the Pressure to Cut the Fat Out of Labor Costs" at 18.

[32]Thomas O'Hanlon, "The Unchecked Power of the Building Trades," *Fortune*, Dec. 1968, at 102; "Breaking Up a Labor Monopoly," *Fortune*, Sept. 1969, at 85, 86.

[33]Although higher construction costs "are an especially important factor in international competition because the United States is forced to rely on modernizing and building new plants and equipment in order to offset the lower wage rates abroad," the amortization period may be so long and output so great that increased construction cost may increase final unit costs only insignificantly. M. Lefkoe, *The Crisis in Construction: There Is an Answer* 111-12 (1970).

[34]Don Sider, "The Big Boondoggle at Lordstown," *Fortune*, Sept. 1969, at 106-109, 196. The magazine provided no hourly conversions of GM executives' incomes.

[35]Sider, "Big Boondoggle" at 196.

[36]Gilbert Burck, "The Building Trades versus the People," *Fortune*, Oct. 1970, at 95. See also Sylvester Petro, "Unions, Housing Cost and the National Labor Policy," 32 *LCP* 329 (1967).

their customers, industrial firms.

By the early 1970s, NCA members had begun to cooperate with the group that *Fortune* had been extolling—the Construction Users Anti-Inflation Roundtable/Business Roundtable, an organization of leading executives of the NCA's largest industrial customers.[37] These industries, and particularly the petroleum industry and power utilities sector, invested the greatest absolute amounts of capital in plant and structures. Because they were also the industries in which such outlays bulked largest in relation to their total fixed capital expenditures, they were peculiarly sensitive to increased construction costs.[38] Although it was unusual for customers to interfere with the way in which their suppliers operated their businesses, instead of buying elsewhere or vertically integrating into that industry, the Roundtable encouraged its members "to intervene in the affairs of suppliers who had lost control of their costs. Contractors soon saw that their long-term interests were served by the arrangement."[39] The NCA had little alternative but to accommodate the Roundtable's cost-cutting antiunionism: constructors experienced the latter's argument that construction unions were a major factor contributing to cost pressures as an expression of their declining competitiveness.[40]

Many firms' desire to eliminate unions and their members from construction sites was in part driven by an effort at belated implementation of a Taylorist program of scientific management, which overlapped with the Roundtable's agitation in favor of the "restoration of the management role in the construction industry."[41] One of Frederick Taylor's guiding tenets was "the very sad fact that almost every workman...who is engaged in anything like coöperative work, looks upon it as his duty to go slow," whereas "[t]here is hardly any worse crime...than that of deliberately restricting output...."[42] In order to reduce workers' power to exercise control over the process of production, Taylor articulated the need for management to wrest from its employees their "rule-of-thumb knowledge," to systematize it, and to formulate and prescribe the new rules as components of managerial prerogatives. Tayloristic management also assumed the task of "scientifically" selecting its workers.[43]

From the outset the open-shop movement aggressively albeit implicitly adopted this agenda. It replaced union journeymen, whose higher wages "embodied [self-]supervisory skills" that enabled them to work independently, with relatively well-paid managerial supervisors who "oversee many other workers

---

[37]Pacific Studies Center, "Black Monday," *Pacific Research & World Empire Telegram*, Nov.-Dec. 1969, at 18, 23; letter from Richard Kibben, Executive Director—Construction, Business Roundtable, to author (Mar. 23, 1976).

[38]"Interindustry Transactions in New Structures and Equipment, 1967," *SCB*, Sept. 1975, at 9, 10-11, 15-17, 21. The petroleum/natural gas industry was both the leading industrial consumer of structures and allotted the greatest share of its fixed capital expenditures to structures (four-fifths in 1967 compared with two-thirds for utilities and three-tenths for manufacturing as a whole).

[39]"A Time of Reckoning for the Building Unions" at 88.

[40]When accused of contributing to inflation, companies like Bechtel had their own methods for deflecting sanctions. Thus on George Shultz's last day in office as Secretary of the Treasury and chairman of the Cost of Living Council (CLC) before entering into Bechtel's employ, the CLC reduced by one-half a penalty that it had imposed on Bechtel for overcharging clients. Conveniently for Bechtel, President Nixon had appointed its owner to the Labor-Management Advisory Committee, which advised the CLC. "Shultz Joins Bechtel Executive Staff," *ENR*, May 16, 1974, at 38; "Wrongdoing Denied in a Bechtel Case," *ENR*, May 30, 1974, at 9.

[41]Business Roundtable, *Coming to Grips with Some Major Problems in the Construction Industry* 51-57 (1975 [1974]).

[42]Frederick Taylor, "The Principles of Scientific Management," in *Scientific Management: Addresses and Discussions at the Conference on Scientific Management, held October 12, 13, 14, 1911*, reprinted in 1 *Some Classic Contributions to Professional Managing: Selected Papers* 37, 38, 40 (1956).

[43]*Id.* at 44-46.

who have lesser skills and are lower paid.''[44] This transition could best be effected on the personnel level by hiring ''a new breed of workers whose goals and needs are substantially different from those of the previous generation. No longer...are young men interested in job and economic security. Rather...they view work as a necessary evil or a means toward achieving other self-oriented goals.''[45] Once wages were restored to a central place in interfirm competition, the race to the bottom quickened. Although at first a firm could ''increase its profit margin by going non-union and bidding against union firms,'' once its competitors ''are also open-shop operators,'' it will ''feel pressured to further reduce worker wages and benefits, increase productivity and lower...profit margins to underbid other non-union firms.'' At the end of this irresistible and irrational spiral, then, the firm's ''profit margin is no better than when the industry was an all-union operation.''[46]

As early as 1980, even Bechtel, the NCA's largest member, had succumbed to this logic and inaugurated so-called double-breasted operations—in which one owner operates two firms, one unionized and the other nonunion—by acquiring Becon Construction Company of Houston, a nonunion firm which had been formed two years earlier by former Bechtel employees as an open-shop firm. Although one of the ''less often mentioned'' reasons for forming the holding company, Bechtel Group, Inc., was to keep it ''well apart from the rest of the organisation, which [wa]s covered by extensive union agreements, the firm publicly stated that Bechtel could perform engineering on the projects for which Becon did the construction.'' This nonunion entity was intended to enable Bechtel to compete in Sunbelt ''areas where open shop construction competition has flourished.'' Yet soon Becon was competing with two leading world market firms, nonunion Brown & Root and Fluor Daniel, in the Northwest, where it built a $40-million project for Weyerhaeuser. And although Bechtel asserted that Becon did not signal a departure from Bechtel's traditional union orientation, especially since its operations were relatively small, by 1982 Becon was already the forty-fourth largest construction firm in the United States; its half-billion dollars in contract awards amounted to almost one-third of Bechtel's domestic total for that year.[47]

Nor was Bechtel alone in this transition to nonunion operations. Unable to persuade the National Labor Relations Board or the federal appellate courts that the common owner of the nonunion firm in double-breasted operations was per se violating its duty to bargain collectively, building trades unions tried but failed to induce Congress to remove this significant obstacle to reunionization of the construction industry.[48] Thus by 1987, NCA membership had dwindled to thirteen firms. Nevertheless in 1992, twelve of its sixteen members still ranked among the twenty-two largest U.S. firms and five ranked among the ten largest in terms of overseas contracts.[49]

---

[44]Boudon & Levitt, *Union and Open-Shop Construction* at 48-49; Leslie Berkman, "Construction Unions Try to Stem Job Losses," *Los Angeles Times*, Mar. 16, 1986, pt. 4, at 1, col. 1 (Nexis).

[45]"The Open Shop Voice Grows Loud and Clear," *ENR*, Nov. 27, 1969, at 44, 45.

[46]Berkman, "Construction Unions Try to Stem Job Losses."

[47]"Bechtel's Dance of the Seven Veils," *Economist*, May 16, 1981, at 93; "Bechtel to Purchase Open Shop Contractor," *ENR*, Jan. 8, 1981, at 53; "Becon Upbeat: Nonunion Builder Expects Workload to Grow by 50%," *ENR*, Feb. 20, 1986, at 59; "The Top Four Hundred Contractors," *ENR*, Apr. 28, 1983, at 64, 69, 72. Because *ENR* during the 1980s listed Becon independently as one of the 400 largest contractors despite indicating that it was a Bechtel subsidiary, the data in table 11.3 for the ten or four largest firms should be adjusted slightly. Although Fluor maintains collective bargaining agreements with unions, Fluor Daniel does not.

[48]29 U.S.C. § 158 (a)(5) (1988). The House of Representatives passed the Construction Industry Labor Law Amendments Act in 1986, but the Senate failed to vote on it. H.R. 281, 99th Cong., 2d Sess., 132 *CR* 7875-76 (1986). The bill has been refiled as H.R. 114, 103rd Cong., 1st Sess., 139 *CR* H103 (Jan. 6, 1993). See generally Stephen Belfort, "Labor Law and the Double-Breasted Employer: A Critique of the Single-Employer and Alter-Ego Doctrines and a Proposed Reformulation," 1987 *WLR* 67.

[49]"NCA Sheds its President," *ENR*, June 4, 1987, at 51; NCA, "1992 Directory of Membership."

## Accumulation and the Transnational Centralization of Capital

The world has become Steve [Bechtel]'s office table; a big chunk of the petroleum, steam power and atomic power industries, his erector set.[50]

Even if the OPEC boom has definitively petered out, its internationalizing impact has survived.[51] The enormous size of the Middle East projects, which precluded competition from smaller firms, and the corresponding level of profits, which, when capitalized, created a new segment of firms, initiated a process that has become detached from its source. As the business press recognized at the height of the boom, the "lure" of "[g]reater profit margins" abroad has made the larger firms increasingly dependent on types of projects that are not inexhaustible. "As a consequence, many competitors fear that the heavy-construction industry is growing so fat through the new ambitions of the energy-rich countries that neither the developing world nor the industrial nations will be able to feed it adequately in the future."[52]

This shrinking market with its concomitant sharp price competition has made visible the operation of the laws of capital accumulation in an industry that some observers are still inclined to regard as standing outside that regime.[53] Thus some construction industry specialists argue that, because industrial consumers demand unique products, there are few scale economies in construction; consequently concentration of capital confers no special advantage with regard to production techniques. This claim, however, is inconsistent with these authors' own admission that firm-size operates to fashion a hierarchy of firms according to market segment, leaving large projects to large companies with "economic power and technical know-how."[54] It is also at odds with trade reports that "mergers and acquisitions were the driving force behind the increased totals for many individual contractors and nationality groups."[55]

This technological stratification is exemplified by Stone & Webster, which on the basis of its proprietary processes has engineered olefins plants accounting for 35 per cent of world capacity. Other firms such as Kellogg, based on patented or proprietary processes and technology for synthetic ammonia, ethylene, and liquified natural and petroleum gas processing, and Impianti in seamless steel pipes, "seem to get all the contracts for certain types of installations, suggesting virtual monopolies."[56] Virtual duopoly characterizes the market for offshore-oil construction, in which in the late 1970s, two U.S. firms, Ray McDermott & Co.,

---

[50]Neill Wilson & Frank Taylor, *The Earth Changers* 288 (1957).

[51]Michael Ball, *Rebuilding Construction: Economic Change and the British Construction Industry* 36-37 (1988), overlooks this impact while failing to explain why construction differs from other industries in opening the way to foreign firms "only...when there is a lack of indigenous...technology and management skills...."

[52]"Where the Constructors Strike it Rich," *BW*, Aug. 23, 1976, at 51, 47, 56. For an examination of the dependence of West German firms on the world market, see the report on Philipp Holzmann AG in *NZZ*, Mar. 12, 1977, at 14, col. 3. On the quondam hope for a new source of inexhaustibility, see "Middle East: A Big Housing Market Begins to Pay Off," *BW*, June 30, 1975, at 43-44.

[53]National Research Council, *Building for Tomorrow* at 49. Strassmann, "The United States," in *Global Construction Industry* at 22, 28, for example, finds that "[o]ddly enough" the concentration ratio "actually" rose "as competition increased with declining business."

[54]Helen Rainbird & Gerd Syben, "Introduction," in *Restructuring a Traditional Industry: Construction Employment and Skills in Europe* 1, 6-7 (Helen Rainbird & Gerd Syben ed., 1991).

[55]"The Top 250 International Contractors," *ENR*, July 13, 1989, at 42.

[56]"Conclusion: Comparison and Analysis," in *The Global Construction Company* at 211, 223; National Research Council, *Building for Tomorrow* at 21; [Brown & Root], *Brownbuilder*, No. 1, 1992, at 11; William Allen, *Stone & Webster: A Century of Service* 20-21 (1989); Stone & Webster, Inc., *1991 Annual Report to Stockholders* 5 (1992); Stone & Webster, "Burgeoning Workload in the Pacific Rim" (n.d.).

which pioneered the building of huge superstructures on land for use in the Gulf of Mexico, and Brown & Root, accounted for 78 per cent of the world market. Their returns were a "phenomenal" 20 to 25 per cent profit margins. A suit by the U.S. Department of Justice forced the owner of Brown & Root, Halliburton Corporation, to divest itself of Ebasco Services, which it had acquired in 1973, because the acquisition would have reduced competition in power plant construction. By the early 1990s, Brown & Root was still "involved in the design and fabrication of 35% of the world's offshore production capacity."[57]

A similar pattern prevails in U.S. nuclear reactor construction. Bechtel's domination of this subsector has been traced back to the fact that John McCone, the chairman of the Atomic Energy Commission—which was responsible for overseeing construction of commercial plants—during the crucial start-up period from 1958 to 1961, was a former partner of Bechtel.[58] As a result of this relationship, Bechtel "got the jump on the rest of the industry in the power business, at one point taking 80 to 85% of [its] income from that market."[59] As of 1981, Bechtel had built 44 per cent of the seventy-five nuclear plants operating in the United States. By 1991 it still maintained "a presence" at more than 40 percent of U.S. nuclear stations. Together with Stone & Webster, United Engineers & Constructors (a subsidiary of Raytheon), and Ebasco Services, it has built 80 per cent of the nuclear plants in the United States.[60]

As these examples suggest, firms commonly specialize in international sub-markets which reflect their technological strengths in their domestic markets. Thus, for example, Dutch firms specialize in dredging and land reclamation, Japanese in high-speed railroads, French in nuclear power plants, Italian in hydroelectric dams, Finnish in pulp and paper mills, and Swiss and Austrian in tunneling.[61]

The laws of capital accumulation have asserted themselves with greater force since the late 1970s. The transnational centralization of capital in the "highly oligopolistic" international construction industry,[62] the competitive interpenetration of the domestic markets in the advanced capitalist countries, the increasing necessity for sellers to grant credit to buyers, and the "development of a world market for all types of construction materials" all testify to the emergence of a world market in construction.[63] This interpenetration within construction mirrors the general "inter-triad" multinational corporate investment among the United States, Japan, and the European Community, which has become the most dynamic aspect of the world economy since the 1980s.[64] In order to support the

---

[57]"Right Place at Right Time—and Lucky," *ENR*, May 8, 1958, at 78; John Huey, "Antitrust Investigation Could Reshape Makers of Offshore-Oil Gear," *WSJ*, July 6, 1978, at 1, col. 6; Shawn Tully, "The Mismatched Merger That Worked," *Fortune*, Apr. 19, 1982, at 166; "The 400," *ENR*, Apr. 12, 1973, at 46; *id.*, May 20, 1976, at 151; Brown & Root, *A World of Services* 18 (n.d. [ca. 1992]).

[58]See Richard James, "For a Family Concern, Bechtel Group Works on Enormous Projects," *WSJ*, Apr. 10, 1979, at 1, col. 6, at 24, col. 2; Robert Ingram, *The Bechtel Story: Seventy Years of Accomplishment in Engineering and Construction* 11, 82 (1968). See also chapter 8 above.

[59]"Bechtel Reorganization Tips Off Market Push," *ENR*, Dec. 11, 1980, at 20, 21.

[60]Kolbenschlag, "Bechtel's Biggest Job—Constructing its Own Future" at 138; "Construction Unions, Contractors Agree to Cut Labor Strife at Nuclear Plant Sites," *WSJ*, Apr. 19, 1978, at 14, col. 2; *1991 Bechtel Report to Employees* at 15.

[61]Jim Antoniou, *Construction in the Middle East* 60 (1978); OECD, *Globalisation of Industrial Activities: Four Case Studies: Auto Parts, Chemicals, Construction and Semiconductors* 114 (1992); Stephen Drewer, "Scandinavia," in *Global Construction Industry* at 160, 169.

[62]Barney Warf, "The International Construction Industry in the 1980s," 43 *PG* 150, 151 (1991).

[63]Steven Setzer, "Materials Markets Going Global," *ENR*, Mar. 29, 1993, at 31 (quotation); "Financial Engineering Wins Jobs," *ENR*, Aug. 2, 1984, at 28; "Introduction," in *The Global Construction Industry* at 5-6. On the connection between credit and competition, see Karl Marx, 1 *Das Kapital: Kritik der politischen Ökonomie* 611-13 (1867).

[64]United Nations Centre on Transnational Corporations, *World Investment Report 1991: The Triad in Foreign Direct Investment* 36-44 (1991).

increasingly crucial financial side of its large-scale operations, Bechtel, which, had it not been the largest privately owned company in the United States, would have ranked twenty-first on the Fortune 500 list, even bought the investment banking firm of Dillon, Read in 1981.[65]

Large international construction firms, confronted with a plethora of fixed capital assets,[66] are in the process of unleashing a further round of internationalization by competing for one another's hitherto relatively sheltered domestic markets in order to amortize their capital.[67] Beginning in the 1970s, the largest Japanese builders, for example, reproducing the U.S. construction firms' model of forming "client-contractor 'alliances' with U.S.-based multinational firms planning production facilities abroad,"[68] followed in the wake of their Japanese manufacturing customers and began constructing the latter's factories in the United States. Ohbayashi's construction of Toyota's plant in Kentucky and Kajima's construction of Mazda's in Michigan in the 1980s were only the most prominent examples. They also raise the possibility of the existence of noneconomic aspects of such Japanese-Japanese relationships between construction and industrial firms overseas inasmuch as the former commonly function merely as general contractors or project managers. Relying on U.S. subcontractors to carry out the actual construction, Japanese constructors in the United States assert that: "Construction is a local business and you have to hire local tradespeople to be cost effective."[69] Even more interestingly, those "tradespeople" often turned out to be the nonunion subsidiaries of the Japanese firms' largest international competitors such as Bechtel and Fluor.[70] Only after a protracted struggle with U.S. construction unions did Ohbayashi, for example, abandon its choice "to do business the American way—merit shop."[71]

Building projects for Japanese manufacturing, trade, and service corporations abroad have continued to form the bulk of Japanese construction firms' worldwide operations.[72] Japanese construction firms, however, have also begun to carry out urban development projects in the United States, Australia, and even the People's Republic of China involving office buildings, hotels, and houses.[73]

---

[65]"Bechtel's Dance of the Seven Veils"; "Construction's Man of the Year: Stephen D. Bechtel, Jr.," *ENR*, Feb. 21, 1974, at 30, 32; Victor Zonana, "Megabuilder Bechtel Tries to Stay on Top by Being Aggressive," *WSJ*, Oct. 16, 1984, at 1, col. 6; "Dillon Read's Managers to Buy Control from Bechtel, Which Will Retain a Stake," *WSJ*, Mar. 8, 1983, at 2, col. 3. In 1991, Bechtel was the eighth largest privately held company. Ronald Henkoff, "Inside America's Biggest Private Company," *Fortune*, July 13, 1992, at 83, 87.

[66]On underutilization of construction capital equipment, see "Factory Builders Find Slim Pickings," *BW*, July 24, 1978, at 51-52.

[67]See Rhonda Rundle, "Rising Sun May Be Too Hot for U.S. Contractors," *WSJ*, Jan. 15, 1988, § 1, at 22, col. 3; "The Top 400 Contractors," *ENR*, May 25, 1989, at 39; Kolbenschlag, "Bechtel's Biggest Job" at 139

[68]"Foreign Markets Rev Up As Domestic Ones Slow," *ENR*, May 24, 1990, at 38, 39. "Multinational manufacturing enterprises establishing a plant abroad commonly reserve the work to a compatriot contractor with whom they have had past experience." "Conclusion: Comparison and Analysis," in *Global Construction Industry* at 211, 222.

[69]Marla Dickerson, "Kajima Builds Up Its Reputation," *Detroit News*, Jan. 21, 1991, sect. F, at 1 (Nexis) (quotation); "Conclusion: Comparison and Analysis" at 250.

[70]Becon and Daniel were major contractors at the Toyota plant. Jay Kraker, "Toyota Plant Plows Ahead with No Sign of Union Pact," *ENR*, Nov. 27, 1986, at 65; Kenneth Noble, "Toyota Agrees on Union Workers to Construct a Plant in Kentucky," *NYT*, Nov. 26, 1986, at B8, col. 1.

[71]"Construction Unions Urged to Stop 'Bullying' Toyota," PR Newswire, Nov. 17, 1986 (Nexis) (telegram from Associated Builders and Contractors Inc. to Toyota).

[72]See Lisa Martineau, "Making Inroads Overseas," *FT*, Dec. 18, 1986, Survey sect. at 37 (Nexis); Fumio Hasegawa, *Built by Japan: Competitive Strategies of the Japanese Construction Industry* 82-83, 148-50 (1988); Sidney Levy, *Japanese Construction: An American Perspective* 2, 9-16, 126 (1990); "The Top 250 International Contractors: Instability Slows Growth Abroad," *ENR*, July 22, 1991, at 30-31.

[73]Hasegawa, *Built by Japan* at 148-50.

The growing force of the world market can be gauged by the fact that international centralization of capital has overtaken national centralization as a vehicle of internationalization. The international accumulation of construction capital has, several decades after similar movements in the extractive and manufacturing industries, finally assumed the form of the international centralization of capital.[74] Refuting the older view according to which "the construction firm...is rarely bought or sold as a unit because it does not generally possess intangible assets, such as location, patents, or a steady clientele,"[75] large European construction firms, in a pattern familiar from earlier international industrial capital movements to the United States,[76] began in the late 1970s to acquire U.S. firms for the purpose of competing in the United States.[77] The collapse of the OPEC boom hastened this process especially for firms that had relied heavily on the Middle East market. Thus, for example, almost 90 per cent of West German firms' $30 billion in orders between 1974 and 1983 originated in oil-exporting countries—Saudi Arabia alone accounting for one-half. It came as no surprise, then, that German firms undertook to diversify their markets geographically.[78]

In the absence of new orders in Saudi Arabia, West German firms began buying their way into the U.S. market. In 1978, Bilfinger & Berger Bau AG acquired the fortieth largest U.S. construction firm, Fru-Con. The next year, the largest West German firm, Philipp Holzmann AG, reoriented itself on the world market by acquiring the then thirteenth largest U.S. firm, J. A. Jones Construction Company. Holzmann proceeded to acquire others in the 1980s. By 1991, North America accounted for more than a quarter of German firms' international contracts—more than the Middle East and the Third World combined.[79]

More major mergers with U.S. firms followed. Shimizu, the largest Japanese firm, acquired 45 per cent of Dillingham, the fifteenth largest U.S. firm in 1987; Tobishima Corporation acquired 48 per cent of George A. Fuller Company, the forty-forth largest firm, in 1988.[80] The same year, the British firm Davy, the then-largest international contractor, acquired Dravo, which had been the thirty-first largest firm in the United States in 1986. The next year the Swedish-

[74]See *National Interests in an Age of Global Technology* 31-32 (Thomas Lee & Proctor Reid ed., 1991); Ernest Mandel, *Der Spätkapitalismus* 292 (1973 [1972]).

[75]Benjamin Kaplan, "Profile of the Contract Construction Industry," *CRev*, Feb. 1957, at 4, 5. By the same token, however, this older view may well explain why U.S. construction firms have engaged in relatively little direct investment in Third World countries. See U.S. Office of Business Economics, *U.S. Business Investments in Foreign Countries: A Supplement to the Survey of Current Business*, tab. 6 at 94 (1960); *idem, U.S. Direct Investments Abroad 1966, Pt. I: Balance of Payments Data*, tab. A-6 at 50 (1970). More recently, multinational firms have established subsidiaries overseas in order to compete for contracts in countries that award them only to domestic firms. See U.N. Centre on Transnational Corporations, *Transnational Corporations in the Construction and Design Engineering Industry* at 11.

[76]See generally Norman Glickman & Douglas Woodward, *The New Competitors: How Foreign Investors Are Changing the U.S. Economy* (1990 [1989]).

[77]See "Overseas Firms Closing in on U.S.," *ENR*, Aug. 2, 1984, at 10; "Foreigners Step Up U.S. Invasion," *ENR*, Nov. 27, 1986, at 12-13.

[78]Erich Gluch & Jürgen Riedel, "The Federal Republic of Germany," in *Global Construction Industry* at 120, 124-25.

[79]National Research Council, *Building for Tomorrow* at 81-84; *BW*, Sept. 18, 1978, at 49; Gluch & Riedel, The Federal Republic of Germany at 127-28; "Both Partners Work for Successful Marriage: Phillip Holzmann and J. A. Jones are Spreading Out," *ENR*, June 3, 1982, at 30; Philipp Holzmann Aktiengesellschaft, *Geschäftsbericht 1992* at 19, 79; Hauptverband der Deutschen Bauindustrie, *BJ 1992* at 36.

[80]"Shimizu Leads Dillingham Buyout," *ENR*, June 4, 1987, at 50; *ENR*, May 12, 1988, at 30; "The Top 250 International Contractors," *ENR*, July 13, 1989, at 42, 45. These acquisitions marked a departure from the large Japanese firms' pattern of starting their own subsidiaries in the United States. See Steven Setzer & Richard Korman, "Are They Better? Japanese Bring More Than Money in Their Quest for U.S. Market Share," *ENR*, Mar. 3, 1988, at 30.

Swiss electrotechnical conglomerate Asea Brown Boveri acquired Lummus Crest, the eighth largest U.S. construction firm.[81] This centralization movement spread even into residential construction at the beginning of the 1980s when the British firm Barratt became one of the largest housebuilders in California by buying American National Housing Corporation and McKeon Construction.[82]

Consequently, whereas until the 1980s "there was virtually no foreign ownership of U.S. construction firms," a decade later "15 of the largest 100 contractors on ENR's Top 400 list are totally or partially owned by foreign interests."[83] Within a few years, these largely German, British, and Japanese firms amassed more than 70,000 employees, almost $10 billion in assets, and $14 billion in sales. In spite of this unprecedented development, however, they still lag far behind their manufacturing counterparts in penetrating the U.S. market. Whereas the latter employ almost 11 per cent of manufacturing workers in the United States, non-U.S.-owned firms employ only one per cent of all U.S. construction workers.[84]

Nevertheless, the surplus in the U.S. international balance of payments for construction services has been reduced. Prior to the 1980s, non-U.S. construction firms' activities in the United States were so mimimal that they were not even identified in the U.S. balance of payments statistics. Since the mid-1980s, however, official but fragmentary data suggest that payments to non-U.S. firms and U.S. affiliates of non-U.S. firms for construction services in the United States have begun to approach the receipts of U.S. firms for construction services performed outside the United States.[85] Thus from 1980 to 1988 the value of contracts

---

[81]"Davy Pittsburgh Sets Sights on Growth," *Allegheny Business News*, Feb. 1991, sect. 1, at 1 (Nexis); *ENR*, May 24, 1990, at 81; "ABB Group Sells Clean Technology," *ENR*, July 5, 1990, at 21.

[82]Ball, *Rebuilding Construction* at 185; Joan Gray, "Specialized Approach to Markets," *FT*, Mar. 5, 1984, § III, at III.

[83]"The Top 250 International Contractors: Instability Slows Growth Ahead," *ENR*, July 22, 1991, at 30, 35.

[84]See Steve Bezirganian, "U.S. Affiliates of Foreign Companies: Operations in 1990," *SCB*, May 1992, at 45, 48, 59, 63, 65, tab. 6 at 52. For further indicators of the enormous gap between manufacturing and construction with regard to the size of foreign investment (in the United States and abroad) and income derived therefrom, see J. Landefeld, Ann Lawson, & Douglas Weinberg, "Rates of Return on Direct Investment," *SCB*, Aug. 1982, at 79, tab. 17 at 113-14; "U.S. Direct Investment Abroad: Detail for Historical-Cost Position and Balance of Payments Flows, 1991," *id.*, at 116, tab. 18 at 143-44; Raymond Mataloni, Jr., "U.S. Multinational Companies: Operations in 1990," *SCB*, Aug. 1992, at 60, tab. 9.1 & 9.2 at 70-71.

[85]Reliable figures are not available because the U.S. Department of Commerce publishes asymmetrical data: those for construction exports are net of merchandise exports and outlays for wages, materials, and other expenses, whereas import data are not netted. John Sondheimer & Sylvia Bargas, "U.S. International Sales and Purchases of Private Services," *SCB*, Sept. 1992, at 82, 116 n.1. The asymmetry derives from the fact that the Department of Commerce collects the import data not from the non-U.S. construction firm, but from the U.S. customer, which reports (on Form BE-20 or BE-22) the total amount (if in excess of $500,000) paid for construction services to foreign firms (but not to U.S. affiliates of foreign firms). See U.S. Bureau of Economic Analysis [BEA], Form BE-20: Benchmark Survey of Selected Services Transaction with Unaffiliated Foreign Persons (Nov. 13, 1991); *idem*, Form BE-22: Annual Survey of Selected Services Transactions with Unaffiliated Foreign Persons (Oct. 21, 1992). On this basis, imports amounted to 35 per cent of exports for the years 1986 to 1991. Calculated according to data in Sondheimer & Bargas, "U.S. International Sales and Purchases of Private Services," tab. 2 at 83. If the "sales of services to U.S. persons by nonbank majority-owned U.S. affiliates of foreign companies" are included, imports actually exceeded exports by wide margins in 1989 and 1990: $2,961,000,000 as against $1,128,000,000 and $1,687,000,000 as against $916,000,000 respectively. Calculated according to data in *id.*, tab. 2 at 83, tab. 12.1-13.2 at 129-32. Presumably the distorting asymmetry also applies to these data, although the group responsible for processing the data at the BEA itself did not know. When confronted with the revelation of the asymmetry, the BEA responded by furnishing gross receipts for construction exports for the years 1987 through 1991 (whereby the BEA was, again, unsure whether they included data for foreign affiliates of U.S. firms). Although these data would show an excess of exports over imports in 1990 ($2,647,000,000 versus $1,687,000,000), they would still leave an implausible deficit for 1989 ($1,917,000,000 versus $2,961,000,000). Telephone interview with Sylvia Bargas (Feb. 2, 1993). A different series of (gross rather than net revenue) data for 1982 and 1983 indicated that U.S. revenues of foreign firms amounted to about half of foreign revenues of U.S. firms. U.S. Congress, Office of

awarded to non-U.S. firms for projects in the United States as a share of the value of overseas contracts awarded to U.S. firms rose from one-sixteenth to one-half (before falling again to one-fifth in 1991).[86]

Nor has the international centralization movement been restricted to the United States. European firms have also acquired construction firms in other countries as well. Hochtief, for example, has acquired almost half of Leighton Holdings Ltd., the most important construction firm in Australia.[87]    Spie Batignolles, one of the largest French firms, acquired an interest in Davy, one of the largest British firms. Both of these firms, which also acquired subsidiaries in the United States, have themselves been subject to centralization movements initiated by their largest domestic competitors—an unsuccessful hostile takeover by Bouygues in 1986 and acquisition by Trafalgar House in 1991 respectively.[88]    In order to secure a base in central and Eastern European markets, in 1992 Trafalgar House, already Britain's largest international construction firm, acquired a half interest in the industrial process engineering companies of Austria's largest international construction firm, Voest-Alpine.[89]

Cross-border construction within the European Community was still limited during the 1980s. As late as 1984, for example, the EC accounted for only two per cent of the value of new British overseas contracts. Yet in Western Europe, too, the "severe crisis" in overseas markets triggered interpenetration and an extensive national and transnational merger and acquisition movement: "European contractors are heading for a shakeout as they withdraw from traditional oil-fired overseas markets that are in deep recession because of oil price cuts. They are finding insufficient work at home and are looking for acquisitions to diversify themselves and to make all of Europe their 'domestic' market."[90]    When demand declined in Northern European markets in 1987, construction firms from those countries entered into intensive competition with local firms for projects in Italy, Spain, Portugal, and Greece.[91]

As British firms' new contracts in the Middle East plummeted from £818 million in 1984 to £125 million in 1987, those that they obtained within the EC increased almost six-fold to £213 million. Thus while the share accounted for by the Middle East dropped from 36 per cent to a mere 5 per cent, the EC's share rose to 9 per cent.[92]    The geographic rediversification of the German construction

---

Technology Assessment, *Trade in Services: Exports and Foreign Revenues* tab. 15 at 60 (1986) (without a source or methodology).

[86]Calculated according to data in James Lee & David Walters, *International Trade in Construction, Design, and Engineering Services*, tab. 2-4 at 27 (1989); "The Top 250 International Contractors," *ENR*, July 13, 1989, at 45; "The Top International Contractors," *ENR*, Aug. 24, 1992, at 36.

[87]Hochtief, *Annual Report 1991*, at 31, 39 (1992); Heiner Radzio, *Die Aufgabe heisst Bauen: 110 Jahre Hochtief* 35 (1985). On Hochtief's acquisition of 50 per cent of Theiss Holding, Ltd., another Australian firm, see "Branching Out," *ENR*, Oct. 1, 1981, at 60.

[88]Spie Batignolles acquired Comstock, one of the largest electrical contractors, while Davy acquired McKee and Dravo. "Bouygues Battle Brewing," *ENR*, Dec. 18, 1986; "France's Bouygues Completes Purchase of Rival," *ENR*, Apr. 17, 1986, at 5; "The French Ascension," *ENR*, Oct. 30, 1986, at 24; Paul Betts, "Bouygues' Expansion Continues," *FT*, Dec. 18, 1986, Survey sect. at 38; Elisabeth Campagnac & Vincent Nouzille, *Citizen Bouygues ou l'histoire secrète d'un grand patron* 157-83 (1988) (also discussing Bouygues' merger efforts with GTM and SCREG); Marc Colombard-Prout, "France," in *The Global Construction Industry* at 104, 109-12; 2 *MIntM* 1991, at 4020 (1991); 1 *MIntM* 1992, at 1773 (1992).

[89]Trafalgar House Public Limited Company, *Report and Accounts* 7 (1992).

[90]Peter Heywood, "European Firms Looking at Their Own Backyard," *ENR*, Nov. 27, 1986, at 67. See also Victor Cox, *International Construction: Marketing, Planning and Execution*, tab. 0.1 at viii (1982); Gluch & Riedel, "The Federal Republic of Germany" at 121; "Europe Set to Open Single Market Doors," *ENR*, Dec. 14, 1992, at 38.

[91]"Riviera Rivalries: European Contractors Compete for Booming Southern Market," *ENR*, June 11, 1987, at 15.

[92]"Civil Engineering Companies Get More New Contracts Abroad," *BB*, July 29, 1988, at 18,20.

industry was even more dramatic. In 1974, at the outset of the OPEC boom, Europe accounted for only 3 per cent of the value of new international contracts and Africa, Asia, and the Middle East for 95 per cent. By 1991, Europe accounted for 44 per cent of new contract value; the EC alone surpassed all of the Middle East, Africa, Asia, and Latin America.[93]

Interpenetration has also spread to relations between the First World and the so-called Newly Industrializing Countries. Construction firms from former Third World countries such as South Korea and Brazil have not only been able to wrest from leading First World firms a significant share of the world market for standard or relatively low-technology cost-sensitive heavy construction with a range of capital-labor substitution, but have even begun to compete in Europe and the United States.[94] Thus Construtora Norberto Odebrecht ("the Bechtel of the Portuguese-speaking world"), a Brazilian conglomerate with large petrochemical holdings and the 40th largest international construction firm in 1991, was forced "'to operate worldwide, if only to know how to fend off our international competition in Brazil.'" Odebrecht has not only secured a contract for the Miami rapid transit system, but also entered into a joint venture with Bechtel to build a refinery in the former Soviet Union.[95] Unlike the Brazilian constructors, South Korean multinational firms were impelled to penetrate the U.S. market by their catastrophic loss of market shares in the Middle East in the mid-1980s. Firms such as Samwhan and Hyundai Engineering and Construction initiated the process by building public works in Alaska.[96]

In the United States, from 1988 to 1990, foreign construction firms acquired seventeen U.S. construction firms in transactions valued at $1.8 billion; during the same period seventy-eight mergers and acquisitions involving only U.S. construction firms took place valued at $1 billion.[97] Although a Bechtel official sought to persuade Congress in 1985 that the forty-two foreign mergers and acquisitions that had taken place since 1978 in the U.S. construction industry had been driven by the foreign firms' interest in gaining U.S. technology and management expertise, a U.S. government report rejected this explanation, focusing instead on the non-U.S. firms' own technological niches and higher research and development expenditures.[98]

By 1987 the rate of import penetration in nonresidential construction in the United States (4.4 per cent) was about the same as in Germany (4.5 per cent) and higher than in France (1.7 per cent) or Japan (0.8 per cent). And although "exports" as a share of U.S. domestic nonresidential construction (9.0 per cent) were considerably lower than in Italy (43.8 per cent), the United Kingdom (33.5

---

[93]Calculated according to data in *BJ 1975* at 51; *BJ 1992* at 36.

[94]"The Top International Contractors," *ENR*, July 16, 1981, at 68, 73; "Brazil Looks Abroad for Work," *ENR*, Apr. 7, 1983, at 17; U.S. International Trade Administration, *A Competitive Assessment of the U.S. International Construction Industry* (1989 ed. [1984]); "The Top 400 Contractors," *ENR*, May 25, 1989, at 80; Josmar Verillo, "Brazil," in *The Global Construction Industry* at 180, 189. On the political-economic contradictions inhering in this new international division of labor, see Ernest Mandel, *The Second Slump: A Marxist Analysis of Recession in the Seventies* 130-40 (rev. ed., Jon Rothschild tr., 1978).

[95]Joel Millman, "You Have to Be an Optimist," *Forbes*, May 24, 1993, at 84 (quotation), 87; Rob McManamy & Armin Schmid, "Odebrecht: Brazil's Giant Beats Adversity," *ENR*, Sept. 20, 1993, at 45, 47 (quoting Odebrecht official); Andrew Wood, "Brazil's Odebrecht Builds a Major Petrochemicals Stake," *CW*, Mar. 31, 1993, at 36; "Big Soviet Job for Brazilian-U.S. Venture," *ENR*, July 15, 1991, at 5; Katherine Molinski, "Brazil's Odebrecht Targets U.S. and Chinese Construction Market," Reuter European Business Report, June 23, 1993 (Nexis).

[96]"Koreans Crack U.S. Market," *ENR*, Dec. 5, 1985, at 46.

[97]*SAUS: 1992*, tab. 854 at 534; *SAUS: 1991*, tab. 889 at 540; *SAUS: 1990*, tab. 884 at 534.

[98]*U.S. International Competitiveness: The Construction Industry: Hearings Before the Subcomm. on International Policy and Trade of the House Comm. on Foreign Affairs*, 98th Cong., 1st Sess. 11-12 (1985) (testimony of Michael Stephenson); U.S. International Trade Administration, *Foreign Builders Target the United States: Implications and Trends* 19-20 (1988).

per cent), or France (27.6 per cent), the share approximated Germany's (11.6 per cent) and far exceeded Japan's (3.5 per cent).[99] In the same year, U.S. affiliates of foreign companies accounted for 6.7 per cent of industrial building in the United States—about 70 per cent of the corresponding level for all of manufacturing.[100]

Protectionist initiatives, prompted by this wave of international centralization of construction capital in the United States, to restrict such foreign investments under the guise of national security have failed to come to fruition.[101] By the same token, however, the Buy American Act was amended in 1988 to forbid the procurement by the federal government of construction services of a contractor owned or controlled by citizens or nationals of a foreign country identified as violating certain provisions of the GATT Agreement on Government Procurement inspite of the fact that the GATT Agreement does not apply to (construction) service contracts unless such services are incidental to the supply of products the value of which they do not exceed.[102] With as yet undetermined consequences, the U.S. trade representative identified Japan as discriminating against U.S. businesses in the procurement of construction services.[103]

More generally, the same kinds of disputes concerning trade barriers and state intervention that have characterized Japanese-American-European manufacturing trade relations have been replicated in the construction industry, in particular with regard to bidding on infrastructure projects.[104] Bemoaning the fact that no U.S. construction firm has been awarded a public works contract in Japan for over four decades[105] or any major contract since the mid-1960s, the U.S. international construction industry has even asserted that Japanese industrial firms' preference for Japanese construction firms on projects in the United States demonstrates that they "have transported the noncompetitive procedures and protectionist barriers they use in Japan to their investments in this country."[106] Such lobbyists fail to mention that U.S. industrial firms have for decades followed the same national-preference practice overseas.[107]

---

[99]OECD, *Globalisation of Industrial Activities*, tab. 34 at 105. Export shares and import penetration levels may be understated to the extent that multinational firms create "a network of autonomous operating companies" abroad. *Id.* at 105.

[100]U.S. Bureau of Economic Analysis & U.S. Bureau of the Census, *Foreign Direct Investment in the United States: Establishment Data for 1987*, tab. 1 at 3-4 (1992).

[101]See "Foreign Bill Planned: Proposed House Bill Seeks to Limit Some Investments," *ENR*, Nov. 18, 1982, at 79.

[102]Buy American Act, 41 U.S.C. §§ 10b-1(a)(2) and (g) (Supp. 1991); Trade Agreements Act of 1979, 19 U.S.C. § 2515 (1980); Agreement on Government Procurement (GATT), Pt. I, ¶ 1(a).

[103] Robert Hershey, "Japan Formally Accused of Bias Against U.S. Contractors," *NYT*, July 1, 1993, at C2, col. 1 (nat. ed.); Martin Tolchin, "U.S. Embassy Work to Japanese," *NYT*, July 27, 1993, at C1, col. 3 (nat. ed.) (U.S. companies complained that Ohbayashi took a loss on bidding for renovating U.S. ambassador's residence in Tokyo in order "to keep U.S. construction companies out of Japan," whereby one of the "U.S." companies was J.A. Jones, a wholly owned subsidiary of Holzmann).

[104]See e.g., "Mixed-Credit Coalition Hopes to Spur Exports," *ENR*, June 21, 1984; "NCA Maps Recovery Plan," *ENR*, Oct. 1, 1987, at 94; "Accord Reached on U.S. Access to 14 Major Projects in Japan," *ENR*, Apr. 7, 1988, at 12; Lee & Walters, *International Trade in Construction* at 82-87; Ralph Folsom, Michael Gordon, & John Spanogle, Jr., *International Business Transactions: A Problem-Oriented Coursebook* 358-59 (2d ed. 1991).

[105]On Japan's yielding to U.S. pressure to make the bidding process more favorable to U.S. firms, see Keith Bradsher, "U.S. Cancels a Plan to BEGIN Sanctions After Japan Acts," *NYT*, Oct. 27, 1993, at A1, col. 3; Andrew Pollock, "Sanctions on Japan Less Likely," *NYT*, Jan. 17, 1994, at A1, col. 6 (nat. ed.).

[106]*United States-Japan Services Trade: Hearing Before the Subcommittee on International Economic Policy, Trade, Oceans and Environment of the Senate Committee on Foreign Relations*, 100th Cong., 2d Sess. 30-34 (quotation at 33) (1988) (statements of Maureen Smith, Dept. of Commerce, and Mark Chalpin, National Constructors Association and International Engineering & Construction Industries Council).

[107]*Business Week* reported that despite technological superiority, U.S. firms have few proprietary processes; instead, their advantage lies in the "close relationship" with the oil and chemical firms from which they license the processes. "Where the Constructors Strike it Rich" at 49.

Although internationalization as a competitive strategy is intended to dampen cyclical downswings for multinational construction firms, the formation of a world market enmeshing previously relatively autonomous national markets could in fact exacerbate world construction depressions.[108]  In the United States and Europe, moreover, where the share of overseas contract volume accounted for by the largest construction firms is almost invariably higher than the latter's share of domestic contract volume, an increase in the relative weight of the world market could contribute to a further concentration of market shares.  In Britain, six firms accounted for more than half of new overseas contract value in 1971 and five for more than three-quarters by 1982, while twenty firms accounted for 93 per cent of all overseas construction work in 1978; by the early 1980s, ten firms accounted for 90 per cent.[109]  As early as 1972 twelve West German firms accounted for 85 per cent of that country's construction export orders.[110]  Even in France, where the degree of concentration is less prominent than in Germany and other countries, by 1978 four firms accounted for a third and ten firms for 58 per cent of foreign construction volume.[111]

This internationally driven domestic centralization of capital was most prominently typified by the acquisition in 1986 and 1991 by Trafalgar House of Britain's two largest internationally oriented construction firms, John Brown Engineers & Constructors, Ltd. and Davy Corporation, respectively.[112]  Purely domestic mergers and acquisitions among the largest multinational firms in other European countries, too, have been driven by the need to furnish the requisite financial base and market niches for firms to compete internationally.  In West Germany in 1981, Hochtief purchased one-fifth of the stock of Holzmann, which in turn bought 15 (later increased to 23) per cent of Dyckerhoff & Widmann.[113]

By the same token, however, to the extent that the largest firms have accumulated large profits in relatively liquid forms or, alternatively, can locate spheres of investment that can accommodate the physical forms of their unutilized capital, some, hedging against a long-term contraction of international construction volume, have attempted to gain access to other industries.  Two of the reasons, for example, that several large construction firms have diversified into coal mining is that they also build mine facilities and that open-pit methods use much of the same earth-moving equipment used in construction.  Utah Construction (which later became Utah Construction and Mining, whose construction division was acquired by Fluor in 1969),[114] was one of the first large construction firms to make the transition from building mines for others to exploiting its own copper and iron ore mines in the United States and Latin America (with the assistance of a loan from

[108]On West German firms, see *Der Spiegel*, Aug. 4, 1975, at 38-39; on Swiss firms, see "Keine Stabilisierung in der Bauwirtschaft," *NZZ*, Sept. 16, 1975, at 15; "Rückbildung im Baugewerbe," *NZZ*, Nov. 19, 1974, at 33; "Bauwirtschaft 1974--wie weiter?" *NZZ*, July 13, 1974, at 17. Karin Behring, Erich Gluch, & Volker Rußig, *Entwicklungstendenzen im deutschen Auslandsbau* 48-49 (1982), find no correlation between domestic and foreign cycles.

[109]"British Construction Work Overseas 1971/72," 9 *TI* 294, 295 (1972); Michael Cassell, "Stepping up Efforts Abroad," *FT*, Nov. 15, 1976, at 25; "Building Big Business Overseas," 33 *TI* 128 (1978); "Going Up--British Building Business Overseas," 37 *TI* 358 (1979); Ball, *Rebuilding Construction* at 140; "Building Up: The Work of UK Construction Firms Overseas," 9 *BB* 256 (1982); "Contractors Fight to Boost Overseas Markets," *IC*, Feb. 1983, at 21, 22.

[110]"West Germany," *IC*, Dec. 1973, at 26, 35.

[111]Behring, Gluch, & Rußig, *Entwicklungstendenzen im deutschen Auslandsbau* at 53.

[112]Trafalgar House Public Limited Company, "Background Information" at 5 (July 1993).

[113]"Holzmann Buys Interest in German Contractor," *ENR*, June 16, 1981, at 46; "German Giants Move Closer," *ENR*, Nov. 26, 1981, at 5; *Directory of the World's Largest Service Companies* at 232, 235; "UK Firms Merger," *IC*, Jan. 1983, at 5; John Kosowatz, "Finnish Seek Help for Foreign Jobs," *ENR*, May 19, 1988, at 54.

[114]On the Fluor acquisition, see *NYT*, July 26, 1969, at 37, col. 2 (Nexis).

the Export-Import Bank) in the 1950s.[115]   Utah Construction and Mining and several large multinational construction companies with longstanding ties to the entities driving natural resource exploitation in the West and Southwest of the United States, including Bechtel, Morrison Knudsen, and Kaiser, began developing plans in the 1960s for building a complex of strip mines, power plants, and coal gasification plants as a regional industrial energy source.[116]   Bechtel and Fluor then acquired 15 and 10 per cent respectively of the largest coal mining firm in the United States, Peabody Coal, in the mid-1970s.  In 1981, "[c]ash heavy" Fluor also acquired St. Joe Minerals for $2.2 billion.[117]

British firms have also diversified into mining.  Costain, "sensing the approaching end of the oil boom," invested heavily to become a major coal producer (also in joint venture with Holzmann's Jones Construction) and exporter in the United States and Australia in the 1980s.[118]   And Wimpey not only operates opencast coal businesses in the United Kingdom and quarries in the United States, Canada, and the Czech Republic, but is also a major producer of lime in the United States.[119]

A further reaction by large construction firms to the pressures of internationally competitive capital accumulation has been the assumption of a financial interest in their own projects.[120]   Replicating the strategic behavior of the mid-nineteenth-century international railway contractors such as Brassey and Peto, the imperious valorization requirements of whose accumulated fixed capital compelled them to finance their own railways in order to forestall the idling of their enormous apparatus, construction firms no longer have the luxury of producing only on order.  Under the pressure of the world construction market crisis, they have been compelled to produce speculatively as well.[121]   One such trend-setting arrangement is the founding of United Infrastructure Company, a joint venture between Bechtel and Kiewit, which will "'fund, build, own and operate elements of infrastructure—highways, bridges, wastewater treatment plants—those kinds of things that are moving toward private ownership....'"[122]   Without offering such "'accommodative equity,'" even large international firms like Brown & Root recognize that it will be impossible to build infrastructure in the United States.[123]

---

[115]Wilson & Taylor, *Earth Changers* at 107-12.

[116]For an undocumented interpretation of this development, see Peter Wiley & Robert Gottlieb, *Empires in the Sun: The Rise of the New American West* 41-45 (1982).

[117][Fluor Corp.], *Heritage*; "Ready to Capitalize on the Hidden Assets in St. Joe," *BW*, Apr. 27, 1981, at 104; Fluor Corporation, *1991 Annual Report* 3, 19 (1992); 1 *IDCH* 569-71 (Thomas Derdak ed., 1988) (explaining Fluor's subsequent partial divestiture of St. Joe); Michael Law, "Mining Surge May Pan Out," *ENR*, Sept. 1, 1988, at 28; "Morrison-Knudsen's Foray into Coal Mining," *BW*, June 20, 1977, at 52; *BW*, Nov. 1, 1976, at 24.  On Bechtel's previous involvement with a planned coal pipeline, see *ibid.*, July 27, 1974, at 36-37; Dec. 15, 1975, at 24.

[118]Costain Group, "Costain Group" (n.d. [ca. 1990]); Costain Group PLC, "Company Milestones" (Sept. 30, 1992); "Building Up" at 260.

[119]*Wimpey: The International Construction Group* 8-9 (n.d.); George Wimpey PLC, *Annual Report 1992*, at 2, 9, 11, 22-25 (1993).

[120]See e.g., "Goodrich, Bechtel Set Chemical Venture," *WSJ*, July 21, 1977, at 11, col. 1; "The New Directions at Dravo," *BW*, Sept. 13, 1976, at 100; "Bechtel: A Builder Moves into Financing and Operations," *BW*, Oct. 22, 1979, at 119-20; Carrie Dolan & Bill Richards, "Bechtel to Cut Its Work Force About 10% in 1984; Nuclear-Power Plant Woes Cited," *WSJ*, Feb. 27, 1984, at 4, col. 2.

[121]Jörn Janssen, "Das Baugewerbe—ein rückständiger Wirtschaftszweig?" in *Bauarbeit in der Bundesrepublik* 27, 34 (Wolfgang Richter ed., 1981) has deduced a trend toward production for inventory from the indicators of increasing capital intensity.

[122]Judy Schriener, "No Grand Plan But Plenty of Cash," *ENR*, Mar. 22, 1993, at 24, 25.

[123]Gary Tulacz, "The Top Owners Are Building, But They Remain Cautious," *ENR*, Nov. 22, 1993, at 34.

# 13

# Multinational Construction
# Firms as Agents of Penetration of
# the Third World

> Many of Morrison's...jobs are in primitive, undeveloped countries, where M-K's
> giant power shovels and 18-ton bulldozers are as much a source of wonder as the
> iron horse was to the Indians a century ago.[1]

In 1954, secure in the worldwide military-economic preeminence that the United
States had been projecting for a decade, *Time* celebrated the contribution of U.S.
construction firms to the establishment and perpetuation of that hegemony. In a
cover story on Morrison-Knudsen's controlling owner at the apogee of the
American Century, *Time* both captured and helped engender the multidimensionally
chauvinist *Zeitgeist* inherent in "helping backward people help themselves":

> U.S. earth movers have shown the world that man need not be a prisoner of his
> surroundings.... He can change much of the unproductive land to suit his needs.
> Part of this change is due to the new machinery: the clanking bulldozers that
> knock down forests, the great draglines that claw house-sized holes at a single
> scoop, the cranes, jumbos, earth movers, power shovels, trenchers and dozens of
> other mechanical giants.... But the biggest part of the change is the revolution in
> construction thinking; today, there is almost no project too big to tackle, no
> reasonable limit to reshaping the earth to make it more productive.[2]

International construction firms have always operated at the cutting edge of
this enterprise designed to realize the dream of subordinating nature to, and
recreating it in the image of, infinitely self-expanding economic value. To be sure,
they are wont to characterize the mammoth changes they have wrought in the
physical environment, especially in the former colonies, as humanitarian
acts—"Subduing nature for the weal of man."[3]  Yet in their attachment to
projects in developing countries with abundant natural resources, multinational
construction firms' microeconomic self-interest drives and is, in turn, impelled by
a certain view of the periphery's role in the world division of labor insofar as "the
exploitation of mineral as well as agricultural products...would demand the
expansion of infrastructures, such as roads, rail, ports, storage facilities required for
the transport of these resources for export."[4]

---

[1]"The Earth Mover," *Time*, May 3, 1954, at 86.

[2]*Id.*

[3]"In Memoriam I. K. Brunel," 17 *Builder* 664 (1859).

[4]Roland Neo, *International Construction Contracting: A Critical Investigation into Certain Aspects of
Financing, Capital Planning and Cash Flow Effects* 96 (1975).

## International Development Aid as a Means of Penetration of the Third World and a Subsidy to U.S. Construction Firms

The weakening of European capital and colonial powers and the concomitant hegemony of U.S. capital and its state brought about by World War II also entailed a new set of relationships with the colonized populations in Africa and Asia, many of which were in rebellion. Britain, for example, was vitally interested in expanding colonial production in order to increase exports to the United States and thus to offset its dollar deficit. "The full exploitation of African minerals," however, depended on an adequate transportation system, which was "the single biggest bottleneck in the drive to tap the Dark Continent's resources."[5]

The power that the United States was able to bring to bear through the Marshall Plan[6] prompted "a growing realization in Europe that African territories are not exclusive, but should be the responsibility (and the opportunity) of the world as a whole."[7] In other words, under the new structure of international relations, "American companies and American private capital will be free to participate on exactly the same terms as British investors."[8] As integration and equal access became the guiding imperialist policy, it finally dawned on the colonial powers that the colonial transportation system had become dysfunctional for the exploiting firms and states because "it is nearly impossible to go from the outer reaches of one colony to another without first going to the coast, taking ship [sic], and reaching the outlet of another railroad or road."[9]

The large capital-intensive infrastructure projects in the Third World, which were prerequisites for the development of profitable industrial investments but not in themselves attractive to investors, came during the 1950s and 1960s to be financed in large part by the International Bank for Reconstruction and Development (IBRD). In addition to examining the engineering feasibility and long-term economic viability of proposed "social overhead capital" projects,[10] the World Bank also maintained a vigilant ideological stance by taking into consideration the borrowing "government's attitude toward private enterprise." This intervention by the IBRD, the bulk of whose loans financed the construction in the Third World of dams, power stations, highways, and ports by First World firms, made it possible for large European and U.S. construction firms to be "Building a Better World—At a Profit."[11] "Because of the World Bank," for example, "Morrison-Knudsen is building a cement plant in Indonesia...."[12]

In particular, however, the World Bank enabled U.S. firms—which had even resorted to building a "loss leader to break into the domination of European companies" in such places as Iraq[13]—to penetrate colonial areas that had largely

---

[5]*ENR*, Oct. 7, 1948, at 8.

[6]See generally Fred Block, *The Origins of International Economic Disorder: A Study of United States International Monetary Policy from World War II to the Present* 70-108 (1978 [1977]).

[7]Frederick Brewster, "Colonial Powers Discuss African Transport Integration," *ENR*, Mar. 22, 1951, at 36, 37.

[8]*ENR*, Oct. 7, 1948, at 8.

[9]Brewster, "Colonial Powers" at 36.

[10]Social overhead capital "can be operationally defined as comprising those activities for the financing of which the International Bank for Reconstruction and Development shows a pronounced preference, just as the behavioral sciences have been said to comprise all those endeavors which manage to obtain financial support from the Ford Foundation." Albert Hirschman, *The Strategy of Economic Development* 83 (1960 [1958]).

[11]"Building a Better World—At a Profit," *ENR*, Jan. 17, 1957, at 21, 23. Morrison-Knudsen and Raymond, for example, built 2,000 miles of highways in Colombia with World Bank financing. Forest Green, "Colombia Modernizes Its Highway System," *ENR*, July 8, 1954, at 30-36.

[12]"Building a Better World" at 23.

[13]"U.S. Contractors Go Global," *BW*, Apr. 14, 1956, at 139, 142.

been protected preserves of British and French construction firms.[14] From 1947 to 1955, almost three-fifths of World Bank disbursements ($1 billion) were spent in the United States for capital equipment and services. Although this share fell by the latter half of the 1950s, it still exceeded the U.S. share of IBRD financing, while the absolute amount spent in the United States rose from $240 million to $280 million.[15] Thus U.S. firms built dams in Ghana and Pakistan in the 1960s while British firms such as Taylor & Woodrow and George Wimpey continued to excel at harbor works in Africa and Europe and Cleveland Bridge and Dorman, Long built bridges throughout the world.[16]

Whereas the World Bank lent only to member governments, the U.S. Export-Import Bank could make loans to private borrowers—both foreign buyers and U.S. suppliers—as well. A very large share of the hundreds of millions of dollars that the Ex-Im Bank had lent for the export of construction equipment and services by the mid-1950s redounded to the benefit of U.S. construction firms such as Morrison-Knudsen. The most important center of Ex-Im Bank lending was Latin America, which was designated a "natural market—wide open for...the U.S. construction industry...."[17] The Third World focus of U.S. construction firms was crystallized in the fact that in the 1950s projects in Western Europe accounted for only 17 per cent of their income generated overseas, whereas Latin America alone accounted for 38 per cent.[18]

The U.S. International Cooperation Administration, operated by the Department of State to provide "civilian" defense support to friendly nations, enabling them to devote more resources to military expenditures, was partial to U.S. firms in its program to improve "internal transport facilities throughout the free world."[19] Utah Construction, for example, received $25 million to build a hydroelectric facility in Pakistan in the mid-1950s.[20] Morrison-Knudsen, Raymond, Brown & Root, and other firms, supported by the U.S. Economic Cooperation Administration, U.S. Department of State Development Loan Fund, Mutual Security Program, and international funds, and frequently supervised by the U.S. Army Corps of Engineers,[21] began early in the postwar period to build airports, highways, dams, and hydroelectric projects in Afghanistan, Thailand, Pakistan, Turkey, Iran, Iraq, the Philippines, and other military client states in order to open up regions to industrial development "in which American private capital

---

[14]See The World Bank, IDA and IFC, *Policies and Operations* viii, 39 (1971); The World Bank, *The Construction Industry: Issues and Strategies in Developing Countries* 19 (1986 [1984]); Marc Linder, 4 *Der Anti-Samuelson: Kritik eines repräsentativen Lehrbuchs der bürgerlichen Ökonomie* 112-15 (1974).

[15]Edward Mason & Robert Asher, *The World Bank Since Bretton Woods*, tab. G-1 at 862 (1973); "World Bank Creating Market for U.S. Construction Goods," *ENR*, Sept. 17, 1953, at 60; "Share of World Bank Work Down, Volume Up," *ENR*, Mar. 5, 1959, at 24.

[16]See e.g., C. Tupholme, "Akosombo: Key to a Stable Future," *IC*, Apr. 1966, at 2 (Kaiser Engineering); "Mangla Dam Scheme—The Largest Water Development Ever Undertaken: Part I," *id.*, Jan. 1968, at 2 (Guy F. Atkinson Co.); *ENR*, Aug. 18, 1949, at 54 (Taylor Woodrow builds harbor in Gold Coast); "World-Wide Dock Service of British Engineers," *ENR*, Sept. 14, 1950, at 54; "Ghana's New £ 26 Million Harbor," *IC*, Sept. 1962, at 2 (Taylor & Woodrow and Wimpey); "New Ore Handling Pier for Sierra Leone," *id.*, Aug. 1964, at 2 (Taylor & Woodrow); *ENR*, June 8, 1950, at 52 (bridge in Siam).

[17]"This Bank Exports U.S. Construction," *ENR*, June 13, 1957, at 35, 36.

[18]Calculated according to data in U.S. Office of Business Economics, *Balance of Payments Statistical Supplement: A Supplement to the Survey of Current Business* tab. 37 at 145 (rev. ed., n.d. [ca. 1961]).

[19]"U.S. Money Aids Foreign Transportation," *ENR*, Mar. 7, 1957, at 61; "Competition Tightens Overseas," *ENR*, Nov. 14, 1957, at 25, 27; Charles Kindleberger, *International Economics* 479-81 (3d ed. 1967 [1953]).

[20]Neill Wilson & Frank Taylor, *The Earth Changers* 115-16 (1957).

[21]See e.g., Lewis McBride & William Tatum, "Two International Civil Airports Under Construction by U.S. Army's Corps of Engineers," *CE*, Sept. 1960, at 45 (Morrison-Knudsen and Kaiser in Iran and Pakistan); *CE*, Oct. 1961, at 103 (Morrison-Knudsen, Jones, and Kiewit build $40 million highway in Afghanistan with International Cooperation Agency funds).

has been invited to participate on favorable terms."[22]    The view from the receiving countries was typically less promising.   Turkey, for example, in burdening itself with speculative loans, "has not hesitated to mortgage its future by borrowing, paying excessively for the privilege if necessary."[23]

Morrison-Knudsen was also in the forefront of a state-private capital program in which "[f]or probably the first time in history, a group of U.S. engineering firms" advised "an admittedly backward nation" on the kinds and amounts of infrastructure it should pay U.S. (and European) construction firms to build for it.[24]  In Iran, where even a landlord-dominated government was impelled from below to institute change, since "the United States was largely responsible for stabilizing the postwar Iranian government, it was natural to turn to an American firm for development aid."[25]   Iran thus commissioned a report from Morrison-Knudsen shortly after World War II on how to spend an estimated $650 million.   Other large U.S. construction firms with a tradition of international activities going back to the turn of the century such as Stone & Webster, Ebasco, and J. G. White Engineering, were represented in another group, Overseas Consultants, Inc., which was supported by the U.S. government's Point Four program in its mission of exporting U.S. know-how assisted by American "venture capital to undeveloped lands."[26]

### Neo-Colonial Infrastructure Projects

The cost of building dams is always underestimated....
There are benefits, of course, which may be countable, but which
Have a tendency to fall into the pockets of the rich,
While the costs are apt to fall upon the shoulders of the poor.
So cost-benefit anaylsis is nearly always sure,
To justify the building of a solid concrete fact,
While the Ecologic Truth is left behind in the Abstract.[27]

Multinational firms building pharaonic works in the Third World have transferred the same model of the domination of nature that they have sought for decades to implement in the First World.  The great dams, for example, that Bechtel, Kaiser, Utah, and Morrison-Knudsen built during the depression were designed to transform the western rivers of the United States into literal regional industrial dynamos.  Thus appropriated and put to work, a river was "constrained to flow against its nature in some rigid, utilitarian straitjacket...abstracted ruthlessly from its dense ecological pattern to become a single abstract commodity having nothing but a cash value."[28]

---

[22]"Thompson-Starrett Co. to Build Big Turkish Dam," *ENR*, Mar. 27, 1952, at 88.  See also Ernie Hood, "Putting a New Face on Old Afghanistan is One of Morrison-Knudsen's Projects," *ENR*, Feb. 21, 1952, at 45, 46; *ENR*, Jan. 15, 1953, at 79; "Foreign Aid: New Look Needed?" *ENR*, July 31, 1958, at 21; Waldo Bowman, "Thailand Sets the Pace for Southeast Asia," *ENR*, Jan. 19, 1961, at 30; *idem*, "Iran Pushes Hard for Development and Defense," *ENR*, Mar. 9, 1961, at 36; *idem*, "Iran's Two Big Dams Promise a Better Life," *ENR*, Mar. 16, 1961, at 38 (Morrison-Knudsen and Impresit).

[23]Waldo Bowman, "Hydro Paces Turkey's Construction Boom," *ENR*, Oct. 10, 1957, at 34.

[24]"U.S. Engineering Group to Advise Iran on Economics of Stabilization Scheme," *ENR*, Oct. 28, 1948, at 73.  For a dissenting view, see Heshmat Ala'i, "How Not to Develop a Backward Country," *Fortune*, Aug. 1948, at 76.

[25]Nikkie Keddie, *Roots of Revolution: An Interpretive History of Modern Iran* 130 (1981).

[26]"Rebuilding a Nation," *ENR*, Nov. 3, 1949, at 34.  See also R. Larkin, "Overseas Consultants Wins Contract for $650-Million Iran Development," *ENR*, Oct. 20, 1949, at 25; "State [Department] Enters Iran Point Four Picture, But Private Consultants Stay," *ENR*, Nov. 9, 1950, at 25.

[27]Kenneth Boulding, "A Ballad of Ecological Awareness," in *The Careless Technology: Ecology and International Development* 157 (M. Farvar & John Milton ed., 1972).

[28]Donald Worster, *Rivers of Empire: Water, Aridity, and the Growth of the American West* 331-32 (1992

The immediate benefits of these environmentally often destructive interventions accrue differentially.[29] Where, for example, a hydroelectric dam is built primarily for the U.S., British, and South African firms owning mines in Rhodesia, but 50,000 to 100,000 indigenous people are dispossessed and resettled,[30] "[m]assive technological development hurts." Because owners and constructors "do not think of themselves as paying...the social costs," they do not count them. This kind of cost accounting is exacerbated when the groups that are forced "to make enormous sacrifices" must do so for the good of groups with which they do not identify themselves.[31] Despite the huge sums spent on irrigation projects, such as gravity dams, in the Third World that have radically altered the environment, lenders have found their impact on agricultural output "disappointing" in part because of the waterlogging and increased salinity that they have caused.[32]

In describing the Cabora Bassa dam and hydro-electric plant that it jointly built with other firms in Mozambique in the 1970s, the German company Hochtief contends that "only yesterday denounced as being the last instrument of colonialism, although it is is indeed only a purely technological enterprise to control the wildest river in Africa, [Cabora Bassa] has by now escaped from the vicious circle of ideology...and now serves, independent from any political interest, as was plannned [sic] from the beginning, the people who live in this country."[33] Yet the Portuguese colonial regime originally conceived the project as part of its strategy of retaining control over the colony by forging an "economic enclave of white-dominated African states" out of South Africa, Rhodesia, and the Portuguese colonies in order to block African independence.[34] Economically Cabora Bassa was designed as a means of securing foreign exchange by selling "the cheapest power in the world" to South Africa: only an insignificant supply of energy was available for whatever industrialization plans the Portuguese government harbored for the colony.[35] Even after Mozambique became independent, it remained clear that, since all the project's earnings flowed to the banks and companies that had provided the $400 million in financing, it would be years "before Mozambique gets anything out of this deal."[36]

Large-scale infrastructure projects in the Third World have typically accommodated the traditional model of semi-colonial capital investments. Illustrative in this regard is the Volta River Project in Ghana. Before that

---

[1985]).

[29]See e.g., Peter Bolton, "Mozambique's Cabora Bassa Project: An Environmental Assessment," in 2 *The Social and Environmental Effects of Large Dams: Case Studies* 156-67 (Edward Goldsmith & Nicholas Hildyard ed., 1986).

[30]See David Brokensha & Thayer Scudder, "Resettlement," in *Dams in Africa: An Interdisciplinary Study of Man-Made Lakes in Africa* 20 (Neville Rubin & William Warren ed., 1968); David Howarth, *The Shadow of the Dam* (1961).

[31]Elizabeth Colson, *The Social Consequences of Resettlement: The Impact of the Kariba Resettlement upon the Gwembe Tonga* 1, 3 (1971).

[32]Vernon Ruttan, "Assistance to Expand Agricultural Production," 14:1 *WD* 39-42 (1986).

[33]*Hochtief 1875-1975*, at 18 (n.d. [ca. 1975]).

[34]"Portuguese Hydro Project Will Put Zambezi to Work," *ENR*, Oct. 12, 1967, at 30. See generally Keith Middlemas, *Cabora Bassa: Engineering and Politics in Southern Africa* (1975); Georg Schreyögg & Horst Steinmann, "Corporate Morality Called in Question: The Case of Cabora Bassa," 8 *JBE* 677, 678 (1989).

[35]Ray Vicker, "Portuguese Are Building Big Dam in Mozambique, But Black Nationalists Call It a Colonialist Ploy," *WSJ*, Aug. 7, 1972, at 20, col. 1 (quotation); Nicholas Woodsworth, "Mozambique Rebels Keep Energy Giant Asleep," *FT*, Aug. 25, 1989, § I, at 3 (Nexis); "Pläne für mehrere Industrievorhaben in Mozambique," *FAZ: Blick durch die Wirtschaft*, Apr. 9, 1974, at 2.

[36]David Ottaway, "Southern Africa: History, Money Tie Odd Couple," *WPost*, Dec. 26, 1977, at A12 (Nexis).

country's independence, the British colonial power saw the project as a means of guaranteeing the United Kingdom a supply of aluminum from a sterling-area, that is, a captive, quasi-domestic source free of the political-economic rigors of the world market. The project was reconceived by the newly independent Ghana in the 1950s and 1960s as a means of initiating a planned process of national economic development rather than as a "simple commercial venture."[37] It failed to do so, however, because Kaiser Aluminum and Reynolds Aluminum succeeded in narrowing the purpose of the hydroelectric dam, which was built by an Italian consortium but which Kaiser Engineers and Constructors, Inc. designed, prepared, and inspected, to the provision of cheap electricity for Kaiser's aluminum smelter.[38]

Not only did Ghana not benefit from the industrial linkages associated with aluminum production in the advanced capitalist countries, but Kaiser chose not even to develop Ghana's abundant bauxite reserves from which to recover the aluminum oxide. Instead, Kaiser, which like the other metropolitan aluminum oligopolists is constantly in search of the cheapest power for an energy-intensive industry, imported the alumina from the Western Hemisphere for smelting.[39] That the Volta River Project achieved the most profitable possible production of aluminum with as little impact on Ghana as possible[40] was a great irony since it confirmed the view of Ghana's then-president, Nkrumah, that the hallmark of neo-colonialism in Africa was the absence of an integrated processing or manufacturing industry for any of its numerous raw materials.[41]

The ample loan provided by the World Bank to Ghana[42] supposedly fit the pattern for infrastructure projects in the developing world insofar as the hydroelectric dam was "less attractive to private capital, either because of the size of the investment required, or the smallness or uncertainty of the returns, or the prospect of government intervention or control."[43] Yet as a virtually single-purpose power generator designed to be used by and to profit one U.S. enterprise, this particular hydroelectric facility scarcely conformed to any meaningful notion of infrastructure as a general condition of production or social overhead capital: its monopoly status contradicted the essence of infrastructure as a public good characterized by indivisibility. In spite of the enormous advantages accruing to Kaiser, the U.S. government delayed funding the project until the last possible moment so that it could answer the vital question: "Is Ghana truly a neutral country?"[44]

That the World Bank extended its theretofore largest loan for the construction of the Kariba hydroelectric dam in Rhodesia in the mid-1950s likewise had more to do with the fact that the copper fields to be served produced one-eighth "of the free world's supply" of the metal than with promoting indigenous

---

[37]"The Volta River Scheme," 5 *WP* 26 (1953); "The Volta River Project," 8 *WP* 366 (1956) (quotation).

[38]See "Ghana Gambles on Aluminum," *BW*, May 2, 1959, at 75.

[39]See Robert Steel, "The Volta Dam: Its Prospects and Problems," in *Dams in Africa* at 63; James Moxon, *Volta: Man's Greatest Lake* (1969); Irving Kaplan et al., *Area Handbook for Ghana* 323 (2d ed. 1971); "For Aluminum, a Shift Overseas," *BW*, Dec. 8, 1980, at 108; Ronald Graham, *The Aluminium Industry and the Third World: Multinational Corporations and Underdevelopment* (1982); idem, "Ghana's Volta Resettlement Scheme," in 2 *The Social and Environmental Effects of Large Dams* at 131-39.

[40]Thomas Balogh, *The Economics of Poverty* 283-92 (1964 [1956]).

[41]Kwame Nkrumah, *Neo-Colonialism: The Last Stage of Imperialism* (1965).

[42]International Bank for Reconstruction and Development, *Seventeenth Annual Report 1961-1962*, at 17 (1962).

[43]International Bank for Reconstruction and Development, *Third Annual Report 1947-1948*, at 18 (1948).

[44]"Mission Gives 'Hard Look' at Aid to Volta Project," *ENR*, Nov. 2, 1961, at 26.

development.[45]     In the end, then, such internationally organized neo-colonial infrastructural development aid recapitulated nineteenth-century colonialism, in which railways "mushroomed...without rhyme or reason, wherever new industries arose." In the post-World War II period, when "[c]heap power and lots of it is needed" for bauxite, copper, and ferro-chrome processing in Africa, hydroelectric plants replaced railways as the centerpiece of infrastructure built by metropolitan firms.[46]

Within two decades, African dams dislocated hundreds of thousands of native people. In addition to producing an irreversible loss of land, the stagnant waters of the gigantic reservoirs necessitated by large dams also generated a large increase in disease, especially of schistosomiasis.[47] In Africa, as elsewhere, large dams also destroy ecological systems, bring about salinization of cropland and siltation behind the dams, and destroy subsistence agriculture, replacing it with cash crops that cannot feed local populations.[48] Perversely, the production of chemical fertilizer needed to maintain the fertility of soil that has been deprived of the silt that dams, which prevent seasonal flooding, hold back, may consume a significant proportion of the power output of those very hydroelectric dams.[49]

In Africa, few inhabitants of rural areas receive the benefits of electrification while the major industrial demand for hydroelectric power derives from foreign-owned mining enterprises—the products of which are exported.[50]     Thus hydroelectric projects in the periphery designed to promote the interests of metropolitan extraction industries are a prime example of a "fundamental conflict": they generate adverse environmental effects for the local population while conferring the benefits of cheap power on far-removed persons and firms.[51] If, despite all these severe defects of large hydroelectric projects as instruments of economic development, the World Bank and other international lenders have continued to lavish loans on them, one major reason has been that countries in the periphery must use much of the money to buy "generators, turbines, transmission facilities, and engineering services from major corporations in the developed world." Because the electricity rates are set low precisely in order to attract energy-intensive firms, the underdeveloped world "derives little immediate economic return" from such projects.[52]

These post-colonial dams are functionally homologous to those built during the era of formal colonial empires. Instructive in this regard is the Sennar Dam, which Weetman Pearson's firm and 20,000 Egyptian and Sudanese laborers built in the Anglo-Egyptian Sudan from 1922 to 1925. The Lancashire cotton industry,

[45]"400-Ft-High Arch Goes Up Across 1800-Ft Kariba Gorge," *ENR*, Sept. 6, 1956, at 71; *ENR*, Mar. 26, 1953, at 78 (quotation); International Bank for Reconstruction and Development, *Eleventh Annual Report 1955-1956*, at 40 (1956).

[46]*ENR*, Oct. 7, 1948, at 8.

[47]See Letitia Obeng, "Should Dams Be Built? The Volta Lake Example," 6 *Ambio* 46, 47, 49 (1977); *idem*, "Environmental Impacts of Four African Impoundments," in *Environmental Impacts of International Civil Engineering Projects and Practices* 29-43 (Charles Gunnerson & John Kalbermattem ed., 1978).

[48]Philip Shabecoff, "Actual Price of High Dams Includes Social Costs," *NYT*, July 10, 1983, sect. 4, at 22, col. 1 (Nexis); A. Biswas & M. Biswas, "Hydropower and the Environment," *IWPDC*, May 1976, at 40. For a comprehensive cataloging of the adverse impact of large dams, see *Man-Made Lakes: Their Problems and Environmental Effects* (W. Ackerman et al. ed., 1973).

[49]Daniel Deudney, *Rivers of Energy: The Hydropower Potential* 16 (Worldwatch Paper 44, 1981).

[50]For good overview, see J. Lazenby, "The Future Role of Hydroelectricity in Sub-Saharan Africa," *IWPDC*, Mar. 1991, at 12.

[51]Robert Stein & Brian Johnson, *Banking on the Biosphere? Environmental Procedures and Practices of Nine Multinational Development Agencies* 97 (1979).

[52]Deudney, *Rivers of Energy* at 27-28. A series of smaller and environmentally less destructive hydrodams can also produce cheaper electricity. See Nicholas Kristof, "China Breaks Ground for World's Largest Dam," *NYT*, June 22, 1993, at B5, col. 2, B6, col. 1 (nat. ed.).

*Projecting Capitalism*

which had been world leaders until the turn of the century, became subject to severe competition from Germany, the United States, and China for markets and raw materials. British firms adapted to this new constellation by shifting to the production of the finer cotton textiles. Such a market strategy, however, required access to a finer raw material—long staple cotton—which was grown chiefly in Egypt. The British Cotton Growers' Association, which, like its German counterpart, was simultaneously promoting imperial cotton growing zones in West Africa insulated from the U.S.-dominated world market, successfully urged the British government to initiate construction of the requisite hydrotechnical infrastructure in the Sudan for a vast expansion in cotton production there. The Sennar Dam thus finally enabled British cotton manufacturers to achieve their long-held objective of bringing an additional 300,000 acres of cotton onto a monopsonized imperial market. The externalities of disease (schistosomiasis, malaria, and yellow fever) and economic disaster which Sennar Dam imposed on the people of the Sudan were not entered into the ledger books of S. Pearson & Son, the cotton capitalists, or the colonial government.[53]

Even in a Newly Industrializing Country such as Brazil, which has attained a sufficient degree of autonomous industrialization to enable its own national firms to build hydroelectric plants, such projects may still be driven by world market compulsions if not more directly by decisions made by metropolitan capitals and their states. The results therefore frequently replicate those just outlined for the most dependent Third World countries.[54] By authorizing non-Brazilian firms to operate only where local firms lack the capacity to undertake projects and preserving the internal market for indigenous firms, the Brazilian state has fostered the development of domestic construction capital.[55] Brazilian (and Paraguayan) firms, for example, built Itaipú, the world's largest dam, although Morrison-Knudsen prepared the engineering plans.[56] Yet Brazil's hydroelectric plants merely reproduce on a higher level of technological development the nineteenth-century pattern of supplying infrastructure to world-market resource extractors. Brazil's dams in effect subsidize the electricity for U.S., European, and Japanese-owned energy-intensive aluminum plants which produce exports for the world market. Brazil is therefore indirectly exporting this energy consumed in the process of producing such raw materials.[57] And like the less-developed periphery, Brazil is therefore also constrained to degrade its own environment to pay the

---

[53]"The Soudan Railway," 15 *Engineering* 149, 176 (1873) (report by engineer John Fowler recommending railway as promoting cotton); Oswalde Prowde, "The Gezira Irrigation Scheme, including the Sennar Dam on the Blue Nile," 222 *MPICE* 81, 82 (1927); J. Spender, *Weetman Pearson First Viscount Cowdray 1856-1927*, at 251-59 (1930); Robert Middlemas, *The Master Builders: Thomas Brassey; Sir John Aird; Lord Cowdray; Sir John Norton-Griffiths* 242-44 (1963); Tony Barnett, "The Gezira Scheme: Production of Cotton and Reproduction of Underdevelopment," in *Beyond the Sociology of Development: Economy and Society in Latin America and Africa* 183, 187-89 (Ivar Oxaal et al. ed., 1975); John Waterbury, *Hydropolitics of the Nile Valley* 64-67 (1979); Nigel Pollard, "The Gezira Scheme—A Study in Failure," *Ecologist*, Jan.-Feb. 1981, at 21, 22-26.

[54]See also Henry Kamm, "Dam Project Brings Little Gain for Sumatra's People," *NYT*, Oct. 2, 1980, at A2, col. 3 (Nexis) (describing a Japanese aluminum smelter built in Sumatra to make use of a hydroelectric plant).

[55]"Brazil Forcing Foreigners Out," *ENR*, Aug. 26, 1982, at 26 (Nexis); Josmar Verillo, "Brazil," in *The Global Construction Industry: Strategies for Entry, Growth and Survival* 180, 181, 185-86, 196 (W. Strassmann & Jill Wells ed., 1988).

[56]"Itaipu Dam Readied for Filling," *ENR*, Aug. 12, 1982, at 29; Peter Kilborn, "Brazil's Hydroelectric Project," *NYT*, Nov. 14, 1983, at D9, col. 1 (Nexis).

[57]See Warren Hoge, "Brazil Taps Amazon Aluminum," *NYT*, Sept. 29, 1980, at D1, col. 3 (Nexis); Joan Todd, "Brazil Goes on Stream with First-Phase Alumina-Aluminum Capacity at Alumar," *Engineering & Mining Journal*, Sept. 1984, at 17 (Nexis); "Brazilian Debt Crisis Threatens Large Projects," *ENR*, Jan. 22, 1987, at 29 (Nexis); Luiz Rosa & Roberto Schaeffer, "Brazilian Energy Policy," in *Hydroelectric Dams on Brazil's Xingu River and Indigenous Peoples* 47, 48 (Leinad Ayer de O. Santos & Lúcia M. M. de Andrade ed., 1990).

Third World's largest foreign debt.[58] Yet promotion of less world market- and energy-dependent industries would not only create employment but also avoid the flooding of enormous areas of agriculturally and environmentally vital land including rain forests and the expulsion and wrenching "resettlement" of tens of thousands of indigenous people—whose small cash compensation often has made it impossible for them to purchase land elsewhere—associated with the creation of huge dam reservoirs.[59]

## Multinational Construction Firms as Transferors of Technology

If there was one thing that distinguished man and gave him almost Divine attributes it was when he conquered Nature to his own uses, and made her power minister to his own wants. Among the most marvellous of his conquests was his ability [sic] to make the very globe he trod upon minister to his happiness, and if by his art and science he could do away with the difficulties which the formation of the world threw in his way he was placed in a position almost divine.[60]

Unlike the traditional model of foreign direct investment by firms from advanced capitalist countries in underdeveloped countries, which is associated with unilateral economic control by the former, so-called new forms of international investment stop short of majority ownership. These operations run the gamut from joint ventures, licensing agreements, franchising, management contracts, turnkey contracts, and production-sharing contracts, to subcontracting. Multinational firms have adopted such methods in part as a reaction to political assertions of sovereignty by Third World countries. In part they also represent accommodations to the autochthonous development of capitalism.[61] This process encompasses the proletarianization of peasants and artisans, leading to the formation of an urban wage-labor force; the emergence of a political-economically potent domestic bourgeoisie dedicated to investment in and management of surplus-producing enterprises; and the growth of a national market for consumer goods and industrial inputs.

Although multinational firms may not always be able to impose their preferred form of investment on Third World countries, wholly owned operations may no longer necessarily be their first choice. Whether the motivation is to shift the responsibility for suppressing labor unrest and containing demands for wage

[58]See Marlise Simons, "Dam's Threat to Rain Forest Spurs Quarrels in the Amazon," *NYT*, Sept. 6, 1987, § 1, at 18, col. 1 (Nexis); Stephen Bunker, *Underdeveloping the Amazon: Extraction, Unequal Exchange and the Failure of the Modern State* 84-89 (1988 [1985]); Elmar Altvater, *Sachzwang Weltmarkt: Verschuldungskrise, blockierte Industrialisierung und ökologische Gefährdung: Der Fall Brasilien* 292-304 (1987). For a similar process in Mexico, see Enrique Peters, "Bye Bye Weltmarkt? Freihandel oder Regionalisierung des Weltmarktes: Das Freihandelsabkommen zwischen Kanada, Mexiko und den USA," *Prokla*, No. 90, Mar. 1993, at 129. See generally World Commission on Environment and Development, *Our Common Future* 74-75 (1990 [1987])

[59]See Paul Aspelin & Silvio Coelho dos Santos, *Indian Areas Threatened by Hydroelectric Projects in Brazil* (1981); E. Monosowski, "The Tucuruí Experience," *IWPDC*, July 1983, at 11, 12; Gerd Kohlhepp, *Itaipú: Basic Geopolitical and Energy Situation* 55-78 (1987); Samuel Florman, "Hegel and the Amazon Basin," *TR*, Oct. 1989, at 19; E. Monosowski, "Lessons from the Tucuruí Experience," *IWPDC*, Feb. 1990, at 29, 33; *Hydroelectric Dams on Brazil's Xingu River and Indigenous Peoples*; Nicholas Lenssen, "Providing Energy in Developing Countries," in *State of the World 1993: A Worldwatch Institute Report on Progress Toward a Sustainable Society* 101, 108, 112 (Lester Brown ed., 1993).

[60]150 *PD* (3d ser.) 1362 (1858) (speech by the Radical John Roebuck in support of his resolution proposing that the British government not oppose construction of the Suez Canal).

[61]Precisely when a settler colony becomes political-economically independent is difficult to determine. When an English firm was selected in the 1920s to build the world's largest arch bridge in Australia, *ENR* observed that: "An English concern will build it, the older community thus becoming the servant of the newer and providing the material response to the dreams and initiative of the South Sea continent." "Australia to Set a Record," 92 *ENR* 433 (1924) (editorial).

increases to "local partners, who are often more efficient in these tasks than even the most ruthless expatriate manager could hope to be," or to avoid the risks of world market overcapacity by entering into agreements that tap into Third World countries' ability to pay that is independent of the profitability of the project in question, multinational producers may prefer to avoid full and direct ownership of new facilities.[62]

Contemporary implantation of capital-intensive technologies is typically a bifurcated process involving both producer and construction-engineering firms. Vertical integration in the form of construction-engineering subsidiaries of large process owners is not uncommon in Europe (Hoechst-Uhde, ENI-SNAM Progetti, and IFP-Technip), and Japan (Mitsui Toatsu Chemicals-Toyo Engineering), but the largest and dominant U.S. firms do not follow this pattern.[63] Nevertheless, producers' in-house engineering divisions still accounted for approximately two-fifths of the value of hydrocarbon processing facilities built in the 1980s.[64] This specialization of function, which is associated with the growing scale and complexity of plants characterized by large capital investment, complex technologies, and "the need to make large numbers of project-specific adaptations to the core processes used," is common to petrochemical, steel, nonferrous metals, continuous process industries such as oil, chemicals, and paper, as well as mining and power generation.[65] Although construction firms as owners of process technologies may transfer them in their own right, they also act as agents of producers in the transfer process.[66]

Producers' and constructors' interests may conflict to the extent that the builders' sole purpose in developing technologies is to sell them in "as large and as packaged a product as possible," whereas producers may impose restrictions on technology transfers in order to avoid depressing world market prices and to protect their worldwide profits and market shares. One such restriction is a limitation on production volume, which implicitly restrains exports since the inability to make use of economies of plant size precludes production at world market competitive prices. Moreover, producers "are under no particular constraint to license their technology" if it is more profitable for them to engage in direct investment and production.[67]

Because the constructors' interests "are served by an increasing output of

---

[62]Charles Oman, *New Forms of International Investment in Developing Countries* 11-21, 71-79 (OECD 1984).

[63]Mariluz Cortes & Peter Bocock, *North-South Technology Transfer: A Case Study of Petrochemicals in Latin America* 25-26, 65 n.5 (1984); C. Freeman, "Chemical Process Plant: Innovation and the World Market," *NIER*, No. 45, Aug. 1968, at 29, 36, 38-39. One seeming exception to the pattern mentioned in the text is Kellogg, which is currently owned by Dresser Industries, which provides oilfield and petroleum services; this acquisition, however, did not take place until 1988—almost ninety years after Kellogg's founding. M.W. Kellogg, "The M.W. Kellogg Company: Service to the Industry Worldwide Since the Turn of the Century," [no pagination (at 6)] (n.d. [1992]).

[64]"U.S. Engineering Firms Losing Global Business," *CEN*, Sept. 14, 1981, at 17.

[65]Cortes & Bocock, *North-South Technology Transfer* at 18-19.

[66]For examples of one large multinational firm's proprietary processes in petrochemical, chemical, and refinery plants, see ABB Lummus Crest, "Technology, Project Management, Engineering, Procurement, and Construction Services for Today's Process Industries" (n.d. [ca. 1992]); idem, "Lummus Olefins Technology for Today's Ethylene Plants" (n.d. [ca. 1992]); idem, "ABB Lummus Crest: Process Technologies and Full-Scope Services" (n.d. [ca. 1992]).

[67]Charles Oman, *New Forms of Investment in Developing Country Industries: Mining, Petrochemicals, Automobiles, Textiles, Food* 91, 92 (OECD, 1989) (chapter written by François Chesnais) (quotations); Cortes & Bocock, *North-South Technology Transfer* at 8, 11, 22, 24-28, 50, 64; Robert Stobaugh, *Innovation and Competition: The Global Management of Petrochemical Products* 79, 82-87 (1988); idem, "Channels for Technology Transfer: The Petrochemical Industry," in *Technology Crossing Borders: The Choice, Transfer, and Management of International Technology Flows* 157, 165-65 (Robert Stobaugh & Louis Wells, Jr. ed., 1984); Scott McMurray & James McGregor, "Asia Targets Chemicals for the Next Assault on Western Industry," *WSJ*, Aug. 4, 1993, at A1, col. 6, at A4, col. 2.

petrochemicals...they will do what they can to assist potential buyers to obtain the necessary finance from sources such as the World Bank."[68]   Multinational construction firms may also be indifferent as to whether they build a plant in the Third World for a First World multinational producer such as Mobil in Singapore, a local (often state-owned) firm such as Petroleos Mexicanos, or a joint venture between the two such as Petronas and Shell in Malaysia.[69]   By the same token, even where construction-engineering firms might wish to resist demands by Third World countries for technology transfers, they may lack the bargaining power of multinational producers, which "are incomparably larger and more powerful financially than even the largest engineering firms."[70]

Deviations from the model of direct investment in the periphery are not, however, synonymous with relinquishment of controls by core-economy firms. Thus when construction-engineering firms introduce First World technologies on a turnkey basis, the local economies may still have to "forego the opportunity of deriving potentially considerable external economies from planning and building the project using local engineers" who are more likely to adopt solutions appropriate to the physical and socioeconomic conditions prevailing in the locality. With multinational construction firms operating as transmission belts of the First World process and production firms, the latter dominate the process of technological transfer by limiting "the free transmissability of know-how and data on process and product within the recipient country." Consequently, developing countries may be required to "accept contractual or proprietorial relationships embodying this domination on a virtually permanent basis...."[71]   Such restraints are reinforced where turnkey petrochemical, electric power, and manufacturing plants are financed by First World states in the form of aid tied to purchases of equipment and materials from firms in the "home country."[72]

The diffusion of these new forms of less direct investment in the Third World does not mean, however, that the profitability of multinational construction firms is determined solely by free competitive forces of the world market. In one of the possible brave new world (dis)orders, the nation-state with the most explosive destruction industry can create privileged access for the largest firms of its construction industry to the periodic processes of reconstruction. U.S. wars in the Third World have frequently provided such opportunities: "No sooner had the shooting stopped in Korea, than some 170 Bechtel men took the field and soon had 900 Koreans putting up the structures that would supply extra kilowatts to revive the country's economy."[73]   Although the war in Vietnam failed to fulfill such

---

[68]John Dunning, *Multinationals, Technology and Competitiveness* 163 (1988). According to a recent calculation, the significance of World Bank loans for multinational construction firms has diminished in large part because three-quarters of the civil works projects are executed by local firms. Consequently only 3 per cent of multinational construction in the Third World is financed by the World Bank. "Conclusion: Comparison and Analysis," in *The Global Construction Industry* at 211, 246-47. This reasoning appears inconsistent with the claim that "under the pressure of the World Bank...to give more freedom to the main international contractors," Third World government agencies have relaxed their own requirement that multinational firms subcontract certain sections of their projects. Ridha Ferchiou, "Tunisia," in *The Global Construction Industry* at 198, 204-205.

[69]See "Big One for Badger," *ENR*, May 13, 1991, at 23); "Mexico: A Tough Nut to Crack, But," *ENR*, June 4, 1981, at 30; "Gas Spurs Malaysian Boom," *ENR*, Aug. 12, 1982, at 32.

[70]Oman, *New Forms of Investment in Developing Country Industries* at 92.

[71]John Roberts, "Engineering Consultancy, Industrialization and Development," in *Science, Technology and Development: The Political Economy of Technical Advance in Underdeveloped Countries* 39, 45, 49-50 (Charles Cooper ed., 1973).

[72]On the role of the U.S. Export-Import Bank, see e.g. U.S. House of Representatives, Ways and Means Committee, 102d Cong., 1st Sess., *Overview and Compilation of U.S. Trade Statutes* 138 (1991 ed.); Peter Behr, "Bechtel Bridging Financing Gap: Builder Forced to Wear Banker's Hat," *WPost*, Oct. 21, 1984, at K1 (Nexis); See also OECD, *Globalisation of Industrial Activities: Four Case Studies: Auto Parts, Chemicals, Construction and Semiconductors* 112-13 (1992).

[73]Wilson & Taylor, *Earth Changers* at 264.

hopes,[74] subsequent U.S. military destruction proved much more constructive. Thus when the U.S. Navy destroyed an Iranian oil production platform, a U.S. firm (McDermott International) received a large contract to reconstruct it.[75] For a conglomerate corporation, such as Raytheon, which combines subsidiaries of destruction (missiles) and war-zone petrochemical construction (Badger Company), the connection may even become direct.[76]

State-capital cooperation can also operate on a much grander and more systematic scale:

> While B-52s of the U.S. Air Force pound Iraqi Republican Guard positions along the Iraq-Kuwaiti border, another branch of the U.S. armed forces [the Army Corps of Engineers] is quietly doing work that could mean billions of dollars for U.S. companies. ... Even as the U.S., Britain, and France cooperate on the Desert Storm battlefield, cutthroat competition is breaking out over who will reap the commercial spoils.[77]

In turn, the profits derived from Bechtel's $2.5 billion firefighting and reconstruction contract with the Kuwait Oil Company may, for example, "enable the Bechtel board, unimpeded by snoopy stockholders, to amass...slush funds" to finance the election of other regimes sympathetic to its interests.[78]

Such state intervention may enable U.S. firms to retain their leading role in servicing multinational petrochemical companies—projects that account for one-third of the world construction market—at "'locations that offer advantages such as an abundant supply of workers, lax environmental controls or labor pricing.'"[79] Acquisition by multinational firms of the largest Third World firms—such as Fluor's purchase in Mexico—offers another way of circumventing potential local competition.[80] The penetration by the new international division of labor of the refining, chemical, and petrochemical industries "has opened the world market, particularly in industrialized countries, to producers with access to cheap feedstocks, advantageous geographic location and a cheap pool of local labor."[81] Consequently, Asian countries such as Indonesia, Malaysia, and Thailand have become "even more attractive to investors." These and other Pacific Rim economies are the projected sites of plant construction by Bechtel, Kellogg, Foster Wheeler, Stone & Webster, and others valued at tens of billions of dollars—if these countries' world market-driven "'staggering national debt'" does not thwart their

---

[74]See e.g., "Vietnam Starts the Long Journey Back," *CW*, Feb. 7, 1973, at 34.

[75]James Tanner, "Iran's Oil Production Is Soaring, With Help from American Firms," *WSJ*, Nov. 25, 1992, at A1, col. 6, A9, col. 4.

[76]See Raytheon Company, *1991 Annual Report* 5, 9-13, 23-27 (1992); Badger, *Lubricating Oil and Wax Production* 5, 18, 19, 24, 26 (n.d. [ca. 1990]).

[77]"To the Victor Go the Spoils," *BW*, Feb. 18, 1991, at 50. See also "US Leads Charge as Allies Fight for Kuwaiti Contracts," *FT*, Feb. 27, 1992, § I, at 4 (Nexis); U.S. General Accounting Office, *Persian Gulf: U.S. Business Participation in the Reconstruction of Kuwait* (NSIAD-93-69, 1992).

[78]"Bechtel Leaves Kuwait, Oil Capacity Restored," *ENR*, Sept. 6, 1993, at 12; Joe Stork, "The Gulf War and the Arab World," 8 *WPJ* 365, 373 (1991) (quotation).

[79]"The Top 400 Contractors," *ENR*, May 24, 1990, at 38 (quoting vice president of ABB Lummus Crest); "The Top 250 International Contractors," *ENR*, July 22, 1991, at 35; "The Top 400 Contractors," *ENR*, May 25, 1992, at 55. See also Lakdasa Wijetilleke & Anthony Ody, *World Refinery Industry: Need for Restructuring* 200-208 (World Bank Technical Paper No. 32, 1984). On U.S. firms' preeminence in the construction of (petro-)chemical plants, see Hugh Hambleton, "The Saudi Petrochemical Industry in the 1980s," in *Saudi Arabia: Energy, Developmental Planning, and Industrialization* 51, 52, 54, 59 (Ragaei El Mallakh & Dorothea Mallakh ed. 1982); "The Top International Contractors," *ENR*, July 15, 1982, at 77; Howard Seymour, *The Multinational Construction Industry* 170 (1987).

[80]By buying 49 per cent of Empresa ICA Sociedad Controladora S.A. de C.V. Mexico, Fluor has become the largest construction engineering firm in Mexico. *ENR*, May 24, 1993, at 5.

[81]Walter Vergara & Donald Brown, *The New Face of the World Petrochemical Sector: Implications for Developing Countries* 69 (World Bank Technical Paper No. 84, 1988).

programs.[82]

More important, however, for the future contours of the world than the national identity of the dominant multinational construction firms is the character of the economic development programs pursued by the Third World. If those countries choose, for example, to promote "export processing zones," "conceived...as a physical, economic and even social enclave," they will continue to discourage horizontal internal linkages that could galvanize more balanced national economic development. By providing not only the infrastructure but even standardized factory buildings for the exporting firms in these zones, international construction firms and their Third World customer-states create a "grotesque" contrast with the surrounding nonextraterritorial areas.[83] This kind of internal unbalanced development is exacerbated by the fact that Third World infrastructure projects such as roads, harbors, and airports are typically financed by redistributions from surpluses created in agriculture and extractive industries, which fail to create a horizontally integrated broad base of production.[84] These programs reproduce the same forms of underdevelopment that nineteenth-century British infrastructural colonialism engendered with the consequence, for example, that by the middle of the twentieth century India possessed one of the world's longest railway systems without having created the corresponding productive forces.[85] Under such circumstances, the populations of the Third World live in another economic world despite sharing the territory in which First World capital valorizes itself.[86]

As major political-economic actors not only operating in their own world market but producing the fixed capital of many other global industries, the multinational construction firms face a future dependent in large part on the life-expectancy of the prevailing fossil-fuel-driven international Fordism and especially of the latter's hold on the newly industrializing dependent nations.[87] The U.S. Agency for International Development advances precisely such an agenda when, for example, it gives a grant to Bechtel to help Morocco, Bangladesh, Costa Rica, Jamaica, and the Economic Community of Western African States to develop their own fossil-fuel energy resources.[88] And even if Bechtel and other companies cannot build fossil-fuel projects, they can still profit from "cleaning up problems" at the nuclear power and weapons plants the construction of which they once monopolized.[89]

The hopes attached to China's emergence as the new center for mega-

---

[82]Stone & Webster, "Burgeoning Workload in the Pacific Rim" (n.d.); Lewis Koflowitz, "A New World Order," *Chemical Marketing Reporter*, July 8, 1991, at S10 (Westlaw-Dialog); Herb Short, "Tough Conditions Shape Plans of Engineering Firms," *ChE*, Nov. 28, 1983, at 26 (Nexis) (quoting Bechtel official); Walter Vergara & Dominique Babelon, *The Petrochemical Industry in Developing Asia: A Review of the Current Situation and Prospects for Development in the 1990s* (World Bank Technical Paper No. 113, 1990); Frank Warren, Jr., "International Construction Markets Hindered by Nations in Debt," *Constructor*, Jan., 1986, at 28 (author is Jones Construction executive).

[83]International Labour Organisation, *Economic and Social Effects of Multinational Enterprises in Export Processing Zones* 109 (1988); Folker Fröbel, Jürgen Heinrichs, & Otto Kreye, *Umbruch in der Weltwirtschaft* 439-41 (1986).

[84]See Folker Fröbel, Jürgen Heinrichs, & Otto Kreye, *Die neue internationale Arbeitsteilung* 568-69, 577, 501-502 (1977); Wolfgang Schoeller, *Weltmarkt und Reproduktion des Kapitals* 186-87 (1976).

[85]Daniel Thorner, "Great Britain and the Development of India's Railways," 11 *JEH* 389, 400-402 (1951).

[86]Rolf Knieper, *Nationale Souveränität* 143-44 (1991).

[87]See generally Elmar Altvater, *Der Preis des Wohlstands oder Umweltplünderung und neue Welt(un)ordnung* (1992).

[88]*WSJ*, Jan. 28, 1982, at 48, col. 6.

[89]See G. Zachary & Susan Faludi, "Bechtel, Hurt By Slide in Heavy Construction, Re-Engineers Itself," *WSJ*, May 28, 1991, at A1, col. 6, A16, col. 1; Victor Zonana, "Megabuilder Bechtel Tries to Stay on Top By Being Aggressive," *WSJ*, Oct. 16, 1984, at 1, col. 6, at 25, col. 1.

projects and the potential integration of a sizable segment of the one-seventh of world construction formerly performed in the centrally planned Comecon states into the world market have also reignited belief in the sustainability of a perpetually rebuilt environment.[90] Thus expectations of an enormous building boom in East Germany are already said to have West German construction firms "salivating."[91] Hochtief, for example, has already acquired East German and Polish construction firms.[92]

Finally, and most portentously, many developing countries, constrained by their debt-driven entanglement in the world market, have reproduced the model of systematic environmental degradation that arose in the advanced capitalist countries in the nineteenth and twentieth centuries. In order, for example, to supply the Weyerhaeusers and final consumers of the First World with the volume of wood products that the depletion of the forests of the Northern Hemisphere (replicating the history of the international petroleum industry) can no longer satisfy, or to conquer Asian markets by driving Japanese and Korean producers out of business, Third World producers and states have embarked on the destruction of the ecologically vital and non-renewable rain forests. Building local pulp mills and massive dams propels the accumulation process for multinational construction firms while impoverishing the Third World's and the whole world's ecosystems.[93] In "waging the equivalent of thermonuclear war upon their own territories,"[94] the former colonialized societies may yet externalize the ultimate costs of exploitation onto what has become one ecologically doomed capitalist world.

[90]See Behr, "Bechtel Bridging Financing Gap"; M.W. Kellogg, "The M.W. Kellogg Company" [no pagination (4, 6)];"Industry Heads East," *ENR*, Feb. 1, 1990, at 27; "Czechoslovakia Moves to Be European Hub," *ENR*, Aug. 19, 1991, at 65; William Krizan, "Low-Octane Domestic Markets Stall Out U.S. Contractors," *ENR*, May 24, 1993, at 36 (Parsons forms joint-stock company with Russian organizations to build infrastructure in Russia).

[91]John Kosowatz & Peter Reina, "Germany Begins the Costly Reconstruction of Its New States," *ENR*, Apr. 27, 1992, at 24. See also "Brown & Root Goes East," *ENR*, Feb. 1, 1993, at 5.

[92]"Hochtief Acquires East German Firm," *ENR*, Apr. 22, 1991, at 5; *Die Baubude*, No. 139, Apr. 1993, at 3 (Hochtief acquires 40 per cent share of Budokor).

[93][Brown & Root], *Brownbuilder*, No. 2, 1992, at 8-9 (characterizing the use of the rain forest in Indonesia to supply a new pulp mill as "environmentally sound"); World Bank, *Indonesia: Sustainable Development of Forests, Land, and Water* 4 (1990) (deforestation also threatens Indonesia's economic objectives); "Nathaniel Nash, "Bolivia's Rain Forest Falls to Relentless Exploiters," *NYT*, June 21, 1993, at A1, col. 2, A6, col. 3-4 (nat. ed.) ("almost limitless demand" for mahogany in the United States). For critiques, see Dan Morgan, "'Slash and Burn' Risks Disaster in Tropical Forests," *WPost*, Nov. 27, 1978, at A1 (Nexis); Val Plumwood & Richard Routley, "World Rainforest Destruction—The Social Factors," *Ecologist* No. 1, 1982, at 4, 11-17; Michael Vatikiotis, "Tug-of-War Over Trees," *FEER*, Jan. 12, 1989, at 41; "A Saw Point for Forestry," *FEER*, Apr. 19, 1990; "Lost in the Forest," *Economist*, Aug. 31, 1991, at 30; Adam Schwarz & Jonathan Friedland, "Green Fingers," *FEER*, Mar. 12, 1992, at 42; "Shades of Green," *Economist*, Apr. 18, 1992, at 34; Adam Schwarz, "Timber is the Test," *FEER*, July 23, 1992, at 36. On the reasons for Weyerhaeuser's withdrawal from Indonesia, see *WSJ*, Oct. 23, 1981, at 41 (Westlaw-Dialog); *id.*, Apr. 11, 1984, at 361; Richard Robison, *Indonesia: The Rise of Capital* 187-88 (1986).

[94]Nicholas Guppy, "Tropical Deforestation: A Global View," *FA*, Spring 1984, at 928, 943.

# Bibliography

Omitted are all newspaper articles and unattributed articles in magazines and trade journals.

## Books and Articles

Aburish, Said. *Pay-Off: Wheeling and Dealing in the Arab World* (1985)

Ackerman, W., et al. (ed.). *Man-Made Lakes: Their Problems and Environmental Effects* (1973)

Addison, John, & K. Hazareesingh. *A New History of Mauritius* (1984)

Adler, Dorothy. *British Investment in American Railways, 1834-1898* (1970)

Akademiia Nauk SSSR. *Postroenie fundamenta sotsialisticheskoi ekonomiki v SSSR 1926-1932 gg.* (1960)

Ala'i, Heshmat. "How Not to Develop a Backward Country." *Fortune*, Aug. 1948, at 76

Albérdi, J. *The Life and Industrial Labors of William Wheelwright in South America* (1877)

Aldcroft, Derek. *From Versailles to Wall Street: 1919-1929* (1981 [1977])

Allen, G., & Audrey Donnithorne. *Western Enterprise in Indonesia and Malaya: A Study in Economic Development* (1957)

Allen, Steven. "Declining Unionization in Construction: The Facts and the Reasons." 41 *ILRR* 343 (1988)

Allhands, J. *Tools of the Earth Mover: Yesterday and Today Preserved in Pictures* (1951)

Altvater, Elmar. *Der Preis des Wohlstands oder Umweltplünderung und neue Welt(un)ordnung* (1992)

———. *Sachzwang Weltmarkt: Verschuldungskrise, blockierte Industrialisierung und ökologische Gefährdung: Der Fall Brasilien* (1987)

———. "Zu einigen Problemen des Staatsinterventionismus." *PK*, No. 3, May 1972, at 1

Amoroso, Bruno, & Ole Olsen. *Lo Stato imprenditore* (1978)

Amuzegar, Jahangir. *Iran: An Economic Profile* (1977)

Anderson, Gordon. "International Labour Standards and the Review of Industrial Law." 11 *NZJIR* 27 (1986)

———, & Peter Brosnan. "Freedom of Association: New Zealand Law and ILO Convention 87." *NZLJ*, Sept. 1984, at 307

Antoniou, Jim. *Construction in the Middle East* (Economist Intelligence Unit Special Rep. No. 55, 1978)

Apgar, Mahlon. "Succeeding in Saudi Arabia." *HBR*, Jan.-Feb. 1977, at 14

Appleton, Nathan. "What the Slaven Dredges are Doing at Panama." 19 *EN* 490

(1888)

Armytage, W. *A Social History of Engineering* (4th ed. 1976 [1961])

Artz, Frederick. *The Development of Technical Education in France 1500-1850* (1966)

Ash, Horace. "Progress on Central Highway of Cuba During 1927." 100 *ENR* 22 (1928)

Ashley, Evelyn. 2 *The Life of Henry John Temple Viscount Palmerston: 1846-1865* (2d ed. 1876)

Askari, Hossein. *Saudi Arabia's Economy: Oil and the Search for Economic Development* (1990)

Aspelin, Paul, & Silvio Coelho dos Santos. *Indian Areas Threatened by Hydroelectric Projects in Brazil* (1981)

Atighetchi, Abolghassem. *Industriepolitik als Versuch der Überwindung ökonomischer Unterentwicklung im Iran* (1983)

Baasch, Ernst. *Holländische Wirtschaftsgeschichte* (1927)

Bailey, Martin. "Freedom Railroad." *MR*, Apr. 1976, at 32

Bairoch, Paul. "International Industrialization Levels from 1750 to 1980." 11 *JEEH* 269 (1982)

Baker, Ray. "The Trust's New Tool—The Labor Boss." 22 *McClure's* 30-43 (Nov. 1903).

Baker Brown, W. 4 *History of the Corps of Royal Engineers* (1952)

Ball, Michael. *Housing Policy and Economic Power: The Political Economy of Owner Occupation* (1983)

———. "The Housing Production Process and the Crisis of Production." [4] *PBE, 1982: Labour in Building and Construction* 2-18 (1983)

———. *Rebuilding Construction: Economic Change and the British Construction Industry* (1988)

Balogh, Thomas. *The Economics of Poverty* (1964)

Baltzer, F. *Die Kolonialbahnen mit besonderer Berücksichtigung Afrikas* (1916)

———. *Kolonial- und Kleinbahnen.* Pt. 2: *Bauliche Ausgestaltung von Bahn und Fahrzeug* (1983 [1920])

Bancroft, Gertrude, & Stuart Garfinkle. "Job Mobility in 1961." 86 *MLR* 897 (1963)

Bandarage, Asoka. *Colonialism in Sri Lanka: The Political Economy of the Kandyan Highlands, 1833-1886* (1983)

Baran, Paul. *The Political Economy of Growth* (1968 [1957])

Barjot, Dominique. "L'Analyse comptable: Un Instrument pour l'histoire des entreprises. La Société Générale d'Entreprises (1908-1945)." 1 *HES*, No.1, 1982, at 145

Barnett, Tony. "The Gezira Scheme: Production of Cotton and Reproduction of Underdevelopment." In *Beyond the Sociology of Development: Economy and Society in Latin America and Africa* 183 (Ivar Oxaal et al. ed., 1975)

Barnwell, P., & A. Toussaint. *A Short History of Mauritius* (1949)

Battelle Memorial Institute. *The State of the Art of Prefabrication in the Construction Industry* (1967)

Bauer, Otto. "Proletarische Wanderungen." 26:1 *NZ* 476 (1907)

Bay, Hermann. "Emil Mörsch: Erinnerungen an einen großen Lehrmeister des Stahlbetonbaus und technischen Mentors der Wayss & Freytag AG." In *Herausragende Ingenieurleistungen in der Bautechnik: Schriftenreihe der VDI-Gesellschaft Bautechnik*, No. 3 (1985)

Bayles, George. "Constructing a 98-Kilometer Water Conduit in Chile." 83 *ENR* 593 (1919)

Beale, Howard. *Theodore Roosevelt and the Rise of America to World Power* (1967 [1956])

Beard, Charles, & Mary Beard. *America at Midpassage* (1939)

Beatty, Charles. *Ferdinand de Lesseps: A Biographical Study* (1956)

Bedale, Caroline, Michael Paddon, & Peter Carter. "Direct Labour: A Form of Socialised Production in the Construction Industry." 1 *PBE* 175 (1980)

Behring, Karin, Erich Gluch, & Volker Rußig. *Entwicklungstendenzen im deutschen Auslandsbau* (1982)

Belfort, Stephen. "Labor Law and the Double-Breasted Employer: A Critique of the Single-Employer and Alter-Ego Doctrines and a Proposed Reformulation." 1987 *WLR* 67.

Bell, Herbert. 2 *Lord Palmerston* (1936)

Bemis, Samuel. *The Latin American Policy of the United States: An Historical Interpretation* (1971 [1943])

Benjamin, Walter. "Geschichtsphilosophische Thesen." In *idem, Illuminationen* 268 (1961)

Bennett, Ira. *History of the Panama Canal: Its Construction and Builders* (1915)

Bergman, Jules. *The United States and Cuba: Hegemony and Dependent Development, 1880-1934* (1977)

Berton, Pierre. *The Impossible Railway: The Building of the Canadian Pacific* (1972 [1970])

Bey, Voisin. 1 *Le Canal de Suez: Histoire administratif et actes constitutifs de la Compagnie*. Pt. I: *Période des études et de la construction 1854 à 1869* (1902)

———. *Le Canal de Suez*. II: *Description des travaux de premier établissement*. Pt. II: *Exécution des travaux* (1904)

Bezirganian, Steve. "U.S. Affiliates of Foreign Companies: Operations in 1990." *SCB*, May 1992, at 45

Bién, Witold. *Ekonomika przedsiebiorstwa budowlanego* (1969)

Birks, J., & C. Sinclair. *International Migration and Development in the Arab Region* (1980)

Bishop, Joseph. *The Panama Gateway* (1913)

Biswas, A., & M. Biswas. "Hydropower and the Environment." *IWPDC*, May 1976, at 40

"Black Monday." *PRWET*, Nov.-Dec. 1969, at 18

Blackwell, William. *The Beginnings of Russian Industrialization 1800-1860* (1968)

Block, Fred. *The Origins of International Economic Disorder: A Study of United States International Monetary Policy from World War II to the Present* (1978 [1977])

Bober, W. "The Construction Industry After the War." 20 *HBR* 427 (1942)

Böhning, W. "International Contract Migration in the Light of ILO Instruments." In *idem, Studies in International Labour Migration* 233 (1984 [1982])

Bolton, Peter. "Mozambique's Cabora Bassa Project: An Environment Assessment." In 2 *The Social and Environmental Effects of Large Dams: Case Studies* 156 (Edward Goldsmith & Nicholas Hildyard ed., 1986)

Bonilla, Heraclio. *Guano y burguesía en el Perú* (1974)

Bonin, Herbert. *Suez: Du Canal à la finance (1858-1987)* (1987)

Boswell, Jonathan. "Sir Arthur Dorman." 2 *DBB* 136 (David Jeremy ed., 1984)

Boulding, Kenneth. "A Ballad of Ecological Awareness." In *The Careless Technology: Ecology and International Development* 157 (M. Farvar & John Milton ed., 1972)

Bourdon, Clinton, & Raymond Leavitt. *Union and Open-Shop Construction: Compensation, Work Practices, and Labor Markets* (1980)

Bower, Tom. *Blind Eye to Murder: Britain, America and the Purging of Nazi Germany—A Pledge Betrayed* (1983 [1981])

Bowley, Marian. *The British Building Industry* (1966)

Bowman, Waldo. "Construction Begins on Aswan Dam—Russian Style." *ENR*, Feb. 23, 1961, at 32

————. "Construction Today in the U.S.S.R." *ENR*, Aug. 30, 1962, at 38
————. "Hydro Paces Turkey's Construction Boom." *ENR*, Oct. 10, 1957, at 34
————. "Iran Pushes Hard for Development and Defense," *ENR*, Mar. 9, 1961, at 36
————. "Iran's Two Big Dams Promise a Better Life," *ENR*, Mar. 16, 1961, at 38
————. "Iraq's Operation Bootstrap—Part One: A Modern Mesopotamia is Molded." *ENR*, Dec. 12, 1957, at 34
————. "Thailand Sets the Pace for Southeast Asia," *ENR*, Jan. 19, 1961, at 30
Brace, James, Frances Mason, & S. Woodard. "The New York Tunnel Extension of the Pennsylvania Railroad: The East River Division." 35 *TASCE* 1045 (1909)
Brand, James. "Working Methods of Engineering Contractors." 89 *Engineer* 262 (1900)
Brassey, Thomas. *Foreign Work and English Wages* (1879)
————. *Work and Wages: The Reward of Labour and the Cost of Work* (1916 [1872])
Breasted, James. *A History of Egypt* (1964 [1905])
Brede, H., et al. *Ökonomische und politische Determinanten der Wohnungs-versorgung* (1975)
Brewster, Frederick. "Colonial Powers Discuss African Transport Integration." *ENR*, Mar. 22, 1951
Briggs, Asa. "Foreword." In Robert Middlemas. *The Master Builders* 13 (1963)
————. *The Making of Modern England 1783-1867* (1965 [1959])
*Britain's Industrial Future: Being the Report of the Liberal Industrial Inquiry* (1928)
Brody, David. *Steelworkers in America: The Nonunion Era* (1969 [1960])
Brokensha, David, & Thayer Scudder. "Resettlement." In *Dams in Africa: An Interdisciplinary Study of Man-Made Lakes in Africa* 20 (Neville Rubin & William Warren ed., 1968)
Brooke, David. *The Railway Navvy: "That Despicable Race of Men"* (1984)
Brooks, Kenneth. "The U.S. Engineering-Construction Industry: Is It Ready for a Building Boom?" *CW*, Mar. 21, 1973, at 33
Brown, Hanbury. "Land Values in Egypt." 114 *Engineer* 456 (1912)
Brown, Jonathan. *Oil and Revolution in Mexico* (1993)
Brown, Robert, Jr. "The Story of M-K." 3:4 *AB* 1 (1954)
"The Brown & Root Story." 3:7 *AB* 1 (1954)
Brünner, E. *De Bagdadspoorveg: Bidrage tot de kennis omtrent het optreden der mogenheden in Turkije 1888-1908* (1957)
Brumlik, Ana. "State Intervention and the Barriers to Accumulation of Capital in Construction, with Special Reference to the Labour Process: Venezuela, 1945-58." [4] *PBE, 1982: Labour in Building and Construction* (1983)
Brunlees, James. "Address of the President." 72 *MPICE* 2 (1883)
Brunot, A., & R. Coquand. *Le Corps des ponts et chaussées* (1982)
Brunton, John. "Description of the Line and Works of the Scinde Railway." 22 *MPICE* 451 (1863)
Brunton, Richard. "The Japan Lights." 47 *MPICE* 1 (1877).
Bucharin, N. *Imperialismus und Weltwirtschaft* (1969 [1929])
Buckley, Peter, & Brian Roberts. *European Direct Investment in the U.S.A. Before World War I* (1982)
Buell, Raymond, et al. *Problems of the New Cuba: Report of the Commssion on Cuban Affairs* (1935)
Bunker, Stephen. *Underdeveloping the Amazon: Extraction, Unequal Exchange and the Failure of the Modern State* (1988 [1985])
Burck, Gilbert. "The Building Trades versus the People." *Fortune*, Oct. 1970, at

95
——. "A Time of Reckoning for the Building Unions." *Fortune*, June 4, 1979, at 82
Burge, C. "The Nile Irrigation Question." 58 *ER* 65 (1908)
Burge, Charles. "The Hawkesbury Bridge, New South Wales." 101 *MPICE* 2 (1890)
Burns, Arthur, & Wesley Mitchell. *Measuring Business Cycles* (1946)
Busch, Klaus. *Die multinationalen Konzerne* (1974)
Busch, [Klaus], [Wolfgang] Schöller, & [Frank] Seelow. *Weltmarkt und Weltwährungskrise* (1971)
Business Roundtable. *Coming to Grips with Some Major Problems in the Construction Industry* (1975 [1974])
Cady, R. "New Deep-Water Port at Cartagena, Colombia." 115 *ENR* 710 (1935)
Calhoun, Daniel. *The American Civil Engineer: Origins and Conflict* (1960)
Cameron, Ian. *The Impossible Dream* (1971)
Cameron, Rondo. *France and the Economic Development of Europe 1800-1914: Conquests of Peace and Seeds of War* (1961)
Campagnac, Elisabeth, & Vincent Nouzille. *Citizen Bouygues ou l'histoire secrète d'un grand patron* (1988)
[Campbell, George John Douglas]. 1 *George Douglas Eighth Duke of Argyll (1823-1900)* (Dowager Duchess of Argyll ed., 1906)
Campbell, Persia. *Chinese Coolie Emigration to Countries Within the British Empire* (1923)
Caplan, Basil. "Decade of Diversification Keep M-K Ahead." *IC*, July 1983, at 26
——"The Japanese Construction Industry: Part 1: Construction Activity." *IC*, June 1969, at 54
——. "The U.K. Construction Industry: Part 1: Construction Activity." *IC*, Oct. 1969, at 49
Cardwell, D. *Turning Points in Western Technology: A Study of Technology, Science and History* (1972)
Caro, Robert. *The Years of Lyndon Johnson: The Path to Power* (1982)
——. *The Years of Lyndon Johnson: Means of Ascent* (1990)
Carr, Edward. *The Twenty Years' Crisis, 1919-1939: An Introduction to the Study of International Relations* (1964 [1939])
——, & R. Davies. *A History of Soviet Russia:* 1 *Foundations of a Planned Economy: 1926-1929* (1974 [1969])
Carter, A. "American Roadbuilding in Liberia." 123 *ENR* 479 (1939)
——. "Building the Interamerican Highway: Part I—History, Survey, Access, and Housing." 131 *ENR* 209 (1943)
Cassimatis, Peter. *Construction and Economic Development* (NTIS, 1975)
——. *Economics of the Construction Industry* (1969)
Castle, Victor. "Well, I Quit My Job at the Dam." 133 *Nation* 207 (1931)
Catholic Institute for International Relations. *The Labour Trade: Filipino Migrant Workers Around the World* (1987)
Caton, John. "Building the 'Road-to-the-Sea' in Colombia." 101 *ENR* 950 (1928)
Chamberlain, J. "From Edison to the Atomic Age: Stone & Webster Rolls Along." *ENR*, May 21, 1953, at 59
Chapman, Maybelle. *Great Britain and the Bagdad Railway 1888-1914*. In 31 *SCSH* (1948)
Chandler, Alfred, Jr. *The Visible Hand: The Managerial Revolution in American Business* (1978 [1977])
Chang, Dae. "The Republic of Korea." In *The Global Construction Industry* 141
Chao, Kang. *The Construction Industry in Communist China* (1968)
*Charter, By-Laws and Regulations, and List of Members of the Institution of*

*Engineers* (1881)
Checkland, S. *The Rise of Industrial Society in England 1815-1885* (1971 [1964])
Chevallier, Raymond. *Les Voies romaines* (1972)
Choucri, Nazli. "Asians in the Arab World: Labor Migration and Public Policy." 22 *MES* 252 (1986)
Clapham, J. *An Economic History of Modern Britain: The Early Railway Age 1820-1850* (1926)
———. *An Economic History of Modern Britain: Free Trade and Steel 1850-1886* (1932)
Clapp, Gordon. *The TVA: An Approach to the Development of a Region* (1955)
Clark, Colin. *The Conditions of Economic Progress* (3d ed. 1957 [1940])
Clark, John Maurice. *Strategic Factors in Business Cycles* (1949 [1935])
Clark, Victor. 3 *History of Manufactures in the United States: 1893-1928* (1929)
———. "Labor Conditions in Cuba." 7 *BDL* 663 (1902)
Clarke, Linda. "The Importance of a Historical Approach: Changes in the Construction Industry." 1 *PBE* 30 (1980)
Cleary, Edward. "Building the World's Biggest Oil Line." 129 *ENR* 915 (1942)
Clerk, J. "Suez Canal." 5 *FR* (n.s.) 80 (1869)
Cleveland, Frederick, & Fred Powell. *Railroad Finance* (1912)
Cleveland, Harold, & Thomas Huertas. *Citibank 1812-1970* (1985)
Cliff, Tony. *Rosa Luxemburg* (1969 [1959])
Coad, Roy. *Laing: The Biography of Sir John W. Laing, C.B.E. (1879-1978)* (1992 [1979])
Coatsworth, John. *Growth Against Development: The Economic Impact of Railroads in Porfirian Mexico* (1981)
Cochran, Thomas, & William Miller. *The Age of Enterprise: A Social History of Industrial America* (rev. ed. 1961 [1942])
Cockburn, Charles. *Construction in Overseas Development* (1970)
Colclough, J. *The Construction Industry of Great Britain* (1965)
Coleman, Terry. *The Railway Navvies* (1967 [1965])
Collins, Robert. *The Waters of the Nile: Hydropolitics and the Jonglei Canal, 1900-1988* (1990)
Colombard-Prout, Marc. "France." In *The Global Construction Industry* 104
Colson, Elizabeth. *The Social Consequences of Resettlement: The Impact of the Kariba Resettlement upon the Gwembe Tonga* (1971)
Commoner, Barry. "Summary of the Conference: On the Meaning of Ecological Failures in International Development." In *The Careless Technology: Ecology and International Development* xxi (M. Farvar & John Milton ed., 1972)
Condit, Carl. *American Building* (1968)
Conniff, Michael. *Black Labor on a White Canal: Panama, 1904-1981* (1981)
Cook, Walter. "Erection of the Nairne Viaducts, near Adelaide, South Australia." 112 *MPICE* 185 (1903)
Cordtz, Dan. "Bechtel Thrives on Billion-Dollar Jobs." *Fortune*, Jan. 1975, at 90
Corey, Lewis. *The House of Morgan: A Social Biography of the Masters of Money* (1930)
Cortes, Mariluz, & Peter Bocock. *North-South Technology Transfer: A Case Study of Petrochemicals in Latin America* (1984)
Cotard, Ch. "Inauguration de la voie ferrée de Lefké à Bilédjik (Ligne d'Anatolie)." 19 *GC* 103 (1891)
Cotter, Arundel. *The Authentic History of the United States Steel Corporation* (1916)
Cottrell, P. "Railway Finance and the Crisis of 1866: Contractors' Bills of Exchange, and the Finance Companies." 3 *JTH* (n.s.) 20 (1975)
———. "Sir Samuel Morton Peto." In 4 *DBB* 644 (David Jeremy ed., 1985)

Cox, Victor. *International Construction: Marketing, Planning and Execution* (1982)
Cronon, William. *Nature's Metropolis: Chicago and the Great West* (1991)
Cuban Economic Research Project. *A Study on Cuba* (1965)
Cudahy, Brian. *Rails Under the Mighty Hudson* (1975)
Cunningham, W. *The Growth of English Industry and Commerce in Modern Times: The Mercantile System* (6th ed. 1925 [1882])
Currie, A. *The Grand Trunk Railway of Canada* (1957)
Curtis, William. "The Railroads of Central America." 10 *RA* 698 (1885)
———. "Railway Construction in Central and South America." 29 *EN* 616 (1893)
Czichon, Eberhard. *Der Bankier und die Macht: Hermann Josef Abs in der deutschen Politik* (1970)
*Dams in Africa: An Interdiscplinary Study of Man-Made Lakes in Africa* (Neville Rubin & William Warren ed., 1968)
Dasent, Arthur. *John Thadeus Delane Editor of "The Times": His Life and Correspondence* (1908)
Davis, Clarence. "Railway Imperialism in China, 1895-1939." In *Railway Imperialism* (Clarence Davis & Kenneth Wilburn, Jr. ed., 1991)
Dawson, William. *The Evolution of Modern Germany* (n.d. [1908])
Day, John. *Railways of Northern Africa* (1964)
Dayer, Roberta. *Bankers and Diplomats in China 1917-1925: The Anglo-American Relationship* (1981)
De Silva, K. *A History of Sri Lanka* (1981)
Deane, Phyllis, & W. Cole. *British Economic Growth 1688-1959: Trends and Structure* (1969 [1962])
[Defoe, Daniel]. *A Plan of the English Commerce* (2d ed. 1967 [1730])
Delmer, A. 1 *Le Canal Albert* (1939)
Dempsey, G. Drysdale. *The Practical Railway Engineer* (1855)
Deniot, Joelle. *Usine et cooperation ouvrière: Métiers-syndicalisation conflits aux Batignolles* (1983)
Depping, Guillaume. "Le Transsaharien." 17 *GC* 105 (1890)
Dernburg, Bernhard. *Zielpunkte des deutschen Kolonialwesens: Zwei Vorträge* (1907)
Deudney, Daniel. *Rivers of Energy: The Hydropower Potential* (Worldwatch Paper 44, 1981)
*Deutsches Kolonial-Lexikon* (Heinrich Schnee ed., 1920)
Devey, Joseph. *The Life of Joseph Locke* (1862)
DiLullo, Anthony. "Service Transactions in the U.S. International Accounts, 1970-80." *SCB*, Nov. 1981, at 29
———, & Obie Whichard. "U.S. International Sales and Purchases of Services." *SCB*, Sept. 1990, at 37
Dobbins, J. "The Imperial Peking-Kalgan Railway and Its Extension." 64 *EN* 191 (1910)
———. "Rebuilt Antung-Mukden Ry., China." 68 *EN* 809 (1912)
Dodge, Norton. *Women in the Soviet Economy* (1966)
Drechsler, Horst. *Südwestafrika unter deutscher Herrschaft* (1966)
Drew, Walter. *Closed Shop Unionism* (n.d. [ca. 1910])
Drewer, Stephen. "Scandinavia." In *The Global Construction Industry* 160
Drucker, Peter. *The New Society: The Anatomy of Industrial Order* (1962 [1949])
Dummett, R. "Joseph Chamberlain, Imperial Finance and Railway Policy in British West Africa in the Late Nineteenth Century." 90 *EngHR* 287 (1975)
Dunham, Arthur. "How the First French Railways Were Built." 1 *JEH* 12 (1941)
Dunlop, John, & Arthur Hill. *The Wage Adjustment Board: Wartime Stabilization in the Building and Construction Industry* (1950)
Dunning, John. *Explaining International Production* (1988)

————. *Multinational Enterprises and the Global Economy* (1993)

————. *Multinationals, Technology and Competitiveness* (1988)

Durham, Henry. "Road Construction in Paraguay." 126 *ENR* 876 (1941)

Dutt, Romesh. *The Economic History of India in the Victorian Age* (1904)

Du Val, Miles. *And the Mountains Will Move: The Story of the Building of the Panama Canal* (1968 [1947])

Earle, Edward. "Egyptian Cotton and the American Civil War." 41 *PSQ* 520 (1926)

————. *Turkey, the Great Powers, and the Bagdad Railway: A Study in Imperialism* (1923)

Eccles, Marriner. *Beckoning Frontiers: Public and Personal Recollections* (Sidney Hyman ed., 1951)

Edgar-Bonnet, George. *Ferdinand de Lesseps: Le Diplomate, Le Créateur de Suez* (1951)

Ellis, John. "Gustave Eiffel: A Biographical Sketch." 112 *JSE* 1404 (1986)

Elton, J. "Management Contracting." In *Management of International Construction Projects: Proceedings of a Conference Organized by The Institution of Civil Engineers* 73 (1985)

Engels, Friedrich. *Herrn Eugen Dührings Umwälzung der Wissenschaft*. In Karl Marx [&] Friedrich Engels, 20 *Werke* (1968 [1878])

Engelund, Anker. "Danes Introduce New Caisson Practice at Little Belt Bridge." 114 *ENR* 841 (1935)

Engler, Robert. *The Politics of Oil: A Study of Private Power and Democratic Directions* (1967 [1961])

Enock, C. "Railway Development in Peru." 53 *EN* 463 (1905)

Ensor, R. *England 1870-1914* (1936)

Esko, Timo. *The Law Applicable to International Labour Relations* (1982)

Eves, Graves. "The Canton-Kowloon Railway: British Section." 192 *MPICE* 190 (1913)

Fainsod, Merle, & Lincoln Gordon. *Government and the American Economy* (rev. ed. 1948 [1941])

Faulkner, Harold. *The Decline of Laissez Faire 1897-1917* (1951)

Fawcett, Brian. *Railways of the Andes* (1963)

Feis, Herbert. *Europe the World's Banker 1870-1914* (1965 [1930])

————. *Three International Episodes: Seen from E.A.* (1966 [1946])

Ferchiou, Ridha. "Tunisia." In *The Global Construction Industry* 199

Ferns, H. *Britain and Argentina in the Nineteenth Century* (1960)

Fichte, Johann. *Der geschlossene Handelsstaat*. In *idem*, 7 *Sämmtliche Werke* 387 (1845 [1800])

Filene, Peter. *Americans and the Soviet Experiment, 1917-1933* (1967)

Fischer, Fritz. *Krieg der Illusionen: Die deutsche Politik von 1911 bis 1914* (1969)

Fitch, Edwin. *The Alaskan Railroad* (1967)

Fite, Emerson. *Social and Industrial Conditions in the North During the Civil War* (1910)

Fitzgerald, Percy. 1-2 *The Great Canal at Suez: Its Political, Engineering, and Financial History* (1876)

Fitzgibbon, Russell. *Cuba and the United States 1900-1935* (1935)

Fitzmaurice, Maurice. "The Nile Reservoir, Assuan." 152 *MPICE* 71 (1903)

Fleming, Philip. "Impoverished Europe Faces Slow Comeback." 136 *ENR* 203 (1946)

Fletcher, Max. "The Suez Canal and World Shipping, 1869-1914." 18 *JEH* 556 (1958)

Flinn, Alfred. "Architecture of Kensico Dam." 74 *EN* 433 (1915)

————. "The New Kensico Dam." 67 *EN* 772 (1912)

Florman, Samuel. "Hegel and the Amazon Basin." *TR*, Oct, 1989, at 19

Foerster, Robert. *The Italian Emigration of Our Time* (1924)

Folsom, Ralph, Michael Gordon, & John Spanogle, Jr. *International Business Transactions: A Problem-Oriented Coursebook* (2d ed. 1991)

Foner, Philip. 5 *History of the Labor Movement in the United States: The AFL in the Progressive Era 1910-1915* (1980)

―――――. 1-2 *The Spanish-Cuban-American War and the Birth of American Imperialism 1895-1902* (1972)

Forbes, Ian. "German Informal Imperialism in South America Before 1914." 31 *EHR* (2d ser.) 384 (1978)

Forchheimer, Prof. Dr. "Die Eisenbahn von Ismid nach Angora." 41 *ZB* 359 (1891)

Foster, Mark. "Giant of the West: Henry J. Kaiser and Regional Industrialization, 1930-1950." 59 *BHR* 1 (Spring 1989)

―――――. *Henry J. Kaiser: Builder in the Modern American West* (1989)

Francis, John. 1-2 *A History of the English Railway: Its Social Relations and Revelations 1820-1845* (1968 [1851])

"The Frederick Snare Corporation." 5:8 *AB* 1 (1959)

Freeman, C. "Chemical Process Plant: Innovation and the World Market." *NIER*, No. 45, Aug. 1968, at 29

French, Samuel. "In the Path of Progress: Railroads and Moral Reform in Porfirian Mexico." In *Railway Imperialism* 85 (Clarence Davis & Kennth Wilburn, Jr. ed., 1991)

Fröbel, Folker, Jürgen Heinrichs, & Otto Kreye. *Die neue internationale Arbeitsteilung* (1977)

―――――. *Umbruch in der Weltwirtschaft* (1986)

Fürstenberg, Carl. *Die Lebensgeschichte eines deutschen Bankiers, 1870-1914* (Hans Fürstenberg ed., 1931)

Full, August. *Fünfzig Jahre Togo* (1935)

Fuller, William. "Dam Building and Bullet Dodging in Mexico." 67 *EN* 1002 (1912)

Furnivall, J., & A. De Graeff. *Netherlands India: A Study of Plural Economy* (1939)

Furtado, Celso. *Formação econômica do Brasil* (12th ed. 1974)

Galeano, Eduardo. *Las venas abiertas de América Latina* (4th ed. 1973 [1971])

Galt, William. *Railway Reform: Its Importance and Practicability* (1865)

Gann, L. "Economic Development in Germany's African Empire, 1884-1914." In 4 *Colonialism in Africa, 1870-1960: The Economics of Colonialism* 213 (L. Gann ed., 1988 [1975])

―――――, & Peter Duignan. *The Rulers of German Africa 1884-1914* (1977)

Gates, Paul. *The Illinois Central Railroad and Its Colonization Work* (1934)

Gentilini, R. "Les Voies de communication en Cochinchine." 9 *GC* 177, 199, 225 (1886)

Ghadar, Faribarz. "The Impact of the New OPEC Downstream Operations on Oil Industry Structure." In *Petroleum Resources and Development: Economic, Legal and Policy Issues for Developing Countries* 232 (Kameel Khan ed., 1988)

Ghosh, Suresh. *Dalhousie in India, 1848-56: A Study of His Social Policy as Governor-General* (1975)

Gibson, Katherine, & Julie Graham. "Situating Migrants in Theory: The Case of Filipino Migrant Contract Construction Workers." 29 *CC* 130 (Summer 1986)

Giedion, Siegfried. *Space, Time, and Architecture* (1959 [1941])

Girard, L. "Transport." In 6 *The Cambridge Economic History of Europe: The Industrial Revolutions and After: Incomes, Population and Technological Change (I)* 212 (H. Habakkuk & M. Postan ed., 1965)

Glazebrook, G.P. de T. *A History of Transportation in Canada* (1938)
Glick, Edward. "The Tehuantepec Railroad: Mexico's White Elephant." 22 *PHR* 373 (1953)
Glickman, Norman, & Douglas Woodward. *The New Competitors: How Foreign Investors Are Changing the U.S. Economy* (1990 [1989])
*The Global Construction Industry: Strategies for Entry, Growth and Survival* (W. Strassmann & Jill Wells ed., 1988)
Gluch, Erich, & Jürgen Riedel. "The Federal Republic of Germany." In *The Global Construction Industry* 120
Goldman, Marshall. *Soviet Foreign Aid* (1967)
Goldsmith, Edward, & Nicholas Hildyard. 1 *The Social and Environmental Effects of Large Dams: Overview* (1984)
Goldthorpe, J. *The Sociology of the Third World: Disparity and Involvement* (1975)
Gormly, James. "Keeping the Door Open in Saudi Arabia: The United States and the Dhahran Airfield, 1945-46." 4 *DH* 189 (1980)
Gradus [pseud]. "A Treatise on Building by Contract." 14 *Builder* 296 (1856)
Graham, Richard. *Britain and the Onset of Modernization in Brazil 1850-1914* (1968)
Graham, Ronald. *The Aluminium Industry and the Third World: Multinational Corporations and Underdevelopment* (1982)
————. "Ghana's Volta Resettlement Scheme." In 2 *The Social and Environmental Effects of Large Dams: Case Studies* 131 (Edward Goldsmith & Nicholas Hildyard eds., 1986)
Grant, Luke. *The National Erectors' Association and the International Association of Bridge and Structural Iron Workers* (1971 [1915])
Greathead, James. "The City and South London Railway; with Some Remarks upon Subaqueous Tunneling by Shield and Compressed Air." 123 *MPICE* 39 (1896)
Greeley, Horace, et al. *The Great Industries of the United States* (1872)
Greif, Martin. *The New Industrial Landscape: The Story of the Austin Company* (1978)
Green, Forest. "Colombia Modernizes Its Highway System." *ENR*, July 8, 1954, at 30
Grier, John. "Construction." In President's Conference on Unemployment, 1 *Recent Economic Changes in the United States* 219 (1929)
Gross, Edith. "Migration Within and Towards the European Community and Its Impact on the Construction Industry." 12 *PBE* (forthcoming 1993)
Grossmann, Henryk. *Das Akkumulations- und Zusammenbruchsgesetz des kapitalistischen Systems (zugleich eine Krisentheorie)* (1929)
Grunwald, Kurt. *Türkenhirsch: A Study of Baron Maurice Hirsch Entrepreneur and Philanthropist* (1966)
Guppy, Nicholas. "Tropical Deforestation: A Global View." *FA*, Spring 1984, at 928
Gurlitt, Friedrich. "Die ersten Baujahre in Deutsch-Ostafrika." 55 *ZB* 57 (1905)
Haber, Stephen. *Industry and Underdevelopment: The Industrialization of Mexico, 1890-1940* (1989)
Haber, William. *Industrial Relations in the Building Industry* (1930)
Hadfield, Charles. *British Canals: An Illustrated History* (1974 [1950])
————. *The Canal Age* (1981)
Hagedorn, Herman. 1 *Leonard Wood: A Biography* (1931)
Hagedorn, Jan. "Economic Initiative and African Cash Farming: Pre-Colonial origins and Early Colonial Developments." In 4 *Colonialism in Africa 1870-1960: The Economics of Colonialism* 283 (L. Gann ed., 1988 [1975])
Haggard, Stephen. *Paths from the Periphery: The Politics of Growth in the Newly Industrializing Countries* (1990)

Hains, Peter. "The Labor Problem on the Panama Canal." 179 *NAR* 42 (1904)
Hallberg, Charles. *The Suez Canal: Its History and Diplomatic Importance* (1931)
Hallgarten, George. 1-2 *Der Imperialismus vor 1914: Die soziologischen Grundlagen der Aussenpolitik europäischer Grossmächte vor dem Ersten Weltkrieg* (2d ed. 1963 [1951])
Halliday, Fred. *Arabia Without Sultans* (1974)
Hambleton, Hugh. "The Saudi Petrochemical Industry in the 1980s." In *Saudi Arabia: Energy, Developmental Planning, and Industrialization* 51 (Ragaei El Mallakh & Dorothea Mallakh ed., 1982)
Hansen, Alvin. *Business Cycles and National Income* (1951)
Hardin, Patrick (ed.). *The Developing Labor Law* (3d ed. 1992)
Hardman, R. "Highway Construction in Panama." 91 *ENR* 594 (1923)
Harrington, Fred. *God, Mammon, and the Japanese: Dr. Horace N. Allen and Korean-American Relations, 1884-1905* (1944)
Harris, Nigel. *The End of the Third World: Newly Industrializing Countries and the Decline of an Ideology* (1986)
Hart, John. *Revolutionary Mexico: The Coming and Process of the Mexican Revolution* (1987)
Harvey, David. *The Urban Experience* (1989 [1985])
Hasegawa, Fumio. *Built by Japan: Competitive Strategies of the Japanese Construction Industry* (1988)
Havas, George. "Foreign Work Has Special Problems." 28 *CE* 905 (1905)
Hay, Peter. *Brunel: His Achievements in the Transport Revolution* (1973)
Headrick, Daniel. *Tentacles of Progress: Technology Transfer in the Age of Imperialism, 1850-1940* (1988)
————. *The Tools of Empire: Technology and European Imperialism in the Nineteenth Century* (1981)
Heckscher, Eli. *Merkantilismen: Ett led i den ekonomiska politikens historia* (1931)
Helfferich, Karl. 3 *Georg von Siemens: Ein Lebensbild aus Deutschlands großer Zeit* (1923)
Hell, Jürgen. *Kurze Geschichte des kubanischen Volkes* (1976)
Helps, Arthur. *Life and Labours of Mr. Brassey: 1805-1870* (1872)
Henderson, W. *Britain and Industrial Europe 1750-1870: Studies in British Influence on the Industrial Revolution in Western Europe* (2d ed. 1965 [1954])
Henkoff, Ronald. "Inside America's Biggest Private Company." *Fortune*, July 13, 1992, at 83
Henry, Arnold. *The Panama Canal and the Intercoastal Trade* (1929)
Herbert, Gilbert. *Pioneers of Prefabrication: The British Contribution in the Nineteenth Century* (1978)
Herodotus. *Historiae*
Hess, A. "Notes on a Costly Brazilian Railway Line." 68 *EN* 578 (1912)
Hesseltine, William. *Ulysses S. Grant: Politician* (1935)
Heywood, Peter. "European Firms Looking at Their Own Backyard." *ENR*, Nov. 27, 1986, at 67
Hicks, John. *Republican Ascendancy, 1921-1933* (1963 [1960])
Hilferding, Rudolf. *Das Finanzkapital: Eine Studie über die jüngste Entwicklung des Kapitalismus* (1968 [1910])
Hill, Forest. *Roads, Rails and Waterways: The Army Engineers and Early Transportation* (1957)
Hillebrandt, Patricia. "La Diversification des entreprises de construction en Europe." In *Les Grands groupes de la construction: De Nouveaux acteurs urbains?* 49 (Elisabeth Campagnac ed., 1992)
Hippo, Yasuyuki, & Saburo Tamura. "Japan." In *The Global Construction Industry* 59

Hirschman, Albert. *The Strategy of Economic Development* (1960 [1958])
*History of Public Works in the United States 1776-1976* (Ellis Armstrong ed., 1976)
Hitchcock, Henry-Russell. 1 *Early Victorian Architecture* (1972 [1954])
Hitchman, James. *Leonard Wood and Cuban Independence 1898-1902* (1971)
Hize, Jimmy. *Construction Contracts* (1993)
Hobsbawm, E. *The Age of Capital 1848-1875* (1977 [1975])
Hobson, C. *The Export of Capital* (1963 [1914])
Hobson, G. "The Great Zambezi Bridge." In 2 *The Story of the Cape to Cairo Railway and River Route, from 1887 to 1922: The Main Line as It Exists To-Day from the Cape to the Nile Delta* 43 (n.d. [1922])
Hobson, George. "The Victoria Falls Bridge." 170 *MPICE* 1 (1907)
Hobson, J. *Imperialism: A Study* (1967 [1902])
Hogan, William. 1 *Economic History of the Iron and Steel Industry of the United States* (1971)
Holley, A., & Lenox Smith. "American Iron and Steel Works: No. XXXVIII—The Works of the Phoenix Iron Company." 29 *Engineering* 103 (1880)
Holm, David. "Thailand's Railways and Informal Imperialism." In *Railway Imperialism* 121 (Clarence Davis & Kenneth Wilburn, Jr. ed., 1991)
Hood, Ernie. "Putting a New Face on Old Afghanistan Is One of Morrison-Knudsen's Projects." *ENR*, Feb. 21, 1952, at 45
Hoskins, Halford. *British Routes to India* (1966 [1928])
Howarth, David. *The Shadow of the Dam* (1961)
Howenstine, E. "Social Consideration in Promoting Construction Work in Developing Countries." *CRev*, June 1972, at 4
Hüber, Reinhard. *Die Bagdadbahn* (1943)
Hungerford, Edward. *Men of Erie: A Study of Human Effort* (1946)
Hunt, Shane. "Growth and Guano in Nineteenth-Century Peru." In *The Latin American Economies: Growth and the Export Sector, 1880-1930*, at 255 (1985)
Hutchinson, Lincoln. *The Panama Canal and International Trade Competition* (1915)
Hyman, Sidney. *Marriner S. Eccles: Private Entrepreneur and Public Servant* (1976)
Hymer, Stephen. "Direct Foreign Investment and the National Economic Interest." In *idem, The Multinational Corporation: A Radical Approach* (1979 [1966])
Institut für die Wirtschaft des sozialistischen Weltsystems an der Akademie der Wissenschaften der UdSSR. 3 *Sozialistisches Weltwirtschaftssystem: Arbeitsteilung und Standortverteilung der Produktion* (1968)
*International Directory of Company Histories* (Thomas Derdak, Adele Hast, & Paula Kepos ed., 1988-92)
Ismael, Jacqueline. *Kuwait: Social Change in Historical Perspective* (1982)
Jagtiani, H. *The Rôle of the State in the Provision of Railways* (1924)
James, E. "Development of the Inter-American Highway." 14 *CE* 5 (1944)
Jameson, Charles. "Notes on the Panama Canal." 16 *EN* 202 (1886)
Janssen, Jörn. "Das Baugewerbe—ein rückständiger Wirtschaftszweig?" In *Bauarbeit in der Bundesrepublik* 27 (Wolfgang Richter ed., 1981)
———. "Unternehmenspolitik der Großkonzerne verantwortlich für Baukostenexplosion." 25 *WSI Mitteilungen* 392 (1972)
Jastrow, Morris. *The War and the Bagdad Railway: The Story of Asia Minor and Its Relation to the Present Conflict* (1918 [1917])
Jaycox, Edward, & Clifford Hardy. "Domestic Construction Industries in Developing Countries." *FD*, Mar. 1975, at 21
Jenks, Leland. "Britain and American Railway Development." 11 *JEH* 375 (1951)

————. *The Migration of British Capital to 1875* (1963 [1927])

Jensen, J. & Gerhard Rosegger. "British Railway Builders Along the Lower Danube, 1856-1869." 46 *SEER* 105 (1968)

Jensen, Per. "Work and Qualifications of Civil Engineers in Relation to the Development of the Labour Process in the Construction Industry." [4] *PBE, 1982: Labour in Building and Construction* 1-23 (1983)

Jeremy, David. "Sir John Jackson." In 3 *DBB* 462 (David Jeremy ed., 1985)

————. "Weetman Dickinson Pearson." In 4 *DBB* 582 (David Jeremy ed., 1985)

Jessop, Arthur. *A History of the Mauritius Government Railways 1864 to 1964* (1964)

Joby, R. *The Railway Builders: Lives and Works of the Victorian Railway Contractors* (1983)

Johany, Ali, Michel Berne, & J. Mixon, Jr. *The Saudi Arabian Economy* (1986)

Johnson, Emory. "The Isthimian Canal in Its Economic Aspects." *AAAPSS*, Jan. 1902, at 1

————. "Report on the Industrial and Commercial Value of the Canal." In *Report of the Isthmian Canal Commission, 1899-1901*, at 515 (1904)

————, et al. 1 *History of Domestic and Foreign Commerce of the United States* (1915)

Jones, Charles. "The San Rafael Bridge in San Domingo." 112 *ENR* 249 (1934)

Julien, Charles-André. *Histoire de l'Algérie contemporaine: La Conquête et les débuts de la colonisation (1827-1871)* (1964)

Kaplan, Benjamin. "Profile of the Contract Construction Industry." *CRev*, Feb. 1957, at 4

Kaplan, Irving, et al. *Area Handbook for Ghana* (2d ed. 1971)

Kazin, Michael. *Barons of Labor: The San Francisco Building Trades and Union Power in the Progressive Era* (1989)

Keddie, Nikki. *Roots of Revolution: An Interpretive History of Modern Iran* (1981)

Keller, Ulrich. *The Building of the Panama Canal in Historical Photographs* (1983)

Kelly, Burnham. *The Prefabrication of Houses* (1951)

Kent, Percy. *Railway Enterprise in China: An Account of Its Origins and Development* (1907)

Kindleberger, Charles. *American Investment Abroad: Six Lectures on Direct Investment* (1971 [1969])

————. *International Economics* (3d ed. 1963 [1953])

————. *The World in Depression 1929-1939* (1975 [1973])

King, Judson. "Open Shop at Boulder Dam." 67 *NR* 147 (1931)

Kirby, Richard, & Philip Laurson. *The Early Years of Modern Civil Engineering* (1932)

Kitchen, Martin. *The Political Economy of Germany 1815-1914* (1978)

Klein, Fritz. *Deutschland von 1897/98 bis 1917* (3d ed. 1972)

Kluger, James. *Turning Water with a Shovel: The Career of Elwood Mead* (1992)

Knapp, Harry. "The Navy and the Panama Canal." In *History of the Panama Canal: Its Construction and Builders* 255 (Ira Bennett ed., 1915)

Knieper, Rolf. *Nationale Souveränität* (1991)

————. "Staat und Nationalstaat: Thesen gegen eine fragwürdige Identität." 23 *Prokla* (No. 90) 65 (1993)

Knoll, Arthur. *Togo Under Imperial Germany 1884-1914: A Case Study in Colonial Rule* (1978)

Knowles, L. *The Economic Development of the British Overseas Empire* (1924)

Kohlhepp, Gerd. *Itaipú: Basic Geopolitical and Energy Situation* (1987)

Kolbenschlag, Michael. "Bechtel's Biggest Job—Constructing Its Own Future." *Forbes,* Dec. 7, 1981, at 138

Kolko, Gabriel. *The Politics of War: The World and United States Foreign Policy,*

*1943-1945* (1970 [1968])

Kolko, Joyce, & Gabriel Kolko. *The Limits of Power: The World and U.S. Foreign Policy, 1945-1954* (1972)

Kondratieff, N. "Die langen Wellen der Konjunktur." 56 *ASS* 573 (1926)

Korman, Richard. "The Other Side of Paradise." *ENR*, June 7, 1993, at 6

Kosowatz, John. "Finnish Seek Help for Foreign Jobs." *ENR*, May 19, 1988, at 54

———, & Peter Reina. "Germany Begins the Costly Reconstruction of Its New States." *ENR*, Apr. 27, 1992, at 24

Kōtsū hakubutsukan. *Tetsudo no nihon: Tokaido shin kansen kaitsū kinen shuppan* (1964)

Kraker, Jay. "Toyota Plant Plows Ahead with No Sign of Union Pact." *ENR*, Nov. 27, 1986, at 65

Krizan, William. "Diversified Firms are Chomping at Market." *ENR*, Apr. 5, 1993, at 34

———. "Low-Octane Domestic Markets Stall Out U.S. Contractors." *ENR*, May 24, 1993, at 36

———. "Ranking Data Rankles Some." *ENR*, May 24, 1993, at 67

Kuczynski, Jürgen. 17 *Die Geschichte der Lage der Arbeiter unter dem Kapitalismus: Zur westdeutschen Historiographie—Schöne Literatur und Gesellschaft im 20. Jahrhundert und andere Studien* (1966)

Kuczynski, Robert. *The Cameroons and Togoland: A Demographic Study* (1930)

Kuntze, A. "The State Railways on the West Coast of Sumatra." 105 *MPICE* 370 (1891)

Kurgan-van Hentenryk, G. *Rail, finance et politique: Les Entreprises Philippart (1865-1890)* (1982)

Kuznets, Simon. *Capital in the American Economy: Its Formation and Financing* (1961)

Lamoreaux, *The Great Merger Movement in American Business, 1895-1904* (1988 [1985])

Läpple, Dieter. *Staat und allgemeine Produktionsbedingungen: Grundlagen zur Kritik der Infrastrukturtheorien* (1973)

Land, Thomas. "Migrant Labour Suffering from Mid-East Cut-Backs." *IC*, June 1984, at 4

Landau, Ralph, and Nathan Rosenberg. "Innovation in the Chemical Processing Industries." In *Technology & Economics: Papers Commemorating Ralph Landau's Service to the National Academy of Engineering* 107 (1991)

Landefeld, J., Ann Lawson, & Douglas Weinberg. "Rates of Return on Direct Investment." *SCB*, Aug. 1982, at 79

Landes, David. *Bankers and Pashas: International Finance and Economic Imperialism in Egypt* (1979 [1958])

Larkin, R. "Overseas Consultants Wins Contract for $650-Million Iran Development." *ENR*, Oct. 20, 1949, at 25

Larson, H. *Guide to Business History* (1948)

Lavis, Fred. "The Part of Inland Waterways in Latin American Transportation." 131 *ENR* 277 (1943)

Law, Michael. "Mining Surge May Pan Out." *ENR*, Sept. 1, 1988, at 28

Lazenby, J. "The Future Role of Hydroelectricity in Sub-Saharan Africa." *IWPDC*, Mar. 1991, at 12

Lee, James, & David Walters. *International Trade in Construction, Design, and Engineering Services* (1989)

Lefkoe, M. *The Crisis in Construction: There Is an Answer* (1970)

Lemke, Heinz. "Die Erdölinteressen der Deutschen Bank in Mesopotamien in den Jahren 1903-1911." 24 *JG* 41 (1981)

———. "Das Scheitern der Verhandlungen über die offizielle Beteiligung

Frankreichs am Bagdadbahnunternehmen 1903." 29 *JG* 227 (1984)

Lenin, V.I. *Imperializm, kak vysshaia stadiia kapitalizma.* In *idem,* 27 *Polnoe sobranie sochinenii* (1962 [1917])

———. *Zamechanie V.I. Lenina na knigu R. Luksemburg "Nakoplenie kapitala."* In 22 *Leninskii Sbornik* (1933 [1913])

Lenssen, Nicholas. "Providing Energy in Developing Countries." In *State of the World 1993: A Worldwatch Institute Report on Progress Toward a Sustainable Society* 101 (Lester Brown ed., 1993)

Leopold, Ellen. "The Costs of Accidents in the British Construction Industry." [4] *PBE, 1982: Labour in Building and Construction* 1-28 (1983)

Le Riverend, Julio. *Historia económica de Cuba* (4th ed. 1985 [1974])

Lesseps, Ferdinand de. *Lettres, Journal et Documents pour servir à servir l'histoire du Canal du Suez (1854-1855-1856)* (1875)

———. *1-2 Recollections of Forty Years* (C. Pitman tr., 1887)

LeTourneau, Robert. *Mover of Men and Mountains* (1967 [1960])

Levin, G., & I. Osmakov. "Reserven der Bauproduktion." In Autorenkollektiv, *Intensivierung und ökonomische Reserven* 285 (Gerhard Krupp tr., 1972 [1970])

Levin, Jonathan. *The Export Economies: Their Pattern of Development in Historical Perspective* (1960)

Levy, Sidney. *Japanese Construction: An American Perspective* (1990)

Lewin, Henry. *The Railway Mania and Its Aftermath 1845-1852* (1936)

Lewinsohn, Richard (Morus). *Die Umschichtung der europäischen Vermögen* (1926)

Lewis, Cleona. *America's Stake in International Investments* (1938)

Lewis, R. "Edwin Chadwick and the Railway Labourers." 3 *EHR* (2d ser.) 107 (1950)

Liebich, Otto. *Organisations- und Arbeitsverhältnisse im Baugewerbe: Eine volkswirtschaftliche Studie* (1922)

Linder, Marc. 4 *Der Anti-Samuelson: Kritik eines repräsentativen Lehrbuchs der bürgerlichen Ökonomie* (1974)

———. *Migrant Workers and Minimum Wages: Regulating the Exploitation of Agricultural Labor in the United States* (1992)

———. *Reification and the Consciousness of the Critics of Political Economy: Studies in the Development of Marx' Theory of Value* (1975)

———, & Larry Zacharias. "Opening Coase's Other Black Box: Why Workers Submit to Vertical Integration into Firms." 18 *JCL* 371 (1993)

Lipietz, Alain. "Building and the Crisis of Fordism: The Case of France." 6 *PBE* 1-13 (1984)

Little, Tom. *High Dam at Aswan* (1965)

Livesay, Harold. *Andrew Carnegie and the Rise of Big Business* (1975)

Locke, Joseph. "Address of the President." 17 *MPICE* 128 (1858)

Long, Clarence Jr. *Building Cycles and the Theory of Investment* (1940)

Louis, Wm. *The British Empire in the Middle East 1945-1951: Arab Nationalism, the United States and Postwar Imperialism* (1984)

——— (ed.). *The Robinson and Gallagher Controversy* (1976)

Lovett, H. *Canada and the Grand Trunk 1829-1924* (n.d. [1924])

Low, Emile. "Economic Analysis of Excavation Methods on a Typical Section of New York State Barge Canal Work." 39 *EC* 583 (1913)

———. "A German Excavator on the New York Barge Canal." 53 *ER* 503 (1906)

Lucas, Chester. *International Construction Business Management* (1986)

Lübbert, Erich. *AGVI 1901-1931* (1963)

Lueder, A. "Experience in the Erection of American Viaducts on the Uganda Railway." 51 *EN* 345 (1904)

Luxemburg, Rosa. *Die Akkumulation des Kapitals: Ein Beitrag zur ökonomischen Erklärung des Imperialismus.* In *idem*, 6 *GW* (1923 [1913])
———. "Riesenwerke des Kapitalismus." In *idem*, 1:1 *GW* 286 (1970 [1898])
———. "Wasserkonstruktionen in Nordamerika." In *idem*, 1:1 *GW* 282 (1970 [1898])
MacAuley, Patrick. "World-Wide Value of New Construction Put in Place." *CRev*, Sept.-Oct. 1986, at 2
MacGill, Caroline, et al. *History of Transportation in the United States Before 1860* (1917)
Mack, Gerstle. *The Land Divided: A History of the Panama Canal* (1944)
Macpherson, W. *The Economic Development of Japan c. 1868-1941* (1987)
Maier, Charles. *Recasting Bourgeois Europe: Stabilization in France, Germany, and Italy in the Decade After World War I* (1975)
Mandel, Ernest. *Die EWG und die Konkurrenz Europa-Amerika* (1968)
———. *The Second Slump: A Marxist Analysis of Recession in the Seventies* (1978)
———. *Der Spätkapitalismus* (1973 [1972])
Mantoux, Paul. *The Industrial Revolution in the Eighteenth Century* (1961 [1928])
Marichal, Carlos. *A Century of Debt Crises in Latin America: From Independence to the Great Depression, 1820-1930* (1989)
Marlowe, John. *The Making of the Suez Canal* (1964)
Marquand, A. "Travaux d'adduction d'eau potable à Valparaiso (Chile)." 32 *GC* 309 (1898)
Marsh. P. "The Dubai Aluminium Smelter Project." In *Management of International Construction Projects: Proceedings of a Conference Organized by The Institution of Civil Engineers* 155 (1985)
Marshall, Alfred. "Fragments on Trade Unions." In 2 *The Early Economic Writings of Alfred Marshall, 1867-1890*, at 346 (J. Whitaker ed., 1975)
Marston, Thomas. *Britain's Imperial Role in the Red Sea Area 1800-1878* (1961)
Martin, Percy. "Arica-La Paz Railway." 112 *Engineer* 452 (1911)
Martin, Philip. *Seasonal Workers in American Agriculture: Background and Issues* (National Commission for Employment Policy, Research Rep. RR-85-04, 1985)
Marx, Karl. "Crédit Mobilier." In Karl Marx & Frederick Engels, 15 *CollW* 270 (1985 [1857])
———. "The Defeat of Cobden, Bright and Gibson." In *id.* at 238 (1857)
———. "The English Election." In *id.* at 226 (1857).
———. "The French Crédit Mobilier." In *id.* at 8 (1856)
———. "The Future Results of British Rule in India." In Karl Marx [&] Friedrich Engels, I:12 *Gesamtausgabe (MEGA)* 248 (1984 [1853])
———. *Grundrisse der Kritik der politischen Ökonomie (Rohentwurf) 1857-1858* (1953)
———. 1 *Das Kapital: Kritik der politischen Ökonomie* (1867 [reprint 1959])
———. 1 *Das Kapital: Kritik der politischen Ökonomie: Der Produktionsprocess des Kapitals* (2d ed. 1872)
———. 1 *Das Kapital.* In Karl Marx [&] Friedrich Engels, 23 *Werke* (1962)
———. 2 *Das Kapital: Kritik der politischen Ökonomie: Der Circulationsprocess des Kapitals.* In Karl Marx [&] Friedrich Engels, 24 *Werke* (1963 [1885])
———. 3 *Das Kapital: Kritik der politischen Ökonomie: Der Gesammtprocess der kapitalistischen Produktion. In Karl Marx [&] Friedrich Engels, 25 Werke (1964 [1894])*
———. "Lord Palmerston." In Karl Marx [&] Friedrich Engels, I:12 *Gesamtausgabe (MEGA)* 357 (1984 [1853])
———, & Friedrich Engels. *Manifest der kommunistischen Partei.* In *idem*, 4 *Werke* 459 (1959 [1848])

Mason, Edward, & Robert Asher. *The World Bank Since Bretton Woods* (1973)

Mataloni, Raymond, Jr. "U.S. Multinational Companies: Operations in 1990." *SCB*, Aug. 1992, at 60

Mathias, Peter. *The First Industrial Nation: An Economic History of Britain 1700-1914* (1969)

May, Glenn. *Social Engineering in the Philippines: The Aims, Execution, and Impact of American Colonial Policy, 1900-1913* (1980)

Mayer, Joseph. "Canals Between the Lakes and New York." 26 *PASCE* 972 (1900)

Mazuzan, George. "'Our New Gold Goes Adventuring': The American International Corporation in China." 43 *PHR* 212 (1974)

McBride, Lewis, & William Tatum. "Two International Civil Airports Under Construction by U.S. Army's Corps of Engineers." *CE*, Sept. 1960, at 45

McCartney, Laton. *Friends in High Places: The Bechtel Story* (1988)

McCormick, Thomas. *China Market: America's Quest for Informal Empire 1893-1901* (1967)

McCullough, Conde. "Bridging the Rio Chiriqui on the Pan American Highway." 117 *ENR* 757 (1936)

McCullough, David. *The Path Between the Seas: The Creation of the Panama Canal 1870-1914* (1977)

McFeeley, William. *Grant: A Biography* (1981)

McGhie, W. "The Industrialisation of the Production of Building Elements and Components." [4] *PBE, 1982: Labour in Building and Construction* 3-21 (1983)

McKay, John. *Pioneers for Profit: Foreign Entrepreneurship and Russian Industrialization 1885-1913* (1970)

McManamy, Rob. "Bigger Firms Busted in Foreign Work." *ENR*, Apr. 14, 1988, at 66

————, & Mary Powers. "Firms Go Along for the Ride as More Clients Begin to Travel." *ENR*, May 24, 1993, at 74

————, & Armin Schmid. "Odebrecht: Brazil's Giant Beats Adversity." *ENR*, Sept. 20, 1993, at 45

McMillen, Carl. *Multinationals from the Second World: Growth of Foreign Investment by Soviet and East European Enterprises* (1987)

McQuade, Walter. "The Arabian Building Boom is Making Construction History." *Fortune*, Sept., 1976, at 112

Mead, Elwood. "The Construction of Boulder Dam." *LD*, Nov. 4, 1933, at 14

Mechkat, Cyrus. "Production d'architecture, concentration du capital et migration du travail dans le golfe arabo-persique." [4] *PBE: 1982, Labour in Building and Construction* 4-8 (1983)

Mehren E. "American Contractors and Labor Conditions in France." 85 *ENR* 340 (1920)

Mejcher, Helmut. "Die Bagdadbahn als Instrument deutschen wirtschaftlichen Einflusses im Osmanischen Reich." 1 *GG* 447 (1975)

*Memoirs of Sir Edward Blount* (Stuart Reid ed., 1902)

Menzenreiter, Johann. *Die Bagdadbahn: Als Beispiel für die Entstehung des Finanzimperialismus in Europa (1872-1903)* (1982)

Merckel, Curt. *Die Ingenieurtechnik im Alterthum* (1969 [1899])

Meyer, Hans. *Die Eisenbahnen im tropischen Afrika: Eine kolonialwirtschaftliche Studie* (1902)

Mi Rucheng. "Deutscher Eisenbahnbau in China, 1870-1938." In *Von der Kolonialpolitik zur Kooperation: Studien zur Geschichte der deutsch-chinesischen Beziehungen* 101 (Kuo Heng-yü ed., 1986)

Middlemas, Keith. *Cabora Bassa: Engineering and Politics in Southern Africa* (1975)

Middlemas, Robert. *The Master Builders: Thomas Brassey; Sir John Aird; Lord Cowdray; Sir John Norton-Griffiths* (1963)
Mill, John Stuart. *Principles of Political Economy* (W. Ashley ed., 1926 [1848])
Miller, Aron. *Search for Security: Saudi Arabian Oil and American Foreign Policy, 1939-1949* (1980)
Miller, Rory. "Transferring Techniques: Railway Building and Management on the West Coast of South America." In Rory Miller & Henry Finch, *Technology Transfer and Economic Development in Latin America, 1850-1930*, at 1 (1986)
Millman, Joel. "You Have to Be an Optimist." *Forbes*, May 24, 1993, at 84
Mitchell, B. *European Historical Statistics 1750-1970* (1970)
Mittag, Albert. "Constructing Highways in Colombia." 5 *CE* 361 (1935)
Molesworth, Guilford. "Address." 159 *MPICE* 5 (1905)
Molesworth, Henry. "American Workshop Methods in Steel Construction." 148 *MPICE* 58 (1902)
Monosowski, E. "Lessons from the Tucuruí Experience." *IWPDC*, Feb. 1990, at 29
———. "The Tucuruí Experience." *IWPDC*, July 1983, at 11
Moody, John. *The Truth About Trusts* (1904)
Moody's Investors Service & U.N. Centre on Transnational Corporations. *Directory of the World's Largest Service Companies* (Ser. I—Dec. 1990)
Moon, Chung In. "Korean Contractors in Saudi Arabia: Their Rise and Fall." 40 *MEJ* 614 (1986)
Mooney, Booth. *Builders for Progress: The Story of the Associated General Contractors of America* (1965)
Morgan, Geo. *Annual Statement of the Trade and Commerce of St. Louis for the Year 1903* (1904)
Morgenstern, Felice. *International Conflicts of Labour Law: A Survey of the Law Applicable to the International Employment Relation* (1984)
Mosse, James. "Ceylon Government Railways." 63 *MPICE* 63 (1881)
———. "The Mauritius Railways—Midland Line." 28 *MPICE* 232 (1868-69)
Mottek, Hans, Walter Becker, & Alfred Schröter. 3 *Wirtschaftsgeschichte Deutschlands: Von der Zeit der Bismarckschen Reichsgründung 1871 bis zur Niederlage des faschistischen deutschen Imperialismus 1945* (1974)
Moulton, Harold. *Waterways Versus Railways* (1912)
Moxon, James. *Volta: Man's Greatest Lake* (1969)
Mühlmann, C. "Die deutschen Bauunternehmungen in der asiatischen Türkei 1888-1914." 24 *WA* 121*, 365* (1926)
Müller, Fritz. *Deutschland-Zanzibar-Ostafrika: Geschichte einer Kolonialeroberung 1884-1890* (1959)
Munasinghe, Indrani. "The Colombo-Kandy Railway." 25 *CHJ* 239 (Nos. 1-4, 1978)
Murray, Martin. *The Development of Capitalism in Colonial Indochina (1870-1940)* (1980)
Myrdal, Gunnar. *Asian Drama* (1968)
Nansouty, Max de. "Travaux du Canal de Panama: Les Excavateurs." 13 *GC* 1 (1883)
*National Interests in an Age of Global Technology* (Thomas Lee & Proctor Reid ed., 1991)
National Research Council. *Building for Tomorrow: Global Enterprise and the U.S. Construction Industry* (1988)
Neo, Roland. *International Construction Contracting: A Critical Investigation into Certain Aspects of Financing, Capital Planning and Cash Flow Effects* (1975)
Neusüss, Christel. *Imperialismus und Weltmarktbewegung des Kapitals* (1972)

Nevin, W. "The Railway Situation in Mexico." 14 *EN* 86 (1885)
Nevins, Allen, & Frank Hill. *Ford: Expansion and Challenge 1915-1933* (1957)
Newell, F. "Federal Land Reclamation: A National Problem: 1. Origin, Problems and Achievements of Federal Land Reclamation." 91 *ENR* 666 (1923)
Newman, W. *The Building Industry and Business Cycles*. In 5:4 *Studies in Business Administration* (1935)
Newton, C. "The Hydro-Electric Development of the Braden Copper Co." 69 *EN* 1041 (1913)
Newton, Velma. *The Silver Men: West Indian Labour Migration to Panama 1850-1914* (1984)
Nirumand, Bahman. *Persien, Modell eines Entwicklungslandes oder die Diktatur der Freien Welt* (1967)
Nkrumah, Kwame. *Neo-Colonialism: The Last Stage of Imperialism* (1965)
Noble, Alfred. "The New York Tunnel Extension of the Pennsylvania Railroad: The East River Division." 35 *TASCE* 888 (1909)
Noda, Masaho, et al. *Nihon no tetsudo: seiritsu to tenkai* (1986)
Norman, E. Herbert. *Japan's Emergence as a Modern State: Political and Economic Problems of the Meiji Period* (1940)
Norsa, Aldo. "Italy." In *The Global Construction Industry* 86
North, Douglass. *Growth and Welfare in the American Past: A New Economic History* (1966)
Northrup, Herbert. *Open Shop Construction Revisited* (1984)
————, & Howard Foster. *Open Shop Construction* (1975)
————, & Margot Malin. *Personnel Policies for Engineers and Scientists: An Analysis of Major Corporate Practices* (1986 [1985])
Nothstein, Gary, & Jeffrey Ayres. "The Multinational Corporation and the Extraterritorial Application of the Labor Management Relations Act." 10 *CILJ* 1 (1976)
Nourse, J. *The Maritime Canal of Suez* (1869)
*Nouvelles Installations maritimes du Port d'Anvers: Notice explicative des travaux projétés et des moyens d'éxécution et des moyens d'éxécution proposés par MM. A. Couvreux & H. Hersent* (1880)
Nwulia, Moses. *The History of Slavery in Mauritius and the Seychelles, 1818-1875* (1981)
OECD. *Globalisation of Industrial Activities: Four Case Studies: Auto Parts, Chemicals, Construction and Semiconductors* (1992)
————. *The Petrochemical Industry: Trends in Production and Investment to 1985* (1979)
Obeng, Letitia. "Environmental Impacts of Four African Impoundments." In *Environmental Impacts of International Civil Engineering Projects and Practices* 29 (Charles Gunnerson & John Kalbermattem ed., 1978)
————. "Should Dams Be Built?" 6 *Ambio* 46 (1977)
O'Connor, A. *Railways and Development in Uganda* (1965)
O'Connor, Gerald. "Foreign Competition in Overseas Construction." *CE*, Feb., 1962, at 56
O'Connor, Harvey. *The Empire of Oil* (1955)
O'Connor, T. "Lord Cowdray: A Study in Personality." 51 *NPMM* 353 (1913)
O'Hanlon, Thomas. "The Unchecked Power of the Building Trades." *Fortune*, Dec. 1968, at 102
Olivier, H. *Great Dams in South Africa* (n.d. [1976])
Oman, Charles. *New Forms of International Investment in Developing Countries* (OECD 1984)
————. *New Forms of Investment in Developing Country Industries: Mining, Petrochemicals, Automobiles, Textiles, Food* (OECD 1989)
Opatrný, Josef. *Antecedentes históricos de la formación de la nación cubana*

(1986)
O'Reilly, Brian. "Your New Global Work Force." *Fortune*, Dec. 14, 1992, at 52
Orren, Karen. *Belated Feudalism: Labor, the Law, and Liberal Development in the United States* (1991)
Owen, E. *Cotton and the Egyptian Economy 1820-1914: A Study in Trade and Development* (1969)
Owen, Marguerite. *The Tennessee Valley Authority* (1973)
Painter, David. *Oil and the American Century: The Political Economy of U.S. Foreign Oil Policy, 1941-1954* (1986)
Pakenham-Walsh, R. 9 *History of the Corps of Royal Engineers: 1938-1948* (1958)
Parry, Albert. *Whistler's Father* (1939)
Parsons, Maurice. "The Philosophy of Engineering." 77 *TASCE* 38 (1914)
Paterson, Peter. "An Account of the Cast-Iron Lighthouse Tower in Gibbs Hall, in the Bermudas." 2 *MPICE* 182 (1843)
Paul, Hans-Holger. *Marx, Engels und die Imperialismustheorie der II. Internationale* (1978)
[Pauling, George]. *The Chronicles of a Contractor: Being the Autobiography of the Late George Pauling* (David Buchan ed., 1926)
Pears, Edwin. "The Bagdad Railway." 94 *ContR* 570 (1908)
Peña, Sergio de la. *La formación del capitalismo en México* (1977 [1975])
Peniston, William. "Public Works In Pernambuco, in the Empire of Brazil." 22 *MPICE* 385 (1863)
Pepperman, W. *Who Built the Panama Canal?* (1915)
Peters, Enrique. "Bye Bye Weltmarkt? Freihandel oder Regionalisierung des Weltmarktes: Das Freihandelsabkommen zwischen Kanada, Mexicko und den USA." *Prokla*, No. 90, Mar. 1993, at 129
Peterson, Charles. "Prefabs in the California Gold Rush, 1849." 24 *JSAH* 318 (1965)
[Peto, Henry]. *Sir Morton Peto: A Memorial Sketch* (1893)
Petras, Elizabeth. *Jamaican Labor Migration: White Capital and Black Labor, 1850-1930* (1988)
Petras, James, & Dennis Engbarth. "Third World Industrialization and Trade Union Struggles." In *Trade Unions and the New Industrialization of the Third World* 81 (Roger Southall ed., 1988)
Petro, Sylvester. "Unions, Housing Cost and the National Labor Policy." 32 *LCP* 329 (1967)
Pettitt, George. *So Boulder Dam Was Built* (1935)
Platt, D. *Foreign Finance in Continental Europe and the United States, 1815-1870: Quantities, Origins, Functions and Distribution* (1984)
Pletcher, David. *Rails, Mines, and Progress: Seven American Promoters in Mexico, 1867-1911* (1958)
Plumwood, Val, & Richard Routley. "World Rainforest Destruction—The Social Factors." *Ecologist*, No. 1, 1982, at 4
Podshivalenko, P., et al. *Ekonomika stroitel'stva: Uchebnik* (1962)
Poidevin, Raymond. *Les Relations économiques et financières entre la France et l'Allemagne de 1898 à 1914* (1969)
Pollard, Nigel. "The Gezira Scheme—A Study in Failure." *Ecologist*, Jan.-Feb. 1981, at 21
Pollard, Sidney. *The Genesis of Modern Management: A Study of the Industrial Revolution in Great Britain* (1968 [1965])
Pollins, Harold. "Railway Contractors and the Finance of Railway Development in Britain." 3 *JTH* 41, 103 (1957)
Pollock, Norman. *Nyasaland and Northern Rhodesia: Corridor to the North* (1971)
Porter, Whitworth. 2 *History of the Corps of Royal Engineers* (1951 [1889])
Potter, Edward. *Freedom of Association, the Right to Organize and Collective*

*Bargaining—The Impact on U.S. Law and Practice of Ratification of ILO Conventions No. 87 & No. 98* (1984)

Potter, William. "Railway Work in Japan." 56 *MPICE* 2 (1879)

Powell, Fred. *Railroads of Mexico* (1921)

Prasad, Amba. *Indian Railways: A Study in Public Utility Administration* (1960)

Prebisch, Raúl. *Transformación y desarollo: La gran tarea de la América Latina* (1970)

Prelini, Charles. "The Erie Canal." 90 *Engineering* 1, 76 (1910)

———. "The New York Subaqueous Tunnels." 83 *Engineering* 297, 367, 667 (1907)

Price, Wright. "Auto Manufacturing Plant Built in Argentina." 27 *CE* 88 (1957)

Pritchard, H. (ed.). 7 *History of the Corps of Royal Engineers: Campaigns in Mesopotamia and East Africa, and the Inter-War Period, 1919-38* (1952)

Pritzkoleit, Kurt. *Bosse Banken Börsen: Herren über Geld und Wirtschaft* (1954)

———. *Männer-Mächte-Monopole: Hinter den Türen der westdeutschen Wirtschaft* (1958 [1953])

Prowde, Oswalde. "The Gezira Irrigation Scheme, including the Sennar Dam on the Blue Nile." 222 *MPICE* 81 (1927)

Pursell, C. Review of McCartney, *Friends in High Places*. 30 *TC* 702 (1989)

Quesada y Miranda, Gonzalo de. 1 *¡En Cuba Libre! Historia documentada y anecdótica del Machadato: 1925-1931* (1938)

"Railway Morality and Railway Policy." *ERev*, Oct. 1854, at 420

Rainbird, Helen, & Gerd Syben. "Introduction." In *Restructuring a Traditional Industry: Construction Employment and Skills in Europe* 1 (Helen Rainbird & Gerd Syben ed., 1991)

Raphael, Lois. *The Cape-to-Cairo Dream: A Study in British Imperialism* (1936)

Rapier, Richard. "Brief Account of the Woosung Railway." 59 *MPICE* 274 (1880)

Rathmann, Lothar. *Berlin-Bagdad: Die imperialistische Nahostpolitik des kaiserlichen Deutschlands* (1962)

Reckman, Bob. "Carpentry: The Craft and Trade." In *Case Studies in the Labor Process* 73 (Andrew Zimbalist ed., 1979)

Regalsky, Andrés. "Foreign Capital, Local Interests and Railway Development in Argentina: French Investments in Railways, 1900-1914." 21 *JLAS* 425 (1989)

Reich, Robert. *The New American Frontier* (1983)

Rein, J. *The Industries of Japan* (1889)

Reina, Pete, & Gary Tulacz. "International Contracts Dip Slightly in 1992." *ENR*, Aug. 23, 1993, at 28

Reisner, Marc. *Cadillac Desert: The American West and Its Disappearing Water* (1987 [1986])

Renty, E. de. 1 *Les Chemins de fer coloniaux en Afrique: Chemins de fer des colonies allemandes, italiennes et portugaises* (1903)

———. 2 *Les Chemins de fer coloniaux: Chemins de fer dans les colonies anglaises et au Congo Belge* (1904)

———. 3 *Les chemins de fer coloniaux en Afrique: Chemins de fer dans les colonies françaises* (1905)

Reutter, Mark. *Sparrows Point: Making Steel—The Rise and Ruin of American Industrial Might* (1989 [1988])

Richardson, Harold. "Alcan—America's Glory Road. Part III: Construction Tactics." 130 *ENR* 63 (1943)

Richter, Winfred. "Middle East Construction: Potentials and Prospects." *IC*, Sept. 1975, at 80

Ridley, William. "The Grand River Viaduct, Mauritius Railways." 25 *MPICE* 237 (1866)

Riegel, Robert. *The Story of the Western Railroads* (1926)
Rigby, Edward, & William Leitch. "Railway Construction in North China." 160 *MPICE* 271 (1905)
Rimmer, Peter. "Japanese Construction Contractors and the Australian States: Another Round of Interstate Rivalry." 12 *IJURR* 404 (1988)
Rippy, J. *British Investments in Latin America, 1822-1949: A Case Study in the Operation of Private Enterprise in Retarded Regions* (1959)
———. *The Capitalists and Colombia* (1931)
Robbins, Michael. "The Balaklava Railway." 1 *JTH* 28 (1953)
———. *George and Robert Stephenson* (1966)
Roberts, John. "Engineering Consultancy, Industrialization and Development." In *Science, Technology and Development: The Political Economy of Technical Advance in Underdeveloped Countries* 39 (Charles Cooper ed., 1973)
Robinson, Herbert. *The Economics of Building* (1939)
Robinson, Joan. *The Accumulation of Capital* (3d ed. 1971 [1956])
Robinson, Michael. *Water for the West: The Bureau of Reclamation 1902-1977* (1979)
Robinson, Tracy. *Fifty Years at Panama 1861-1911* (2d ed. 1911 [1907])
Robison, Richard. *Indonesia: The Rise of Capital* (1986)
Rolt, L. *Great Engineers* (1962)
———. *The Railway Revolution: George and Robert Stephenson* (1962 [1960])
———. *Thomas Telford* (1962 [1958])
[Roosevelt, Theodore.] 5 *The Letters of Theodore Roosevelt* (Elting Morison ed., 1952)
Rosa, Luiz, & Roberto Schaeffer. "Brazilian Energy Policy." In *Hydroelectric Dams on Brazil's Xingu River and Indigenous Peoples* 47 (Leinad Ayer de O. Santos & Lúcia M.M. de Andrade ed., 1990)
Rose, J. (ed.) 2 *Cambridge History of the British Empire: The Growth of the New Empire 1783-1870* (1968 [1940])
Rosenberg, Hans. *Die Weltwirtschaftskrise 1857-1859* (1974 [1934])
Rowland, John. *George Stephenson: Creator of Britain's Railways* (1954)
Rudin, Harry. *Germany in the Cameroons 1884-1914: A Case Study of Modern Imperialism* (1938)
Ruegnitz, W. "Building Bridge Substructures on the Canadian Trunk Ry." 72 *EN* 710 (1914)
Ruiz Williams, E. "Cuba Begins New Central Highway 700 Miles Long." 98 *ENR* 558 (1927)
Ruttan, Vernon. "Assistance to Expand Agricultural Production." 14:1 *WD* 39-42 (1986)
"San Francisco Bridge Co." 5:4 *AB* 1 (1958)
Sanderson, Steven. *Agrarian Populism and the Mexican State: The Struggle for Land in Sonora* (1981)
———. *The Politics of Trade in Latin American Development* (1992)
Sawyer, G. "The Transandean Railway from Arica, Chile, to La Paz, Bolivia." 70 *EN* 1059 (1913)
Scheiber, Harry. "World War I as Entrepreneurial Opportunity: Willard Straight and the American International Corporation." 84 *PSQ* 486 (1969)
Scherer, F. *Industrial Market Structure and Economic Performance* (2d ed. 1980)
Schinzinger, Francesca. *Die Kolonien und das Deutsche Reich: Die wirtschaftliche Bedeutung der deutschen Besitzungen in Übersee* (1984)
Schivelbusch, Wolfgang. *Geschichte der Eisenbahnreise: Zur Industrialisierung von Raum und Zeit im 19. Jahrhundert* (1977)
Schlesinger, Arthur, Jr. *The Age of Roosevelt: The Politics of Upheaval* (1960)
Schmidt, Hermann. *Das Eisenbahnwesen in der asiatischen Türkei* (1914)
Schoeller, Wolfgang. *Weltmarkt und Reproduktion des Kapitals* (1976)

Schott, Joseph. *Rails Across Panama: The Story of the Building of the Panama Railroad 1847-1855* (1967)

Schrecker, John. *Imperialism and Chinese Nationalism: Germany in Shantung* (1971)

Schreyögg, Georg, & Horst Steinmann. "Corporate Morality Called in Question: The Case of Cabora Bassa." 8 *JBE* 677 (1989)

Schriener, Judy. "No Grand Plan But Plenty of Cash." *ENR*, Mar. 22, 1993, at 24

Schulte, Dieter. "Die Monopolpolitik des Reichskolonialamts in der 'Ära Dernburg' 1906-1910: Zu frühen Formen des Funktionsmechanismus zwischen Monopolkapital und Staat." 24 *JG* 7 (1981)

Schumpeter, Joseph. *Business Cycles: A Theoretical, Historical, and Historical Analysis of the Capitalist Process* (1939)

———. *Capitalism, Socialism and Democracy* (1966 [1942])

Schuyler, Hamilton. *The Roeblings: A Century of Engineers, Bridge-Builders and Industrialists* (1931)

Schwartz, Adam. "Timber is the Test." *FEER*, July 23, 1992, at 36

———, & Jonathan Friedland. "Green Fingers." *FEER*, Mar. 12, 1992, at 42

Searles, P. "Difficulties of Construction Work on the Island of Guam." 97 *ENR* 106 (1926)

Semmel, Bernard. *Imperialism and Social Reform: English Social-Imperial Thought 1895-1914* (1968 [1960])

Serageldin, Ismail, et al. *Manpower and International Labor Migration in the Middle East and North Africa* (1983)

Setzer, Steven. "Materials Markets Going Global." *ENR*, Mar. 29, 1993, at 31

———, and Richard Korman. "Are They Better? Japanese Bring More Than Money in Their Quest for U.S. Market Share." *ENR*, Mar. 3, 1988, at 30

Seymour, Howard. *The Multinational Construction Industry* (1987)

Shaw, R. "Migration and Employment in the Arab World: Construction as a Key Policy Variable." 118 *ILR* 589 (1979)

Sheehan, Robert. "Steve Bechtel: Born to Build." *Fortune*, Nov. 1955, at 142

Shelford, Frederic. "Some Features of the West African Government Railways." 189 *MPICE* 1 (1912)

Sibert, William, & John Stevens. *The Construction of the Panama Canal* (1915)

Sider, Don. "The Big Boondoggle at Lordstown." *Fortune*, Sept. 1969, at 106

Sill, Van Renssaler. *American Miracle: The Story of War Construction Around the World* (1947)

Sitterson, J. *Sugar Country: The Cane Sugar Industry in the South, 1753-1950* (1953)

Skelton, Oscar. *The Life and Times of Sir Alexander Tilloch Galt* (1920)

———. *The Railway Builders: A Chronicle of Overland Highways* (1920)

Smart, John. "Saudi Demand for Filipino Workers: Labor Migration Issues in the Middle East." *APCF*, Aug. 1982, at 1

Smiles, Samuel. *The Life of George Stephenson and of His Son Robert Stephenson* (1868)

———. 1-2 *Lives of the Engineers* (1861)

Smith, Adam. *An Inquiry into the Nature and Causes of the Wealth of Nations* (Edwin Cannan ed., 1937 [1776])

Smith, Richard. "The Fifty-Million-Dollar Man." *Fortune*, Nov. 1957, at 176

Smith, Robert. *The United States and Cuba: Business and Diplomacy, 1917-1960* (1960)

Smith, V. "African Airbases—A Job Well Done." *ENR*, Aug. 11, 1955, at 34

Smith, Wilson. "Excavation and Foundation Work for the Kensico Dam." 71 *EN* 763 (1914)

Smyth, Hedley. *Property Companies and the Construction Industry in Britain* (1985)

Sohn-Rethel, Alfred. *Ökonomie und Klassenstruktur des deutschen Faschismus* (1973)

Sombart, Werner. 1 *Der moderne Kapitalismus* (1902)

———. 3 *Der moderne Kapitalismus: Das Wirtschaftsleben im Zeitalter des Hochkapitalismus* (1927)

Sondheimer, John, & Sylvia Bargas. "U.S. Sales and Purchases of Private Services." *SCB*, Sept. 1992, at 82

Southall, Roger. "Introduction." In *Trade Unions and the New Industrialization of the Third World* 1 (Roger Southall ed., 1988)

Southard, Frank. *American Industry in Europe* (1931)

Spender, J. *Weetman Pearson First Viscount Cowdray 1856-1927* (1930)

Spiller, John. "The Respective Merits of Roads and Railways for Colonial Development." 237 *MPICE* 546 (1935)

Spitz, Peter. *Petrochemicals: The Rise of an Industry* (1988)

Spohn, Willfried. *Weltmarktkonkurrenz und Industrialisierung Deutschlands 1870-1914: Eine Untersuchung zur nationalen und internationalen Geschichte der kapitalistischen Produktionsweise* (1977)

Stallings, Barbara. *Banker to the Third World: United States Portfolio Investment in Latin America, 1900-1986* (1987)

Stallworthy, E., & O. Kharbanda. *International Construction* (1986)

Starrett, Paul. *Changing the Skyline: An Autobiography* (1938)

Stead, W. *The Americanization of the World: The Trend of the Twentieth Century* (1902 [1901])

Steel, Robert. "The Volta Dam: Its Prospects and Problems." In *Dams in Africa: An Interdisciplinary Study of Man-Made Lakes in Africa* 63 (Neville Rubin & William Warren ed., 1968)

Steele, E. *Palmerston and Liberalism, 1855-1865* (1991)

Stein, Robert, & Brian Johnson. *Banking on the Biosphere? Environmental Procedures and Practices of Nine Multinational Development Agencies* (1979)

Steinhaus, Kurt. *Soziologie der türkischen Revolution: Zum Problem der Entfaltung der bürgerlichen Gesellschaft in sozioökonomisch schwach entwickelten Ländern* (1969)

Stephenson, George Robert. "Address of the President." 44 *MPICE* 2 (1876)

Stevens, G. 1 *Canadian National Railways: Sixty Years of Trial and Error (1836-1896)* (1960)

Stevens, H. "Some Road Building in the Philippines." 50 *ER* 535 (1904)

Stevens, Joseph. *Hoover Dam: An American Adventure* (1988)

Stewart, Watt. *Chinese Bondage in Peru: A History of the Chinese Coolie in Peru, 1849-1874* (1951)

———. *Henry Meiggs: Yankee Pizarro* (1968 [1946])

Stobaugh, Robert. "Channels for Technology Transfer: The Petrochemical Industry." In *Technology Crossing Borders: The Choice, Transfer, and Management of International Technology Flows* 157 (Robert Stobaugh & Louis Wells, Jr. ed., 1984)

———. *Innovation and Competition: The Global Management of Petrochemical Products* 79 (1988)

Stoecker, Helmuth. "The German Empire in Africa Before 1914: General Questions." In *German Imperialism in Africa: From the Beginnings Until the Second World War* 185 (Helmuth Stoecker ed., Bernd Zöllner tr., 1986)

———, & Peter Sebald. "Enemies of the Colonial Idea." In *Germans in the Tropics: Essays in German Colonial History* 59 (Arthur Knoll & Lewis Gann ed., 1991)

Stoff, Michael. *Oil, War, and American Security: The Search for a National Policy on Foreign Oil, 1941-1947* (1980)

Stone, Charles. "Engineer's Relation to Foreign Expansion." 75 *ER* 5 (1917)

Stork, Joe. "The Gulf War and the Arab World." 8 *WPJ* 365 (1991)

Strassmann, W. "Construction Productivity and Employment in Developing Countries." 101 *ILR* 503 (1970)

———. "The Construction Sector in Economic Development." 18 *SJPE* 391 (1970)

———. Review of McCartney, *Friends in High Places.* 23 *JEI* 275 (1989)

———. "The United States." In *The Global Construction Industry* 22

Straub, Hans. *A History of Civil Engineering: An Outline from Ancient to Modern Times* (E. Rockwell tr., 1952 [1949])

Strode, Hudson. *The Pageant of Cuba* (1936 [1934])

Sun, E-tu Zen. *Chinese Railways and British Interests 1898-1911* (1971 [1954])

Sutton, Anthony. *Western Technology and Soviet Economic Development 1917 to 1930* (1968)

———. *Western Technology and Soviet Economic Development 1930-1945* (1971)

Suviranta, A. *Labour Law and Industrial Relations in Finland* (1987)

Sweezy, Paul. *The Theory of Capitalist Development: Principles of Marxian Political Economy* (1968 [1942])

Taylor, Frank. "Builder No. 1." *SEP*, June 7, 1941, at 9

Taylor, Frederick. "The Principles of Scientific Management." In *Scientific Management: Addresses and Discussions at the Conference on Scientific Management, held October 12, 13, 14, 1911.* Reprinted in 1 *Some Classic Contributions to Professional Managing: Selected Papers* 37 (1956)

Taylor, George. *The Transportation Revolution, 1815-1860* (1968 [1951])

Thackwell, H. "Tunnel Building in Nicaraguan Jungles." 86 *ENR* 821 (1921)

Thobie, Jacques. *Intérêts et impérialisme français dans l'empire ottoman (1895-1914)* (1977)

Thomas, Hugh. *Cuba or the Pursuit of Freedom* (1971)

Thompson, A. "The Labour Problem of the Panama Canal." 83 *Engineering* 589 (1907)

Thompson, Virginia. *French Indo-China* (1968 [1937])

———, & Richard Adloff. "French Economic Policy in Tropical Africa." In 4 *Colonialism in Africa 1870-1960: The Economics of Colonialism* 127 (L. Gann ed., 1988 [1975])

Thompson, Wells. "Modern Factory Built in Korea." 1 *CE* 1275 (1931)

Thorner, Daniel. "Great Britain and the Development of India's Railways." 11 *JEH* 389 (1951)

Thorup, Cathryn. "La competencia económica británica y norteamericana en México (1887-1910): El caso de Weetman Pearson." 31 *HM* 599 (1982)

Tincauzer, Eugen. "Der Bau des Panamakanals." 61 *ZB* 611 (1911)

Tomlin, Robert, Jr. "American Road-Building in French War Zone Organized." 80 *EN* 198 (1918)

Townsend, Mary. *The Rise and Fall of Germany's Colonial Empire 1884-1918* (1930)

Treblicock, Clive. *The Industrialization of the Continental Powers 1780-1914* (1981)

Trimmer, John. "ABC: Profile of Philosophy." *MSC*, Jan. 1976, at 15

Trollope, Anthony. *Doctor Thorne* (1858)

———. *North America* (1951 [1862])

Tugan-Baranowsky, Michael von. *Studien zur Theorie und Geschichte der Handelskrisen in England* (1901)

Tulacz, Gary. "The Top Owners Are Building, But They Remain Cautious." *ENR*, Nov. 22, 1993, at 34

Tully, Shawn. "France's Master Builder is on the March." *Fortune*, May 2, 1983, at 210

———. "The Mismatched Merger That Worked." *Fortune*, Apr. 19, 1982, at 166
Tupholme, C. "Akosombo: Key to a Stable Future." *IC*, Apr. 1966, at 2
———. "Cabora Bassa." *IC*, Apr. 1970, at 24
Turchaninova, Svetlana. "Trends in Women's Employment in the USSR." 112
   *ILR* 253 (1975)
Turner, John. "The Construction of the Yokohama Water-Works." 100 *MPICE*
   277 (1890)
"Turner Construction Company." 2:6 *AB* 1 (1954)
University of Ceylon. 3 *History of Ceylon* (K. de Silva ed., 1973)
Vail, Leroy. "The Making of an Imperial Slum: Nyasaland and Its Railways,
   1895-1935." 16 *JAH* 89 (1975)
Valentine, John. "Description of the Line and Works of the Railway from Lisbon
   to Santarem." 21 *MPICE* 1 (1859)
Vallenilla, Nikita Harwich. "El modelo economico del liberalismo amarillo:
   Historia de un fracaso, 1888-1908." In *Politica y economia en Venezuela
   1810-1976*, at 203 (Alfredo Boulton ed., 1976)
Varga, E. *Osnovye voprosy ekonomiki i politiki imperializma (posle vtoroi mirovoi
   voiny)* (1953)
Vasil'ev, L. *Mezhdunarodnye trudovye kollektivy stroitelei stran-chlenov SEV:
   praktika i perspektivy razvitii* (1987)
Vatikiotis, Michael. "Tug-of-War Over Trees." *FEER*, Jan. 12, 1989, at 41
Vaughan, Adrian. *Isambard Kingdom Brunel: Engineering Knight-Errant* (1991)
Vaughan, Walter. *The Life and Work of Sir William Van Horne* (1920)
Vergara, Walter, & Dominique Babelon. *The Petrochemical Industry in Developing
   Asia: A Review of the Current Situation and Prospects for Development in
   the 1990s* (World Bank Technical Paper No. 113, 1990)
———, & Donald Brown. *The New Face of the World Petrochemical Sector:
   Implications for Developing Countries* (World Bank Technical Paper No. 84,
   1988)
Verillo, Josmar. "Brazil." In *The Global Construction Industry* 180
Vernon, Raymond. "The American Corporation in Underdeveloped Areas." In *The
   Corporation in Modern Society* 237 (Edward Mason ed., 1966 [1959])
Vernon-Harcourt, L. *Achievements in Engineering During the Last Half Century*
   (1892)
Vevier, Charles. *The United States and China 1906-1913: A Study of Finance and
   Diplomacy* (1955)
Vignoles, Olinthus. *Life of Charles Blacker Vignoles: Soldier and Civil Engineer*
   (1889)
Wakeman, Frederic, Jr. *The Fall of Imperial China* (1977 [1975])
Wald, Lillian, & Frances Kellor. "The Construction Camps of the People." 23
   *Survey* 449 (Jan. 1, 1910)
Walker, Charles. *Thomas Brassey: Railway Builder* (1969)
Wallace, H. "The Way to Abundance." *NR*, Mar. 27, 1944, at 414
Waltershausen, A. Sartorius Freiherr von. *Das volkswirtschaftliche System der
   Kapitalanlage im Ausland* (1907)
Wanamaker, W. "Vast and Varied Engineering Works Develop Venezuelan Iron-
   Ore Deposits." 23 *CE* 807 (1953)
Wáng Jing-chūn. *Railway Loan Agreements of China* (1922)
Warf, Barney. "The International Construction Industry in the 1980s." 43 *PG* 150
   (1991)
Warne, William. *The Bureau of Reclamation* (1973)
Warren, Frank, Jr. "International Construction Markets Hindered by Nations in
   Debt." *Constructor*, Jan., 1986, at 28
Warren, Kenneth. *The American Steel Industry 1850-1970: A Geographic
   Interpretation* (1973)

Waterbury, John. *Hydropolitics of the Nile Valley* (1979)
Watson, Charles. 3 *History of the Corps of Royal Engineers* (1954 [1914])
Weaver, Leon. "Raymond Concrete Pile Company." 4:6 *AB* 1 (1957)
Webb, Sidney, & Beatrice Webb. *The History of Trade Unionism* (new ed. 1902 [1894])
Webb, Edward. "On the Means of Communication in the Empire of Brazil." 19 *MPICE* 240 (1860)
Wehler, Hans-Ulrich. *Bismarck und der Imperialismus* (1976 [1969])
Weidmann, H. *Hochtief: Aktiengesellschaft für Hoch- und Tiefbauten vorm. Gebr. Helfmann* (1931)
Weiss, John. *The Making of Technological Man: The Social Origins of French Engineering Education* (1982)
Wellhöne, Volker. *Großbanken und Großindustrie im Kaiserreich* (1989)
Wells, David. *Recent Economic Changes* (1890)
Wennas, C. "Erecting the Bridge in the Heart of the Sudan." 40 *ER* 526 (1899)
Westwood, J. *A History of Russian Railways* (1964)
Whichard, Obie. "U.S. Sales of Services to Foreigners." *SCB*, Jan. 1987, at 22
White, Gilbert. "Organizing Scientific Investigations to Deal with Environmental Impacts." In *The Careless Technology: Ecology and International Development* 914 (M. Farvar & John Milton ed., 1972)
White, Lazarus. *The Catskill Water Supply of New York City: History, Location, Sub-Surface Investigations and Construction* (1913)
White, Leonard. *The Jeffersonians: A Study in Administrative History 1801-1829* (1965 [1951])
Whitford, Noble. "New York State Barge Canal." 108 *SA* 377 (1913)
Wiener, Jonathan. *Social Origins of the New South: Alabama, 1860-1885* (1981 [1978])
Wiener, Lionel. *Les Chemins de fer coloniaux de l'Afrique* (1930)
———. *L'Égypt et ses chemins de fer* (1932)
Wijetilleke, Lakdasa, & Anthony Ody. *World Refinery Industry: Need for Restructuring* (World Bank Technical Paper No. 32, 1984)
Wiley, Peter, & Robert Gottlieb. *Empires in the Sun: The Rise of the New American West* (1982)
Wilgus, Horace. *A Study of the United States Steel Corporation in Its Industrial and Legal Aspects* (1973 [1901])
Wilkins, Myra. *The Emergence of Multinational Enterprise: American Business Abroad* (1970)
———. *The Maturing of Multinational Enterprise: American Business Abroad from 1914 to 1970* (1974)
———, & Frank Hill. *American Business Abroad: Ford on Six Continents* (1964)
Wilkinson, Joseph. "Raymond International, Inc. Goes Up on the Big Board." *ENR*, June 16, 1960, at 44
Willcocks, W. 2 *Egyptian Irrigation* (3d ed. 1913)
Willes, Day. "The Enlargement of the Erie Canal." 95 *SA* 45 (1906)
Williams, Archibald. *How It Is Done; Or, Victories of the Engineer* (1908)
Williams, William. "Plant and Material of the Panama Canal." 19 *TASCE* 273 (1888)
Williams, William. *The Contours of American History* (1966 [1961])
———. *The Roots of Modern American Empire: A Study of the Growth and Shaping of Social Consciousness in a Marketplace Society* (1970 [1969])
Williamson, Harold, & Kenneth Myers. *Designed for Digging: The First 75 Years of Bucyrus-Erie Company* (1955)
Wilson, Edmund. "Hoover Dam." 68 *NR* 66 (1931)
Wilson, Joan. *Ideology and Economics: U.S. Relations with the Soviet Union, 1918-1933* (1974)

Wilson, Neill, & Frank Taylor. *The Earth Changers* (1957)
Wines, Richard. *Fertilizer in America: From Waste Recycling to Resource Exploitation* (1985)
"Winston Bros. Company—1875-1950." 1:1 *AB* 1 (Sept. 1952)
Wolf, John. *The Diplomatic History of the Bagdad Railroad.* In 11:2 *UMS* (Apr. 1, 1936)
Wolfe, J. "Engineering Construction Work Under Foreign Laws." 89 *ENR* 559 (1922)
Wood, Andrew. "Brazil's Odebrecht Builds a Major Petrochemicals Stake." *CW*, Mar. 31, 1993, at 36
Woodruff, William. "The Emergence of an International Economy 1700-1914." In 4 *The Fontana Economic History of Europe: The Emergence of Industrial Societies Part Two* 656 (1973)
Woods, Edward. "Address of Mr. Edward Woods, President." 87 *MPICE* 1 (1886)
*Works of Isambard Kingdom Brunel: An Engineering Appreciation* (Alfred Pugsley ed., 1976)
World Commission on Environment and Development. *Our Common Future* (1990 [1987])
Worster, Donald. *Rivers of Empire: Water, Aridity, and the Growth of the American West* (1992 [1985])
Woytinsky, W., & E. Woytinsky. *World Commerce and Governments* (1955)
Wright, Winthrop. *British-Owned Railways in Argentina: Their Effect on Economic Nationalism, 1854-1918* (1974)
Yates, Ray. "New York State Barge Canal." 111 *SA* 492 (1914)
Yergin, Daniel. *The Prize: The Epic Quest for Oil, Money, and Power* (1992)
Young, Desmond. *Member for Mexico: A Biography of Weetman Pearson, First Viscount Cowdray* (1966)
Yu Fai Law. *Chinese Foreign Aid* (1984)
Zahlan, A. *The Arab Construction Industry* (1984)
Zander, Kurt. "Das Eisenbahnwesen der Türkei mit Berücksichtigung der wirtschaftlichen Entwicklungsmöglichkeiten der Bagdadbahn." In *Das Türkische Reich* 48 (Josef Hellauer ed., 1918)
Ziebura, Gilbert. *Weltwirtschaft und Weltpolitik 1922/24-1931: Zwischen Rekonstruktion und Zusammenbruch* (1984)
Ziegler, Philip. *The Sixth Great Power: A History of the Greatest of All Banking Families, The House of Barings, 1762-1929* (1988)
Zimmerman, James. *Extraterritorial Employment Standards of the United States: The Regulation of the Overseas Workplace* (1992)


## Newspapers, Periodicals, and Serials

*America's Builders.* 1952-1959
*Barge Canal Bulletin.* 1908-1919
*Baustatistisches Jahrbuch.* 1975, 1992
*Board of Trade Journal.* 1956-1970
*Bradshaw's Shareholders' Guide, Railway Manual and Directory.* 1855, 1864
*British Business.* 1982-1989
*Builder.* 1842-1863
*Business Week.* 1930-1993
*Civil Engineering.* 1930-1969
*Construction Review.* 1966, 1970
*Dod's Parliamentary Companion: New Parliament.* 33d ed., 1865
*Economist.* 1859-1992
*Engineer.* 1856-1939

*Engineering.* 1866-1940
*Engineering-Contracting.* 1908-1915
*Engineering News.* 1874-1917
*Engineering News-Record.* 1917-1994
*Engineering Record.* 1877-1917
*Far Eastern Economic Review.* 1990
*Financial Times.* 1976-1990
*Financial World.* 1976-1977
*Frankfurter Allgemeine Zeitung.* 1963, 1974
*Fortune.* 1933-1993
*Génie Civil.* 1880-1915
*Handelsblatt.* 1974
*International Construction.* 1962-1984
*International Water Power and Dam Construction.* 1970-1991
*Minutes of the Proceedings of the Institution of Civil Engineers.* 1842-1935
*Moody's International Manual.* 1991
*Moody's Manual of Investments* [various titles]. 1903-1964
*Monthly Labor Review.* 1935
*National Cyclopædia of American Biography*
*Neue Deutsche Biographie.*
*Neue Zürcher Zeitung.* 1974, 1977
*New York Times.* 1875-1994
*Poor's Fiscal Records.* 1941
*Poor's Fiscal Volume.* 1938
*Poor's Industrial Volume.* 1937
*Proceedings of the American Society of Civil Engineers.* 1876-1955
*Railway Age.* 1881-1903
*Schweizerische Bauzeitung.* 1883-1935
*Spiegel.* 1975
*Survey of Current Business.* 1975, 1993
*Time.* 1931-1954
*Times* [London]. 1855-1919
*Trade and Industry.* 1972-1979
*Transactions of the American Society of Civil Engineers.* 1867-1939
*Wall Street Journal.* 1963-1993
*Water Power.* 1949-1970
*Zeitschrift für das Bauwesen.* 1888-1911

## Government Documents

*France*

"Rapport fait au nom de la commission du budget chargée d'examiner le projet de loi portant fixation du budget général de l'exercice 1905 (chemins de fer colonies)." In 66 *ACDDP*, Annéxes No. 1959 et 1960, at 1867 (Session ordinaire de 1904, Pt. 2, July 4-13, 1904, 1905) (written by M. Bourrat)

*Germany*

*Die Eisenbahnen Afrikas: Grundlagen und Gesichtspunkte für eine koloniale Eisenbahnpolitik in Afrika.* In *SBVR*, 12th Legis. Per., 1st Sess., 241 *ASB*, Doc. No. 262 (1907)
Reichstag. *SBVR*, 11th Legis., 1st & 2d Sess. (1904-1906)

Statistisches Bundesamt. *SJ 1976 für die Bundesrepublik Deutschland* (1976)
*SJ der DDR 1974* (1974)

Great Britain

*Ceylon Railway* (45 *PP* 1860 [111])
*Correspondence Relating to Railway Construction in Niger* (Cd. 2787, 78 *PP* 1906
    [21])
*General Act of the Brussels Conference, 1889-90* (Cd. 6048, 50 *PP* 1890 [1])
"Minute by His Excellency Sir John Lawrence, Governor General, dated 9th
    January 1869: Railway Extension in India." In *East India (Railways)* (47
    *PP* 1868-69 [129])
"Minute by the Most Noble the Governor-general; dated the 20th April 1853." In
    *Railways (India)* (76 *PP* 1852-53 [481])
*Papers Relating to the Affairs of the Ceylon Railway* (C. 289, 47 *PP* 1871 [605])
*Papers Relating to the Construction of Railways in Sierra Leone, Lagos, and the
    Gold Coast* (Cd. 2325, 56 *PP* 1905 [361])
*Papers Respecting Proposed Railway from Mombasa to Lake Victoria Nyanza* (C.-
    6560, 16 *PP* 1892 [27])
*Parliamentary Debates* (Hansard). 1854-1900
*Private Enterprise in British Tropical Africa* (Cmd. 2016, 8 *PP* 1924 [195])
*Report from the Select Committee on East India (Railways)* (14 *PP* 1857-58 [161])
*Report from the Select Committee on Eurphrates Valley Railway* (9 *PP* 1872).
*Report from the Select Committee on Railway Enactments* (14 *PP* 1846 [590])
*Report from the Select Committee on Railway Labourers* (13 *PP* 1846 [530])
*Report from the Select Committee on the Growth of Cotton in India* (9 *PP* 1847-48
    [1])
*Report on the Construction and Working of the Mombasa-Victoria (Uganda)
    Railway and Steamboat Services on Lake Victoria, 1903-1904* (Cd. 2332, 13
    *PP* 1905 [317])
*Report to the Board of Trade of the Empire Cotton Growing Committee* (Cmd.
    523, 16 *PP* 1920 [16])
*Reports of Her Majesty's Colonial Possessions for the Year 1862: Part II* (40 *PP*
    1864 [3309-I])
*Reports Showing the Present State of Her Majesty's Colonial Possessions for the
    Year 1865: Pt. I—West Indies and Mauritius* (58 *PP* 1867 [3812])
*Reports Showing the Present State of Her Majesty's Colonial Possessions for the
    Year 1868: Pt. III* (C. 151, 59 *PP* 1870)
*Reports Showing the Present State of Her Majesty's Colonial Possessions for the
    Year 1867, Part III: Eastern Colonies* (43 *PP* 1868-69 [4090-I])
Central Statistical Office. *AAS 1975* (No. 112, 1975)
Department of the Environment. *Private Contractors' Construction Census 1973*
    (1975)


Iran

Statistical Centre of Iran. *Statistical Yearbook of Iran 1352 (March, 1973-March,
    1974)* (1976)


Iraq

Central Statistical Organization. *Annual Abstract of Statistics 1976* (n.d.)

*New Zealand*

*Report of the Committee of Inquiry into Industrial Relations on the Whangarei Refinery Expansion Project at Marsden Point* (1985)


*Saudi Arabia*

Central Department of Statistics. *Statistical Year Book* (1978, 1983, 1988)


*U.S.S.R.*

Tsentral'noe Statisticheskoe Upravlenie pri Sovete Ministrov SSR. *Narodnoe khoziaistvo SSSR v 1974 g.: Statisticheskii ezhegodnik* (1975)


*United Nations*

*Yearbook of Construction Statistics 1973-1980* (1982)
Centre on Transnational Corporations. *Transnational Corporations in the Construction and Design Engineering Industry* (1989)
———. *World Investment Report 1991: The Triad in Foreign Direct Investment* (1991)
Economic & Social Council. Committee on Housing, Building & Planning. 5th Sess. *Industrialization of Building* (1967)
International Bank for Reconstruction and Development. *Eleventh Annual Report 1955-1956* (1956)
———. *Seventeenth Annual Report 1961-1962* (1962)
———. *Third Annual Report 1947-1948* (1948)
Industrial Development Organization. *UNIDO Monographs on Industrial, Industrialization of Developing Countries: Problems and Prospects*. No. 2: *Construction Industry* (1969)
International Labour Organisation. *Building for Tomorrow: International Experience in Construction Industry Development* (1991) (written by Derek Miles & Richard Neale)
———. "Contract Migration in the Republic of Korea" (International Migration for Employment Working Paper 4, 1982) (written by Sooyong Kim)
———. "Contract Migration Policies in the Philippines" (International Migration for Employment Working Paper 3, 1982) (written by L. Lazo, V. Teodosio, & P. Sto. Thomas)
———. *Economic and Social Effects of Multinational Enterprises in Export Processing Zones* (1988)
———. "International Contract Migration in the Light of ILO Instruments, with Special Reference to Asian Migrant-Sending Countries" (International Migration for Employment Working Paper 8, 1982) (written by W. Böhning)
———. "International Labour Migration and the Asean Countries" (International Migration for Employment Working Paper 13, 1982) (written by C. Stahl)
———. *Meeting of Experts on Problems of Foreign Construction Workers Employed in European Countries* (1979)
———. "Tripartite Declaration of Principles concerning Multinational Enterprises and Social Policy." 66 *OB*, Ser. A, No. 1 (1978)
———. 1 *World Labour Report: Employment, Incomes, Social Protection, New Information Technology* (1984)

————. Building, Civil Engineering & Public Works Committee. 6th Sess. Report II: *International Migration of Labour in the Construction Industry* (1959)
————. 7th Sess., Report II: *Technological Changes in the Construction Industry and Their Socio-Economic Consequences* (1964)
————. Sectoral Activities Programme. Building, Civil Engineering and Public Works Committee. 11th Sess. *General Report* (1987)
————. *Measures to Overcome Obstacles to the Observance in the Construction Industry of ILO Standards* (1986)
————. 12th Sess. Report I: *Recent Developments in Building, Civil Engineering and Public Works* (1992)
————. International Labour Office. *International Labour Conventions and Recommendations, 1919-1981* (1982)
————. *The Rights of Migrant Workers: A Guide to ILO Standards for the Use of Migrant Workers and Their Organisations* (1986)
————. International Labour Conference. 75th Sess. Report III (Part 5): *List of Ratifications of Conventions (as at 31 December 1987)* (1988)
Secretariat of the Economic Commission for Europe. *Economic Survey of Europe in 1971.* Pt. I: *The European Economy from the 1950s to the 1970s* (1972)
World Bank. *The Construction Industry: Issues and Strategies in Developing Countries* (1986 [1984])
————. *Indonesia: Sustainable Development of Forests, Land, and Water* (1990)
————, IDA, & IFC. *Policies and Operations* (1971)


                                  *United States*


U.S. *National Study on Trade in Services: A Submission by the United States Government to the General Agreement on Tariffs and Trade* (n.d. [1984])
[Army Corps of Engineers]. *Report of the Chief of Engineers U.S. Army, 1908.* Pt. I (1908)
Bureau of Economic Analysis. *Business Statistics, 1963-91* (27th ed. 1992)
————. *Fixed Nonresidential Business Capital in the United States, 1925-73* (1974)
————. *National Income and Product Accounts of the United States: 1959-88* (1992)
————. U.S. *International Trade and Investment in Services: Data Needs and Availability* (Staff Paper 41, 1984) (written by Obie Whichard)
————, & Bureau of the Census. *Foreign Direct Investment in the United States: Establishment Data for 1987* (1992)
Bureau of Labor Statistics. *Construction During Five Decades* (Bull. No. 1146, 1954)
————. *Labor Law and Practice in Saudi Arabia* (Rep. No. 269, 1964)
————. *Labor Law and Practice in the Kingdom of Saudi Arabia* (Rep. No. 407, 1972)
————. *The Structure of the U.S. Economy in 1980 and 1985* (Bull. No. 1831, 1975)
Bureau of the Census. *CCI, 1987: Industry Series: Heavy Construction Contractors, Not Elsewhere Classified* (1990)
————. *CCI, 1982: Industry Series: Heavy Construction Contractors, N.E.C.* (1984)
————. 1 *CCI, 1977: Industry and Area Statistics* (1981)
————. 1 *CCI, 1972: Industry and Special Statistics* (1976)
————. 1 *CCI, 1967: Industry Statistics and Special Reports* (1971)
————. *County Business Patterns: U.S. Summary, 1974-1990* (1977-1993)
————. *Fifteenth Census of the United States: 1930: Construction Industry* (1933)

———. *Historical Statistics of the United States, Colonial Times to 1970* (1975)
———. *1987 CoM: Concentration Ratios in Manufacturing* (1992)
———. *1987 CoM: Subject Series: General Summary: Industry Product Class, and Geographic Area Statistics* (1991)
———. *1982 CoM: Subject Series: General Summary*. Pt. 2: *Industry Statistics by Employment Size of Establishment* (1985)
———. *1987 Enterprise Statistics: Large Companies* (1990)
———. *1982 Enterprise Statistics: General Report on Industrial Organizations* (1986)
———. *1977 Enterprise Statistics: General Report on Industrial Organizations* (1981)
———. *1972 Enterprise Statistics: General Report on Industrial Organizations* (1977)
———. *1967 Enterprise Statistics: General Report on Industrial Organizations* (1972)
———. *Statistical Abstract of the United States*. 1975-1992
Bureau of Foreign and Domestic Commerce. *The Construction Industry* (Market Research Ser. No. 10.1, 1936) (written by H. Bookholtz & C. Judkins)
———. *Railways of Central America and the West Indies* (Trade Promotion Ser. No. 5, 1925) (written by W. Long)
———. *Railways of South America*. Pt. I: *Argentina* (Trade Promotion Ser. No. 32, 1926) (written by George Brady)
———. *Railways of South America*. Pt. II (1927) (written by W. Long)
———. *Railways of South America*. Pt. III: *Chile* (Trade Promotion Ser. No. 93, 1930).
Bureau of Reclamation. *Boulder Canyon Project Final Reports*. Pt. I: *Introduction*. Bull. 1: *General History and Description of Project* (1948)
———. *The Story of Boulder Dam* (Conservation Bull. No. 9, 1941)
Congress. *Congressional Record*. 1986, 1993
———. Office of Technology Assessment. *Trade in Services: Exports and Foreign Revenues* (1986)
Department of the Army. *The History of the US Army Corps of Engineers* (n.d. [1986])
———. *Vietnam Studies: U.S. Army Engineers 1965-1970* (1974) (written by Robert Ploger)
Department of the Navy. *Southeast Asia: Building the Bases, The History of Construction in Southeast Asia* (n.d. [1975]) (written by Richard Tregaskis)
General Accounting Office. *Persian Gulf: U.S. Business Participation in the Reconstruction of Kuwait* (NSIAD-93-69, 1992)
House of Representatives. *Activities of the United States Army Corps of Engineers in Saudi Arabia: Hearing Before the Subcommittee on Europe and the Middle East of the House Committee on Foreign Affairs*. 96th Cong., 1st Sess. (1979)
———. *U.S. International Competitiveness: The Construction Industry: Hearing Before the Subcommittee on International Policy & Trade of the House Committee on Foreign Affairs*. 98th Cong., 1st Sess. (1985)
———. Ways & Means Committee. *Overview and Compilation of U.S. Trade Statutes*. 102d Cong., 1st Sess. (1991 ed.)
International Trade Administration. *A Competitive Assessment of the U.S. International Construction Industry* (1989 [1984])
———. *Current Developments in U.S. International Service Industries* (1980)
———. *Foreign Builders Target the United States: Implications and Trends* (NTIS PB88172457, 1988)
Isthmian Canal Commission. *Annual Report of the Isthmian Canal Commission*. 1911-1914

————. *Report of the Isthmian Canal Commission, 1899-1901*. S. Doc. No. 222, 58th Cong., 2d Sess. (1904)
National Export Expansion Council. *Report of the Industry Committee on Engineering and Construction Services* (1970)
Office of Business Economics. *Balance of Payments Statistical Supplement* (rev. ed., n.d. [ca. 1961])
————. *U.S. Business Investments in Foreign Countries: A Supplement to the Survey of Current Business* (1960)
————. *U.S. Direct Investments Abroad 1966, Pt. I: Balance of Payments Data* (1970)
Office of Management and Budget. *Standard Industrial Classification Manual 1987* (1987)
Senate. *Electric-Power Industry: Control of Power Industries*. S. Doc. No. 213, 69th Cong., 2d Sess (1927)
————. *Foreign Assistance and Related Agencies Appropriations for 1964: Hearings Before the Senate Committee on Appropriations*. 88th Cong., 1st Sess (1963)
————. *Panama Canal Equipment*. S. Doc. No. 258, 63d Cong., 1st Sess. (1914)
————. 1 *Report of the Committee of the Senate upon the Relations Between Labor and Capital* (1885)
————. *Sale of Foreign Bonds or Securities in the United States: Hearings Before the Senate Committee on Finance*. 72d Cong., 1st Sess. (1931-32)
————. 6 *Testimony Taken by the United States Pacific Railway Commission*. S. Exec. Doc. No. 51, 50th Cong., 1st Sess. (1887)
————. *To Amend the National Labor Relations Act, 1947, with respect to the Building and Construction Industry: Hearings Before the Subcommittee on Labor and Labor-Management Relations of the Senate Committee on Labor and Public Welfare*. 82d Cong., 1st Sess. (1951)
————. *United States-Japan Services Trade: Hearing Before the Subcommittee on International Economic Policy, Trade, Oceans and Environment of the Senate Committee on Foreign Relations*. 100th Cong., 2d Sess. (1988)
State of New York. *Report of the Commission on Barge Canal Operation* (1913)

## Conventions, Statutes, and Regulations

*New Zealand*

Whangarei Refinery Expansion Project Disputes Act 1984, N.Z. Stat. 1984, No. 2
Labour Relations Act 1987, N.Z. Stat. 1987, No. 77

*Saudi Arabia*

Labor Code (Royal Decree No. M/21, Nov. 15, 1969). In ILO, *LS*, 1969—Saudi Arabia 1

*United Arab Emirates*

Federal Law to Regulate Employment Relationships (No. 8, Apr. 20, 1980). In ILO, *LS*, 1980—United Arab Emirates 1

*United Nations*

ILO Convention No. 87: Convention Concerning Freedom of Association and Protection of the Right to Organise (1948)
ILO Convention No. 97: Concerning Migration for Employment (1949)
ILO Convention No. 98: Convention Concerning the Application of the Principles of the Right to Organise and to Bargain Collectively (1949)

*United States*

Act of Mar. 2, 1901, ch. 803, 31 Stat. 895
S. Res. 169. 63d Cong., 1st Sess. (1913)
Act of Mar. 12, 1914, ch. 37, 38 Stat. 305
Boulder Canyon Project Act, ch. 42, 45 Stat. 1057 (1928)
Act of June 19, 1934, ch. 648, 48 Stat. 1021
40 U.S.C. §§ 321, 324 (1934)
Philippine Trade Act of 1946, ch. 244, 60 Stat. 141
Foreign Assistance Act of 1961, Pub. L. No. 87-195, 75 Stat. 424
Foreign Assistance Act of 1963, Pub. L. No. 88-205, 77 Stat. 379
Foreign Assistance Act of 1964, Pub. L. No. 88-633, 78 Stat. 1009
Trade Agreements Act of 1979, 19 U.S.C. § 2515 (1980)
Military Construction Authorization Act, 1984, Pub. L. No. 98-115, § 803, 97 Stat. 757 (1983)
Buy American Act, 41 U.S.C. §§10b-1(a)(2) and (g) (Supp. 1991)
29 U.S.C. §§ 157-158 (1991)

NLRB General Counsel Advice Memorandum, Case No. 19-CC-1300, 1981 NLRB GCM Lexis 95

**Cases**

*Finland*

*Työtuomioistuimen Vuosikirja.* TT 1979 No. 169
————. TT 1980 No. 135

*New Zealand*

Whangarei Refinery Expansion Project, Arbitration Court, Decision No. 162/82, [1982] *NZILR* 597
————. Arbitration Court Decision No. 198/82, [1982] *NZILR* 605

*United States*

Benz v. Compania Naviera Hidalgo, S.A., 353 U.S. 138 (1957)
Dowd v. International Longshoremen's Ass'n, 975 F.2d 779 (11th Cir. 1992)
Empire Engineering Corp. v. Mack, 111 N.E. 475 (N.Y. 1916)
Freeport Transport Inc. v. Carr, 220 N.L.R.B. 833 (1975)
GTE Automatic Electric Inc. v. International Bhd. of Elec. Workers, 226 N.L.R.B. 1222 (1976)
Great Lakes Dredge & Dock Co. v. United Marine Division, 240 N.L.R.B. 197 (1979)
Huntley v. Empire Engineering Corp., 211 F. 959 (2d Cir. 1914)

International Longshoremen's Ass'n v. Coastal Stevedoring Co., 313 N.L.R.B. No. 53 (1993)
S. Pearson & Son, Inc. v. State, 182 N.Y.S. 481 (Ct. Cl. 1920)
RCA OMS, Inc. (Greenland) v. International Bhd. of Elec. Workers, 202 N.L.R.B. 228 (1973)
Rodgers v. H.S. Kerbaugh, Inc., 161 N.Y.S. 1016 (Sup. Ct., App. Div. 1916)
Shannahan v. Empire Engineering Corp., 98 N.E. 9 (N.Y. 1912)
Six Companies, Inc. v. Stinson, 58 F.2d 649 (D. Nev. 1932)
Six Companies v. Stinson, 2 F. Supp. 689 (D. Nev. 1933)
In re Warren Bros. Co., 43 F. Supp. 173 (D. Mass. 1942)
Windward Shipping v. American Radio Ass'n, 415 U.S. 104 (1974)


**Privately Published Firm Histories and Materials**

ABB Lummus Crest. "ABB Lummus Crest: Process Technologies and Full-Scope Services" (n.d. [ca. 1992])
———. "Lummus Olefins Technology for Today's Process Industries" (n.d. [ca. 1992])
———. "Technology Process Management, Engineering, Procurement, and Construction Services for Today's Process Industries" (n.d. [ca. 1992])
Aberthaw Construction Company. *Aberthaw Construction Company: A Quarter Century of Fulfilment* (1919)
Allen, William, Jr. *Stone & Webster: A Century of Service* (1989)
Badger. "Construction Services" (n.d.)
———. *Lubricating Oil and Wax Production* (n.d. [ca. 1990])
Bechtel Corp. *The Arab Lands: An Age of Change* (n.d. [ca. 1979])
———. *Facts About Bechtel* (n.d. [ca. 1968])
———. *1991 Bechtel Report to Employees*
Bonny, J. *Morrison-Knudsen Company, Inc.: "Fifty Years of Construction Progress"* (1962)
Brown & Root. *Brownbuilder: The First 50 Years* (1969)
———. *Brownbuilder*. No. 1 & 2, 1992
———. *A World of Services* (n.d. [ca. 1992])
Christiani & Nielsen. *75 Years of Civil Engineering 1904-1979* (Leif Nielsen ed., 1979)
Costain Group PLC. "Company Milestones" (Sept. 30, 1992)
———. "Costain Group" (n.d. [ca. 1990])
Dravo. *A Company of Uncommon Enterprise: The Story of the Dravo Corporation 1891-1966* (1974)
DYWIDAG. *Dyckerhoff & Widmann AG 125 Years* (n.d. [1990])
Fluor Corporation. *Heritage* (n.d. [ca. 1989])
———. *1991 Annual Report* (1992)
Foster Wheeler Corporation. *Annual Report*. 1990, 1991
Freeport-McMoRan. *1992 Annual Report* (1993)
George A. Fuller Company. *George A. Fuller Company: General Contractors 1882-1937* (1937)
Hochtief. *Annual Report 1991* (1992)
———. *Die Baubude*, No. 139, Apr. 1993
———. *Hochtief 1875-1975* (n.d. [1975])
Holzmann, Philipp, Aktiengesellschaft. *1849-1974 H[olzmann]: Ansprachen beim Festakt anläßlich des 125jährigen Bestehens der Firma Philipp Holzmann* (1974)
———. *Ausbau des Trinkwasser-Systems der libyschen Hauptstadt Tripolis* (1984)
———. *Geschäftsbericht 1992*

————. *Hafen Damman Saudi Arabien* (n.d. [1976])
————. *Medizinisches Zentrum in Riyadh Saudi-Arabien: Schlüsselfertige Planung und Ausführung* (1980)
————. *Philipp Holzmann Aktiengesellschaft im Wandel von Hundert Jahren 1849-1949* (Hans Meyer-Heinrich ed., n.d. [1949])
————. *Das umfassende Leistungsangebot der Holzmann-Gruppe* (1992)
Ingram, Robert. *The Bechtel Story: Seventy Years of Accomplishment in Engineering and Construction* (1968)
————. *A Builder and His Family: 1898-1948* (1961 [1949])
Jones, Edwin. *J.A. Jones Construction Company* (1965)
Kaiser Industries Corporation. *The Kaiser Story* (1968)
M.W. Kellogg. "The M.W. Kellogg Company" (n.d.)
————. "The M.W. Kellogg Company: Service to the Industry Worldwide Since the Turn of the Century" (n.d. [1992])
Morrison Knudsen Corporation. "History, 1912-1993." (n.d. [1993])
————. "MK's Major Projects" (n.d. [ca. 1993])
————. "Partial Listing of Countries with MK Projects" (n.d [ca. 1992])
National Constructors Association. "1992 Directory of Membership"
"The Parsons Story" (mimeo, n.d. [ca. 1970])
Radzio, Heiner. *Die Aufgabe heisst Bauen: 110 Jahre Hochtief* (1985)
Raytheon Company. *1991 Annual Report* (1992)
*Samsun Harbour in Turkey: A Joint Enterprise of the Companies Rar-Insaat Türk, Philipp Holzmann, Hochtief* (n.d. [1961])
Seidenzahl, Fritz. *100 Jahre Deutsche Bank 1870-1970* (1970)
*Seventy Years: The Foley Saga* (n.d.)
Sociéte de Construction des Batignolles. *L'Oeuvre d'un siècle 1846-1946* (1952)
Stone & Webster, Inc. "Burgeoning Workload in the Pacific Rim" (n.d.)
————. *1991 Annual Report to Stockholders* (1992)
Trafalgar House Public Limited Company. "Background Information" (July 1993)
————. *Reports and Accounts* (1992)
Warren Brothers Company. *Historical Review of the Warren Brothers Company Contract with the Government of Cuba for Construction of a Part of the Cuban Central Highway* (n.d. [1936])
————. *The Largest Highway Contract in History* (n.d. [ca. 1929-30])
————. "Reflections: 1900-1975." *The Spreader*, Fall 1975, at 2
Warren, Herbert 3d. "The Warren Story: A History of Warren Brothers Company and Its Founders." (1969 [1965])
Wayss & Freytag. *100 Jahre Wayss & Freytag 1875-1975* (n.d. [1975])
White, Valerie. *Wimpey: The First Hundred Years* (1980)
*Wimpey: The International Construction Group* (n.d.)
Wimpey, George, PLC. *Annual Report 1992* (1993)


**Dissertations and Theses**

Cassimatis, Peter. "The Performance of the Construction Industry" (Ph.D., New School for Social Research, 1967)
Lapkin, David. "Building Construction and Business Cycles 1870-1938" (Ph.D., Columbia University, 1957)
Mills, Daniel. "Factors Determining Patterns of Employment and Unemployment in the Construction Industry of the United States" (Ph.D., Harvard University, 1967)
Visvanathan, Shanmugan. "International Construction Industry" (M.A., University of Texas at Austin, 1990)

# Index

Abbas Pasha, 46
Abs, Hermann, 80
Actiengesellschaft für Hoch- und
  Tiefbauten, 87; *see also* Hochtief
Adams, Edward Dean, 92
Aden, 130, 136
Afghanistan, 53, 129, 209
AFL-CIO Building & Construction
  Trades Dept., 192
Aird, John, 84-85, 109
Aird, John & Sons, 49
Aktiengesellschaft für
  Verkehrswesen, 83
Alaska, 3
Alaskan-Canadian Highway, 127
Albert Canal, 90
Algeria, 71
Allgemeine Elektrizitäts-
  Gesellschaft, 82, 87
Alton, William, 46
Aluminum Co. of Canada, 129
American & Foreign Power Co., 103
American Bridge Co., 98-99, 103,
  115, 129
American Contracting & Dredging
  Co., 105
American International Corp., 107-
  10, 112, 113
American National Housing Corp.,
  200
Amsterdam Chamber of Commerce,
  69
Anatolia, 73, 77
Andes: construction of railways in,
  51
Anglo-Iranian Oil Co., 136
Antiunionism, 190-95
Aramco, 126, 130
Argentina: construction of railways

in, 38-39, 51
Arrowrock Dam, 121
Asea Brown Boveri, 199-200
Aspinwall, William, 95
Associated General Contractors of
  America (AGCA), 121, 122
Aswan Dam, 49, 85, 109
Aswan High Dam, 143-44
AT&T, 177, 188
Atchison, Topeka, & Santa Fe
  Railroad, 96
Atlantic & Great Western Ry, 43, 91
Atlantic, Gulf & Pacific Co., 103
Atlas Constructors, 129-30
Austin Co., 110, 111
Australia: construction of railways
  in, 43; exports of prefabricated
  structures to, 10; proletarianization
  of settlers in, 11
Azores, 130

Badger Co., 110, 128, 130, 164, 218
Baghdad Railway, 73-75, 77-80; and
  German-British conflicts, 79
Bahia & San Francisco Ry, 45
Bahrain, 130
Balaklava, 39
Balfour, Beatty & Co., 90
Balloon frame wooden house, 10
Banana line, 83
Barbados: export of prefabricated
  lighthouse to, 10; shipment of
  workers from to Africa to build
  railway, 46; workers from on
  Panama Canal, 106
Baring & Glyn, 42
Barratt, 200
Bechtel, Stephen, 119, 131, 196
Bechtel, Warren A., 125, 131; as